Equity and Tru

'Undergraduate law students traditionally find equity and trusts one of the most difficult subjects which they have to study. The straightforward and down-to-earth approach of this book should help to make the subject more accessible and enjoyable. I will certainly recommend it to my students.'

> Robert Collinson LL.B, BCL (Oxon), Solicitor, Module Leader for Equity and Trusts, Edge Hill University.'

'Atkins writes in a pleasant, accessible style which involves the reader. There is no other textbook which gives such detailed explanation of the cases.'

> Judith Riches, LL.M, Barrister, Senior Lecturer in Law, Brighton University'

Atkins' *Equity and Trusts* is an ideal choice for all undergraduate and GDL students looking for a comprehensive yet accessible core textbook. The author's clear writing style and focus on modern case law demystify difficult concepts and help to bring this complicated and dry subject to life.

The author provides students with a clear understanding of the law through the use of vital pedagogic methods such as flow-charts, diagrams and highlighted text-boxes, whilst keeping the focus on recent case law. Equity and Trusts is shown to be a live, growing and developing subject, with an important historical underpinning that ensures students gain a sound grasp of key material and understand both its history and current application. Features include:

- **As you read** aids deeper understanding by highlighting key points to bear in mind whilst working through each chapter
- **Key learning points** help students clarify complex issues and draw attention to important concepts
- **Explaining the law** assists in placing principles in a wider context by focussing attention on important individual cases
- **Key Glossary terms** help readers by providing on the spot definitions of key terms
- **Useful things to read** signposts the way to further understanding and achieving higher marks by providing an invaluable annotated guide to primary and secondary further reading.

Scott Atkins (LL.B, Dip LP, FHEA, Solicitor (non-practising)) is a Senior Lecturer in Law at the University of Derby and a Visiting Professor at the Institute of Law, Jersey. Scott has enjoyed teaching both Contract Law and Equity and Trusts to students for a number of years and views learning law as a partnership between student and tutor.

Equity and Trusts

Scott Atkins,

(LLB, Dip LP, FHEA)
Solicitor (non-practising)
Senior Lecturer in Law
University of Derby
Visiting Professor at the Institute of Law, Jersey

Routledge
Taylor & Francis Group

LONDON AND NEW YORK

First published 2013
by Routledge
2 Park Square, Milton Park, Abingdon, Oxon OX14 4RN

Simultaneously published in the USA and Canada
by Routledge
711 Third Avenue, New York, NY 10017

Routledge is an imprint of the Taylor & Francis Group, an informa business

British Library Cataloguing in Publication Data
A catalogue record for this book is available from the British Library

Library of Congress Cataloging in Publication Data
A catalog record for this book has been requested

ISBN: 978-0-415-81861-2 (hbk)
ISBN: 978-0-415-60372-0 (pbk)
ISBN: 978-0-203-57627-4 (ebk)

Typeset in Joanna
by RefineCatch Limited, Bungay, Suffolk

Printed and bound in Great Britain by
TJ International Ltd, Padstow, Cornwall

Outline Contents

Detailed Contents

Preface

Equity and trusts. Three words which usually conjure up a heady concoction of fear, loathing and, dare I say it, boredom in law students. This book aims to be a tonic to those ills.

How have these aims been achieved? Through the following mechanisms:

- Take a glance through this book. You will see clear diagrams of key information and principles. Each Chapter contains 'As you read' guidance notes at the start which act as signposts to point out key themes. Boxes entitled 'Key Learning Points' appear in important places throughout the Chapters to continue that directed reading and to ensure that you really appreciate the absolutely essential legal concepts;
- Glossaries are used to explain essential terminology. I know from personal experience that students often struggle with terminology used in Trusts' courses, so I have tried to ensure that you are not lost in jargon as you progress onto new topics;
- Sections on 'Applying the Law' show you how the law is actually used in real life and in worked examples so you should not feel that principles are being discussed in a vacuum;
- As equity and trusts is often a second, or final year subject, your ability to think about concepts critically will be tested. Boxes in the text headed 'Analyzing the Law' draw your attention to issues which you should consider critically before moving on further; and
- Each Chapter closes with sections entitled 'Points to Review' and 'Useful things to read'. Reflection is an essential skill in your learning and the former heading ensures that you can join the key concepts in the Chapter together. I am not a big fan of undirected further reading, so the 'Useful things to read' sections contain what I believe are relevant primary and secondary sources for you to develop your knowledge and understanding of each area.

This book is different to other textbooks in many ways — and deliberately so. One important area where it is different is in the detail of the cases which I have chosen to incorporate. Too often, in my view, case details are omitted for what are no doubt sensible reasons, but the effect can be to take the emotion out of the subject. It has always been my view that if students can appreciate the facts of cases, they are more likely to understand the principle from the decision in the case and it is, after all, the principle which is important to grasp. So I make no apology for writing a textbook which takes perhaps a smaller number of cases than other textbooks would normally do but looks at them in more detail. Equity and trusts is a subject which can involve, for instance, family disputes, theft, shady corporate transactions and sexual impropriety (see Chapter 11) and to omit case details would be to deny the reader the chance to see the rounded, controversial and everyday nature of the subject material.

In writing this book I have been assisted by a number of individuals and I must take this opportunity to thank them. The team at Routledge have been outstanding. The commissioning editor, Fiona Briden, had faith in my writing from the very start of the project and an enthusiasm for this textbook that surpassed even mine! My editor for the vast majority of the time I have been working on this book, Russell George, was a great help. I greatly valued his calming presence and patience. Seven academics at other UK universities took the trouble to read the manuscript in draft form and I am immensely grateful to them for their comments throughout and I have attempted to incorporate as many of their suggestions as possible in this final version.

My former colleague at Derby, Charlotte Woodhead, kindly offered to read the manuscript and her many thoughtful suggestions have improved the text immeasurably. Students in both Derby and Jersey have read the book in draft form and made useful comments; in particular, Rita Salem, who took the time and trouble to critique the text from a student's perspective. Two individuals have offered great help with the companion website. Carla Plater in Jersey has drafted the multiple choice questions and Gregory Allan, Senior Lecturer at the University of Wolverhampton, has written problem-based questions. My thanks are due to them both.

Certain authorities used in this book strained at the limits of my research capabilities and I am grateful to the librarians at Derby for helping me: Jane Robinson (now enjoying a happy retirement), Chris Martindale and Jane's able successor, Caroline Ball. I also troubled Lisa Anderson, librarian at the Harding Law Library at the University of Birmingham, and abused my status as an alumnus of that university on more than one occasion. I am grateful to her for finding authorities as well as pulling the 1935 edition of the Weekly Notes out of storage.

Other people have assisted me too. Bryn Perrins, formerly Senior Lecturer at the University of Birmingham and whose enthusiasm for his subjects will never be forgotten by those of us fortunate enough to be taught by him, introduced me to equity's 'rose-tinted glasses' and my 3-D version in Chapter 1 is perhaps an updated metaphor with him in mind. My colleagues at Derby have been kind, offering me support and encouragement throughout the writing process. Professor Michael Gunn, Vice-Chancellor at Staffordshire University and Professor Andrew Le Sueur, Director of Studies at the Institute of Law, Jersey, both offered wise counsel to me, particularly at the start of this project.

Finally, I owe thanks and love to my wife, Julie, and son, Harry, who have both been tremendously supportive and offered their own particular words of wisdom whilst I have been writing. They have had to endure the worries and stresses associated with this project and I am in their debt.

I hope that this book dispels those three attributes that I mention at the start. The historical development of Equity is interesting and its modern use today fascinating and I hope this comes across when you read this book. The law is as I understand it at 1 August 2012 and, despite all of the assistance offered by others, any errors within the text are mine alone.

Scott Atkins
Derby, 1 August 2012

Table of Cases

Table of UK Legislation

Table of Statutory Instruments

Table of European and International Legislation

Guide to the Companion Website

www.routledge.com/cw/atkins

Visit *Equity and Trusts* Companion Website to discover a comprehensive range of resources designed to enhance the teaching and learning experience for both students and lecturers.

A video Introduction from the author

In this video, the author, Scott Atkins, gives a brief introduction to the book and to the subject of Equity and Trusts. He outlines his approach to teaching this sometimes challenging subject and explains why he decided to write the book.

Problem Questions and Answers

This set of practice essay and problem questions is designed to give you invaluable exam practice and help you to hone your technique. The questions are organised according to each Part of the book.

A testbank of Multiple Choice Questions

Ordered by chapter, these MCQs have been written to allow instructors to test students' knowledge and understanding of each subject in the book.

Updates

Keep on track with the latest subject developments with text updates written by the author.

List of Figures

Chapter 1

Equity: Its Meaning, History and Maxims

Chapter Contents

This chapter deals with the very essence of equity: what it is, how it came about, its development over the centuries and the guiding principles which govern its operation today. The contents of this chapter contain the foundations upon which your study of equity will be built, so it is essential that you have a good understanding of its contents.

As You Read

Look out for the following key issues:

- How equity developed over the years, how it became discredited in the nineteenth century but how it escaped the jaws of defeat through the Supreme Court of Judicature Acts 1873 and 1875 to become even more important than ever before;
- What the term 'equity' means – how initially it might appear to be a vague concept involving fairness, justice and doing what is right according to good conscience but appreciate how such concepts have solidified over the centuries into principles applied today; and
- What those guiding principles – or 'maxims' – of equity entail and how they operate.

'Equity' – What is it?

The word 'equity' has different meanings for different people. In the wider world, people talk of 'the equity in their homes' as meaning the surplus of money which is their own in their houses after the sum borrowed on mortgage from their lender has been repaid. In recessionary times, if the sum borrowed from the lender is more than the actual overall value of the house itself, then there is no surplus or 'equity' in the house, thus giving rise to the phrase 'negative equity'. Another meaning of 'Equity' would be the trade union which represents performers and artists.

In this book, however, 'equity' is considered in a different light entirely. 'Equity' in our sense is derived from the Latin phrase *aequitas equitas* which means fairness or justice. Equity means something which might generally be considered to be positive. It means acting fairly, in good conscience, or perhaps doing what would generally be thought of as right. Doing what is 'equitable' is commonly understood to mean doing what is fair.

A common misconception amongst people is that the law in general does what is morally right. That is not necessarily the case. The law largely provides functionality to situations ensuring, for instance, that contracts are entered into and upheld or that people are punished after committing a criminal offence. Morality may or may not be part of the law as a whole, but it forms part of equity.

Equity in practice

Take an example of equity's operation in the real world. Today, there are two key instances of where equity operates:

(a)   the trust; and
(b)   in offering bespoke remedies to the legal system.[1]

---

1   See Chapter 17 for a full discussion of equitable remedies.

Suppose you enter into a contract to buy a new house. You then change your mind and decide not to proceed with the purchase itself. The law provides that if you fail to pay for the property under a contract in which you have promised to pay for it, you can be sued by the person to whom you owe money. In our example, this is the house-builder. The common law gives the builder the right to sue you for damages, not because it feels that it is morally right to give him that right, but more so because in general terms, the law should be seen to be enforcing contracts. Contracts are freely made and should be upheld. In practical terms, the builder would sue you for his loss: the difference between what you had agreed to pay for the house and the amount the builder could now get from selling the house to someone else.

The common law gives the builder a remedy. In reality, though, it might not be that useful for the builder. He is the entirely innocent party. To sue you for damages, he will need to re-market the house and sue you only for the difference between the amount he would have received from you had you proceeded with the purchase and the (lower) amount he actually achieved on another sale after you had pulled out. The builder can only sue you for the main loss he has sustained together with other, subsidiary, consequential losses.

However, it seems unfair that the builder should have to market the property again and wait until he can receive his money given that he has done nothing wrong. In this case, equity may come to the assistance of the builder. Equity can provide another remedy to the builder: that of specific performance.

Glossary: Specific performance

This is a court order which ensures that a defaulting party must adhere to the terms of a contract that they have entered into. Such an order is usually only given when the subject matter of the contract has a unique identity – for example, where a contract concerns a piece of land. See Chapter 17 for a detailed discussion of this equitable remedy.

The equitable remedy of specific performance will mean that the court can compel you to buy the house from the builder. The builder asks the court for an order stating that you must specifically perform the contract. If such an order is given, then you must go ahead and buy the property.

Arguably, this equitable remedy of specific performance is fairer to the builder. It is probably objectively fairer to the entire situation, since it is right that you are made to go ahead with a contract into which you freely entered.

What this example shows is that:

(a)   the remedy equity provides can give a fairer result than the law;
(b)   equity is far more flexible than the law and its remedies are capable of tailoring themselves to specific situations. The common law is comparatively inflexible, taking more of a 'broad brush' approach to all situations. Damages in this example will suffice for the builder as after all, they do give him a remedy. But equity is more akin to a made-to-measure suit than the answer which the law gives, which is more off-the-peg in that it will fit the vast majority of situations before it. Specific performance in our example is a bespoke remedy which is capable of giving the innocent party exactly what they want, whilst making sure the defaulting party is no worse off than under the original agreement that they entered into; and
(c)   equity can be seen to be grafted upon the law. More than this, it takes precedence over the law in certain situations. The remedy the law gives is similar to watching a movie in 3-D without the special glasses. You will still see the 'gist' of the movie, but you will not

really understand it or see it all. Equity is the equivalent of putting the glasses on. Suddenly a more rounded view is brought into focus. It enables you to see everything clearly and takes into account all of the subtleties in the film. It is the same with equity: equity can take into account the subtleties in the case and award an appropriate remedy.

To understand why equity in our context means fairness and why it is capable of providing bespoke remedies, it must be understood how equity developed into such an important legal concept.

Our Civil Court System in the Twenty-First Century

The court system in England and Wales has been shaken up in recent years. The Constitutional Reform Act 2005 created a new Supreme Court for the United Kingdom.[2] This new court replaced the House of Lords as the highest appellate court. It heard its first case in October 2009.

Making connections

One of the reasons for abolishing the House of Lords (as the forerunner of the Supreme Court) was that not only did its members decide important cases which had reached the highest appellate court but those same Law Lords could also take part in debates which led to the enactment of legislation.[3] There was, therefore, a potential conflict of interest as the same set of people were both making the law and deciding on its interpretation. This arguably offended the separation of powers of the legislature and the judiciary.

Although, by convention, the Law Lords did not take part in political debates in the House of Lords during its law-making processes, they were permitted to speak out on matters if giving their own personal views.

To avoid any possible conflicts of interest, the government decided to establish an entirely separate final court of appeal, called the 'Supreme Court'. The Law Lords would hear final appeals in that court and would no longer take part in debates in the House of Lords.

Below the Supreme Court, the Court of Appeal retains its appellate jurisdiction, hearing civil appeals from both the county court and the High Court. These last two are, of course, courts of first instance.

What is important for our purposes, however, is the system of law that the courts currently apply. As seen in the example with the building contract,[4] the courts apply both law and equity to determine the outcome of cases. Ultimately equity can take precedence over the law. Yet the important point remains that nowadays we have one combined system of 'law' in general terms comprising both common law and equity. The courts apply whichever system gives the most appropriate result.

This combined system is a relatively recent development. In order to understand how the courts have this ability, we need to take a look back at the historical development of equity.

---

2 Constitutional Reform Act 2005, s 23(1).
3 See http://www.judiciary.gov.uk/about_judiciary/judges_and_the_constitution/supreme_court/index.htm
4 See above: p 3.

History of Equity

Stepping back in time – the development of the common law

1066. The year, for most people, is significant as being the year in which William of Normandy defeated King Harold at the battle of Hastings. What happened in the years following the battle was the spread of what is known as the 'common law'.

❖ EXPLAINING THE LAW

Students traditionally nowadays think of the phrase 'common law' as meaning law made by the judges (i.e. law which is not made by Parliament).

Originally, however, 'common law' meant law which was common across the country. Common law was encouraged by William the Conqueror as a means of ensuring that the whole country was subject to the same laws. It was a way of unifying the country and ensuring that the monarch kept control.

The development of the court structure through the Middle Ages cannot be set out precisely. It is hard to pin down exactly when each court was set up since 'court' is not an easily definable term.[5]

Aside from a system of local courts, what we can say is that, probably by the thirteenth century,[6] three main courts, trying common law matters, were established in Westminster, London: the Court of King's Bench, the Court of Exchequer and the Court of Common Pleas. These are detailed in Figure 1.1 below, although there appears to have been a great deal of overlap of the subject matter dealt with by each court.

Court of King's Bench	Court of Exchequer	Court of Common Pleas
This court appeared to exercise two main functions: (i) hearing actions between private citizens in both civil and criminal cases (except in relation to actions concerning land) and (ii) supervising other inferior courts.	Originally, this court was used to enforce rights that the King enjoyed against citizens – for instance, actions could be brought by the King for debts owed to him. Later, this court also heard personal actions (i.e. those not involving claiming land) brought by a private individual against another citizen. It had, for the majority of the time it existed, the ability to administer both common law and some limited remedies in equity.	If a claim involved land, then this was the only court that could hear the case. Personal actions were also permitted but appeared to be infrequent, as the costs of pursuing litigation in this court were higher than the other two main courts.

Figure 1.1 The jurisdiction of the common law courts.

---

5   F Pollock and F W Maitland, *History of English Law* (2nd edn, Cambridge University Press, 1898), Vol I at p 190.
6   Ibid.

> ❖ **EXPLAINING THE LAW**
>
> The original Exchequer was established by the reign of Henry III (1216–1272) with two main functions: (i) a financial office and (ii) a court.[7] Later, the two functions would be separated into the two distinct entities that would form part of what we know today as HM Treasury and the court system of England and Wales.

The courts trying common law matters had therefore been in existence for roughly 600 years until their abolition by the Supreme Court of Judicature Acts of 1873 and 1875.

Beneath the surface of the common law courts, however, lay a number of problems. These took the form of:

(a)   the procedure for initiating an action; and
(b)   the use of juries in deciding facts in an action.

Procedural defects with the common law courts

The main form of commencing an action against another party was by issuing a writ.

Glossary: A writ

This was a formal document that was used by a claimant to start a case. Though it changed in form and content over the centuries, it was only abolished comparatively recently, by the Civil Procedure Rules 1998. It was replaced by the 'claim form' which remains in use today.

Writs were issued by a common law court. The objective of issuing a writ was to ensure that defendants came to court to hear the case against them. The common law had a rather harsh way of ensuring that occurred, however. To give an example with regard to an action for land, if the defendant did not appear before the court, his land would be seized for the King; if he still did not appear, then the land would be given to the claimant.[8] In other claims, it appears that the defendant could be arrested if he did not voluntarily attend the court.

That was not the only difficulty with writs, however. Lawyers, even today, like to use precedents – or templates – before they draft any document. It gives a practising lawyer a sense of security that someone before them has drafted a similar document. At the time of Henry III, there were 'some thirty or forty' types of writ in use but there were 'large differences' between them[9] so that the total number of writs in use could have been in the hundreds. This may not have been a bad system in itself, given lawyers' fondness for precedents, but the Provisions of Oxford, issued in 1258, specified that no writ could be issued unless the case followed a writ that had previously been issued. This meant that a party whose case was substantially different from a previous case could not make use of the common law to help them find a remedy, given the need to find a former writ to start the action. It could mean that a party was effectively remedy-less, which is hardly a fit state for the law to be in!

In addition, two causes of action could not be contained within the same writ: there had to be separate writs. This invariably added expense for the party who wished to start an action.

---

7   Ibid at p 191.
8   Op cit. Pollock and Maitland fn 5, vol II at p. 592.
9   Ibid at 565.

The use of juries in deciding facts in an action

The use of juries became more common in civil actions from the thirteenth century onwards. Trial by jury has practically been abolished in civil matters today. The main danger of trial by jury was the lack of certainty in the outcome, especially as it was possible for members of juries to be bribed, cajoled or threatened into finding certain facts in favour of one of the parties.

The end result of these difficulties was delay. Frustration no doubt followed on the part of not only claimants but also defendants. Even if the claimant's case was eventually heard and he was successful, the remedy he had to accept was given from the common law. As the example of the building contract shows,[10] the successful claimant might not necessarily want a common law remedy but might instead want a more specific remedy, tailored to his needs.

Fortunately, a separate system also existed and worked alongside the common law, to mitigate its harsh effects. That was the system of equity.

Stepping back in time – the development of the court of equity

Following the Norman Conquest and even by the thirteenth century, there was no *separate* court which simply administered equitable principles of fairness and doing what was right according to good conscience. The main courts were able to dispense justice as they saw fit. Most times, this would lead to a result which was derived from the common law, but the courts had the ability to give an equitable result if they felt it right to do so.

If the common law was unable to grant a remedy, however,[11] claimants had another avenue available to them. The claimant could petition – or ask – the King directly. The King could grant relief even if the common law was unable to assist. The courts were the courts of the King and he could step in to grant a remedy when his courts did not.

History illustrates, however, that English Kings had more pressing matters to deal with than petitions from their subjects. These other matters of both domestic and foreign policy were time-consuming. It no doubt became impractical for the King himself to deal with petitions from his subjects and so, gradually, he transferred the responsibility of dealing with the petitions to his Chancellor. Edward III's Order of 1349 to this effect regularised this procedure for the first time.

Glossary: The Chancellor

The Chancellor was the most important of the King's ministers. The Chancellor was the head of Chancery. Two of the most famous Chancellors in history, Thomas Wolsey (who was Chancellor 1515–1529) and Sir Thomas More (Chancellor 1529–1532), both of Henry VIII's reign, effectively ran the country's entire domestic policy and aspects of foreign policy as well as the Chancery.

Nowadays, the Chancellor is head of the Chancery Division of the High Court.

Chancery as an institution was not originally a court. It has been described as 'a great secretarial bureau, a home office, a foreign office and a ministry of justice'.[12] Originally, the

---

10 Above, p 3.
11 For example, perhaps there was no previous writ that was of assistance to the claimant's case, thus preventing a new claim from commencing.
12 Op. cit. Pollock and Maitland, fn 5, Vol I p 193.

Chancery issued its own writs, called 'original' writs, but these developed a more informal slant as it grew used to dealing with petitions to the King. Over time, the Chancellor gained his own court, called the Court of Chancery. This court had been established long before Wolsey's time. It was in this court that the Chancellor considered the petitions sent to him.

How did the Chancellor decide upon matters presented to him? It seems that by the time of More as Chancellor, decisions of the Chancellor and the court were made according to matters of 'conscience' since the role of the Chancellor was that of the 'keeper of the King's conscience' due to early Chancellors being members of the clergy. The Chancellor did what he thought was objectively the right thing to do. He applied rules of equity.

Moreover, decisions could be based on conscience because the Court of Chancery was the only court to examine the parties on oath.[13] It was, consequently, thought that since evidence was effectively a product of someone's conscience – since their conscience would govern what they said in court – the decision given to them could similarly be based on conscience.

The Chancery Commissioners' Report of 1826[14] gave examples of the Court of Chancery's equitable jurisdiction concerning, amongst other matters:

(a)   managing trusts;
(b)   managing the powers of disposing property by will or the laws of intestacy through the control of personal representatives; and
(c)   providing more bespoke remedies in actions where the common law could not assist, such as the remedy of specific performance.

Equity's fall from grace

As described above, equity sounds like a good idea in theory. The principle that a claimant's legal problem can be resolved according to good conscience creates a nice, warm feeling. It also, in theory at least, leads to the right result in a case. That, coupled with the concept that a relatively informal procedure can be applied – of petitioning the King or his Chancellor – in order to obtain a remedy, should lead to a highly flexible system of justice, capable of responding to all types of legal case.

Arguably, for the first few centuries of the existence of the Court of Chancery, the court applied its equitable principles in a flexible manner. This approach was summarised by John Selden as 'being as variable as the length of each Chancellor's foot'.[15] His expression clearly meant that equity was not a fixed concept.

Yet the point of having a flexible system implies that it must be used in a malleable manner. Applying equitable principles in a flexible manner can be good, but it rests on the assumption that the person who is Chancellor is content to adopt such an approach. Lord Eldon is arguably the best example of a Chancellor who was not content to apply equitable principles flexibly. He was Chancellor from 1801–1827 and was proud of the fact that:

> The doctrines of this Court ought to be as well settled and made as uniform almost as those of the common law, laying down fixed principles. . . . I cannot agree that the doctrines of this Court are to be changed with every succeeding judge. Nothing would inflict on me greater pain, in quitting this place, than the recollection that I had done any thing to justify the reproach that the Equity of this Court varies like the Chancellor's foot.[16]

---

13 Report by the Commissioners appointed to inquire into the practice of Chancery (No. 56) (1826) at 7.
14 Ibid.
15 Selden J, *Table Talk of John Selden* (F Pollock (ed), Quaritch, 1927) at p 43.
16 *Gee v Pritchard* (1818) 2 Swanst 404, 414; 36 ER 670.

Lord Eldon was the high-water mark of the Court of Chancery's inflexibility. But he was not the first Chancellor to wish to bring more 'fixed principles' to the court of equity. In the late sixteenth century, Lord Ellesmere (1596–1617) appears to have been the first Chancellor who started the process of applying principles to cases, instead of applying the more flexible notion of conscience.

In addition, the background of Chancellors began to change after Wolsey. They no longer tended to have a church background, but instead, most of them were lawyers. As mentioned above, English lawyers to this day tend to like precedents but, from Ellesmere to Eldon, Chancellors used it to the disadvantage of equity. As a consequence, the flexibility at the heart of equity began to be eroded, and was replaced by the certainty of applying the same principles in each case.

The inflexible, rigid application of applying fixed principles to cases by the nineteenth century had other consequences. Delays in cases became notorious in the Court of Chancery as successive Chancellors grappled with applying increasingly fixed principles to the varying facts of each case. With delays came additional expenses for the litigating parties, as their lawyers were linked to the case for longer periods of time. This became well known, so much so that Charles Dickens wrote *Bleak House*, which focused on the delays in the Court of Chancery in his fictional case of *Jarndyce v Jarndyce*. Indeed, Dickens describes the Court of Chancery as being the 'shining subject of much popular prejudice' and whilst the case in his book was fictional, his preface gives an example of a real-life case:

> there is a suit before the Court that was commenced nearly twenty years ago; in which from thirty to forty counsel have been known to appear at one time; in which costs have been incurred to the amount of seventy thousand pounds . . . and which is (I am assured) no nearer to its termination now than when it was begun.[17]

That having been said, however, it is probably worth mentioning that not everyone thought that delays in court were a bad thing. The Report of the Chancery Commissioners in 1826 acknowledged that the court had been subjected to criticisms of delay, but said that the notion of delay had been 'so frequently misapplied, as to convey a very incorrect idea'. The Report even went on to say that delay could be useful in some situations, such as in applications for dealing with the property of children under a trust:

> It is obvious that, in the common case of bills filed for the protection of the property of infants, the suit must last until such infants attain their ages of 21 years (i.e. until the infant reached the age of majority, where they could take the property themselves).[18]

It is interesting to note that the chair of the Chancery Commissioners was none other than Lord Eldon!

Applying fixed principles was not the only cause of the delay. The actual procedure which governed the mechanics of the workings of the Court of Chancery was effectively broken too. From commencing a case in the Court of Chancery until after judgment was given, the system in the nineteenth century was far harder than it should have been.

From petitioning the King as a relatively informal process which avoided the more formal requirements of the common law writ, the start of an action in Chancery had developed into the need for the claimant to draft a rather complex bill to the Chancellor. In Manchester's view,

---

17 Charles Dickens, *Bleak House* (Bradbury and Evans 1853) p vi.
18 Report by the Commissioners appointed to inquire into the practice of Chancery No. 56 (HC 1826, 143) at 9.

the bill 'consisted of nine parts and was of an impressive length'.[19] It was hardly something that the layman could have drafted by himself. Taking evidence from witnesses was a long process, with the danger that witnesses could be led into giving certain answers by solicitors who had usually to take the witnesses through the questions asked of them. A curious rule was that if any of the parties were to marry or die during the litigation, then new bills had to be filed on each occasion. Rather interestingly, pretty much every stage in the process depended on a fee being paid to the court. The court clerks were paid out of these fees, so it was in their personal interests to encourage more steps to be taken in the litigation process so that more money would be generated for them. Nowadays such behaviour would invariably feature on a consumer-focused television programme!

Judgment being given was a triumph, but – fairly unbelievably for modern students of law – any issue could be raised in an appeal.

Clearly, reform was needed for both the Chancery and the common law courts. The whole court system needed to (a) operate more cheaply and efficiently and (b) deal with cases more quickly. Reform came in the Supreme Court of Judicature Acts of 1873 and 1875.

Reform of the Court of Chancery – and the triumph of equity

The Supreme Court of Judicature Acts 1873 and 1875 were a direct result of the reports of the Judicature Commission which was established in 1867.

The main effects of the Acts were:

(a) the abolition of the three common law courts;[20]
(b) the abolition of the Court of Chancery;
(c) the establishment of one Supreme Court of Judicature consisting of:

- the Court of Appeal; and
- the High Court, with five divisions: Queen's Bench, Chancery, Probate, Divorce and Admiralty

(d) the delivery of both common law and equity by the Supreme Court of Judicature; and
(e) under s 25 of the 1873 Act, in the event of conflict between the provisions of law and equity, equity was to prevail.[21]

Coming Full Circle – Back to the Twenty-First Century

The establishment of the Supreme Court of Judicature lasted until the effects of the Constitutional Reform Act 2005 when, rather helpfully (!), the name 'Supreme Court' was given to the body that replaced the Judicial Committee of the House of Lords.

The court system now considers and applies principles of both common law and equity together, to the benefit of the parties to the litigation. That, in any event, is the theory.

The fusion debate

Members of the academic community and the courts have disagreed amongst themselves over whether the Supreme Court of Judicature Acts really intended to join – or fuse – together common law and equity in one of two forms:

---

19 Manchester, A H *Modern Legal History* (Butterworths, 1980) at p 139.
20 See Figure 1.1.
21 Supreme Court of Judicature Act 1873, s 25(11).

(a) substantively, so that there are no longer two separate bodies of legal rules in place but only one with the courts applying the most appropriate remedy from either body to the case in question; or

(b) procedurally, so that there remain two distinct bodies of both common law and equity, but they are dispensed as justice demands by one unified court system.

Ashburner was the first academic to believe that the systems of common law and equity had not mixed together substantively, but only procedurally:

> the two streams of jurisdiction, though they run in the same channel, run side by side and do not mingle their waters.[22]

Judges have usually disagreed with this view and have shown that they believe that the two systems were fused together substantively as well as procedurally by the 1873 and 1875 Acts. In *United Scientific Holdings Ltd v Burnley Borough Council*,[23] Lord Diplock went so far as to describe Ashburner's view as 'mischievous and deceptive'[24] and carried on to say that 'there should continue to be, as there had been since 1875, only one set of rules for judges to apply'.[25]

In the same case, Lord Simon of Glaisdale made it plain that:

> the object of section 25 of the Supreme Court of Judicature Act 1873 was to reconcile the differences between common law and equity so that the two systems . . . could form a single coherent code.[26]

Lord Simon then gave the example of the equitable doctrine of estoppel 'permeat[ing] the whole of our law' following its origins in *Hughes v Metropolitan Railway Company*[27] as developed by Denning J in *Central London Property Trust Ltd v High Trees House Ltd*.[28]

In *Central London Property Trust Ltd v High Trees House Ltd*, the claimant let out a newly built block of flats in London to the defendant company which was, in fact, a subsidiary of the claimant. Rent was payable at the rate of £2,500 per year. The main lease was granted from 29 September 1937. The defendants then sub-let the flats to individual tenants. The problem was that, due to the Second World War, the block of flats had been unoccupied from 1939, when war was declared, as many people had decided to leave London. As many of the flats were unoccupied, the claimant agreed to reduce the rent by half to £1,250 per year. No time limit was placed on how long this revised agreement was to last.

The defendant honoured the revised agreement and paid the reduced amount of rent. By the start of 1945, all of the flats in the block were occupied. In September 1945, the receiver of the claimant company noticed that the claimant was receiving only half of the originally agreed rent. The receiver, therefore, claimed both the full amount of the rent going forwards into the future and, as a means of testing whether all of the arrears accumulated since 1937 could be claimed, half the year's rent for 1945. The defendant said that the claimant was estopped from changing its mind and going back on its promise to charge only half-rent.

---

22 Walter Ashburner, *Principles of Equity* (Butterworths, 1902) p 23.
23 *United Scientific Holdings Ltd v Burnley Borough Council* [1978] AC 904.
24 Ibid at 925.
25 Ibid at 927.
26 Ibid at 943.
27 *Hughes v Metropolitan Railway Company* (1877) 2 App Cas 439.
28 *Central London Property Trust Ltd v High Trees House Ltd* [1947] KB 130.

❖ **EXPLAINING THE LAW**

> *High Trees* is a well-known case in both the law of contract and equity but it was not really an adversarial case in the way that we think of traditional court proceedings. It is described in the law report as 'friendly', in the sense that the case was brought to test the legal position of whether reneging on the promise to accept half-rent was permissible.

The problem for the defendant was this. There was an original contract – or lease, in this case – under which the defendant had promised to pay £2,500 per year to the claimant. The later agreement to reduce the rent by half was a variation of that contract. Variations to contracts have to be supported by consideration in English law unless the variation is made by deed. It has long been held that, at common law, there is no consideration in paying less than is due under a contract – *Foakes v Beer*.[29]

The defendant admitted in argument that such a variation would probably not be thought of as complying with the rules of consideration as known by the common law. Nonetheless, the defendant argued that a court of equity would enforce such an agreement as that arrived at between the two parties. Counsel for the defendant sought to emphasise the practical advantages that the claimant had attained from the variation to the contract. He argued that the reduction in rent enabled the defendant to continue managing the block of flats which, in his view, would have been a practical benefit sufficient for a court of equity to enforce the variation, despite there being no consideration for the variation.[30]

The issue for Denning J to resolve was whether equity could take precedence over the common law doctrine of consideration.

Denning J believed that 'when law and equity have been joined together for over seventy years, principles must be reconsidered in the light of their combined effect'.[31]

He held that the courts 'have refused to allow the party making [the promise] to act inconsistently with it'.[32] That meant an estoppel was created: the claimant could not go back on the promise to accept reduced rent payments. This equitable principle of estoppel could, on the facts, take priority over the common law principle that there was no consideration in an agreement to accept less money than was originally due. Denning J believed this triumph of equity was 'a natural result of the fusion of law and equity'[33] and that the ingredients to maintain a successful defence of promissory estoppel were:

> a promise intended to be binding, intended to be acted on and in fact acted on [which would then be] binding so far as its terms properly apply.[34]

Provided those ingredients were shown and proven, a defendant would be estopped – or prevented – from going back on their promise. They would have to honour it. In principle, this seems entirely fair and logical. A party should not be allowed to change their mind and go back on their promises, provided that those promises have been freely given.

---

29 *Foakes v Beer* (1884) 9 App Cas 605.
30 *Central London Property Trust Ltd v High Trees House Ltd* [1947] KB 130 at 132.
31 Ibid at 135.
32 Ibid at 134.
33 Ibid.
34 Ibid at 136.

Yet this did not sit comfortably with the common law rule in *Foakes* v *Beer*[35] that a promise to accept less money than was actually due did *not* discharge the entire debt owed. This rule itself had largely developed by historical accident through *Pinnel's Case*.[36] However, Denning J had no difficulty in his own mind with that rule, that the common law was subject to the equitable doctrine of estoppel:

> The logical consequence, no doubt, is that a promise to accept a smaller sum in discharge of a larger sum, if acted upon, is binding notwithstanding the absence of consideration and *if the fusion of law and equity* leads to this result, so much the better.[37]

Such was the power of equity following the reforming Acts of 1873 and 1875.

High Trees shows that equity was now capable of overpowering the common law, even in such established doctrines as consideration provided that conditions for its operation were satisfied. Equity had shown that it was malleable enough to balance the competing interests between the two parties. The result of *High Trees* was that the claimant could not claim for the amount of rent through the years of the Second World War, but was able to claim for future rent after the war had ended. Each party received justice: the claimant was bound to his original promise not to claim the rent from 1937, but the defendant could not keep him to his promise to claim only half of the rent due in the future. Equity truly had triumphed over the common law and continues to do so today.

What must now be considered is *how* equity works: the principles that guide its operation. Let's see how they have developed and been applied by the courts.

Equity's Guiding Principles – Its Maxims

Equity's maxims were developed over the centuries as the principles under which the Court of Chancery would reach decisions in cases before it. *Snell's Equity*[38] lists 12 maxims as follows:

- equity will not suffer a wrong to be without a remedy;
- equity follows the law;
- where there is equal equity, the law shall prevail;
- where the equities are equal, the first in time shall prevail;
- he who seeks equity must do equity;
- he who comes to equity must come with clean hands;
- delay defeats equities;
- equality is equity;
- equity looks to the intent rather than to the form;
- equity looks on that as done which ought to be done;
- equity imputes an intention to fulfil an obligation;
- equity acts in *personam*.

The 12 maxims are guiding principles that the courts still use to make decisions in cases today. They overlap to a degree and it is, on occasions, difficult to pigeonhole cases as falling squarely within one equitable maxim. Bear this in mind as you study equity.

---

35 *Foakes v Beer* (1884) 9 App Cas 605.
36 *Pinnel's Case* (1602) 5 Co Rep 117a; 77 ER 237.
37 *Central London Property Trust Ltd v High Trees House Ltd* [1947] KB 130 at 135 (emphasis added).
38 McGhee, J *Snell's Equity* (32nd edn, Sweet & Maxwell, 2010) p 105.

Making connections

Being able to spot which equitable maxim(s) are at work in the judgments of decided cases will lead to a greater understanding of the reasons behind the judgments.

Initially, the maxims of equity look rather like a collection of mystical sayings which do not mean an awful lot. It is hard to see how the courts can apply them to cases. In order to see how that is done, each maxim is considered, using decided cases or illustrations as examples.

Equity will not suffer a wrong to be without a remedy

This maxim is the first one listed, because logically it arises from the origins of equity. Equity was founded because the common law was defective both in terms of procedure and, on occasions, in terms of remedies available.

The mechanism of the trust is perhaps the biggest asset that equity has given to the English legal system. This is considered in depth throughout the majority of the remainder of this book but, for the moment, a fundamental understanding of the express trust will suffice. A trust is where one person, the settlor, transfers property to another person, the trustee. That trustee is instructed by the settlor to hold that property for the benefit of a third person (the beneficiary).

In an express trust, there is a type of agreement between the settlor and the trustee that the trustee will hold certain property for the beneficiary. Suppose the trustee does not honour that agreement and wants to claim the property for himself. Suppose, also, the settlor does not wish, for whatever reason, to enforce that agreement. Can the beneficiary take any action against the trustee to enforce the trust?

The common law will not help the beneficiary. Although the settlor and the trustee entered into an agreement with each other to benefit a third party, it is a form of agreement made between the settlor and trustee. The common law tells us that a third party cannot generally enforce a contract made between two other people (through the doctrine of privity of contract). Only those people who make the contract with each other can enforce it. The common law, through the law of contract, traditionally offers no remedy to the beneficiary if the trustee refuses to honour the original trust.

Under the common law, the beneficiary was stuck, entirely unable to do anything but watch as the trustee disappeared with what is rightfully his property. Nowadays, since the enactment of the Contracts (Rights of Third Parties) Act 1999, the beneficiary may be able to sue the trustee, but only if the original contract made between the settlor and the trustee specifically mentions the beneficiary either by name or as a member of a group.[39] That is a rather recent change in the law and until that Act came into force in 2000, the common law would not help a beneficiary where the trustee would not honour the terms of a trust agreement.

Fortunately, way before the Contracts (Rights of Third Parties) Act 1999 was even dreamed about, equity was willing to step in and help the beneficiary. Equity recognised the concept of a trust existing from the Middle Ages. Equity permits the beneficiary to enforce the terms of a trust largely because it is not fair in good conscience that, having agreed to look after property on behalf of someone else, the trustee should be permitted to renege on that arrangement. It is instead fair that the trustee should be obliged to honour the terms of the arrangement and the Court of Chancery enforced that initial arrangement. Through its

---

39 The Contracts (Rights of Third Parties) Act 1999, s 1.

recognition of the trust, equity grabbed hold of the concept that it would not suffer a wrong to be without a remedy and would help a beneficiary out by giving effect to the settlor's intention.

Equity follows the law

The problem with dealing with this maxim next is that it illustrates perfectly how having explained one maxim, the next one appears to contradict it. In fact, this is not quite true but it appears to be so, at least at first sight.

This maxim is that equity will try, wherever possible, to give the same result as that which would have been achieved at common law. This, again, is as a result of the historical development of equity. Until the time of Sir Thomas More as Chancellor, the remedies given out by both the common law courts and the courts of equity did, to a certain degree, overlap. It was only really during and after More's time that the attitudes of the common law and equity courts started to develop separately.

In theory, it makes a lot of sense that there is overlap between the common law and equity. The maxim makes it clear that the preference is that equity will give the same result as the common law. Where the two systems divide is where the common law will not help the claimant. In such a situation, we return to the first maxim in that equity will then step in and give an appropriate remedy.

Nowadays, we can see that the equitable remedy of an injunction[40] is a good example of where equity will step in if the common law will not help. All breaches of contract give the innocent party an automatic right to damages at common law. The innocent party is entitled to nominal damages for the breach of contract itself and 'real' damages to reflect the loss they have suffered. The vast majority of innocent parties will be awarded damages. Equity will not step in to help those parties since the common law gives an appropriate remedy in the circumstances. There is no need for equity to intervene. On these occasions equity follows the (common) law. Equity will only intervene where damages will not give the innocent party an appropriate remedy.

Suppose you accept a job in a business where you have access to a large amount of confidential information – say, you are a designer of cars for a motor-racing team, Atkins Racing. You decide to leave the team and go to work for a rival team. Atkins Racing will be keen that you do not use the confidential information you learned during your employment with your new team. Suppose Atkins Racing discovers that you do plan to use some of that information to benefit your new team. In order to prevent you from doing so, it will sue you for breach of contract – assuming your contract actually contains a clause preventing you from using confidential information after you have left Atkins Racing.

Here, the common law remedy of damages is of little use to Atkins Racing. It would be hard to quantify the loss suffered to that team by you using the information elsewhere. Also, the remedy of damages would merely compensate Atkins Racing. This does not achieve Atkins Racing's objective, which is to stop you using that information to the other team's advantage. Atkins Racing is trying to pre-empt a loss that it will suffer by you working for another team. It needs a remedy that will stop something happening in the future, rather than trying to 'right' a past 'wrong'.

The equitable remedy of the court granting a prohibitory injunction may assist. That remedy would compel you not to use the confidential information that you acquired when working for your new team. On such an occasion, equity would not follow the law but

---

40 See Chapter 17 for a full discussion.

would depart from it. Equity adds to the common law by providing Atkins Racing with a more appropriate remedy, which is more flexible for that innocent party's needs.

Where there is equal equity, the law shall prevail

This maxim applies when there is more than one claimant and where multiple claimants have effectively the same entitlement to a claim. In this situation, equity will not step in. There is no need for it to do so – both claimants have the same claim and there is nothing to choose between them. The law can sort the claims out by itself, so there is no need for equity's intervention.

Suppose an individual is made bankrupt. You and I both lent him £10,000. Rather foolishly, neither of us asked the individual for any security in return for our money.[41] We are both unsecured creditors. There is nothing to differentiate our claims. In due course, we may be paid out from his bankruptcy and we will both receive either £10,000 if there is enough money left for all creditors to be paid in full, or we will receive a proportion of that amount if, as in most bankruptcies, there is not enough money to pay all creditors in full.[42] Equity will not intervene in this case since the law can sort out the claims all by itself. It would not be fair for equity to prefer to help one of us and not the other, since our claims are exactly the same. Our claims are equal, so the law takes precedence.

Where the equities are equal, the first in time shall prevail

Similar to maxim (iii), this principle again deals with the situation where there is more than one claimant. This time it is about having multiple claimants where their claims are similar but they were not created at the same time. There is thus an order of priority in the claims. This maxim recognises that order of priority and seeks to give priority to the claimant with the earliest claim. Another way of expressing it would be 'first come, first served' (but only where the claims are otherwise equal).

To illustrate this, take the example, again for maxim (iii), but now alter the facts a little. Suppose you and I still lend the individual £10,000 each. I lend him £10,000 on Monday and you lend him a further £10,000 on Tuesday. This time, both of us are more cautious and we ask for security. He agrees to give us a charge over his house. Knowing a little about the law, we each write down the basic terms of the deal, to comply with the statutory requirements that all dispositions of land must be made in writing and include all of the terms which the parties to the agreement have made.[43] We insist that the borrower (on the lender's behalf) registers each charge at HM Land Registry as his title to the house is registered.

We have each created an equitable mortgage. It is not a legal mortgage because the document did not take the form of a deed.[44] But equity will recognise our attempts to try to have some security for our loans as valid because of the ninth equitable maxim – that equity looks on that as done which ought to be done. Even though our document does not comply with the requirements of a deed,[45] we have tried to give ourselves security for our loans and equity will still recognise that.

Suppose, then, that the borrower goes bankrupt and that there is just £10,000 in total to pay out from his bankruptcy. Should we share it equally? Not this time. The reason is due to

---

41 For example, a charge by way of legal mortgage on a house.
42 Insolvency Act 1986, s 328.
43 Law of Property (Miscellaneous Provisions) Act 1989, s 2(1).
44 As required by Law of Property Act 1925, s 52.
45 Set out under Law of Property (Miscellaneous Provisions) Act 1989, s 1.

this equitable maxim – that where the equities are equal, the first in time shall prevail. Remember that I created my charge with the borrower the day before you created yours. My claim, says this equitable maxim, is stronger than yours, because mine is first in time. Consequently, applying this maxim to our situation means that I will have the £10,000 in settlement of my claim and you will receive nothing.

Glossary: A Deed

People often talk about the 'title deeds' to their house with reverence. Nowadays, a deed is simply a document which has the word 'deed' on it, usually at the place where the parties sign it. The person signing the document must 'sign it as a deed' and their signature must be witnessed. It must then be 'delivered', which doesn't mean that it has to be handed over to the other person, but instead means that you intend to be bound by it. There are special privileges that documents drawn up as deeds enjoy:

(a)   they need no consideration to support them; and
(b)   each party's limitation period to sue the other for breach of contract is doubled.

He who seeks equity must do equity

This maxim reflects the development of equity. Equity is all about doing what is right, according to fairness and good conscience. This maxim reflects that by saying that if you want equity to help you, then you must be prepared to act fairly yourself in your dealings with the other party. It prevents hypocrisy. You cannot claim equity's assistance unless you are willing to be honest. It is closely related to the sixth maxim.

He who comes to equity must come with clean hands

The difference between this maxim and the previous maxim is simply one of timing: the previous maxim looks to the future whilst this maxim looks to the past. The exact phraseology of the two maxims spells this out: this current maxim looks at what the claimant has actually done. The claimant has come to the court seeking an equitable remedy but has the claimant been fair in their dealings with the other party? Only if that can be answered in the affirmative will this maxim be satisfied and equity will intervene.

An illustration of this maxim working can be shown in the famous case of *D & C Builders Ltd v Rees*.[46]

The claimants were, in Lord Denning's words, 'a little company . . . [who were] . . . jobbing builders'.[47] The defendants, Mr and Mrs Rees, were husband and wife who owned a shop in which they sold building materials. The defendants wanted some work done to the shop and contracted the claimants to do the work. The total cost of the work came to just over £746. The defendants paid some of the money owed to the claimants, but there was a balance remaining of approximately £482.

Mrs Rees made an arrangement with the claimants to pay them a total of £300 in full satisfaction of the sum owed. In reality, Mrs Rees was putting the claimants over a barrel. The claimants were in a very difficult financial situation and Mrs Rees knew that. She effectively

---

46   *D & C Builders Ltd v Rees* [1966] 2 QB 617.
47   Ibid at 621.

offered them the £300 on a 'take it or leave it' basis. The claimants had to take the money offered. Mrs Rees insisted that the claimants write her a receipt saying that the money was in 'completion of the account', which they duly did.

After taking the money offered, the claimants sued Mr and Mrs Rees for the balance of the money owed.

As part of their defence, Mr and Mrs Rees tried to invoke promissory estoppel. They said that the claimants had made a promise to accept £300 in full satisfaction of the work done and they were now estopped from going back on that promise.

The problem for Mr and Mrs Rees is that promissory estoppel is an equitable doctrine. In the form revived by Denning J in *Central London Property Trust Ltd v High Trees House Ltd*,[48] it is designed to mitigate the harsh effects of the common law doctrine in *Foakes v Beer*[49] that a creditor can still sue for the balance of the money he is owed even if he has accepted a lower sum. But for promissory estoppel to apply, the person relying on it must come to equity with clean hands. In other words, they must show that they have acted fairly throughout in their dealings with the other party. This was Mr and Mrs Rees' downfall. They could not show that they had acted fairly towards the claimants. In fact, the reverse was true. They knew that the claimants were in financial difficulty and sought to take advantage of that by offering them a lower amount of money than that which was due to them. Equity would not help them. The rule of the common law prevailed, from *Foakes v Beer*,[50] which provided that the claimants could recover the whole amount due to them.

Lord Denning MR emphasised in the case that there had to be a true agreement, freely made between the parties before equity would intervene with promissory estoppel.[51] That really sums up this maxim: that any claimant wanting to rely on equity must arrive at the court having treated the other party fairly. It is, after all, what equity is all about.

Delay defeats equities

Generally the law has time limits in which a claimant can bring a claim against a defendant. The policy reason behind this is one of fairness. There comes a point where delay turns into the claimant actually acquiescing in the wrong that has been done to him. If he acquiesces in or affirms the wrong done to him, by taking no legal action, it is unfair to a defendant for the claimant to change his mind and subsequently bring an action.

The Limitation Act 1980 provides a series of limitations for certain actions. To give an example, a claimant has six years to sue for breach of a contract, commencing on the date the breach occurred.[52] The time limit is doubled if the contract was made in the form of a deed.[53]

Glossary: Limitation periods

Memories fade. It is seen to be unfair that defendants should run the risk that they could be subject to litigation forever. Consequently, for a number of actions, the Limitation Act 1980 provides that claimants may only bring a claim within a certain period of time. After that time has ended, the claimant may generally not bring his claim against the defendant.

---

48 *Central London Property Trust Ltd v High Trees House Ltd* [1947] KB 130.
49 *Foakes v Beer* (1884) 9 App Cas 605.
50 Ibid.
51 *D & C Builders Ltd v Rees* [1966] 2 QB 617 at 625.
52 Limitation Act 1980, s 5.
53 Ibid, s 8.

Section 36 of the Limitation Act 1980 provides that a number of the time limits in the Act 'shall not apply to any claim for specific performance of a contract or for an injunction or for other equitable relief'. This means that the statute has not provided a time limit by which actions for equitable remedies will be time barred. Where there are no time limits for a claim, equity comes in, because of this seventh equitable maxim – that delay in bringing an action will, in any event, defeat equity. In other words, even where statute does not give a specific time limit for seeking an equitable remedy, equity will step in to prevent a claim being successful if the court feels that the claimant has delayed for too long in bringing their claim. This is sometimes known as the doctrine of laches.

This doctrine was recently invoked by the court in *Azaz v Denton and Self-Realization Meditation Healing Centre*.[54]

This case concerned a claim for undue influence. Dr Azaz was a medical doctor who developed an interest in alternative medicine and wanted to embrace it wholeheartedly. He met the first defendant, Mrs Denton, who had established the Self-Realization Meditation Healing Centre. Dr Azaz went to live and work at the Centre. Significantly, he agreed to transfer all of his property to the centre, which was a registered charity. The amount of money handed over was around £100,000 plus his other possessions. Dr Azaz also abandoned his medical career and worked from mid-1992 until the end of 2003 without any proper payment.

Dr Azaz claimed the return of all of his money and possessions and compensation for the work he had carried out for the Centre for the 11 years or so that he was based there. To achieve this result, he brought claims against the two defendants to set aside two contracts he had signed on the basis that he had only signed them due to the undue influence of the defendants. The first contract was dated 23 January 1996 and the second was when he left the centre. Both contracts made it clear that he had given away his possessions willingly and without undue influence.

Without reaching a definitive conclusion on whether Dr Azaz had been subject to undue influence or not, Judge Richard Seymour QC held that Dr Azaz had simply waited too long to bring his claim. There was a gap of nearly 16 years between Dr Azaz first meeting the defendants and issuing his claim at the court. There was a gap of nearly four years between him signing the second contract and issuing the claim form. Dr Azaz had, in the meantime, secured alternative employment and, by all accounts, had started to rebuild his life. In other words, there was no reason why he could not have initiated court proceedings much earlier than he did. He had left it too late to seek equity's help in setting the contracts aside through the equitable doctrine of undue influence. In his case, his delay had defeated equity.

Equality is equity

This maxim is arguably a logical furtherance of maxims three and four: where there is equal equity, the law shall prevail and where the equities are equal, the first in time shall prevail. This time, however, the maxim implies that where the law cannot assist and the equitable claims that people have were both created at the same time and are worth the same, then equity will intervene, in as fair a manner as possible, by holding that equal claims are treated equally.

The concept of the law recognising a constructive trust of the family home in modern cases such as *Stack v Dowden*[55] can illustrate this maxim.

In this case, Barry Stack and Dehra Dowden started a relationship in 1975. They lived in a couple of houses during their relationship, which lasted until 2002. The second house is

54 *Azaz v Denton and Self-Realization Meditation Healing Centre* [2009] EWHC 1759, QB.
55 *Stack v Dowden* [2007] 2 AC 432.

significant for our purposes here. They bought it in 1993. When they bought it, the property was transferred into their joint names. That meant that they both owned the legal title to the property. The only way legal title can be owned by more than one owner is as joint tenants,[56] but property ownership is recognised by both law and equity. The problem with the transaction in this case, however, was that there was no express declaration of what was to happen to the interest in the property in equity and whether it was to be held by them as either joint tenants or tenants in common.

Glossary: Joint Tenants or Tenants in Common in equity?

Joint tenants – this means that the parties do not have shares in the property but they both own all of it. If one party should die, the whole property belongs to the other party, regardless of the contribution they each made. Say two people buy a house for £100,000. One party contributes £80,000 and the other the remaining £20,000. If they choose to own the property as joint tenants, these shares are not recognised as such. Often it is said that the parties own everything and yet nothing. The consequence is that if one of them dies, the other will automatically own all of the property entirely and the property is not subject to the deceased party's will.

Tenancy in common – where the parties each own shares in the property. The amount of these shares can – and should – be expressly agreed between the parties when they purchase the property and stated categorically in the purchase deed. This is what did not occur in *Stack v Dowden*. If the parties do not state the shares they own, it is for the court to work out, based on the principles in *Stack v Dowden*. On one party's death, their share will pass to whomever they have left it in their will or, if they have not made a will, according to the general law of intestacy contained in the Administration of Estates Act 1925.

The result of the case was that the House of Lords, by majority, held that where a residential property was transferred into joint names at law then, prima facie, equity would follow the law by holding that the equitable interest was also held as joint tenants. That, of course, is an example of the operation of maxim two, that equity follows the law.

Significantly for our purposes now, Baroness Hale also held that 'at least in the domestic consumer context, a conveyance into joint names indicates both legal and beneficial joint tenancy, unless and until the contrary is proved'.[57] So not only will equity follow the law but also, unless the parties are able to prove that equal division of the equitable ownership of their home was not the right course of action, equity would operate on the basis of giving them equal entitlement to the property by recognising that they have a joint tenancy in equity. The two parties bought the house at the same time and unless they are able to prove that they have contributed different amounts in terms of either time or money to the property,[58] equity's starting point is that they have the same interest in it.

Equity looks to the intent rather than to the form

Equity essentially developed as a response to the inflexibility of the common law. Part of the problem with the common law was its insistence on claims being commenced by writ and the

---

56 Law of Property Act 1925, s 34.
57 *Stack v Dowden* [2007] 2 AC 432 at 454.
58 For further examples of what can count towards valuing an equitable interest, see para 69 of Baroness Hale's speech in *Stack v Dowden* (ibid) and Chapter 14.

need for the claimant to find a precedent writ before a new writ could be issued. Equity developed a more flexible procedure, which originally involved claimants petitioning the King directly. Whilst this simple procedure has become more formal over the years, it illustrates how informal equity was originally.

This maxim reflects that same type of informality. Traditionally, common law was as concerned as much about the claim as it was about the procedure for bringing that claim. Statute has often followed that line of thought. For example, if two parties wish to create a legal lease for a term of over three years, then it has to be created by deed.[59] The law will not recognise a lease which is over three years and has not been created by deed. But equity will. Equity recognises that the parties have attempted to create a lease and so will see the lease as valid.[60] The reason is due to this maxim: equity is more concerned with the parties' intentions than whether they have properly complied with the form of the document required by the law.

Equity looks on that as done which ought to be done

This maxim goes against the saying that the road to hell is paved with good intentions since, effectively, equity will recognise those good intentions.

The case of *Walsh v Lonsdale*[61] is a good illustration of this maxim. It concerned an agreement made between the parties on 29 May 1879 under which the defendant was to grant to the claimant a lease of a property known as Providence Mill. The agreement said that a solicitor was to draw up a lease formally and the lease was to contain such provisions as were included in another lease dated 1 May 1879. The relevant parts of that lease included the important provision that the claimant would have to pay one year's rent in advance if the defendant demanded it. The claimant took possession of the mill and paid his rent, as agreed, in arrears.

Nearly three years after the agreement between the parties was made, the defendant demanded his full year's rent to which he felt he was entitled. The claimant did not pay and so the defendant tried to distrain for the rent. (Distraining for rent is when the landlord goes into the property, seizes the tenant's goods to the amount of rent owed and sells them to recover the amount due.)

The claimant, though, had an answer. He said that the defendant could not distrain for the year's rent because no formal lease had actually been drawn up by the solicitor. There had to be a legal lease to distrain for rent. Instead, there was only ever the basic agreement that the parties had reached on 29 May 1879. This was intended to lead to a formal lease being created, but no such lease had ever been entered into.

Giving the leading judgment in the Court of Appeal, Sir George Jessel MR held:

> There is only one Court, and the equity rules prevail in it. The tenant holds under an agreement for a lease. He holds, therefore, under the same terms in equity *as if a lease had been granted*, it being a case in which . . . relief is capable of being given by specific performance.[62]

In other words, equity would treat the lease as having been granted because there was an agreement to grant the lease, which was capable of being enforced by an order of specific performance. That meant that either party could rely on the terms of the agreement and enforce it against the other and require the other to have the actual lease formally drawn up.

---

59 Law of Property Act 1925, ss 52 and 54.
60 *Walsh v Lonsdale* (1882) LR 21 ChD 9.
61 Ibid.
62 Ibid at 14–15 (emphasis added).

Since it was possible that either party could have forced an actual lease to be drawn up and entered into, equity was effectively circumventing that procedure by saying that it would treat the lease as having already been drawn up. That was what the parties had actually agreed and equity was giving effect to their agreement. Equity was looking on something as having been done because it ought to have been done.

Equity imputes an intention to fulfil an obligation

This maxim is an example of equity looking kindly on a person's actions. The idea here is that if you are bound by an obligation and you do something to perform that obligation, equity will look benevolently upon your actions as being undertaken in fulfilment of your original obligation.

Suppose you lend a friend £100. You both agree that your friend would repay the money to you. Later on, however, you change your mind and you want to write off the debt. You tell your friend not to repay you the money. In addition, you appoint your friend to be the executor of your will. After your death, the debt your friend owed you is extinguished. By appointing him executor, you are confirming that you want the debt written off as it would make no sense for your friend (in his capacity of executor) to sue himself for the debt (in his capacity as debtor). Equity sees your action of appointing your friend as executor as meaning that you did not intend him to sue himself for the debt and hence that you intended to give the money to him.

This procedure is known as the rule in *Strong v Bird*[63] and is considered further in Chapter 7.

Equity acts *in personam*

This final maxim again reflects the development of equity. Equity's by-words are 'fairness', 'conscience' and generally doing what is thought to be right.

This maxim shows that equitable rights affect the person, as opposed to legal rights which are said to be rights in *rem*, which are valid as against the whole world. Equity affects parties' consciences – it affects them personally. This explains why equity recognises the concept of a trust.

Think about it like this. I transfer my car to you and ask you to hold it on trust for our mutual friend, Ulrika. The common law does not recognise a trust. At common law, I have transferred my car to you. You are the legal owner of it. But that is only half of the picture. Equity, as we have already seen, is akin to putting on 3-D glasses and seeing all of the movie, not just half of it. So, in this scenario, equity recognises the trust and, if you fail to hold the car on trust for Ulrika, she can take action to enforce the trust. She can sue you for breach of trust. The underlying rationale for allowing Ulrika to take this course of action is because equity acts in *personam* or against your conscience. It recognises that it is not right, in good conscience, that you should enjoy the car since it is not rightfully yours to enjoy.

Points to Review

You have seen:

- what 'equity' is as a concept – how it is a doctrine of fairness and good conscience;
- the history of equity and and how it developed, its downfall and its resurgence following the Supreme Court of Judicature Acts 1873 and 1875; and
- the guiding maxims of equity as developed over the centuries.

---

63 *Strong v Bird* (1874) LR 18 Eq 315.

Making connections

Before you move on, make sure you are comfortable with the contents of this chapter. Re-read it if you are not sure about any topics.

As you move on, keep the equitable maxims in mind since they underpin the case law and, to an extent, statute law that has developed. Knowing where equity has come from and the principles that guide it are essential to a good understanding of the coverage of this book.

 Useful Things to Read

A number of secondary sources are listed here, which you may wish to read to gain additional insight into the areas considered in this chapter.

Secondary sources

Legal history
J H Baker *An Introduction to English Legal History* (Butterworths Lexis-Nexis, 2002) Chapter 6. This contains an interesting summary of the history and development of the Court of Chancery.

Rt Hon Lord Denning *Landmarks in the Law* (Butterworths, 1984) Pt 3. This looks at Sir Thomas More, Thomas Wolsey and John Scott from the judge arguably most responsible for the development of equity in the twentieth century.

A H Manchester *Modern Legal History* (Butterworths, 1980) Chapter 6. This chapter contains a detailed discussion of the superior common law courts and the Court of Chancery, along with the background that led to the Supreme Court of Judicature Acts 1873–1875.

Joint tenancies/Tenancies in common
K Gray and S F Gray *Land Law* (Oxford University Press, 2009) Chapter 7. This goes into some depth as to the differences between joint tenancies and tenancies in common and should serve as a useful refresher if you have already studied land law.

Equitable maxims
Simon Gardner, 'Two maxims of equity' (1995) CLJ 54(1), 60–68. A rare modern article that considers some of equity's maxims; in this instance, the maxims that equity looks on that as done which ought to be done and equity follows the law.

Alastair Hudson *Equity & Trusts* (7th edn, Routledge-Cavendish, 2012) Chapter 1. This chapter contains more information on the equitable maxims.

J A McGhee *Snell's Equity* (32nd edn, Sweet & Maxwell, 2010) Chapter 5. This contains a look at the maxims of equity from a practitioner's point of view.

Chapter 2

Classification of Trusts and Powers

This chapter builds upon the meaning and history of equity considered in Chapter 1. The focus now shifts to the single biggest item that equity has created in the English and Welsh legal system: the trust. It is the trust which now remains the subject of the remainder of this book (except for Chapter 17), so its importance to equity cannot be overstated.

As You Read

As you read this chapter, look out for:

- what a trust is: its concept, how it grew up from its origins in the Middle Ages to today and the different types of property that can be left on trust;
- the different types of trust within the two over-arching areas of express trusts and implied trusts; and
- how a trust can be compared to and distinguished from something that may, at first glance, look very similar to it – a power of appointment.

The Trust

As has been seen in Chapter 1, equity's history is long. It has grown up over centuries into what it is today: a set of legal principles that contributes meaningfully to the English legal system to mitigate the otherwise harsh effects of the common law. The principles – or maxims – of equity are applied in cases today to give results that are designed to be fair and in good conscience.

But equity is not just a series of maxims that are applied by the courts. Those are only the underlying *ideas* that guide equity. Equity has more structure to it than the maxims suggest.

As has been mentioned in Chapter 1, equity has also given the legal system a set of bespoke remedies when common law damages are not adequate. Those remedies include orders of specific performance, injunctions and the rectification of documents.[1]

There is, however, one item that equity has given the legal system which far surpasses all of the other items – remedies or maxims – which it has also provided. That item is the trust. It is the greatest asset that equity has bestowed on the legal system. The word 'asset' is not used lightly, for as we shall see, it is the concept of a trust that enables the legal system to recognise more subtle shades of ownership than the common law permits.

Definition

Snell's Equity defines a trust as being formed when:

> a person in whom property is vested (called 'the trustee') is compelled in equity to hold the property for the benefit of another person (called 'the beneficiary'), or for some legally enforceable purposes other than his own.[2]

This concise definition demonstrates that:

---

1 See Chapter 17.
2 J H Baker, *Snell's Equity* (32nd edn, Sweet & Maxwell, 2010) at p 623.

- it is equity – not the common law – that recognises the trust;
- due to equity being the body that recognises the trust, the basis of the recognition is likely to be conscience and fairness;
- there are normally three parties to the trust, those being the person who originally owns the property, the trustee and the beneficiary; and
- there does not, in fact, have to be a human beneficiary to benefit from the trust, since the trustee can hold the trust property for some other 'legally enforceable purposes'.[3,4]

All of these issues are explored later in this chapter.

The parties typically involved in the creation of an express trust

In a simple, expressly declared trust, there are three parties involved in the matter. They are:

- *The settlor*. This is the person who creates the trust. He 'settles' the property on trust. In order to do this, he transfers the legal ownership of the property to the second person in the arrangement, the trustee.
- *The trustee*. This is the person who administers the trust. The trustee will hold the trust property for the benefit of the third party in the arrangement, the beneficiary. When the trust comes to an end, the trustee must transfer the legal ownership to the beneficiary, but until that time he retains it. Usually it is a good idea to have more than one trustee so that, for example, the burden of trusteeship can be shared. The maximum permitted number of trustees where the trust involves land is four.[5]
- *The beneficiary*. This is the person who benefits from the trust. They will enjoy the equitable interest in the property which is the subject matter of the trust. The beneficiary's easy task is to reap the rewards of being the person the settlor has chosen to benefit from his generosity. As we shall see, however,[6] the beneficiary's harder task is as the enforcer of the trust, making sure the trustee completes his obligations by, if necessary, forcing him to do so. There can be any number of beneficiaries.

The simple trust arrangement can be illustrated by the diagram in Figure 2.1.

Since the trust is a creature recognised by equity, the trustee is obliged to hold the equitable ownership on trust for the beneficiary due to the requirements of fairness and good conscience. By willing to recognise and enforce the trust, equity gives the trustee no other option but to adhere to its terms and will, if necessary, force the trustee to comply with the trust.[7]

In order to understand those issues, it is essential to have an understanding of how the trust originated.

Where It All Began . . .

It may have begun like this . . .

This story of the beginnings of the trust may be real or apocryphal, but it remains a nice tale.

---

3 Ibid.
4 See also the discussion of the beneficiary principle in Chapter 6 for a fuller analysis of who, apart from a human beneficiary, may benefit from a trust.
5 Trustee Act 1925, s 34.
6 See Chapter 6.
7 Through the mechanism of the implied trust: see Chapter 3.

Settlor

transfers entire ownership
in trust property

Trustee: retains legal ownership

holds equitable ownership for

Beneficiary

Figure 2.1 How a trust is formed: the concept of split ownership.

The origins of the trust may be linked to the crusades. The crusades occurred in the time of the Middle Ages and did not just involve English people but also those from other European countries. The crusades were a number of holy wars whose objective was to reclaim the Holy Land around Jerusalem for the benefit of Christians from the Muslims living there.

In all, the crusades led to hundreds of thousands of people, both members of the nobility and those from the lower classes of society, taking up arms to join in the fight for recapturing the Holy Land.

Those crusaders who owned land had a problem. They could – and often would – be away from tending their land for years at a time. What those crusaders needed was someone who could look after their land, manage it and farm it, whilst they were away. Those crusaders did not want to give their land away but instead wanted someone to take temporary custody of it. The land had to be returned to the original landowner on his return from the crusade. The land needed to be given away on a metaphorical piece of elastic, so that its ownership would always bounce back to the original landowner.

The common law, with its blinkered view of matters, could not help the landowner. Even today, if you give something away, the common law sees a change in ownership of the property from you to the recipient. You are no longer the owner at common law. You have given the property away. You have relinquished all claims to it. The common law could not assist the landowner who went away on crusade because the common law was not subtle enough to help with the landowner's problem. The common law would simply say that the landowner had given his land away to someone else.

Equity, though, with its 3-D glasses, could assist. Equity was capable of looking at the entire situation and seeing that the landowner only wanted to transfer his land to someone else on a time-limited basis. Equity would see that the land was to be, effectively, loaned out and that it was always to be returned to the landowner at the end of the loan period. Equity achieved that outcome through creating and developing the medium of the trust. The landowner would remain the true owner of the land whilst passing the day to day management of the land to someone else whilst he was away on crusade. That manager would then return the land to its rightful owner upon his return. The landowner, it might be said, trusted the manager to look after the land for him during his absence and return it to him on his return. The trust was born.

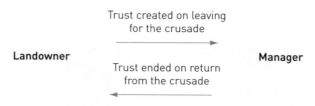

Figure 2.2 The (apocryphal?) crusader's trust.

Note that this crusader's trust differed from the majority of today's trusts by only having two parties to it. The manager would take the role of trustee holding the land on trust for the person setting up the trust who was also the beneficiary.

But it probably began like this . . .

As the victor at the Battle of Hastings in 1066, William the Conqueror had a new prize that he could distribute to his friends and associates who had supported him: England. He began to divide the country up into parcels of land and gave it away to those friends and associates – his chief lords. In turn, those chief lords sub-divided their pieces of land to lords and those lords gave it to other people who did the same until the land found itself being owned by a peasant tenant, at the very end of the chain. Each layer of people made money from it, down to the individual at the bottom of the chain who perhaps farmed the land. This was the concept of feudalism that was established in the early years after the Norman conquest and which grew up over the centuries. The King remained the technical owner of all of the land.

Originally, in return for land being granted from the King to his chief lords and so on, the chief lord would demand services from his lord and each lord from his tenant.

By the beginning of the thirteenth century, actual services being provided by one party to his lord in return for the land were dying out in favour of the tenants paying cash for the privilege of holding their interest in the land. This would enable their immediate successor to purchase any services they actually required. Cash was becoming more and more important in England's economy.

Related to this concept of each person in the feudal system preferring cash to services was the concept of inheritance. Chattels were not subject to inheritance but land was. The idea of inheritance provided that when a tenant died, the land would pass to his heir. The tenant would not get any choice about this and the concept of the common law recognising a will for a piece of land was anathema.

Death also carried with it another consequence. When the tenant died, privileges became due to the lord or, if it was the chief lord who died, to the King. These privileges were some of the 'incidents of tenure'. They included:

- Customary dues – local customs that were recognised and had to be performed on death. Baker[8] gives the example of the 'custom of heriot' where the lord could 'seize the best beast or chattel of a deceased tenant'.
- The concept of escheat – if the tenant died without leaving an heir, then his land would go to his lord.

---

8 J H Baker, *An Introduction to English Legal History* (4th edn, Butterworths Lexis-Nexis, 2002) at p 240.

Clearly, if a chief lord owned a lot of land, and with the King owning all of the land, the chief lords and the King could be in receipt of a great deal of money upon a tenant's death.

Probably since the beginning of time, people have tried to circumvent paying any more than they absolutely must to either the King or to whomever they owe money. Whilst tenants could not find a way around death, what they set out to do was to find a way around the inheritance requirements that their land must go to their heir. That is probably where the concept of the trust first arose.

The first use of the trust

The first use of the trust, then, was really to find a way around the rules of inheritance – in other words, to circumvent the requirement that your land had to go to your heir.

It was not possible to make a will of land. The owner of the land had to find some other way to rid himself effectively of his land before he died. If he was able to achieve that objective then, critically, the incidents of tenure applicable on his death would not become due. The tenant would also have some say over who would actually receive his land. This ability to state who should have your land after your death should not be understated and remains a concept of vital importance to most people today.

The key appeared to be that the tenant should take steps to deal with how his land was going to be administered during his life and not wait for the law of inheritance to strike after his death.

The main way that was developed was the concept of the 'use'.

Glossary: The 'use'

The 'use' has nothing to do with the English verb, to use. It comes from the old French word 'oeps'. For our purposes, the words 'use' and 'trust' can be used interchangeably.

A tenant could give the land to his friends on the explicit direction that, after his death, the friends should give the land to whomever the tenant chose. The tenant trusted his friends to honour his instructions hence the concept of the 'trust'. The concept stopped short of imposing an absolute obligation on the friends that they had to deal with the land as instructed for, if it did this, it would have circumvented the rules on wills too crudely. The arrangement can be represented by Figure 2.3.

Original tenant ———————————→ Directs friends ———————————→ New tenant
                                    to hold land on trust

Figure 2.3 The probable first trust.

This trust reflects the classic tri-partite arrangement described in *Snell's Equity*.[9]

The idea of giving something as serious as a piece of land to someone else on the basis of trust alone was far too flimsy a concept for the common law to recognise. Equity, however, would recognise trusting as a concept since, in the end, it is based on what good conscience should do – good conscience says that if you have been asked to hold a piece of land on behalf of someone else, you should not be allowed to renege on that arrangement. The Court of

---

9   At p 25 above.

Chancery, therefore, began to manage trusts and by the 1400s, it consumed much of the court's time.[10]

It may have been a bit of both . . . or something else entirely!

It is not impossible that both the crusades and the wish to avoid inheritance duties both spurred on the development of the trust. The crusades had ended by the closing years of the thirteenth century and we know that, by that stage, the incidents of tenure associated with feudalism were pretty much in full swing. Both crusaders and tenants wanted mechanisms to avoid the common law consequences of what would happen to their land. Both needed to rely on the idea of trusting others to look after their property, which was far too subtle for the common law to appreciate.

Other writers talk about the trust being descended from Franciscan monks who needed property to be held on trust for their benefit but who could not themselves own it due to their vow of poverty.[11] In truth, we simply do not know what the facts were which surrounded the creation of the very first trust. Some people like to believe the crusading version of events. History supports the tax evasion version with more facts, but it is by no means impossible that the first trust was used for any version of occurrences.

Split Ownership

The common law was not willing to recognise the concept of a trust. The common law likes definites: someone either owns property or they do not. It had no time for equity's recognition of ownership of property being based on conscience.

What is left by the two systems running parallel with each other is the concept that it is possible to split ownership of *property*. As will be seen, this includes *all* types of property, not just land. At common law, it is possible to have one person owning the property, whilst equity will recognise that the actual benefit of the property is being held for another. Equity does this by saying that the owner has an equitable interest. This is a proprietary interest – an interest in the property which is the subject of the trust – and can be relied upon against the whole world.

Key Learning Point

This is key to understanding a trust. The trust is built upon the basis that ownership of the property is split between the owner of the interest of the property at common law (the trustee) and the owner of the interest in equity (the beneficiary).

Owning the legal interest results in the trustee managing the trust. The equitable interest ensures that the beneficiary can enjoy the fruits of the trustee's labour.

To try to understand this idea, think of a cream cake. A cream cake consists of cake and fresh cream. Without both cake and fresh cream, the end product is not complete. The trust is like that insofar as it is a mixture of the common law and equity and, without one

---

10 J H Baker, *An Introduction to English Legal History* (4th edn, Butterworths Lexis-Nexis 2002) at p 251.
11 See, for example, Alastair Hudson's *Equity and Trusts* (7th edn, Routledge-Cavendish, 2012) Chapter 2.

part, the whole trust is not complete. Yet when looking at a cream cake, it is still possible to identify which part of the object is cake and which part is fresh cream. Depending on your eating preferences, it is possible to separate one from the other. That is true of the trust too: you can identify who owns the property at common law and who owns the property in equity. You can also separate the ownership of the different interests.

The Different Types of Trust

The expressly created trust is not the only type of trust that is recognised by equity. Figure 2.4 below shows what we might term a 'family tree' of trusts.

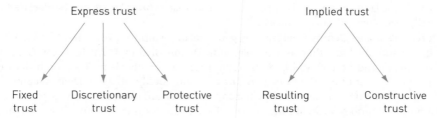

Figure 2.4 The family tree of trusts.

Each of these must be considered in a little more detail.

Express trusts

The fixed trust

The fixed trust is so called because the interests of the beneficiaries are determined expressly by the settlor when the trust is created. The interests are, therefore, fixed. The trustees must give to each beneficiary what the settlor has expressly provided. So the settlor has deliberately – or expressly – created a trust and fixed the beneficial interests.

If the settlor does not himself define the beneficial shares in a fixed trust, the maxim 'equity is equality' applies so that each beneficiary will have an equal equitable share in the trust property.

❖ EXPLAINING THE LAW

Scott appoints Thomas as his trustee and transfers £1,000 to him to hold on trust for the benefit of Ulrika. That is an express, fixed trust. It is an express trust because Scott has deliberately created it and it is fixed because Scott has provided that Ulrika is solely entitled to the benefit of the trust property – the money.

This trust is not confined to having just one beneficiary. For example, suppose another time Scott transfers the same amount to Thomas for Thomas to hold on trust for Ulrika and Vikas in equal shares. That means that Ulrika and Vikas will equally enjoy the trust property. It is still an example of an express, fixed trust because Scott has deliberately created it and the equitable interests are still fixed: Ulrika and Vikas are each to have 50 per cent shares in the money.

The example above demonstrates the classic, three-party arrangement in creating a trust.

There is also another way to declare an express trust, just involving two parties. The settlor can say that he himself is a trustee and declare that he holds certain trust property on trust for the beneficiary. Both ways were recognised as equally good alternatives by Turner LJ in *Milroy v Lord*.[12] There is still the three-party arrangement even in this alternative – it is just that one party is wearing two 'hats' of both the settlor and trustee.

Declarations of express trusts can be written down but, if the property of the trust is land, they must be evidenced in writing and signed by a person able to declare the trust.[13] If the trust property is not land, it may be surprising to know that express trusts can be declared quite informally, as occurred in *Paul v Constance*.[14]

Doreen Paul and Dennis Constance began a relationship in 1967. They moved into the same house and lived together, as a couple, until Dennis died in 1974. In 1969, Dennis was injured at work and he received £950 as compensation for his claim. They both decided to open a bank account to put the money in. The account would only be in Dennis' name.

From the time the account was opened to Dennis' death, more money was paid into it. A small amount of money was withdrawn from the account for them to buy Christmas presents and food and for them to each treat themselves. By the time Dennis died, the account still had the compensation money of £950 remaining in it.

Dennis had been married prior to meeting Doreen. Dennis died without leaving a will so his widow, Bridget, wound up his estate. Bridget claimed that, as the bank account was in Dennis' sole name, the entire contents of it belonged solely to him. That money, she argued, became part of Dennis' estate which she was bound to administer according to the laws of intestacy, as opposed to any of it belonging to Doreen.

Doreen disagreed. She argued that, whilst the legal title of the money had been in Dennis' sole name, a trust had been created by him. That meant that the equitable interest in the money was held by both her and Dennis. Doreen argued that Dennis had declared an express trust of the money. The difficulty that she faced was that the trust had been declared only orally and informally.

The Court of Appeal upheld the trial judge's finding that there was an express declaration of trust by Dennis in favour of both himself and Doreen. In his judgment, Scarman LJ pointed out that:[15]

> one should consider the various things that were said and done by the [claimant] and the deceased during their time together *against their own background and in their own circumstances.*

Certain facts led to the conclusion that Dennis had orally declared an express trust. These were that they had only opened the account in Dennis' sole name due to their embarrassment of having an account in joint names when they were not married, that they had paid in joint

---

12 *Milroy v Lord* (1862) 4 De G F & J 264; 45 ER 1185. See the more detailed discussion of this case in Chapter 7.
13 Law of Property Act 1925, s 53(1)(b). See Chapter 4 for a discussion of this complex topic.
14 *Paul v Constance* [1977] 1 WLR 527.
15 Ibid at 530 (emphasis added).

earnings, they had both enjoyed the money that was withdrawn and, crucially, that Dennis had said to Doreen on more than one occasion 'This money is as much yours as mine' led to the conclusion that an express trust had been declared.

Scarman LJ emphasised the case was near the borderline. It must be clear when an express trust is formed and it was not entirely clear here: was it, for instance, at the time the bank account was opened or at some later point when Dennis had promised Doreen that the money was theirs to share equally?

But the comments of Scarman LJ quoted above illustrate that equity will look at all the circumstances of each situation to decide if a declaration of an express trust has been made. Equity will not blithely permit informal declarations of trust without considering the full factual surrounding circumstances, as shown by Jones v Lock.[16]

Robert Jones lived in Pembroke. He went on a business trip to Birmingham and when he returned, he was told off by his child's nanny for failing to bring a present back for his nine-month old son. His reply was to present the child with a cheque for £900, saying to the nanny: 'Look you here, I give this to baby; it is for himself, and I am going to put it away for him . . .'. Robert's wife then warned him that the child was about to tear the cheque up and his response was to put the cheque in his safe.

The issue for the court to decide was whether Robert's words and actions were enough to declare a trust.

Lord Cranworth LC held that there was no express declaration of trust because he thought that:

> it would be of very dangerous example if loose conversations of this sort, in important transactions of this kind, should have the effect of declarations of trust.[17]

Again, the court looked at the evidence surrounding the actual words used by the alleged settlor. Lord Cranworth LC thought it highly unlikely that Mr Jones would have considered that he had made a once-and-for-all decision to part with such a large amount of money by such a conversation. This crucial fact surrounding the words spoken by Robert showed that a trust had not been declared.

The case also shows that equity will not use a trust as a 'second-best' alternative to save a failed gift. As will be seen in Chapter 7, the general rule is that where a gift fails, a trust cannot step in to rescue it.[18]

Express fixed trusts can be made easily, but the court will look at all of the evidence surrounding the oral declaration to be confident that a trust truly was intended.

The discretionary trust

This is still a type of express trust since it is deliberately created by the settlor. This time, however, the settlor leaves some issues of choice up to the trustees. The settlor may, for example, give the trustees a choice over who should benefit from the trust (within a defined group) and/or to the extent that those whom the trustees choose should benefit. The settlor might prefer to use a discretionary trust if he cannot himself decide who should benefit from a particular group of people.

---

16 Jones v Lock (1865-66) LR 1 Ch App 25.
17 Ibid at 29.
18 Although now see the decision of the Court of Appeal in Pennington v Waine [2002] 1 WLR 2075, which arguably erodes that principle (for a detailed discussion, see Chapter 7).

❖ **EXPLAINING THE LAW**

Scott is feeling generous again and appoints Thomas as his trustee and transfers £1,000 to him to hold on trust for the benefit of those people who live in the same road as Scott. Scott provides that Thomas should use his absolute discretion to choose those people who are to benefit and the amounts by which they are to benefit.

This is again a type of express trust since Scott has deliberately created it. The beneficial interests are not fixed. Instead, Scott has said that Thomas must choose who will benefit from a particular group of people and the extent to which they will benefit. This is a discretionary trust. Problems can arise where the settlor fails to define the group with sufficient precision.[19]

Trustees of a discretionary trust must choose a recipient (or recipients) from the class of people the settlor has defined. The trustees must then consider how much such a recipient should receive from the trust fund.

The rights of people falling into the group as defined by the settlor under a discretionary trust are interesting. They were considered by Walton J in *Vestey v IRC (No. 2)*.[20]

Walton J said that, individually, such potential recipients had no 'relevant right whatsoever' to enjoy any equitable entitlement from the trust. Instead, as a whole, all of the members of the defined group of the trust could join together and collectively enforce a right to ensure the trustees kept to the terms of the trust. The reason for none of the individuals having rights personally under the trust is, of course, because of the very nature of the trust that has been created. The settlor has created a discretionary trust, to benefit a defined group. Any individual within that group may, or may not, eventually be chosen by the trustees to benefit. Until that individual is chosen, he is not a true beneficiary and has no individual rights. Collectively, however, all of those individuals can join together to enforce the trust against the trustees since – by definition – some of them must be chosen from the group. Once an individual is chosen by the trustee to benefit from the trust, he becomes a true beneficiary and only at that point does he have an equitable interest in the trust property. Until that stage, all he has is a hope of being chosen to benefit.[21]

The protective trust

This is our third type of express trust. As its name suggests, it is an example of equity acting paternalistically again. It seeks to protect beneficiaries from themselves. It ensures that the beneficiary can enjoy the trust property for their lifetime, but if the beneficiary infringes the trust during their life, it is converted into a discretionary trust.[22] This can be shown by an example.

---

19 See Chapter 5 Certainty of Object.
20 *Vestey v IRC (No. 2)* [1979] Ch 198.
21 *Re Munro's Settlement Trusts* [1963] 1 WLR 145 at 149 per Wilberforce J.
22 Trustee Act 1925, s 33.

❖ **EXPLAINING THE LAW**

Scott transfers a house to Thomas, his trustee, to hold on protective trust for Ulrika. Scott is concerned that Ulrika has an alcohol dependency which is out of control, but he wants Ulrika to have a home in which to live. Consequently, Scott makes the trust protective by providing that if Ulrika does not seek treatment for alcoholism, the trust will come to an end and will be replaced with a discretionary trust in favour of other people whom Scott defines.

This trust should give Ulrika the incentive to control her alcohol habit by providing that the trust in her favour will end should she continue to consume it to extremes.

Section 33 of the Trustee Act 1925 provides that if the protective trust comes to an end during the original beneficiary's lifetime, the income from the trust will be held on trust for the original beneficiary, their spouse/civil partner, or their issue as the trustees decide. The trustees have discretion to choose who will benefit from the trust if the original beneficiary infringes its terms. Hopefully, it is that sanction that will ensure the original beneficiary adheres to the terms of the protective trust.

Protective trusts are, at first glance, ideal for avoiding bankruptcy. In an ideal world, a settlor might wish to settle property on trust for himself as a beneficiary, but provide that if he goes bankrupt, a discretionary trust will take its place and the equitable interest in the property will pass to others. Such protective trusts are difficult to create nowadays due to legislation which seeks to protect creditors and disallow trusts to be created which seek to put assets beyond their reach.[23]

In reality, protective trusts are used rarely, not only due to anti-avoidance insolvency legislation, but also because it is hard to prevent an adult beneficiary from claiming an absolute interest in the trust property. The basic rule is that adult beneficiaries have a right to terminate the trust and enjoy the absolute interest in the property themselves.[24] If, in the example above, Ulrika and the other beneficiaries joined together, they would stand a good chance of terminating the trust. We return to this theme in Chapter 10.

Implied trusts

All implied trusts are so called because they are implied by equity into particular situations. They are not expressly created by the settlor. They fill gaps.

Implied trusts are a major topic in their own right and the reader is referred to Chapter 3 for a full discussion.

As Figure 2.4 illustrates, there are two types of implied trust: the resulting trust and the constructive trust.

The resulting trust

This type of trust may occur on either one of two occasions:

(a)   when a gift is made by one person to another; or
(b)   when the entire equitable interest has not been used up.

---

23 See, for example, Insolvency Act 1986, s 423. Creating a protective trust for your own benefit was disallowed much earlier in *Re Burroughs-Fowler* [1916] 2 Ch 251.
24 This is known as the rule in *Saunders v Vautier* (1841) 4 Beav 115; 49 ER 282. See Chapter 10.

(i) when a gift is made by one person to another

In life, we often make gifts to other people. On occasions, though, equity takes a cynical and perhaps protectionist view of such gifts. Equity says that the equitable interest should remain with the giver (the 'donor'). To achieve this result, equity implies a resulting trust into the situation.

❖ APPLYING THE LAW

Re Northall (Dec'd)[25]

This case involved Mrs Northall and her family. In December 2006, she sold her house for nearly £55,000. The house was registered in her name together with Dennis, one of her six sons, as he helped her buy the property. When it was sold, the problem that she had was that she did not have a bank account in which to pay the cheque for the sale proceeds. Another one of her sons, Christopher, opened a joint account in his name and Mrs Northall. The money was paid into it.

Mrs Northall died on 23 January 2007. Between the time the account was opened and her death, Christopher had withdrawn over £28,600 from the account. The day after his mother died, Christopher transferred the remaining money in the account into his own personal bank account.

Action was taken by two of the other siblings against Christopher. His defence was that his mother had told him that she wanted to use the sale proceeds as she desired and that anything left over was to go to him. He claimed that she was giving him the remaining money in the account.

David Richards J held that there was, on the facts, no evidence that Mrs Northall had wanted to make a gift of any of the money to Christopher. Rather, the evidence pointed to the conclusion that she wanted to spend the money herself. She had only put the money into a joint bank account with Christopher for administrative convenience, not because she wanted to give half of her money away to him.

A resulting trust was implied by equity. The presumption to be applied here was that Mrs Northall's actions of putting the money into her name and her son's should not be assumed to be giving the money away. Equity could act paternalistically and protect Mrs Northall from losing all control of her money. The common law might recognise the transfer of ownership of the legal title in the money but equity would not. Equity would see the money as still truly belonging to Mrs Northall.

The case is a good example of equity acting according to good conscience. Mrs Northall was a frail woman whom equity would protect. Christopher was ordered by the court to account for the money he had taken from the account, except for some small amounts he was able to prove were withdrawn on his mother's instructions.

---

25 *Re Northall (Dec'd)* [2010] EWHC 1448 (Ch).

Equity says that even though the legal interest in the gift has been transferred to the recipient, the person giving the gift did not really intend to give their interest away.

(ii) when the entire equitable interest has not been used up

A further equitable principle, but which is perhaps not so settled as to be a maxim, is that equity abhors a vacuum. In other words, equity does not like gaps. As we have mentioned, equity fills gaps with implied trusts and arguably the best example of this occurring is this second species of resulting trust.

If a party successfully shows that they have given property away but that they have not disposed of the entire equitable interest, there is a gap which equity fills by implying a resulting trust.

This was shown on the facts of *Vandervell v IRC*.[26] Mr Vandervell wished to benefit the Royal College of Surgeons and, to do so, he instructed his trustee to transfer his interest in certain shares to the Royal College. An option was retained for the trustee to repurchase the shares from the Royal College at some future point. It was the presence of this option that led the House of Lords to decide that Mr Vandervell had not successfully divested himself of his entire equitable interest in his shares. This meant that he had not successfully transferred any of his equitable interest in the shares to the Royal College. A gap in the equitable ownership resulted: the trustee clearly held the legal title, but the Royal College had never enjoyed the equitable interest. The only logical conclusion was that the trustee held the equitable interest for Mr Vandervell on a resulting trust. The resulting trust could fill in the gap of the equitable ownership.

We return to this in greater depth in Chapter 3.

The constructive trust

The constructive trust is the second type of trust that equity implies.

The constructive trust again reflects the origins of equity in terms of its ideals of fairness and doing what is right according to good conscience. The constructive trust applies when it would be unconscionable to permit a person to claim an equitable interest in property which really belongs to another party.

❖ EXPLAINING THE LAW

Profits made by trustees and other parties where there is a relationship of trust and confidence has been a fruitful area for the use of constructive trusts over the years.

The fundamental idea is that if you are in a relationship of trust and confidence with another person, you should not be allowed to make any profit from that relationship in a secretive manner.[27] The relationship between trustee and beneficiary is one of trust and confidence.

The relationship between a solicitor and a client is also one where trust and confidence is implied. So if, in my former life when I was a solicitor in private practice, I decided to make money for myself by gambling my clients' money that they gave me to purchase their

---

26 *Vandervell v IRC* [1967] 2 AC 291. This case is considered in greater depth in Chapter 3 at pp 61/64.
27 *Keech v Sandford* (1726) 2 Eq Ab 741; 25 ER 223.

house or office, I would have had to account to my clients for any proceeds (or more likely, losses) that I made. Equity would not have allowed me to keep any secret profit that I made as a result. It would have imposed a constructive trust on me and I would have been a constructive trustee of the money with my clients having the equitable interest in it. With my clients as the equitable owners of the money, they would have been able to compel me to hand the money over to them.

Equity would have imposed a constructive trust on me because it would have been unconscionable for me to retain the proceeds of the winnings as those winnings really belonged to my clients. I would not have made the winnings unless I had used my clients' money to do so.

But, as will be seen in Chapter 3, bad faith on the trustee's part is not needed for a constructive trust to be imposed upon him. It is the fact that the trustee has made a gain (and such gain can be made entirely honestly) that means he is made a constructive trustee of the gain.

What Type of Property Can Be Left on Trust?

The fundamental principle is that any type of property can be left on trust. 'Property' can be split into two different broad categories:

(a)   real property which is sometimes shortened to 'realty'. This is essentially freehold land. The ability to leave realty by trust was a device which has existed since the Middle Ages; and

(b)   personal property, which is sometimes shortened to 'personalty'. This encompasses every other type of property. For instance, it therefore includes chattels and goods. These are called 'choses in possession' – they are things that a person possesses which are tangible, such as a car or a vase.

Personalty also includes leasehold land and choses in action. Choses in action are rights that are not tangible such as bank accounts or shares in a company. They are called 'choses in action' because they are rights which depend on you taking action should you wish to enforce them.

❖ EXPLAINING THE LAW

Think about your own bank account. If you walk into the local branch of your bank, you cannot ask to see your own personal bank account because it does not exist in a physical sense. It would be impractical to expect a bank to keep everyone's account physically in their own local branch – the banks would need far larger buildings to do so. Instead, the amount in your account is a debt that the bank owes to you. You have a right to demand the balance from your bank, by legal action if necessary.

A similar concept is applied to company shares. If you own shares in a company such as British Gas plc, you cannot physically see those shares. You may have a share certificate, but that is just a formal piece of paper stating how many shares you own. You do not

> physically possess the actual shares in the company. Rather, you have a right against the company for a sum of money to the amount of shares that you own. Your right is a chose in action as it depends on you taking action to obtain anything from it.

Trusts can be created of both realty and personalty and, of course, a mixture of the two.

The Express Trust

When can express trusts be created?

There are two occasions on which a settlor can deliberately create a trust:

(a) *During his lifetime.* A trust created by the settlor to take effect whilst he is alive is also known by its Latin name as being created *inter vivos*; and

(b) *Upon his death.* A trust created by the settlor to take effect on his death is one that the settlor creates in his will or, if he fails to make a will, by the laws of intestacy.

Trusts created during the settlor's lifetime can, if they consist just of personalty, be made entirely orally. Best practice must be for the settlor to write down the terms of the trust so that each party can be sure that a trust has been created and the nature of its terms.

Trusts of land expressly created by the settlor during their lifetime must be evidenced in writing and signed by some person who is able to declare the trust.[28] Any trust expressly created by the settlor's will, whether consisting of realty, personalty or both, must comply with the formal requirements set out in section 9 of the Wills Act 1837. Such trusts created by will are subject to far more formal requirements than those created during the settlor's lifetime, simply because they are contained in a will and there is no opportunity to question the settlor about such trusts when they take effect, since they take effect on the settlor's death.

Section 9 of the Wills Act 1837 provides that the will containing the trust must be:

(a) in writing;

(b) signed by the settlor or some other person at his direction and in his presence;

(c) witnessed by at least two witnesses present at the same time; and

(d) each witness must then either sign the will or acknowledge his signature in the settlor's presence.

It's not all that straightforward: the different types of equitable interest

Trusts exist because equity recognises the concept that the legal and equitable interests in property can be split and owned by different people at the same time. There can, of course, be more than one beneficiary enjoying the ownership of the equitable interest. If there are two or more beneficiaries, their interests should be set out by the settlor. The settlor has a number of different options from which he can choose and these are set out below.

---

28 Law of Property Act 1925, s 53(1)(b).

First, the beneficiary's interest can be either in possession or in remainder. If the former, the beneficiary will be able to enjoy the trust property straightaway; if the latter, he must wait for a current beneficiary's interest to end before he can enjoy it.

Second, the beneficial interest can be either vested or contingent. This is all about whether the beneficiary must fulfil any condition before he enjoys the trust property. If he has no condition to fulfil, his interest is vested; if he must meet a condition, he enjoys a contingent interest. As soon as any condition is met, the beneficiary's interest changes from vested to contingent.

Lastly, the beneficiary can enjoy an absolute or limited interest. An absolute interest means the beneficiary can enjoy the capital of the trust property and therefore it is his to do with as he wishes. A limited interest is more restrictive and means the beneficiary usually enjoys the interest for his lifetime only. He cannot spend the capital of the trust property and it is invested on his behalf for him to enjoy the products of that investment instead.

The settlor must choose one option from each of the three discussed when creating the trust. The following example shows an illustration of a settlor creating a trust having chosen from the options discussed.

❖ EXPLAINING THE LAW

Scott settles £1,000 on trust. He appoints Thomas as his trustee and instructs Thomas to hold the money on trust for:

(a) Ulrika for her lifetime, provided she qualifies as a solicitor but if not or thereafter, as the case may be; or
(b) Vikas absolutely.

This example shows that Ulrika's equitable interest has the following characteristics:

(a) it is in possession, because she is the first beneficiary who can benefit from the trust property and she has no other beneficiary whose interest is before hers;
(b) it is a contingent interest because to be entitled to any of the trust property, she must qualify as a solicitor. If she does not qualify as a solicitor, then she is not entitled to benefit; and
(c) it is a limited interest because she can only enjoy the trust property for her lifetime. This means she can only have the income from the £1,000 and cannot generally have access to the capital sum itself.

Vikas' interest has the following characteristics:

(a) it is in remainder, because the interest has a prior one before it (Ulrika's). Only when Ulrika has died or fails to become a solicitor is Vikas entitled to the trust property;
(b) it is a vested interest, because there is no condition that Vikas must fulfil before he becomes entitled to the trust property; and
(c) it is an absolute interest because it is not limited in any way. This means that, when he becomes entitled to the interest, he will have full access to the trust property and may do with it as he wishes.

What are the uses of express trusts?

Trusts are deliberately created nowadays for a variety of purposes. Significant practical uses of trusts include:

- houses;
- pensions;
- charities; and
- taxation avoidance.

Houses

Where more than one person owns their home, they are obliged to hold it under a trust.[29] Section 36(2) of the Law of Property Act 1925 provides that two or more people who own the house must own the legal estate as joint tenants. The law, this time in the form of a statute, is typically inflexible.

Equity is more flexible. Equity enables the co-owners of the property to have a choice. The co-owners can hold the equitable interest in the property either as joint tenants or as tenants in common. As has been seen,[30] holding the property as tenants in common is the more flexible method of ownership of the two, since the parties are then free to leave their share to whomsoever they choose in their will. Equity permits the maximum possible choice for co-owners to decide the proportions in which they each own the property. Their choice should be recorded on the purchase deed.[31]

If co-owners do not record their main choice as to whether to hold the property in equity as joint tenants or tenants in common, then equity will, *prima facie*, follow the law in holding that the parties hold the equitable interest as joint tenants. Equity will, however, depart from this presumption in a number of situations. The most common are:

(a) if the parties pay unequal contributions to the purchase of the property. If two people make unequal contributions to the purchase of the home, then the presumption must be that they intended their equitable interests to reflect those unequal contributions;

(b) if the parties hold the property not as a family home but as a business. Equity presumes that business parties prefer a more commercial relationship and would not want their shares to pass automatically to their business partner upon their death; or

(c) if there are any words which go against the idea that the parties intended to own the property as joint tenants in the purchase deed. These are known as 'words of severance'.

Pensions

Often people save for their retirements by paying into a pension scheme. There are a number of different schemes available, from pension schemes which are entirely dependent on the individual's contributions to those entirely provided by a person's employer as a perk of the job. Lots of people who are employed enjoy a pension which is perhaps a mixture of the two – so the individual will make contributions to it from their monthly salary but the employer will also make payments to it.

---

29 Law of Property Act 1925, s 34.
30 See Chapter 1, p 20.
31 Usually on Land Registry form TR1.

Pensions are a modern use of the trust in practice. In straightforward terms, the money which is paid into each scheme is transferred to trustees. Those pension trustees then hold the money on trust for the individual who benefits from the pension. When an individual retires and reaches the age prescribed by the scheme, they can start to claim the benefits from the trust. In reality, nowadays, pension administration is big business.

❖ **EXPLAINING THE LAW**

Large companies, such as Standard Life plc, act as pension trustees and administer pension funds. They do this by endeavouring to grow pension funds by investing them in a wide range of opportunities which will hopefully secure growth of funds for the beneficiaries. That is why often nowadays you see business parks with words akin to 'a Standard Life investment' at the foot of the entrance sign. Have a look next time you go past a business park to see evidence of trusts in action.

Pensions are types of express trusts, since they are deliberately created by the individual or their employer. Schemes provided by employers are known as occupational pension schemes. These schemes are also types of discretionary trusts. The amount the individual will benefit from in retirement depends on a number of variables, such as how many other beneficiaries there are in the pension scheme and how successfully the money that has been paid in over the years has been invested. People join and leave pension schemes all the time as, for example, they change employers. It is consequently not practicable to make use of the express fixed trust as far as pensions are concerned. There has to be flexibility built into the scheme for when new people join it. Remember that a fixed express trust dictates that trustees must hold property on trust for clear, fixed beneficiaries. Whilst a discretionary trust must still define its beneficiaries clearly, it is the mechanism used for typical occupational pension schemes because it enables beneficiaries to be defined by reference to a group.[32] As more people join the group, they can be included in the beneficiaries who will be entitled to benefit from the scheme because they form part of a group.

There are restrictions on who can be a trustee for an employer-funded scheme. The Pensions Act 2004 seeks to protect such schemes by providing that at least one-third of the trustees of the scheme are nominated by the beneficiaries.[33] Such nominated trustees must come from either the current members of the scheme who are still making payments into the scheme or those who have retired.[34] Once appointed, a member-nominated trustee can only be removed if all of the other trustees agree.[35]

Charities

Charities have been in existence since at least the time of Elizabeth I.[36] Some of the main charities in England and Wales are very well known – charities such as the Royal Society

---

32 See Chapter 5 for a detailed discussion on the requirements of certainty of object.
33 Pensions Act 2004, s 241(1).
34 Ibid, s 241(2).
35 Ibid, s 241(6).
36 The Preamble to the Statute of Charitable Uses 1601 is arguably the starting point of a discussion of the modern law of charities.

for the Prevention of Cruelty to Animals (RSPCA) and Barnardo's are examples of national charities. The law of charities is an area of law in its own right,[37] but for now, we can see that they are examples of the use of the trust, albeit a use of the trust with slight twists to it.

Property is held by charitable trustees. There is no maximum number of charitable trustees who can hold land,[38] unlike non-charitable trustees.[39] Charities are also an exception to the typical arrangements of trusts where there is a settlor, a trustee and a beneficiary. A settlor will still have originally created the charitable trust and trustees still hold the property on trust, but unusually in English law, there does not have to be any human beneficiary for the trust to be valid. Instead, it is permissible (and, indeed, entirely usual) to leave property on trust for a charitable purpose. These purposes are now set out in the Charities Act 2011,[40] but the list in that Act is not exhaustive since all charitable purposes decided as charitable before the Act came into force will continue to be charitable.[41]

Taxation avoidance

The probable first use of the trust was as a means of avoiding taxation. That use remains today as one of the main uses of a trust. Taxation is a highly complex subject with volumes of books devoted to it so some very introductory principles only can be given here.

Tax is generally payable by the person in whose hands money is made. For example, income tax is payable on income that you receive. Income may be generated through different methods – for instance, as a result of being employed, as a result of dividend payments received on shares that you own or perhaps you receive rent from property that you let out to tenants. The income that you receive is taxed in bands, with a certain amount of money earned being free of tax and the remainder being charged at different rates.

> ❖ **EXPLAINING THE LAW**
>
> In the tax year 2012–2013, the amount of income those aged under 65 can earn before tax is charged is £8,105. After that, income tax is payable at the basic rate of 20 per cent for money earned between £0 and £34,370 and at the higher rate of 40 per cent for money earned between £34,371 and £150,000. Those earning above £150,001 must pay income tax at the additional rate of 50 per cent.

As you can see from the above example, the more income you have, the more income tax you pay.

A trust may help you to minimise those tax charges, as illustrated in the following example.

---

37 See Chapter 15.
38 Trustee Act 1925, s 34(3).
39 Where the maximum number is four: Trustee Act 1925, s 34(2).
40 Charities Act 2011, s 3(1).
41 Ibid, s 3(1)(m).

❖ **EXPLAINING THE LAW**

Suppose Scott owns several large houses that he rents out. He also has a significant shareholding in a private company that is doing very well. His income through employment is sufficient to mean that he is already a higher rate taxpayer. He wishes to minimise his tax liabilities if possible.

What he could do is set up a trust and settle the houses and shares on trustees for, say, the benefit of his children. His children are under 18 so are not taxpayers. That means that any income from the houses and shares are treated as theirs since income tax is payable by the recipients of the money.

What that means is that the taxation liabilities are minimised. The disadvantage for him is that he cannot claim interests in the houses and shares once he has placed them on trust. If he continues to enjoy interests in them, then he will be taxed accordingly.[42]

A word of warning about using a trust to minimise tax. It is lawful to seek to minimise tax liabilities by proactively seeking to set your affairs in order so that your charges to tax are reduced. You cannot seek to retrospectively re-order your affairs once the tax is due, however. That is called tax evasion and is something upon which HM Revenue & Customs is not too keen!

A related concept to the trust is the power of appointment.

Powers of Appointment

The central feature of a trust is that it is an obligation. It obliges a trustee to hold property on trust for a beneficiary. Naturally, depending on the terms of the trust, the trustee may have some room for manoeuvre when managing the trust or even deciding who will benefit. The Trustee Act 2000 significantly enlarged trustees' decision-making powers of investment[43] and a trustee can go so far as to be able to choose the beneficiaries in a discretionary trust.[44] In the end, though, the trustee has no choice that he must hold property on trust and someone or something, in the case of a trust for a purpose,[45] must benefit from the trust.

A power of appointment is fundamentally different from a trust. A power of appointment gives the trustee the ability to choose whether someone else will benefit from it. The trustee is not obliged to ensure that someone will benefit.

---

42 *Vandervell v IRC* [1967] 2 AC 291.
43 Trustee Act 2000, s 3 and see Chapter 9.
44 Above, pp 33–34.
45 See Chapters 6 and 15.

Glossary

The terminology changes a little for powers of appointment as opposed to trusts:

Trust

Settlor ⟶ Trustee ⟶ Beneficiary

(Creator) (Manager) (Recipient)

Power of appointment

Donor ⟶ Donee ⟶ Object

(Creator) (Manager) (Potential Recipient)

The Potential Recipient under a power of appointment will only become an object if chosen to benefit by the donee.

Trust or power of appointment?

In drafting terms, there is often a thin line between creating a trust, or creating a power of appointment. Tomlin J in *Re Combe*[46] said that, in cases of difficulty in deciding whether a provision was a trust or a power of appointment, the matter had to be resolved in accordance with the 'ordinary principles of construction'.[47] That would involve giving the language used in the drafting its ordinary and natural meaning.

This is easier said than done, though, as is shown by comparing two cases which featured provisions which, at first glance, look very similar in terms of their actual wording.

In *Re Sayer*,[48] the governing director of Sayers (Confectioners) Ltd wished to provide 'grants allowances annuities or payments' for a group of people which included his employees, ex-employees or their dependants. A committee was 'empowered at its discretion' to administer payments to anyone who fell within that group. Upjohn J held that the ability of the committee to distribute the money took the form of a power. By the wording used, the committee had the right, but not the obligation, to benefit individuals.

Similar wording of a clause can have a different result, as illustrated by *Re Saxone Shoe Co Ltd's Trust Deed*.[49] The case again concerned a fund which was to provide benefits for employees, ex-employees or their dependants. Clause 6 of the deed provided that the fund and income from it 'shall in the discretion of the directors be applicable for' such people. The question again arose as to whether this wording made the directors subject to a power or whether they were under an obligation to distribute the fund in the form of a trust.

This time, the High Court's decision was that a trust had been created. Again, the decision turned upon the actual words used, as had been suggested in *Re Combe*. Cross J believed[50] that the words 'shall be applicable', together with other provisions of the deed setting up the fund, pointed towards an obligation being imposed upon the directors of the company.

---

46 *Re Combe* [1925] Ch 210.
47 Ibid at 218.
48 *Re Sayer* [1957] Ch 423.
49 *Re Saxone Shoe Co Ltd's Trust Deed* [1962] 1 WLR 943.
50 Ibid at 951.

The difficulty is that there is not usually a nice, neat distinction between trusts and powers of appointment. The impression given so far is that there is: that there are two distinct types of document that a person might create: one a trust and the other a power of appointment.

Instead, what usually happens is that there is a mixture of the two concepts in the one document. This, in fact, occurred in both *Re Sayer* and *Re Saxone Shoe Co Ltd's Trust Deed*. In both cases, a settlor established an overarching trust which then went on to contain the provisions discussed above. As we have seen, the High Court reached differing results as to whether these internal provisions within the overarching trusts took the form of either a power of appointment or a trust. Which of these two results is reached will depend on the wording used, coupled with the context in which the relevant provision sits in the document.

The distinction over whether there is a power or a trust matters because a power by itself may be exercised fairly freely by the donee. The donee has a lot of discretion and may even choose not to exercise the power at all. These powers of appointment – where the donee has a great discretion as to whether anyone from a class should benefit at all – may be called 'mere' or 'bare' powers.

Key Learning Point

To understand the difference between a power of appointment and a trust, you need to grasp that:

● a power of appointment *may* be exercised by the donee; but
● a trust *must* be executed by the trustee.

The rights of the eventual recipient under a mere power or a trust differ too. Under a mere power, the potential object has no rights over the property itself, since they may or may not be chosen by the donee to benefit from the property. In *Vestey v IRC (No. 2)*,[51] Walton J held that a potential object has three limited rights under a power:

> (i) the right to be considered by the person exercising the power when he comes to exercise it; (ii) the right to prevent certain kinds of conduct on the part of the person so exercising the power – e.g., by distributing part of the assets to not within the class – and (iii) the right to retain any sums properly paid to him by the trustees in exercise of their discretionary powers. But beyond that he has no relevant 'right' of any description . . . .[52]

Megarry V-C summarised the issue succinctly in *Re Hay's Settlement Trusts*[53] when he said:

> The essence of that difference [between a trust and a power of appointment], I think, is that beneficiaries under a trust have rights of enforcement which mere objects of a power lack.[54]

---

51 *Vestey v IRC (No. 2)* [1979] Ch 198.
52 Ibid at 206.
53 *Re Hay's Settlement Trusts* [1982] 1 WLR 202.
54 Ibid at 213–214.

The concept to which Megarry V-C was referring is also known as the beneficiary principle. This is considered in Chapter 6 but, for now, understand that the beneficiary also acts as an enforcer of the trust, ensuring that the trustee honours the terms of the trust. An object of a power has no such comparable role.

What types of powers of appointment can be given to trustees?

A power given to a trustee can either take the form of a mere power or, alternatively, may impose on the trustee some form of obligation. The mere power gives the trustee a wide right of discretion, as occurred in Re Sayer. There the trustees had the ability to make grants to certain people but in the end, it was entirely at their discretion over whether they did so. In contrast, a settlor may give a power to a trustee under which a trustee must exercise his discretion. This type of power was the type given in Re Saxone Shoe Co Ltd's Trust Deed. The trustees still had some discretion – as to who benefited from the trust fund – but fundamentally they had to choose people who would benefit. Such powers are known as 'trust powers' or, in more modern terminology, discretionary trusts.

The court can control the exercise of a trust power by, if necessary, forcing the trustees to exercise it or exercising it in place of the trustees if they fail to do so. All of the beneficiaries can collectively force the trustees to pay the fund to them, provided they are 18 years old or over and have mental capacity. A mere power cannot be controlled by the court in such a manner since the operation of it is at the entire discretion of the donee.[55] Lord Upjohn set out what he described as the 'basic difference' between a mere power and a trust power in Re Gulbenkian's Settlement as follows:

> in the first case [that of a mere power] trustees owe no duty to exercise it and the relevant fund or income falls to be dealt with in accordance with the trusts in default of its exercise, whereas in the second case [that of a trust power] the trustees must exercise the power and in default the court will.[56]

Yet, if a mere power is given to a trustee, the trustee is under more duties than if a power of appointment was simply given to a non-trustee. Trustees are duty bound to act in accordance with their fiduciary duties of trusteeship.[57] Megarry V-C set out some of those obligations in relation to mere powers in Re Hay's Settlement Trusts.[58] He said the trustees had to:

(a)   consider actively whether to exercise the power from time to time;

(b)   exercise the power in a responsible manner by considering the 'range of objects' within the power (in other words, by considering the size of the group that the settlor has defined); and

(c)   consider whether it was appropriate for particular individuals to benefit from the power.

The latter two obligations on trustees arise by virtue of their being trustees and the nature of the office of trusteeship being fiduciary. By contrast, a non-trustee donee of a mere power has a much easier time of it. Such a donee has complete freedom over whether or not even to

---

55   Re Gulbenkian's Settlement [1970] AC 508.
56   Ibid at 525.
57   See Chapter 8.
58   Re Hay's Settlement Trusts [1982] 1 WLR 202 at 209.

exercise the power in favour of a potential beneficiary, let alone be obliged to undertake the activities that Megarry V-C suggests.

Types of powers

Powers which are either of the mere or trust type can be one of three categories:

- general;
- special; or
- intermediate/hybrid.

General powers of appointment

A general power of appointment is the widest one possible. It enables the donee to choose anyone in the world to benefit from the power. As anyone at all can benefit from the power, that means that the donee could conceivably simply choose himself alone! Clearly, that would be akin to the donor just giving the donee the property for his own benefit. Presumably if the donor had intended that course of action all along, he would not have set up a power at all but would simply have given away the property straightforwardly to the donee.

Special powers of appointment

This power of appointment is at the other end of the spectrum to the general power. The special power of appointment is where the donor restricts the donee's choice over who can benefit from the power. The choice is restricted to a particular group.

Intermediate/hybrid power of appointment

This is a combination of the other two types of power. It was described by Harman J in *Re Gestetner's Settlement*[59] as 'something betwixt and between' the other two. Here the donor gives the donee the ability to choose from anyone at all but specifically excludes people if they fall into a particular group.

The facts of *Re Hay's Settlement Trusts*[60] are an example of the intermediate power of appointment. In the case, a settlement was created by Lady Hay for the benefit of such people as the trustees were to decide – in other words, the trustees could choose anyone in the world to benefit. Specifically excluded in the trust deed, however, were Lady Hay herself, her husband and any present or past trustee. These exclusions turned the otherwise general power of appointment into an intermediate one.

Any of these types of powers can be created as mere powers or, if given to trustees, can take the form of trust powers.

The operation of a power

The difficulty that arises is how a donee actually exercises a power. This issue can arise because it is often not clear who the donor actually wants to benefit from the power. The whole purpose of a power is to give the donee some discretion over which members of a group – or class – will benefit. The donor will hopefully have assisted to some extent by creating a general, special or intermediate power, but it is still often unclear how the donee is to decide whether a potential beneficiary actually falls within that class or not.

---

59 *Re Gestetner's Settlement* [1953] Ch 672 at 685.
60 *Re Hay's Settlement Trusts* [1982] 1 WLR 202.

Lord Upjohn laid down guidelines in *Re Gulbenkian's Settlement*.[61] In the case itself, a philanthropist called Calouste Gulbenkian created two trusts, one in 1929 and the other in 1938. In effect, the wording of both trusts was identical. Both trusts sought to leave property on trust for the maintenance and support of a particular class of people: Mr Gulbenkian's son, Nubar, his son's wife and issue (if any) and anyone that Nubar either resided with, or employed, but those who were to benefit were to be at the trustees' discretion. This was a mere power as the trustees were under no duty to exercise it.

The facts are summarised in the diagram at Figure 2.5.

Figure 2.5 The facts of *Re Gulbenkian's Settlement*.

In order that they should even be able to consider exercising the power, the trustees had to know in whose favour the power should be exercised. The question for the House of Lords, therefore, was whether the mere power was valid in the sense of whether the class that was defined was sufficiently certain so that the power could be operated by the trustees knowing which type of people were entitled to benefit.

Lord Upjohn said that the court had to:

(a) try to ascertain the settlor's intention. To do this, the court would start by giving the words used their natural meaning; but

(b) if the words used were not clear, then the court would try to make sense of the settlor's intentions in order to give a reasonable meaning to the language used. The court would use its 'innate common sense'[62] to do so.

The test then to be applied was the following one:

> a mere . . . power of appointment among a class is valid if you can with certainty say whether any given individual is or is not a member of the class; you do not have to be able to ascertain every member of the class.[63]

Key Learning Point

The test enunciated by Lord Upjohn in *Re Gulbenkian's Settlement* is known as the 'individual ascertainability' or 'given postulant' test, since it focuses on the concept of asking whether an individual can fall within the group defined by the settlor.

---

61 *Re Gulbenkian's Settlement* [1970] AC 508.
62 Ibid at 522.
63 Ibid at 521.

In the case of a power to benefit those from a class, therefore, the donees' job was to focus on the individual and ask if it is possible to say that, hypothetically, a person could be a member of the class as defined by the donor. If the answer to that is a definitive 'yes' or 'no', the given postulant test is fulfilled and there is sufficient certainty in the description of the class as defined by the settlor. The power is valid. If, on the other hand, it is impossible to say that any one person is definitely in the class or not because the wording of the class by the settlor is too vague, then the defined class will not pass the given postulant test. In this case, the class will not be sufficiently certain and the power will be void. The given postulant test demands a concrete answer as to whether any person can or cannot definitely fall within the class and if there is any doubt as to whether one person could or could not, the class fails and the power is void.

The focus is on the individual. The donee does not have to draw up a complete list of all those people who might be entitled to benefit from the trust.[64] Donees do not have to 'worry their heads to survey the world from China to Peru, when there are perfectly good objects of the class in England'[65] in order to draw up a definitive and complete list of beneficiaries of the power. There is no point in them doing this, since each potential beneficiary is almost certainly not eventually going to benefit from the power in any event. All the donee has to do is to consider that the class of people, as defined by the settlor, is reasonably certain in terms of saying that a given person definitely can or cannot fall within the class.

Some classes will usually be regarded as too uncertain in their definition to be capable of being enforced. Lord Upjohn gave the example of a donor leaving property to be divided equally amongst a class being defined as 'my old friends'.[66] Such a class is uncertain because it is normally impossible to say who is a friend of somebody else's. For instance, you might say that someone is definitely your friend and that another person definitely is not. You probably know a number of people whom you regard neutrally – they are neither your friends nor 'non-friends'. They may be simply people you have met and whom you get along with quite well. As there are such people who it is impossible to say whether they are your friends or not, a class of 'my old friends' must be, by definition, uncertain.

Yet a class of 'friends' was held to be sufficiently certain in Re Barlow's Will Trust.[67]

Helen Barlow died in 1975, leaving a valuable collection of paintings. In clause 5(a) of her will, she provided that her 'friends' could purchase these paintings at a price that was lower than the present valuation. The issue was whether this clause was valid as it was argued that 'friends' had previously been held to be an uncertain concept.

Browne-Wilkinson J held that, in this situation, 'friends' was conceptually uncertain but that the dispositions did not fail because of this. The reason was because the case did not revolve around one gift to a group of people that either stood or failed in its entirety. Instead, the option to purchase the paintings at a discounted price represented a series of gifts to those people who were friends of the testatrix. It was not relevant to try to ascertain whether one class of people that could be defined as 'friends' of Ms Barlow was certain, since she had never intended to leave the paintings simply to one class of people. Instead, she wanted her friends to benefit on an individual basis, not on the basis that they formed one class for the purpose of taking one gift.

Whilst not wishing to lay down any hard rules, Browne-Wilkinson J gave some guidance[68] as to when a person could be seen to be a 'friend' of another. He described the following as the 'minimum requirements':

---

64 Harman J in Re Gestetner's Settlement [1953] Ch 672 at 684.
65 Ibid at 688–89.
66 Re Gulbenkian's Settlement [1970] AC 508 at 524.
67 Re Barlow's Will Trust [1979] 1 WLR 278.
68 Ibid at 282.

(a) a long-standing relationship was needed;

(b) the relationship had to be social, as opposed to professional; and

(c) the two parties must have met 'frequently' when circumstances permitted.

This case is, however, deciding a different issue from that in *Re Gulbenkian's Settlement*, as Browne-Wilkinson J was at pains to justify. It was not necessary to identify all the members of the class in this case since the gift was never intended to go to all members of the class. Instead, the case decided that a gift to 'friends' could be valid, but only where a series of gifts was left to a series of friends.

❖ ANALYSING THE LAW

Has the concept of 'friend' changed since 1979? In an age of amassing 'friends' through social networking sites would someone who you have never met, but who you contact frequently online, fall within the category of friends in a *Re Barlow*-type situation?

Would these online friends meet Browne-Wilkinson J's requirement that there should be a long-standing relationship? Would regular correspondence through social networking sites on a regular basis amount to meeting frequently?

Browne-Wilkinson J also suggested that the relationship needs to be a social rather than professional one. However, nowadays much more socialising goes on with work colleagues and even bosses – would people who you have got to know through work but who are now friends be excluded? The obiter comments of Browne-Wilkinson J about "minimum requirements" are unlikely to be seen as being set in stone. If a court were faced with a *Re Barlow*-style situation in the future it may well take a much more modern approach to the concept of friend.

The operation of trust powers is considered in Chapter 5, under its more modern name of 'Discretionary Trusts'.

Points to Review

We have seen:

- how the trust grew up from the Middle Ages;
- the fact that there are different types of trust, of both express and implied varieties. Express trusts are deliberately created by the settlor. Implied trusts are not so deliberately created but exist to fill gaps in the equitable ownership of property;
- how express trusts are created and used today; and
- how powers of appointment, whilst outwardly a similar concept to a trust, are actually different from the trust.

Making connections

Before you move on, you will benefit from having a good understanding of this chapter. It is essential that you understand the basics of trusts and powers, since these form the foundations upon which the main building blocks of trusts law are constructed. So, please, take a minute now to ask yourself whether you really grasp the material on the different types of trust that can be created, the tri-partite arrangement typically involved in creating a trust and the subtleties of powers of appointment.

If you do not grasp that material in particular, make sure you go back through this chapter and re-read it. The different types of implied trust are examined in greater depth in the next chapter. You need to know the people who are involved in the typical trust arrangement as this forms the basis of the material in Chapters 4 to 7. Understanding powers of appointment underpins the operation of the discretionary trust, which is examined in Chapter 5.

Useful Things to Read

A number of additional things to read are set out below, which you may wish to read to gain additional insights into the areas considered in this chapter.

Secondary sources

J H Baker *An Introduction to English Legal History* (4th edn, Butterworths Lexis-Nexis, 2002) chs 13 and 14. This contains a good account of the nature of both feudal tenure and the concept of the original 'use', the predecessor to the trust.

Roy T Bartlett, 'When is a "trust" not a trust? The National Health Service Trust' (1996) Conv May-June 186–192. This article considers a contemporary use of the trust by the NHS and asks whether it can truly be considered a trust under equity's jurisdiction or whether it is an example of a corporate body.

David Hayton, 'Pension trusts and traditional trusts: drastically different species of trusts' (2005) Conv May/Jun 229–246. This explores pension trusts in more detail than this chapter and compares the differing obligations on trustees of such trusts with the obligations on trustees of traditional family trusts. For an update on the principle of *Re Hastings-Bass*, please see Chapter 12.

A Hudson, *Equity & Trusts* (7th edn, Routledge-Cavendish, 2012) ch 2.

Maurizio Lupoi, 'Trust and confidence' (2009) LQR 125 (Apr) 253–287. This article looks at the history of trusts in England and argues that European learning played an important role in the development of the trust.

J A McGhee, *Snell's Equity* (32nd edn, Sweet & Maxwell, 2010) chs 9, 19 and 20. This considers the issues raised here from a practitioner's viewpoint.

M Macnair, 'Equity and conscience' (2007) OJLS 27(4) 659–681. This article considers the role of conscience in the development of equity from the fifteenth to the eighteenth centuries.

Mohamed Ramjohn, *Text, Cases & Materials on Equity and Trusts* (4th edn, Routledge-Cavendish, 2008) ch 1.

Chapter 3

Implied Trusts

Chapter Contents

Having introduced implied trusts in Chapter 2, it is important that you understand the nature and workings of such trusts before your study of the overall law of trusts can continue in more detail. Implied trusts are gap-fillers and will arise when there is no valid express trust to regulate the relationship between the settlor, trustee and beneficiary.

As You Read

In this chapter, the types and characteristics of implied trusts are addressed. Accordingly, as you read, you should look out for the following issues:

- what implied trusts are;
- the resulting trust: the occasions on which this type of trust can arise, how it operates and what its effect is; and
- the constructive trust: again, when it arises, its effects and the issue of whether it can be taken forward outside its traditional remit into some sort of general remedial device.

The Background to Implied Trusts

The requirement of form

It is probably fair to say that usually trusts created under English law are done so deliberately. As was shown in Chapter 2,[1] most trusts are formed involving three parties:

(a) the settlor, who creates the trust;

(b) the trustee, who holds the legal interest in the trust property and who administers the trust; and

(c) the beneficiary, who holds the equitable interest in the trust property, who enjoys the trust but who also acts as an 'enforcer' of the trust, ensuring that the trustee honours the terms of the trust.[2]

Most trusts that are formed deliberately – or expressly – do not have to comply with any requirements as to form. That means that they can, for the most part, be created entirely orally. For example, a settlor can simply instruct a trustee to hold property for a beneficiary's benefit. The hallmark of such express trusts is that they are created by the settlor's intention.

A major exception to this principle exists, however, for trusts which have land as their subject matter. All trusts which are expressly created and have land as all, or part, of their subject matter are caught by a statutory provision which means that they must be evidenced in writing. There is no option for settlors to circumvent this requirement,[3] for the wording of s 53(1)(b) of the Law of Property Act 1925 is prescriptive. It provides:

> a declaration of trust respecting any land or any interest therein must be manifested and proved by some writing signed by some person who is able to declare such trust or by his will. . . .

---

1 See Figure 2.1 at p 27.
2 The latter point is known as the 'beneficiary principle' and is considered in depth in Chapter 6.
3 Unless the trustee commits fraud by denying the existence of the trust, when the rule in *Rochefoucauld v Boustead* [1897] 1 Ch 196 will apply (see Chapter 4 at p 97).

For most legal rules there are exceptions and the provision in s 53(1)(b) follows that tradition. The exception is contained in the next sub-section, which provides that '[t]his section does not affect the creation or operation of resulting, implied or constructive trusts'.[4]

Section 53(2) of the Law of Property Act 1925 consequently permits all implied trusts to be created entirely orally, even where their subject matter is land. Implied trusts can, therefore, be created by the parties quite informally and flexibly. As we shall see in this chapter, though, that is not necessarily the case and the courts have restricted the growth of what appears to be, at first glance, a highly malleable form of trust.

Implied Trusts – A Definition

If express trusts are created by the deliberate intention of the settlor, implied trusts are generally not. Instead, they arise by operation of law: through equity deciding that a trust should apply to a particular situation. There are two main types of implied trust: the resulting trust and the constructive trust.

The resulting trust

The name 'resulting' is derived from the Latin word *resalire* which means 'to jump back'. This means that if a resulting trust exists, the equitable interest jumps back to the settlor instead of remaining permanently with a different beneficiary. The consequence is the settlor wears two hats – one as settlor and the second as beneficiary.

Resulting trusts are said to arise in one of two circumstances. These two circumstances were set out by Lord Browne-Wilkinson in *Westdeutsche Landesbank Girozentrale v Islington LBC*.[5]

He explained that a resulting trust would arise in the first case ('Category A'):

> where A makes a voluntary payment to B or pays (wholly or in part) for the purchase of property which is vested either in B alone or in the joint names of A and B . . .[6]

There are, in fact, three separate situations occurring in Lord Browne-Wilkinson's first example. For clarity, they are set out in Figure 3.1.

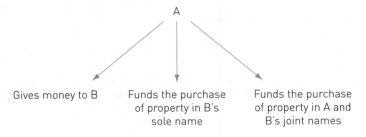

Figure 3.1 Lord Browne-Wilkinson's first resulting trust.

---

4   Law of Property Act 1925, s 53(2).
5   *Westdeutsche Landesbank Girozentrale v Islington LBC* [1996] AC 669.
6   Ibid at 708.

In all of these instances, there is a presumption that a resulting trust will arise of the equitable interest in the property in A's favour.

This means that equity will presume that A did not really intend to make some sort of gift to B, but instead really wanted to keep hold of the property for himself. Equity takes a cynical view of each of these transactions. Equity cannot quite believe that, in these situations, A would deliberately wish to give their money away to B. Equity acts in a paternalistic, protective manner for A's benefit.

Before we get too carried away and assume that equity will never allow one person to give something to another, as Lord Browne-Wilkinson stressed in the case, it is only a presumption that equity makes in such transactions. This presumption can be overturned − or rebutted − by, for example, evidence that A really did wish to transfer property to B. In *Vandervell v IRC*,[7] Lord Upjohn emphasised that the presumption of a resulting trust in these cases was 'no more than a long stop to provide the answer when the relevant facts and circumstances fail to yield a solution'.[8]

The second situation ('Category B') in which Lord Browne-Wilkinson said that a resulting trust would arise was '[w]here A transfers property to B *on express trusts*, but the trusts declared do not exhaust the whole beneficial interest . . .'[9]

This essentially arises where A has made a mistake in creating an express trust. Instead of establishing a trust of the entire equitable interest in the property, A has created a trust of part only of the equitable interest. Since equity abhors a vacuum, the remaining part of the property cannot exist in limbo. The device of the resulting trust is used to fill in that gap and the entire equitable interest will be held on resulting trust for the settlor.[10]

Divergence of views of the basis of a resulting trust

Aside from Lord Browne-Wilkinson's belief that a resulting trust arises from the parties' intentions, there have been other views expressed as to the basis of such trusts. Megarry J in *Re Vandervell's Trusts* (No. 2)[11] thought that the first type of resulting trust arose by what were presumed to be the intentions of the settlor. Such resulting trusts could be categorised as 'presumed resulting trusts'.[12] The second type, in his view, arose automatically by operation of law. His view was that any express trust which accidentally failed to dispose of the entire equitable interest in property would not contain evidence of the settlor's intentions as to what should occur to the remaining non-disposed part of the equitable interest. He labelled the second type of resulting trusts as 'automatic resulting trusts'.[13]

This theoretical distinction as to the basis for both types of resulting trust was rejected by Lord Browne-Wilkinson in *Westdeutsche Landesbank Girozentrale v Islington LBC*.[14] Lord Browne-Wilkinson believed that both types of resulting trust operated by 'giving effect to the common intention of the parties'.[15] That means that, as his Lordship stated, '[a] resulting trust is not imposed by law against the intentions of the trustee . . . but gives effect to his presumed intention'.[16]

It could not be said, thought Lord Browne-Wilkinson, that if a settlor had abandoned an equitable interest that a resulting trust would step in automatically in his favour and return the

---

7 *Vandervell v IRC* [1967] 2 AC 291.
8 Ibid at 313.
9 *Westdeutsche Landesbank Girozentrale v Islington LBC* [1996] AC 669 at 708.
10 *Vandervell v IRC* [1967] 2 AC 291. See later at pp 61−64 for a full discussion of this case.
11 *Re Vandervell's Trusts* (No. 2) [1974] Ch 269 at 289.
12 Ibid.
13 Ibid.
14 *Westdeutsche Landesbank Girozentrale v Islington LBC* [1996] AC 669.
15 Ibid at 708.
16 Ibid.

equitable interest to him. If the court could not ascertain the settlor's intentions in such a situation, then the logical inference had to be that such property would pass on a *bona vacantia* basis to the Crown.[17] The basis for resulting trusts had to be the settlor's presumed intention.

Glossary: *Bona vacantia*

The Treasury Solicitor's website reminds us that *bona vacantia* means 'empty goods'. It arises where no-one owns the goods and so they pass to the Crown, as a type of 'default' position. More modern terminology might refer to the goods as 'ownerless'. The Treasury Solicitor administers the goods on behalf of the Crown. Have a look at www.bonavacantia.gov.uk for a modern insight as to what this part of the Treasury Solicitor's Department undertakes.

The approaches of Megarry J and Lord Browne-Wilkinson were arguably linked together by Lord Millett in *Air Jamaica Ltd v Charlton*[18] where he said, '[l]ike a constructive trust, a resulting trust arises by operation of law, though unlike a constructive trust it gives effect to intention'.[19]

❖ ANALYSING THE LAW

Do you prefer the views of Lord Browne-Wilkinson or Megarry J for the basis of a resulting trust? The difficulty with Lord Browne-Wilkinson's notion that the resulting trust is founded on a settlor's intention is exemplified in his Category B type of resulting trust. How can it be said that in the case of a failed express trust, the settlor still intended to have the equitable interest returned to him? Surely his intention of a settlor is merely to create an express trust and a settlor usually gives no thought to the consequences of his express trust failing.

In the discussion which follows, for the sake of consistency, Lord Browne-Wilkinson's classification of the types of resulting trust is followed.

Category A resulting trusts: From a voluntary transfer

In this category, it is the intentions of the donor (A) which are paramount: if A truly intended to benefit B, then the gift will stand in B's favour. If A's intentions cannot be proven, equity will step in with a resulting trust in A's favour.[20] When equity steps in with a resulting trust, the fundamental idea at work is that A did not intend to benefit B in any way, despite first appearances from the transaction which has taken place. B receives the property as a volunteer since he provided no consideration for the property he received. Equity will not assist a volunteer. This type of resulting trust was found to occur on the facts of *Re Vinogradoff*.[21]

The case concerned a transfer of War Loan shares by a grandmother into hers and her granddaughter's joint names. By her will, the grandmother purported to leave her interest in

---

17 In support of this proposition, Lord Browne-Wilkinson cited *Re West Sussex Constabulary's Widows, Children and Benevolent (1930) Fund Trusts* [1971] Ch 1.
18 *Air Jamaica Ltd v Charlton* [1999] 1 WLR 1399.
19 Ibid at 1412.
20 *Aroso v Coutts & Co* [2001] WTLR 797.
21 *Re Vinogradoff* [1935] WN 68.

the shares to a third party. The executors of the grandmother's will brought an action to ascertain whether the granddaughter had any interest in the shares or whether they were rightly left by the terms of the will. That, of course, depended on whether the grandmother had truly intended to make a gift of the shares into hers and her granddaughter's joint names. If such clear intention could not be shown, equity would step in with a resulting trust in favour of the grandmother's estate.

The court held that the intention was to create a resulting trust in favour of the grandmother which would now clearly benefit her estate. The shares would, therefore, go to the third party under the will, not to the granddaughter.

This presumption of a resulting trust can easily be rebutted if evidence can be led which shows that A did, in fact, intend to benefit B.

Alternatively, it used to be the case that the presumption of a resulting trust could be rebutted by a different presumption: the presumption of advancement. As will be shown, the presumption of advancement will be abolished[22] so the only way to rebut the presumption of a resulting trust being imposed in the future will be to show evidence that a true gift was intended. It is necessary, however, to consider what the presumption of advancement is and how it operates to defeat the presumption of a resulting trust. Whilst it is due to be abolished, the presumption of advancement is explicitly preserved for anything done, or obligations incurred, before s 199 of the Equality Act 2010 comes into effect.[23]

The presumption of advancement

The presumption of advancement provided that, where A and B enjoyed a certain type of relationship, any gift of property by A for B would be recognised by equity as being a true gift in B's favour. A resulting trust would not, therefore, be implied. B's equitable interest in the property would be recognised and secure. This can be shown in Figure 3.2.

A ————————▶ B
transfers the legal interest
in the property to

IF a resulting trust applies, the equitable interest bounces back to A

BUT

IF the presumption of advancement applies, the equitable interest is assigned to B.
B therefore holds the absolute interest in the property.

Figure 3.2 The presumption of advancement.

The presumption of advancement applied to gifts between husband and wife and father and child.[24] Note that the presumption was like going down a one-way street in that it only applied to gifts going in a particular direction. It applied only for gifts given by husbands to wives and by fathers to children. It did not apply for gifts given by wives to husbands or children to fathers.

---

22 When s 199 of the Equality Act 2010 is brought into force.
23 Equality Act 2010, s 199(2).
24 See *Dyer v Dyer* (1788) 2 Cox Eq Cas 92; 30 ER 42.

The presumption of advancement applied to a gift between a fiancé and fiancée where they were later married: *Moate v Moate*.[25] In 1930, a man and woman agreed to purchase a home together. The purchase of the property was completed whilst the parties were engaged, but some three weeks before they married. At the man's request, the legal ownership of the property was put into the woman's name. The actual purchase price of the property was paid by the man, subject to a mortgage. Whilst the wife was contractually bound to pay the mortgage, the man always paid the instalments as they fell due and eventually paid off the mortgage in its entirety.

Some 16 years after the property was purchased, the parties' relationship broke down. The issue for the court to resolve was who enjoyed the equitable ownership of the property. The man's argument rested on the basis that he had effectively paid for the property in its entirety and so a resulting trust should be found in his favour.

Jenkins J held that the presumption of advancement applied in favour of the woman. The husband had originally intended the house to be a gift to his wife providing the marriage actually took place which, of course, had occurred. The mortgage repayments also benefited from the presumption of advancement working as the man had failed to discharge the presumption that they were not made as gifts to his wife.

The case effectively extended the presumption of advancement from applying between husbands and wives to those intending to be married. Jenkins J had no difficulty with this. He believed the presumption of advancement would be stronger between fiancées in any event. It would be entirely natural for a man to give a woman a gift of a property as a wedding present before the wedding took place.

The presumption of advancement rested upon what might now be seen to be old-fashioned beliefs that certain people would naturally wish to provide for others. It was natural for a husband to wish to take care of and provide for his wife. Pragmatically, it was necessary for husbands to do so, since the majority of married women could not own property in their own right before 1882.[26] Similarly, it was natural for a father to wish to take care of and provide for his child. But the presumption of advancement was fairly narrowly constrained. For example, it was originally not the case that the presumption of advancement would apply as of right to gifts between mothers and their children, as *Bennet v Bennet*[27] illustrated.[28]

The case concerned a loan of £3,000 from Ann Bennet to her son, Philip which was made in 1869. In 1875, Philip predeceased his mother with the amount of the loan still owing to her. She claimed that she was a creditor of his estate. The defendant, another creditor, argued that she had no claim, since the presumption of advancement applied between a mother and child which meant that the money had been given to Philip. Nothing was repayable to the mother, since it was a gift by virtue of this presumption. Jessel MR held that no gift had been intended. There was no moral duty for a mother to provide for her child. As such, the presumption of advancement could not apply. Philip's estate had to repay the loan.

By the late twentieth century, the presumption of advancement had become very weak, as explained by Lord Hodson in *Pettitt v Pettitt*:

> Reference has been made to the 'presumption of advancement' in favour of a wife in receipt of a benefit from her husband. In the old days when a wife's right to property was limited, the presumption, no doubt, had great importance and today, when there

---

25 *Moate v Moate* [1948] 2 All ER 486.
26 Married Women's Property Act 1882.
27 *Bennet v Bennet* (1878–79) LR 10 ChD 474.
28 It was only recently in *Close Invoice Finance Ltd v Abaowa* [2010] EWHC 1920 (QB) that the High Court recognised *obiter* that the presumption of advancement could now apply to a gift from a mother to her child.

are no living witnesses to a transaction and inferences have to be drawn, there may be no other guide to a decision as to property rights than by resort to the presumption of advancement. I do not think it would often happen that when evidence had been given, *the presumption would today have any decisive effect.*[29]

Indeed, the presumption itself had always been able to be rebutted by evidence to the contrary, as occurred on the facts in the well-known case of *Marshal v Crutwell*.[30]

Henry Marshal's health was failing. He went to the London and County Bank, withdrew all of his money from his own personal account and placed it in a new joint account in his own name and that of his wife. He told his bank to honour any cheques drawn on the new account by either of them.

In fact, after these events occurred, Henry never drew a cheque on the account, but his wife did so, using the money for household purposes. After Henry's death, his wife argued that all of the money left in the account belonged to her. She argued that the presumption of advancement applied: that it could be presumed that Henry had intended to benefit her with the money.

Sir George Jessel MR held that the presumption of advancement was rebutted on the facts. Taking into account all of the facts and especially Henry's ill health, he said that the opening of the joint account was a 'mere arrangement of convenience'[31] as opposed to a case where Henry was giving the money to his wife. The arrangement that Henry set up enabled his wife to draw cheques on the account whilst he was alive; this was different from giving her the money for her use absolutely after his death.

The presumption of advancement, therefore, had lost much of its impetus over the years. The Equality Act 2010 was enacted, amongst other reasons, to reduce 'socio-economic inequalities' and to 'amend the law relating to rights and responsibilities in family relationships'.[32] The presumption of advancement offends principles of equality by benefiting women to the exclusion of men. Consequently, the whole principle of the presumption of advancement, having generally been reduced in importance by successive case law since its heyday in the nineteenth century, has been abolished in its entirety in s 199(1). By way of exception, s 199(2) permits the presumption to survive for anything done before section 199 commences or anything done pursuant to an obligation incurred before the section commences.

Category B resulting trusts: Created where the entire equitable interest is not exhausted

This was the second category of resulting trusts recognised by Lord Browne-Wilkinson in *Westdeutsche Landesbank Girozentrale v Islington LBC*.[33]

This second category of resulting trust can itself be created in one of two situations:

(a) where, upon creation of the trust, the settlor made an error by failing to transfer all of their equitable interest to the trustee; or

(b) where, although the trust was created properly, it was created with a condition attached to it and that condition has come to an end.

We need to consider each of these two instances in turn.

---

29 *Pettitt v Pettitt* [1970] AC 777 at 811 (emphasis added).
30 *Marshal v Crutwell* (1875) LR 20 Eq 328.
31 Ibid at 330.
32 Equality Act 2010, Introductory Text.
33 *Westdeutsche Landesbank Girozentrale v Islington LBC* [1996] AC 669.

Category B: Where the settlor makes an error

Key Learning Point

It is essential that you understand the next cases of *Vandervell v IRC* and *Re Vandervell's Trusts (No. 2)* if you are to fully grasp this type of resulting trust. These cases are perhaps the most famous litigation in the entire law of trusts.

This type of resulting trust was found to have occurred on the facts in *Vandervell v IRC*.[34]

The case itself concerned some of the taxation affairs of Mr Guy Vandervell. He was the controlling shareholder in Vandervell Products Ltd, an engineering company. The company had various categories of shares, amongst which were 100,000 'A' ordinary shares. As a wealthy man, Mr Vandervell had some concerns about his estate being liable for a large amount of tax when he died. He could afford to divest himself of some of his property so that his estate would not be subject to so much tax upon his death.

The Royal College of Surgeons, coincidentally and at the same time as Mr Vandervell was worried about his taxation, was seeking donations. In response to this, Mr Vandervell decided to give the Royal College the sum of £150,000 to establish a Chair of Pharmacology.

Mr Vandervell was not simply going to write a cheque for this amount to the Royal College, however. Instead, his financial advisor suggested giving the Royal College all of the 'A' shares in Vandervell Products Ltd. The company could then declare a dividend on these shares to the sum of £150,000. The Royal College would still get its funds. At the same time, by giving the shares away to the Royal College, Mr Vandervell would have divested himself of some of his property for tax purposes.

The plan thus far seemed solid enough. The problems for Mr Vandervell began when his financial advisor recommended that he include an option to buy back the shares in the arrangement with the Royal College, in case Vandervell Products Ltd was ever converted into a public limited company. The financial advisor thought that it would be awkward to potential outside investors for the Royal College to have such a significant shareholding in the company. An option would clearly give Mr Vandervell the right to buy back the shares before any public flotation of the company occurred.

An option was, therefore, granted in favour of another of Mr Vandervell's companies, Vandervell Trustees Ltd. This was a company whose object was really just to manage trusts.

The arrangement was put into effect. The Royal College became the legal owner of the 'A' shares in Vandervell Products Ltd. As promised by Mr Vandervell, dividends were declared on the shares, to the net amount of £157,000, for the benefit of the Royal College.

The Royal College was a charitable trust. As such, it decided to reclaim the tax that had already been paid on the dividends declared to it. That meant that the Inland Revenue started to look into the arrangement that had been made between Mr Vandervell, Vandervell Trustees Ltd and the Royal College. The Inland Revenue claimed that the effect of the option agreement to buy back the shares meant that Mr Vandervell had never really relinquished control of those shares. He still owned the equitable interest in them. If he had never relinquished control of them, they were still owned by him and he was liable to pay a large amount of additional 'surtax' on them which amounted to £250,000.

---

34 *Vandervell v IRC* [1967] 2 AC 291.

Part of the argument of the Inland Revenue was that a resulting trust existed with Mr Vandervell as beneficiary. Their argument is set out diagrammatically in Figure 3.3 below.

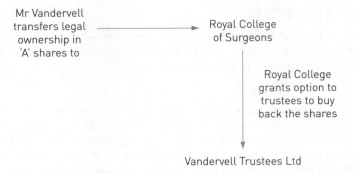

Figure 3.3 The *Vandervell* litigation.

The case went to the House of Lords. On this issue, the House of Lords agreed with the Inland Revenue. The Royal College did indeed hold the shares on resulting trust.

What is particularly interesting about the case is that Vandervell Trustees Ltd had no firm idea of who would benefit from the shares if they decided to buy them back from the Royal College by exercising the option. This did not cause any difficulty for the House of Lords to find a resulting trust. Lord Wilberforce said:

> The conclusion, on the facts found, is simply that the option was vested in the trustee company as a trustee on trusts, not defined at the time, possibly to be defined later.[35]

Lord Wilberforce then acknowledged the potential difficulty with that concept which was that the equitable interest could, if the trusts were not defined, simply remain in the air. For reasons of certainty,[36] it is generally not possible to have a trust with no equitable interest vesting in a beneficiary. His response to that difficulty was, 'the equitable, or beneficial, interest cannot remain in the air: the consequence in law must be that it remains in the settlor'.[37]

This conclusion for Lord Wilberforce was a pragmatic operation of this category of resulting trust:

> There is no need to consider some of the more refined intellectualities of the doctrine of resulting trust, nor to speculate whether, in possible circumstances, the shares might be applicable for Mr Vandervell's benefit: he had, as the direct result of the option and of the failure to place the beneficial interest in it securely away from him, not divested himself absolutely of the shares which it controlled.[38]

The difficulty with Lord Wilberforce's opinion, however, is that he held that the equitable interest remained with Mr Vandervell at all times. This seems not to fit instinctively with the orthodox principle of a resulting trust that the equitable interest jumps back to the settlor.

---

35 Ibid at 328v.
36 See Chapter 5.
37 Ibid.
38 Ibid.

Once the Inland Revenue began looking into the arrangement with the Royal College, Vandervell Trustees Ltd was advised to exercise the option to buy back the shares. It duly exercised the option in October 1961. The intention was that Vandervell Trustees Ltd would hold the shares on trust for Mr Vandervell's children. A letter to this effect was sent to the Inland Revenue by the trustee company. The cash sum of £5,000 needed to exercise the buy-back option was taken from the children's trust.

From 1961 until early 1965, dividends of over £769,000 net of tax were declared on the shares. In early 1965, Mr Vandervell formally executed a Deed of Release. This document released any interest that Mr Vandervell may still have had in the shares to Vandervell Trustees Ltd. The issue now became as to the operative effect of that document and precisely when it released Mr Vandervell from liability to taxation. Was it in 1961, so that its effect was retrospective, or only from 1965, when it was executed?

This became the issue in what was actually the third part of the Vandervell litigation – *Re Vandervell's Trusts* (No. 2).[39] The Inland Revenue was of the view that, despite the letter indicating that the shares were to be held for the children's trust, it was only by the formal Deed of Release that Mr Vandervell's equitable interest was transferred to that trust.

❖ APPLYING THE LAW

Somewhat sadly, Mr Vandervell did not live to see the outcome of the case. He died in 1967 and judgment was only given by the Court of Appeal in 1974.

The Court of Appeal held that the resulting trust that had been found by the House of Lords in the earlier case[40] had come to an end when Vandervell Trustees Ltd had exercised the option in 1961 to buy back the shares. At that time, legal ownership in the shares was transferred to the trustee company. Due to this, the trustee company could (and did) then declare a trust in favour of the children. Lord Denning MR highlighted[41] three important points of evidence which supported this conclusion:

(a)   the money to buy back the shares came from the children's trust which would have been a breach of that trust, unless something (i.e. the shares) were to be put into that trust;

(b)   the existence of the letter from the trustee company to the Inland Revenue, in which it was explained that the shares would, from the date of the exercise of the option, be held for the children's trust; and

(c)   all dividends on the shares after the option had been exercised were paid by the trustee company to the children's trust.

Lord Denning MR explained how the resulting trust came to an end in the case:[42]

A resulting trust for the settlor is born and dies without any writing at all. It comes into existence whenever there is a gap in the beneficial ownership. It ceases to exist whenever that gap is filled by someone becoming beneficially entitled.

---

39 *Re Vandervell's Trusts* (No. 2) [1974] Ch 269.
40 *Vandervell v IRC* [1967] 2 AC 291.
41 *Re Vandervell's Trusts* (No. 2) [1974] Ch 269 at 319.
42 Ibid at 320.

The resulting trust, which had been designed to fill in the gap of the missing equitable owner-ship of the shares, had been discharged by the trustee company declaring a new trust.

The judgment of the Court of Appeal arguably reached a satisfactory result for the Vandervell family but not, perhaps, for the law of trusts. The House of Lords had decided that Mr Vandervell was the equitable owner of the shares under a resulting trust. Yet, somehow, the Court of Appeal decided that the trustee company could end that resulting trust by declaring an express trust in the children's favour. This goes against the basic premise that it is the settlor – not the trustee – who must declare an express trust.

Category B: Where a condition to the operation of the trust has come to an end

The defining case on this second type of resulting trust is *Barclays Bank Ltd v Quistclose Investments Ltd*.[43]

The case concerned a loan of money to a company called Rolls Razor Ltd. That company was in financial difficulties. It had exceeded its overdraft with its bank, Barclays, by a large sum. It wanted to borrow further money from another financier. The financier was prepared to agree to this, but on the basis that Rolls Razor paid a large dividend that it had already declared. Rolls Razor could not afford to pay this dividend (a sum well in excess of £200,000) from its own reserves, so approached Quistclose Investments Ltd for a further loan of this amount to pay the dividend. An arrangement was entered into with Quistclose to lend Rolls Razor the money. Quistclose only lent the money on the basis that it was to be used to pay the dividend that Rolls Razor had declared.

A cheque was sent from Quistclose to Rolls Razor for the amount required to pay the dividend. Rolls Razor sent the cheque to Barclays, so that it could be paid into its account with them. Rolls Razor sent a letter with the cheque, explaining that the money was only to be used to pay the dividend already declared. The cheque was duly paid into the account.

Some six weeks' later, Rolls Razor went into liquidation. The money from Quistclose had not yet been used to pay the dividend. Barclays saw the money sitting in the account and wanted to offset it against the overdraft and other amounts that Rolls Razor owed.

Quistclose was presumably not pleased at this turn of events and brought an action against both Rolls Razor and Barclays, arguing that Rolls Razor had held the money on resulting trust for Quistclose. It argued that the trust had been created with a particular condition attached to it: that the money could only be used to pay the dividend due. If that condition was not met, then the money had to be returned to Quistclose. As Barclays had been told of the purpose for which the money was being held, Quistclose said that Barclays had *constructive notice* of the trust.

The matter reached the House of Lords.

Glossary: Constructive notice

Constructive notice means the recipient should have known about the existence of something.

Lord Wilberforce, giving the substantive opinion of the House, held that the money was only to be used to pay the dividends due. He also said that arrangements, as had occurred on the facts, gave rise to a fiduciary relationship or trust. He said there were two trusts in issue here: a primary trust in favour of the creditors of Rolls Razor (i.e. the shareholders who were

---

43 *Barclays Bank Ltd v Quistclose Investments Ltd* [1970] AC 567.

due to receive their dividends) and, if that trust failed, a second trust arose in favour of the original lender of the money.

As it had not been paid to the shareholders who were due to receive the dividends, the money should be returned to the lender. The primary trust of the money being for the benefit of the creditor had failed. The secondary trust of the money being returned to the lender would be effective. Quistclose could, therefore, receive its money back.

Lord Wilberforce justified this approach not only on the basis of previous case law but also on the basis of policy. It would have been wrong to say that a lender lent money to a company such as Rolls Razor on the basis that Rolls Razor had to pay its creditors and if it did not, the money would then be owned by the creditors if Rolls Razor went insolvent. He did not think that a lender would ever agree to such an arrangement. The lender would want some protection when advancing the loan: if it was not to be used for the purpose specified, then it would want the money returned. The lender achieved this by acquiring an equitable right to see that the money was used for its primary purpose; if that failed, the secondary trust of the money being held for the lender would operate.

On the final point in the case, Lord Wilberforce held that Barclays did have constructive notice of the trust because of the letter that had been sent to Barclays by Rolls Razor when the cheque was paid in. The letter supported an oral conversation between the two parties to the same effect.

Lord Wilberforce's analysis has caused much consternation amongst academics. The difficulty is that the primary trust to which he refers is a purpose trust – a trust for the purpose of paying the dividend. As will be seen in Chapter 6, English law dislikes private purpose trusts and generally holds that they are void. Such a primary trust should arguably never have been recognised by Lord Wilberforce as it seems to infringe this principle of English law.[44]

It may be that this type of resulting trust is really just another variety of the first type of resulting trust that we have discussed: where the trust arises due to a failure to dispose of all of the equitable interest. Remember the lender lends the money to the borrower on the basis that it will be used for a certain obligation. When that obligation is no longer possible, the money is returned to the lender. It could be said that the lender does not part with his entire equitable interest in the first instance when the loan is originally made.

This was certainly the analysis put forward by the House of Lords in *Twinsectra Ltd v Yardley*.[45] On this basis, there are not really two trusts operating, but simply one. Lord Millett pointed out that Lord Wilberforce's view that there were two trusts had received little academic support. Lord Millett was of the view that the *Quistclose* resulting trust was a 'simple commercial arrangement' under which the money remained the lender's property until it was applied according to his wishes. If it was not so applied, it had to be given back to the lender. This was simply the operation of a resulting trust. The equitable interest remained with the lender throughout the transaction until the borrower paid the money over.[46]

A *Quistclose*-type of resulting trust can also operate in a non-commercial context, as illustrated by the facts of *Hussey v Palmer*.[47]

Mrs Emily Hussey was an elderly widow. Her own house was in a very poor state of repair, so she sold it and went to live with her daughter and son-in-law. She paid, in effect, for the construction of a 'granny flat', which took the form of an extra bedroom. It cost her £607, which she paid to the builder. Unfortunately, Mrs Hussey and her daughter could not live

---

44 Otherwise known as the 'beneficiary principle' (see Chapter 6).
45 *Twinsectra Ltd v Yardley* [2002] UKHL 12 per Lord Millett at para 69.
46 For a more detailed discussion of Lord Millett's opinion in *Twinsectra Ltd v Yardley*, see Chapter 7 at pp 199–201.
47 *Hussey v Palmer* [1972] 1 WLR 1286.

together and Mrs Hussey moved out. She wrote to her son-in-law, Mr Palmer, and asked for a small weekly allowance to help her out. This was not paid, so Mrs Hussey brought an action claiming repayment of the £607.

She argued that the money was held by Mr Palmer for her on a resulting trust. Effectively, her case was that she had paid the money over for the construction of an extra bedroom in which she would live. If she could not live there, then the operation of the condition under which she gave the money came to an end and she was entitled to the money back, by means of a resulting trust. Mr Palmer, on the other hand, argued that there was no trust in her favour. He said that Mrs Hussey had provided the money by way of a gift.

Giving the leading judgment in the Court of Appeal, Lord Denning MR rejected the idea that the money had been lent. He brought into operation the concept found in contract law that this was a family arrangement between the parties where there was no intention to create legal relations such that would support a formal loan agreement between Mrs Hussey and her son-in-law.

Yet he also held that there was no gift of the money from Mrs Hussey to Mr Palmer. Instead, there was a trust in favour of Mrs Hussey of the money. Phillimore LJ held that it was a resulting trust for the amount of money that Mrs Hussey had paid.

Effectively, Mrs Hussey had wished to live in the property and, once she was unable to do so, the original trust under which she provided the money for the extension came to an end and a resulting trust arose in her favour.

Lord Denning MR thought that the case probably did not concern a resulting trust but a constructive one. In doing so, he emphasised the close connections between the two types of implied trusts. Arguably, he somewhat blurred the line of distinction between the two:

> Although the plaintiff alleged that there was a resulting trust, I should have thought that the trust in this case . . . was more in the nature of a constructive trust: but this is more a matter of words than anything else. The two run together.[48]

He emphasised equity's origins behind both types of trust:

> By whatever name it is described, it is a trust imposed by law whenever justice and good conscience require it. It is a liberal process, founded upon large principles of equity . . .[49]

Key Learning Point

Despite Lord Denning's words about the blurring of the distinction between resulting and constructive trusts, it is easier and better to keep the two trusts separate. Lord Denning largely describes the creation of a constructive trust which, as we shall see, can be created more informally than a resulting trust which should be kept in its boundaries as discussed in this chapter.

We now turn to the second type of implied trust: the constructive trust.

---

48 Ibid at 1289.
49 Ibid at 1290.

The Constructive Trust

A concise definition of a constructive trust was given by Millett LJ in *Paragon Finance plc v D B Thakerar & Co (a firm)*[50] as follows:

> A constructive trust arises by operation of law whenever the circumstances are such that it would be unconscionable for the owner of property (usually but not necessarily the legal estate) to assert his own beneficial interest in the property and deny the beneficial interest of another.

This definition highlights two important points:

(a) a constructive trust is derived from the origins of equity – from the concepts of what is fair and in good conscience; and
(b) this trust will affect the conscience of the property owner for it is seeking to right the wrong that is occurring by the owner of the legal interest in the property denying another their rightful equitable interest.

As Millett LJ pointed out,[51] the constructive trust itself covers two entirely different situations. The first is:

(a) Where a party has assumed the role of a trustee by a lawful transaction which occurred before a breach of trust.

❖ EXPLAINING THE LAW

This first type of constructive trust can occur where two or more parties buy a home together and the legal title is registered in one party's name only. If the parties then separate, any claim the other party may have in the property is based on the idea that the legal owner owns the property on trust for both of them. The constructive trust is the device used to advance that argument.

As Millett LJ explained,[52] a true trust always existed. The recipient of the legal interest in the property was obliged to hold the property, not as an absolute owner, but as a trustee. However, the recipient breached the trust by, effectively, denying that he was a trustee and sought to claim the equitable ownership of the property for himself.

The second situation where a constructive trust arises is:

(b) Where the recipient of the property has acted in breach of his fiduciary duty.[53] In this instance, a trust was never specifically established but the recipient is said to be, as Millett LJ put it,[54] 'liable to account as constructive trustee' to the true owner of the property.

---

50 *Paragon Finance plc v D B Thakerar & Co (a firm)* [1999] 1 All ER 400.
51 Ibid.
52 Ibid.
53 Fiduciary duties are discussed in detail in Chapter 8.
54 Ibid.

> ### ❖ EXPLAINING THE LAW
>
> This second type of constructive trust can occur whenever there is a fiduciary relationship between parties. It could, for example, occur between a company director and his company. If the director makes a secret profit through his role as director, he will be liable to pay the company the money he has made. He is said to be a constructive trustee of that money.

The difference between the first and second types of constructive trust is that the recipient of the property was never appointed to the position of trustee. As Millett LJ said, '[s]uch a person is not in fact a trustee at all, even though he may be liable to account as if he were. He never assumes the position of a trustee . . .'[55]

Millett LJ went further in describing this second type of constructive trust:[56]

> In such a case the expressions 'constructive trust' and 'constructive trustee' are misleading, for there is no trust and usually no possibility of a proprietary remedy . . .

Essentially, the first type of constructive trust is based on a type of trust that was probably unwritten between the parties, but which the parties to the particular type of transaction mutually understood. It would be unconscionable for the person who is supposedly the trustee to deny the existence of the trust.

The second type of constructive trust is based on equity providing a remedy against one person's fraud. This type of trust is imposed on the situation to do justice between the parties.

Constructive trust – where one party is the legal owner of the property

The first instance of the constructive trust is considered in detail in Chapter 14. What follows here is an introduction to the subject.

The background to the case law of this type of constructive trust is as follows. Two people form a relationship and decide to live together. The legal title to the home that is bought is usually registered in one of their names only – usually the man's. The relationship breaks up. The woman wishes to claim an interest in the home. She can only do so by claiming that the man holds the legal title on constructive trust for them both in equity.

According to the Court of Appeal in *Grant v Edwards*,[57] this type of constructive trust requires two issues to be proven:

(a)   both parties had a common intention that they should both enjoy the equitable interest in the home; and

(b)   the claimant then needs to have acted to her detriment on the basis of that common intention.

---

55 Ibid.
56 Ibid.
57 *Grant v Edwards* [1986] Ch 638.

Not surprisingly, these types of constructive trusts are often referred to as 'common intention' constructive trusts.

The common intention can itself arise in one of two ways:

(a)   through express discussions between the parties; or
(b)   where the claimant relies on the conduct of both of the parties alone.

In each case, the claimant must show that, through her conduct, she acted upon the common intention. There is a higher requirement for the conduct to meet in the second type of common intention because of the lack of any type of firm agreement through express discussion between the parties. All the claimant has is the parties' conduct to show that there is a trust; the court is sceptical about relying on it alone where there is no evidence of an agreement.

These two ways of establishing common intention were analysed further by Lord Bridge in *Lloyds Bank plc v Rosset*.[58] Although his comments were *obiter dicta*, they were seen to be a decided view of the law for the establishment of a common intention constructive trust.

Lord Bridge said that where there was a claim that the common intention constructive trust was based on express discussions of the parties, those express discussions could be 'imperfectly remembered' and their terms 'imprecise'.[59] Once such discussions forming an agreement between the parties were proven, then the claimant would need to go on to show that she had acted to her detriment or 'significantly altered . . . her position in reliance on the agreement'[60] to show that a constructive trust existed. The claimant's detrimental actions must, in the words of Nourse LJ in *Grant v Edwards*, be 'conduct on which the woman could not reasonably have been expected to embark unless she was to have an interest in the house'.[61] Such conduct included the claimant wielding a 14lb sledgehammer to break up concrete in *Eves v Eves*[62] and the claimant making significant contributions to household expenses in *Grant v Edwards*.[63] Both cases involved an agreement to share the equitable interest in the home and, in both cases, the claimant would have only embarked on such conduct if she had believed she was entitled to a share in the house.

For the second type of constructive trust, where the claimant has to rely on evidence of the parties' conduct alone to establish the trust as no express discussions ever took place, there was only one type of conduct that the court would accept to show that a constructive trust existed. That was by the claimant making direct contributions to the purchase price of the property. Those direct contributions could only be when the property was first purchased or, alternatively, through paying the mortgage.

Such a precise requirement for this second method of establishing a constructive trust meant that, in reality, there seemed to be little difference between this type of trust and a resulting trust. The basis of a Category A resulting trust is usually that a party has funded the purchase of property which he has then, allegedly, given away.

Indeed, Lord Bridge's stringent requirement for the conduct required for the second type of common intention constructive trust was commented on in *Stack v Dowden*.[64] Lord Walker[65]

---

58   *Lloyds Bank plc v Rosset* [1991] 1 AC 107.
59   Ibid at 132.
60   Ibid.
61   Ibid at 648.
62   *Eves v Eves* [1975] 1 WLR 1338.
63   *Grant v Edwards* [1986] Ch 638.
64   *Stack v Dowden* [2007] UKHL 17.
65   Ibid at para 26.

questioned whether such a restrictive view of the type of conduct giving rise to the second instance of a common intention constructive trust was needed at the time of *Lloyds Bank v Rosset* and thought that such a restrictive view was needed less still at the time of the present case. Baroness Hale believed that many factors other than just pure financial contributions could be relevant to ascertaining what she described as the 'parties' true intentions'.[66] These factors included whether the parties took advice, or had discussions about, their intentions when they bought the property, the purpose for which the property was bought, how the purchase of the property was financed, as well as the parties 'individual characters and personalities'.[67]

Since *Stack v Dowden* itself did not directly concern the establishment of a constructive trust but what the parties' interests were worth, the comments of Lord Walker and Baroness Hale were, once again, *obiter dicta*. Subsequent Court of Appeal cases[68] have shown a preference for Lord Bridge's requirements to establish either type of common intention constructive trust.

Constructive trust – from where equity will not suffer a wrong to be without a remedy

This type of constructive trust arises from the first of equity's maxims. Equity imposes a constructive trust where otherwise a wrong would be committed. The most common scenario is where someone in a fiduciary position over another takes advantage of that position to make a secret profit. In these cases, equity holds that the maker of the secret profit is a constructive trustee of it and must account to the innocent party for that profit. This is an instance of equity acting in good conscience according to the demands of justice. It is not because there is initially a trust between the two parties.[69]

As liability is imposed on a fiduciary, the first issue here is for us to define someone who is a fiduciary. In *Bristol & West Building Society v Mothew*,[70] Millett LJ said that a fiduciary is:

> someone who has undertaken to act for or on behalf of another in a particular matter in circumstances which give rise to a relationship of trust and confidence.[71]

And he added that '[t]he distinguishing obligation of a fiduciary is the obligation of loyalty'.[72]

Millett LJ said that this loyalty meant that the fiduciary, in practice, had to:

(a)   act in good faith;
(b)   not make a profit out of the trust;
(c)   not place himself in a position where his duty to the principal and his self-interest could conflict; and
(d)   not act for his own benefit (or for the benefit of someone else) without his principal's consent.

---

66   Ibid at para 69.
67   Ibid.
68   See, for example, *James v Thomas* [2007] EWCA Civ 1212 and *Morris v Morris* [2008] EWCA Civ 257.
69   It is, arguably, the case that there is no 'true' constructive trust here at all. In *Paragon Finance plc v D B Thakerar & Co (a firm)* [1999] 1 All ER 400, Millett LJ thought that to describe this situation as being that of a constructive trust was misleading. It is probably more accurate to say that the individual who has made a secret profit is merely liable to account for it and to refrain from describing him as a constructive trustee.
70   *Bristol & West Building Society v Mothew* [1998] Ch 1.
71   Ibid at 18.
72   Ibid.

Who, then, are fiduciaries in the real world? The following are examples of fiduciary relationships, where one party is a fiduciary because they owe loyalty to the other:

- Trustee/beneficiary
- Doctor/patient
- Solicitor/client
- Company director/company.

As Lord Browne-Wilkinson pointed out in *Henderson v Merrett Syndicates Ltd*,[73] it is not the
label of their profession or employment that makes such people fiduciaries. Rather, it is
because, on the facts of each case, such people have voluntarily said that they will be
responsible for the affairs of another person.

The core reason why a fiduciary is obliged to act out of loyalty for their principal and is
obliged also to adhere to those requirements listed by Millett LJ was explained by Lord
Herschell in *Bray v Ford*.[74] Lord Herschell explained the reason as not coming from ideas of
morality but rather pragmatism:

> human nature being what it is, there is a danger . . . of the person holding a fiduciary
> position being swayed by interest rather than by duty, and thus prejudicing those
> whom he was bound to protect.

This may, however, be somewhat circular. True, equity seeks to protect the fiduciary's principal
by ensuring that the fiduciary remains loyal to him, but the reasons underpinning that must
be based on justice and conscience. These are, after all, the foundations of the whole of equity
and its various remedies.

The mechanism that equity uses to ensure that a fiduciary maintains loyalty to his principal
is that of the constructive trust. A constructive trust has been held to apply to various types
of fiduciaries.

One of the earliest twentieth century cases in which fiduciaries were held liable to account
was *Regal (Hastings) Ltd v Gulliver*.[75] This concerned the fiduciary nature of company directors.

The claimant was a company which operated cinemas. The claimant was interested
in expanding its business by buying or taking leases on two additional cinemas, one in
Hastings and the other in St Leonards. The claimant set up a subsidiary company to take leases
of those two cinemas. The subsidiary was named 'Hastings Amalgamated Cinemas Ltd'
('Amalgamated').

Amalgamated had an initial offering of 5,000 shares. The claimant took 2,000 of them.
The remaining shares were split between different individuals and companies but, significantly, four of the directors of Regal (who were, importantly, also directors of the subsidiary)
agreed to purchase 500 shares each.

---

73 *Henderson v Merrett Syndicates Ltd* [1995] 2 AC 145.
74 *Bray v Ford* [1896] AC 44.
75 *Regal (Hastings) Ltd v Gulliver* [1967] 2 AC 134.

The leases for the cinemas were entered into in favour of Amalgamated. Regal was sold. As a result of the sale agreement, the shares in Amalgamated were sold at a considerable profit from which they were originally bought.

The facts of the case are shown in the flowchart at Figure 3.4 below.

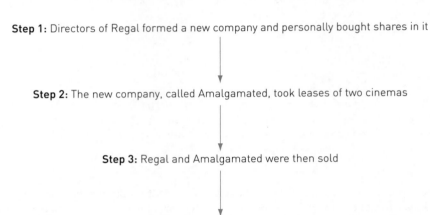

Step 1: Directors of Regal formed a new company and personally bought shares in it

Step 2: The new company, called Amalgamated, took leases of two cinemas

Step 3: Regal and Amalgamated were then sold

Step 4: The consequence: the shares in Amalgamated were sold at over a 200% profit from which they were originally bought. The new owners wanted to recover that profit element, which they had paid, from the former directors.

Figure 3.4 Regal (Hastings) Ltd v Gulliver.

The new owners of the claimant company sued the former directors of Regal, arguing that they were constructive trustees of the profits that they had made.

There was no suggestion that the directors of Regal/Amalgamated had acted anything other than honourably. Regal could only afford to buy the first 2,000 shares. All of the remaining shares in Amalgamated had to be bought. The directors thought that they had no real choice but to purchase them.

This cut little ice with the House of Lords. In giving his opinion, Lord Russell of Killowen held that the shares acquired by the original directors of Regal were only acquired because they were directors of Regal. Such directors, he thought, undoubtedly stood in a fiduciary position to their company. They owed obligations of loyalty and honesty to their company. For those reasons, the directors were accountable to Regal for the profits they had made when they had sold their shares in Amalgamated to the new owners of Regal. It was irrelevant that they had acted honestly throughout. It did not matter that Regal could not afford to purchase the shares itself and the directors were in an ideal position to do so. All that mattered was they had put themselves in a position where their duty to their company and their self-interest was placed in a position of conflict. The potential conflict was that their duty to the company was to obtain the best price for the shares whilst their self-interest was to pay the lowest price. For that reason, the directors were accountable for the profits they had made.

Lord Russell cited the old case of *Keech v Sandford*[76] with approval, a decision which appears to be even harsher than the facts before him.

---

76 *Keech v Sandford* (1726) 2 Eq Ab 741; 25 ER 223.

This case concerned breach of the obligation of loyalty by a trustee. A lease of the profits of a market was due for renewal. The lease was held on trust and the beneficiary was a child. The trustee asked for the lease to be renewed but the landlord refused, on the basis that a child could not be liable for non-payment of rent. The trustee consequently entered into a lease for his own benefit.

The Lord Chancellor, Lord King, held that the trustee had to transfer – or assign – the benefit of the lease to the child. This was even though the landlord specifically refused to grant the lease for the benefit of the child on renewal. The reason for the decision was that the trustee had to act for the entire benefit of the beneficiary under the trust. He owed absolute loyalty to the beneficiary. Equity had to remove the temptation from a trustee not to act in the trust's best interests. Trustees might have been tempted to seek out personal gain for themselves in future cases by, for example, requesting leases to be renewed in their favour rather than for their beneficiaries. If the trustee did not show that absolute loyalty voluntarily, he would effectively be made to be a constructive trustee of the lease for the benefit of the beneficiary.

This principle was reaffirmed by the House of Lords in the landmark case of Boardman v Phipps,[77] which is, perhaps, the high-water mark of constructive trusteeship.

The case concerned a solicitor to a trust. The trust itself had a minority shareholding in a textile business that had two factories in the English Midlands and one in Australia. The solicitor, Mr Boardman, believed that the business was not being operated as profitably as it might be. He, along with Tom Phipps, one of the beneficiaries of the trust, tried to cajole the company into trading more profitably. The company generally resisted these attempts. Eventually, in 1959, Mr Boardman and Tom Phipps agreed to buy a controlling interest in the company from the current shareholders, but they did so in their own personal capacities and not in the name of the trust. The trust would have needed the rather cumbersome approval of the court before it could buy additional shares in the company.

Mr Boardman and Tom Phipps proceeded to reorganise the company. One of the factories in the Midlands, together with the Australian operation, was sold. These sales generated substantial income for the business. Mr Boardman and Tom Phipps distributed some of this money to each shareholder. This included the trust but it also included themselves.

At that point, Tom Phipps tried to purchase the shares from one of the other beneficiaries of the trust, John Phipps. John took legal advice and soon afterwards issued a claim against Mr Boardman and Tom. John's case was that Mr Boardman and Tom Phipps were agents for the trustees at all times and that they were in a fiduciary position vis-à-vis the trust. He said that they should be seen to be constructive trustees of their share of the profits for the beneficiaries of the trust since it was only in their position that they were able to invest in the company personally. In short, his argument was that they had placed themselves in a position where their duty to the trust and their self-interest had come into conflict. The only remedy for that was for them to account to the trust for the profits they had made and to hand over their personal shares to the trust.

By a bare majority, the House of Lords agreed with John Phipps' argument. In the majority, Lord Cohen placed great weight on the fact that Mr Boardman and Tom Phipps were only able to invest in the company due to their being agents for the trustees of the trust. Mr Boardman obtained information as to how well the company was trading by virtue of his being the solicitor to the trust. It was this unique position in which Mr Boardman found himself that presented him with the ability to look into the company in greater depth and eventually purchase the additional controlling shares. He used the trust's original shareholding as, in the

---

77 Boardman v Phipps [1967] 2 AC 46.

words of Lord Hodson,[78] a 'weapon', with which to obtain the information about the company which he put to profitable use.

The trust would have needed the court's consent to purchase the shares and at that stage, Mr Boardman would have found himself in a position where his duty to the trust and his self-interest may have conflicted. Due to this possible conflict between duty and self-interest, Mr Boardman was liable to account for the profits he made in his personal capacity. Both he and Tom Phipps were in fiduciary positions to the trust and would only have been able to purchase shares in their own capacities with the true and informed consent of the beneficiaries.

Again, as in *Regal (Hastings) Ltd v Gulliver*,[79] the honesty and integrity of Mr Boardman and Tom Phipps were not doubted. Lord Cohen remarked[80] that John Phipps was a 'fortunate man in that the rigour of equity enables him to participate in the profits' that Mr Boardman and Tom Phipps had made personally.

The only practical saving grace for Mr Boardman and Tom Phipps was that the majority believed that they should be rewarded for all of their hard work in transforming the company for the benefit of the trust. Indeed, payment was due to them both on a 'liberal scale'.[81]

Before the decision in *Boardman v Phipps* causes too much alarm, it should be noted that their Lordships were willing to attach criteria to their remarks as to when constructive trusteeship would be imposed on fiduciaries.

Lord Cohen, echoing the trial judge, Wilberforce J, stated that it was not simply knowledge that came to the attention of the fiduciary which made him liable to account for profits. He said that had the company in the case been a public limited company, with information about it and its shares available for sale on the open market, Mr Boardman and Tom Phipps would not have been accountable for the profits. What made a vital difference in this case was that the company was private. The information surrounding the company's performance and the opportunity to buy the shares only arose due to the fact that Mr Boardman and Tom Phipps were agents for the trustees, since they could only access such information by virtue of their positions.

Lord Hodson explained that not everyone would be imposed with constructive trusteeship unless they received trust property or, alternatively, dishonestly assisted in a breach of trust. He quoted Lord Selborne in *Barnes v Addy*:[82]

> strangers are not to be made constructive trustees merely because they act as the agents of trustees in transactions within their legal powers ... unless those agents receive and become chargeable with some part of trust property, or unless they assist with knowledge in a dishonest and fraudulent design on the part of the trustees.

Two of their Lordships dissented. Lord Upjohn focused on the concept that there had to be a 'real sensible possibility of conflict' between a fiduciary's duty and his self-interest. He further said[83] that a trustee could use information acquired by him as a trustee, provided that such information did not 'injure' the trust.

Lord Upjohn said that in his initial dealings with the textile company, Mr Boardman had tried to have Tom Phipps appointed as a director. When this failed, any notion that Mr Boardman and Tom Phipps were agents of the trustees also came to an end. The trust was not able

78 Ibid at 107.
79 *Regal (Hastings) Ltd v Gulliver* [1967] 2 AC 134.
80 *Boardman v Phipps* [1967] 2 AC 46 at 104.
81 Ibid, quoting trial judge Wilberforce J with approval.
82 *Barnes v Addy* (1874) 9 Ch App 244.
83 *Boardman v Phipps* [1967] 2 AC 46 at 129.

to purchase further shares itself in the company. There could be no conflict between their duty to the trust and their interests to themselves since, by that stage, the trust was itself not able to have any more input into the company. Mr Boardman and Tom Phipps were entirely free to purchase the shares in the company in their own capacities. He summed up the case as follows:

> [Mr Boardman and Tom Phipps] have bought for themselves at entirely their own risk with their own money shares which the trustees never contemplated buying and they did so in circumstances fully known and approved of by the trustees.[84]

Regal (Hastings) Ltd v Gulliver[85] could be distinguished on the basis that the original idea in that case was that Regal would make a profit on the shares in Amalgamated, but what in fact happened was that the directors made that profit by purchasing the shares themselves instead of Regal doing so. This case was not the same. Here the trustees were unwilling to purchase the controlling shareholding in the company, and never intended to do so and so Mr Boardman and Tom Phipps stepped up to the mark.

The decision in *Boardman v Phipps*[86] can be seen to be a very black-and-white application of the rule that duty to the trust and self-interest must not conflict. Certainly, it seems not to encourage those in a fiduciary position to assist the trust where there might even be a possibility of the fiduciary also benefiting, even if the benefit is subsidiary to the trust also benefiting. Mr Boardman and Tom Phipps went to a lot of personal expense and invested a lot of their own time in making a success of the company for the benefit of the trust, only for their personal rewards to be removed from them.[87]

All of their Lordships felt the issue of whether duty and interest did conflict depended on the circumstances of each case.

This view was reflected in the decision in the Australian case of *Queensland Mines Ltd v Hudson*.[88]

Here, the managing director of the claimant company had had issued to him two licences for mining exploration. He had obtained those licences due to the strength of the claimant company's resources and solid reputation. Before the licences were issued by the Tasmanian government, a decision had been taken to 'mothball' (i.e. close down temporarily) the claimant company and consequently, the company itself had no funds with which the licences could be implemented.

The managing director made a profit as a result of the licences being issued to him. The claimant company claimed against him for breach of fiduciary duty and for an account of the profits that he had made.

The Privy Council said that he was not liable to account for the profits made. He had made the profit due to his original position in the claimant company but he had fully advised the company of his intention to make use of the licences. The company had consented to his use of them. There was no 'real sensible possibility'[89] of conflict between his duty to the company and his self-interest.

The rule that a fiduciary's duty to his principal and his interest to himself must not conflict remains absolute but the courts will examine the facts of each case to determine if there was a real risk of this occurring. It seems as though the court has perhaps moved away from the

---

84 Ibid at 133.
85 *Regal (Hastings) Ltd v Gulliver* [1967] 2 AC 134.
86 *Boardman v Phipps* [1967] 2 AC 46.
87 Subject, of course, to the 'liberal' reward that they were promised by the majority in the Lords.
88 *Queensland Mines Ltd v Hudson* (1978) 18 ALR 1.
89 Lord Upjohn in *Boardman v Phipps* [1967] 2 AC 46.

harshness of *Keech v Sandford* to ascertain more pragmatically not only whether duty and interest will conflict in theory, but also whether the two concepts would conflict in practice. Providing that trusts do not lose out to fiduciaries feathering their own nests, such a move is to be welcomed. This movement is bolstered by the *obiter* comments of Arden LJ (with whom Jonathan Parker LJ agreed) in *Murad v Al-Saraj*[90] who said:

> It may be that the time has come when the court should revisit the operation of the inflexible rule of equity in harsh circumstances, as where the trustee has acted in perfect good faith and without any deception or concealment, and in the belief that he was acting in the best interests of the beneficiary.[91]

As Arden and Jonathan Parker LJJ recognised, however, any such revision to equity's 'inflexible rule' would, due to the doctrine of precedent, have to come from the Supreme Court.

The constructive trust as a remedial device

It has been shown that a constructive trust may be used by equity on two occasions:

(a) through holding that one party must, due to an agreement reached or contributions made, hold property for other(s) in equity; or

(b) by ensuring that, although no formal trust was created, it is right for equity to compel someone in a fiduciary position to hold property for someone else.

These two types of constructive trust are, however, examples of equity responding to what the party at fault originally agreed to do. In the first type of constructive trust, the party at fault can be said to have originally intended to hold the property on trust for another beneficiary. In the second type, the defaulting party should have acted in the best interest of the party with whom they were in a fiduciary relationship.

There appears to be, in theory at least, another use of the constructive trust: as a remedy on a given set of facts. This is less a case of equity responding to the parties' intentions. It is really a question of equity imposing a constructive trust onto a set of facts because equity thinks that that is the right thing to do. This is known as the remedial constructive trust. It entails equity imposing a constructive trust onto a recipient of another's property where the recipient has unlawfully retained that property. This type of constructive trust has already been developed in other Commonwealth jurisdictions, most particularly in decisions handed down by the Supreme Court of Canada.[92]

Key Learning Point

The remedial constructive trust is equity looking backwards over the parties' relationship and imposing a constructive trust on it to act as a remedy for their present difficulties. The trust gives an equitable right in property to the successful party.

---

90 *Murad v Al-Saraj* [2005] EWCA Civ 959.
91 Ibid at 82.
92 See, for example, *Murdoch v Murdoch* (1973) 41 DLR (3d) 367, *LAC Minerals Ltd v International Corona Resources Ltd* (1989) 61 DLR (4th) 14 and *Korkontzilas v Soulos* (1997) 146 DLR (4th) 214.

This contrasts with the usual type of constructive trust (sometimes referred to as an 'institutional' constructive trust) which is simply recognised by the court as giving effect to what the parties originally intended should be their relationship. The institutional constructive trust, therefore, is traditionally seen as working from the circumstances that caused it to arise.

The chance to introduce this remedial type of constructive trust into England and Wales has met with mixed judicial favour.

In *Eves v Eves*,[93] Lord Denning MR described a remedial constructive trust as 'a constructive trust of a new model'.[94] He developed this theme from *Hussey v Palmer*,[95] where he described that it would be 'a trust imposed by law whenever justice and good conscience require it'.[96] It was of little surprise that Lord Denning MR was keen on the development of the remedial constructive trust since it would have enabled the courts to award very flexible types of remedy, whenever justice required it.

Whilst Lord Browne-Wilkinson in *Westdeutsche Landesbank Girozentrale v Islington LBC*[97] expressly left the door open to the remedial constructive trust being developed in English law, other English decisions have shown a reluctance to pursue such a doctrine.

Re Polly Peck International plc (in administration) (No. 2)[98] was one of a series of cases concerned with the collapse of Polly Peck International ('PPI'), a substantial company which owned over 200 subsidiary companies.

❖ APPLYING THE LAW

Polly Peck was controlled by Asil Nadir, who fled the UK to the Turkish part of Cyprus whilst awaiting trial on criminal fraud charges. He remained out of the country until 2010 when he returned to face the allegations and to attempt to prove his innocence. His trial resulted in a sentence of 10 years' imprisonment for stealing nearly £29 million from his companies.

The case concerned the invasion of the northern part of Cyprus by Turkish forces. That part of Cyprus unilaterally declared itself to be the Turkish Republic of Northern Cyprus. All immovable property belonging to Greek Cypriots was seized and transferred to the ownership, initially, of that Turkish state. Later on, certain properties, including a hotel, an apartment complex and a warehouse, were occupied by subsidiaries of PPI. The action was brought against PPI and their administrators for the money that those companies had received as a result of occupying the properties.

Amongst other claims, the claimants alleged that they should benefit from the court imposing a remedial constructive trust against the administrators of PPI in order that the claimants should have their properties returned to them. Underneath this argument lay the

---

93 *Eves v Eves* [1975] 1 WLR 1338.
94 Ibid at 1341.
95 *Hussey v Palmer* [1972] 1 WLR 1286.
96 Ibid at 1289–1290.
97 *Westdeutsche Landesbank Girozentrale v Islington LBC* [1996] AC 669 at 716.
98 *Re Polly Peck International plc (in administration) (No. 2)* [1998] 3 All ER 812.

idea that the claimants should not stand in the line of unsecured creditors of PPI and simply wait their turn to claim in PPI's insolvency. If they were to benefit from a remedial constructive trust, this would mean that they had equitable ownership of the various properties *before* PPI became insolvent. PPI's administrators would not be able to claim that those properties were assets of PPI, because the claimants would have a prior equitable interest over them. The claimants would take priority over the other unsecured creditors of PPI.

The Court of Appeal rejected the opportunity to impose a remedial constructive trust. The reasoning was largely due to the effects of what would have occurred had such a trust been imposed. The court recognised that it would have created an equitable right in the properties for the claimants and, therefore, it would have given them priority in the insolvency of PPI over all other unsecured creditors. To give the claimants this right would be to go against the wishes of Parliament, which had enacted a specific statutory scheme in the Insolvency Act 1986 for dealing with claims by unsecured creditors. It would not be fair to prioritise the claimants over the other creditors and it would not be right to go against Parliament's intention to deal with creditors as set out in that Act. Equity did not have the power to go against the will of Parliament. In the words of Mummery LJ, '[equity] cannot be legitimately moved by judicial decision down a road signed "No Entry" by Parliament'.[99]

As Nourse LJ recognised, awarding one party a proprietary interest would necessarily mean someone else's proprietary interest being decreased. Varying equitable interests in that manner required an Act of Parliament. Parliament had stepped in before to vary equitable interests such as through the Variation of Trusts Act 1958[100] and it would, believed Nourse LJ, need to do so here if the remedial constructive trust were to be developed in English law.

Consequently, it appears that English law has shied away from the opportunity taken by the Supreme Court of Canada to develop a remedial constructive trust. It has done so for good reasons, not least because it is seen to be unfair to a creditor that a particular party might be awarded an equitable interest in property through a remedial constructive trust when the creditor may have had no knowledge at all that the other claimant party even existed. That having been said, since *Re Polly Peck International plc (in administration) (No. 2)*[101] did concern an insolvent company, perhaps it should remain open for the English courts to develop a remedial constructive trust in cases which do not concern insolvency – for example, as it was initially developed in Canada – through cases concerning family breakdowns. Arguably, this might not be a huge leap from the cases recognising constructive trusts in those instances.

❖ ANALYSING THE LAW

How far do you think that the remedial constructive trust should play a role in English law, either by the courts in appropriate cases or by Parliament?

---

99 Ibid at 827.
100 See Chapter 10.
101 *Re Polly Peck International plc (in administration) (No. 2)* [1998] 3 All ER 812.

Points to Review

You have seen:

- how implied trusts arise generally by operation of law and are often used to fill gaps in the ownership of the equitable interest;
- how implied trusts are often based upon moral desires by equity to protect an innocent party; and
- how the constructive trust has been attempted to be developed into a more generic equitable remedy but how that door appears to have been closed by recent case-law developments.

Making connections

Learning about implied trusts is often the basis to learning about express trusts. If you understand how equity will step in with an implied trust, you can see how equity can manage scenarios where express trusts have been imperfectly formed or, alternatively, not formed at all. This can often occur where people buy a house together and, in the excitement of the occasion, do not explicitly state in what proportions they will share the equitable interest in the property. This is considered in more detail in Chapter 14.

The next four chapters consider how the express trust is formed. This is where the settlor deliberately sets out the equitable interest(s) in the trust property with the consequence that, hopefully, a beneficiary will not have to rely on an implied trust to fill in any gaps.

 Useful Things to Read

The best reading is contained in the primary sources listed below. It is always good to consider the decisions of the courts themselves as this will lead to a deeper understanding of the issues involved. A few secondary sources are also listed, which you may wish to read to gain additional insights into the areas considered in this chapter.

Primary sources

Boardman v Phipps [1967] 2 AC 46.
Barclays Bank Ltd v Quistclose Investments Ltd [1970] AC 567.
Eves v Eves [1975] 1 WLR 1338.
Re Polly Peck International plc (in administration) (No. 2) [1998] 3 All ER 812.
Re Vandervell's Trusts (No. 2) [1974] Ch 269.
Twinsectra Ltd v Yardley [2002] UKHL 12.
Vandervell v IRC [1967] 2 AC 291.
Westdeutsche Landesbank Girozentrale v Islington LBC [1996] AC 669.

Secondary sources

Michael Bridge, 'The *Quistclose* Trust in a World of Secured Transactions' (1992) 12 (3) OJLS 333. This article considers using the resulting trust, in its *Quistclose* form, as a form of security in commercial transactions.
Robert Chambers, *Resulting Trusts* (OUP, 1997). This book is devoted to the subject of the resulting trust. Chambers' view is that resulting trusts arise because of unjust

enrichment on the part of the recipient of property. This is a controversial view which is contradicted by other academics, notably William Swadling.

Alastair Hudson *Equity & Trusts* (7th edn, Routledge-Cavendish, 2012) chs 11 and 12.

Mohamed Ramjohn, *Text, Cases and Materials on Equity and Trusts* (4th edn, Routledge-Cavendish, 2008) chs 8 and 9.

Irit Samet, 'Guarding the fiduciary's conscience: a justification of a stringent profit-stripping rule' (2008) OJLS 28(4) 763–781. This article suggests that the notion that a fiduciary who has made gains should be stripped of all of those gains, regardless of whether he has acted in good faith or whether any harm has occurred to the trust, can be justified.

P St J Smart and Lusina Ho, 'Re-interpreting the *Quistclose* trust: A critique of Chambers' analysis' (2001) 21(2) OLJS 267–285. Chambers argues that the *Quistclose* trust is not a true trust, but one in which the borrower receives the entire equitable interest in the funds, subject to a contractual right of the lender to enforce the use which has been agreed between the two of them. This article critiques that view.

William Swadling, 'Explaining resulting trusts' (2008) LQR 124 (Jan) 72–102. This is a good overview of the subject of resulting trusts together with the presumptions that exist.

Chapter 4

Trust Formation: Capacity and Formalities

Chapter Contents

This, together with the next three chapters, considers arguably the most fundamental part of trusts law: how to form an express trust. It is essential that you grasp how the requirements to form an express trust operate as this is key to understanding this most vital area.

As You Read

In this chapter, you start to consider how the most widely used type of trust, the express trust, is formed. The express trust is a like a jigsaw: only when all of the pieces of the jigsaw are placed together will you see the main picture. It will take until (and including) Chapter 7 to understand how each component part of the express trust comes together. Here, look out for:

- the fundamental requirements to form an express trust. An understanding of these component parts is essential;
- capacity: who can declare a trust, who may be trustees and who can benefit from a trust; and
- formalities: how, in some types of trust, the law imposes formal requirements if the declaration of trust is going to be enforceable.

The Fundamental Requirements Needed to Form an Express Trust

The nature of an express trust was discussed in Chapter 2.

The diagram showing how an express trust is formed is set out below, in Figure 4.1.

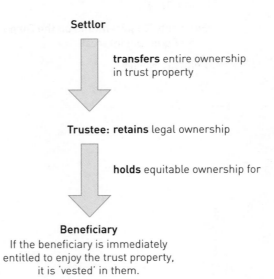

Settlor

transfers entire ownership
in trust property

Trustee: retains legal ownership

holds equitable ownership for

Beneficiary
If the beneficiary is immediately
entitled to enjoy the trust property,
it is 'vested' in them.

Figure 4.1 How a trust is formed: the concept of split ownership.

The diagram at Figure 4.1 is a straightforward illustration of how an express trust is formed. The key transactions in the diagram need to be examined.

The settlor transfers the entire ownership in the trust property to a trustee

This part of the setting up of the express trust can be broken down into two critical stages, in which the settlor:

(a)   declares the express trust; and
(b)   constitutes the express trust.

Both stages need to be done properly if a valid express trust is created. Again, both stages have several parts to them. When the settlor declares an express trust, they need to adhere to four requirements. The express trust must comply with:

● formal requirements;
● the three certainties;
● the beneficiary principle; and
● the rules against perpetuity.

Formal requirements

The formal requirements needed for a trust depend upon the type of property which is to be the subject matter of the trust. To take the following examples:

(a)   if the trust property is a chattel, that chattel needs to be delivered to the trustee and there must be an intention by the settlor to give the chattel to him;
(b)   in the case of shares, any shares must be transferred to the trustee by making use of a Stock Transfer Form;[1] and
(c)   if the trust property is land, the terms of the trust must be evidenced in writing and declared by some person able to declare the trust.[2] This requirement is considered later in this chapter.

The three certainties

It must be clear that there is certainty that the settlor intended to create a trust rather than simply intending to give the property away to someone. This is known as 'certainty of intention'. It must also be certain what the subject matter of the trust is, or in other words, precisely what property the settlor placed on trust. Finally, the requirements of certainty mean that it must be possible to say who is going to benefit from the trust or, in legal parlance, certainty of object must be present. These certainty requirements are known as 'the three certainties'. They are considered in detail in Chapter 5. As we shall see, the requirements of certainty are largely present to help the trustees administer the trust. The trustees must be able to be sure that the settlor intended to create a trust, what property the settlor expected his trustees to administer for the beneficiaries and lastly, who the beneficiaries are who will benefit from the trust.

---

1   Pursuant to the Stock Transfer Act 1963, s 1.
2   Law of Property Act 1925, s 53(1)(b).

The beneficiary principle

This principle requires that trusts in English law should usually be established for the benefit of ascertained or ascertainable beneficiaries. This means that they have already been identified, or are capable of being identified, as individuals or as being a member of a class of persons. In practical terms, this means that a trust should normally benefit an individual or individuals. Sometimes a trust may benefit a company because, in law, a company is generally seen to be a legal individual. A trust cannot normally be set up for a purpose, as opposed to an individual. Trusts for purposes generally do not comply with the beneficiary principle and will be void. There are exceptions to this requirement to have an ascertained or ascertainable beneficiary and these exceptions are considered, along with the beneficiary principle itself, in more detail in Chapter 6.

The rules against perpetuity

These are three rules which exist to ensure that a trust will start and come to an end at some point in the future. It is generally thought to be a bad thing to allow a trust to last forever. In the past, trusts were often used to manage property (usually vast estates of land) for wealthy families. The intention behind such trusts was to ensure the land remained in the same family. The danger with this intention is that, if this practice were widespread, it would be difficult for property to circulate freely in the economy. In a market economy, it is important that all types of property, both land and personal property, are allowed to be bought and sold easily and that there are as few restrictions on this ability to buy and sell as possible. The rules against perpetuity are considered in a chapter on the companion website.

Provided the settlor meets these four requirements, the express trust will have been declared successfully.

The settlor then needs to go on to ensure the trust is constituted. In theory, this is a relatively simple requirement. It means that the property of the trust must be properly transferred to the trustee. Constitution of a trust is needed so that the ownership of the trust property can be placed with the trustee and then the trustee can start to hold the equitable interest in the property on behalf of the beneficiary. Without transferring the property to the trustee, there can be no constitution, since the trustee would not own any property to administer on behalf of the beneficiary.

Of course, nowadays most express trusts are professionally drawn up by solicitors or accountants. This means that the requirements that the trust is properly declared and constituted should all be capable of being met in a document drawn up by the adviser. For such professionally drawn-up trusts, it is artificial to see the stages needed to declare a trust as coming one after the other: in truth, all the requirements to declare the trust and constitute it will be recorded in the same document. Nevertheless, to understand how such a modern trust may be drawn up, it is important to break down the separate requirements of declaring and constituting a trust and examine them in depth in the following chapters. The following four chapters, then, are all connected with this central theme of forming an express trust.

The trustee holds the property on behalf of the beneficiary

Once the trust has been validly declared and constituted by the settlor, it is ready to be used. That means that the trustee is subject to a number of duties and obligations, but enjoys some rights too in terms of administering the trust. The duties that the trustees are under, together with the rights that they enjoy, can be found in Chapters 8 and 9.

Correspondingly, as soon as the trustee holds the equitable ownership in the property for the beneficiary, the beneficiary can, provided his interest is vested, start to enjoy the property. If he is only entitled to enjoy the property for his lifetime, he is said to have a 'life interest' and can enjoy just the income from it. If, on the other hand, the beneficiary is entitled to enjoy the trust property entirely, he is said to have an 'absolute interest' in the property and can benefit from both the income from the trust property and enjoy the proceeds from its capital too.

This begs the question: what type(s) of property can be left on trust?

Trust Property

Figure 4.1 illustrates the settlor transferring trust property to the trustee to hold on trust for the beneficiary's enjoyment.

An express trust can be declared of virtually any property in which the settlor holds a legal interest. As mentioned, from the advent of trusts being first used, often trust property would amount to land. Wealthy families have made use of the trust for centuries as an attempt to ensure that land remained in their hands. But trusts do not have to have land as their property. 'Trust property' is used in a very wide sense.

Trust property may, for example, include the following, as well as land:

(a)   *Chattels.* Sometimes these are known as 'choses in possession'. They can be taken into the possession of someone or they are capable of being possessed. They are items which are not fixed to a piece of land, but are instead independent. In other legal systems, such as in France, they are known as 'movables' precisely because they can be moved about rather than being immovable, like land. This book that you are currently reading is a chattel, as is the chair upon which you are sitting to read it. If something is affixed to the land with the intention that it enhances the land, it ceases to be a chattel. For example, the washbasin and bath in your bathroom would not be seen as chattels since they are fixed to the land with the objective of enhancing the land.

(b)   *Money.* Often trusts are set up with just money as their property.

(c)   *Choses in action.* These are things which are dependent on the holder of them taking legal enforcement action (as opposed merely to taking physical possession of them) in order to obtain the rights associated with them. For instance, a share in a company is a chose in action. To obtain the money that it is worth, you would have to take legal action against the company and the company would pay you the value of it. The share certificate that you may have in your possession is merely evidence that you own a certain share in the company. Another example of a chose in action would be an insurance policy. Again, you would need ultimately to take legal action against the insurance company to enforce it.

All of these types of property are forms of 'personal' property, or 'personalty', so called because the rights in the property are enjoyed personally by the owner. The other type of property is known as 'real' property, or 'realty', which consists only of freehold land. This is called real property because the rights in it are real – they are rights that are enjoyed in the property itself, as against the whole world.

Often the property of a trust will be a mixture of all these different types of property. It is important to understand that not every trust will have land as its property.

❖ **EXPLAINING THE LAW**

Suppose Scott writes his will. He appoints Thomas and Vikas to be his trustees and provides that they are to hold on trust:

- his gold watch for his cousin, Amy;
- all of his shares in British Airways plc for his sister, Bethany;
- £100,000 in his bank account for his son, Charlie; and
- the house known as 4 Barlow Close, Derby, for his wife, Deborah.

These are examples of Scott declaring four express trusts: one in favour of each of the four beneficiaries. Providing the four requirements for a valid declaration are fulfilled, constitution of the trust will occur after Scott's death. Each of the four trusts has a different type of property. Only the final one has land as its trust property.

Capacity

It must be asked whether anyone can declare a trust, whether anyone can administer a trust and whether anyone can benefit from a trust. The capacity of each of the three main parties to an express trust – the settlor, the trustee and the beneficiary – must be examined.

The issue of capacity focuses on two concerns: whether the person under consideration has to be a particular age and whether the person must have mental stability in order to have capacity.

Capacity of the settlor

The general principle is that anyone can be a settlor of a trust and thus create a trust, provided they are at least 18 years old and are not mentally incapable. Of course, the settlor must own property and therefore must own the legal (or at least the equitable) interest in the property which they wish to settle on trust.

Children

It is possible for a child to settle personalty on trust. This trust is, however, voidable by the child, either before the child reaches 18 years old or within a reasonable time of reaching that age. This was shown in *Edwards v Carter*.[3]

Here, Albert Silber declared a trust in contemplation of a marriage between his son, Martin Silber and Lady Lucy Vaughan. The terms of the trust were that Albert was to pay the trustees the sum of £1,500 each year whilst Lady Lucy or any of their children were alive. The trustees were to pay that money, in turn, to Martin during his life and then, after his death or bankruptcy, to Lady Lucy and their children. The trust went on to say that if Albert left Martin further property under his (Albert's) will, that property was to be held by the trustees in place of the annual sum of £1,500. This trust was declared by Albert whilst Martin was still a child. Approximately one month after the trust was declared, Martin became an adult.

---

3   *Edwards v Carter* [1893] AC 360.

The terms of the trust effectively gave Martin a life interest in the money only, with remainder to his wife and any children that they might have. It obviously also provided that any further property Martin might acquire from his father upon his father's death was to be held on the same basis. Martin was, consequently, declaring a trust of property that he might acquire in the future.

Albert died in May 1887, nearly four years after declaring the trust. Martin attempted to repudiate the trust in July 1888 which, by then, was nearly five years after the trust had been declared.

The House of Lords held that Martin could not repudiate the trust. Whilst they affirmed the rule that a contract was voidable before a child reached 18 years old, or within a reasonable time of reaching 18 years old, their Lordships held that Martin had waited too long before repudiating the contract. Lord Watson explained the issue of repudiation as:

> If he [the former child] chooses to be inactive, his opportunity passes away; if he chooses to be active, the law comes to his assistance.[4]

For our present purposes, the case illustrates that a child can be a settlor of a trust of personalty. The child also has the ability to repudiate the trust, either before he reaches 18, or within a reasonable time of reaching 18. What is a reasonable time will be a question of fact for the court to resolve: the House of Lords found it unnecessary in the case to set down what period of time was reasonable in every case.

A child cannot own the legal estate in realty. Under Sched 1, para 1 of the Trusts of Land and Appointment of Trustees Act 1996, any realty conveyed to a child will be held automatically on trust for them, so they will only be able to enjoy an equitable interest in the property. Since a child is himself a beneficiary of such a trust and is unable to deal with the legal estate in the realty, the most a child can do with realty is to declare a trust of their equitable interest.

Mentally incapacitated individuals

Whether or not a person suffering from mental capacity has the ability to declare a trust was considered in *Re Beaney*.[5] The High Court held that whether a trust would be recognised depended on the size of the property being given away.

In the case, Mrs Maud Beaney owned her own home in Cranford, Middlesex. She had three children: Valerie (the eldest), Peter and Gillian. Mrs Beaney suffered from an 'advanced state of senile dementia'[6] from October 1972 until her death in 1974.

In May 1973, Mrs Beaney was admitted to hospital. Whilst there, Valerie claimed that her mother had decided to give her house to her. Valerie explained that this was in case the house needed to be sold at a future point to provide funds for the cost of her mother's care. Valerie asked a solicitor to draw up a document, formally transferring the house into her name. The solicitor brought the document to Mrs Beaney and explained to her that if she signed it, its effect would be to give the house to Valerie absolutely. The solicitor asked Mrs Beaney twice whether she understood the nature of the document and on both occasions, Mrs Beaney confirmed that she did. The solicitor, Valerie and a third witness believed that Mrs Beaney understood what she was doing when she signed the transfer document.

After her death, Peter and Gillian argued that Mrs Beaney had lacked capacity to transfer the house to Valerie. They said that their mother was confused, as illustrated by her calling her

---

4   Ibid at 366.
5   *Re Beaney* [1978] 1 WLR 770.
6   Ibid at 772.

family by incorrect names, having a tendency to get into the wrong bed whilst in hospital and by her handwriting being practically illegible. Valerie maintained that her mother did have capacity to transfer the house to her. She argued that the house was now hers, to the exclusion of Peter and Gillian.

Judge Martin Nourse QC held that the transfer of the property to Valerie was void due to a lack of capacity on Mrs Beaney's part.

He said that there were different degrees of understanding required for lifetime transfers of property. The degree of understanding required was related to the actual transfer which was proposed. How much the individual transferring the property had to understand about the transaction varied depending on the value of the property being transferred and its relation to that individual's other assets. He said:

> at one extreme, if the subject matter and value of a gift are trivial in relation to the donor's other assets a low degree of understanding will suffice. But, at the other extreme, if its effect is to dispose of the donor's only asset of value and thus, for practical purposes, to pre-empt the devolution of his estate under his will or on his intestacy, then the degree of understanding required is as high as that required for a will . . .[7]

When writing a will, Martin Nourse QC reminded the court that the degree of understanding required was that the testator had to understand the claims of all potential recipients of his property and the extent of the property of which he was disposing. The requirements for understanding are summarised in Figure 4.2 below.

Degree of understanding the donor must have for the transaction to be valid

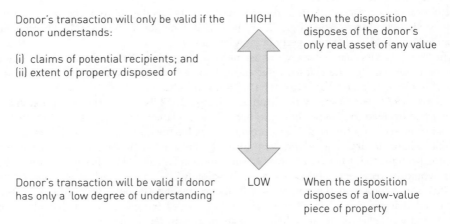

Donor's transaction will only be valid if the donor understands:

(i) claims of potential recipients; and
(ii) extent of property disposed of

HIGH — When the disposition disposes of the donor's only real asset of any value

Donor's transaction will be valid if donor has only a 'low degree of understanding'

LOW — When the disposition disposes of a low-value piece of property

Figure 4.2 The nature of 'understanding' a disposition of property.

---

7   Ibid at 774.

Applied to the facts here, Mrs Beaney was disposing of her home, which was her only real asset. The degree of understanding she needed to have for that transaction to be effective was as high as if she were writing her will. The reason for this was that she was effectively circumventing the need for a will, by divesting herself of her only real property by the transfer to her daughter. Mrs Beaney needed to understand first, that her other children might have at least moral claims to her home and second, that she was giving away her only real asset. She had effectively no other property of her own. The evidence of her confusion led to the conclusion that she could not have understood these two crucial issues. At best, the judge found that all she could have grasped was that the transfer had 'something to do with the house' and that the effect of it was 'to do something which her daughter Valerie wanted'.[8]

Re Beaney was applied by the High Court in the more recent case of Re Sutton.[9] This latter case illustrates how the test of whether the donor understands the nature of his gift is applied. Here, Norman and Rosalie Sutton lived in a bungalow in Tangmere, West Sussex. The house was in Norman's sole name. He transferred it in August 1997 to his son, Mark, who later transferred it into his and his wife's joint names. Norman and Rosalie continued to live in the bungalow. Norman died in 2005. Afterwards, Rosalie brought an action, claiming that the transfer of the house should be set aside. She argued that Norman lacked capacity when he signed the transfer.

The judge, Christopher Nugee QC, found that, unlike Mrs Beaney, the bungalow that was transferred was not Norman's only real asset. He had several other investments. Yet the judge found that the house was his main asset. As such, the degree of understanding that Norman had to have to show capacity was a high one. It had to be shown that he understood not only the 'general nature of the transaction but also the claims of other potential donees'.[10]

The judge pointed out that the burden of proof that a person lacked capacity lay with the person seeking to prove that the document was invalid. The evidence in this case was that Rosalie had to help Norman physically sign the document transferring the property to Mark. Mark admitted that he did not discuss the transaction with Norman and he was concerned that his father did not understand the effect of the document he was signing. Various entries from a diary kept by Rosalie confirmed Norman's deteriorating mental health before and around the time that he signed the transfer document. A consultant neurologist's view was that by the summer of 1997, Norman had significant cognitive decline which would have impaired his ability to understand a legal document and he did not believe that Norman would have had the high degree of understanding required from Re Beaney to ensure that the transfer he signed was valid.

Christopher Nugee QC accepted this evidence and held that Norman lacked capacity. In terms of the concrete proof that was needed for the transfer to have been valid, he said that Norman would have needed to understand that he was giving away the bungalow to Mark and that, as a consequence, neither he nor Rosalie would have had any right to remain in the house. To deprive himself and his wife of their matrimonial home was a serious consequence and, as such, Norman needed to demonstrate a high degree of understanding. The evidence showed that he did not have this.

The parties in the case not only wanted the judge to declare the transaction invalid but also that it was void.

---

8 Ibid at 777.
9 Re Sutton [2009] EWHC 2576 (Ch).
10 Ibid at [10].

Glossary: Void or Voidable?

If a document is void, that means that the document was never valid. It was of no effect at any time. Everything goes back to square one: it is as though there never was a transaction at all.

If, on the other hand, a document is voidable, this means that a document is valid, but that it may be set aside at the bequest of the innocent party. A good example occurs if the document was made as a result of a misrepresentation. The innocent recipient of the misrepresentation may well wish to have the document set aside – or, alternatively, they may be content to leave the document to have its normal legal effect. Such is possible if a document is voidable. 'Voidable' gives the innocent party some flexibility over whether they wish to rely on the document or not.

By the time of the hearing, Rosalie and Mark had been reconciled. The hearing was really about taxation and, in particular, the payment of capital gains tax.

Glossary: Capital Gains Tax

This tax is generally payable whenever an item is sold which has increased in value since it was purchased. A typical example might be a rare painting that was bought in 2000 for £1 million and is sold today for £3 million. Capital gains tax (CGT) is charged on the gain made – £2 million.

Reliefs exist and exemptions apply which mean that often no CGT is charged on everyday transactions. For instance, if a house is bought and then later sold, the principal private residence exemption will apply to the gain made. This means that no CGT is payable on the gain, provided that the owner used the house as his main residence whilst he owned it.

For more information on capital gains tax, see www.hmrc.gov.uk/cgt/

Rosalie and Mark feared that if the transaction was held to be valid, Mark would have acquired the bungalow in 1997. That would mean that, by the hearing date in 2009, he would have owned the property during the 12 years in which house prices increased significantly. In turn, that would mean that he would have made a large gain on the property so that when he sold it, CGT would be due from him. He would not have been able to make use of the principal private residence exemption since he had remained living in his own house. If, on the other hand, the transaction could be declared void, then the property had never been transferred to him, he did not own it now and so he would not be liable for any CGT when the property was eventually sold.

The court in Re Beaney had seemingly declared the transaction void. But Christopher Nugee QC pointed out that the judge in the earlier case had emphasised that it made no difference on the facts whether the transaction was void or voidable. Re Beaney could not be taken as authority that lack of capacity made a lifetime transfer void.

Christopher Nugee QC found that he did not need to express a decided view about whether the gift here by Norman to Mark was void or voidable. Such a declaration was only required by the parties in their efforts to avoid tax. Holding the transaction as invalid due to incapacity and that it should consequently be set aside was enough to dispose of the case. But he reviewed contradictory English and Australian authorities. He preferred the argument from the Australian courts[11] that lack of capacity made the gift voidable, as opposed to void. Being

---

11 As set out in *Gibbons v Wright* (1954) 91 CLR 423 and *Craigo v McIntyre* [1976] 1 NSWLR 729.

an equitable issue, a gift being voidable would enable the doctrine of laches to be applied if the innocent party took too long to apply to the court for a declaration that the document was voidable.

Glossary: Laches

The doctrine of laches (delay) applies where an equitable remedy is sought. It may prevent the innocent party from seeking their remedy if they have delayed too long in applying for it, after their right to pursue their remedy has arisen. This principle is discussed further in Chapter 1 (under equitable maxim (vii) that delay defeates equities) and in Chapter 12.

If laches applied, gifts such as those made here could be kept alive, notwithstanding the lack of the donor's capacity, because the donor failed to take action to set the gift aside within a reasonable period of time. Tantalisingly, by expressing no firm view, the High Court left this consequence open as a possibility if such gifts were seen to be voidable, as opposed to being void.

The usual practice, if possible, is to avoid scenarios such as those found in Re Beaney and Re Sutton. An alternative mechanism exists under the Mental Health Act 1983 where someone suffering from mental incapacity can place their affairs under the control of the Court of Protection. A disposition of their property then requires the court's permission for that disposition to be valid. In that manner, a person suffering from mental incapacity may have their affairs controlled so that there will be no questions raised if dispositions do have the permission of that court.

Capacity of the trustee(s)

Generally, anyone can be a trustee of a trust provided they are 18 years of age or older and of sound mind. Section 34(2) of the Trustee Act 1925 provides that the maximum number of trustees of land at any one time is four. Where more than four people are named as trustees, the trustees will consist of the first four named only. As an exception, charitable or ecclesiastical trusts of land may have an unlimited number of trustees.[12]

Normally, it is good practice to have at least two trustees, so that one may both assist and keep a watchful eye over the other.

❖ APPLYING THE LAW

Having at least two trustees is useful if the trust property contains land. If the land is sold, the purchase money will be paid to the trustees and then the buyer can overreach the equitable interests of the beneficiaries under the trust.[13] That means that the buyer will buy the land free from the trust, which is his objective. Overreaching the beneficial interests can only occur provided that there are at least two trustees of the trust or the trust is managed by a trust corporation.

---

12 Trustee Act 1925, s 34(3).
13 Law of Property Act 1925, ss 2 and 27.

Children as trustees

It appears that a child cannot be deliberately appointed to be a trustee, under s 20 of the Law of Property Act 1925. This section provides that:

> The appointment of an infant to be a trustee in relation to any settlement or trust shall be void, but without prejudice to the power to appoint a new trustee to fill the vacancy.

This applies to all express trusts, regardless of the type of property left by the settlor on trust. The decision in *ReVinogradoff*[14] would seem to suggest, however, that a child can be a trustee of an implied trust.

Here, a grandmother decided to transfer War Loan shares into hers and her granddaughter's joint names. Rather contradicting this transfer, the grandmother then purported to leave the same shares to another recipient in her will. After she died, the grandmother's executors brought an action seeking to ascertain whether the granddaughter did have any interest in the shares. The court held that she enjoyed no equitable interest in the shares and instead, the granddaughter held the shares on resulting trust for the grandmother's estate. The granddaughter was just four years old and must surely be one of the youngest trustees ever known.

Section 36 of the Trustee Act 1925 provides that a trustee who is an infant may be replaced as a trustee. For the draftsman of the Act to provide that an infant trustee is capable of being replaced confirms that it must be possible to have children as trustees. It appears, however, that the combined effect of this provision, s 20 of the Law of Property Act 1925 and *ReVinogradoff* is that children can be trustees of implied trusts only and are liable to be replaced by adult trustees.

Trust corporations

The reasons why settlors place property on trust have changed over the centuries. In its original form, the *use* was probably a means by which paying tax could be avoided. The trust became a device in the eighteenth and nineteenth centuries where this aim could still be achieved but could also be a mechanism for retaining property within the same family (subject to perpetuity requirements being met). More modern functions of the trust have been discussed in Chapter 2, but perhaps the general focus of the trust nowadays has reverted to its original function: to be used as a means of tax avoidance.

Due to this, it is becoming an increasingly common practice that settlors do not appoint individuals to manage trusts but instead use trust corporations.

Section 68(18) of the Trustee Act 1925 defines a 'trust corporation' as:

> the Public Trustee or a corporation either appointed by the court in any particular case to be a trustee, or entitled by rules made under subsection (3) of section four of the Public Trustee Act, 1906, to act as custodian trustee . . .

In practice, trust deeds usually give a wider meaning to the term than the Trustee Act 1925. This means that trust corporations are generally large organisations such as banks, insurance

---

14 *Re Vinogradoff* [1935] WN 68.

companies and other financial institutions which are incorporated in the UK. Such organisations have specialist staff who invest in and manage property on a daily basis. The theory is a trust managed by such a trust corporation will be managed more effectively and, perhaps, more professionally than a trust managed by individual trustees who, despite being well-meaning, may not naturally have the skills required to administer property for the benefit of others.

The appointment of a trust corporation to administer a trust has a convenient legal consequence if the trust wishes to dispose of property which is land. Section 14(2)(a) of the Trustee Act 1925 provides that a trust corporation, as a sole trustee, can give a valid receipt for the money arising from a sale of land. The beneficial interests under the trust are then overreached and the buyer of the land will take the land free from the trust. If individual trustees are appointed instead of a trust corporation, the same sub-section of the Act provides that the valid receipt is needed from at least two trustees in order that the beneficial interests under the trust are overreached.

It is possible to appoint a trust corporation to be a trustee alongside an individual or individuals. Due to the legal advantage of appointing a trust corporation in relation to the sale of trust property, however, such a dual appointment is rare.

Member-nominated trustees

The general rule is that anyone may be a trustee provided they are over 18 years of age and are of sound mind, so that they may hold property.

An exception exists in relation to occupational pension schemes. These are pension schemes which are established by employers to provide benefits to their employees when the employee retires. Benefits are usually paid to person(s) the employee chooses through a Letter of Wishes if the employee dies during the time he is a member of the scheme albeit that the trustees are not bound to follow the employee's choice in the Letter of Wishes and may pay the proceeds to the employee's personal representatives instead. Occupational pension schemes are a form of discretionary trust.

At least one-third of all of the trustees of an occupational pension scheme must be member-nominated, pursuant to s 241 of the Pensions Act 2004. This type of trustee must be appointed following a process of election in which the members of the scheme – both presently paying into the pension and those in retirement – may participate. Usually member-nominated trustees will be members of the pension scheme themselves.[15] Section 241(7) specifically states that member-nominated trustees enjoy exactly the same rights to manage the trust as the other trustees.

❖ APPLYING THE LAW

The requirement of occupational pension schemes to contain member-nominated trustees was as a result of the circumstances surrounding Robert Maxwell and the occupational pension scheme of the *Daily Mirror* newspaper.

---

15 Although non-members may be appointed to be member-nominated trustees, providing the employer's consent is obtained if the employer requires it to be obtained: s 241(5)(c).

Robert Maxwell was a publisher who owned the Mirror group of newspapers in the 1980s and early 1990s. He was found dead in the sea off the Canary Islands in November 1991, after which his media empire began to unravel. It appears that he took money (approximately £400 million) from the *Daily Mirror's* occupational pension scheme to fund both his businesses and his own personal lifestyle. This resulted in the amount of money in the scheme being reduced and left some of his employees with a greatly reduced retirement provision.

As a result of this, member-nominated trustees were introduced to give members of occupational pension schemes a greater sense of security that their retirement funds were being protected by people who were in the same position as themselves – members of the scheme–and who would, therefore, have a natural interest in safeguarding and administering the trust.

Capacity of the beneficiaries

Anyone can be a beneficiary. This means that children can benefit from a trust, as can mentally incapacitated individuals. Even if the property of the trust is land, children are only prevented from holding a legal estate in land and not an equitable one.[16] Companies may also benefit from a trust.

Having considered who create, administer and benefit from a trust, it is time now to turn to the first of the requirements that will be considered over the creation of an express trust: requirements as to formality.

Formalities

As a preliminary point, the difference between creating an express trust and assigning an equitable interest under a trust must be understood. That is illustrated in Figure 4.3 below.

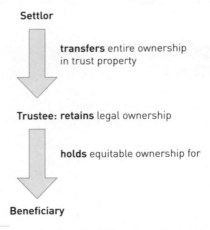

Declaring a trust

Settlor

transfers entire ownership in trust property

Trustee: retains legal ownership

holds equitable ownership for

Beneficiary

---

16 Law of Property Act 1925, s 1(6).

Assigning an equitable interest

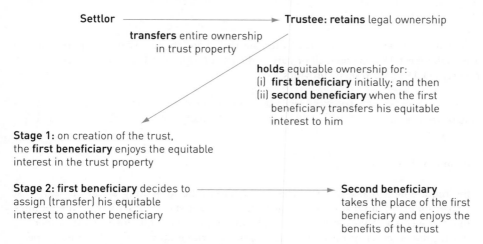

Figure 4.3 The difference between declaring an express trust and assigning an equitable interest.

Assigning an equitable interest, then, is an act undertaken by the beneficiary once the trust is in existence. The reason for drawing this distinction between the creation of a trust and the assignment of an equitable interest under a trust that already exists is because, generally speaking, there are no written formality requirements that must be fulfilled on the declaration of a trust, unless the trust property consists of land. There are, however, always requirements of formality[17] that must be met on the assignment of an equitable interest.

Formality Requirements on the Declaration of a Trust

The fundamental position is that there are no requirements of writing that a settlor must meet when he declares a trust. That means that a trust can be declared entirely orally. Provided the other requirements to declare an express trust are met (three certainties, beneficiary principle and the rules against perpetuity), then the trust will be effectively declared. Naturally, proving that an express trust which has been declared orally actually exists is a practical problem that a settlor would have to address if required but declaring a trust orally is legally possible.

Making connections

Think back to the facts of *Paul v Constance*,[18] that was considered earlier in Chapter 2. Both the trial judge and the Court of Appeal had little difficulty in finding that Mr Constance had

---

17 See pp. 191 onwards.
18 *Paul v Constance* [1977] 1 WLR 527.

declared a trust orally of money in his bank account by the words 'This money is as much yours as mine'. Mr Constance held the money as trustee on behalf of himself and Mrs Constance.

There is, however, an exception to the rule that there are no writing requirements to declare a valid trust. That is when all or part of the trust property is land. In that case, the Law of Property Act 1925 s 53(1)(b) provides:

> a declaration of trust respecting any land or any interest therein must be manifested and proved by some writing signed by some person who is able to declare such trust or by his will . . .

This paragraph shows:

(a) the requirement that a declaration of trust should be in writing applies to any trust concerning land, no matter what tenure of land is at issue. In other words, the require-ment of writing applies to both freehold and leasehold land that forms trust property;

(b) strictly, the exact terms of the trust need not be written down when the trust property concerns land. As more and more trusts are professionally drawn up nowadays, it will frequently be the case that the exact terms of the trust are written down in a formal document. That is not necessary to comply with the requirements of the Law of Property Act 1925. All that is needed is that the terms of the trust must be 'proved' or evidenced in writing. It is possible, for instance, that a trust of land could meet the requirements of the Act by having its main terms embodied in a simple note written by the settlor to the trustee. It would, for example, be possible for the settlor to write the terms of a trust on a 'post-it' note;

(c) the requirement that the terms of a trust concerning land must be written down applies to trusts declared both during the settlor's lifetime and in his will. Of course, s 9 of the Wills Act 1837 already imposes more strict requirements on the writing of a will, including the requirement that the signature of the testator is witnessed by at least two witnesses present at the same time as the testator. These stricter requirements of the Wills Act 1837 apply to a trust declared in a will; and

(d) if an express trust of land is not evidenced in writing, it will be unenforceable as opposed to void. This effectively means that the trust does exist but the beneficiary is dependent on the trustee's moral integrity to honour the terms of the trust. A court will generally not enforce an express trust of land which does not meet the requirements set out in this sub-section.

The Law of Property Act 1925 s 53(1)(b) applies only to a trust of land declared as an express trust. It does not apply to constructive or resulting trusts, even if they contain land as their property. This is set out in s 53(2), '[t]his section does not affect the creation or operation of resulting, implied or constructive trusts'.

This has the effect that all constructive and resulting trusts of land can still be valid without their terms being written down.

The effect of a trust involving land being declared only orally was considered in *Rochefoucauld v Boustead*.[19]

---

19 *Rochefoucauld v Boustead* [1897] 1 Ch 196.

The facts concerned land owned in Sri Lanka by the Comtesse de la Rochefoucauld. The land was sold by the mortgagee (lender) to the defendant in 1873. The land was used for coffee production and, in the years following the sale, the defendant accounted to the Comtesse for some of the profits made from the coffee growing. The Comtesse's claim was that the defendant owned the lands on trust for her, using this account of profits to her as evidence for her claim. The defendant went bankrupt in 1880. The defendant's trustee in bankruptcy claimed the lands as belonging to the defendant absolutely, so that they could be used in order to pay the defendant's creditors. The lands were sold. The Comtesse brought an action in 1894, claiming that the defendant owned the land on trust for her from when he bought them in 1873 and, as such, he now owned the proceeds of sale from the land for her in the same capacity. In response to her claim, the defendant argued that the land had been originally transferred to him as absolute owner and, in any event, the equivalent then of s 53(1)(b) of the Law of Property Act 1925[20] applied to the claimant's claim. This meant that any trust of the land would have been required to have been set out in writing and, since it was not, there could be no trust of the land in the claimant's favour.

The Court of Appeal disagreed with the trial judge and held that there was an express trust in favour of the claimant. She had transferred the land to the defendant subject to the terms of a trust. In delivering the judgment of the Court of Appeal, Lindley LJ explained:

(a)   section 7 of the Statute of Frauds 1677 (the predecessor to s 53(1)(b) of the Law of Property Act 1925) did not require a trust to be declared in writing when it was first established by the settlor. It only required that the trust should be *proved* in writing by a written document signed by the settlor. Such a document could be dated at any time:[21] it did not have to be contemporaneous with the date the trust was established;

(b)   the requirement that the trust must be proved in writing could not outweigh a fraud. The requirement of writing would not be allowed to 'trump' the maxim that equity will not permit a statute to be used as an instrument of fraud. The defendant could not, consequently, hide behind s 7 and argue that no written document meant the trust was invalid when he knew the land was transferred to him as a trustee. As Lindley LJ said:

> Consequently, notwithstanding the statute, it is competent for a person claiming land conveyed to another to prove by parol (i.e. oral) evidence that it was so conveyed upon trust for the claimant, and that the grantee, knowing the facts, is denying the trust and relying upon the form of conveyance and the statute, in order to keep the land himself;[22] **and**

(c)   Letters written between the claimant and defendant could establish that a trust actually existed. Those would fulfil s 7. Once the actual existence of a trust had been established, the exact terms of it could be added to by the claimant's oral evidence.

The principles which arise in this case are equally applicable to s 53(1)(b). Overall, the case illustrates the principle that equity will not permit someone to deny the existence of a trust just because the precise requirements of a statute have not been met.

---

20 Statute of Frauds 1677, s 7.
21 See also *Gardner v Rowe* (1828) 5 Russ 258; 38 ER 1024.
22 *Rochefoucauld v Boustead* [1897] 1 Ch 196 at 205.

The principle arising from *Rochefoucauld v Boustead* was taken one stage further in the decision of the High Court in *Hodgson v Marks*.[23] Here, the beneficiary's action was not against the actual person who had defrauded her, but against a third party. The High Court held that the principle in *Rochefoucauld* could still apply.

In this case, Mrs Beatrice Hodgson was an elderly widow who took a lodger, John Evans, into her home. It seems that Mr Evans was of a controlling nature, for example, following Mrs Hodgson when she went out shopping and also persuading her to give him, over time, her life savings for him to invest. Twelve months after taking him in, Mrs Hodgson trusted him so much that she transferred her home into his name. According to Mr Evans, this was done to allay his fear of Mrs Hodgson's nephew from evicting Mr Evans from the house.

Mrs Hodgson believed that she had verbally agreed with Mr Evans that the house would continue to be hers, albeit registered at HM Land Registry in his name. Four years later, Mr Evans sold the house (allegedly with vacant possession) to Mr Marks. Mr Marks and Mrs Hodgson then slowly realised that each of them had competing claims in the house. Mr Marks' view was that he had bought the property from the registered proprietor with vacant possession and he was entitled to it. Mrs Hodgson's case was that she still owned the equitable interest under a trust. Her difficulty was that since this was a trust of land, s 53(1)(b) required the trust to be proved in writing and signed by some person able to declare the trust. There had, of course, been nothing written down by either her or Mr Evans to evidence the creation of a trust. She wanted a declaration from the court that Mr Marks was bound to transfer the house to her.

Ungoed-Thomas J found that Mrs Hodgson had transferred the house to Mr Evans but that she had never intended to make a gift of the property to him entirely and that she had always intended to retain the beneficial interest in the house. He held that Mr Evans possessed only the legal interest in the property for himself and that he held the equitable interest for Mrs Hodgson.

Counsel for Mr Marks had argued that the principle in *Rochefoucauld v Boustead* only applied where the individual who had caused the fraud was trying to deny the existence of a trust. That was not the position here. Here, it was not Mr Evans being subjected to the principle in *Rochefoucauld v Boustead* but instead a third party, Mr Marks. Mr Marks was an entirely innocent buyer of the house.

Ungoed-Thomas J rejected this submission. He said whoever relied on s 53(1)(b) to deny the existence of a trust in circumstances like those in the case was, by definition, using the statute as an instrument of fraud – they were using the statute to try to prevent any recognition of the trust. It was not necessary that that principle should be confined simply to those who had committed the fraud. Ungoed-Thomas J held that Mrs Hodgson's oral evidence would be allowed to clarify the written conveyance of the house to Mr Evans because to exclude her oral evidence would be to hide behind the writing requirements of s 53(1)(b) and permit the statute to be used as an instrument of fraud. As Ungoed-Thomas J put it,[24] 'extrinsic evidence is always admissible of the true nature of any transaction'. His decision actually went further than that in *Rochefoucauld v Boustead* on this issue of the type of evidence needed to establish a trust. In *Rochefoucauld*, it was the letters written between the parties that were relied on primarily

---

23 *Hodgson v Marks* [1970] 3 WLR 956.
24 Ibid at 969.

to establish the trust whereas in *Hodgson v Marks*, the verbal evidence of Mrs Hodgson was accepted on its own to create a trust.

The actual result in the High Court went against Mrs Hodgson, since it was held that she had failed to satisfy the requirements of being in 'actual occupation' of the property under the terms of s 70(1)(g) of the Land Registraton Act 1925. Her occupation of the property had not been apparent to Mr Marks when he had visited the property before he bought it. As such, she had no overriding interest to remain in the house. She appealed to the Court of Appeal.[25]

Mrs Hodgson was successful at the Court of Appeal. The decision of the Court largely rested upon the fact that she was in actual occupation of the property under s 70(1)(g) of the Land Registration Act 1925 and did enjoy an interest in the land which overrode that of the buyer, Mr Marks.

In delivering the only substantive opinion of the court, Russell LJ did not disagree with the trial judge that there was an express trust but offered alternative solutions:

(a) Since Mrs Hodgson never intended to give the house away to Mr Evans, he must have held it on trust for her. Instead of that being an express trust, it could be said to be an implied resulting trust. Section 53(2) of the Law of Property Act 1925 specifically states that resulting trusts of land do not have to be proved in writing. The oral evidence of Mrs Hodgson would be more than sufficient to establish a resulting trust of her home in her favour. If an attempted express trust had failed due to it not being evidenced in writing, that presented an opportunity for a resulting trust to apply; or

(b) A resulting trust might arise due to Mrs Hodgson never actually giving the equitable interest in her house away. There was therefore no 'disposition' of the equitable interest or any declaration of trust within the meaning of s 53(1)(b). Russell LJ merely offered this as a suggestion but declined to hold that it was directly applicable to the facts in the case.

Russell LJ did not answer the question as to whether the principle in *Rochefoucauld v Boustead* applied only to those in direct receipt of the property. Mr Marks did not, on the facts, know about Mrs Hodgson's interest in the property and relying on s 53(1)(b) in such circumstances probably could not be seen to be acting fraudulently. As Russell LJ put it,[26] '[q]uite plainly Mr Evans could not have placed any reliance on section 53, for that would have been to use the section as an instrument of fraud'.

No opinion was offered on whether a third party would, in theory, be prevented from relying on s 53(1)(b) to deny the existence of a trust if in fact they had knowledge of the trust.

Summary of the main principles of s 53(1)(b) of the Law of Property Act 1925

A trust with its property as land must, therefore, be proved in writing as a general rule, to comply with s 53(1)(b). There are exceptions to that principle:

(a) The principle in *Rochefoucauld v Boustead* applies the equitable maxim that equity will not permit a statute to be used as an instrument of fraud. It is submitted that this principle would extend to third parties, such as Mr Marks, if they had knowledge of the fraud which had been committed. The equitable maxim itself is phrased generally and

---

25 *Hodgson v Marks* [1971] Ch 892.
26 Ibid at 933.

there is nothing in it to limit it simply to those who have personally committed the fraud; and

(b) a trust of land created by an implied (resulting or constructive) trust is not required to be evidenced in writing due to s 53(2) of the Law of Property Act 1925.

Formality Requirements on the Disposition of an Equitable Interest

Consider again the diagram showing the lifetime disposition of an equitable interest in Figure 4.3. The nature of this transaction, of course, is fundamentally different from the declaration of an express trust. An express trust may be declared orally unless, as we have seen, the trust property consists of land.

The requirements of the disposition of an equitable interest are more strict than declaring a trust. Any disposition of an equitable interest must be in writing, under s 53(1)(c) of the Law of Property Act 1925. This provides:

> a disposition of an equitable interest or trust subsisting at the time of the disposition, must be in writing signed by the person disposing of the same, or by his agent thereunto lawfully authorised in writing or by will.

The important requirements of this paragraph are:

(a) Any disposition of an equitable interest has to be in writing. This is different from s 53(1)(b), where the declaration of a trust merely had to be *proved* in writing. This requirement enabled the trust in *Rochefoucauld v Boustead* to be established because there was enough to indicate the existence of a trust in letters passing between the parties in the case to meet the statutory requirement that the trust could be proved through writing. Yet under s 53(1)(c) the actual disposition itself must be in written form;

(b) The disposition of the equitable interest must be signed by the person disposing of it. Again, this is a more onerous requirement than in s 53(1)(b) where the writing required for a trust of land to be declared could be signed by 'some person who is able to declare such trust'. Section 53(1)(b) does not necessarily mean that the settlor has to sign the written document declaring the trust; and

(c) When disposing of an equitable interest, the actual nature of the property which is the subject of that equitable interest is irrelevant. All dispositions of equitable interests in any type of property − not just land, as under s 53(1)(b) (regarding declaration of trusts) − must be in writing.

Once again, s 53(2) may 'save' some equitable dispositions if they have not been written down since that sub-section confirms that the requirements of s 53(1)(c) do not apply to the operation of resulting or constructive trusts. It is due to s 53(2) that there is cross-over between the case law which is considered under s 53(1)(c) and which has already been considered in the context of implied trusts in Chapter 3.

The policy reason underpinning s 53(1)(c) is that the trustees ought to know who owns the equitable interest in the trust property. If their task is to administer the trust, it is probably useful if they know for whom they are administering it! Requiring each disposition of an equitable interest to be in writing helps to keep a track of who owns the equitable interest which, in turn, assists the trustees in administering the trust. If the court has to step in to administer the trust because the trustees fail to do so, such evidence again is vital so that the court can see who the current beneficiaries are.

Most of the case law in this area is concerned with whether or not there has been a 'disposition' within s 53(1)(c). It is only if there has been a disposition of the equitable interest that the requirement of writing applies. It is clear that where a beneficiary transfers his equitable interest to another person directly, as shown in Figure 4.3, that will be a disposition of the equitable interest and it will only be valid if it has been written down. There are, however, variations on this straightforward transfer that have occurred and now need to be considered. The question is always whether what has been done amounts to a disposition.

Where the beneficiary asks the trustee to hold their equitable interest for another person

In this scenario, the beneficiary does not transfer their equitable interest directly to a recipient but instead asks the trustee to hold the equitable interest on trust for that other person. This situation is shown in Figure 4.4 below.

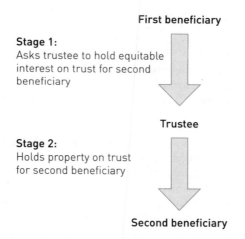

First beneficiary

Stage 1:
Asks trustee to hold equitable interest on trust for second beneficiary

Trustee

Stage 2:
Holds property on trust for second beneficiary

Second beneficiary

Figure 4.4 The beneficiary instructs the trustee to hold the trust property on trust for another.

The literal view: *Grey v Inland Revenue Commissioners*[27]

This situation arose in *Grey v Inland Revenue Commissioners*. The case concerned six trusts that Mr Hunter had declared. Five of the trusts were for the benefit of each of Mr Hunter's grandchildren; the sixth was for the benefit of any grandchildren that might be born in the future. Some years after declaring the trusts, Mr Hunter transferred to the trustees 18,000 shares in a company. He then orally instructed the trustees to split the shares into six equal parts and to hold the shares on each of the six trusts that he had previously established. This verbal instruction was later confirmed in a document.

The Inland Revenue wanted stamp duty to be paid on the document confirming the transfer of the shares. They argued that the document effected the disposition of the shares

---

27 *Grey v Inland Revenue Comissioners* [1960] AC 1.

from Mr Hunter to the trusts for his grandchildren. As the document operated in this way, stamp duty was payable on it.

Glossary: Stamp Duty

Stamp duty was a tax payable on documents which transferred land or shares. It was charged on the value of the transaction which the paper document effected. It was, for the vast majority of transactions, replaced on 1 December 2003 by Stamp Duty Land Tax for transfers of land and Stamp Duty Reserve Tax for shares purchased electronically. Stamp duty itself only exists nowadays for shares purchased using a paper form. Such instances will be rare. These changes were made due to the increasing use of electronic forms for the transfer of land and shares.

The trustees of the trusts argued that no stamp duty was due to the Inland Revenue because the document which Mr Hunter subsequently entered was merely confirmatory of the oral transfer of the shares which had taken place earlier. Since stamp duty applied only to documents, nothing was due since the transfer had occurred verbally and the document merely operated as a confirmation that the transfer had taken place. The Inland Revenue's response to that was that the transfer consisted of a disposition of an equitable interest and, under s 53(1)(c), such disposition was only effective if done in writing. That meant that the document recording the transfer of the shares was actually doing something and was not merely confirmatory in nature, if the shares were to be effectively transferred. As the document was active, stamp duty could be charged upon it.

The case reached the House of Lords. Viscount Simonds held that 'disposition' in s 53(1)(c) had to be given its natural meaning. That meant that the direction from Mr Hunter to his trustees to hold the shares on the trusts of his grandchildren was a 'disposition'. To be valid, such a disposition had to be in writing. Thus the document which Mr Hunter later entered into was the only effective act to transfer the shares to the grandchildren. As the document was effective and not merely confirmatory, stamp duty was due.

Lord Radcliffe mused that the oral actions of Mr Hunter could, in theory, amount to a declaration of trust and, since the trust property was not land, such declaration could be valid even though it was not in writing. But he thought that where the beneficiary exhausted his equitable interest by his oral direction to the trustees, as had occurred here, that could *also* amount to a disposition of the equitable interest which, to be valid, had to be in writing to comply with s 53(1)(c).

❖ ANALYSING THE LAW

Viscount Simonds applied the literal rule of interpretation to the word 'disposition' in *Grey v IRC*. Remember, however, the policy reason underpinning s 53(1)(c): that dispositions of equitable interests should be in writing so that the trustees always know who owns the equitable interest. Why was writing needed on the facts of this case? Mr Hunter had instructed the trustees explicitly to transfer the equitable interest to his grandchildren so they already knew the new owners of the equitable interest. In light of this, do you think that *Grey v IRC* was rightly decided? Was Viscount Simonds' interpretation of 'disposition' too one-dimensional? Should the House of Lords have reflected more deeply on the policy reasons behind the sub-section?

A potential shift away from the literal view: *Oughtred v Inland Revenue Commissioners*[28]

This issue was considered again by the House of Lords, in an opinion delivered just two days after those in *Grey v IRC* in the case of *Oughtred v Inland Revenue Commissioners*. The facts concerned a mother and son's shareholding in a private company. Shares were held by trustees for the mother, Phyllis Oughtred, as to 100,000 ordinary shares and a further 100,000 preference shares for her life, with remainder to her son, Peter. In order to save tax, Peter agreed that he would surrender his remainder interest in all of those shares, in return for which he would be entitled to 44,190 ordinary shares and 28,510 preference shares from his mother's separate personal shareholding. This agreement was made orally. Eight days later, documents were executed formalising the transaction: the first being a document in which the trustees acknowledged that they now held Peter's former shares on trust for Mrs Oughtred; the second being an actual transfer of those shares to Mrs Oughtred.

The Inland Revenue claimed stamp duty on the document transferring the shares to Mrs Oughtred. Their view was that Peter had disposed of his equitable (reversionary) interest in the 200,000 shares by transferring his equitable interest to the trustees. Transfers of equitable interests had to be in writing under s 53(1)(c) and this was the only document available which would satisfy that requirement. It therefore fell within the meaning of 'disposition' within that paragraph.

Lords Radcliffe and Cohen were in the minority in their opinions. Lord Radcliffe analysed the matter in this way:

(a) Originally, Peter owned a reversionary interest in the shares (i.e. an interest that he was entitled to enjoy at a later point in his life, after his mother had died);

(b) He orally agreed to transfer those shares to Mrs Oughtred. This oral agreement gave his mother an equitable interest in his reversionary interest;

(c) Mrs Oughtred now had a right in the shares. The shares were a unique item, such that if Peter had refused to transfer them, his mother could have obtained the remedy of specific performance in relation to the agreement reached with him;

(d) In being subjected to this theoretical action of specific performance, Peter became a trustee *sub modo* (i.e. subject to a condition or qualification) of that right for his mother. He had no option but to transfer the shares to her from that point onwards and had he not done so, she could have sued him for breaching that trust. Such a trust which arose was an implied constructive trust, arising by operation of law;

(e) Section 53(2) of the Law of Property Act 1925 specifically permitted such implied trusts to circumvent the requirements of writing in s 53(1);

(f) Peter's trusteeship was confirmed as fully established when he received the promised shares from his mother; and

(g) As such, Peter continued to hold the shares on trust for his mother, a trust that was never required to be in writing due to it not consisting of land. The written documents did not, in Lord Radcliffe's view, confirm that the trustees had been instructed to dispose of Peter's equitable interest to his mother because the trustees never had any rights to dispose of at all. Peter always retained the rights in the shares, which he transferred to his mother.

---

28 *Oughtred v Inland Revenue Commissioners* [1960] AC 206.

The majority of their Lordships took a different view. Lord Denning took, for him, a rather strict view in that he believed that s 53(1)(c) required a disposition of an equitable interest to be in writing and such a requirement could not be circumvented by s 53(2). The written document transferring the shares to Mrs Oughtred therefore fell within the confines of s 53(1)(c).

Lord Jenkins, giving the leading speech of the majority, believed that even if Peter was a constructive trustee of the shares for his mother, this would not prevent a subsequent written transfer of the shares taking place. On the facts, a written transfer of the shares had taken place; since it had actually occurred, it was this document that was liable to stamp duty. To explain his view, Lord Jenkins used the analogy of a typical conveyancing transaction. When a house is agreed to be sold, at the point the agreement is made between the seller and buyer, the seller becomes a constructive trustee of the house for the buyer. It remains standard practice for the parties later to execute a formal transfer document. That latter document attracts stamp duty. Stamp duty does not become unpayable just because a constructive trust has already risen of the rights in the house in favour of the buyer. That analogy could be applied here. Even if Peter was a constructive trustee of the shares for his mother, the fact that they then entered into a transfer document in which he transferred his shares to the trustees for them to hold on trust for her meant that such a document could be considered to attract stamp duty.

Lord Jenkins believed that a beneficiary who enjoyed rights in property by virtue of a constructive trusteeship had a 'lower' category of rights than a beneficiary who had had an equitable interest properly transferred to them:[29]

> In truth, the title secured by a purchaser by means of an actual transfer is different in kind from, and may well be far superior to, the special form of proprietary interest which equity confers on a purchaser in anticipation of such transfer.

To support this view, he explained that a purchaser of shares in a private company, as here, only enjoyed rights such as being able to vote at general meetings of the company when he was a full owner of the shares, as opposed to being entitled to them under a constructive trust.

Lord Jenkins was of the view that if the subject matter of the transaction could only be transferred by a written document, then *any* instrument executed in performance of the transaction would be subjected to stamp duty. This caught the documentation that had been executed in the case.

It appears, then, that it will not be sufficient to transfer an equitable interest orally if a written document is a normal and integral part of the means necessary to transfer that interest. The shares here were intended to be transferred by written document and the oral disposition by Mrs Oughtred to Peter was not sufficient to fulfil s 53(1)(c).

The minority view given credence: *Re Holt's Settlement*[30]

That having been said, Megarry J appears to have been sympathetic to the views of the minority in *Re Holt's Settlement* and did believe that it was possible to transfer some equitable interests orally, due to the transferor becoming a constructive trustee of them.

The facts concerned the variation of a trust (considered in more detail in Chapter 10). A settlor established a trust with a life interest for his daughter (a Mrs Wilson) with remainder

---

29 Ibid at 240.
30 *Re Holt's Settlement* [1969] 1 Ch 100.

interests for Mrs Wilson's children equally provided they reached the age of 21. Mrs Wilson wished to vary the trust by, amongst other matters, surrendering her interest in half of the income from the trust and increasing the contingency age that her children might enjoy the trust property by nine years. That meant that the children would have to reach the age of 30 before they could enjoy the property, assuming that by then Mrs Wilson herself had died.

The three children were all infants. As will be seen,[31] under the Variation of Trusts Act 1958, the court must approve a variation of a trust on behalf of an infant, since the child has no capacity to give their own consent.

In approving the variation of the trust, Megarry J accepted that such a variation did create a 'disposition' of an equitable interest by Mrs Wilson to her children. He realised that the House of Lords had given a wide meaning to that word in *Grey v Inland Revenue Commissioners*.[32] But he thought that such disposition did not have to be in writing under the terms of s 53(1)(c). He thought that there was 'considerable force'[33] in the argument advanced by Lord Radcliffe in *Oughtred v Inland Revenue Commissioners*.[34] He said that where the equitable interest passed under an agreement that could be enforced by a court order of specific performance, the equitable interest passed when that agreement was made. The means by which the equitable interest passed was by a constructive trust. Since constructive trusts did not have to be in writing by virtue of s 53(2), no writing was needed to pass the interest.

❖ ANALYSING THE LAW

Megarry J appears to confirm in *Re Holt's Settlement* that the transfer of an equitable interest need not be in writing if it passes by virtue of an agreement which would be specifically enforceable by a court order. A constructive trust is the mechanism by which the equitable interest passes and that species of trust is exempt from writing requirements under s 53(2).

Does this albeit limited exception go against the main principle underlying s 53(1)(c)? The concept behind the paragraph was to ensure that it is possible to say with certainty who owns the equitable interest at any point in time, since there should be a written document in evidence to prove that fact. If exceptions such as the transfer of an equitable interest by an unwritten constructive trust are allowed to exist, does this not make establishing the identity of the equitable owner harder on some occasions?

In addition, Megarry J's view cannot be reconciled with that of Lord Denning in *Oughtred v Inland Revenue Commissioners*, who said that:

I should have thought that the wording of section 53 (1) (c) . . . clearly made a writing necessary to effect a transfer; and section 53 (2) does not do away with that necessity.[35]

Which view do you think is right?

---

31 See Chapter 10.
32 *Grey v Inland Revenue Commissioners* [1960] AC 1.
33 *Re Holt's Settlement* [1969] 1 Ch 100 at 116.
34 *Oughtred v Inland Revenue Commissioners* [1960] AC 206.
35 Ibid at 233.

A more modern view on the relationship between s 53(1)(c) and s 53(2)

The relationship between s 53(1)(c) and s 53(2) was considered more recently by the Court of Appeal in *Neville v Wilson*.[36] The facts concerned a family dispute over a company's shares. A company named J E Neville Ltd took over another company, Universal Engineering Co (Ellesmere Port) Ltd, in the late 1950s by buying all of its issued shares, which numbered 1,640. One hundred and twenty of those shares in Universal were held by two of its directors on trust, with J E Neville Ltd as the beneficiary.

In 1965, the directors of Universal met and, at the request of J E Neville Ltd, agreed to transfer all of the shares in Universal to the shareholders of J E Neville Ltd. The problem was that the 120 shares were not included within this transfer and the equitable interest in them remained in J E Neville Ltd.

Four years later, the shareholders of J E Neville Ltd informally agreed to dissolve that company. This occurred in the following year. Its assets were distributed between its shareholders. The issue for the court was whether the company still owned the equitable interest in the 120 shares at that point in time. If it did, they passed to the Crown as *bona vacantia* under s 354 of the Companies Act 1948. The alternative argument was that the informal agreement to dissolve the company disposed of all of J E Neville Ltd's assets, including those 120 shares. The problem was that this agreement was not in writing. Insofar as the agreement purported to transfer the equitable interest in those 120 shares, it had to be in writing to comply with s 53(1)(c).

The Court of Appeal held that the agreement reached in 1969 was to dissolve J E Neville Ltd and that, from that point onwards, it was never intended that the company should be left with any assets. For this reason, the agreement to dissolve the company must have included the 120 shares in dispute.

Whilst the agreement was not in writing, the Court of Appeal held that it could be saved by s 53(2). When making the agreement to dissolve the company, each shareholder of J E Neville Ltd became a constructive trustee of their shareholding for the recipients of the assets of that company. That meant that s 53(2) could apply and the agreement did not need to be in writing.

Giving the judgment of the Court of Appeal, Nourse LJ examined the decisions of the various courts in *Oughtred v Inland Revenue Commissioners*.[37] He accepted Lord Radcliffe's view that s 53(2) could effectively override s 53(1)(c), although he recognised Lord Denning's rejection of that concept. Overall, he thought that as a matter of policy s 53(2) should be able to apply in certain cases to override s 53(1)(c). He said:

> Why then should subsection (2) not apply? No convincing reason was suggested in argument and none has occurred to us since. Moreover, to deny its application in this case would be to restrict the effect of general words when no restriction is called for, and to lay the ground for fine distinctions in the future. With all the respect which is due to those who have thought to the contrary, we hold that subsection (2) applies to an agreement such as we have in this case.[38]

Consequently, it seems as though the view that s 53(2) can override s 53(1)(c) and can prevail where it is possible to hold that an agreement to transfer an equitable interest is capable

---

36 *Neville v Wilson* [1997] Ch 144.
37 *Oughtred v Inland Revenue Commissioners* [1960] AC 206.
38 *Neville v Wilson* [1997] Ch 144 at 158.

of being specifically performed and a constructive trusteeship is created. Such agreements, which transfer only the equitable interest, appear not to have to be in writing, following *Neville v Wilson*.

Does s 53(1)(c) apply where the legal estate is transferred from one trustee to another recipient?

The final transaction to be considered in relation to s 53(1)(c) is whether a legal estate, transferred by one trustee to another recipient, constitutes a 'disposition' within the meaning of the section, given that it also transfers with it the equitable interest in the trust property. This arose in *Vandervell v Inland Revenue Commissioners*.[39]

The facts of this case have been considered in detail in Chapter 3. In brief, Mr Vandervell wanted to sponsor the establishment of a Chair in Pharmacology with the Royal College of Surgeons. He asked his bank, as trustee, to transfer the shares in which he owned the equitable interest to the Royal College. A right was retained for Vandervell Trustees Ltd to repurchase the shares from the Royal College for £5,000. One issue for the House of Lords was whether s 53(1)(c) applied to the transaction to transfer the shares to the Royal College. This depended on whether there was a transfer of the equitable interest by the bank when it transferred the shares to the Royal College.

Lord Upjohn explained the reasoning behind the enactment of s 53(1)(c):

> the object of the section . . . is to prevent hidden oral transactions in equitable interests in fraud of those truly entitled, and making it difficult, if not impossible, for the trustees to ascertain who are in truth his beneficiaries.[40]

Lord Upjohn said that s 53(1)(c) did not apply to the situation that Mr Vandervell found himself in. It did not apply to where an equitable owner, owning under a bare trust, asked his trustee to deal with the whole legal and equitable interest together.

Glossary: Bare trust

A bare trust exists where the equitable owner is over 18 years old, enjoys mental capacity and owns the absolute interest in the trust property but the property is still managed by a trustee. The equitable owner has a right, under *Saunders v Vautier*,[41] to bring the trust to an end and enjoy the trust property themselves. For some reason, the equitable owner chooses not to exercise that right but to leave the trust subsisting.

Section 53(1)(c) had no application to the situation where the legal and equitable interests were 'glued' together. The section only applied where the equitable interest was being dealt with on its own, separately from the legal estate. Consequently, an oral direction by Mr Vandervell to the bank as his trustee was sufficient to transfer the equitable ownership in the case. It was because the legal estate was also being transferred at the same time. There was no requirement, where the two interests were transferred together, for the writing requirements

---

39 *Vandervell v Inland Revenue Comissioners* [1971] AC 912.
40 Ibid at 311.
41 *Saunders v Vautier* (1841) 4 Beav 115; 49 ER 282.

of s 53(1)(c) to be fulfilled. By being asked to transfer the equitable interest to another bene-ficiary, the trustees would know the new location and ownership of the equitable interest.

❖ **ANALYSING THE LAW**

Lord Upjohn took into account the policy reasoning behind s 53(1)(c) in *Vandervell v IRC* and, in so doing, applied the 'mischief' rule of statutory interpretation and asked what was the mischief the statute was designed to prevent? It was to prevent hidden oral transac-tions. Yet the mischief rule generally only applies if the literal meaning of the statute is not clear. In *Grey v IRC*, Viscount Simonds thought that the literal meaning of the statute was perfectly clear: all dispositions of equitable interests had to be in writing to fulfil s 53(1)(c). Whilst there seems to have been no legal reason to apply the mischief rule in *Vandervell v IRC*, it is suggested that its application gives a more sensible result to the facts and reflects the policy behind the statute. Do you think that rules of statutory inter-pretation should be 'bent' in this almost Machiavellian manner where the end justifies the means?

The result, however, of the first case was that Mr Vandervell still owned the equitable interest in the shares, due to the existence of a resulting trust in his favour. In 1961, Vandervell Trustees Ltd exercised the option to buy back the shares from the Royal College. The trustees used £5,000 from Mr Vandervell's children's trust. The Royal College transferred the shares to the trustee company which then held them on the trusts for the children. The trustee company advised the Inland Revenue of this transaction. In *Re Vandervell's Trusts* (No. 2),[42] the Inland Revenue claimed that despite this transaction occurring, Mr Vandervell had not divested himself of the equitable interest in his shares. It claimed that it was not until four years later, when Mr Vandervell executed a formal document transferring the equitable interest to the trustee, that he had complied with s 53(1)(c).

In the Court of Appeal, Lord Denning MR held that the resulting trust on which the shares had been held for Mr Vandervell came to an end when the trustees exercised the option to buy back the shares and the shares were registered in the children's names. This was a declaration of a new trust by the trustees in favour of the children – not the disposition of an equitable interest. Since the trust property was money, this declaration could be created orally since s 53(1)(b) only applied to declaring trusts of land.

❖ **ANALYSING THE LAW**

The decision of the Court of Appeal in *Re Vandervell's Trusts (No. 2)* is peculiar. Lord Denning MR held that the resulting trust in favour of Mr Vandervell was brought to an end by the trustee declaring a trust in favour of the children. Yet the principles of basic trusts mean that a trustee cannot declare a trust: that task can only be undertaken by the settlor.

---

42 *Re Vandervell's Trusts* (No. 2) [1974] Ch 269.

It could be questioned whether the decision of the Court of Appeal was influenced by the actions of the Inland Revenue. The feeling the judges shared may have been that the Inland Revenue had already enjoyed a large taxation windfall from Mr Vandervell's actions. He had tried to put a stop to the Inland Revenue's activities through telling the trustee to hold the shares on trust for his children and the feeling may have been that he deserved to succeed by his oral instructions to the trustees to hold the shares on his children's trusts. Certainly such a feeling is borne out in Lord Denning MR's views that 'even now Mr Vandervell had not shaken off the demands of the revenue authorities'.

Lord Denning's judgment ended with an interesting view on the case, supporting the idea that he had sympathy to Mr Vandervell's plight:

> Every unjust decision is a reproach to the law or to the judge who administers it. If the law should be in danger of doing injustice, then equity should be called in to remedy it. Equity was introduced to mitigate the rigour of the law. But in the present case it has been prayed in aid to do injustice on a large scale – to defeat the intentions of a dead man – to deprive his children of the benefits he provided for them – and to expose his estate to the payment of tax of over £600,000. I am glad to find that we can overcome this most unjust result.[43]

What do you think was the real reason for the decision in the case?

Does s 53(1)(b) or (c) apply?

Suppose a beneficiary himself declares a trust of his equitable interest. The issue here is whether s 53(1)(b) applies (as it is a declaration of trust) or whether the transaction is caught by s 53(1)(c) (as it is a disposal of an equitable interest). Assuming the trust property is not land, the transaction would only have to be in writing if s 53(1)(c) applied. This issue was considered by the Court of Appeal in *Re Lashmar*.[44]

The answer depends on whether the beneficiary declared a 'proper' trust giving the trustee proper trust management functions. This would be a true declaration of trust and would only fall within s 53(1)(b) (and therefore need to be evidenced in writing and signed) if the property was land. On the other hand, if the trustee did not perform any functions of a trustee (as occurred on the facts of the case) then in reality he was disposing of his equitable interest and such a transaction had to be in writing to conform to s 53(1)(c).

Summary of the main principles of s 53(1)(c) of the Law of Property Act 1925

The main principle continues to be that a disposition of an equitable interest has to be in writing in order to comply with s 53(1)(c). Exceptions exist to this rule:

(a)   If the contract under which the equitable interest is transferred is specifically enforceable so that one party becomes a constructive trustee of the interest, then the interest may be transferred orally: *Neville v Wilson*;[45]

---

43 Ibid at 322.
44 Re Lashmar [1891] 1 Ch 258.
45 Neville v Wilson [1997] Ch 144.

(b)   If the equitable interest is transferred together with the legal estate, then such a disposition may be done orally and s 53(1)(c) has no application: *Vandervell v Inland Revenue Commissioners;*[46] and

(c)   If a new trust is declared by a trustee at the direction of the beneficiary, it will fall within s 53(1)(b) where no writing will be required if the trust property is personalty. Section 53(1)(c) has no application: *Re Vandervell's Trusts (No. 2).*[47]

Points to Review

This chapter has discussed:

- how an express trust is formed;
- that it is not just land that can be left on trust, but personalty too;
- that anyone can be a settlor, trustee or beneficiary, but there are restrictions on children and those mentally incapacitated setting up trusts or being trustees of them;
- that there are certain formal requirements that must be met depending on the type of property left on trust. Arguably, the most important of these is land as trusts of land must be evidenced in writing and signed by a person able to declare the trust, pursuant to s 53(1)(b) of the Law of Property Act 1925; and
- that dispositions of an equitable interest of any type of property generally have to be in writing in order to be valid, following s 53(1)(c) of the Law of Property Act 1925.

Making connections

It is important that you understand how an express trust is formed. Most trusts in English law are expressly made. This chapter has explored the formality requirements that trusts of land must fulfil, as well as examining the formality requirements for the disposition of an equitable interest.

The following chapters on the three certainties (Chapter 5), the beneficiary principle (Chapter 6) and the rules against perpetuity (on the companion website) look at each of the other requirements to declare an express trust. Constitution of that declared trust is then considered in Chapter 7. Together, all of these chapters will enable you to have a rounded understanding of how an express trust is formed.

 ## Useful Things to Read

The best reading is contained in the primary sources listed below. It is always good to consider the decisions of the courts themselves as this will lead to a deeper understanding of the issues involved. A few secondary sources are also listed, which you may wish to read to gain additional insights into the areas considered in this chapter.

---

46 *Vandervell v Inland Revenue Commissioners* [1967] 2 AC 291.
47 *Re Vandervell's Trusts (No. 2)* [1974] Ch 269.

Primary sources

Grey v Inland Revenue Commissioners [1960] AC 1.
Hodgson v Marks [1970] 3 WLR 956.
Neville v Wilson [1997] Ch 144.
Oughtred v Inland Revenue Commissioners [1960] AC 206.
Re Beaney [1978] 1 WLR 770.
Re Holt's Settlement [1969] 1 Ch 100.
Re Sutton [2009] EWHC 2576 (Ch).
Re Vandervell's Trusts (No. 2) [1974] Ch 269.
Rochefoucauld v Boustead [1897] 1 Ch 196.
Vandervell v Inland Revenue Commissioners [1971] AC 912.

Secondary sources

Graham Battersby, 'Formalities for the disposition of equitable interests under a trust' (1979) Conv 17–38. This contains a useful view of the key cases in the area of formalities: *Grey v IRC*, *Oughtred v IRC*, *Re Holt's Settlement* and the *Vandervell* litigation. If you struggled to understand these cases whilst reading this chapter, this article is highly recommended.

Brian Green, '*Grey, Oughtred* and *Vandervell* – A contextual reappraisal' (1984) MLR 385–421. This article considers the scope of s 53(1)(c) of the Law of Property Act 1925 through an analysis of the key decisions in these three cases.

Alastair Hudson, *Equity & Trusts* (7th edn, Routledge-Cavendish, 2012) ch 5.

Mohamed Ramjohn, *Text, Cases & Materials on Equity & Trusts* (4th edn, Routledge-Cavendish, 2008) ch 3.

Timothy G. Youdan, 'Informal trusts and third parties: A response' (1988) Conv Jul/Aug 267–274. This article explores whether the doctrine in *Rochefoucauld v Boustead* allows a third party to enforce a trust declared in his favour.

Chapter 5

Trust Formation: The Three Certainties

Chapter Contents

Chapter 4 considered the first two main requirements to form an express trust: that the settlor must have mental and legal capacity and that, for certain types of property, formalities must be fulfilled. This chapter moves on to consider the next requirement: that the trust must be certain. The requirement of certainty can itself be split into three parts: intention, subject matter and object.

As You Read

In this chapter, the focus is on the three certainties, all of which are required in order for the trust to be properly declared. When reading this chapter, pay particular attention to:

- *certainty of intention* – it must be clear that the settlor truly wanted to establish a trust. The case law on this point focuses on settlors using vague words and, through their use, not evidencing a true intention to set up a trust;
- *certainty of subject matter* – this focuses on the actual property that the settlor wishes to leave on trust. Obviously, in order for the trustee to administer the trust properly, it must be clear both what property is being left on trust and also, if there is more than one beneficiary, the shares in which those beneficiaries are to enjoy the trust property; and
- *certainty of object* – arguably, this is the most difficult certainty for students to grasp. Read this section of the chapter particularly carefully, focusing on the difficulties settlors have met when trying to be clear over who is to benefit in a discretionary trust.

Formation of an Express Trust

Central to how any type of trust is formed is an understanding of how an express private (as opposed to charitable) trust is created. Implied trusts, as has been seen,[1] exist to fill in gaps and, on a number of occasions, have been recognised because settlors have failed to create an express trust properly.[2]

By way of a brief reminder, to be created properly, an express private trust must be both correctly declared and constituted by the settlor. For the settlor to declare a trust correctly, he must ensure that the following issues have been dealt with properly:

(a) the trust is certain, or clear, in terms of:

  (i) the settlor evidencing a clear intention to set up the trust;
  (ii) the subject matter (or property) which is to be placed on trust can be said to be clear and the proportions in which the beneficiaries are to enjoy the property are equally clear; and
  (iii) who is to enjoy the property;

(b) the settlor must adhere to any formality requirements in establishing the trust. These have been considered in detail in Chapter 4. As you have seen, whether there are any formal requirements to set up a trust depends on what the property being left on trust is. For instance, if the trust property is shares, they must be transferred to the trustee using a stock transfer form.[3] If the property being left on trust is land, then the effect of

---

1 See Chapter 3.
2 See, for example, *Vandervell v Inland Revenue Commissioners* [1967] 2 AC 291.
3 Stock Transfer Act 1963, s 1.

s 53(1)(b) of the Law of Property Act 1925 means that the settlor must evidence his declaration of trust by using a written document, which he signs;

(c) the settlor must adhere to the beneficiary principle. Again, this is a topic which should be considered in its own right,[4] but the basic concept is that a trust must have someone who can enjoy the benefit of it. As will be seen,[5] English law generally dislikes trusts which benefit no clearly defined beneficiary; and

(d) the settlor must ensure that the trust he creates does not last forever. This is usually expressed by saying that the settlor must comply with the rules against perpetuity.[6] The fundamental principle behind the rules is to ensure that trusts do not last forever, thus tying up property in trusts instead of it being able to be used freely in the economy.

Together with ensuring that the trust is properly declared, the settlor must also ensure that the trust is constituted. This entails the settlor properly transferring the property he intends to settle on trust to the trustee, so that the trustee can then hold it on trust for the beneficiary. Constitution of a trust is considered in detail in Chapter 7.

The Three Certainties

The basics . . .

The three certainties comprise:

- certainty of object;
- certainty of subject matter; and
- certainty of intention.

> ## Key Learning Point
>
> All three certainties are as vital as each other in creating an express trust. It is not possible to choose a supermarket 'any 3 for 2' style offer: all three certainties are needed for the trust to be validly formed.

The three certainties were explained by Lord Langdale MR in *Knight v Knight*.[7] A family tree setting out the relationships in this family is shown below at Figure 5.1.

The case concerned the will of Richard Payne Knight. He had inherited land from his grandfather and his grandfather's wish in his will was that the land should pass down to his male heirs. Richard left the land in his will to his brother, Thomas Andrew Knight. At the end of his will, however, Richard stated the following words, in which he asked for the lands to continue to be left to the male descendants of his grandfather, Richard Knight:

> I trust to the liberality of my successors . . . to their justice in continuing the estates in the male succession, according to the will of the founder of the family, my above-named grandfather, Richard Knight.

---

4   See Chapter 6.
5   Ibid.
6   See chapter on companion website for a detailed discussion.
7   *Knight v Knight* (1840) 3 Beav 148; 49 ER 58.

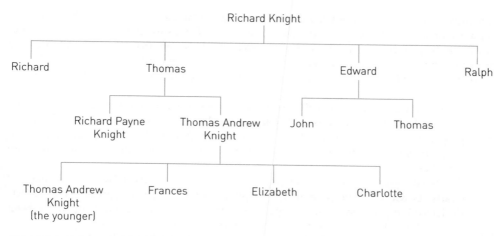

Figure 5.1 Knight v Knight family tree.

Thomas Andrew duly inherited the land from Richard upon Richard's death. Thomas Andrew himself had a son, but his son predeceased him. In his will, Thomas explained that he wanted to give effect to his own son's wishes by leaving the lands to his son's three sisters, Frances, Elizabeth and Charlotte. Such a direction brought Thomas Andrew into conflict with other male members of the family, who were descendants of Richard's grandfather. The claimant in the case was John, one of those other male members of the family. John's case was that the lands could not be left by Thomas Andrew to his daughters. Instead, John argued that Richard Payne Knight had created a trust of the lands in his will through the use of the words quoted above and consequently, he should enjoy the lands as a beneficiary under the trust. The argument to the contrary was that no trust was created by Richard Payne Knight by those words. A trust could only be created by a settlor imposing a clear obligation on the trustee to hold property for a beneficiary's benefit and the words Richard used fell far short of imposing an obligation on any trustee.

In giving the judgment of the Court of Chancery, Lord Langdale MR stated that where property was given to another person and the recipient had been 'recommended, entreated or wished' by the giver to hold the property for a third party, then a trust would be created. Crucially, however, he said that this was subject to three requirements:

> First, if the words are so used, that upon the whole, they ought to be construed as imperative;[8]

> Secondly, if the subject of the recommendation or wish be certain; and

> Thirdly, if the objects or persons intended to have the benefit of the recommendation or wish be also certain.[9]

The point was that not all instructions by one person to another to hold land for the benefit of a third party would create a trust. The instructions had to fulfil the requirements of certainty.

---

8   I.e. that they impose an *order* upon the recipient to hold the property for another person.
9   *Knight v Knight* (1840) 3 Beav 148, 173; 49 ER 58.

Certainty could be broken down into the three parts that the Master of the Rolls set out: certainty of the words that the settlor used, certainty of the subject matter of the trust and lastly, certainty of the person who it was intended should benefit from the trust. All three key areas of a trust had to be certain before the trust would be recognised.

On the facts of the case, it was held that Richard Payne Knight had not created a trust:

(a) he had not used words which showed a clear intention to create a trust. Instead, he had left it to the successors in his family to do 'justice' in continuing to leave the property to the male descendants of his grandfather. Such wording suggested that the recipients had a discretion over whether or not to continue the succession to future male heirs;

(b) by describing the property left in his will as 'the estates', Richard Payne Knight had not clearly shown which property that description related to. It was impossible on the facts to determine precisely which property Richard meant and consequently, the subject matter of the alleged trust was not certain; and

(c) whilst Richard Payne Knight had described whom he wished to benefit, this was not enough since he had not set out their beneficial entitlements in terms of precisely what equitable interest he wanted them to have. He had not, for example, clearly set out that each beneficiary should have a life interest in property left to them.

Why does English law insist on the need for the three certainties?

The court must be able to recognise a trust as intended by a settlor and cannot write a trust for him. The court uses the three certainties as a means of ascertaining the terms of the trust: whether, crucially, the settlor actually intended to set up a trust, what the subject matter (or property) of the trust is and who the settlor intended should benefit from the trust. The function of the court is simply to recognise the trust that the settlor created, not to invent a trust for the settlor's benefit.

Additionally, the three certainties help to ensure that a trustee can properly manage a trust. The trustee must be sure that a trust has been created, be clear what property is expected to be held on trust and must be confident that he is managing the trust on behalf of beneficiaries that are the people whom the settlor intended.

It is this requirement of certainty, or clarity, that ensures that not only the court but also all of those involved in the trust – the settlor, the trustee and the beneficiary – can be sure of the fundamental terms of a trust.

Certainty of Intention

This certainty considers whether the settlor showed sufficient intention to set up a trust. As such, it focuses on the words used by the settlor. Indeed, as we have seen in *Knight v Knight*,[10] Lord Langdale MR specifically mentioned that the settlor's words had to be 'construed as imperative'.

---

10 *Knight v Knight* (1840) 3 Beav 148; 49 ER 58.

Key Learning Point

The key to understanding this certainty is that the settlor must express an intention, *when viewed in the context of the words he uses*, to subject another person to a binding *obligation* to hold property for the benefit of a third party.

No special words have to be used to display intention

Ultimately, it is not necessary for every settlor to use a particular set of 'special' words to satisfy this certainty. Remember the equitable maxim that equity looks to the substance and not the form of actions or words used. This has the consequence here that equity will look to see if the words used contain an intention by the settlor to make sure that the recipient of the property has no option but to hold the property on trust for the benefit of a third party. It is only if the recipient is under an obligation to hold the property for someone else's benefit that this certainty will be met. Equity looks to find the settlor's intention by considering the words the settlor used in establishing the alleged trust. Due to equity focusing on the words used, this certainty is sometimes referred to as the 'certainty of words'.

If the settlor uses the word 'trust' then that may be a good indication that he intended to create a trust, but it all depends on the context in which that particular word is used. As we have seen, in *Knight v Knight* itself, the settlor used the word 'trust' but, in fact, no trust was deemed by the court to have been intended to have been created. The case is a good illustration of the maxim[11] of equity looking to the substance and not the form of the precise word(s) used. Even though the settlor had used the word 'trust', when viewed in the context of the other words used – that the recipients of the property could leave it to their own 'justice' to decide who would take the lands after themselves – it was not clear that the settlor had intended to impose a binding obligation on the recipient of the property.

❖ APPLYING THE LAW

Many legal precedents (templates) used by lawyers for creating express trusts do, of course, contain the word 'trust' in them. It is, therefore, considered to be good practice to mention the word 'trust' when a settlor sets up an express trust because that very word gives a good indication of the settlor's intentions at the time the arrangement is set up.

Settlors have not always used words which show a clear intention to subject the recipient of the property to a binding obligation to hold that property on trust for a beneficiary. Where the courts have not been able to deduce a clear and certain intention by a settlor to impose such a binding obligation on another, then no trust has been held to have been created.

The leading case in this area remains *Re Adams and the Kensington Vestry*.[12]

The facts of the case concerned a conveyancing dispute over a piece of land in Notting Hill, London. A lease had been granted in 1819 giving the tenant the right to purchase the

---

11 See Chapter 1, p 20.
12 *Re Adams and the Kensington Vestry* (1884) LR 27 Ch D 394.

freehold interest in the land. The tenant – Charles Adams – duly bought the freehold in July 1877. In the meantime, the original freehold owner (George Smith) had made a will, in which he left everything to the 'absolute use of my dear wife':

> in full confidence that she will do what is right as to the disposal thereof between my children, either in her lifetime or by will after her decease.

Charles Adams tried to sell the land to the Vestry of the parish of St Mary Abbotts, Kensington. The Vestry was concerned that he had no legal right to sell the land, as the Vestry feared that it had been subjected to a trust by George Smith in his will, in the terms of the words set out above.

The Court of Appeal focused on the need to ascertain the intentions of George Smith. A trust would only be found if it could clearly be shown that he had intended to create a trust by considering the words used.

The court held that no trust had been intended by the words used, when looked at in their entirety. Instead, George Smith had intended to give the property to his wife entirely. By being confident that she would use the property for the benefit of their children, he may have placed her under a *moral* obligation to make such use of the property, but he had never intended to put her under a binding legal obligation to do so. As she had not been placed under a legal obligation, there could be no trust of the land in favour of her children. As the absolute owner, she was free to sell the land to whomever she chose. She had chosen to sell it to Charles Adams and, in turn, he was entirely free to sell it to the Vestry.

'Precatory' (or 'begging') words do not create a trust

In terms of the historical development of the law of trusts, *Re Adams and the Kensington Vestry* continued the turning point when construing a settlor's intention. The case confirmed the move away from earlier cases in which the court placed emphasis on the precise word(s) used by the settlor.

Previously, the Court of Chancery had recognised a trust, even though a certain type of 'precatory' word had been used. These gave rise to so-called 'precatory trusts'.[13] Precatory words were merely words which begged, asked, or requested recipients to look after property on behalf of a third party. The Court of Chancery had wanted to recognise such trusts as, if no trust was found, the executors of the deceased's will would have been personally entitled to the deceased's property!

The change in judicial thought as to the types of trust that ought to be recognised occurred in *Lambe v Eames*.[14]

John Lambe left his property in his will to his widow 'to be at her disposal in any way she may think best for the benefit of herself and family'. One of John's sons had an illegitimate son, Henry Lambe. The widow left the property on trust for her daughter, Elizabeth Eames, but with an annual sum for Henry's benefit. Elizabeth failed to pay Henry his allowance, so Henry brought an action. Elizabeth's defence was that there was no trust at all because all the widow could ever do was leave the property to her family, according to the terms of John's will. Her argument was that the widow had acted outside of her power by leaving an allowance to Henry as, being illegitimate, he was not a family member.

---

13 'Precatory' is derived from the Latin *precari*, which means 'to beg'.
14 *Lambe v Eames* (1870–71) LR 6 Ch App 597.

The Court of Appeal in Chancery held that John had not created any trust by the words he had used in his will. John had no intention of creating a trust. Instead, his intention was to give his widow the ability to deal with the property as she saw fit. The widow had received an absolute gift from John and it was then her property to deal with as she wished, both during her lifetime and upon her death. The trust she created in favour of both Elizabeth and John was, therefore, valid.

The case shows the court construing the testator's intention from his will. John had not imposed an obligation on his widow to deal with his property in a particular manner and consequently, no trust could be found.

The Court of Appeal in *Re Adams and the Kensington Vestry* continued this development and preferred not to look at individual words used on their own but to place them in the context in which they appeared in the document. Only then could the settlor's true intention be ascertained. As Cotton LJ said:

> [W]e must not . . . rely upon the mere use of any particular words, but, considering all the words which are used, we have to see what is their true effect, and what was the intention of the testator as expressed in his will.[15]

Looking at the words in the context of their use enabled the court to obtain a more rounded picture of what the settlor really intended. Such a rounded picture was likely to be far more reflective of the settlor's true intentions as opposed to taking a word out of its context and deciding its meaning in the abstract.

This development against the use of precatory words was reaffirmed in another decision of the Court of Appeal just four years later – *Re Diggles*.[16] In this case, Mary Ann Diggles made a will in which she left all of her property to her daughter but said that she had a 'desire' that an annual sum of £25 should be paid by her executors to her companion, Anne Gregory, for the rest of Anne's life. Ms Diggles died and, for eleven years after her death, £25 was paid each year to Anne. The payments then stopped. Anne brought an action against the executors. The basis of her action was that the executors were under a binding obligation to pay her the annual sum. Anne argued that she was the beneficiary of a life interest under a trust which Ms Diggles had established and the executors were the trustees.

Cotton LJ reminded the court that the task was to construe the trust as a whole to ascertain Ms Diggles' true intention. The task was not just to focus on particular words. Ms Diggles' true intention was to give all of her property to her daughter. She had merely added a wish that her daughter should provide for Anne. As Bowen LJ explained,[17] imposing a mere 'desire' gave the daughter a choice over whether Anne should receive the annual sum or not. Such a desire was entirely different from imposing a binding obligation on her daughter. And, of course, a trust could only have been said to have been created if a binding obligation was imposed.

Fry LJ pointed out the inconvenient consequences if the court had held that there was a trust. Ms Diggles had not provided a separate sum of money for the annual payment to Anne. Consequently, the daughter would have had to fund the payment from the property left to her, all of which would have been held under a trust in favour of Anne for life, remainder to the daughter. The daughter would have had to sell some of the trust property to fund the annual payment. This made no sense in terms of Ms Diggles merely expressing a desire, or wish, for

---

15 *Re Adams and the Kensington Vestry* (1884) LR 27 ChD 394 at 409.
16 *Re Diggles* (1888) LR 39 ChD 253.
17 Ibid at 257.

Anne to receive the money. Such precatory words would have to be construed in the context of the document as a whole as to whether a trust would be created. On the facts here, there was no intention by Ms Diggles to subject her daughter to an obligation.

The court is always trying to ascertain if the settlor expressed clear enough wishes to amount to an obligation to place the recipient of the legal estate in the property under an obligation to hold the property on trust for a beneficiary. There are situations where what initially appear to be precatory words can amount to a trust because, construed in the context of the document as a whole, it can be said that the settlor intended to subject a recipient to binding trustee obligations. Such a situation arose in *Comiskey v Bowring-Hanbury*.[18]

The case concerned the will of a Member of Parliament, Mr Hanbury, in which he left all of his property (which consisted of a number of valuable collieries) to his wife, Ellen, 'in full confidence that she will make such use of it as I should have made myself' and that, when Ellen died, she was to leave the property to whichever of Mr Hanbury's nieces she chose. Crucially, the will provided that if Ellen made no choice, the property was to be split equally between the nieces when Ellen died. Following Mr Hanbury's death, Ellen brought an action before the court, in which she wanted to know whether her husband had created a trust in his will, or whether the words used showed insufficient certainty of intention to bind her to an obligation to give the property to his nieces when she died. If the latter was the case, then there would be no trust and Ellen would have taken the property for herself absolutely.

Both the trial judge and the Court of Appeal held that Mr Hanbury's words did not subject his widow to an obligation to hold the property on trust for the nieces. As such, she took the property absolutely. The nieces appealed to the House of Lords.

The House of Lords, by a majority, reversed the Court of Appeal's decision and held that the words were sufficient to subject Ellen to a binding obligation.

Lord James reminded the House[19] that its 'only duty' was to ascertain the testator's intention and that could only be ascertained from the words of the will. The House had to give the 'natural and ordinary meaning' to the words used by the testator.[20] The words had to be considered overall, without special focus on any particular words on their own. As Lord Davey explained:

> The words which have been so much commented upon, 'in full confidence', are, in my opinion, neutral. . . . They are words which may or may not create a trust, and whether they do so or not must be determined by the *context* of the particular will in which you find them.[21]

In this context, the words 'in full confidence' did merely express a hope, or desire, by Mr Hanbury that Ellen would use it as he would have done and leave it to his nieces when she died. If she did not dispose of the property by choosing which of his nieces were to receive it, then the final words of this part of the will would be crucial:

> I hereby direct that all my . . . property . . . shall at her death be equally divided among the surviving said nieces.

It was not possible to separate 'in full confidence' from those final words of that part of the will. They had to be read together. When read together, they meant that Ellen could use the

---

18 *Comiskey v Bowring-Hanbury* [1905] AC 84.
19 Ibid at 91.
20 Ibid at 88 *per* Earl of Halsbury LC.
21 Ibid at 89 (emphasis added).

property for her lifetime only and that, on her death, the property had to go to Mr Hanbury's nieces. She could choose which niece(s) was to receive it, but if she made no choice, Mr Hanbury's instructions were clear: the property had to be split equally between those nieces still living. Ellen's only real choice in this arrangement was which niece might get the property on her death. The words therefore imposed an obligation on Ellen to look after the property during her lifetime and, on her death, to pass it on to the nieces. Due to an obligation being imposed, a trust had been created of the property. Ellen was to have a life interest and the nieces, either chosen by Ellen or all of them equally if she made no choice, were to have the remainder interest.

If a settlor chooses to use exactly the same words which have been given meaning in a decided case already, however, the court will assume that the settlor wanted those words to be given the same meaning in his particular case. The settlor must have had a reason for using precise words which had previously been adjudicated upon. Whilst the court is trying to ascertain the settlor's intention, it will hold that, by using particular words that had already been held to have a precise meaning, the settlor intended to have that meaning applied to his settlement. This principle can be shown in *Re Steele's Will Trusts*.[22]

The case involved a diamond necklace belonging to Mrs Adelaide Steele. She wrote her will, in which she left the necklace to her son and then to his eldest son and, in turn, to his eldest son and so on as far as she was legally permitted to do. The relevant provision of the will ended with the words, 'and I request my said son to do all in his power by his will or otherwise to give effect to this my wish'.

The trustees of Mrs Steele's will brought an action to the High Court to determine if Mrs Steele had created a trust by imposing an obligation on her son to pass the necklace down the family line. Their query was whether those final words used by Mrs Steele were precatory in nature since she merely requested her son to do everything he could to give effect to her 'wish'. If no obligation had been imposed upon him by those words, there could be no intention by Mrs Steele to subject her son to a trust, so he would take the necklace as an absolute gift.

Wynn-Parry J noted that the words used by Mrs Steele in her will were the same as had been used by a previous testatrix in *Shelley v Shelley*[23] and the court had held in that case that a valid trust had been created. The difficulty was that *Shelley v Shelley* was a case which pre-dated *Re Adams and the Kensington Vestry* and was decided at a time when courts of equity were, of course, more inclined to declare trusts, even though they involved precatory words in their creation.

Yet Wynn-Parry J was able to reconcile the decision in *Shelley v Shelley* with the 'new' direction the courts had taken since *Re Adams and the Kensington Vestry*. He said that he followed the decision in *Re Adams and the Kensington Vestry* as he recognised that his task was to discover Mrs Steele's true intentions by looking at all of the words she used in her will in their context. Her will had been professionally prepared and no doubt the lawyer who drew up the will was familiar with the decision in *Shelley v Shelley*. By adopting the same words, Wynn-Parry J held that Mrs Steele's true intention was for her property to be subjected to the same result as the property left by will in *Shelley v Shelley*. In this manner, Wynn-Parry J was still giving pre-eminence to finding Mrs Steele's intention.

It is submitted that this decision is not without its difficulties. *Shelley v Shelley* was a decision in which certainty of intention was not given as much prominence as it was later to receive after the decision in *Re Adams and the Kensington Vestry*. The judge in *Shelley v Shelley*, Sir W Page Wood V-C, gave prominence not so much on ascertaining the testatrix's intentions as instead focusing

---

22 *Re Steele's Will Trusts* [1948] Ch 603.
23 *Shelley v Shelley* (1868) LR 6 Eq 540.

on the fact that the objects of the trust were certain. Whilst the judge considered the testatrix's intention 'clear and precise',[24] he seems to have done so on the basis that the court should recognise that a trust exists as the beneficiaries could be easily ascertained. Much weight was placed on the beneficiaries of the trust being certain. As the beneficiaries were certain, that had to mean that there was a trust. The decision in *Re Adams and the Kensington Vestry* later placed more weight on ascertaining the settlor's true intentions independently of whether the beneficiaries of the trust were certain. It gave ascertaining the settlor's intentions more prominence and brought the task of ascertaining those intentions up to the same level of importance as finding out if the beneficiaries were certain.

> ### ❖ ANALYSING THE LAW
>
> How close do you think the words used in a present will have to be to those used in a will in a previously reported decision? They were exactly the same in *Re Steele's Will Trusts* but do you think that they have to be? Would it be sufficient to use similar words? Would similar words clearly show an intention to have the same consequence as the words used in the earlier decision?

By relying heavily on *Shelley v Shelley*, arguably the decision in *Re Steele's Will Trusts* does not take into account the spirit of the decision in *Re Adams and the Kensington Vestry* in trying to ascertain this particular testatrix's intentions. Instead, it relies on this testatrix having the same intention as the testatrix in *Shelley v Shelley*, but the intention of the testatrix in that case was barely mentioned and her intention to create a trust was simply assumed to exist. Notwithstanding this, the principle in *Re Steele's Will Trusts* remains good law.

Actions can speak as loud as words

If the facts of the individual case support it, it will not just be the settlor's words, but also their actions in support of their words, that the court will keep in mind in ascertaining whether the settlor expressed sufficient certainty of intention to create a trust.

This has been shown in Chapter 2[25] in the discussion of *Paul v Constance*[26] and *Jones v Lock*.[27]

In *Paul v Constance*, a settlor paid several sums of money into a joint bank account. The question for the Court of Appeal was whether the settlor had declared a trust of those sums. It was held that he had created a trust through a combination of his words and his actions. He often told the claimant that '[t]his money is as much yours as mine'. His actions involved opening a bank account which was only in his sole name because of the embarrassment he and the claimant would have felt in asking the bank to open an account in their joint names when they were living together whilst not being married. The actions of opening the bank account and paying in joint sums of money could be seen as bolstering an intention to create a trust, albeit that Scarman LJ could not be sure *when* that intention to create a trust came into existence.

The case can be contrasted with *Jones v Lock*. There the settlor handed over a cheque to his baby son with the words 'I give this to baby . . . .' After rescuing the cheque from the child

---

24 Ibid at 546.
25 Chapter 2, pp 32–33.
26 *Paul v Constance* [1977] 1 WLR 527.
27 *Jones v Lock* (1865–1866) LR 1 Ch App 25.

when it was about to be torn up, the settlor placed the cheque in his safe. The court held that the settlor had not declared a trust of the money. His words and actions did not indicate he had ever intended to do so. The court found that the settlor had no intention to burden himself with the responsibilities of trusteeship. The settlor's action of placing the cheque in the safe was neutral. It did not bolster an oral intention to declare a trust.

The settlor's actions can be as relevant as their words in determining whether a trust has been created. The court will look at all the circumstances surrounding the creation of the trust to determine whether the settlor has expressed sufficient intention to declare it.

Certainty of intention in trusts involving businesses

What has been discussed so far with certainty of intention has involved considering the matter in relation to traditional, family trust cases. The requirement that the settlor must clearly intend to create a trust applies to all types of trust, however, not just those involving families. In cases involving businesses, it can be more difficult to pinpoint that a settlor intended to establish a trust since the trust is not typically created by the settlor at such a momentous time as when an individual testator writes his will.

❖ APPLYING THE LAW

Think about why it is important to establish if a trust is created in a business setting. This issue can be vital if a business has monetary difficulties.

When a company becomes insolvent, the property that the business owns passes to the liquidator. The liquidator's task is to settle the business's debts and to pay the creditors (the people to whom the creditor owes money) the amounts that they are owed from the remaining money. Usually there is insufficient money remaining to pay each creditor in full. The reason the company has become insolvent is because it does not have sufficient money to pay its debts.

A trust is an attractive proposition from a creditor's point of view because, if successful, it ring-fences property in favour of the creditor. If the successful creditor can establish a trust in their favour, he will own the equitable interest in the property and will be entitled to have it returned to him. That means that the liquidator cannot use that property to pay creditors in general.

The difficulty of pinpointing certainty of intention in a business context was highlighted by Megarry J in *Re Kayford Ltd (In Liquidation)*.[28]

The case concerned a mail-order company that specialised in soft furnishings. It received orders from members of the public, who would either pay in full, or provide a deposit for the goods when they placed their orders. Kayford Ltd depended on another company to supply it with the soft furnishings. That supplier became insolvent. Fearing that Kayford Ltd would also get into financial difficulties, the managing director of the company sought advice from its accountants over how to keep its customers' prepayments safe and secure in the event that it too became insolvent.

---

28 *Re Kayford Ltd (In Liquidation)* [1975] 1 WLR 279.

The accountant advised Kayford Ltd to tell its bank to open a separate account for the customers' prepayments and to pay all of those sums of money into that new account, which was to be called a 'Customers' Trust Deposit Account'. The company did just that, but a mistake was made: instead of opening up a new separate account, the bank and the company agreed that one of the company's dormant accounts would be used instead.

Kayford Ltd then went into liquidation. The company's liquidator argued that the money in the separate account – which totalled nearly £38,000 – belonged to the company and so, on liquidation, to the company's creditors. Against that stood the customers, who argued that a trust had been created by the company of the money in the account in their favour.

Megarry J held that a trust had been created. As far as certainty of intention was concerned, he acknowledged the issue was whether 'in substance a sufficient intention to create a trust has been manifested'.[29] But unlike the cases involving individuals, Megarry J did not have the advantage of being able to construe the precise words that the company had used in the context of a larger document. Instead, he had to construe the company's actions as well as the few words it had used in its intended description of the account.

He found that the entire purpose of the company putting the customers' prepayments into a separate bank account was to ensure that the equitable interest in those prepayments remained with the customers and did not transfer to the company. As he put it, 'a trust is the obvious means of achieving this'.[30] The company had successfully showed an intention to create a trust by its words and actions. It had:

(a) considered very carefully how to protect its customers' prepayments in the event of its insolvency;

(b) instructed its bank to use a separate account (which Megarry J described as 'useful (though by no means conclusive))';[31] and

(c) asked that the name of that account reflect that the company was a trustee of the money for the customers.

In the context of a business relationship, therefore, not only the words but also the actions of the settlor (business) may be used to ascertain whether there is an intention manifested to create a trust.

The decision of Megarry J appears to have been influenced by reasons of policy. He made it clear at the end of his judgment that he supported the actions of a company, such as Kayford Ltd, which tried to act in its customers' best interests by endeavouring to keep their money safe in a separate bank account. He seems to have had sympathy with the individual customers who had made the prepayments to Kayford Ltd and wished to assist those customers. He made it clear that his decision only applied where the court was dealing with individuals who had made such prepayments saying that 'different considerations' may apply in relation to businesses who had made such prepayments to companies who later became insolvent. He hinted that the court may not so readily hold that a trust had been established in such a case.

Such a case arose, however, in Re Lewis's of Leicester Ltd.[32] Lewis's was a national chain of department stores. The chain became insolvent in 1991. From that insolvency, the management and staff of the store in Leicester formed a company (Lewis's of Leicester Ltd) to operate that single store. The store made heavy losses and, in order to try to make some money, areas

---

29 Ibid at 282.
30 Ibid.
31 Ibid.
32 Re Lewis's of Leicester Ltd [1995] BCC 514.

of the store were licensed to other types of businesses. These businesses were independent organisations who traded in their own right within the store, selling different types of goods. One group of these businesses' takings from the public were paid into cash tills owned by Lewis's. Lewis's took all of the money from the tills but then, either on a weekly or monthly basis, paid a sum to each business which represented its takings less an average 25 per cent commission for Lewis's.

In January 1994, Lewis's of Leicester went into administration. Knowing that it was in financial difficulties, Lewis's took the advice of its accountants and ensured that the takings from the tills were paid into a separate bank account from December 1993.

The businesses argued that a trust had been created by Lewis's opening up that separate bank account in December 1993. They argued that those actions were enough to demonstrate an intention to create a trust.

Robert Walker J held that Lewis's of Leicester Ltd had shown sufficient intention to create a trust of the money in the separate bank account. In keeping with *Re Kayford Ltd*, he relied on the actions and words of the settlor of the trust:

(a) Compelling evidence from one of Lewis's directors showed that the money was regarded to be held on trust for the benefit of the businesses. Lewis's did not regard the money in the separate bank account as its own. The fact that Lewis's segregated money which it did not believe to be its own reinforced its view that the money was really money which was to be held on trust; and

(b) Lewis's had opened a separate bank account in which the money was to be placed. This, in itself, would not provide sufficient evidence of intention to establish a trust but, taken together with the other evidence in the case, bolstered the conclusion that Lewis's had intended to create a trust.

The main beneficiaries of the trust were the businesses. But, in this case, Lewis's of Leicester Ltd was also held to be a beneficiary of the trust, in proportion to the amount of money it would have received as its commission had it still been solvent and trading.

Despite having sympathy for creditors of an insolvent company, whether those creditors are individuals or businesses, it is not in every case that a court will find that there is a trust. It may be that the settlor did not do enough to show an intention to create a trust and the court will not be afraid to hold that is the case, even in cases which invoke a high degree of public sympathy such as *Re Farepak Food and Gifts Ltd (in Administration)*.[33]

This case concerned the collapse of Farepak Food and Gifts Ltd, which made national headlines when it entered administration in October 2006. Farepak operated a year-long savings scheme in which people made regular savings for spending at Christmas time. The customers would pay a Farepak agent (who would often be one of the customer's friends, work colleagues or relatives) each week for 45 weeks of the year and the agents would pay all of their customers' money into a bank account owned by Farepak. Each individual customer made total contributions for the year of approximately £250–£300. Near Christmas, the customers' savings would be converted into either a food hamper, gifts or shopping vouchers, at the choice of each customer.

In the two-day period between when it stopped trading, but before it entered into administration, Farepak's directors attempted to protect their customers' money by purporting to declare that the company held it in trust for the customers. This culminated, on 12 October

---

33 *Re Farepak Food and Gifts Ltd (in Administration)* [2008] BCC 22.

2006, with the directors executing a formal deed of trust to record this. The deed referred to a bank account into which the customers' money had been paid.

Mann J held that no express trust was created in favour of customers who had paid money to Farepak's agents. A trust could exist for customers who had paid money to the agents on or after 12 October 2006, since it was only at that stage that Farepak had evidenced sufficient intention to create a trust, through the actions of its directors. Before that crucial October date, there was no clear intention, either by Farepak's words or its actions, to create a trust in favour of its customers.

As an alternative argument, the customers alleged that a Quistclose[34] trust had been established in their favour. Their argument was that they had effectively lent Farepak their money on the specific purpose that it would be returned to them, albeit in a slightly different form, as either a hamper, shopping vouchers or gifts. As that specific purpose had failed, the money was held by the company on a Quistclose-type resulting trust for the customers.

Mann J rejected that proposition. He pointed out that the customers had each paid in varying amounts of money, but only into one main bank account. Whilst he held that this would not necessarily be fatal to the existence of a trust, Farepak had taken no action to demarcate its customers' money from its general funds. That failure to separate customers' money from Farepak's general funds was fatal to the establishment of a Quistclose trust. Indeed, it would not have made any sense to Farepak's business model for customers' money to have been kept separate from its general funds as then Farepak would not have been able to access such a large total sum of money until it converted the cash into hampers, vouchers or gifts. Companies would not generally operate in such a way as to have a large amount of cash simply lying there in an account which they could not touch for most of the year. There was no trust relationship between Farepak and its customers: the customers were simply making advance payments towards buying hampers, goods or vouchers at some future point in time. Mann J described[35] this as a 'contractual relationship' as opposed to trustee–beneficiary.

The consequence if certainty of intention is missing

If the settlor has not demonstrated, by his words or actions (or a combination of the two) in their context that he intended to create a trust, the recipient of the property will take it not as a trustee but as an absolute gift for himself.[36] This means that the property is entirely at the disposal of the recipient for him to use as he wishes.

Certainty of Subject Matter

The requirement that the subject matter of a trust be certain is there, as with the other aspects of the requirement of the three certainties, primarily to assist the trustee:

(a) when creating the trust, the settlor must ensure that he correctly identifies the trust property, so that the trustee can be sure what property he is expected to hold on trust and administer for the benefit of the beneficiary; and

(b) the interests of the beneficiaries in the subject matter of the trust must be certain so that the trustee can be sure what interest each beneficiary enjoys. Again, without such knowledge, the trustee would find it impossible to administer the trust.

---

34 Barclays Bank Ltd v Quistclose Investments Ltd [1970] AC 567. See Chapters 3 (pp 64–65) and 7 (pp 198–201) for further discussion.
35 Re Farepak Food and Gifts Ltd (in Administration) [2008] BCC 22 at 34.
36 See Lambe v Eames (1870–71) LR 6 Ch App 597.

The responsibilities and duties of trustees are onerous[37] and it is only reasonable that if a trustee is to be burdened by such onerous obligations, he is at least sure over which property those obligations attach and the interest that each beneficiary enjoys. Ultimately, if the trustee fails to administer the trust correctly, the court will step in and it must be clear to the court that the property and the beneficial interests in the property are certain.

❖ EXPLAINING THE LAW

A trustee has a duty to invest the trust property and, under s 4 of the Trustee Act 2000, to keep those investments under review. The aim is to produce the best return for the beneficiaries. In order for the trustee to undertake those duties, it is essential that he knows which property his duties affect and what interests each beneficiary enjoys. Sometimes the beneficial interests will verge on competing with each other in a trust so that the trustee needs to balance those interests when making investment decisions.

Suppose Scott establishes a trust. Scott appoints Terry as the trustee and settles £100,000 on trust for Ulrika for life, remainder to Vikas.

Terry understands his duty to invest the £100,000 for the benefit of the beneficiaries. Since bank interest rates are low, he contemplates investing in real property (freehold land) instead of simply paying the money into a bank. In making that decision, he needs to balance up the interests of both beneficiaries. The rental income might be suitable for Ulrika since, as life tenant, she is entitled to the income from the property for her life. The property might be suitable for Vikas' interest too, as the capital value of the property should increase in the long term.

The trustee must be able to balance the interests of the life tenant and the remainderman. The only way of ensuring that can occur is if the subject matter of the trust – in terms of both the property being left on trust and the beneficial interests – are certain.

Identification of the trust property

The property that the settlor leaves on trust must be clearly identified so that the trustee can administer that property for the benefit of the beneficiaries.

The trust property will not be certain if it is unclear what property is being left on trust, as occurred in *Sprange v Barnard*.[38]

In this case, Susannah Sprange made a will in which she left £300 to her husband, Thomas. This gift was expressed to be 'for his sole use'. Her will then provided that on Thomas' death:

the remaining part of what is left, that he does not want for his own wants and use, to be divided equally between my brother, John Crapps, my sister Wickenden, and my sister Bauden . . . .

---

37 See Chapters 8 and 9.
38 *Sprange v Barnard* (1789) 2 Bro CC 585; 29 ER 320.

After Susannah died, Thomas claimed that the words she used were not certain enough to create a trust of the money and that, in fact, the money should go to him as an absolute gift.

Sir R P Arden held that no trust had been created of the money. For a trust to be created, the property of the trust had to be certain when it was created. The property here for Susannah's siblings was only what was left over when Thomas died and which he had not used for his own benefit. It was not possible to say, when the trust was created, how much property would be left over at Thomas' death. Consequently, it was impossible to say how much of the £300 should be for Thomas' benefit and how much for Susannah's siblings. It all depended on how much of the £300 Thomas spent during his lifetime. Such an imprecise approach could not create a valid trust. The court recognised that such a trust would be impossible for a trustee to administer. The trustee could never be sure precisely how much property was supposed to be for Thomas' benefit and how much was for Susannah's siblings. It was clearly not right to place a trustee in such an awkward position. No trust was established and, instead, Thomas was to enjoy the entire property absolutely.

A similar result was reached in *Palmer v Simmonds*.[39] Here, Henrietta Rosco provided in her will that the residue of her estate was to be left to her nephew, Thomas Harrison, on the basis that if he died without having had children, he would use a sufficient amount of the money to provide for his widow. After using such an amount for his widow, the will continued that, 'the bulk of my residuary estate' should be left to her other relatives. The issue for the court was whether 'the bulk' was a sufficiently certain description of property to be left on trust.

The Vice-Chancellor held that there was no trust because the property to be left on trust had not been sufficiently clearly defined. There was no certainty in what was meant by using the word 'bulk'. The Vice-Chancellor pointed out[40] that 'bulk' meant 'the greater part' of something, but that very definition of the word ensured that the testatrix had not defined the trust property with any certainty. Again, it would have been impossible to say when the alleged trust was created how much property was to be held on trust for Thomas Harrison and how much should be held for the other relatives. The trust could not have been administered. There was no trust and, instead, the property went to Thomas absolutely.

These two cases illustrate that the settlor must describe the trust property with accuracy otherwise the court will hold that no trust has been created.

❖ EXPLAINING THE LAW

Often a testator leaves the 'residue' of their property to a recipient in their will. This gift will be certain. The residue of a testator's estate is everything that remains after expenses have been met and all other gifts distributed.

Do not confuse 'residue' with the principle in *Sprange v Barnard* and *Palmer v Simmonds*. Those cases held that where it was impossible to say how much would be left over for a recipient, there would be no certainty of subject matter. But it is always possible to say how much will be left over as far as the residue of a testator's estate is concerned.

As with every rule, there are exceptions. In this instance, it seems that if the trust property forms part of a larger identical 'batch' of intangible property, then it does not need to be

---

39 *Palmer v Simmonds* (1854) 2 Drew 221; 61 ER 704.
40 Ibid at 227.

precisely identified by the settlor when creating the trust. Such was the decision of the Court of Appeal in *Hunter v Moss*.[41]

The case concerned a purported declaration of trust by the defendant, Robert Moss, in favour of the claimant, David Hunter. Robert owned 950 out of 1,000 issued shares in his family's business, Moss Electrical Co Ltd. David was employed as the Finance Director. In a conversation between the two men in June 1986, Robert stated his intention to give David 50 shares in the company. Later, in September 1986, the company was sold to a larger company for a considerable sum.

The trial judge held that the conversation between the two men amounted to Robert declaring a trust of those 50 shares for David. The shares amounted to five per cent of the company's total number of issued shares. That entitled David to a five per cent share of the sale proceeds when Moss Electrical was sold. That sum amounted to over £112,000. Robert appealed the judge's decision. One of his grounds of appeal was that there was no declaration of trust because the subject matter of the trust was not certain. There had been no proper identification of which of the 50 shares Robert should hold on trust for David which, Robert maintained, was needed so that it could be said with certainty what the subject matter of the trust was.

The Court of Appeal dismissed Robert's appeal and held that there was sufficient certainty with regard to the subject matter of the trust. In giving the only substantive judgment of the court, Dillon LJ held that it did not matter that the 50 shares were not precisely identified because all of the issued shares in the company were exactly the same. They were all identical to one another. It made no difference as to which 50 shares Robert should hold on trust for David.

The case shows that the subject matter of the trust need not be segregated from a larger whole provided that:

(a) the property of the trust is precisely defined by the settlor (Robert had made it clear he would hold exactly 50 shares on trust for David). Where the extent of the property is not precisely defined, the decisions in *Sprange v Barnard* and *Palmer v Simmonds* remain good law;

(b) the property forms part of a larger identical whole mass of the same property; and

(c) the property is intangible.

> ### ❖ ANALYSING THE LAW
>
> In *Hunter v Moss*, Dillon LJ used the analogy of a will to hold that part of intangible goods could be held on trust. But there the entire estate of the deceased is vested in his executors after his death. This was not the case which Dillon LJ faced which was an *inter vivos* (lifetime) declaration of trust. On the facts, the property always remained vested in Robert and was not transferred to anyone else.
>
> On this basis, do you think that the part of the property for David should have been segregated so that it could be clearly seen the extent of property which was to be held on trust for him?

---

41 *Hunter v Moss* [1994] 1 WLR 452.

It appears, however, that the principle in *Hunter v Moss* has been limited to apply only to the position where the trust property forms part of an overall amount of property which is precisely identical. This limitation was illustrated first in *Re London Wine Co (Shippers)*[42] and later by the Privy Council in *Re Goldcorp Exchange Ltd (In Receivership)*.[43]

In *Re London Wine Co (Shippers)*, the company supplied wines to customers. Customers ordered their chosen wine from the company mainly as an investment, as opposed to for consumption. The wine often remained in the warehouses of the London Wine Company. Instead of receiving the actual bottles of wine, the customers would be sent a document which stated that each buyer was the sole, equitable owner of the bottle(s) of wine that they had bought. No bottles of wine were ever set aside specifically for each customer's order. The company entered receivership and the question for the High Court was whether the customers could claim a trust of their bottle(s) of wine. That depended on whether it could be said, with certainty, which bottle(s) of wine belonged to each customer.

With *Hunter v Moss* in mind, it might be argued that it did not matter that there was no segregation of the trust property for each customer. Each customer simply bought wine of a particular vintage. If the company had a number of bottles of wine on its shelves of that particular vintage, then arguably it might not matter precisely which bottle(s) each customer was entitled to, since each bottle of each vintage would be the same as each other.

Oliver J rejected this argument. It could not be argued that a particular bottle of wine in a warehouse should be held for a particular customer's order. All that the document that was sent to each customer confirmed was that the customer was entitled to a quantity of wine of a particular description, as opposed to a particular bottle of wine actually lying down in a warehouse. In addition, it was open to the London Wine Company – and this did occur in some instances – to source alternative wine to fulfil customers' orders after the wine had been sold to the individual customers. It was not possible to say that a customer was entitled to a *particular* bottle of wine in a warehouse.

The customers could not argue that it did not matter which bottle of wine was appropriated to their order since all bottles of wine of a particular vintage were not of the same type. Even if two bottles of wine were of the same type and vintage, one bottle would contain wine which would be slightly different from that in the other bottle. No two bottles of wine, unlike the shares in *Hunter v Moss*, could contain wine which could be considered as identical to each other.

The decision in *Re London Wine Co (Shippers)* was applied by the Privy Council in *Re Goldcorp Exchange Ltd (In Receivership)*.

Goldcorp Exchange Ltd was a company which dealt in gold and other precious metals. Customers bought gold coins and/or ingots from it, but left them with the company for safe storage. The intention was that if they notified Goldcorp, the company would send them their gold. When they purchased the gold, Goldcorp sent each customer a certificate stating that their gold was being held on a 'non-allocated' basis. In other words, each customer's gold was part of a larger amount of gold which contained every other customer's gold and any gold awaiting sale. There were no demarcations between the different categories of gold.

Goldcorp began to experience financial difficulties and one of its creditors, the Bank of New Zealand, appointed a receiver of the company to recover money owed to it. Goldcorp did not have sufficient levels of gold or other assets to pay all of its creditors, including its customers, in full.

---

42 *Re London Wine Co (Shippers)* [1986] PCC 121.
43 *Re Goldcorp Exchange Ltd (In Receivership)* [1994] 3 WLR 199.

The customers sought to argue that their gold was safe as a trust had been created of it. They argued that it did not matter that no actual gold had been physically appropriated to each customer's order. There was sufficient certainty of subject matter as it made no difference precisely which pieces of gold were allocated to each customer.

The Privy Council rejected the arguments in favour of a trust. In delivering the advice of the Board, Lord Mustill set out the reality of Goldcorp's business which was the amount of gold it had was constantly changing as it continuously bought and sold gold. A separate stock of gold which was available to fulfil the customers' orders simply did not exist. As Goldcorp's stock of gold constantly changed, it could not be said that any particular piece of gold was held on trust for any particular customer. There was no sufficient certainty of subject matter in the gold to establish a trust for the customers.

It can be questioned whether the judgments in *Hunter v Moss* and *Re Goldcorp Exchange* are compatible. The Privy Council delivered its judgment in the latter in May 1994 which was some five months after the Court of Appeal had handed down its judgment in *Hunter v Moss*. Yet, intriguingly, the Privy Council makes no mention of *Hunter v Moss* in its decision. This may be down to a simple misfortune in timing in that argument in *Hunter v Moss* had still to be heard when the appeal in *Goldcorp* was argued before the Privy Council, so the attention of the Privy Council could not be drawn to the decision in *Hunter v Moss* in the appeal process.

The two cases do, at first glance, appear to give different results as to whether non-segregated property can give rise to sufficient certainty of subject matter to establish a trust. *Hunter v Moss* appears to confirm that there may be sufficient certainty of subject matter as long as the property forms part of an identical whole. All of the shares in that case were identical. It therefore made no difference which ones were to form the subject matter of the trust. *Re Goldcorp Exchange*, following *Re London Wine Company*, seems to say that there is no sufficient certainty of subject matter in a situation where the actual trust property forms part of a greater whole even when the property appears to be the same since surely all of the gold was identical.

It is possible, however, to distinguish the cases. Both cases rely heavily on their own individual facts. *Hunter v Moss* may still be taken as good law for the proposition that there can be sufficient certainty of subject matter where the trust property has not been segregated provided that all of the wider amount of the property is absolutely identical and is intangible in nature. All of the issued shares in that case were precisely the same and they remained untouched. In *Re Goldcorp Exchange* there could be no certainty of subject matter since the wider whole of the property was being constantly bought and sold. Different gold was being added all of the time. The whole amount of gold was not, therefore, necessarily identical to what the customers had originally bought. The same is true of the facts in *Re London Wine Company*: that company constantly bought and sold wine so that it was not possible to say that any particular wine was held for any particular customer at any one time. The shares in *Hunter v Moss* remained constant. They were not bought and sold. It therefore made sense to hold that a trust could be declared over a proportion of them, but not in the other two cases, where the property which formed part of the wider whole was being changed constantly.

The Sale of Goods (Amendment) Act 1995[44] has brought relief to buyers of tangible goods and thus effectively reverses the decisions in *Re London Wine Company* and *Re Goldcorp Exchange*. Buyers are now to be treated as tenants in common of tangible goods before the goods are delivered to them. This, therefore, gives them priority over creditors which the buyers in those two cases did not enjoy.

---

44 Sale of Goods (Amendment) Act 1995 s 1(3) inserting s 20A into the Sale of Goods Act 1979.

Identification of the beneficial interests

In addition to ensuring that the actual property to be held on trust is sufficiently certain, the settlor must also ensure that the beneficial interests are clearly expressed. This – and the consequences of failing to do so – were illustrated in *Boyce v Boyce*.[45]

Richard Boyce made a will in which he purported to establish a trust of two of his properties in Southwold. Both houses were to be held on trust for his wife for her life and, after her death, the absolute interest in one house was to be given to his eldest daughter Maria and the absolute interest in the other house was to be given to another of his daughters, Charlotte. Crucially, the will provided that Maria had to choose which of the two properties she wished to have. She was to make this choice after her mother had died.

Rather tragically, all of Richard's children (with the exception of Charlotte) and his wife predeceased him. Significantly, of course, that meant that Maria had not chosen which of the two properties she wished to have before she died. The issue for the court was whether the trust of one house for Charlotte could still be valid.

The Vice-Chancellor held that there could be no valid trust of either property in Charlotte's favour. The trust of the property in favour of Charlotte depended entirely on Maria making a choice of which property she wanted for herself. As Maria had not made a choice, it was simply not possible for Charlotte to have the property that Maria did not want for herself.

In essence, there was no certainty of subject matter in the arrangement that Richard Boyce had created. It was not possible to say with any degree of certainty which property should be held on trust for Charlotte. That all depended on Maria making an election over which property she wanted for herself. As no choice had been made, there was no certainty of subject matter and no trust in favour of Charlotte existed.

It appears, though, that the decision in the court was partly based on law and partly on pragmatism. In terms of the former, Charlotte owning a house was always subject to a condition – that she could not enjoy a property unless and until Maria had chosen her own. Pragmatically, Maria never did make a choice with the consequence that it was not possible for the court to say with certainty which house Charlotte should enjoy.

❖ ANALYSING THE LAW

Change the facts of *Boyce v Boyce* a little and suppose Maria had outlived her father by one minute. In that event, her equitable interest, incorporating the right to choose the house, would probably have vested in her. That would have meant that her personal representatives could have made a choice on her behalf and so the trust would have been certain.

The decision in this case can, however, be contrasted with that in *Re Golay's Will Trusts*.[46]

Here, Adrian Golay made a will in which he provided that a friend of his, Tossy, was to be allowed, 'to enjoy one of my flats during her lifetime and to receive a reasonable income from my other properties . . .'.

The question for the court was whether it could be said that the phrase 'reasonable income' was sufficiently certain for the trust to be administered.

---

45 *Boyce v Boyce* (1849) 16 Sim 476; 60 ER 959.
46 *Re Golay's Will Trusts* [1965] 1 WLR 969.

Ungoed-Thomas J held that it was sufficiently certain. The testator's deliberate use of the word 'reasonable' meant that the testator wanted a wholly objective assessment of what was a suitable income for Tossy. There was sufficient certainty of subject matter for the income.

Interestingly, the court seems not to have considered the question that the testator did not specify which particular flat Tossy was to enjoy. Again, perhaps pragmatism was key here. Tossy was alive and able to choose which flat she wished to enjoy. There was, unlike in *Boyce v Boyce*, no reason why that trust should fail.

The decision in *Boyce v Boyce* should, therefore, be seen to be peculiar to its own unfortunate facts. Provided that the beneficiary is able to exercise a choice, it would appear that there is no reason why beneficial interests cannot be made conditional upon a beneficiary choosing from which trust property they wish to benefit.

Of course, there is a major exception to the principle that the settlor must set out precisely the extent of the beneficial interests of the trust. That is the creature known as the discretionary trust. There the settlor gives a power to the trustees to decide who will benefit (from a defined group) and usually the amount by which each beneficiary will benefit. There is no conflict with certainty of subject matter in such an arrangement for, as we have seen, underpinning the whole principle of certainty is the policy that the trustees must be able to administer the trust effectively. The requirements of certainty are there to assist the trustees to do their job. If the trustees have been given a discretion over who will benefit from the trust and the amount by which they can benefit, then the trustees need some room to manoeuvre in terms of choosing beneficiaries and quantifying their amounts. Being too prescriptive over setting out the beneficial interests of each beneficiary would actually hinder, as opposed to help, trustees in such a trust.

The consequences if certainty of subject matter is absent

If the settlor has not adequately defined the property to be left on trust, there cannot be a trust and the recipient will take the whole property as an absolute gift.[47] If the settlor, whilst defining the property, has not set out the beneficial interests with sufficient clarity, the property will return to his estate on resulting trust.[48]

Certainty of Object

What is usually dealt with by lecturers as the final certainty concerns the objects of the trust (i.e. the beneficiaries). The settlor must define the beneficiaries of the trust with sufficient clarity when he declares the trust. It is this which is meant by 'certainty of object'. This requirement is imposed to ensure that the trustees have no doubts over who the beneficiaries are. It is of vital importance that the trustees administer the trust correctly by investing the funds and distributing the capital and income to the right recipients. If the trustees do not administer the trust correctly, then they are at risk of being held liable for breach of trust. It works the other way too: only true beneficiaries have certain rights such as the right to claim for the interest or capital from the trust. In the end, however, the requirement that the objects of the trust be certain is imposed to assist the trustees in their functions.

---

47 *Sprange v Barnard* (1789) 2 Bro CC 585; 29 ER 320.
48 *Boyce v Boyce* (1849) 16 Sim 476; 60 ER 959.

Key Learning Point

It is essential that you grasp that 'object' = beneficiary.

We need to consider this topic in relation to both fixed and discretionary trusts.

Fixed Trusts

The concept of a list

❖ APPLYING THE LAW

I give £10,000 to my trustees to hold the money on trust for Julie Smith and Harry Benjy in equal shares. This is a fixed trust. The trustees have no choice but to hold the money for the two named beneficiaries.

In a fixed trust, so that the trustees know what they are to do with the trust fund and for whom, ultimately, they are to manage it, it must be possible for them to draw up a complete list of the beneficiaries. This was set out by Jenkins LJ in *Inland Revenue Commissioners v Broadway Cottages Trust*.[49] This means the trustees must be able to state categorically who is and who is not a beneficiary. This is possible in the example above as the trustees are able to draw up a list of the beneficiaries since only the beneficiaries are explicitly named. If the trustees cannot draw up such a list, then the particular trust is said to fail for certainty of objects. In such a situation, the trustees will simply hold the property on trust for the original settlor, under a resulting trust.[50]

OT Computers Ltd v First National Tricity Finance Ltd[51] is a relatively recent illustration of the principle that the trustees must be able to draw up a list of beneficiaries for it to be valid.

OT Computers traded as Tiny Computers. It started to make heavy losses. The company told its bank to open up two separate trust accounts to try to protect customers' deposits and money due to its urgent suppliers if the company went into insolvency. The first account, called the 'Customer Trust Account', was to be for the deposits received from its customers. The second account, named the 'Supplier Trust Account', was for money due to urgent suppliers. The company drew up a formal Trust Deed, which contained two lists: the first list had on it the names of its customers and the second list had on it the names of its suppliers. The company then entered administration. The company sought a declaration from the court that the money in the two bank accounts fell outside its assets available for the administration, on the basis that the money was held on trust for two distinct groups. The question for the High Court was whether the accounts were valid. That depended on whether it could be said that the objects of each trust account were certain.

Pumfrey J held that the trust for the customers was valid since it was possible to say who the beneficiaries were. The customers could be identified and a list made of them. The second

---

49 *Inland Revenue Commissioners v Broadway Cottages Trust* [1955] Ch 20.
50 See Chapter 3.
51 *OT Computers Ltd v First National Tricity Finance Ltd* [2003] EWHC 1010 (Ch).

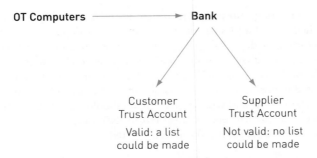

Figure 5.2 OT Computers Ltd v First National Tricity Finance Ltd.

purported trust, however, for the urgent suppliers was not valid since it was not possible to say who an 'urgent supplier' was. That term was too vague to be defined.

This case was applied by the Court of Appeal in *Brazzill v Willoughby*.[52] This is a contemporary example of trusts law being applied on a grand scale, since the amount of money in dispute in the case was over £147 million!

The background to the case was the near-collapse of the financial markets in 2008. Kaupthing Singer & Friedlander Ltd (KSF) was an English bank, owned by an Icelandic parent company. It offered internet bank accounts to corporate and retail customers. The market lost confidence in KSF which resulted in the Financial Services Authority issuing a formal Notice requiring the bank to open a Trust Account with the Bank of England. KSF was instructed by the Financial Services Authority to credit the account with amounts equal to deposits it received from its customers on particular dates. The Notice, however, did not define what was meant by 'deposits' or 'customers'. The money placed into the Trust Account was transferred by the Bank of England to a second bank, ING Direct NV (ING) and ING then assumed KSF's obligations to its customers. KSF later went into administration. The questions for the court included whether a trust had been created and, if so, who the beneficiaries of the trust were, given that 'customers' had not been defined in the Notice. Were the beneficiaries – or objects – sufficiently certain for a trust to be recognised?

In the High Court,[53] Peter Smith J held that a trust was created by the Notice. The beneficiaries of the trust were the customers who had paid money as deposits into KSF in the period between the Notice being issued and the date KSF was placed into administration. Although 'deposits' and 'customers' were not defined in the Notice, they could be given their ordinary meanings.

Figure 5.3 Brazzill v Willoughby.

52 *Brazzill v Willoughby* [2010] EWCA Civ 561.
53 *Brazzill v Willoughby* [2009] EWHC 1633 (Ch).

Lloyd LJ, giving the only substantive judgment in the Court of Appeal, agreed that a trust had been established by KSF in favour of its customers over deposits they made. But he disagreed over the meaning of 'deposits', giving it a more restricted meaning than at first instance. 'Deposits' in this case could only mean deposits which were classed as regulated under the Financial Services and Markets Act 2000. The customers were a class of beneficiaries who had made such regulated deposits. As such, it was possible for a list to be drawn up of customers who had made such deposits and who were entitled (should sufficient money remain) to the deposits in the account that had been transferred to ING. Consequently, there was sufficient certainty of object in the trust for it to be validly created.

The list need not be absolutely definitive

Our next point with regard to fixed trusts might be considered to be something of an exception to what has been said so far. It is this:

Key Learning Point

The trustees do not have to know the exact number of beneficiaries as long as the number of them is ascertainable.

You could have, for instance, a trust which says '£10,000 to my trustees to hold on trust for my fellow employees (as at the date of first publication of this book) in equal shares in the School of Law & Criminology at the University of Derby'. This would be a valid trust. The trustees might not know how many fellow employees there are, but this does not present a difficulty for the requirements of certainty. If we remember the reasoning behind certainty of object, it was to enable the trustees to understand the number of beneficiaries and their identity so that they could correctly administer the trust. If I set up a trust for the benefit of my fellow employees, it is still possible for the trustees to identify them because they form part of a group and it is clear who can and who cannot be included in such a group. This is implicit from the decisions in *Broadway Cottages* and *OT Computers*. The requirement, therefore, that the trustees need only know the number of beneficiaries is not, when analysed a little deeper, an exception to the premise that the trustees must be able to draw up a list of beneficiaries.

Untraceable beneficiaries in a fixed trust

What if the trustees cannot trace someone in the class? Suppose that one fellow employee was last heard of on a sabbatical in a far flung country and there is no way of contacting him, simply because his whereabouts are unknown. The trust is still certain because he is, at least, ascertainable: he still falls into the class of colleagues in the school. In such a situation, the trustees have two choices. They can either:

(a) apply to the court for a Benjamin Order. This comes from *Re Benjamin*.[54] This Order permits the trustees to distribute the trust fund to those beneficiaries that they can trace. This will include the missing beneficiary's share. If the missing beneficiary subsequently returns, he can claim his share from the other beneficiaries; or

---

54 *Re Benjamin* [1902] 1 Ch 723.

(b) alternatively, an often cheaper and quicker alternative for trustees instead of applying to court for a Benjamin Order is simply to take out 'missing beneficiary' insurance. This insures against the risk of the missing beneficiary later claiming his share. The trustees still distribute the trust to those beneficiaries they can trace. The policy will then pay out if the missing beneficiary returns.

To take this matter to its next logical stage, what if the trustees do not actually know if there are any other beneficiaries? This is different from where the beneficiary is just not contactable.

In this case, s 27 of the Trustee Act 1925 provides that the trustees can distribute the trust fund to those beneficiaries they know about and they can ignore claims of which they have no notice. To comply with s 27, however, the trustees must place advertisements in local newspapers and in the *London Gazette* notifying the public of their intention to distribute the trust fund and they must also give at least two months in which interested parties can submit their claim to the trustees.[55]

Discretionary Trusts

Where the requirement for the objects to be certain causes more difficulty is where the settlor declares a trust but does not name the beneficiaries specifically and instead leaves it to the trustees to decide who will benefit. This is the position in a discretionary trust.

❖ EXPLAINING THE LAW

I give £10,000 to my trustees to hold on trust for such of those students studying Law on a full-time basis in the final year of the LLB undergraduate degree at the University of Derby as my trustees shall choose.

This is a discretionary trust. It gives the trustees the ability to choose who in the particular group (or class) of students will benefit and the extent to which they will benefit.

Discretionary trusts are highly flexible. The trust will define a class of possible beneficiaries. Who in that class is to benefit and the terms upon which they will benefit is not decided until the trustees choose one or more of them as beneficiaries. Until a person is so chosen by the trustees, he has no beneficial interest in the trust property – all he has is a hope of being chosen to be a beneficiary.

Key Learning Point

This is all about drafting a trust. The settlor must give a clear enough definition of the beneficiaries so the trustees can choose them without any question marks over who is entitled to benefit from the trust.

---

55 Trustee Act 1925, s 27(1).

Certainty of objects also applies to discretionary trusts. The reasons for this with regard to discretionary trusts are two-fold:

(a)   as with fixed trusts, the trustees always need to know the identity of the beneficiaries so that they can execute and administer the trust; and

(b)   a trust must always be able to be controlled by the court, because if the trustees fail to administer the trust correctly, the court would have to step in to do so. In order for the court to administer the trust, the beneficiaries would have to be ascertained already so that the court could distribute the trust property amongst them. The court cannot choose the beneficiaries itself so rules must already exist by which objects can be chosen. This reasoning comes from Lord Eldon's speech in *Morice v Bishop of Durham*.[56]

Originally, the test for the objects to be certain in a discretionary trust meant that the trustees had to draw up a complete list of possible beneficiaries. Only then, as a second stage test, would they be required to choose people to benefit from that list. If they could not draw up a complete list initially, the trust would be void for uncertainty.

This approach to discretionary trusts was confirmed by the Court of Appeal in *IRC v Broadway Cottages Trust*.[57]

In 1950, Alan Timpson executed a Deed of Trust which declared that £80,000 was to be held on trust for his wife, Ethel, and certain other beneficiaries who were set out in a schedule to the document. The income was to be held on trust for such beneficiaries in such shares as the trustees themselves decided. This trust was of a discretionary nature. The other beneficiaries included numerous variations of former employees (or their wives or widows) of the settlor and his various relatives, and two charitable organisations, one of which was the Broadway Cottages Trust.

The difficulty was that, in view of the numerous possible types of beneficiary, it was impossible to draw up a complete list of all those people who were eligible to benefit from the trust. It would have been possible to determine whether any particular individual in their own right would fall into the category of being a beneficiary – it was just not possible to make a complete list of people who could be beneficiaries. The question was whether that was enough to make both the trusts certain.

The Court of Appeal held that it was not. For the objects to be certain, the trustees had to be able to draw up a complete list of all of the beneficiaries. Jenkins LJ, giving the judgment of the court, followed the reasoning given by Lord Eldon in *Morice v Bishop of Durham*.[58] If necessary, the court had to be able to take the place of the trustees and administer the trust. The only way the court could do this would be if it was quite clear who the beneficiaries were supposed to be. The only way it could be clear who the beneficiaries were supposed to be was if the trustees could draw up a complete list of them. The definition of the beneficiaries in the Trust Deed had to lend itself to that task. The definition in the Trust Deed in this particular case did not lend itself to that particular task and, as such, the objects of the trust were uncertain.

The requirement in *Broadway Cottages* that trustees draw up a fixed list of beneficiaries does not make a lot of sense. There is little point in making trustees of a discretionary trust draw up a complete list of potential beneficiaries when it was never the settlor's intention for every possible person to benefit from the trust. If the settlor did have such an intention, then presumably he would have created a fixed trust, not a discretionary one. The whole point about a discretionary trust is that the trustees have some flexibility over who should benefit. In

---

56 *Morice v Bishop of Durham* (1805) 10 Ves 522; 32 ER 947.
57 *IRC v Broadway Cottages Trust* [1955] Ch 20.
58 *Morice v Bishop of Durham* (1805) 10 Ves 522; 32 ER 947.

practical terms, even if it would be possible for a complete list of beneficiaries to be drawn up in a small discretionary family trust, it becomes impossible to do that when considering a trust with a large number of potential beneficiaries, as *Broadway Cottages* shows.

Broadway Cottages created a further difficulty. The Court of Appeal rejected a submission that, if a trust was void for certainty of objects, a valid power of appointment could be found instead. Jenkins LJ said that '[w]e do not think that a valid power is to be spelt out of an invalid trust'.

Instead, since the trust was void, an implied resulting trust would apply under which the trustees would hold the trust property for the settlor.

The effect of this meant that there could be no 'fall-back' provision in documents of a power of appointment being found where a trust was lacking. As such, the only way around the inconvenience of the decision in the case was for settlors not to declare discretionary trusts but instead to create powers of appointment, under which donees had the power – but not the obligation – to benefit people chosen at their discretion.

Why is a power of appointment different from a discretionary trust?

❖ EXPLAINING THE LAW

I give £10,000 to my donees to hold so that they may give the money to such of those students studying Law on a full-time basis in the final year of the LLB undergraduate degree at the University of Derby as my donees may choose.

This is a power of appointment. My donees *may* give the money away to people who fall within that group (or class) or they may not. It is entirely up to them. As such, I have given my donees a power to appoint recipient(s) of the money, hence the name 'power of appointment'.

A power is a different creature from a trust. The donor of a power is the same person as a settlor of a trust. The donor gives a power to appoint to the donee, who stands in the shoes of the trustee in a trust. The donee has the ability, if he chooses, to appoint someone in a class defined by the donor to benefit from the property left by him. Yet unlike a trust, the donee has a complete discretion over not only who benefits but whether anyone in the class should benefit at all.

A trustee under a discretionary trust is, however, obliged to distribute the trust fund. His discretion lies in the person to whom he distributes the fund. The trustee also has a discretion over how much to award to the chosen beneficiaries. The trustee, as part of his fiduciary duties, must consider whether to exercise his discretion.

As can be seen, a power of appointment is a far more relaxed concept for a donee to manage than a discretionary trust, at least under the law as established by *Broadway Cottages*.

Indeed, the use of a power in place of a discretionary trust was an attractive alternative following the decision in *Broadway Cottages* since there was, as confirmed by the House of Lords in *Re Gulbenkian's Settlement Trusts*,[59] no obligation on the donee to draw up a complete list of beneficiaries whom the donee believed fell within the class as defined by the donor. Lord Upjohn in *Re Gulbenkian's Settlement Trusts* confirmed the earlier decision of Harman J in *Re*

---

59 *Re Gulbenkian's Settlement Trusts* [1970] AC 508.

Gestetner's Settlement[60] that the correct test to determine whether the objects under a power were certain was:

> . . . if you can with certainty say whether any given individual is or is not a member of the class; you do not have to be able to ascertain every member of the class.

Re Gestetner's Settlement[61] concerned a settlement entered into by Sigmund Gestetner whom Harman J described as 'a man of great wealth'. In 1951, Mr Gestetner entered into a declaration of trust settling £100,000 on trustees to hold various trusts for a large and relatively diverse number of beneficiaries. Many of the trusts gave the trustees a power to determine who should benefit.

Harman J explained the difference between a power and a trust. In his view, a mere power did not mean that it was 'necessary to know of all the objects in order to appoint to one of them'.

In other words, in the case of a power of appointment, the donee simply had to consider whether each particular candidate for a share in the property left by the donor fell within the defined class. The focus was on the individual claimant, not on drawing up a list of all potential claimants.

The position with discretionary trusts and powers at the end of the 1960s

By the end of the 1960s, what resulted were two different tests to determine whether settlors' directions were valid or not. If a settlor chose to put his trustees under an obligation to distribute the property to beneficiaries that they might choose, then a discretionary trust had been created. The test in *Broadway Cottages* applied which meant that the trustees had to be able to draw up a complete list of potential beneficiaries. If a complete list could not be drawn up of all potential beneficiaries, the trust was void for the objects being uncertain.

On the other hand, if a donor chose to give his donees discretion over whether to choose anyone to benefit from his property, a power had been created. Following *Re Gulbenkian's Settlement Trusts*, no list had to be compiled of all potential recipients since it was never within the donor's original intention that all potential recipients could benefit from the power. Instead, the *Gulbenkian* test was simply whether any given person fell within the class defined by the donor.

This can be shown in the following diagram:

It was unfortunate that two separate tests existed and each one applied – giving a completely different result over whether a particular settlement was valid – depending on the

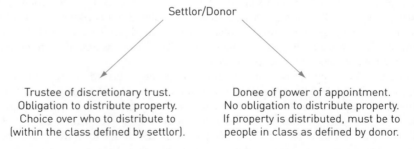

Settlor/Donor

| Trustee of discretionary trust. Obligation to distribute property. Choice over who to distribute to (within the class defined by settlor). | Donee of power of appointment. No obligation to distribute property. If property is distributed, must be to people in class as defined by donor. |

Figure 5.4 Summary of different tests for discretionary trusts and powers.

60 *Re Gestetner's Settlement* [1953] Ch 672.
61 Ibid.

exact wording that the settlor/donor had chosen to use in his document. In turn, this meant that more settlors were choosing to create a power rather than a trust as the threshold for creating a power was far easier to overcome than the one for a trust.

The House of Lords takes stock . . .

These two tests, fortunately, were reviewed by the House of Lords in *McPhail v Doulton*.[62]

In the case itself, Mr Bertram Baden created a trust of shares in a company. He was of a benevolent nature and his idea was that these shares would form the basis of a trust fund for the benefit of his company's staff and their families.

Clause 9(a) of the trust deed provided:

The trustees shall apply the net income of the fund in making at their absolute discretion grants to or for the benefit of any of the officers and employees or ex-officers or ex-employees of the company or to any relatives or dependants of any such persons in such amounts at such times and on such conditions (if any) as they think fit.

The question was whether Mr Baden intended to create a trust or a power.

If a trust, then following *Broadway Cottages*, the trustees would have had to have drawn up a complete list of possible beneficiaries. This would have been a difficult task since there were over 1,300 employees, let alone anyone else in the class. However, the real problem was whether the terms 'relatives' or 'dependants' of the officers, employees etc could be said to be sufficiently certain concepts. Could the trustees draw up an entire list of relatives and dependants of officers, employees, ex-officers and ex-employees of the company? If they could not, the trust would have been void for uncertainty.

Alternatively, if the document had created a power, then it would be valid as *Re Gestetner's Settlement* had decided that such a list need not be compiled and the trustees could assess whether any given person would fall within the class established by the settlor.

Mr Baden died in 1960. The background to the litigation was that his executors were seeking to have the trust declared void, so that the funds tied up in it would be available for Mr Baden's estate. The trustees of the trust, not unnaturally, resisted this. They sought to put into effect the terms of the trust which had, in their view, been Mr Baden's desire when he established the trust. The litigation itself lasted over nine years and Sachs LJ in the Court of Appeal in *Re Baden's Deed Trusts (No. 2)*[63] was quite scathing over the conduct of the executors saying that they had, by the end of the litigation:

caused much time and money to be devoted to their efforts to destroy the [trust] fund and frustrate the intentions of the man who appointed them executors.

Both Goff J in the High Court and the majority of the Court of Appeal held that Mr Baden had created a power in clause 9(a). This neatly stepped around the list requirement.

The House of Lords, however, held that a discretionary trust had been created. By a 3:2 majority, the decision was that the test applicable to powers would, in future, also be applicable to certainty of objects for discretionary trusts. This was a key defining moment. The test for whether the objects in a discretionary trust were certain had now been made the same as for assessing whether the objects in a power of appointment were sufficiently certain.

62 *McPhail v Doulton* [1971] AC 424.
63 *Re Baden's Deed Trusts (No. 2)* [1973] Ch 9.

The leading opinion of the majority was given by Lord Wilberforce. He explained that:

> [i]t is striking how narrow and in a sense artificial is the distinction, in cases such as the present, between trusts or as the particular type of trust is called, trust powers, and powers. It is only necessary to read the learned judgments in the Court of Appeal to see that what to one mind may appear as a power of distribution coupled with a trust to dispose of the undistributed surplus . . . may to another appear as a trust for distribution coupled with a power to withhold a portion. . . . A layman and, I suspect, a logician, would find it hard to understand what difference there is.[64]

He went on to say:

> It does not seem satisfactory that the entire validity of a disposition should depend on such delicate shading[65]

and later that:

> the wide distinction between the validity test for powers and that for trust powers is unfortunate and wrong . . . .[66]

Lord Wilberforce thought that, in practice, a trustee who has been handed either a power or a discretionary trust would undertake the same investigation as to who should benefit from the trust. It was, in reality, unrealistic to say that a trustee under a discretionary trust would draw up a complete list of all those beneficiaries who might benefit from an exercise of the trustee's discretion. Similarly, it was equally unrealistic to say that a donee of a power would not exercise his power responsibly and carefully.

Given that there were few differences in practice between those possessing a trust and those possessing a power, there should be just one test which addressed both situations. As there was just one test, that left him free to decide that clause 9(a) in the trust deed was not truly a power but was a trust since it contained an obligation on the trustee to distribute the trust fund.

Lord Wilberforce said that one test should apply for the validity of both trusts and powers. The test was that enunciated by the House of Lords in the earlier powers case of *Re Gulbenkian's Settlement Trusts*, namely 'the trust is valid if it can be said with certainty that any given individual is or is not a member of the class'.[67]

The court would, he said, exercise the power under a discretionary trust to choose beneficiaries if the trustees failed to use the power themselves. Consequently, by using this test, the court would be able to control discretionary trusts.

Key Learning Point

Objects in a Discretionary Trust = Certain

if:

'it can be said with certainty that any given individual is or is not a member of the class'

---

64 *McPhail v Doulton* [1971] AC 424 at 448.
65 Ibid at 449.
66 Ibid at 456.
67 Ibid.

At the end of his opinion, Lord Wilberforce made some additional points too vis-à-vis certainty:

(a) If the court could not resolve linguistic conceptual uncertainty in a declaration of trust, then the trust would be declared void. By contrast, the court could assist with where trustees simply could not locate particular beneficiaries through making a *Benjamin* Order.

(b) The meaning of the words used to describe a class of beneficiaries could be clear but if the result was to create a class which was massive in scale then the trust would be 'administratively unworkable'. Lord Wilberforce gave as an example of this 'all the residents of Greater London'. It would be clear who would fall into such a class of beneficiaries but the class would be administratively unworkable as it would be impracticable for trustees to consider the range of people who would fall into it.

Not too long after Lord Wilberforce's views on this latter issue came the facts facing the court in R v District Auditor ex parte West Yorkshire Metropolitan County Council.[68]

The West Yorkshire Metropolitan County Council was being split up. It had some surplus funds for which it had no defined plans. Consequently, the Metropolitan County Council proposed to set up a trust fund for the benefit of 'any or all or some of the inhabitants of West Yorkshire'.

Taylor J held that the trust was void given that there were potentially 2.5 million people within its class. Even though people could prove whether or not they lived in West Yorkshire, the trust was administratively unworkable.

Re Baden's Deed Trusts (No. 2) – the sequel . . .

After deciding that Mr Baden had actually declared a discretionary trust and not a power in his document, the House of Lords remitted the case to the High Court to apply the new test that Lord Wilberforce had set out. The issue for the High Court was whether, on the facts, Mr Baden's trust did satisfy Lord Wilberforce's test: namely, could it be said with certainty that any individual was or was not a member of the class of people described in clause 9(a) of the document. This secondary piece of litigation was known as *Re Baden's Deed Trusts* (No. 2).

In fact, the precise problem between Mr Baden's executors and the trustees of his trust was whether it was possible to say with certainty that any given individual was or was not a 'relative' or 'dependant' of an employee or ex-employee of the company.

As an initial point, Sachs LJ reiterated the difference between conceptual and evidential uncertainty. Conceptual uncertainty occurs where the description of a class of objects is in itself unclear or uncertain. Conceptual uncertainty in a trust would render the trust void. He cited an example put forward by counsel for the executors that a trust expressed to be for the benefit of 'someone under a moral obligation' would be void as it would be impossible to identify such a beneficiary. Evidential uncertainty would not defeat a trust, however. The court simply needed to see evidence to ascertain whether a potential beneficiary fell within a defined class that was evidentially uncertain. Again, Sachs LJ cited an example given by counsel for the executors, this time of 'first cousins'. This was a phrase that would be conceptually certain as the class of people who would benefit from the trust was clearly and precisely defined. Before benefiting from the trust, however, such first cousins would have to provide evidence that they really were first cousins of the settlor. Evidential uncertainty would not defeat a trust since the matter could be proved definitively with the necessary evidence.

In the end, all three members of the Court of Appeal decided that the terms 'relatives' and 'dependants' were sufficiently certain to make the trust in clause 9(a) valid. The difficulty with the case is that all three Lords Justice gave slightly different interpretations as to whether a person could be a 'relative' or 'dependant' of another. Their views are summarised in the following table:

68 R v District Auditor ex parte West Yorkshire Metropolitan County Council [1986] RVR 24.

	Sachs LJ	Megaw LJ	Stamp LJ
How should 'given postulant' test from *McPhail v Doulton* be applied?	Only conceptual certainty needed. Evidential difficulties do not invalidate the trust as the court is never defeated by evidential issues. A person who 'is not' a member of the class is not interpreted strictly and the 'don't knows' are part of the 'is not' category.	The trust will not fail just because one cannot prove one 'is not' a relative or dependant of another. A substantial number needs to be in the class for the class to be conceptually certain. There must be some evidential certainty for this substantial number.	Both conceptual and evidential certainty are needed so any 'don't knows' will invalidate the trust.
Was 'dependants' certain?	Quoted with approval Collins LJ in *Simmons v White Brothers*:[1] '"Dependant ... means dependant for the ordinary necessaries of life for a person of that class and position in life."'	'Dependants' was used in Acts of Parliament without being defined or explained (e.g. s 46 Administration of Estates Act 1925) and it would, he thought, be 'odd' if the word was then declared uncertain by a court.	The word meant being financially dependant on another person.
Was 'relatives' certain?	Approved Brightman J in the High Court: a person was a relative of another if 'both trace legal descent from a common ancestor'. Although this could produce a potentially huge class, he believed in practice trustees would select those people whom another might introduce as their relative as opposed to a '"kinsman" or "distant relative"'.	The test laid down by Lord Wilberforce in *McPhail* was satisfied if 'as regards a substantial number of objects, it can be said with certainty that they fall within the trust'. This would render the term certain.	The term meant someone's legal next-of-kin.

Figure 5.5 Table summary of the judgments in *Re Baden's Deed Trusts* (*No. 2*).

❖ ANALYSING THE LAW

To what extent do the views of the three members of the Court of Appeal in *Re Baden's Deed Trusts (No. 2)* reflect the looser objective that Lord Wilberforce was trying to achieve in *McPhail v Doulton*?

Sachs LJ believed only conceptual certainty was required so, in theory, one beneficiary could validate the trust. But this one-person idea was rejected in *McPhail v Doulton*.

Megaw LJ seemed to graft on an additional test to that of Lord Wilberforce: why should the trust only be valid if a substantial number of objects can fall into the definition?

Stamp LJ seemed to return to the 'list' test by the back door, by forcing trustees to categorise potential beneficiaries rigidly into those who fall within the class and those who do not.

❖ EXPLAINING THE LAW

I leave £1 million on trust for my trustees to distribute amongst such of my relatives and good friends as they think fit.

I have attempted to create a discretionary trust: I have given the trustees an obligation to distribute the money but they have discretion over who will receive a share of it. The objects must, however, fall into one of two classes: they must either be a relative of mine or one of my good friends.

To be valid, we know that the objects must be both conceptually and evidentially certain. Is the class of 'my relatives' certain in both respects?

The test to apply is the test set out by Lord Wilberforce in *McPhail v Doulton*, namely whether it 'can be said with certainty that any individual is or is not a member of the class'. The decision in the Court of Appeal in *Re Baden's Deed Trusts (No. 2)* decided that the word 'relatives' was conceptually certain (see Figure 5.5 for how the members of the Court of Appeal thought 'relatives' should be interpreted). To satisfy the requirements of evidential certainty, potential beneficiaries would need to adduce sufficient evidence to prove that they are, in fact, one of my relatives.

Is the class of my 'good friends' certain both conceptually and evidentially?

No. Again we need to apply the test in *McPhail*. This time, however, it is impossible to say that any individual is or is not a good friend of mine. Such people might fall anywhere in the spectrum of being an acquaintance, a friend, a good friend through to your best friend. As a concept, therefore, 'good friends' is incapable of definition. As that phrase is conceptually uncertain, whether it is evidentially certain or not becomes irrelevant.

Final note – a cautionary case . . .

Thus far, it has been shown that a discretionary trust in favour of 'friends' will fail, since the term is conceptually uncertain.

In Chapter 2,[69] *Re Barlow's Will Trusts*[70] was discussed as an example of where the term 'friends' was held to be a valid concept. The High Court held that the clause in Ms Barlow's will bequeathing paintings to her 'friends' was valid. It is important to note that the case does not decide that 'friends' is a certain concept for discretionary trusts. There was no trust found in that case. Instead, Browne-Wilkinson J found that a series of gifts had been created as opposed to one trust. As the case did not concern a trust, it was unnecessary (and it would have been wrong) to apply the 'given postulant' test. *Re Barlow's Will Trusts* leaves the issue of 'friends' being uncertain in a discretionary trust untouched.

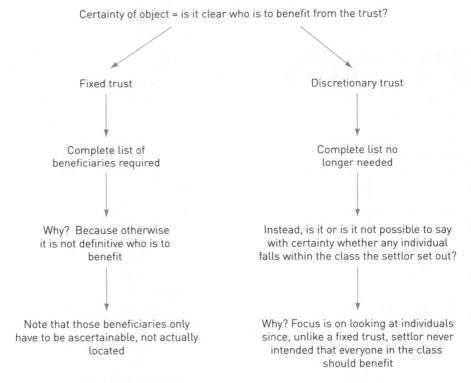

Figure 5.6 Summary of certainty of object.

---

69 See Chapter 2, p 50–51.
70 *Re Barlow's Will Trusts* [1979] 1 WLR 278.

Points to Review

We have seen:

- how all three certainties must be present as part of the requirements to form a valid trust;
- that certainty of intention involves looking at whether the settlor expressed a sufficient intention to establish a trust, by considering their words and actions;
- that certainty of subject-matter involves looking at two issues: whether it is possible to say that the property of the trust is sufficiently well defined and whether the beneficial interests in the property are clear;
- that certainty of object focuses on whether the beneficiaries themselves have been clearly identified; and
- that all of the certainties are there primarily to assist the trustee(s) in administering the trust. It would be an impossible task for a trustee to administer a trust if they did not know that (i) there was a trust (ii) what the trust property was and (iii) who the beneficiaries of the trust were. The requirements of the three certainties ensure that these key areas are clearly set out.

Making connections

An understanding of the three certainties has both long- and short-term consequences. In the long term, an understanding of this area is essential if you are to have a solid grasp of how a trust is formed. In the short term, this area very often features in assessments at undergraduate level – some might even say that it is a favourite of examiners!

This area is one piece of the jigsaw of trust formation. The chapters on the beneficiary principle (see Chapter 6), formalities (see Chapter 4) and the rules against perpetuity (on the companion website) look at the other requirements to declare a trust and those must be seen as the logical next steps in your learning development.

 Useful Things to Read

The best reading is contained in the primary sources listed below. It is always good to consider the decisions of the courts themselves as this will lead to a deeper understanding of the issues involved. A few secondary sources are also listed, which you may wish to read to gain additional insights into the areas considered in this chapter.

Primary sources
Lambe v Eames (1870–71) LR 6 Ch App 597.
Comiskey v Bowring-Hanbury [1905] AC 84 (Opinions of Earl of Halsbury LC and Lord James).
Re Kayford Ltd (in Liquidation) [1975] 1 WLR 279 (Judgment of Megarry J).
Hunter v Moss [1994] 1 WLR 452 at 457–459.
Re Goldcorp Exchange Ltd (in Receivership) [1994] 3 WLR 199.
IRC v Broadway Cottages Trust [1955] Ch 20.
Re Gulbenkian's Settlement Trusts [1970] AC 508 (Opinion of Lord Upjohn).
McPhail v Doulton [1971] AC 424 (Opinion of Lord Wilberforce).
Re Baden's Deed Trusts (No. 2) [1973] Ch 9.

Secondary sources

David Hayton, 'Uncertainty of subject matter in trusts' [1994] LQR 335. This article critiques *Hunter v Moss* and is a brief, useful read on the Court of Appeal's controversial decision.

Alastair Hudson, *Equity & Trusts* (7th edn, Routledge-Cavendish, 2012) ch 3.

Paul Matthews, 'A heresy and a half in certainty of objects' (1984) Conv 22–31. A fascinating article which argues that *McPhail* was not a revolutionary decision and that the decision in the case is applicable also to fixed trusts.

Mohamed Ramjohn, *Text, Cases and Materials on Equity & Trusts* (4th edn, Routledge–Cavendish, 2008) ch 3.

Sarah Worthington, 'Sorting out ownership interests in a bulk: gifts, sales and trusts' (1999) JBL Jan 1–21. This looks at the factors to be taken into account as to when an individual may be said to have a share in an undivided bulk of property.

Chapter 6

Trust Formation: The Beneficiary Principle

The task of understanding the components needed to form an express trust continues in this chapter with a discussion of another essential element: the beneficiary principle and its exceptions. The beneficiary principle is the notion that, generally speaking, an express trust must exist for the benefit of an individual (or individuals) as opposed to a purpose or cause.

As You Read

As you read, focus on the following:

● the definition of the beneficiary principle: the central idea that English law prefers trusts to be for the benefit of an ascertained or ascertainable beneficiary rather than for a defined purpose;

● how the beneficiary principle links in to the other requirements needed to declare an express trust; and

● exceptions to the beneficiary principle: what they entail, how they apply and their relevance to today's world.

Definition of the Beneficiary Principle

The beneficiary principle is the concept that a private, express trust must be for the benefit of a beneficiary who the trustees can either ascertain or is at least ascertainable. In practical terms, this means that the settlor must settle property on trust for the benefit of an individual or individuals (or, on some occasions, a company[1]) who are sufficiently well defined so that the trustees can understand the identity of the people for whom they are administering the trust.

This requirement can be contrasted with a trust being set up to pursue a purpose. English law traditionally frowns upon trusts being for the benefit of a purpose. As a general rule, a trust set up for a purpose instead of ascertained or ascertainable beneficiaries will be void. These principles can be illustrated by Re Astor's Settlement Trusts.[2]

Viscount Astor purported to declare a trust in February 1945 of most of the issued shares in The Observer Limited, a company owning a national newspaper. The trust provided that the shares were to be held for a number of purposes including, for instance, 'the establishment, maintenance and improvement of good understanding sympathy and co-operation between nations' and 'the preservation of the independence and integrity of newspapers'. Crucially, the trust was only established for purposes and it was not possible to say that any human beneficiary would directly benefit from the trust.

Roxburgh J held that the trust was void since there was no human beneficiary who could benefit from the trust. He relied on the earlier leading case of Bowman v Secular Society Ltd[3] in which Lord Parker had said:[4]

A trust to be valid must be for the benefit of individuals . . . or must be in that class of gifts for the benefit of the public which the courts in this country recognize as charitable in the legal as opposed to popular sense of that term.

---

1 See the comment of Viscount Simonds in Leahy v A-G for New South Wales [1959] AC 457 at 478.
2 Re Astor's Settlement Trusts [1952] Ch 534.
3 Bowman v Secular Society [1917] AC 406.
4 Ibid at 441.

Roxburgh J examined the reasoning behind Lord Parker's statement. He pointed out that at the heart of a trust was a series of equitable rights that a beneficiary enjoyed. These equitable rights had been 'hammered out'[5] in litigated cases over many years. Taken as a whole, the people who enjoyed the equitable rights under a trust – the beneficiaries – had the ability to enforce them against the trustees if the trustees refused to honour these rights voluntarily. Human beneficiaries could take court action against recalcitrant trustees. Roxburgh J confirmed that a trust required that there had to be a physical person who was a beneficiary and who could, if necessary, take such court action against the trustees to enjoy their equitable rights. Trusts for purposes, as Viscount Astor had declared, gave rise to no single individual enjoying equitable rights which meant there was no human person who had the right to take court action against the trustees if they failed in their duties as trustees.

❖ EXPLAINING THE LAW

Suppose Scott settles £100,000 on trust. He appoints Thomas as his trustee. Scott provides in the declaration of trust that he wants the money to be invested by Thomas and the proceeds to be used each year for the development of world peace.

No doubt this is a worthwhile purpose, but such a trust would be void since it infringes the beneficiary principle. Suppose Thomas refused to invest the money according to Scott's wishes. Who would then enforce the trust against him? There is no-one to do so because there is no human beneficiary who could take court action against him. Remember that, as settlor, Scott cannot take action against the trustee for breach of trust because the settlor (unless he has expressly reserved such a power to himself in the trust documentation) has no involvement in the trust once it has been established.

Rationale of the beneficiary principle

The main reason behind the requirement that a trust should have a human beneficiary benefiting from it has been shown in the examination of the judgment of Roxburgh J in Re Astor's Settlement Trusts.[6] His view, echoing that of Lord Parker in Barlow v Secular Society Ltd,[7] reaffirmed the long-established position set out in Morice v Bishop of Durham[8] that, as far as a trust was concerned, '[t]here must be somebody, in whose favour the court can decree performance'.

In this sense, equity is acting with a mixture of both pragmatism and pre-planning. Equity realises that not all trustees may act in the best interests of the beneficiaries but they may instead act to benefit themselves. For example, some trustees may simply fail in their obligations towards the trust by, for example, failing to take proper advice before investing trust money. If the trustees fail in their duties towards the trust, regardless of whether the trustees themselves benefit personally from their failings, there has to be someone who can take action against them. That person cannot be the settlor for, as we have seen, the settlor generally steps out of the trust once he has set it up. By almost a process of elimination, the only person left in the relationship to ensure that the trustees keep to the right track is the beneficiary. There is

---

5 Re Astor's Settlement Trusts [1952] Ch 534 at 541.
6 Ibid.
7 Bowman v Secular Society [1917] AC 406.
8 Morice v Bishop of Durham 9 Ves 399 at 405; 32 ER 656.

no-one else to take action against the trustees: for example, the court will not of its own instigation take action; neither is there an officer of the government whose job it is to hold trustees of private trusts accountable.

English law, therefore, embodies the idea that there must be someone who can take action against the trustees into one of the ingredients required to declare a trust: the beneficiary principle. The corollary of the principle, as illustrated by the facts of *Re Astor's Settlement Trusts*, is that English law does not like trusts for purposes as a general concept.

There is a second reason for the law of trusts embodying the beneficiary principle. It is more of a legalistic reason. In Chapter 2 you saw how the concept of a trust involves split ownership: that the trustee holds the legal title to the property and the beneficiary enjoys the equitable interest. An equitable interest will, therefore, always exist in a trust. There must be someone who can enjoy that equitable interest as it cannot exist without it attaching to a beneficiary. An equitable interest cannot simply 'float' around without being owned because, of course, equity abhors a vacuum. The beneficiary principle, therefore, ensures that someone owns the equitable interest in the property of the trust. It is possible to see this second reason as being tied to the same underlying principle as certainty of object that was considered in Chapter 5. At their heart, both concepts require a beneficiary to be present in a valid trust.

The third reason given for the existence of the beneficiary principle is related to the rules against perpetuity.[9] The rule against perpetuity which is relevant here is the rule against inalienability. This provides that the capital of the trust must reach the beneficiaries for them to enjoy at some point in the future. The idea behind this rule is that a trust must come to an end at some point. If the trust does not come to an end within the time period contemplated by this rule, it will be void for offending the rule against inalienability.

Trusts which do not have any identifiable beneficiaries but are instead for a purpose offend the rule against inalienability. This is because a purpose may well last forever, which will require the money to be reinvested time and again. As such, the money is tied up for the purpose instead of being available in the wider economy. The beneficiary principle thus supports the rule against inalienability by ensuring that there should be an identifiable beneficiary who will eventually take the legal title in the trust property and use the trust property in the wider economy.

Exceptions to the Beneficiary Principle

The general rule is that there must be a human beneficiary for there to be a valid declaration of trust. However, for almost every rule there is an exception. There are five main exceptions, see Figure 6.1.

Charitable trusts

Charitable trusts are a major topic of the law of trusts in their own right and are considered separately in Chapter 15.

There are two key requirements for a trust to be charitable under the Charities Act 2011:

(a)   there must be a charitable purpose as defined under s 3(1) of that Act; and
(b)   the charity must be able to demonstrate, through its activities, a sufficient benefit to the public or a section of it, under s 2(1)(b) of the Act.

---

9   This topic is addressed in depth on the companion website.

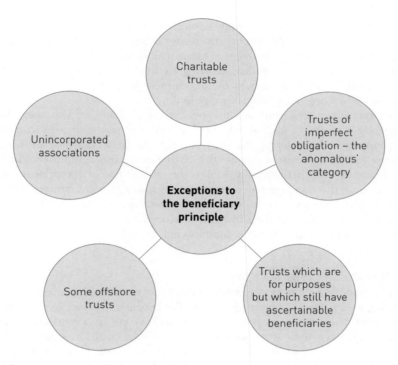

Figure 6.1 Exceptions to the beneficiary principle.

Most trusts which meet these requirements of charitable status do not, of course, have defined human beneficiaries and some, at first glance, do not directly benefit humans at all.

❖ **APPLYING THE LAW**

Consider some of the most well-known charities in England and Wales such as the Royal Society for the Prevention of Cruelty to Animals (RSPCA), Barnardo's or Cancer Research UK.

It cannot be said that any of these charitable trusts have defined human beneficiaries. Instead, they exist to benefit society as a whole through their daily activities.

Yet such trusts are permitted to exist and, in addition, can be granted charitable status which, as will become apparent,[10] enables them to enjoy significant tax-saving advantages.

The reasons why such trusts are permitted even though they infringe the beneficiary principle are two-fold:

---

10 See Chapter 15.

(a)   as a matter of public policy, charities should be encouraged to exist due to the good works that they undertake. If charities were not allowed to exist, their good works would either fall to the government to implement or simply lapse. Either may not be as beneficial to society as a whole as allowing a charity which understands its respective area to exist. In addition, should the government have to provide such services, the increased cost would fall to the tax-payer; and

(b)   The main reason underpinning the beneficiary principle is that there has to be somebody who can, if needed, take legal action to force the trustees to honour their obligations in administering the trust correctly. As far as charities are concerned, a separate mechanism exists to ensure that charitable trustees administer their charitable trust correctly. The Charity Commission is the relevant body responsible for overseeing charities and, if action is required to be taken against a charity's trustees, such action is taken by the Attorney-General, one of the government's legal officers. The Attorney-General acts on behalf of the Crown, whose overall responsibility it is to ensure that property belonging to a charity is administered correctly.

Trusts of imperfect obligation

A trust of an imperfect obligation is a trust which has no defined human beneficiary and which would, at first glance, appear to infringe the beneficiary principle since such a trust is for a purpose. These trusts are permitted to exist. They are an 'anomalous'[11] category of trusts which may, albeit sometimes quite loosely, benefit the public in some way. The reason why such purpose trusts are permitted to exist has not been fully explained judicially. In *Re Astor's Settlement Trusts*,[12] Roxburgh J acknowledged that the explanation put forward by the well-regarded academic Sir Arthur Underhill that such trusts were judicial 'concessions to human weakness or sentiment'[13] may well be correct. In addition, these types of trust are usually of small enough scope to be able to be controlled by the court if necessary.

Such trusts fall into three main categories:

(a)   trusts relating to tombs and monuments;
(b)   trusts for the provision of masses in private; and
(c)   trusts benefiting a specific animal.

These purpose trusts are trusts which still, however, need to meet the other requirements to form a valid express trust. So they must comply with any requirements of formality, adhere to the principles of certainty and meet the rules against perpetuity. It would seem that the only requirement which is relaxed in their favour is the need to have a human beneficiary benefiting from the trust.

Trusts relating to tombs and monuments

These types of trust arise where property is left on trust with the purpose of providing for the establishment and/or upkeep of specific memorials in churches.

In *Re Hooper*,[14] Harry Hooper left £1,000 on trust for trustees to invest and use the income for four purposes:

---

11   Roxburgh J in *Re Astor's Settlement Trusts* [1952] Ch 534 at 541.
12   *Re Astor's Settlement Trusts* [1952] Ch 534.
13   Ibid at 547, quoting from Underhill's *Law of Trusts*, 8th edn, p 79.
14   *Re Hooper* [1932] 1 Ch 38.

(a)   the upkeep of his parents' grave in Torquay cemetery;
(b)   the upkeep of a vault and monument, also in Torquay cemetery, in which his wife and daughter were buried;
(c)   the upkeep of a grave and monument in a churchyard near Ipswich in which his son was buried; and
(d)   the care of a tablet and a window in a church at Ilsham, which were devoted to the memories of some of his family members.

The issue for the High Court was whether this trust was valid. Clearly, there could be no defined human beneficiaries of the trust, as all the people to whom the trust referred had already predeceased Mr Hooper.

Maugham J held that the trust overall was valid. In a short judgment, the reasoning why the trust was valid was not especially detailed. He followed an earlier High Court decision[15] which had reached the same result and Maugham J was guided by matters of pragmatism:

> The case does not appear to have attracted much attention in text-books, but it does not appear to have been commented upon adversely, and I shall follow it.[16]

The fourth part of the trust was, however, held to be charitable. Again, there is no explanation given by Maugham J but it may be presumed that he felt that it was for a valid charitable purpose (presumably for the advancement of religion) and could be said to benefit a section of the public through their enjoyment of viewing the tablet and the window in the church.

This latter part of the decision illustrates that the courts prefer, if possible, not to recognise valid trusts of imperfect obligation, but instead hold them to be valid charitable trusts. Indeed, the courts have no wish to extend these categories of purpose trust and prefer to keep them within narrow confines as illustrated by Re Endacott.[17]

In this case, Albert Endacott wrote his will in which he left his residuary estate (worth approximately £20,000) to North Tawton Devon Parish Council for them to provide 'some useful memorial to myself'. The Court of Appeal held that the obligatory nature of Mr Endacott's bequest meant that a trust had been created. The issue was whether such a trust could be valid given that there was no human beneficiary who could enforce the trust. It was clearly a trust for a purpose.

The Court of Appeal held that the trust could not be valid. It was a type of trust which left far too much open to be decided in the future. No-one could police this type of trust over what the North Tawton Devon Parish Council chose to spend the money on.

Lord Evershed MR believed that the categories of trusts of imperfect obligation ought not to be extended in the future. A cardinal principle in English law was that a trust required an ascertained or ascertainable beneficiary to enforce it. Trusts of imperfect obligation were an exception to that requirement but, as an exception, they had to be kept within narrow confines. Harman LJ went further, saying that all categories of trusts of imperfect obligation:

> stand by themselves and ought not to be increased in number, nor indeed followed, except where the one is exactly like another.[18]

---

15 Pirbright v Salwey [1896] WN 86.
16 Re Hooper [1932] 1 Ch 38 at 40.
17 Re Endacott [1960] Ch 232.
18 Ibid at 250–251.

He summed up his true feelings on cases of trusts of imperfect obligation, calling them 'troublesome, anomalous and aberrant'.[19]

The decision also illustrates that the courts will have little sympathy for purpose trusts of a capricious nature.

It appears, then, that trusts involving the establishment or upkeep of memorials will be permitted, but only when such trusts are well defined so that they can be said to be managed by the court if necessary. Widely drafted trusts involving awarding the recipient a great deal of discretion over the type of memorial to be established will not be permitted.

Trusts for the provision of Masses in private

This second type of trust of imperfect obligation is based upon a particular type of ceremony in the Catholic Church: the Mass.

Typically, a settlor will set up a trust in which money is left to the Catholic Church which helps to meet the additional costs of a priest being available to conduct a separate Mass for the soul(s) of the person named in the trust. The souls who are usually mentioned in the trust are those of the settlor's spouse, family and friends and perhaps the settlor themselves. These types of trust are usually created in the settlor's will and so only take effect on the settlor's death. There is no living beneficiary who would be able, if necessary, to enforce the trust. This is a further example of a trust for a purpose: the purpose being to pray for the souls mentioned in the trust.

That this type of trust could exist as a trust of imperfect obligation was decided by the House of Lords in *Bourne v Keane*.[20] This area had been wrapped up in the historical development of the Church of England in its break-away from the Catholic Church. Previous case law, especially *West v Shuttleworth*,[21] had decided that leaving property to the Roman Catholic Church to pay for a priest to say Masses constituted a 'superstitious use' which was not permitted under the preamble to the Chantries Act 1547. By way of departure from this previous jurisprudence, the House of Lords in *Bourne v Keane* decided that the Chantries Act 1547 had not been enacted with the intention to prevent property being left for such masses to be said.

In the case itself, Edward Egan made a will in which he left £200 to Westminster Cathedral and his residuary estate to the Jesuit Fathers. In both instances, the money was left for Masses to be said.

The House of Lords held that such gifts were valid. As Lord Birkenhead LC pointed out, gifts to the Catholic Church to build a new church or provide for an altar in an existing church had long been held to be valid (albeit as valid charitable gifts). He said that it would be an 'absurdity' if:

> a Roman Catholic citizen of this country may legally endow an altar for the Roman Catholic community, but may not provide funds for the administration of that sacrament which is fundamental in the belief of Roman Catholics, and without which the church and the altar would alike be useless.[22]

A more recent case which has considered this issue is *Re Hetherington*.[23] The case concerned the will of Margaret Hetherington. She was described as a 'devout Roman Catholic',[24] so it was not surprising that she desired to benefit the Catholic Church in her will. Two clauses of her will

---

19 Ibid.
20 *Bourne v Keane* [1919] AC 815.
21 *West v Shuttleworth* 2 My & K 684; 39 ER 1106.
22 *Bourne v Keane* [1919] AC 815 at 861.
23 *Re Hetherington* [1990] Ch 1.
24 Ibid by Sir Nicolas Browne-Wilkinson V-C at 7.

are relevant here. First, she left £2,000 to the Roman Catholic Church Bishop of Westminster 'for the repose of the souls of my husband and my parents and my sisters and also myself when I die'. Second, she left her residuary estate to the Roman Catholic Church St Edward's Golders Green 'for Masses for my soul'. The issue for the High Court was whether such provisions in the will could validly take effect as trusts of imperfect obligation.

Sir Nicolas Browne-Wilkinson, V-C, held that the provisions of Mrs Hetherington's will could take effect as valid charitable trusts. They were plainly for the benefit of religion. In addition, there was nothing in the will which provided the Masses had to be said in private. Where a gift for the benefit of religion could be celebrated either privately or publicly, the Vice-Chancellor followed the earlier decisions in Re White[25] and Re Banfield[26] and held that the service should be carried out in public. Through attending the service, members of the public could benefit from the spiritual nature of the religious rite. This public benefit meant that Mrs Hetherington's trusts could be seen to be of a charitable nature and were valid on this basis.

The decision again illustrates the reluctance of the courts in modern times to find examples of trusts of imperfect obligation. Sir Nicolas Browne-Wilkinson again referred to trusts of imperfect obligation as 'trusts of the anomalous class'[27] which suggests he had little appetite to keep this category of trust alive by adding further examples to it. On the facts, it was not necessary to hold that Mrs Hetherington's were further examples of trusts of imperfect obligation and the Vice-Chancellor instead preferred to recognise the trusts as examples of more soundly-established charitable trusts.

❖ ANALYSING THE LAW

Think about whether the decision in *Re Hetherington*, to prefer the trust as being of a charitable nature, is necessarily consistent with the House of Lords decision in *Bourne v Keane*. Whilst the House of Lords did not extensively consider the issue of whether Edward Egan's gift could have charitable status, Lord Buckmaster did appear to rule out that possibility when he said that '[i]n the present case, no general charitable intention is disclosed'.

The Vice-Chancellor in *Re Hetherington* held that where the trust was silent on whether the Masses could be said in public or in private, they should be said in public since this would provide sufficient benefit on members of the public who attended to mean that the trust could have charitable status.

Yet the facts in neither case suggested that the settlor had made any express intention clear as to whether the Masses were to be said in public or private.

The House of Lords in *Bourne v Keane* appears to have assumed that the Masses were to be said in private and that there was no public benefit to be attained from the services. At the very least, the decision in *Re Hetherington* stretches the settlor's intentions by providing that the Masses can be said in public where the settlor has not provided that the service must be held in private. Lord Buckmaster in *Bourne v Keane* had presumably thought that such a development was not a possibility on the facts before him.

---

25 Re White [1893] 2 Ch 41.
26 Re Banfield [1968] 1 WLR 846.
27 Re Hetherington [1990] Ch 1 at 10.

Trusts to benefit a specific animal

Trusts established to benefit animals in general (e.g. the RSPCA) will usually have charitable status as enhancing animal welfare is a charitable purpose under s 3(1)(k) of the Charities Act 2011. Public benefit in protecting animals was explained by Swinfen Eady LJ in *Re Wedgwood*[28] in that such a trust:

> tends to promote and encourage kindness towards [animals], to discourage cruelty
> . . . and thus to stimulate humane and generous sentiments in man towards the
> lower animals, and by these means promote feelings of humanity and morality
> generally, repress brutality, and thus elevate the human race.[29]

Trusts set up to benefit only one particular type of animal – for example, the Royal Society for the Protection of Birds – are usually considered charitable too for the same reasons.

The category of trust considered here is that which is established to protect the settlor's personal animals. These trusts cannot be charitable as they do not benefit the public but rather just the settlor. Such trusts were recognised as valid trusts of imperfect obligation in *Re Dean*.[30]

Mr William Dean was an animal lover. He provided in his will that his freehold land should be held on trust. It was to be subjected to an annual sum of £750 being taken out of the income from it and given to his trustees so that they would have sufficient money to be able to look after his eight horses and his dogs. The trust was to last for 50 years from his death.

North J held that the trust could take effect as a valid trust. He said that there had been other cases in which sums of money had been validly left on trust despite the trusts having had no beneficiary to enforce them. He quoted a trust to build a monument as an example. He did not see any reason why a similar type of trust which could not be enforced should not be valid.

The more general comments that North J made to the effect that a trust could be valid despite having no beneficiary to enforce it should probably be treated with caution nowadays, given the Court of Appeal's reluctance in *Re Endacott*[31] to sanction the recognition of further categories of trusts of imperfect obligation. Nevertheless, the principle in *Re Dean* still stands and it is possible, therefore, to have a valid trust in favour of the settlor's personal animals.

It seems that North J entirely ignored the perpetuity point in the case. This trust could have come into effect more than 21 years from Mr Dean's death, so should have been held to have been invalid.

❖ APPLYING THE LAW

People often leave large sums of money in their wills for the benefit of their pets. In 2010, it was reported in America that multi-millionaire Gail Posner had bequeathed Conchita, her pet Chihuahua, a house worth $8.3 million and a separate sum of $3 million for her maintenance. Her son, Bret, had been left $1 million and he is in the process of bringing an action to try to increase his share of his mother's estate, at Conchita's expense.

Prima facie, such a trust in favour of Conchita would be valid in English law pursuant to *Re Dean*.

---

28 *Re Wedgwood* [1915] 1 Ch 113.
29 Ibid at 122.
30 *Re Dean* (1889) LR 41 ChD 552.
31 *Re Endacott* [1960] Ch 232.

Other categories of trust of imperfect obligation?

The main categories of trust of imperfect obligation which have been recognised by the courts have been considered. There are other examples where such trusts have been held to be valid, but these are mostly one-off situations and are peculiar to the facts of the individual cases. Such examples include:

- A trust for the promotion and furtherance of fox hunting as occurred in *Re Thompson*.[32] Here the testator left £1,000 to his friend, George Lloyd, in order that the money should be applied in whatever manner Mr Lloyd thought fit to promote and further fox hunting. In a short judgment, Clauson J took the pragmatic consideration that the gift to Mr Lloyd was 'of a nature to which effect can be given'.[33] The overriding points in the case seem to be that the gift was clearly defined by the testator and the judge thought that it should be upheld. Nowadays, as indicated in *Re Endacott*, unless a further case had precisely the same facts as *Re Thompson*, it is likely that the court would be more inquisitive as to whether the trust should be valid than just considering whether the trust had been clearly defined. Given that hunting wild mammals with dogs has now been banned by Parliament,[34] it is unlikely that a future trust which promotes traditional fox hunting with hounds would be upheld.
- A trust for the promotion of non-Christian religious ceremonies: *Re Khoo Cheng Teow*.[35] Here, clause 5 of Mr Khoo Cheng Teow's will directed that a building at 56 Church Street, Singapore, be rented out and the money raised should be used for the furtherance of 'religious ceremonies according to the custom of the Chinese called *Sin Chew*'. Terrell J held that there was no reason why such a trust should not be valid:

> it is fitting and proper that the same validity should be accorded to gifts for the performance of ceremonies which are an essential feature of the religious rites of the Chinese . . .[36]

The decision illustrates that equity will not distinguish between different faiths and religions. A trust for the private performance of any recognised religious ceremony can thus be valid.

The categories of case that will be upheld as trusts of imperfect obligation are now closed, following *Re Endacott* and, following *Re Hetherington*, it seems that the courts will, wherever possible, prefer to recognise a trust which can be interpreted as having a public element to it as charitable rather than as a further example of a non-charitable purpose trust. This is all part of the general principle which is to dissuade settlors from establishing trusts without ascertained or ascertainable beneficiaries to enforce them.

Purpose trusts but which nonetheless have ascertainable beneficiaries

As has been considered, the main reason why purpose trusts are not upheld in English law is because there is no-one who can compel the trustees to administer the trust if they refuse to

---

32 *Re Thompson* [1934] Ch 342.
33 Ibid at 344.
34 Hunting Act 2004, s 1.
35 *Re Khoo Cheng Teow* [1933] 2 MLJ 119.
36 Ibid at 122.

do so. Unless the trust has charitable status or can be seen to fall within one of the 'anomalous' categories of trusts of imperfect obligation, the general principle used to be that any other trust established for a purpose would fail. This was shown in *Leahy v Attorney-General for New South Wales*.

The facts involved the will of Francis Leahy. Under clause 3, he left his property called 'Elmslea' in Bungendore, Australia, together with his furniture, on trust:

> for such order of nuns of the Catholic Church or the Christian Brothers as my executors and trustees shall select . . .

The Privy Council held that the trust created by Mr Leahy was a trust for a purpose. It did not benefit specific individuals, but instead was a trust of property which was to be held on trust for the purpose of whichever order of nuns or Christian Brothers that the trustees actually selected. To hold that the trust was for the benefit of individuals would be to go against the evidence available on the facts in three ways:

(a)   the wording used by Mr Leahy spoke of the property being held for an 'order' of nuns or Christian Brothers. This suggested the property being held on trust for the order's purposes as opposed to the individual members of such an order;

(b)   if the trust was a trust benefiting individuals, as opposed to a purpose, the trust would have to benefit all of the members of the chosen orders of nuns or Christian Brothers who were living, no matter where they were located across the world. It was thought that this was unlikely to have been Mr Leahy's intention. No doubt he wished to benefit nuns or members of the Christian Brothers who were based closer to him in New South Wales; and

(c)   Elmslea was a substantial property, consisting of approximately 730 acres of land, a 20-room main building and several outbuildings. It was unlikely that Mr Leahy's intention was to divide that size of property up between individuals. It was unlikely he would have seen that the nuns or Christian Brothers would have themselves personally owned the equitable interest in his property. Instead, it was far more likely that, as a whole, the property might be used for the purpose of benefiting an entire order of nuns or Christian Brothers.

Overall, Mr Leahy's intention was to benefit an order to help secure and further its work in the future. As such, Mr Leahy had created a purpose trust. Such a trust would be invalid in law.[37] Despite Mr Leahy seemingly setting out that the trust was for individuals, the court would look to the substance of the trust and see that it was essentially a trust for purposes. After all, equity looks to the substance and not the precise form in which a document is drafted. As the trust was for purposes, it had to fail.

This point was, however, reconsidered by Goff J in *Re Denley's Trust Deed*[38] where he suggested that not every purpose trust would automatically fail.

The facts concerned a trust deed made in August 1936 by Charles Denley and others in which land located in Gloucestershire was settled on trust for the purpose of a sports or recreation ground. Under clause 2(c) of the trust deed, the land could be used by two categories of person:

---

37   Although, on the facts, s 37D of the Conveyancing Act 1919–1954 (New South Wales, Australia, legislation) saved the provision in the case itself.
38   *Re Denley's Trust Deed* [1969] 1 Ch 373.

primarily for the benefit of the employees of [a company] and secondarily for the benefit of such other person or persons (if any) as the trustees may allow.

As in *Leahy v Attorney-General for New South Wales*, the provision seemed, at first sight, to benefit individuals. But, as in that previous case, it could be argued that the trust was a trust for a purpose – namely, that the land had been placed on trust to be used as a sports and recreation ground.

Goff J, however, held that the trust was valid. In doing so, he held there was a distinction between two different types of purpose trust:

(a)   a type of purpose trust where, although it does benefit an individual, the benefit is 'so indirect or intangible . . . as not to give those persons any *locus standi* to apply to the court to enforce the trust'.[39] In such a case, the purpose trust would fail since it would infringe the beneficiary principle. There would be, in practical terms, no-one who had sufficient authority to ensure the trustees honoured the terms of the trust as it could not be said that any beneficiary directly benefited enough from the trust to be able to take court action; and

(b)   a type of purpose trust which will be enforced by the court because the trust is 'directly or indirectly for the benefit of an individual or individuals'.[40] Goff J felt that this type of purpose trust was 'outside the mischief of the beneficiary principle'.[41]

The beneficiary principle existed to ensure that there was someone who could force the trustees to honour the terms of the trust. In this trust, Goff J believed that the court could force the trustees to administer the trust in the two ways fundamental to the trust's existence:

(a)   by restraining any use of the land which the court felt was improper; and/or

(b)   by ordering the trustees to allow the employees and such other persons to use the land as a recreation or sports ground.

❖ ANALYSING THE LAW

Who were the beneficiaries in *Re Denley's Trust Deed*?
The result reached by Goff J in *Re Denley's Trust Deed* was perhaps the right one on the facts. It enabled Mr Denley's wish that the land be left to a club for the benefit of others to be carried out. Yet the decision in the case is not without difficulty.

As will be seen in Chapter 10, the rule in *Saunders v Vautier*[42] enables all adult beneficiaries, provided they are of sound mind and together absolutely entitled to the trust property, to join forces to bring the trust to an end. Who could bring the trust to an end if they so desired in *Re Denley's Trust Deed*?

Goff J accepted the first group of people, the employees of the company, were correctly regarded as beneficiaries. He held that the second group of people were the objects of a power of appointment. As discussed in Chapter 2, such people have a hope of being

---

39   Ibid at 383.
40   Ibid.
41   Ibid.
42   *Saunders v Vautier* (1841) 4 Beav 115; 49 ER 282.

chosen to be able to benefit from the power and only once chosen do they became full beneficiaries of the trust.

The only people who could bring the trust to an end in *Re Denley's Trust Deed* would be those people who fell within the first category of beneficiaries – the employees. Those who fell within the second category – anyone else whom the trustees may permit to use the land – would not be beneficiaries unless and until they were so chosen by the trustees to benefit from the trust.

The consequence this has is that all of the beneficiaries in the first category could bring the trust to an end under the rule in *Saunders v Vautier* because only they would (together) be absolutely entitled to the trust property. This cannot have been Mr Denley's intention when setting up the trust. As those in the second category may not yet have all been chosen, they would not be classed as beneficiaries and therefore would have no right to bring the trust to an end.

Any such action by the employees would mean the employees would defeat the purpose for which the land had been left on trust, which was not only to benefit them but also anyone else that the trustees decided could use the land. The settlor's wishes in setting up the trust would then be ignored. Such a result would be surprising, but such a consequence appears to be the logical result of the decision in the case.

The decisions in *Leahy v Attorney-General for New South Wales* and *Re Denley's Trust Deed* seem to be contradictory. The first followed traditional jurisprudence in holding that a trust for purposes was void, whilst the second took a more subtle approach, in finding that there could be two types of purpose trust. Where there were sufficiently defined people who could benefit from the purpose trust so that it could be said that they would have standing to bring a court action to enforce the trust against the trustees, such purpose trust would be valid.

The approach in *Re Denley's Trust Deed* was applied by the High Court in *Re Lipinski's Will Trusts*.[43] This suggests that the more modern approach is indeed to recognise purpose trusts if it can be said that they benefit sufficiently well-defined individuals.

Re Lipinski's Will Trusts concerned the will of Harry Lipinski, in which he left half of his residuary estate on trust for the Hull Judeans (Maccabi) Association. The Association was a club which provided social, cultural and sporting activities for young people of the Jewish faith in Hull. The Association was obliged by the terms of the will to use the money for constructing new buildings and/or making improvements to its existing buildings. Clearly, this was a trust for a purpose and so would, at first glance, seem to be void.

Applying *Re Denley's Trust Deed*, Oliver J held that the trust was valid. He made the same distinction in terms of the two types of purpose trust as Goff J had done:

There would seem to me to be, as a matter of common sense, a clear distinction between the case where a purpose is prescribed which is clearly intended for the benefit of ascertained or ascertainable beneficiaries ... and the case where no beneficiary at all is intended (for instance, a memorial to a favourite pet) or where the beneficiaries are unascertainable ...

---

43 *Re Lipinski's Will Trusts* [1976] 3 WLR 522.

A trust for the purpose of ascertained or ascertainable beneficiaries would be valid; a trust where no beneficiary was intended at all or where the beneficiary was unascertainable would generally be void.

The trust in the case was valid. The members of the Association were entirely ascertainable – they were the people who had joined the Association. They had the necessary connection with the Association that they would have been able to bring court action against the trustees of the Association had the trustees failed to administer the trust correctly.

In summary, the more recent cases of *Re Denley's Trust Deed* and *Re Lipinski* suggest a more pragmatic approach is taken by the court in order to recognise some purpose trusts. Such an approach is to be welcomed, since it upholds the settlor's intentions in declaring the trust. The decision in *Leahy v Attorney-General for New South Wales* will, however, still stand if the purpose of the trust has no ascertainable beneficiaries (i.e. it is of an abstract nature and it cannot be said that any beneficiary at all has any standing to enforce the trust before the court).

Offshore trusts

Certain trusts may be governed in offshore jurisdictions. These generally involve islands located in various parts of the world whose residents and organisations based there may enjoy lower taxation than, say, in England and Wales. Trusts established in such jurisdictions may benefit from those lower rates of taxation.

The Cayman Islands has been at the forefront of developing a trust known as the 'Special Trusts Alternative Regime' or 'STAR' trust. These trusts, which must be created in writing containing a declaration stating that the law is to apply to them, allow trusts to be established specifically for a purpose to be carried out. The trust may also be for the benefit of people or it can be for the benefit of a mixture of persons and purposes. The trust may be charitable or non-charitable.

Whilst specifically designed to permit non-charitable purpose trusts, then, STAR trusts still have one eye to the beneficiary principle in English law. All STAR trusts must have an 'enforcer' as one of their parties, in addition to the settlor and trustee(s). The central idea in the beneficiary principle is that there has to be someone who can compel the trustees to perform the trust. In a STAR trust, regardless of whether there are individual beneficiaries, the person whose task it is to compel performance of the trust is the enforcer. The beneficiaries, in fact, may not themselves enforce the trust unless they happen to be the enforcers of the trust as well. It is the presence of the enforcer which deals with the same aim as the main reason for the beneficiary principle in English law.

In order to keep the trustees on the straight and narrow road of administering the trust correctly, s 9 of the Special Trusts Alternative Regime states that the enforcer enjoys the following rights:

(a) to bring applications to court to enforce the trust; and
(b) to be advised about the terms of the trust and to have information about the trust given to them. The enforcer may also inspect and take copies of the trust documents.

The STAR trust is gaining in popularity in offshore jurisdictions. The Channel Island of Jersey has adopted a similar trust regime to STAR in the Trusts (Amendment No. 3) (Jersey) Law 1996 and it is likely that Guernsey will follow the lead set by Jersey in the near future.

English law, however, seems wedded to the beneficiary principle, albeit with significant exceptions applying on a legal and practical level on a day-to-day basis.

Unincorporated associations

Re Lipinski's Will Trusts showed that a trust for the purposes of an unincorporated association could be valid. There has been much debate over the years as to how unincorporated associations can hold their property.

First, a preliminary issue: what is an unincorporated association? In *Conservative and Unionist Central Office v Burrell*,[44] Lawton LJ defined it as:

> two or more persons bound together for one or more common purposes, not being business purposes, by mutual undertakings each having mutual duties and obligations, in an organisation which has rules which identify in whom control of it and its funds rests and upon what terms and which can be joined or left at will.[45]

In straightforward terms, an unincorporated association is a club or society, which has members. We are considering here such associations which have not been established for charitable purposes. Associations established for charitable purposes will enjoy charitable status (see Chapter 15) and since they enjoy charitable status, can validly hold property. Non-charitable associations would seem to be examples of purpose trusts: they are clubs set up for a purpose in which officers of the club hold property. These types of purpose trust are permitted in English law, as an exception to the beneficiary principle.

The principle of how an unincorporated association can hold property was considered by Cross J in *Neville Estates Ltd v Madden*.[46] He believed that there were three possibilities:

(a) the property could be held between the members of the association as joint tenants in equity. That would mean that any member could sever his share and claim a part of it as his own personal property. This would seem to be a little odd and go against the concept that all of the property in total is held for the purposes and benefit of the association;

(b) the property could be a gift to the existing members of the association and be governed by the association's rules. Such rules formed a contract between the members. This would have the result that each member's share would pass to the other members on his death or resignation from the association. Each member would not be allowed to claim it for himself personally; or

(c) the property could be given to the association on the basis that it was to be given for the association itself and not for the members' benefit. A gift of property on this basis would be void since it would constitute a purpose trust.

This discussion was taken further by Brightman J in *Re Recher's Will Trusts*.[47] The case concerned the will of Eva Recher. She left part of her residuary estate to an organisation she described as 'The Anti-Vivisection Society, 76 Victoria Street, London, SW1'. The issue for the High Court was whether such a trust could be valid. It seemed at first sight that such a trust would be void as it was a trust for the purposes of the society, instead of ascertained or ascertainable individuals.

Building on Cross J's analysis in *Neville Estates Ltd v Madden*, Brightman J summarised counsels' arguments that suggested that a gift to an unincorporated association could be held in four possible ways:

---

44 *Conservative and Unionist Central Office v Burrell* [1982] 1 WLR 522.
45 Ibid at 525.
46 *Neville Estates v Madden* [1962] Ch 832.
47 *Re Recher's Will Trusts* [1972] Ch 526.

(a) as a gift to the existing members of the association. The present members would need to hold their shares in equity as joint tenants or tenants in common. If they held the gift as tenants in common, then each member could take his share of the association with them if they decided to leave. The same result would be reached if they held their shares as joint tenants, as a leaving member could decide to sever their share. Brightman J did not think Mrs Recher's intention in this case was to benefit the members of the association personally in this way so that they could personally take an individual benefit from her gift. Instead, she had decided to benefit the association itself. Cases which fall in this category are rare as the donor of the gift (like Mrs Recher) does not usually wish to benefit the members of the association personally;

(b) as a gift to all of the members of the association, both now and in the future. Yet as Brightman J pointed out, such a gift would fail since it would infringe the rules against perpetuity as potentially the effects of the gift would never come to an end. Construing the gift in this way would, again, defeat the testatrix's intentions of wishing to benefit the association;

(c) as a gift to the trustees or other officers of the association so that they might hold the gift on trust for the purposes of the association. This type of gift too would fail since it would, as a purpose trust, breach the beneficiary principle; or

(d) as a gift to the members of the association in equity but on the basis that the gift is held according to the rules of the association. Individual members would not be able to take their share if they left the association and their property would simply accrue to the other members if they died or resigned from the association. The rules of the association would form a contract between the members.

Brightman J held that the gift to the Association should be considered to be held on the basis of the fourth proposition, perhaps due to reasons of policy:

> It would astonish a layman to be told that there was a difficulty in his giving a legacy to an unincorporated non-charitable society which he had . . . supported without trouble during his lifetime.[48]

Brightman J was guided by the concept that an association would be governed by a set of rules. Such rules would form a contract between the members of the association. As with any other contract, the one between the members could be varied even to the extent that the members could agree to wind up the association. The gift to the association should be seen here to be a type of gift to the members, to be held on the terms of the contract between them. The money should be seen to be an addition to the association's funds.

❖ ANALYSING THE LAW

There is now a presumption that this fourth category is the one that governs gifts to unincorporated associations following the effective approval of *Re Recher's Will Trusts* by the House of Lords in *Universe Tankships Inc of Monrovia v International Transport Workers' Federation (The Universe Sentinel)*.[49]

---

48 Ibid at 536.
49 Universe Tankships Inc of Monrovia v International Transport Workers' Federation (The Universe Sentinel) [1983] 1 AC 366.

> But, surely this category infringes s 53 (1)(c) of the Law of Property Act 1925 as when one member leaves, their share accrues to the new member joining. But, to comply with s 53(1)(c), should there not be a requirement that the assignment of this equitable interest should be in writing?

The logical extent of the contract between the members was that the members could, if they so desired, agree between themselves to close the association permanently. In that event, the members would be entitled to divide the assets of the association between themselves. Brightman J thought that whilst such a possibility was remote and Mrs Recher undoubtedly would not have known that such a possibility existed when she wrote her will, such a conclusion had to stand as the logical consequence of finding that the gift was held on the basis of a contract between the association's members.

In fact, the consequence that the members of the association had to have the right to divide the association's funds between themselves was of vital significance. This prevented the gift to the association being void for infringing perpetuity, as Cross J explained in *Neville Estates Ltd v Madden*.[50]

Any gift to an unincorporated association can, therefore, be valid provided that it is seen to be a gift not to the association for its purposes but instead as a gift to its members. To be seen as a gift to its members, on the terms of the contract between them, the members have to have the right to dissolve the association and split its assets between them.

If the members cannot divide the association's assets between themselves then it will not be possible to say that the gift is to the members but instead the gift will be to the association itself. Such a gift will infringe the beneficiary principle and will be void, as illustrated by *Re Grant's Will Trusts*.[51]

Wilson Grant was a long-term member of the Labour Party. By his will, he left all his property to the 'Labour Party property committee for the benefit of the Chertsey Headquarters of the Chertsey and Walton Constituency Labour Party'. This Chertsey and Walton Constituency Labour Party was an unincorporated association. Crucially, the rules of the association provided that its rules could only be changed to ensure that they reflected those made by the central Labour Party at its annual party conference or by its National Executive Committee. The actual members of the association did not have the power to alter the rules of the association by their own choice.

Vinelott J held that Mr Grant's property could not be said to have been left to the members of the Chertsey and Walton Constituency Labour Party with the intention that they should benefit from it on the basis of their contractual membership. The members did not have complete freedom to do as they liked with property left to them, since their rules were governed by the national Labour Party. This meant that, for example, the national Labour Party could have requested that the Constituency Party's property be transferred to it and the members would not have had the contractual right to resist such a transfer. The members also had no contractual right to divide the property amongst themselves in equity. The gift from Mr Grant was void. It was a trust for the purposes of the Labour Party and infringed the beneficiary principle.

Re Grant's Will Trusts illustrates that not every gift to an unincorporated association will be construed as a gift to its members according to the terms of their contractual relationship with each other. The contractual relationship must be a genuine one, giving the members the

---

50 *Neville Estates Ltd v Madden* [1962] Ch 832 at 849.
51 *Re Grant's Will Trusts* [1980] 1 WLR 360.

ultimate freedom to dispose of the property if they so choose. The default principle from *Leahy v Attorney-General for New South Wales* will apply if this is not the case.

This means that a gift left on trust for the association's purposes will rebut the fourth category of how the property should be held and so the settlor will have (inadvertently) created a private purpose trust.

Dissolution of an unincorporated association

The issue which must be considered now is who owns the property of an unincorporated association when it is dissolved. It should be borne in mind that often the cases concern a mixture of donations, where the property of the association has been given by both members and non-members.

Donations primarily by non-members

The first modern case on funds given by predominently non-members was *Re Gillingham Bus Disaster Fund*.[52]

The facts concerned a serious road traffic accident in December 1951, when a bus ran into a column of Royal Marine cadets marching along a road in Gillingham, Kent. Twenty-four of the cadets were killed and a number of the others were injured. The mayors of the neighbouring towns launched an appeal through the *Daily Telegraph* for donations to offset the cost of the funerals of those cadets who had died and to help provide care for those who had been left disabled. A total of nearly £9,000 was raised. Most of the money had come from anonymous donors through street collecting boxes. Only £2,400 was spent from the money as the cadets pursued successful legal claims against the bus company for compensation.

The issue was what should happen to the surplus funds.

Making connections

The fund in *Re Gillingham Bus Disaster Fund* was not charitable as it had no charitable purpose (as defined in law) and neither did it provide a general benefit to the public.

Had it been charitable, it is likely that the surplus money could have given instead to a charity with a similar object as the fund had. This is known as the cy-près doctrine and is discussed in Chapter 16.

The choice faced by Harman J was whether the funds should be returned to the donors under a resulting trust or instead be paid to the Crown as *bona vacantia* (ownerless property). He held that the donations should be returned to the original donors under a resulting trust.

Harman J stated that the general principle was that where money was held upon trust and the trust did not exhaust the whole of the money, it had to be returned to the original settlor under the doctrine of the resulting trust. This was based on the settlor not parting with the beneficial interest in the money. He parted solely with the legal title and only to the extent that his wishes were carried out – that the money was used for the purposes for which he gave it. If those purposes failed, the money had to be returned to him.

It made no difference that each donor was anonymous and could not be found. The resulting trust in his favour still existed. The money could not, as Harman J put it, 'change its destination and become *bona vacantia*'.[53] If the donor could not be found, the trustees had to pay the money into court and wait for the beneficiary to come forward.

---

52 *Re Gillingham Bus Disaster Fund* [1958] Ch 300 (affirmed at [1959] Ch 62 (CA)).
53 Ibid at 313.

> ### ❖ APPLYING THE LAW
>
> The trustees did pay the surplus funds into court. The money remained there until the late 1990s when, eventually, the money that remained was spent on renovating the cadets' graves and in constructing a new memorial to them.

The decision in *Re Gillingham Bus Disaster Fund* might well be seen to be a logical application of the resulting trust. But the difficulty with the decision of Harman J is two-fold. First, the decision leads to the practical problem that the money has to be returned to anonymous donors and must be paid into court until those donors come forward. Quite how an anonymous donor can remember, let alone prove, years after the event that they donated a sum into a street collecting box must be open to debate. The donations will (and, on the facts of the case, did) remain in the court's control for decades after the court's decision. Second, the imposition of a resulting trust – for, as Harman J admitted, it is imposed – goes against the donor's intentions when they gave the money. When placing money in a collecting box, the donor never expects to see it again. It is odd that a trust can be imposed which entirely contradicts the settlor's intentions.

Donations by both members and non-members

The imposition of a resulting trust was considered again by Goff J in *Re West Sussex Constabulary's Widows, Children and Benevolent (1930) Fund Trusts*.[54] This case considered funds contributed by both members and non-members.

Here the West Sussex Constabulary's Widows, Children and Benevolent (1930) Fund existed to provide benefits to widows, children and dependent widowed mothers of officers of the West Sussex Constabulary police force. On 1 January 1968, the force was merged with other forces to form a singular Sussex Constabulary. The trustees brought an action seeking the court's approval to its scheme to wind up the unincorporated association pursuant to a meeting of its members in June 1968. Goff J held that that meeting was abortive as by that time, the association had no members given that the force had already been merged. The issue was what was to happen to the property of the association.

The association had raised its funds by four methods:

(a) members' subscriptions;
(b) entertainment proceeds;
(c) collecting boxes; and
(d) donations from other parties, including legacies from others' wills.

The members of the association argued that the doctrine of the resulting trust should govern the ultimate destination of the funds. This would mean that money raised by the first method would be held on trust for the present (and possibly past) members.

Goff J rejected this proposition. He reiterated that the basis of the holding of property between members of an unincorporated association was the law of contract, not trusts. Contractually, all members who had died had received their contractual entitlement from the association, either because their widows and dependants had received benefits or because

---

54 *Re West Sussex Constabulary's Widows, Children and Benevolent (1930) Fund Trusts* [1971] Ch 1.

they did not leave a widow and/or dependant. The present members held the property of the association on a contract between themselves so it was not appropriate for a resulting trust to apply when the association was dissolved. The subscriptions had to go *bona vacantia* to the Crown. Goff J left open the possibility of the surviving members making a claim that the contract had been frustrated or, alternatively, that there had been a total failure of consideration,[55] when the association was dissolved. Goff J then dealt with the contributions from non-members.

For the money raised from entertainment, he chose not to follow the judgment of Harman J in *Re Gillingham Bus Disaster Fund*[56] and held that there was no resulting trust of the money to those who made the contributions. He held that in this situation again, the relationship between the donor and the association was one based on the law of contract, not trusts. The donor had donated money in return for being entertained not on the basis of any trust. The donor had, once again, received their contractual entitlement by being entertained.

Donors who had given the money through street collecting-boxes were taken to have parted with all property in the money once they placed it in the box. Goff J followed Upjohn J in *Re Hillier's Trusts*,[57] who decided that such a donor had no intention of having the money returned to him if there was a surplus after the object of the association had been achieved. This remained the case even if the association's objects had never been achieved. When placing his donation in the street collecting box, the donor's intention was to part entirely with all property in the money. As such, there was no room later to argue that he should have it returned to him under a resulting trust. Goff J quoted Denning LJ in the Court of Appeal in *Re Hillier's Trust*[58] who had explained the position with characteristic clarity that '[w]hen a man gives money on such occasion, he gives it, I think, beyond recall. He parts with his money out-and-out.'

The resulting trust doctrine was only appropriate for the fourth category of donations, by specific (traceable) donors, including legacies in wills. Such donations could be returned to them under a resulting trust on the basis that those donors could be seen to be giving a donation for a specific purpose. If that purpose failed, then the money should be held on resulting trust for them.

The decision in *Re West Sussex Constabulary's Widows, Children and Benevolent (1930) Fund Trusts* was distinguished by Walton J in *Re Bucks Constabulary Widows' and Orphans' Fund Friendly Society (No. 2)*.[59] The facts were similar to the *Re West Sussex* case in that funds were contributed to a scheme which benefited widows and orphans of the deceased members of the scheme who had worked as police officers. The fund was dissolved and the issue was what happened to the surplus.

Walton J adopted Brightman J's analysis of how an unincorporated association held property in *Re Recher's Will Trusts*.[60] The members held it between themselves according to the contract which existed between them – known as the rules of the association. It made no difference whether the members had contributed property to the association or it came from a non-member. A donation from a non-member would be treated as a gift to the association's funds which would be held between the members according to the contract between them.

Given that the members held the property of the association on a contract between them whilst the association existed, it followed that when the association was dissolved, the assets of the society would continue to be held by that contract for the now former members. The

---

55 Nowadays this would be seen as a restitutionary claim as opposed to a claim in the law of contract.
56 *Re Gillingham Bus Disaster Fund* [1958] Ch 300.
57 *Re Hillier's Trusts* [1954] 1 WLR 9.
58 *Re Hillier's Trust* [1954] 1 WLR 700 at 714.
59 *Re Bucks Constabulary Widows' and Orphans' Fund Friendly Society (No. 2)* [1979] 1 WLR 936.
60 *Re Recher's Will Trusts* [1972] Ch 526.

funds were not ownerless property (*bona vacantia*) which had to go to the Crown: the members still owned the property of the association. The property had to be distributed to the members who were still alive. Deceased members could have no claim as their membership of the association would have terminated automatically on their death.

Walton J said that he was 'wholly unable to square [the decision of Goff J in *Re West Sussex*] with the relevant principles of law applicable' as far as the contributions from the members were concerned.

❖ ANALYSING THE LAW

It is suggested that the decision in *Re Bucks Constabulary* is to be preferred over *Re West Sussex* and *Re Gillingham Bus Disaster*. It is surely beyond argument now that the law of contract governs the ownership of the property of an unincorporated association. It is, therefore, hard to see why this contract should terminate once the association was dissolved and either a resulting trust imposed or the concept of *bona vacantia* dictate the destination of the association's property.

Walton J held that all members of the association should receive the property in equal shares. If the contract between the members (the rules of association) was silent on the issue, then all members of the fund had an equal entitlement to it.

Walton J considered what would happen to an association's funds if the members of the association dwindled to just one. He thought that:

> if a society is reduced to a single member neither he, nor still less his personal representatives on his behalf, can say he is or was the society and therefore entitled solely to its fund.[61]

In such a scenario, therefore, the society's assets would become ownerless and had to go to the Crown as *bona vacantia*.

This last point has, however, been considered expressly by the High Court in *Hanchett-Stamford v Attorney-General*.[62]

Mrs Hanchett-Stamford was the last surviving member of the Performing and Captive Animals Defence League, an unincorporated association formed in 1914 in order to prevent the use of animals performing in circuses or in films. The League was not charitable as its objects were political in nature.

The League had had many members, particularly during the 1960s but slowly membership had declined to where the claimant was the only member. She was elderly and lived in a nursing home. The League, however, still had assets worth over £2 million. The issue was what would happen to the association's property at this point.

Lewison J held that as the last surviving member of the association, the assets belonged to Mrs Hanchett-Stamford absolutely.

Lewison J rejected Walton J's *obiter* view that, where an association had only one member remaining, its property could not belong to that member. Such a view led to an inconsistent

---

61 *Re Bucks Constabulary Widows' and Orphans' Fund Friendly Society (No. 2)* [1979] 1 WLR 936 at 943.
62 *Hanchett-Stamford v Attorney-General* [2009] Ch 173.

conclusion which seemed to depend simply on chance as to how many members of the association remained:

> It leads to the conclusion that if there are two members of an association which has assets of, say £2m, they can by agreement divide those assets between them and pocket £1m each, but if one of them dies before they have divided the assets, the whole pot goes to the Crown as *bona vacantia*.[63]

Such a conclusion could make no logical sense: the ultimate ownership of the money could not depend on the numbers of members of the association.

Lewison J restated that the assets of an unincorporated association belong to its members whilst they are alive. If the association is dissolved, those members are entitled to share in the assets of the property. This principle would not change if the number of members of the association fell to one.

In addition, Lewison J considered the application of Article 1 of the First Protocol of the European Convention for the Protection of Human Rights and Fundamental Freedoms. This provides that 'No one shall be deprived of his possessions except in the public interest and subject to the conditions provided for by law . . .' He felt that if he was to decide the case other than by holding that Mrs Hanchett-Stamford was entitled to the assets of the association, there would be a breach of Article 1.

Lewison J's views are, with respect, sensible. The views of Walton J in *Re Bucks Constabulary* on the notion that if the membership of an association fell to one the assets of that association should go to the Crown as *bona vacantia* were *obiter* and seemingly contradicted the logical principle that if the members hold the association's property between them on the basis of a contract, it should ultimately make no difference at all quite how many members there are.

Summary

It therefore seems that the following conclusions may be reached about the destination of property when an unincorporated association is dissolved:

(a) that the association's trustees hold the property on trust for the members during its existence. The equitable interest held by the members is held on the basis of the contract between them;

(b) funds contributed to the association (if given by the members or by anonymous donors) should be seen as given to the members to be held on the terms of their contract on a once-and-for-all basis;

(c) on a dissolution of the association, subject to any rule of the association to the contrary, the funds should be returned to the surviving members in equal shares; and

(d) it makes no difference if there is only one surviving member of the association.

---

63 Ibid at 185.

Points to Review

You have seen:

- What the beneficiary principle is: how English law generally insists that trusts must be for the benefit of ascertained or ascertainable beneficiaries;
- How the beneficiary principle is an essential part of an express, non-charitable trust in English law. Exceptions do exist but these exceptions are self-contained and are usually only permitted where there is at least someone who has standing to enforce the trust against the trustees; and
- How STAR trusts are a comparatively new device which allow trusts to be established for a purpose without any ascertained or ascertainable beneficiary. If such trusts were to be embraced by English law, there would be a great number of permitted purpose trusts. Such trusts are, however, yet to be considered by the English courts or Parliament in any real depth. The beneficiary principle, as we have seen, seems too well entrenched to be subjected to the STAR regime displacing it.

Making connections

This chapter considered another piece of the jigsaw in trust formation and, specifically, in the requirements to a valid declaration of trust.

There is a close connection between the concept of there being an ascertained or ascertainable beneficiary in a trust and certainty of object. In both cases, there has to be someone who should benefit from the trust so that, in turn, that person can enforce the trust against the trustees if necessary. That circular system enables the trust to be administered correctly since it provides an in-built control over the trustees' powers.

The rules against perpetuity have also been hinted at during this chapter. These are considered in detail in the chapter on the companion website. The rule of perpetuity which addresses inalienability, that provides that the property must pass to the beneficiaries within a certain time, is of particular relevance.

Chapter 7 discusses the final requirement to form an express trust: that the trust must be constituted.

 Useful Things to Read

The best reading is contained in the primary sources listed below. It is always good to consider the decisions of the courts themselves as this will lead to a deeper understanding of the issues involved. A few secondary sources are also listed, which you may wish to read to gain additional insights into the areas considered in this chapter.

Primary sources
Re Astor's Settlement Trusts [1952] Ch 534.
Re Denley's Trust Deed [1969] 1 Ch 373.
Re Endacott [1960] Ch 232.
Re Grant's Will Trusts [1980] 1 WLR 360.
Re Horley Town Football Club [2006] EWHC 2386 (Ch).

Leahy v Attorney-General for New South Wales [1959] AC 457.
Re Recher's Will Trusts [1972] Ch 526.

Secondary sources

Simon Baughen, 'Performing animals and the dissolution of unincorporated associations: The 'contract-holding theory' vindicated' (2010) Conv 3, 216–233. This article reviews how an unincorporated association holds property and how its property should be distributed when it is wound up. It also looks at when assets can be distributed to non-members.

James Brown, 'What are we to do with testamentary trusts of imperfect obligation?' (2007) Conv Mar/Apr 148–160. A look at trusts of imperfect obligation and their interaction with the rules against perpetuity together with a practical demonstration of the extent to which such trusts are used today.

Simon Gardner, 'A detail in the construction of gifts to unincorporated associations' (1998) Conv Jan/Feb 8–12. This article was written in response to that by Professor Paul Matthews (below) and looks specifically at the relevance of the donor's intentions to how the gift to the unincorporated association should be construed. You are advised to read Professor Matthews' article before this one.

B Heape, 'Non charitable purpose trusts in the Channel Islands' (2008) JLR February. An interesting look at how Jersey and Guernsey treat private purpose trusts.

Alastair Hudson, *Equity & Trusts* (7th edn, Routledge-Cavendish, 2012) ch 4.

Paul Matthews, 'A problem in the construction of gifts to unincorporated associations' (1995) Conv Jul/Aug 302–308. This considers the decision in *Re Denley* and compares how a gift may be given to the members of an association with it being given to the association itself, as an addition to its funds.

Mohamed Ramjohn, *Text, Cases and Materials on Equity & Trusts* (4th edn, Routledge-Cavendish, 2008) ch 13.

Chapter 7

Constitution of a Trust

This chapter addresses the final ingredient necessary to form an express trust: that the trust must be constituted. At its most fundamental level, all this means is that the settlor must transfer legal ownership in the trust property to the trustee (or, alternatively, hold it on trust for the beneficiary himself). The trustee will then hold the property on trust for the beneficiary. Yet settlors have often failed either to transfer the ownership of the trust property to a trustee clearly or confirm that they are now holding the property as a trustee. The issue is to what extent equity is prepared to step in and recognise a trust despite its two maxims that it will not perfect an imperfect gift or assist a volunteer.

As You Read

Look out for the following key issues:

- what is meant by a trust being 'completely constituted' and how that has changed from a rigid, objective requirement in the nineteenth century to a more flexible concept in contemporary case law;
- how this topic is underpinned by two equitable maxims: that equity will not perfect an imperfect gift and will not assist a volunteer; and
- how and when a trust can be completely constituted.

Constituting the Trust and the Relationship with Creating a Trust

The essential requirements for the creation of an express trust are that the trust must be both declared and constituted. The requirements to declare a trust have been considered in the previous three chapters. They are that the trust must:

(a) be established by a settlor with mental and physical capacity who must, if the type of trust property requires it (for example, land[1]), adhere to any necessary formalities;[2]
(b) comply with the three certainties. The settlor must intend to declare a trust, that the trust property and the intended beneficial interests in it must be sufficiently certain and that the objects of the trust must also be clear, so that in all cases the trust can be administered by the trustees;[3]
(c) adhere to the beneficiary principle which, as a general rule, provides that the trust must be intended to benefit ascertainable human beneficiaries, as opposed to pursue a purpose;[4] and
(d) not infringe the rules against perpetuity. The most significant of these is that the trust property must nowadays vest in its intended beneficiaries within a fixed perpetuity period of 125 years from when the trust comes into effect.[5]

---

1   Law of Property Act 1925 s 53(1)(b).
2   See Chapter 4.
3   See Chapter 5.
4   See Chapter 6.
5   Perpetuities and Accumulations Act 2009, s 5. See chapter on the companion website for further discussion.

Complying with these four requirements ensures that the express trust has been properly declared. In addition, the trust must be completely constituted. The trust will not be valid unless it has been constituted.

Constitution of a Trust

Key Learning Point

A trust is constituted when the trust property is transferred from the settlor to the trustee or the settlor holds the property on trust for the beneficiaries. At this point, the trustee becomes the legal owner of the property and holds it on trust for the beneficiary who, of course, has an equitable interest in it.

To understand why a trust must be completely constituted, the relationship between the trust and a gift has to be examined. Equity has two maxims which underpins its treatment of gifts and these also apply to trusts. Those are:

(a)   equity will not perfect an imperfect gift; and
(b)   equity will not assist a volunteer.

The relationship between a gift and a trust

There is a relationship between a gift and a trust, which was explained by Arden LJ in *Pennington v Waine*:[6] '[a] gift can be made either by direct assignment, by a transfer to trustees or by a [self] declaration of trust.'[7]

This *dictum* can be illustrated by Figure 7.1. In all of the following examples in Figure 7.1, assume that the benefactor wishes to benefit the recipient by the amount of £10,000.

Both the second and third examples in Figure 7.1 involve the settlor setting up a trust. In Arden LJ's first method of declaring a trust, the property which forms the subject of the gift (£10,000) is transferred to trustees, whereas in her second method, the settlor physically keeps hold of the money himself but on the basis that he declares himself to be a trustee of it.

---

6   *Pennington v Waine* [2002] 1 WLR 2075.
7   Ibid at 2085.

Gift

transfers £10,000

Donor ────────────────► Donee

This is a gift. The donor simply gives property to the donee. This is what Arden LJ calls 'direct assignment'.

Trust

There are two ways in which a trust may be created. According to Arden LJ, the first is 'by a transfer to trustees' whilst the second is by a 'declaration of trust':

First method: by a 'transfer to trustees'

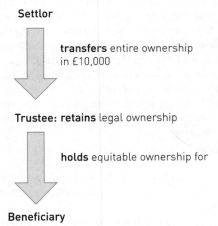

Settlor

transfers entire ownership in £10,000

Trustee: **retains** legal ownership

holds equitable ownership for

Beneficiary

Second method: 'by a declaration of trust'

Settlor
Declares himself to be the trustee
so retains legal ownership in £10,000 but
holds equitable ownership for

Beneficiary

Figure 7.1 Gift or trust?

Key Learning Point

There are fundamental differences between a gift and a trust. As can be seen from Figure 7.1, a gift involves the donor giving away the property entirely. The donor thus gives away all rights and liabilities in the property to the donee. The donee receives both legal and equitable interests in the property and it becomes his to do with as he generally wishes. The donee is the absolute owner of the property.

A trust, on the other hand, means that whilst the settlor gives away the rights and liabilities in the property to a trustee, the ownership in the property is split. The trustee retains the legal interest and the beneficiary acquires an equitable interest. The trustee then administers the trust for the beneficiary's benefit. The beneficiary's rights in the property are limited to the interest he enjoys. If, for instance, the beneficiary has only a life interest in the property, he can enjoy only the income from the trust property for his lifetime. If this was the case in Figure 7.1, the beneficiary would simply receive the interest on the £10,000, rather than the capital sum of £10,000. It is only when a beneficiary becomes entitled to the absolute interest in the trust property that he may seek, provided he is over 18 years of age and mentally capable, to call for the legal interest in the trust property to be transferred to him, merge the legal and equitable interests together and end the trust. This is known as the rule in *Saunders v Vautier*.[8] It is not until that point that the interests will be joined together again.

As trusts are effectively part of the overarching notion of a gift, the equitable maxim that equity will not perfect an imperfect gift applies to all trusts in the same way as making a straightforward gift.

The notion that equity will not perfect an imperfect gift illustrates that equity will not assist everyone on each occasion.[9] Equity will not 'right' a 'wrong'. If a trust has not been constituted correctly by a settlor, equity will not finish the job of setting up the trust correctly for them. The trust will not, therefore, have been completely constituted by the settlor and, as such, it will not have been validly created.

Equity will also not assist a volunteer. A volunteer is someone who has not provided any consideration in the transaction. Again, if a settlor has failed to constitute the trust completely, the beneficiary, albeit wholly innocent, will not be allowed to claim any beneficial interest in the trust property. The beneficiary in these circumstances is a volunteer. He has provided no consideration for the transaction and equity will not help him. This appears to flow from part of the general principles of the law of consideration where, to enjoy rights in English law, one must generally have given something to acquire those rights. If the trust is not completely constituted, the beneficiary will have acquired no rights in the trust property and has no basis on which to enforce any such rights.

Constitution of a trust can be broken down into two distinct parts:

● When is a trust completely constituted?
● How is a trust completely constituted?

---

8   *Saunders v Vautier* (1841) Cr & Ph 240.
9   See *Jones v Lock* (1865–66) LR 1 Ch App 25.

When is a Trust Completely Constituted?

As You Read

When you read this part of the chapter, bear in mind:

- the fundamental concept that, whilst it is equity that recognises a trust, equity traditionally took the position of an onlooker as opposed to an intervener. Due to its equitable maxims, equity would not assist a defective trust to be created because to do so would infringe the principles of not assisting a volunteer and perfecting an imperfect gift;
- the original — and objective — principle for equity to recognise a trust as having been completely constituted was that the settlor must have done 'everything necessary' to transfer the trust property to the trustees;
- how that objective principle has been eroded over the years by the inclusion of a more subjective element which meant that a trust would be constituted if the settlor had done 'everything in his power' to create the trust; and
- the more recent development of the Court of Appeal in the key case of *Pennington v Waine* which appears to develop a new test based on the equitable concept of 'unconscionability' to ascertain whether the trust should be seen to be constituted or not. This test seems to result in equity taking an interventionist approach to the constitution of a trust and infringe its two guiding maxims in this area.

The original test – has the settlor done 'everything necessary' to constitute the trust?

Originally, a trust would only be completely constituted when the settlor did everything necessary for the trust property to be transferred to the trustee or to declare himself a trustee. It is only when it could be said that the settlor had taken all necessary steps that the trust could be considered binding on the settlor. What was required was an objective assessment of whether all necessary steps had been taken by the settlor: it is only if they were taken that the trust would have been completely constituted.

This test of whether the settlor had taken all necessary steps to transfer the property to a trustee or to declare himself trustee of it was set out in Milroy v Lord.[10]

The case concerned an attempt by a resident of New Orleans, Thomas Medley, to set up a trust of 50 of the shares that he owned in the Bank of Louisiana. By a deed dated 2 April 1852, Thomas purported to transfer the shares to his father-in-law, Samuel Lord, so that Samuel would hold the shares on trust for Thomas' English niece, Eleanor Dudgeon. That meant that the income from the shares — the dividends that the Bank may declare — would be paid to Eleanor. Acting upon this declaration of trust, Thomas gave the share certificates to Samuel. Thomas also gave Samuel both a general power of attorney to act on his behalf in relation to his financial affairs and a specific power of attorney in relation to the dividends which may have been paid by the Bank of Louisiana.

---

10 Milroy v Lord (1862) 4 De G F & J 264; 45 ER 1185.

Glossary: Power of Attorney

A power of attorney is a document in which a person (the donor) may appoint another to act on their behalf. The recipient thus stands in the donor's shoes and acts as if he was the donor.

The power might be general or specific. A general power of attorney enables the recipient to act on the donor's behalf to manage all of the donor's affairs. A specific power of attorney is where the donor limits the recipient to acting for him in relation to defined property.

The problem in the case arose because the Bank of Louisiana's constitution provided that for shares to be transferred into the name of a recipient, the actual share certificates being transferred had to be sent to the Bank. In addition, if a transfer was to be made by a person using a power of attorney, the original power of attorney also had to be lodged with the Bank when the application to transfer the shares was made.

The share certificates were never sent to the Bank. But Samuel Lord acted as though the trust had been properly established. He received the dividends declared by the Bank and paid them over to Eleanor, who by now had married and had become Eleanor Milroy.

Thomas Medley died in 1855. Samuel Lord continued to be willing to honour the trust. It was Thomas' executor, Mr Otto, who objected to the trust. His argument was that there had been no successful creation of a trust, but instead simply an incomplete gift. This was based on the fact that the share certificates had never been transferred fully into the trustee's name. All that had occurred was that the settlor had physically handed over the share certificates to the trustee. No legal transfer had taken place. Such a transfer could only be undertaken by the Bank of Louisiana receiving the old share certificates in Thomas Medley's name and issuing new ones in the name of Samuel Lord. Equity could not perfect this imperfect gift. In addition, Eleanor had provided no consideration for the gift of the shares from her uncle and, as such, she was a volunteer. Equity should not assist a volunteer.

The Court of Appeal agreed with Mr Otto's argument. The legal ownership in the shares had never passed to Samuel. As the trust had not been constituted, he could not be considered to be a trustee of the shares for Eleanor.

In a well-known dictum, Turner LJ set out when a trust could be considered to be completely constituted:

> I take the law of this Court to be well settled, that, in order to render a voluntary settlement valid and effectual, the settlor must have done everything which, according to the nature of the property comprised in the settlement, *was necessary to be done* in order to transfer the property and render the settlement binding upon him.[11]

Of course, Samuel Lord had had the benefit of two powers of attorney granted by Thomas Medley under which Samuel could have stepped into Thomas's shoes and instructed the Bank of Louisiana to transfer the shares into his name. But Samuel had not actually used his authority under either of the powers of attorney to transfer the legal ownership of the shares into his name.

It also made no difference that Samuel had considered himself a trustee of the shares from the moment that the 'trust' had been declared by Thomas, by paying the dividends declared by

---

11 Ibid at 1190 (emphasis added).

the Bank to Eleanor. This action, too, was irrelevant. It could not 'right' the 'wrong' of the trust being incompletely constituted by Thomas when it was originally set up.

Equity would not intervene to correct the imperfections of this attempted trust. To do so would infringe its two maxims. The trust had to be completely constituted by the settlor himself for it to be recognised by equity. It would only be completely constituted if the settlor had done 'everything necessary' to transfer the legal title in the trust property to the trustee.

Making connections

Look again at the *dictum* Turner LJ uses for what a settlor must do to create a valid trust in *Milroy v Lord*. There appear to be two requirements:

(a) the settlor must have done everything 'necessary to be done' to transfer the property. This appears to be an objective test, focussing on whether the settlor has done everything physically necessary to transfer the legal title to the trustee; and

(b) the settlor's actions must be undertaken with the mental element that his actions undertaken should be done with an intention that the trust should becoming binding upon him.

Do you think there is an element of cross-fertilisation with certainty of intention here? At its roots, certainty of intention requires the settlor to display an intention to create a valid trust. It appears that the actions the settlor takes in constituting the trust must be undertaken with a similar intention. Perhaps, however, there is a distinction that can be made. Certainty of intention focuses on an objective intention by the settlor to declare a trust. Intention in constituting the trust requires the settlor to acknowledge that he is, in effect, putting the trust property beyond his own reach. He can do this either by transferring the property physically to a trustee or, alternatively, retaining the legal interest for himself whilst confirming that the beneficial interest is held on trust for the beneficiary.

It is the words of Turner LJ that the settlor must have done 'everything necessary' for the trust to be completely constituted and therefore be recognised by equity that the courts have focused on in succeeding cases.

The next significant case in which Turner LJ's words were examined was *Re Fry*.[12] Ambrose Fry was an American resident who owned shares in Liverpool Borax Ltd. He wanted to give his shares away. He signed transfer documents to transfer 2,000 shares to his son, Sydney and the remainder to Cavendish Investment Trust Ltd ('the Investment Trust'). The transfer documents eventually found their way to Liverpool Borax Ltd who refused to register the transfer of the shares due to wartime restrictions then in place. Before any shares in the company could be registered in a new owner's name, the consent of the United Kingdom Treasury had to be obtained. This required Mr Fry to complete and return a number of supplementary documents. Although he did so, he died before the Treasury had given its consent to the transfers of the shares.

The action came before Romer J. Sydney and the Investment Trust argued that Mr Fry had done everything he could possibly have done to affect the transfers of the legal interests in the

---

12 *Re Fry* [1946] Ch 312.

shares to those two recipients. It was out of Mr Fry's control that the Treasury had not given its consent. The case could, they argued, be distinguished from *Milroy v Lord* where the share certificates had never reached the company for them to be transferred into the recipient's name.

Romer J cited the test propounded by Turner LJ in *Milroy v Lord* and asked[13] '[H]ad everything been done which was necessary to put the transferees into the position of the transferor?' He answered the question almost immediately:

> [I]t is impossible, in my judgment, to answer the questions other than in the negative. The requisite consent of the Treasury to the transactions had not been obtained, and, in the absence of it, the company was prohibited from registering the transfers. In my opinion, accordingly, it is not possible to hold that, at the date of the testator's death, the transferees had . . . acquired a legal title to the shares in question. . . .[14]

As an alternative, Sydney and the Investment Trust argued that Mr Fry had done enough to transfer just the equitable interest in the shares to themselves. Applying Turner LJ's test again to this argument, Romer J again came to the conclusion that everything necessary to be done to transfer the shares into the names of Sydney and the Investment Trust had not been done. The Treasury's consent had not been obtained to the transfer taking place. Until that consent was given, 'everything necessary' to be done had not been done.

Re Fry appears to be a straightforward application of the principle set out in *Milroy v Lord*, albeit with a harsh result. Romer J himself confessed that he arrived at his conclusion that there was an imperfect gift 'with regret',[15] but found that there was no other logical decision at which he could arrive. Mr Fry had indeed done everything that he could have done: the share certificates had been sent to the company and all necessary forms completed to obtain the Treasury's consent to the transfer had been completed and despatched to the Treasury. But 'everything necessary' to be done had not been done. The Treasury's consent was the final piece of the jigsaw and that piece had not been put into place.

The case illustrates the objectivity of the test in *Milroy v Lord*. The number of steps to effect the gift or create the trust that the settlor may have taken are irrelevant. So too is the fact that the settlor may not, as Mr Fry was, be in a position to take any additional steps to complete the gift or constitute the trust. The key is whether 'everything necessary' to be done to transfer the legal title in the property to the trustee has been done or not. There are no shades of grey in the answer: just a black-and-white 'yes' or 'no'. If the answer is 'no', equity will not step in to help claimants in the place of Sydney and the Investment Trust because equity will not assist a volunteer or perfect the imperfect gift.

The changing concept of 'everything necessary'

The courts, however, started to shift from this solidly objective approach to whether 'everything necessary' to be done to transfer the property had been done to a test which encapsulated a more subjective element to it. The first case in which this shifting approach was seen was *Re Rose*.[16]

---

13 Ibid at 316.
14 Ibid.
15 Ibid at 319.
16 *Re Rose* [1952] Ch 499.

The facts concerned two transfers of shares in a company by Eric Rose. In the first transfer, he gave 10,000 shares to his wife, Rosamond, by way of gift. In the second, he gave a further 10,000 shares to his wife and another recipient, so that they could be held on trust for his wife and his son. Both transfer documents were executed on 30 March 1943, but the transfers were not registered by the company until 30 June 1943. When Mr Rose died, the Inland Revenue claimed tax on the transfers. A new tax had become effective on 10 April 1943.

Counsel for Mrs Rose argued that no tax should be payable on either of the transfers as they were effective when the documents to transfer the shares were executed on 30 March 1943. The difficulty with this argument was that it seemed to run contrary to the principle in Milroy v Lord. According to Turner LJ's dictum in Milroy v Lord, the transfers would not be effective until 'everything necessary' to be done to transfer the property had been done. Until that point, the property would remain in the hands of Mr Rose. 'Everything necessary' to be done in the case of a share transfer included the company registering the transfer of the shares from the former to the new owner. This step was not taken until the end of June, by which time the new tax had come into operation.

The Court of Appeal distinguished Milroy v Lord, holding that its ratio did not apply in the present case. Mr Rose's transfer was always intended to take effect immediately upon its execution on 30 March 1943. As such, the transfer was a way of signalling that he was willing to give away all of his rights in the shares. Between the execution of the transfer and the date of registration of it by the company, Mr Rose became a trustee of the legal interest for the transferees. Evershed MR quoted with approval the decision of Jenkins J in a different case entitled Re Rose; Midland Bank Executor and Trustee Co Ltd v Rose,[17] in which he said that the decisions in Milroy v Lord and Re Fry:

> turn on the fact that the deceased donor had not done *all in his power*, according to the nature of the property given, to vest the legal interest in the property in the donee. In such circumstances it is, of course, well settled that there is no equity to complete the imperfect gift.[18]

The decision of the Court of Appeal in Re Rose[19] was, therefore, to add a twist to the decisions in Milroy v Lord and Re Fry. It made a distinction between gifts made where there were potentially more steps for the donor to take and those where the donor had taken all of the steps that he personally could take. Milroy v Lord and Re Fry were examples of the former situation. In Milroy v Lord, there was more for the donor to do to perfect the transfer: he needed to use the correct form and start the procedure again. In Re Fry, the donor needed to obtain the Treasury's consent to the proposed transfer of the shares, which he failed to obtain. Jenkins J had explained in Re Rose; Midland Bank Executor and Trustee Co Ltd v Rose that both of those earlier cases had actually focused on whether the donor had done everything he could possibly do to perfect the gift. In that manner, the facts in both Re Rose; Midland Bank Executor and Trustee Co Ltd v Rose and Re Rose could be distinguished from Milroy v Lord and Re Fry. In both of those former cases, the donor had, in fact, done everything he could have done to perfect the gift. The remaining steps needed to be undertaken to perfect the gifts were to be undertaken by other individuals.

The decisions in both Re Rose; Midland Bank Executor and Trustee Co Ltd v Rose and Re Rose brought a subjective element into Turner LJ's dictum by asking whether the donor had done everything

---

17 Re Rose; Midland Bank Executor and Trustee Co Ltd v Rose [1949] Ch 78,
18 Re Rose [1952] Ch 499 at 511–512 (emphasis added).
19 Re Rose [1952] Ch 499.

that he could do in order to constitute the gift or trust. If he had done so, then the gift would be perfected or the trust constituted.

In either situation, equity's maxims of not perfecting an imperfect gift and not assisting a volunteer would still be honoured. There was no need for equity to intervene to perfect the gift or assist the beneficiary as the trust had been completely constituted by the settlor doing everything in his power to transfer the legal title in the property to the trustee.

The difficulty is that such a subjective approach does not sit easily with the decision in either Milroy v Lord or Re Fry. There is no hint in Turner LJ's test in Milroy v Lord of a subjective element being mentioned: the test seems entirely objective. In Re Fry, it is arguable that Mr Fry had indeed done everything in his power that he could have done to bring about the transfers of the shares, but still Romer J held that the objective test in Milroy v Lord had not been satisfied. Whilst bringing in an element of subjectivity may have led to the 'right' result on the facts in both Re Rose; Midland Bank Executor and Trustee Co Ltd v Rose and Re Rose, it is hard to see how it is supported by previous authority. The decision in Re Rose was, however, approved obiter by Lord Wilberforce in Vandervell v IRC[20] where he said that Mr Vandervell had done everything in his power to constitute the trust when he orally directed his trustees to transfer the shares to the Royal College of Surgeons.

The beginnings of equity's interventionist approach: a new test based on 'conscience'

A more interventionist approach was started by the decision of the Privy Council in T Choithram International SA v Pagarani.[21]

The facts revolved around Thakurdas Choithram Pagarani, an Indian man who established a chain of supermarkets around the world. He became very wealthy as a result and, having made provision for his family, wanted to leave much of his money to charity. To do so, he established a charitable foundation, Choithram International Foundation. On the same day, he confirmed orally that he wanted to give all of his wealth to the Foundation, which the Foundation could use for various charitable purposes.

The difficulty arose because the shares and money he instructed to be transferred to the Foundation were not transferred. Mr Pagarani gave instructions to his accountant to undertake the transfers but some of the transfers were never made until after his death. The issue for the court was whether the gifts made by Mr Pagarani could be perfected by those transfers entered into after his death. The High Court of the British Virgin Islands and the Court of Appeal of the British Virgin Islands had both held that Mr Pagarani had made incomplete gifts to his Foundation. The Privy Council disagreed.

In delivering the opinion of the judicial Board, Lord Browne-Wilkinson found that the facts did not fall squarely within the principle of Milroy v Lord. There was no complete gift effected by Mr Pagarani to another recipient nor did he declare himself a trustee of the property for the Foundation. Instead, when Mr Pagarani had expressed the desire to give the money and shares to the Foundation, he intended to give that property to the trustees of the Foundation for them to hold on trust for the Foundation's charitable purposes. That was the only logical way to construe Mr Pagarani's words. Lord Browne-Wilkinson explained that the maxim that equity would not assist a volunteer was a simplification of that principle as far as trusts were concerned:

---

20 *Vandervell v IRC* [1967] 2 AC 291.
21 *T Choithram International SA v Pagarani* [2001] 1 WLR 1.

> Until comparatively recently the great majority of trusts were voluntary settlements under which beneficiaries were volunteers having given no value. Yet beneficiaries under a trust, although volunteers, can enforce the trust against the trustees. Once a trust relationship is established between trustee and beneficiary, the fact that a beneficiary has given no value is irrelevant.[22]

This explained why a beneficiary had standing to enforce a trust against a trustee, despite the beneficiary having given no consideration and therefore being a volunteer, 'the donor has constituted himself a trustee for the donee who can as a matter of trust law enforce that trust'.[23]

By holding the shares and money designed for the Foundation in his own name, Mr Pagarani had effectively appointed himself a trustee of that property for the Foundation. This trust was completely constituted even though the trust property was not also vested in the names of the other trustees of the Foundation. Lord Browne-Wilkinson explained that the issue depended on conscience:

> There can in principle be no distinction between the case where the donor declares himself to be sole trustee for a donee or a purpose and the case where he declares himself to be one of the trustees for that donee or purpose. In both cases his conscience is affected and it would be unconscionable and contrary to the principles of equity to allow such a donor to resile from his gift.[24]

The issue as to whether the gift was perfect therefore depended on whether it would be conscionable for the donor to change his mind and reclaim the gift from the donee. If it would be unconscionable for the donor to do so, the gift would be constituted.

Decisions of the Australian courts have followed this line of thinking. Comments of Young CJ in the Supreme Court of New South Wales decision in *Blackett v Darcy*[25] confirmed that the maxim that 'equity will not assist a volunteer' did not completely sum up the maxim in its entirety:

> It must always be remembered that the rule that equity does not assist a volunteer is not a complete statement of the law and is only relevant if the donee requires the assistance of a court of equity in order to gain the property.[26]

An illustration of the point made by Young CJ arose on the facts of *Djordjevic v Djordjevic*.[27] A father gave his son two cheques, totalling AUS $120,000. The son paid the cheques into his own account. Later, the father tried to reclaim the money from his son. He alleged that he only ever intended to lend his son the money, so that his son could pay for a house for his father at an auction that he was to attend. The son's evidence was that his father gave him the money so that he could buy himself a property in which to live whilst at university.

Simos J preferred the son's evidence and held that there was a complete gift of the $120,000 to the son. As the cheques were paid by the father's bank, the gift was complete.

---

22 Ibid at 12.
23 Ibid.
24 Ibid.
25 *Blackett v Darcy* [2005] NSWSC 65.
26 Ibid at 31.
27 *Djordjevic v Djordjevic* [1999] NSWSC 1223.

Although the son was a volunteer in that he had provided no consideration for the money from his father, equity would recognise the gift. However, equity was not assisting a volunteer and did not need to assist a volunteer because the gift was already perfect. His father had transferred both legal and equitable interests in the money to the son. All equity had to do was to recognise the gift as perfect.

Equity's interventionist approach taken further: The key case of *Pennington v Waine*[28]

This test, based on conscience, has been developed further by the decision of the Court of Appeal in *Pennington v Waine*. The Court of Appeal focused heavily on the broad principle of unconscionability underpinning equitable principles to come to the conclusion that this broader test could be used to determine if a gift should be perfected or a trust completely constituted.

The facts concerned a family transaction between an aunt and her nephew. Ada Crampton wanted to give 400 shares in Crampton Bros (Coopers) Ltd to her nephew, Harold. She also wanted to make him a director of the company which, as the majority shareholder, she had the power to do. In September 1998, Ada instructed Mr Pennington, one of the company's auditors, to prepare the necessary forms to make Harold a director of the company and to transfer the shares to him. Mr Pennington duly prepared the forms, Harold signed them and returned them to him. Mr Pennington confirmed in writing to Harold that there were no further steps that Harold had to undertake. The problem arose because the stock transfer form, used to transfer the shares from Ada to Harold, should have been sent to the company for registration. This was never done; instead, it remained on Mr Pennington's file.

Ada wrote her will in November 1998 in which she left the balance of her shares in the company to other individuals. She made no mention of the 400 shares, presumably because she thought she had transferred them to Harold. Shortly after she had executed her will, Ada died.

The issue for the Court of Appeal was whether or not the gift to Harold of the 400 shares was effective. If it was not effective, the gift would fall into the residuary estate under her will and would go to those residuary beneficiaries. The problem was, of course, that Ada had not done 'everything necessary' which should have been done to complete the gift. 'Everything necessary' here would have involved the company registering the transfer of shares into Harold's name. If the more subjective test in *Re Rose* had been applied, arguably Ada could not show that she had met that either – she had not done everything 'in her power' to transfer the shares to Harold as this would have entailed sending the form to the company for registration, rather than sending it to her accountant.

In giving the leading judgment of the court, Arden LJ reviewed the authorities and concluded that the test underpinning them all was based on unconscionability. If it would be unconscionable, as against the donee of the gift, for the donor to change his mind, then equity would perfect the imperfect gift. Arden LJ quoted[29] a *dictum* from Lord Browne-Wilkinson in *T Choithram International SA v Pagarini*:[30] '[a]lthough equity will not aid a volunteer, it will not strive officiously to defeat a gift.'

---

28 *Pennington v Waine* [2002] 1 WLR 2075.
29 Ibid at 2089.
30 *T Choithram International SA v Pagarini* [2001] 1 WLR 1 at 11.

Arden LJ said that:

There can be no comprehensive list of factors which makes it unconscionable for the donor to change his or her mind: it must depend on the court's evaluation of all the relevant considerations.[31]

Here the relevant considerations were that it was Ada's decision to give the shares to Harold, she advised Harold she was going to give him the shares, she executed the relevant transfer forms and Mr Pennington had specifically advised Harold that he need do nothing more to receive them. Given these circumstances, it would have been unconscionable, as against Harold, for Ada to have changed her mind and revoked her gift. As such, equity would intervene and perfect the imperfect gift. It would also, of course, assist Harold as a volunteer who had provided no consideration for the gift. Ada became a constructive trustee of those shares in Harold's favour from the point she signed the transfer form due to the fact that by that stage, it would have been unconscionable for her to revoke the gift.

Pennington v Waine is a landmark decision. The Court of Appeal sanctioned equity's intervention for the first time both to perfect an imperfect gift and assist a volunteer. Before this decision, the courts took the view that equity merely recognised a gift or trust that a settlor had to constitute correctly himself. But there can be no doubt that the gift in *Pennington v Waine* was not completely constituted, as the documents never reached the company for the legal title to be transferred.

❖ ANALYSING THE LAW

Do you think that Arden LJ was right to apply the principle of conscience from the decision of the Privy Council in *T Choithram International SA v Pagarini*?

In the latter case, Mr Pagarini had always owned the trust property himself. It was perhaps not surprising that when he declared that he wanted the property to go to the Foundation, that wish should be sufficient to hold that the property was held by him on trust and also vested in the Foundation's other trustees. Mr Pagarani's situation was novel but there was, ultimately, an express declaration of trust and a trustee of that trust. But in *Pennington v Waine*, there was no question of a trust being set up. There was, unlike in *T Choithram International SA v Pagarini*, no declaration of trust and no trustee. Ada definitively wished to gift the shares to Harold. It was a much bigger step in *Pennington v Waine* for the court to hold that the entire transfer of the gift should be recognised on the basis of conscience than it was in *T Choithram International SA v Pagarini* to hold that property already vested in one trustee should also be seen to be held by the other trustees.

Arguably, the Court of Appeal in *Pennington v Waine* wrongly applied the principle from *T Choithram International SA v Pagarini* to the same situation that had been addressed clearly on a number of occasions (for example, in both *Milroy v Lord* and even *Re Rose*). On this basis, can you support the decision in *Pennington v Waine*?

---

31 *Pennington v Waine* [2002] 1 WLR 2075 at 2091.

Pennington v Waine was considered by the High Court in *Curtis v Pulbrook*.[32]

The case concerned purported transfers of shares in Farnham Royal Nurseries Ltd by Henry Pulbrook to his wife and daughter. Henry was a director of the company. He was also a trustee of a trust of whom the Towns family were beneficiaries. Henry transferred 14 shares in the company to his daughter, Alice. He issued a new share certificate with her name on it and signed a stock transfer form transferring the shares to her, albeit that the stock transfer form only came to light some two years after the purported transfer had occurred. He transferred a further 300 shares in the company to his wife, Anucha using similar documentation. In the meantime, Henry had (unlawfully) made substantial payments from Mr and Mrs Towns' personal joint bank account, using a power of attorney that had been executed appointing him their attorney. Henry and Anucha then emigrated to Thailand. The Towns sought the return of these share transfers, arguing that the shares had never been transferred to the recipients. The issue was whether legal and/or equitable title to the shares had been successfully transferred to Alice and Anucha.

Briggs J found that one of the reasons Henry tried to transfer the shares to Anucha was fear of a claim by the Towns against him that he had misused the power of attorney to withdraw money from their personal joint account. Henry thought they would sue him, and so he tried to divest himself of what he thought were assets that he owned.

Briggs J held that legal title to the shares had not been transferred to Alice or Anucha. Although a director of the company, Henry had had no authority to issue new share certificates to anyone or record their names as new shareholders on the company's register. On the facts of the case, a minimum of two directors' approval was needed to transfer legal title in shares to a new recipient.

Equitable title had not been transferred either. Briggs J analysed the judgment of Arden LJ in *Pennington v Waine* as stating that equitable title could be transferred on one of three occasions:

(a)   the principle in *Re Rose*: where the donor had done everything necessary to transfer title to the donee so that further assistance of the donor to perfect the transfer was not needed;

(b)   where the donee had undertaken an act of detrimental reliance, so that it could be said that the donor's conscience was affected and a constructive trust could be imposed. Briggs J held that this category is what the facts of *Pennington v Waine* seemed to fall into; and

(c)   where 'by a benevolent construction an effective gift or implied declaration of trust may be teased out of the words used'.[33] This is the category that Briggs J held that the decision of the Privy Council in *T Choithram International SA v Pagarini* fell into.

It could not be said that categories (i) or (iii) applied to the transfer of shares here. In terms of category (i), the critical stock transfer forms transferring the titles to either recipient were omitted at the time the transfer of the shares purportedly took place. Briggs J did not feel that any 'benevolent construction' could be applied in Henry's favour here, presumably because of his alleged motivation for the transfer of the shares at least to his wife. Category (ii) could not be relied upon by either Alice or Anucha because neither of them had undertaken any reliance on the purported transfer of the shares to themselves. As such, the equitable interests in the shares had not been transferred to Alice or Anucha.

---

32 *Curtis v Pulbrook* [2011] EWHC 167 (Ch).
33 Ibid at 43.

It seems that Briggs J felt that the decision in *Pennington v Waine* had to fall into the 'detrimental reliance' category largely because it did not fall into either of the other categories he listed. But it is hard to see how Harold relied to his detriment in the earlier case. Whilst it might be said that Harold may well have been happy to receive notification that he was to receive a gift of shares from his aunt, it is hard to see how he relied on such a letter to his detriment.

It is, therefore, interesting to note that Briggs J felt that he could not see that:

> the existing rules about the circumstances when equity will and will not perfect an apparently imperfect gift of shares serve any clearly identifiable or rational policy objective.[34]

He also felt that this area of law might need to be examined further by a higher court.

❖ ANALYSING THE LAW

Briggs J's analysis of *Pennington v Waine* is interesting, as it confirms the case as equity preparing to intervene to perfect an imperfect gift on the basis of detrimental reliance. He was clear that the decision in *Pennington v Waine* led to an entirely separate method of equity perfecting an imperfect gift than had been allowed by the Privy Council in *T Choithram International SA v Pagarini*.

Do you think Arden LJ in *Pennington v Waine* would have regarded her judgment as developing an entirely separate method of perfecting an imperfect gift to that set out by the Privy Council in *T Choithram International SA v Pagarini*? Or do you think her judgment merely applies the principle from *T Choithram International SA v Pagarini*?

Summary of when a gift will be perfect

There have been significant inroads made to the original principle in *Milroy v Lord* that 'everything necessary' must be done to perfect a gift or constitute a trust. The test is based on the idea that if it would be unconscionable for the donor to recall the gift, the gift is perfect. The donor will hold the gift as a constructive trustee for the donee. Using the fundamental equitable doctrine of unconscionability (as occurred in *Pennington v Waine*) may accord with basic notions of equitable justice and fairness but does little to create the certainty afforded by the decision in *Milroy v Lord*. It rails against the two equitable maxims that equity will not perfect an imperfect gift or assist a volunteer and it must be asked to what extent those two maxims now have any application in relation to the constitution of a trust. The key case law in this area is summarised in Figure 7.2.

---

34 Ibid at 47.

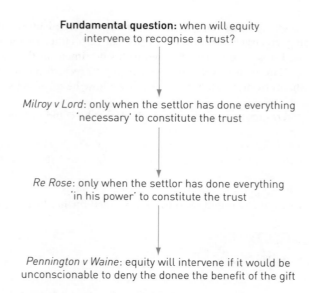

Fundamental question: when will equity
intervene to recognise a trust?

Milroy v Lord: only when the settlor has done everything
'necessary' to constitute the trust

Re Rose: only when the settlor has done everything
'in his power' to constitute the trust

Pennington v Waine: equity will intervene if it would be
unconscionable to deny the donee the benefit of the gift

Figure 7.2 Summary of case law developments of when a trust will be completely constituted.

How a Trust is Completely Constituted

A trust may be constituted in either of the two ways described by Arden LJ in *Pennington v Waine* and illustrated in Figure 7.1. They are:

(a)   transfer of legal ownership in the trust property to a trustee; or
(b)   retention of the legal ownership in the trust property by the settlor where the settlor declares that he himself is the trustee.

The aim of either method is to help establish the trust properly. If complied with, both methods provide that the beneficiary should have the benefit of an equitable interest in the trust property and that the trustee should administer the trust in the beneficiary's favour.

Each method must be considered in turn.

Transfer of legal ownership to a trustee

Normally this should be a straightforward transaction between the settlor and trustee. If there are any formalities to be observed in the transfer of a particular type of trust property, then they must be complied with. For example, if the trust property is land, s 53(1)(b) of the Law of Property Act 1925 provides that any declaration of trust of land must be in writing and signed by a person able to declare the trust, who will normally be the settlor. If the trust property is shares, they must be transferred using a stock transfer form[35] If the property is a chattel, delivery of that chattel must be undertaken.

The key, however, is that legal title to the trust property must be vested in the trustee. Again, the equitable maxims that equity will not assist a volunteer and will not perfect an imperfect gift underpin this area.

---

35 Stock Transfer Act 1963, s 1.

There are three ways in which the legal title may be vested in the trustee which may be seen to be out of the ordinary. Provided, however, that the trustee receives the legal title to the trust property, the trust will still be constituted. It does not matter, therefore, that these ways look, at first glance, a little out of the ordinary. These three ways are:

(a)   where the trust property is vested in the trustee by circumstance;
(b)   the rule in *Strong v Bird*;[36] and
(c)   the doctrine of *donatio mortis causa*.

It is only in (c) that equity really does perfect the imperfect gift. As will be seen, in the first two situations, the courts have argued in successive decisions that the gift has already been perfected so that there is no need for equity to intervene.

Where the trust property is vested in the trustee by circumstance

It seems not to matter how the trust property gets to the trustee, provided that the legal title to the property is actually vested in him, as the facts in *Re Ralli's Will Trusts*[37] illustrate. A family tree of the relevant parties in *Re Ralli's Will Trusts* is set out in Figure 7.3 below.

Trust 1: Mr Ralli (trustee of his trust
= Pandia Calvocoressi)

Widow for life

Helen   Irene

Trust 2: Helen declares a trust
(trustee: Pandia Calvorcoressi)

Helen's children/Irene's children

Figure 7.3 Re Ralli's Will Trusts.

Mr Ralli left his residuary estate on trust with a life interest for his wife and remainder in equal shares to his two daughters, Helen and Irene. Irene's husband, Pandia Calvocoressi, was appointed as a trustee of that trust.

---

36 *Strong v Bird* (1874) LR 18 Eq 315.
37 *Re Ralli's Will Trusts* [1964] Ch 288.

Separately, just before she married, Helen declared a trust in which she was to have a life interest with remainder to any children she might have or, in default, to Irene's children. She promised to transfer any property she might acquire above the value of £500 to that trust. Pandia Calvocoressi was one of the trustees of the trust.

Helen died in 1956, followed by Mr Ralli's widow four years later. Pandia Calvocoressi brought an action for directions in the High Court. Certain investments, representing Helen's share of Mr Ralli's estate, had matured. The question was whether the money should be held on Helen's trust, or whether the money fell outside that trust and should be given to Helen's personal representatives for them to administer on behalf of her estate. Helen had never transferred her residuary interest in her father's trust to her trustees; instead, all she had done was promise to transfer the property to them. The beneficiaries under the trust were, of course, mere volunteers.

Buckley J held that the money belonged to the beneficiaries under Helen's trust, not to the beneficiaries of Helen's estate. The money had originally come from the estate of Mr Ralli. The legal ownership of the money had been vested in Pandia Calvocoressi as personal representative for Mr Ralli. It did not matter that he may have held the money originally in his capacity as personal representative for Mr Ralli as opposed to his other capacity as trustee of Helen's trust. All that mattered was that Mr Calvocoressi had legal title to the money: '[h]e is at law the owner of the fund, and the means by which he became so have no effect upon the quality of his legal ownership.'[38]

In this manner, legal ownership of the fund had been transferred to Mr Calvocoressi. He could now hold the money on trust for the beneficiaries of Helen's trust.

Buckley J did not believe that his decision meant that equity was assisting volunteers. Equity was not intervening. The beneficiaries under Helen's trust were entitled to the money as of right in equity because their trustee enjoyed the legal interest as the money had been vested in him.

Re Ralli's Will Trusts illustrates that it is really a matter of fact whether the trustee has the legal ownership of the trust property. As long as he does, the trust is constituted. Even if he holds the legal title by accident, that seems not to matter. The fact that the legal title in the trust property had been transferred was in issue here; not the motive that may have led to the change of ownership.

The rule in *Strong v Bird*[39]

The rule in Strong v Bird was summed up by Young CJ in the Australian case of Blackett v Darcy[40] as:

> if a testator intends to make a gift but does not make a complete gift before his or her death and still has the intention of making the gift at the time of death and appoints the donee as executor, then equity will assist the donee [in recognising the gift].[41]

This can be illustrated by the flowchart in Figure 7.4.

In Strong v Bird, the defendant lived with his stepmother in his house. She paid him £212 each quarter for her board and lodgings. He needed to borrow money so she lent him £1,100. She was to pay £100 less per quarter for her board and lodgings until the loan had been completely repaid. For the next two quarters following the making of the loan, the stepmother

---

38 Ibid at 301.
39 Strong v Bird (1874) LR 18 Eq 315.
40 Blackett v Darcy [2005] NSWSC 65.
41 Ibid at 32.

1. Scott intends to make a gift to Thomas

2. Scott still wants to make that gift to Thomas when Scott dies

3. Scott appoints Thomas to be the executor of his will

4. The gift is perfected when Thomas proves (administers) Scott's will

Figure 7.4 The rule in *Strong v Bird*.

paid £100 less from her board and lodgings money. Then she changed her mind and said that she would prefer to pay the full amount. The defendant accepted this. Four years later, the step-mother died, having continued to pay the full amount of her board and lodgings money. She appointed the defendant the sole executor of her will. The issue for the Court of Chancery was whether the defendant still owed the £900 to his step-mother's estate.

Sir George Jessel MR held that the £900 debt was extinguished and that the defendant could retain the money. He relied on the old common law concept that the defendant in appointing the executor was, in this action, releasing him from the money owed. Equity would follow the law's conclusion provided the defendant could show his step-mother had a 'continuing intention to give' the money to him which Jessel MR found that there was, on the facts of the case, by the stepmother always paying full board and lodgings to him.

Jessel MR did not believe this was a case of equity perfecting an imperfect gift:

> the transaction is perfected, and he does not want the aid of a Court of Equity to carry it out, or make it complete, because it is complete already, and there is no equity against him to take the property away from him.[42]

Equity was not perfecting the gift. The gift was perfected by the *process* of the testator choosing the same person to be his executor as the donee of the gift and that same individual then proving the testator's will. Legal title to the gift had been transferred by that process. As the gift is perfect, there was no remit for equity to interfere and take it away from the donee. But on the facts, it is surely the case that the defendant was a volunteer to the gift as he had not provided any consideration for his step-mother's release of him from the debt he owed.[43] The decision in the case, however, is probably right on its facts. Had the stepmother's estate wanted to recover the £900, ultimately it would have had to sue for it. That would have meant the defendant — as her executor — suing himself, in his capacity of debtor. Such an action would have been absurd.

---

42 *Strong v Bird* (1874) LR 18 Eq 315 at 319.
43 The defendant had effectively paid part only of the debt he owed to her. Part-payment of a debt is not good consideration for a promise to be discharged of the whole amount: *Foakes v Beer* (1884) 9 App Cas 605.

The rule in *Strong v Bird* has been considered in more recent cases such as in *Re Ralli's Will Trusts*[44] and applied, somewhat reluctantly, by the decision of the Supreme Court of New South Wales in *Blackett v Darcy*[45] where Young CJ said:

> My view is that the rule in *Strong v Bird* should not in this 21st century be extended at all . . . I am bound to apply it, but as I say, it seems to me the prevailing view is that it is an anomalous rule and should not be extended.[46]

The rule was extended by the decision in *Re James*[47] to apply to administrators as well as executors. This was a strange extension of the rule. Any executor is deliberately chosen by the testator. It is this deliberate act of choice that helps to perfect the gift to the donee/executor. An administrator is someone appointed by the court to administer the estate of the deceased who has died without making a will (intestate). It is therefore good fortune if someone is appointed an administrator who also happens to owe money to the deceased. The act of the deceased deliberately choosing an individual to administer his estate is missing entirely if the deceased dies intestate. This point was made by Walton J in *Re Gonin*:[48]

> It is often a matter of pure chance which of many persons equally entitled to a grant of letters of administration finally takes them out. Why, then, should any special tenderness be shown to a person so selected by law and not the will of the testator, and often indifferently selected among many with an equal claim?[49]

Walton J did, however, apply the rule leaving it to a higher court to address whether his doubts over the extension of the rule in *Re James* were well-founded or not.

Donatio mortis causa

This is the third example of how a trust may be constituted or a gift perfected in an unconventional manner.

Buckley J described *donatio mortis causa* as follows in *Re Beaumont*:[50]

> It may be said to be of an amphibious nature, being a gift which is neither entirely *inter vivos* nor testamentary. It is an act *inter vivos* by which the donee is to have the absolute title to the subject of the gift not at once but if the donor dies.[51]

Here equity probably is perfecting an imperfect gift. The donor has made it clear to the donee that the property is to be his if the donor dies. The executor of the donor's will becomes a trustee of the property for the donee. The donee merely has an equitable interest in the property whilst the donor's executor holds the legal title on trust for the donee.

Three requirements for *donatio mortis causa* to apply were set out by Nourse LJ in *Sen v Headley*:[52]

---

44 *Re Ralli's Will Trusts* [1964] Ch 288.
45 *Blackett v Darcy* [2005] NSWSC 65.
46 Ibid at 37.
47 *Re James* [1935] Ch 449.
48 *Re Gonin* [1979] Ch 16.
49 Ibid at 35.
50 *Re Beaumont* [1902] 1 Ch 889.
51 Ibid at 893.
52 *Sen v Headley* [1991] Ch 425.

First, the gift must be made in contemplation, although not necessarily in expectation, of impending death. Secondly, the gift must be made upon the condition that it
is to be absolute and perfected only on the donor's death, being revocable until that
event occurs and ineffective if it does not. Thirdly, there must be delivery of the
subject matter of the gift, or the essential indicia of title thereto, which amounts to
parting with dominion and not mere physical possession over the subject matter of
the gift.[53]

The third requirement in *Sen v Headley* was not met on the facts of *Re Beaumont* itself.

Mr Beaumont was very ill and expected to die. He called his niece to his room and
instructed her to write a cheque for £300 in favour of Mrs Ewbank. He duly signed the cheque
but did so in shaky handwriting. The cheque was not cashed by Mr Beaumont's bankers
because the bank manager was not sure that the signature was genuine. He asked for evidence
that it was. Before that evidence could be presented, Mr Beaumont died. The issue was whether
the gift of the cheque to Mrs Ewbank was perfect.

Whilst it had been made in contemplation of death, the gift was held not to be perfect
because it did not concern any property of the donor's. A cheque could not be described as
property as it did not pass any rights to the recipient. It was described by Buckley J as only a
'revocable mandate'.[54] Mr Beaumont could have changed his mind and stopped the cheque at
any point during his lifetime. As such, he had not transferred any rights – legal or equitable –
to Mrs Ewbank which she could enforce against Mr Beaumont's executor after his death.

Donatio mortis causa is a doctrine which must be applied with care. If successful, it permits
gifts to be made without the need to comply with s 9 of the Wills Act 1837. Section 9 provides,
inter alia, that an individual's will must be in writing, have been signed by the testator and the
signature must be witnessed by at least two witnesses present at the same time as each other
and the testator. These requirements are stringent because the testator is undertaking a process
by which he is giving away all of his property. The process needs careful consideration by the
testator and it must be clear that the testator was not unduly pressured into disposing of his
property to recipients that he would rather not benefit. In addition, the testator must have
mental capacity to write his will.

At first glance, *donatio mortis causa* appears to circumvent the requirements to create a valid
will with ease. But the requirements of the Court of Appeal in *Sen v Headley* restrict it. At the same
time, however, the decision also extended the doctrine to apply to land as well as personal
property.

The facts concerned a house in Ealing, London, owned by Bob Hewitt. He had married
but he and his wife had divorced. During their lengthy separation period, Mr Hewitt had lived
with Mrs Sen, as man and wife, for 10 years. Whilst this ended in 1964, they continued to have
a close relationship. In November 1986, Mr Hewitt was cared for in hospital and Mrs Sen
visited him every day. Whilst he was there, he instructed her to bring him a set of his keys from
his house. Unbeknownst to her, he put them into her handbag and she found them after his
death. Shortly before he died, he had told her that she was to have the house and its contents.
She was to find the deeds to the house in a steel box, the only key for which was on the key
ring that he had put in her bag.

Mr Hewitt died intestate. Mrs Sen claimed that the doctrine of *donatio mortis causa* should
apply to the gift of the house to her. The problem was that Mr Hewitt had not directly given
Mrs Sen any property. He had not given her the title deeds to the house. Instead, he had simply

53 Ibid at 431.
54 *Re Beaumont* [1902] 1 Ch 889 at 894.

given her the only key to the box in which the deeds were kept. At first instance, Mummery J held that that fact was fatal to Mrs Sen's claim.

In giving the judgment of the Court of Appeal, Nourse LJ did not doubt that Mr Hewitt had parted with dominion of the title deeds. The questions, he said, were whether in doing so, Mr Hewitt had parted with dominion of the house and whether land could pass by way of a *donatio mortis causa*.

Nourse LJ stressed that a parting of dominion was needed, not just a parting of possession of the property. Parting of dominion implied that the donor parted with control of the property, not just physical possession of it. Moreover, parting with dominion was different when dealing with tangible and intangible property. When dealing with intangible property, such as a chose in action, parting with the title document of the property would be sufficient to indicate a parting with dominion. Such was the case here. Mr Hewitt had parted with dominion of the title deeds to the house by giving Mrs Sen her own keys to the house and the only one to the steel box and in doing so, he had parted with dominion of the house.

Land could be the subject of a *donatio mortis causa*. There was no policy reason preventing this, according to Nourse LJ:

> A *donatio mortis causa* of land is neither more nor less anomalous than any other. Every such gift is a circumvention of the Wills Act 1837. Why should the additional statutory formalities for the creation and transmission of interests in land [contained in sections 52 and 53 Law of Property Act 1925] be regarded as some larger obstacle?[55]

The issue of certainty in relation to wills fulfilling the requirements of s 9 of the Wills Act 1837 or an *inter vivos* declaration of trust containing land complying with s 53(1)(b) of the Law of Property Act 1925 was not a vital consideration in the doctrine of *donatio mortis causa* as the doctrine was relied upon so infrequently. Mrs Sen could, therefore, enjoy the house under the doctrine.

❖ ANALYSING THE LAW

The facts of *Sen v Headley* concerned unregistered land. The decision of the Court of Appeal is probably therefore confined to unregistered, as opposed to registered, land. As physical title documents (the Land Certificate) were abolished in registered land by the Land Registration Act 2002, do you think that registered land could be subject to a *donatio mortis causa* as there is nowadays nothing physically to hand over to a recipient?

Donatio mortis causa is really the only doctrine in which the courts acknowledge that equity does perfect an imperfect gift. Equity also assists a volunteer. As Nourse LJ stated in *Sen v Headley*, the doctrine is 'anomalous' to those equitable maxims. In all other instances, the courts regard gifts as already perfected by the donor and there is no need for equity to intervene to perfect them.

---

55 *Sen v Headley* [1991] Ch 425 at 440.

Do you think the court is really only perfecting an imperfect gift and assisting a volunteer where the doctrine of *donatio mortis causa* applies? Read again the sections on where the trustee simply happens to become the legal owner of the property through circumstance and the rule in *Strong v Bird*. Do you think the court may be perfecting imperfect gifts and assisting volunteers in both of those situations?

Retention of the legal ownership in the trust property where the settlor declares that he himself is the trustee

This was the second way in which Arden LJ described that a trust may be constituted in *Pennington v Waine*. The settlor changes hats to become the trustee. He assumes the duties, rights and obligations of a trustee. Whilst he will always remain the settlor of the trust, from this point going forwards, he is the trustee. Obviously, there is no transfer of legal title in the trust property: it remains with the one and same person.

Perhaps the best way of the settlor declaring himself to be a trustee and constitute the trust is to execute a written document, regardless of whether a written document is actually required as a matter of law. This brings certainty to the transaction and it is not only clear that the settlor is now the trustee of the trust, but also when he assumed the duties, rights and obligations of being a trustee.

In normal life, however, many trusts are declared informally by both individuals and businesses.

Self-declaration by an individual

Equity will recognise an individual declaring themselves to be a trustee. This occurred in *Paul v Constance*.[56]

Doreen Paul and Dennis Constance were in a relationship together. They were embarrassed to open a bank account in joint names as they were not married. The bank opened the account in Dennis' name alone. Doreen could still withdraw from the account provided she showed the bank staff a note of authorisation from Dennis. They paid what they regarded as money belonging to both of them into the account and also made withdrawals for both their benefits.

Dennis had been married to, and was not divorced from, Bridget before meeting Doreen. Dennis died intestate so his widow, Bridget, was responsible for administering his estate. Bridget claimed that, as the bank account was in Dennis' sole name, the entire contents of it belonged solely to him. That money, she argued, became part of Dennis' estate which she was bound to administer according to the laws of intestacy, as opposed to any of it belonging to Doreen.

Doreen disagreed. She argued that whilst the legal title of the money had been in Dennis' sole name, a trust had been created of it with her and Dennis owning the beneficial interests.

The Court of Appeal upheld the trial judge's finding that there was an express self-declaration of trust by Dennis in favour of both himself and Doreen. Dennis had then held the trust property (the money) as trustee on trust for himself and Doreen. In his judgment, Scarman LJ pointed out that:

---

56 *Paul v Constance* [1977] 1 WLR 527.

> one should consider the various things that were said and done by the [claimant] and the deceased during their time together against their own background and in their own circumstances.[57]

Certain facts led to the conclusion that Dennis had orally declared an express trust. The key fact was that Dennis had said to Doreen on more than one occasion 'This money is as much yours as mine'.

Equity will look at all the circumstances of each case to decide if the settlor has declared himself to be a trustee. There must be sufficient evidence of a self-declaration of trusteeship and there are limits to how informal a declaration of trust can be. This was illustrated in *Jones v Lock*.[58]

The case concerned a businessman who, after being admonished by his son's nanny for failing to bring his son a present from his business trip said, 'Look you here, I give this [cheque for £900] to baby; it is for himself, and I am going to put it away for him . . .'. He then placed the cheque in his safe.

The issue was whether these words could be seen to be a declaration of himself as a trustee. The court held the words were not sufficient to declare the businessman a trustee of the money. The words were, according to Lord Cranworth LC, simply a 'loose conversation'[59] that the businessman had had with his son's nanny.

❖ ANALYSING THE LAW

Jones v Lock can be said to be authority for the proposition that the court will not treat a failed gift as a declaration of trust. Look back again at the facts of *Re Rose*. Did the Court of Appeal not treat a failed gift as a valid declaration of trust in that case?

Declaring oneself to be a trustee means that one retains no equitable rights in the trust property. The legal right in the trust property is retained, but the equitable interest is held on trust for the new beneficiary. The court has to be absolutely sure that there was a true declaration of trust: that the settlor truly intended to give away all the equitable interest he enjoyed in the property for the benefit of another. This was not the position in *Jones v Lock*: it could not be said that the father intended to assume all of the duties and responsibilities of a trustee.

Self-declaration by a business

Equity will recognise a declaration by a business that it now holds property on trust even if that trust is declared informally. This was illustrated in *Barclays Bank Ltd v Quistclose Investments Ltd*.[60]

The facts concerned a company called Rolls Razor Ltd that was in financial difficulties. It approached Quistclose Investments Ltd for a loan that it could use to pay dividends to its shareholders. Quistclose agreed to make the loan, but only on the basis that the money had to be used for the payment of Rolls Razor's dividends. It then sent Rolls Razor a cheque representing the loan money. Rolls Razor duly paid the cheque into its bank, Barclays. Barclays was aware that the money was only to be used for one specific purpose. Before Rolls Razor could use the

---

57 Ibid at 530, although Scarman LJ admitted to the difficulty of pinpointing exactly when there was a declaration of the express trust on the facts of the case.
58 *Jones v Lock* (1865–66) LR 1 Ch App 25.
59 Ibid at 29.
60 *Barclays Bank Ltd v Quistclose Investments Ltd* [1970] AC 567.

money to pay the dividends, it became insolvent. Barclays sought to use the money located in Rolls Razor's account in part payment of Rolls Razor's overdraft. Quistclose objected, arguing that Rolls Razor had declared itself to be a trustee of the money, with Quistclose as the beneficiary. The trust was declared by Rolls Razor making the purpose of the loan money clear to Barclays when the cheque was paid into its account.

In the House of Lords, Lord Wilberforce held that there were two types of trust on the facts. The 'primary' express trust arose in favour of the shareholders to whom the dividends were due. This trust had failed, as Rolls Razor had not paid the shareholders before it went insolvent. Consequently, a 'secondary' trust applied, which was a resulting trust of the money in favour of Quistclose.

The *Quistclose* decision was analysed by Lord Millett in *Twinsectra Ltd v Yardley*.[61] The facts concerned a loan of £1 million from Twinsectra Ltd for the purposes of enabling an entrepreneur, Mr Yardley, to purchase land in the Midlands. Mr Yardley was dealing with two solicitors, unconnected to each other, in relation to the loan. He first instructed a solicitor called Mr Leach but, during the transaction, approached a second solicitor, Mr Sims, to act on his behalf. Mr Sims was also a business associate of his. The money was advanced to Mr Sims, who transferred it to Mr Leach. Part of the money was in fact used to buy property but a substantial amount (over £357,000) was not. Twinsectra brought proceedings to recover that sum from Mr Leach. Their argument was that a *Quistclose* trust had been created when they advanced the money to Mr Sims. They had made it clear that the money was only to be advanced for the purpose of enabling Mr Yardley to buy property. When that purpose was not fulfilled, following *Quistclose*, the money should be returned to them.

The House of Lords held that a *Quistclose* trust had, indeed, been created.

Lord Millett pointed out that a court would not hold that there was a self-declaration of trust in every case where money was advanced for a particular purpose. Lenders were often interested in knowing the purpose of a loan simply to decide whether they should take a commercial risk in lending the money. Indeed, the general rule was that money lent to a borrower was free from a trust and it was at the borrower's discretion to do with the money as he wished. To ascertain if there had been a self-declaration of trust by the lender, '[t]he question in every case is whether the parties intended the money to be at the free disposal of the recipient. . . .'[62]

There was clear evidence here that the money was not to be at the free disposal of Mr Sims. Twinsectra had made it clear that the money was only to be used for purchasing property. Equity would recognise the trust because, according to Lord Millett: '[i]t is unconscionable for a man to obtain money on terms as to its application and then disregard the terms on which he received it.'[63]

Twinsectra had, therefore, created a trust with itself as the beneficiary.

Lord Millett then went on to explain the true nature of the *Quistclose* trust and where the equitable interest lay while the purpose of the trust is being put into effect. He said that there were 'formidable difficulties'[64] in holding that there were two successive trusts in *Quistclose*. For example, there was no clear answer to the question of what would happen to the equitable interest in the trust property if the primary trust was for a purpose and that purpose failed. He thought there were four possibilities as to where the equitable interest may be. These are set out in Figure 7.5.

Lord Millett rejected the idea that the equitable interest had passed to the borrower. If the borrower had the equitable interest as well as the legal title to the money, they would have

61 *Twinsectra Ltd v Yardley* [2002] 2 AC 164.
62 Ibid at 185.
63 Ibid at 186.
64 Ibid at 187.

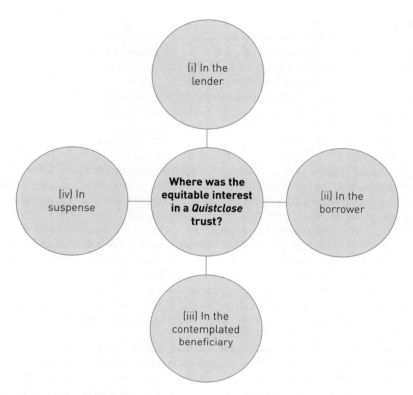

Figure 7.5 Lord Millett's hypotheses on where the equitable interest in a *Quistclose* trust lay.

absolute ownership of it and would be able to use the money as they wished. This was plainly not the case in such arrangements: the borrower is able to use the money only for the purposes expressly stated by the lender. The money would also be part of the borrower's estate if the borrower became insolvent. The arrangement between the borrower and lender was designed to protect the lender from this risk.

The equitable interest could not have passed to the contemplated beneficiary. The facts of *Twinsectra* showed that such a possibility was not capable of being fulfilled. The details of the trust were too imprecise to pinpoint quite who was to benefit from this particular trust, so: '[i]t is simply not possible to hold money on trust to acquire unspecified property from an unspecified vendor at an unspecified time.'[65]

The equitable interest could not be held in suspense. Lord Millett said that such an assertion failed to take into account the role of the resulting trust. The main task of the resulting trust was to fill in a gap in beneficial ownership. This meant that equitable interests could not be suspended.

Instead, Lord Millett held that the equitable interest remained throughout with the lender. That was the reason why the lender could enforce the trust. He said:

---

65 Ibid at 189.

As Sherlock Holmes reminded Dr Watson, when you have eliminated the impossible, whatever remains, however improbable, must be the truth. I would reject all the alternative analyses, which I find unconvincing for the reasons I have endeavoured to explain, and hold the *Quistclose* trust to be an entirely orthodox example of the kind of default trust known as a resulting trust. The lender pays the money to the borrower by way of loan, but he does not part with the entire beneficial interest in the money, and in so far as he does not it is held on a resulting trust for the lender from the outset.[66]

The borrower was under a duty to use the money according to the lender's wishes. If that purpose failed, the money had to be returned to the lender.

In the *Quistclose* arrangement, then, there was only one trust: a resulting trust in the lender's favour. Within the trust, the borrower enjoys a power to apply the money for a particular purpose.

As we have seen, it is possible for there to be a self-declaration of trust by both an individual and a business. The courts are cautious about holding that a declaration of trust has occurred, especially where money has been advanced. The courts' inclination is to state that legal and equitable interests in the money have been transferred by way of a gift to the recipient, rather than a trust created. If, however, the evidence clearly points to a trust being created, it will be recognised.

Points to Review

You have seen that:

- to be properly formed, an express trust must be (a) constituted and (b) declared. In its most basic form, constituting the trust means the settlor either transferring the property to the trustee or the settlor himself holding the property on trust for the beneficiary;
- constitution of a trust revolves around the two equitable maxims that equity will not assist a volunteer and that equity will not perfect an imperfect gift; and
- the two key issues are when and how a trust is properly constituted. For the former, the courts have moved from a narrow interpretation of the settlor having to do 'everything necessary' (*Milroy v Lord*) to a looser, more flexible (but less certain) test of whether it would be 'unconscionable' for the court to deny the beneficiary's interest (*Pennington v Waine*). The question now is to what extent the equitable maxims survive in relation to when a trust is constituted. For the latter, the courts will recognise both formal and informal ways of self-declarations of trust, in both business and non-business scenarios.

Making connections

This chapter considered when and how a trust may be constituted. Constitution is one of the two essential ingredients in forming an express trust. The other essential ingredient is that the settlor must declare the trust. Declaration involves the settlor having capacity, complying with any necessary formalities, adhering to the three certainties, fulfilling the beneficiary principle and ensuring that the trust meets the requirements of the rules against perpetuity. These

---

66 Ibid at 192–193.

requirements are discussed in Chapters 4 to 6 (together with the chapter on perpetuities on the companion website). If you are unsure about any of these requirements, you should re-read those respective chapters.

The discussion of how to form a trust is now at an end. Now is the time to consider how the trust is properly managed. This involves looking at the managers of the trust, the trustees. The structure of how they are appointed to the trust must be considered, together with the powers that they enjoy and duties and responsibilities to which they are subject. These matters are considered in the next chapter.

Useful Things to Read

The best reading is contained in the primary sources listed below. It is always good to consider the decisions of the courts themselves as this will lead to a deeper understanding of the issues involved. A few secondary sources are also listed, which you may wish to read to gain additional insights into the areas considered in this chapter.

Primary sources

Barclays Bank Ltd v Quistclose Investments Ltd [1970] AC 567.
Curtis v Pulbrook [2011] EWHC 167 (Ch).
Re Fry [1946] Ch 312.
Jones v Lock (1865–66) LR 1 Ch App 25.
Milroy v Lord (1862) 4 De G F & J 264; 45 ER 1185.
Paul v Constance [1977] 1 All ER 195.
Pennington v Waine [2002] 1 WLR 2075.
Re Rose [1952] Ch 499.
Sen v Headley [1991] Ch 425.
Strong v Bird (1874) LR 18 Eq 315.
T Choithram International SA v Pagarani [2001] 1 WLR 1.
Twinsectra Ltd v Yardley [2002] 2 AC 164.

Secondary sources

Alastair Hudson, *Equity & Trusts* (7th edn, Routledge-Cavendish, 2012) chs 5 and 22.
Joseph Jaconelli, 'Problems in the rule in *Strong v Bird*' (2006) Conv Sep/Oct 432–450. This article looks at the origins of the rule in *Strong v Bird* and discusses issues with it to explain the logic behind it.
Peter Luxton, 'In search of perfection: The *Re Rose* rule rationale' (2012) Conv 1, 70–75 (note). This article considers the recent High Court decision of *Curtis v Pulbrook* and its treatment of *Pennington v Waine* as a case of detrimental reliance.
Barrie Lawrence Nathan, 'In defence of the primary trust: *Quistclose* revisited' (2012) T & T 18 (2) 123–131. This article considers *Quistclose* in the light of *Twinsectra* and examines the usefulness and limitations of recognising a first, primary trust in *Quistclose*.
Mohamed Ramjohn, *Text, Cases and Materials on Equity & Trusts* (4th edn, Routledge-Cavendish, 2008) ch 4.
J W A Thornely, 'Laying Lord Eldon's ghost: *Donatio mortis causa* of land' (1991) CLJ 50(3) 404–407. This article looks at the decision of the Court of Appeal in *Sen v Headley* in more depth.

Chapter 8

Trustees' Appointment and Removal; Trustees' Fiduciary Duties

Having considered how an express trust is formed, it is now time to discuss how that type of trust is managed. The managers of the trust are the trustees. Trustees are subject to a number of duties of both a fiduciary and non-fiduciary nature. They enjoy a number of powers. To gain a holistic view of the trustees' obligations and powers, you should read Chapter 9 immediately after this chapter.

As You Read

Look out for the following themes:

- how a trustee can be appointed and removed;
- how a trustee is under a number of obligations imposed upon him but enjoys a number of powers; and
- how the core obligations of a trustee are 'fiduciary'. See these as red lines beyond which a trustee must not cross.

Role of a Trustee

The trustee's role in the trust may be explained simply in the now-familiar diagram in Figure 8.1.

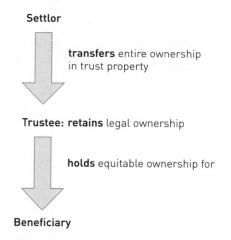

Figure 8.1 Setting up an express trust.

Figure 8.1 shows the most frequently used way of setting up an express trust: the settlor transfers legal ownership in property to a recipient to hold on trust for the beneficiary. As was seen in Chapter 7, however, it is also equally satisfactory to create an express trust by the settlor declaring themselves to be the trustee and holding the trust property on trust for the beneficiary. In both cases, the beneficiary enjoys an equitable interest in the trust property.

Whether or not a separate trustee is involved, the rights, duties and obligations that trustees enjoy and are subjected to remain the same. The trustee holds the legal title to the trust property and manages the trust. The task is mainly administrative.

Appointment of Trustees

Trustees may be appointed by one of four means, as shown in Figure 8.2.

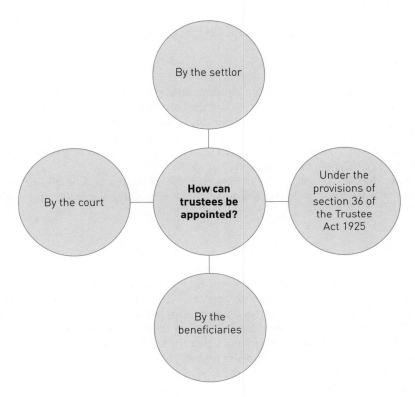

Figure 8.2 How trustees can be appointed.

There can be any number of trustees of a trust, except where the trust property is land. Where the trust property is land, s 34(2) of the Trustee Act 1925 provides that the maximum number of trustees permitted is four. Should more than four trustees be appointed, the first four trustees willing and able to act will be the only trustees of the trust. An exception exists in s 34(3) of the Trustee Act 1925 which provides that the number of trustees for a trust of land used for ecclesiastical, charitable or public purposes can be unlimited.

A single trustee would be the minimum number of trustees permissible although having a single trustee may often be unwise. If any of the trust property is land and a decision is taken to sell it, at least two trustees are needed to sell the land free from the interests of the beneficiaries in it.[1] This is known as the principle of overreaching (you will have learned about this in Land Law). Even if the trust property does not consist of land, a second trustee can always assist in the administration of the trust and in taking decisions that trustees need to take, such as how and where to invest the trust fund.

---

1   Law of Property Act 1925 ss 2, 27(2).

Alternatively, or perhaps in addition to individual trustees, many trusts are now administered by a trust corporation. These are often specialist businesses or departments of large organisations (such as banks) whose task it is to administer trusts. Appointing a trust corporation to administer a trust has the advantage that it should always bring specialist skills and knowledge to the often complex task of trust management. In addition, if the trust property is land, sale of it by a trust corporation also fulfils the requirements of overreaching.[2]

Appointment by the settlor

This is, of course, the usual way in which trustees are appointed when the trust is first created. Best practice must be for the settlor to declare the trust in a written document, so that there can be no doubt over its exact terms. A trust can be declared orally, providing there are no special formalities that must be fulfilled due to the type of property being left on trust (for example, in the case of land, a trust for which must be evidenced in writing to fulfil the provisions of s 53 (1)(b) of the Law of Property Act 1925).

Whether the trust is declared in writing or orally, the settlor will usually either choose trustees, or alternatively, appoint himself to be a trustee, possibly in combination with other people.

Appointment under s 36 of the Trustee Act 1925

Section 36(1) of the Trustee Act 1925 sets out when new trustees may be appointed. New trustees can be appointed under this section either by a power contained in the trust document providing that someone has the ability to appoint a new trustee (such person could be the original settlor, for example) or, if no such power exists in the trust document, by the existing trustees. If all of the existing trustees have died, then the personal representatives of the last surviving trustee enjoy the power to appoint a new trustee. The power to appoint new trustees is always subject to the maximum number of trustees of land not exceeding four. Any appointment of a new trustee under this section must be in writing.

The power to appoint new trustees under s 36(1) arises when a current trustee:

- has died;
- is outside the United Kingdom for a period of more than 12 months;
- wishes to resign from the trust;
- refuses to act as a trustee;
- is unfit to act as a trustee;
- is incapable of acting as a trustee; or
- is a child.

In addition, s 36(2) allows there to be an express power to remove a trustee in the trust document. If such a power exists and is exercised so that a trustee is removed, a replacement trustee can be appointed.

Some of the scenarios listed in s 36(1) have given rise to interesting case law.

Re Walker[3] concerned a trust declared in the will of John Walker. He had appointed his wife and a Mr Summers as his trustees. Mr Summers decided to live abroad in April 1899 and

---

2 Ibid.
3 Re Walker [1901] 1 Ch 259.

when he had not returned by 1 June 1900, Mrs Walker appointed a new trustee in his place. Mr Summers objected. His argument was based on the fact that he had returned to London for a week in November 1899. No power to replace him had arisen in the predecessor to s 36 of the Trustee Act 1925,[4] as he had not been absent from the UK for a period of 12 months.

Farwell J agreed with Mr Summers. He rejected Mrs Walker's argument that the legislation should not be construed literally and said that it was a matter of fact whether the trustee had been absent from the UK for a period of 12 months or more. As he had returned, albeit for a week, he had not been absent for a continuous period of one year, so the power to replace him under this provision had not arisen.

Chitty J considered an example of a trustee being 'incapable to act' in *Re Lemann's Trusts*.[5]

The case concerned a trust declared in the will of Frederick Lemann who appointed his wife, Harriet, to be a trustee. The trust provided that a new trustee could be appointed if any trustee was 'incapable to act'. Harriet had become incapable of acting as a trustee, due to old age and consequent infirmity. She was physically unable to sign a document appointing a new trustee. Chitty J held that she was incapable of acting and that, as she could not appoint a replacement trustee, it was expedient for the court to do so in her place.

Section 36(7) provides that any person appointed as a replacement trustee under s 36 will enjoy all of the same 'powers, authorities, and discretions' as the original trustees. The replacement trustee is viewed as though he was an original trustee.

Appointment by the beneficiaries

The beneficiaries of a trust effectively enjoy a right to appoint a new trustee in one particular circumstance. This right is set out in s 19 of the Trusts of Land and Appointment of Trustees Act 1996.

Provided that no-one is nominated in the trust for appointing a new trustee and the beneficiaries are all of full age, enjoy mental capacity and are together all absolutely entitled to the trust property, they may give a direction in writing to trustees to retire from the trust and nominate someone to take their place. It is the retiring trustee who actually appoints their successor. There is no limit on how many trustees the beneficiaries can force to retire and replace in this manner, provided the maximum number of trustees does not exceed four if the trust property is land. The retiring trustee(s) must do everything they can to ensure that the legal title to the trust property is transferred to the new trustee(s) under s 19(4).

Whilst this right might be seen to be useful to the beneficiaries, it will hardly ever be exercised. It depends on the beneficiaries all being of full age, mentally capable and together absolutely entitled to the trust property. The beneficiaries enjoy their interests under a bare trust. In such a case, the beneficiaries probably will not wish to appoint a new trustee(s) but instead will wish to exercise their rights under the rule in *Saunders v Vautier*.[6] This rule provides that in these circumstances, the beneficiaries can collectively bring the trust to an end. The trust ends and the legal title is transferred by the trustees to the beneficiaries for them to enjoy as they wish.

---

4   Trustee Act 1893, s 10(1).
5   *Re Lemann's Trusts* (1883) LR 22 Ch D 633.
6   *Saunders v Vautier* (1841) 4 Beav 115; 49 ER 282. See Chapter 10 (pp 265–266) for a full discussion.

Appointment by the court

The most important power for the court to appoint a new trustee is contained in s 41 of the Trustee Act 1925. Section 41(1) provides:

> The court may, whenever it is expedient to appoint a new trustee or new trustees, and it is found inexpedient difficult or impracticable to do so without the assistance of the court, make an order appointing a new trustee or new trustees either in substitution for or in addition to any existing trustee or trustees, or although there is no existing trustee.

Section 41(1) then goes on to give some examples of when the court may appoint a new trustee under this section. These are when an existing trustee lacks capacity, has been declared bankrupt or, if a company, has been liquidated or dissolved.

For the provision in s 41 to operate, it must be 'inexpedient difficult or impracticable' to appoint a new trustee without the court's assistance. This was seen to be the case in *Re Lemann's Trusts*,[7] where Harriet Lemann was not physically capable of signing any documentation herself to appoint a new trustee and the court had to appoint a replacement for her.

A further example, albeit on more unusual facts, of it being 'inexpedient difficult or impracticable' to appoint a new trustee without the court's assistance was given by the facts of *Re May's Will Trusts*.[8] Unlike in *Re Lemann's Trusts*, there was no evidence in this case that the trustee was incapable of acting as a trustee within the meaning of s 36(1) of the Trustee Act 1925.

The facts concerned the trust declared in the will of Herbert May. He appointed three trustees: George May, Frederick Stanford and his wife, Marguerite May. Marguerite was in Belgium when the German forces invaded at the beginning of the Second World War. She was therefore unable to return to the UK. The two other trustees brought an action claiming that she was 'incapable of acting' within the meaning of s 36(1) and that a different individual be appointed as a trustee within her place.

Counsel for Mrs May pointed out that all of the previous authorities on trustees being 'incapable' tended to define the term as the trustee being mentally or physically incapable of acting. Crossman J appeared to accept that definition as applying to s 36(1) in his short judgment, as he said that he could find no evidence that Mrs May was 'incapable' of acting within s 36(1) as it had previously been interpreted. He did, however, hold that the court was able to appoint a new trustee in place of Mrs May under the power contained in s 41. It appears that his judgment was as a result of a pragmatic decision that the trust would benefit from the appointment of a trustee who was in a position to act as such.

The case illustrates that the power given to the court in s 41 is a stand-alone power and that, provided it is 'inexpedient difficult or impracticable' for a new trustee not to be appointed without the court's assistance, the court will appoint a new trustee.

Termination of Trusteeship

The office of trustee may be terminated in any one of three main ways, as shown in Figure 8.3.

---

7 *Re Lemann's Trusts* (1883) LR 22 Ch D 633.
8 *Re May's Will Trusts* [1941] Ch 109.

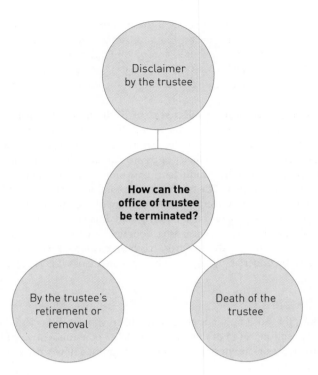

Figure 8.3 How trusteeship can be terminated.

Disclaimer by the trustee

Being a trustee is not compulsory! When chosen by the settlor, there is no obligation on the individual or corporation to accept the office of trustee. The office of trustee may be disclaimed, but it must be disclaimed before any acts associated with being a trustee (for example, investing the trust property) are undertaken.

Disclaiming being a trustee cannot be undertaken in part. The entire office of trustee must be disclaimed, as was shown in *Re Lord and Fullerton's Contract*.[9]

The facts concerned a trust declared in the will of Samuel Lord. He appointed various people to be his trustees, including his son, Samuel Lord the younger. The trust property consisted of real and personal property both within the United States of America and outside it. Samuel Lord the younger purported to disclaim all of the property located outside of the United States. When land was sold in England by the remaining trustees, the buyer brought an action claiming that good title to the property had not been proven to him. His case was that Samuel Lord the younger could not disclaim part only of the trust – that he was either a trustee of the entire trust or he was not a trustee at all.

The Court of Appeal agreed with the buyer. Lindley LJ explained his reasoning as follows:

> A testator intends when he makes such a will as this that his . . . trust shall have
> the joint judgment of all the trustees . . . and I do not think that it is competent for

---

9   *Re Lord and Fullerton's Contract* [1896] 1 Ch 228.

> any trustee to say, 'I will attend to some of the trusts, and I will not attend to others'. It is competent for him to say that he will have nothing to do with the trusts; otherwise a testator would be able to saddle people with duties of an onerous description without their having any opportunity to get rid of them. But it is not competent for him to accept the office as to some part of the estate and not accept it as to the rest.[10]

If a trustee wishes only to administer selected parts of the trust, his wish to do so should be discussed with the settlor when the trust is created. If he wishes to have that individual as a trustee for part only of his property, the settlor would have to create more than one trust of his various property, or have more than one set of trustees to administer the property.

The reason behind this inability to disclaim part only of a trust appears to be certainty in favour of any buyer of trust property. The buyer must be confident that he is dealing with the right trustees. It would not be fair for a buyer to have to enquire of each trustee whether or not he had disclaimed the particular trust property that is being sold. It is far simpler if those who appear to be the trustees actually are the trustees. The trustee does not have to accept his office when the trust is created and may disclaim it even after the trust has been created, provided he has not effectively ratified his own office by undertaking any act which is consistent with being a trustee.

Death of the trustee

When a trustee dies, the surviving trustees assume his responsibilities and continue to be the trustees of the trust. Section 36(1) of the Trustee Act 1925 contains a power for either a person so nominated in the trust or the surviving trustees to appoint a new trustee in their place. Such appointment must be in writing.

If the trustee is the last one of the original trustees to die, his personal representatives will become the new trustees of the trust under ss 1–3 of the Administration of Estates Act 1925 until they appoint a new trustee under s 36(1) of the Trustee Act 1925.

By the trustee's retirement or removal

A trustee may decide to retire from the trust or be removed from it. The distinction is conceptual: retirement suggests that the trustee has voluntarily stepped down from their office, whilst removal implies he was obliged to leave his position.

Retirement

There are five main ways in which a trustee can retire:

(a)   under an express provision in the trust deed;
(b)   under s 36 of the Trustee Act 1925;
(c)   under s 39 of the Trustee Act 1925;
(d)   by a court order; or
(e)   under s 19 of the Trusts of Land and Appointment of Trustees Act 1996.

(a) Under an express provision in the trust deed

It is always possible for a trust deed to contain an express clause permitting a trustee to retire. A trustee may, for example, be given the right to retire when he feels like it, providing a suitable replacement can be found. In such a situation, the retiring trustee simply needs to comply with the provisions of the relevant clause.

---

10 Ibid at 232.

(b) Under s 36 of the Trustee Act 1925

A trustee may retire under s 36 if he 'desires to be discharged from all or any of the trusts or powers reposed in or conferred on him'. In this case, the retiring trustee can be replaced by someone chosen either by a person nominated in the trust deed to choose a replacement trustee or (if there is no such power) by the remaining trustees.

(c) Under s 39 of the Trustee Act 1925

Whilst s 36 of the Trustee Act 1925 provides that a retiring trustee should be replaced, s 39 sets out a provision enabling a trustee to retire and not be replaced. This provision can be exercised providing there are at least two individual trustees or a trust corporation who remain to administer the trust. Under s 39, the trustee must retire by deed.

(d) By a court order

The court has an inherent jurisdiction to sanction the retirement of any trustee.

(e) Under s 19 of the Trusts of Land and Appointment of Trustees Act 1996

This little-used provision means that beneficiaries of full age, mental capacity and together absolutely entitled to the trust property can effectively force a trustee to retire and be replaced with someone of their own choosing. This is rarely used because beneficiaries who find themselves in this position usually prefer to bring the trust to an end under the rule in *Saunders v Vautier*[11] so that they can enjoy their property themselves, free from the restrictions of the trust.

Removal

There are five ways in which a trustee can be removed from office:

(a)   by express provision in the trust deed;
(b)   under s 36 of the Trustee Act 1925;
(c)   under s 41 of the Trustee Act 1925; or
(d)   under the court's inherent jurisdiction.

(a) By express provision in the trust deed

Again, an express clause in the trust deed setting out circumstances in which a trustee must step down from his office is permitted. This may occur if, for example, the trustee breaches a fiduciary duty.

(b) Under s 36 of the Trustee Act 1925

Section 36 sets out when a trustee can be removed from office without obtaining their consent. Such instances include when the trustee is located outside of the UK for more than 12 months, or he refuses to act as a trustee, or is unfit or incapable of acting as a trustee. A child appointed as a trustee can also be removed under this section, although children can only be trustees of implied trusts in any event.[12]

(c) Under s 41 of the Trustee Act 1925

The power of the court under s 41 to appoint a new trustee is a power to appoint 'either in substitution for or in addition to' the existing trustees. The section, therefore, allows the court to remove a trustee from office, if it decides to appoint a new trustee in their place.

---

11 *Saunders v Vautier* (1841) 4 Beav 115; 49 ER 282. See Chapter 10 (pp 265–266) for a full discussion.
12 See Chapter 4 at p 92 for a full discussion.

(d) Under the court's inherent jurisdiction

Again, the court enjoys an inherent jurisdiction to force a trustee out of office. Guidance on this ability was offered by the Privy Council in *Letterstedt v Broers*.[13]

The case concerned the will of Jacob Letterstedt who owned a successful brewing business in South Africa. He declared a trust in his will, in which he left the business to his daughter. Until she reached 25 years old, the trust of the business was to be administered by a board of trustees and the business itself by a manager. The daughter was to be entitled to two-thirds of the profits of the business until she reached 25. She brought an action as she believed the board of trustees had taken too much money for themselves. She claimed just over £28,500. Importantly, she also wanted the board of trustees replaced by new trustees as she had lost confidence in the current trustees. The issue for the Privy Council was in what circumstances the court should exercise its inherent jurisdiction to replace trustees and whether the trustees of this particular trust should be replaced.

In delivering the opinion of the Privy Council, Lord Blackburn thought that the jurisdiction of a court to replace trustees was part of its overall jurisdiction to ensure that trusts are properly executed by the trustees. He found it impossible to lay down definitive guidelines as to when the court should order the removal of trustees, other than the court's 'main guide must be the welfare of the beneficiaries'.[14]

The court had to consider whether it was in the best interests of the beneficiaries to order the removal of the trustees. On the facts of the case, it was. The beneficiary had not proved that the trustees had acted fraudulently towards her by taking such sums from her entitlement and failing to ensure that the accounts of the trust were independently checked. Nonetheless, the relationship of trust and confidence which had to exist between a trustee and a beneficiary had broken down, so it was in her interests that the trustees be removed from office.

The trustees were wholly innocent in this case as allegations against them by the beneficiary had not been proven. That was not thought to matter. It was the claimant's welfare that was the key issue; if her welfare would be improved by the trustees being replaced, then the court would order their removal and replacement.

The issue arose again in *Re Wrightson*.[15] The trustees of a trust had, according to the beneficiaries, effectively invested the trust fund in an investment which was not authorised according to the terms of the trust. The beneficiaries brought an action seeking a declaration from the court that the investment was a breach of trust and wanting relief from it. This was duly granted. In a later action, some of the beneficiaries also sought the trustees' removal from their office.

After quoting from Lord Blackburn's test of whether the removal of the trustees would be for the 'welfare of the beneficiaries' in *Letterstedt v Broers*, Warrington J summed up the position when the court could order the trustees' removal as:

> You must find something which induces the Court to think either that the trust property will not be safe, or that the trust will not be properly executed in the interests of the beneficiaries.[16]

On the facts, the life tenant had died, thus leaving solely beneficiaries in remainder, whose interests had vested in them. All that remained was for the trust to be wound up and the legal title in the property transferred to the remainder beneficiaries. Taking this into account and

---

13 *Letterstedt v Broers* (1883–84) LR 9 App Cas 371.
14 Ibid at 387.
15 *Re Wrightson* [1908] 1 Ch 789.
16 Ibid at 803.

also the time and money involved in replacing trustees, Warrington J held that it was not in the beneficiaries' welfare that the trustees be replaced. Even though the trustees in the case were clearly guilty of a breach of trust, they were not replaced, as the welfare of the beneficiaries was the overriding concern that could trump every other issue.

❖ **ANALYSING THE LAW**

Do you think the decisions in *Letterstedt v Broers* and *Re Wrightson* are compatible? In the former, the trustees were replaced, although there was no objective reason for doing so. The beneficiary had merely lost confidence in them. In the latter, the trustees had breached the trust, but pragmatic reasons appeared to justify their retaining office. Do you think there is any guiding principle behind these decisions or are both just examples of pure pragmatism by the courts?

Having seen how trustees are appointed and how they can leave their office, their obligations whilst in office must now be considered.

Managing the Trust

Once appointed, the trustees' main obligation is to manage the trust fund for the benefit of the beneficiaries. The trustees will have been carefully chosen by the settlor to fulfil their role. Administering the trust is their responsibility.

Whilst administering the trust, the trustees have a number of duties. These can be split into two types: fiduciary and non-fiduciary.

The nature of the relationship between the trustee and beneficiary is fiduciary. 'Fiduciary' was defined by Millett LJ in *Bristol & West Building Society v Mothew*[17] as follows:

A fiduciary is someone who has undertaken to act for or on behalf of another in a particular matter in circumstances which give rise to a relationship of trust and confidence. The distinguishing obligation of a fiduciary is loyalty.[18]

❖ **APPLYING THE LAW**

Look again at Millett LJ's definition of fiduciary. Consider where you may have come across other types of relationship that might be classed as 'fiduciary' in nature either in studying your other legal subjects or perhaps everyday life. One example would be the relationship between a doctor and their patient. The doctor has undertaken effectively to act on their patient's behalf and owes the patient trust and confidence in that relationship.

Would you describe your relationship with your lecturers as 'fiduciary'?

---

17 *Bristol & West Building Society v Mothew* [1998] Ch 1.
18 Ibid at 18.

Fiduciary duties flow from the duty of loyalty that the trustee owes to the beneficiaries. The fiduciary duties the trustee must undertake were set out by Millett LJ that the trustee must:

(a)   act in good faith;
(b)   not make a profit from the trust;
(c)   not put himself into a position where his duty to the trust and his own interest may conflict; and
(d)   not act for his personal benefit or for the benefit of a third party without the consent of the beneficiaries.

He then made clear that, '[t]his is not intended to be an exhaustive list, but it is sufficient to indicate the nature of fiduciary obligations. They are the defining characteristics of the fiduciary'.[19]

Millett LJ quoted[20] with approval the comments of Ipp J in the Australian case of *Permanent Building Society v Wheeler*[21] to illustrate that not every duty that a fiduciary found themselves subject to was a fiduciary duty:

> It is essential to bear in mind that the existence of a fiduciary relationship does not mean that every duty owed by a fiduciary to the beneficiary is a fiduciary one. In particular, a trustee's duty to exercise reasonable care, though equitable, is not specifically a fiduciary duty.

There are other non-fiduciary duties that a trustee must also fulfil. The trustee must:

(a)   undertake various obligations upon appointment;
(b)   act unanimously and personally;
(c)   account to the beneficiaries with relevant information about the trust; and
(d)   distribute the trust fund.

In addition, a trustee enjoys several powers during the operation of the trust. These include:

(a)   a power to invest the trust property;
(b)   a power to maintain the beneficiaries; and
(c)   a power to advance capital to the beneficiaries.

A trustee's fiduciary duties are considered in this chapter. Non-fiduciary duties and powers are considered in Chapter 9.

The difference between fiduciary duties, non-fiduciary duties and powers

The difference between a trustee's fiduciary duties, non-fiduciary duties and powers can be summarised in Figure 8.4.

The reason that it matters why each particular duty that a trustee finds himself subject to is fiduciary or not is related to the remedies used against the trustee if he breaches a duty. If the duty is fiduciary in nature, such as the duty not to profit for himself from the trust, the remedy for its breach has its origins peculiarly in equity. The trustee will hold any gain he

---

19 Ibid.
20 Ibid at 17.
21 *Permanent Building Society v Wheeler* (1994) 14 ACSR 109 at 157.

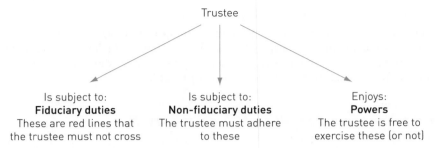

Figure 8.4 Fiduciary duties, non-fiduciary duties and powers.

makes personally on constructive trust for the beneficiaries of the main trust. If, on the other hand, the trustee breaches a non-fiduciary duty, the remedy available against him is monetary, which although called 'equitable compensation' is akin to damages at common law. Trustees cannot generally be held liable for failing to exercise a power, as they have discretion over whether to exercise them or not. Failing to consider whether to exercise a power would, however, be *prima facie* breach of the fiduciary obligation to act in good faith.

❖ **EXPLAINING THE LAW**

Scott has set up a trust, appointing Thomas as his trustee with a life interest for Ulrika and remainder to Vikas.

Suppose Thomas commits two breaches of trust. The first breach is the breach of a fiduciary duty that a trustee must not make a personal profit from the trust. Suppose Thomas makes £10,000 for himself from the trust. Thomas' second breach is that he negligently (but not deliberately) invests the trust funds in investments that Scott had forbidden in the trust deed and the trust fund has suffered loss as a result.

As the first breach is a fiduciary one, the remedy for the beneficiaries is that Thomas should hold the profit he has made as a constructive trustee for the trust. This purely equitable device of an implied trust is used for breach of a fiduciary duty to ensure that Thomas must give the profit to the trust.

The second breach is not a fiduciary one, as Thomas has simply made a mistake. He has misused a power that he enjoys, as opposed to breaching a fiduciary duty. He will be bound to pay equitable compensation to the trust fund, so that the fund recoups the loss. Whilst equitable compensation is still part of equity, it is very similar in nature to common law damages. Effectively, Thomas will be liable for damages to the trust fund for the cost of his error.

The Trustee's Fiduciary Duties

The key to understanding a trustee's fiduciary duties is to remember that a fiduciary's core obligation is one of loyalty towards his principal. This loyalty must not be eroded by the fiduciary or called into question by any acts undertaken by him.

A trustee must act in good faith

This duty flows from the central theme underpinning trusteeship – the trustee must act honestly and with the utmost loyalty to the beneficiaries. Indeed, Millett LJ regarded this duty as so important to the office of trustee in *Armitage v Nurse*,[22] that he did not believe that a trust would be properly established if this duty was not part of it.

A trustee must not make a profit from the trust

This fiduciary duty has two parts:

(a)   that a trustee has no right in equity to charge the beneficiaries for administering the trust; and

(b)   that a trustee must not purchase trust property for his own benefit.

A trustee has no right to charge for administering the trust

This principle comes from *Williams v Barton*.[23] The defendant was a stockbroker, employed by a firm called George Burnand & Co. Part of his salary was made up of one-half of any commission which the firm earned as a result of new business introduced to it by the defendant. The defendant was appointed a trustee of the will of Sir John Roper Parkington. He recommended his employer as the firm which should carry out a valuation of the shares owned by Sir John at the date of his death. The firm duly carried out a valuation of the shareholding and charged the estate of Sir John a fee for doing so. Half of this fee was then paid to the defendant.

The defendant's co-trustee claimed the fee for the estate. His argument was that the defendant, as a trustee, was not allowed to make a profit from the trust and had done so, in breach of this fiduciary duty. As such, he held the profit for the trust.

Russell J agreed that the defendant was not allowed to keep the remuneration he had earned. He said, '[a] person who has the management of property as a trustee is not permitted to gain any profit by availing himself of his position. . . .'[24]

The defendant had done just that. He had recommended the firm for which he worked to carry out the valuation of Sir John's shareholding because he would gain a fee through his contract of employment with the firm. The underlying principle here was that the defendant had allowed his duty of loyalty to the trust to conflict with his own personal interests. Such a conflict could not be allowed.

As this was a breach of a fiduciary duty, the defendant retained the money he had earned in breach of his obligations as a constructive trustee for the trust.

Russell J also laid down a principle that a trustee 'has no right to charge for his time and trouble'.[25] This was part of the more general notion that for a trustee to do so would result in the trustee making a profit from the trust.

This *dictum* was a product of its time when trusts were predominantly used by wealthy families to manage their own wealth. Trustees would be chosen who would often have some familial connection to the settlor. They would be volunteers, usually well-meaning amateurs who had no professional skill in managing a trust. They were seen to be acting as trustees, perhaps almost as a gesture of goodwill for the settlor, and should not be rewarded for doing so.

---

22   *Armitage v Nurse* [1998] Ch 241.
23   *Williams v Barton* [1927] 2 Ch 9.
24   Ibid at 11.
25   Ibid.

As trusts evolved in the twentieth century into being used for different purposes (for example, pensions) and as the number of investment opportunities increased significantly, settlors wanted to appoint professional trustees, who would bring their specialist skills to manage the trust. Professional trustees, such as banks, would wish to be paid for their services. As a consequence, trust deeds started to contain express charging clauses in them, enabling a trustee to charge for their services.

Section 29 of the Trustee Act 2000 specifically permits professional trustees of non-charitable trusts to receive a 'reasonable remuneration' for the services that they provide to the trust.[26]

Section 29(1) provides that a trust corporation is entitled to receive a reasonable remuneration for services it provides to a non-charitable trust. Section 29(2) provides the same for an individual professional trustee as long as they are not a sole trustee and have obtained the written consent of all other trustees that they may receive such remuneration.

Despite the enacting of s 29, the vast majority of trust deeds appointing professional trustees continue to contain an express remuneration clause. This is because s 29 talks about professional trustees receiving 'reasonable' remuneration. Professional trustees have no desire to have a later dispute with the beneficiaries over whether their charges are 'reasonable' or not so do not wish to rely on the statutory permit to charge their fees but instead to an express contractual provision.

Trustees have, however, always been able to claim for any expenses they incur in managing the trust. Being reimbursed for expenses is not an example of the trustees making a profit from the trust. This right is retained in s 31 of the Trustee Act 2000 provided the expenses have been 'properly' incurred by the trustee in administering the trust.

A trustee must not purchase trust property for his own benefit

This fiduciary duty is sometimes known as the 'self-dealing' rule. Megarry V-C described the rule in *Tito v Waddell* (No. 2)[27] as follows:

> The self-dealing rule is (to put it very shortly) that if a trustee sells the trust property to himself, the sale is voidable by any beneficiary *ex debito justitiae* [as a debt of justice, i.e. as of right] however fair the transaction.[28]

The reason for the rule was first mentioned by Lord Eldon LC in *ex parte Lacey*[29] where he stated:

> A trustee, who is entrusted to sell and manage for others, undertakes in the same moment, in which he becomes a trustee, not to manage for the benefit and advantage of himself.[30]

Again, the notion of the duty is to prevent a trustee being placed in the position whereby his duty to the trust and his own interests could be put into conflict. It is to prevent the trustee's obligation of loyalty to the beneficiaries from being eroded. For example, if the trustee was able to buy trust property from the trust, he may pay a lower price than the property is actually worth, to save his own money. Exceptions exist whereby the trustee may sell trust property to

---

26 Trustee Act 2000, s 29(1), (2).
27 *Tito v Waddell* (No. 2) [1977] Ch 106.
28 Ibid at 241.
29 *Ex parte Lacey* (1802) 6 Ves 625.
30 Ibid at 626.

himself (i) if the trust deed expressly authorises it, (ii) if a court order permits it, or (iii) if all of the beneficiaries, being of full age and of mental capacity, consent to it.

A modern example of the rule against self-dealing occurred in *Kane v Radley-Kane*,[31] albeit concerning a personal representative. James Radley-Kane died intestate. Under s 46 of the Administration of Estates Act 1925, his widow, Jeanette, was entitled to a statutory legacy of £125,000 together with a life interest in half of the deceased's residuary estate. James died leaving shares which, for the purposes of the administration of the estate, had been valued at £50,000. His entire net estate was worth £93,000. Jeanette, therefore, took the whole estate, including the shares, in satisfaction of her entitlement to the £125,000. Less than three years later, she sold the shares for over £1.1 million. One of her stepsons, who would have been entitled to a share in his father's estate had the estate exceeded the sum of £125,000, brought an action that his stepmother's appropriation of the shares was invalid. Effectively, she had bought the shares from the estate herself and then sold them at a vast profit.

Sir Richard Scott V-C found that Jeanette's duty as personal representative to her late husband's estate to administer the estate and her interest to herself conflicted when she took the shares as her own property. Her duty as personal representative meant she had to obtain as much money as possible for the shares as she could for the benefit of the estate. Her own interest in purchasing the shares meant she wished to pay as little as possible for them. She effectively paid only £50,000. She had not obtained the beneficiaries' or the court's consent for the transaction. The self-dealing rule could apply to personal representatives just as much as trustees. The sale proceeds of the shares that Jeanette obtained were still to be treated as part of the assets of the estate. Jeanette had to account to the estate for the proceeds of £1.1 million. She was, however, entitled to her full statutory legacy of £125,000 as the assets of the estate were now more than sufficient to pay this sum to her.

The courts have, however, been known not to apply the self-dealing rule if the circumstances of the case mean that it can be logically disapplied. The facts of *Holder v Holder*[32] provide an example. Frank Holder left farmland in his will, which provided that it should be held on trust equally for his widow, his eight daughters and two sons. Victor, the younger son, enjoyed tenancies granted by Frank of two of the farms. He was appointed an executor along with one of his sisters and Frank's widow. After Frank's death, all of the executors opened a bank account at Lloyds Bank and drew cheques on it in order to meet various debts of the estate.

Victor decided that he wanted to purchase the two farms of which he was a tenant. He therefore renounced his executorship and probate was granted to his mother and sister only. The farms were then auctioned, with Victor successfully bidding. He was not able to arrange mortgages in time to complete the purchases as required by the auction, but eventually purchased them a year later.

Victor's older brother, Frank William Holder, objected to Victor buying the farms. He claimed that Victor had infringed the self-dealing rule. As a personal representative of his father's estate, he said that Victor was a fiduciary. He said that Victor's renunciation of his executorship had occurred too late, after he had already taken steps in connection with the administration of the estate by opening the bank account and signing the cheques.

In delivering the leading judgment of the Court of Appeal, Harman LJ thought that all Victor had done was sign a small number of cheques. He had not otherwise taken any steps to administer his father's estate. He then said that where 'the reasons behind the rule [as to self-dealing] do not exist I do not feel bound to apply it'.[33] There was no conflict of duty and

31 *Kane v Radley-Kane* [1999] Ch 274.
32 *Holder v Holder* [1968] Ch 353.
33 Ibid at 392.

interest here. Victor never acted to protect the beneficiaries' interests under the estate; the entire family was well aware that he wished to purchase the farms for his own benefit. In addition, Frank William Holder had attended the auction and had not raised any objection to the sale of the farms to Victor, so had effectively given his permission (through his acquiescence) to the transaction.

Danckwerts LJ went further than Harman LJ, describing the rule against self-dealing as simply 'no more than a practice that the court should not allow a trustee to bid'.[34] This seems to be going too far. Whilst the consent of the court can always be obtained to a trustee's self-purchase of trust property, the rule appears to have a more solid foundation than simply being one of practice of the courts.

The rule against self-dealing is based on not tempting the trustee to profit from the trust. A trustee's duty to the trust and his own interest must not be allowed to conflict in any small possibility. It is impossible for a trustee to deal fairly with both the trust and for his own interests. The trust must be given priority. *Holder v Holder* may well be a decision on its own facts: essentially, the claimant sought to reverse a transaction to which he had earlier agreed, through attendance at the auction. If the rule is breached, the transaction may be set aside by a beneficiary, providing it is still possible for the parties to be returned to their original positions.

The trustee must not put himself into a position where his duty to the trust and his own interest may conflict

This fiduciary duty was described by Viscount Sankey in *Regal (Hastings) Ltd v Gulliver*:[35]

> The general rule of equity is that no one who has duties of a fiduciary nature to perform is allowed to enter into engagements in which he has or *can have* a personal interest conflicting with the interests of those whom he is bound to protect.

Viscount Sankey's description of this fiduciary duty makes it plain that equity is not simply regulating the clash of a fiduciary's *actual* personal interests with his fiduciary duty. Equity also protects the principal against the *possibility* of a conflict of interests that the fiduciary may have.

Equity has traditionally taken a hard line against any fiduciary – not just trustees – who places himself in a position where his duty to his principal and his own self-interest may have come into conflict with each other. The fiduciary has not been allowed to keep or enjoy any advantage he may have obtained by reason of this conflict of interest. To regulate the fiduciary, equity imposes a constructive trust upon them in relation to the gain he has acquired. This can be shown in the following example.

❖ EXPLAINING THE LAW

Scott sets up a trust, appointing Thomas as his trustee with Ulrika and Vikas as the beneficiaries. The trust property is £100,000.

Thomas decides to invest the money in TrustsBooks plc, a company he became aware of whilst investigating potentially suitable investments for the trust. TrustsBooks plc has a

---

34 Ibid at 398.
35 *Regal (Hastings) Ltd v Gulliver* [1967] 2 AC 134 at 137 (emphasis added).

rule that any one individual or organisation can only buy a maximum of £50,000 of its shares. Thomas invests £50,000 of the trust money. Seeing that the shares of TrustsBooks plc are rising, Thomas also decides to invest £50,000 of his own money in the company.

Prima facie, the trust would be entitled to recover any profit that Thomas makes on his own personal investment. At first glance, this appears odd. The trust could not have invested any more than £50,000 of its own money in the company. Yet it is allowed to recover the profit that Thomas makes on his personal investment. Equity will impose a constructive trust over the profit that Thomas has made personally in favour of the trust and its beneficiaries.

The reason equity treats the trustee harshly is to act as a deterrent to ensure that a trustee's duty to the trust and his own self-interest cannot come into conflict with each other. Equity seeks to put the risk of this happening beyond the trustee's reach. After all, Thomas only came to invest his own money due to the knowledge that he had gained about TrustsBooks plc in his capacity as trustee.

This fiduciary duty first appeared in *Keech v Sandford*.[36] The facts concerned a lease of a market, which was due to be renewed. The lease was held on trust and the beneficiary was a child. The trustee asked for the lease to be renewed but the landlord refused, on the basis that a child could not be liable for non-payment of rent. The landlord did not wish to take the risk that the child may not pay the rent and the landlord would not have any remedy against him. The trustee entered into a lease for his personal benefit.

The Lord Chancellor held that the trustee had to assign the benefit of the lease to the beneficiary. The trustee could not benefit personally: he owed absolute loyalty to the beneficiary. In words which have subsequently become well-known, the Lord Chancellor said:

> This may seem hard, that the trustee is the only person of all mankind who might not have the lease: but it is very proper that rule should be strictly pursued, and not in the least relaxed. . . .[37]

The reasoning in the decision in the case shows that the court was concerned to make an example of this trustee to warn other trustees who might find themselves in a similar position. Other trustees might be tempted to seek out personal gain for themselves in future cases by requesting leases to be renewed in their favour rather than for their beneficiaries. Equity had to remove the temptation from a trustee not to act in the trust's best interests. A constructive trust was imposed over the trustee of the profits that the trustee had made from the market since the lease was renewed in his favour.

The rationale underpinning this fiduciary duty was restated by Lord Herschell in *Bray v Ford*:[38]

> human nature being what it is, there is a danger . . . of the person holding a fiduciary position being swayed by interest rather than by duty, and thus prejudicing those whom he was bound to protect.[39]

---

36 *Keech v Sandford* (1726) 2 Eq Cas Abr 741; 25 ER 223.
37 Ibid.
38 *Bray v Ford* [1896] AC 44.
39 Ibid at 51.

Lord Herschell explained that this fiduciary duty was rigid in its application:

> It is an inflexible rule of a Court of Equity that a person in a fiduciary position . . . is not, unless otherwise expressly provided, entitled to make a profit; he is not allowed to put himself in a position where his interest and duty conflict.[40]

The strictness of the application of the rule means that it does not matter if the fiduciary is behaving entirely innocently. Behaving dishonestly is not a requirement for the fiduciary to infringe this duty, as *Regal (Hastings) Ltd v Gulliver*[41] illustrates.

The facts concerned a subsidiary company which was established to take the leases of two cinemas. The claimant company acquired some of its subsidiary's shares, but so too did the claimant's directors. When the claimant company was sold, its new owners brought an action for the profit that the former directors had made on the sale of the shares in the subsidiary company.

The House of Lords held that the former directors had to account to the claimant for the profit they had made. They were constructive trustees of that profit for the claimant. As original directors of the claimant, they had stood in a fiduciary position to that company. They were only able to buy the shares in the subsidiary company because they were former directors of the claimant. Only in this position did they gain the knowledge that the shares in the subsidiary company were available to purchase. As a consequence, they were liable to account to the claimant for the profit element they had made on the shares.

Over the years, the courts have managed to find a method of rewarding the fiduciary where the beneficiary has made a profit which he would otherwise not have made but for the fiduciary's efforts. Whilst the fiduciary has still had to account to the beneficiary for the personal profit made, the courts have allowed the fiduciary a claim in restitution for a *quantum meruit* (a reasonable sum) for the work undertaken by the fiduciary. Such a policy of the courts arguably goes some way to redressing the balance of the position where a fiduciary may have expended considerable time and effort in administering the trust, but has also made an incidental personal profit. The concept of a fiduciary being awarded a *quantum meruit* was first allowed by the House of Lords in *Boardman v Phipps*.[42]

The case concerned a solicitor to a trust. The trust had a minority shareholding in a textile business that had two factories. The solicitor, Mr Boardman, believed that the business was not being operated as profitably as it might be. He, along with Tom Phipps (one of the beneficiaries of the trust) tried to cajole the company into trading more profitably. The company generally resisted these attempts. Eventually, Mr Boardman and Tom Phipps agreed to buy a controlling interest in the company from the current shareholders, but they did so in their own personal capacities, not in the name of the trust. The trust would have needed the rather cumbersome approval of the court before it could buy additional shares in the company. This would have taken additional time.

Mr Boardman and Tom Phipps proceeded to reorganise the company. One of the factories was sold. The sale generated substantial income for the business. Mr Boardman and Tom Phipps distributed some of this money to each shareholder. This included the trust, but they also paid themselves, as they had bought the additional shares.

At that point, Tom Phipps tried to purchase the shares from one of the other beneficiaries of the trust, John Phipps. John took legal advice and soon afterwards issued a claim against both Mr Boardman and Tom. John's case was that Mr Boardman and Tom Phipps were agents

---

40 Ibid.
41 *Regal (Hastings) Ltd v Gulliver* [1967] 2 AC 134.
42 *Boardman v Phipps* [1967] 2 AC 46.

for the trustees at all times and that they were in a fiduciary position vis-à-vis the trust. He said that they should be seen to be constructive trustees of their share of the profits for the beneficiaries of the trust since it was only in their position that they were able to invest in the company personally. In short, his argument was that they had placed themselves in a position where their duty to the trust and their self-interest had come into conflict. The only remedy for that was for them to account to the trust for the profits they had made and to hand over their personal shares to the trust.

By a bare majority, the House of Lords agreed with John Phipps' argument. In the majority, Lord Cohen placed great weight on the fact that Mr Boardman and Tom Phipps were only able to invest in the company due to their being agents for the trustees of the trust. Mr Boardman obtained information as to how well the company was trading by virtue of his being the solicitor to the trust. It was this unique position in which Mr Boardman found himself that presented him with the ability to look into the company in greater depth and eventually purchase the additional controlling shares.

Mr Boardman's duty to the trust was to purchase the shares in the name of the trust. His self-interest meant that he had purchased them in his own name. Due to this possible conflict between duty and self-interest, Mr Boardman was liable to account for the profits he made in his personal capacity. The honesty and integrity of Mr Boardman and Tom Phipps were not doubted, but were irrelevant.

Mr Boardman and Tom Phipps were, however, allowed to claim for the work they had undertaken in transforming the company for the benefit of the trust. Indeed, payment was due to them both on a 'liberal scale'.[43]

Their Lordships were willing to attach criteria to their remarks as to when constructive trusteeship would be imposed on fiduciaries.

Lord Cohen, echoing the trial judge, Wilberforce J, stated that it was not simply knowledge that came to the attention of the fiduciary which made him liable to account for profits. For constructive trusteeship to be imposed on the fiduciary, the fiduciary had to have acquired the knowledge due to the fiduciary relationship. The information surrounding the company's performance and the opportunity to buy the shares only arose because Mr Boardman and Tom Phipps were agents for the trustees. They could only have accessed such information by virtue of their position.

Two of their Lordships dissented. Lord Upjohn favoured a more pragmatic approach, asking whether there had been a 'real sensible possibility of conflict'[44] between a fiduciary's duty and his self-interest. He further said[45] that a trustee could use information acquired by him as a trustee, provided that such information did not 'injure' the trust.

Lord Upjohn took a pragmatic view of the facts. The trust was not able to purchase further shares itself in the company, so there could be no conflict between the fiduciaries' duty to the trust and their interests to themselves. Mr Boardman and Tom Phipps were entirely free to purchase the shares in the company in their own capacities.

❖ ANALYSING THE LAW

Both the majority and minority in *Boardman v Phipps* thought that a strict liability approach was the correct way to determine a trustee's liability. Where they differed was where the

---

43 *Boardman v Phipps* per Lord Cohen at [1967] 2 AC 46 at 104, quoting trial judge Wilberforce J with approval.
44 Ibid at 124.
45 Ibid at 129.

threshold was to be set for a conflict of interest actually occurring. The majority thought that a trustee should be liable for a mere possibility of a conflict; the minority believed that there had to be a real sensible possibility of a conflict. Which do you believe to be the correct approach?

The decision in *Boardman v Phipps* shows that the fiduciary's duty to the trust and his self-interest must not conflict. But it also shows that, whilst preserving this fiduciary duty, the House of Lords was willing to allow an exception to it to develop. Fiduciaries who made a profit for themselves, not at the trust's expense, but in addition to any profit the trust may have made, were to be allowed to be rewarded by a *quantum meruit* for the work they had undertaken.

The idea of a fiduciary being awarded a *quantum meruit* for work undertaken was allowed in *O'Sullivan v Management Agency and Music Ltd*.[46] The facts concerned a dispute between a professional singer and his management company. Gilbert O'Sullivan was a young singer and composer. He approached the defendant, a company managing well-known artistes and, in 1970, the two parties entered into a series of contracts with each other, under which the defendant would manage Gilbert and produce and arrange for his records to be published. Gilbert was never advised to take independent legal advice before signing the contracts. The contracts entered into between Gilbert and MAM Ltd were biased heavily in favour of MAM Ltd in terms of which party would benefit from them most financially. In 1975, the parties had a series of disagreements, concerning the artistic direction of the records being produced. During this time, Gilbert had attained significant success in both the UK and the USA.

Following their disagreements, Gilbert brought an action claiming that he only entered into the contracts as a result of the defendant's undue influence and that the contracts should be set aside. He wanted the copyright in his recordings returned to him, together with the profit element that the defendants had made as a result of these unfair contracts.

The Court of Appeal held that the defendant was in a fiduciary relationship with Gilbert. The evidence pointed strongly to that conclusion: all of Gilbert's affairs were run by the defendant, they had taken it upon themselves to look after Gilbert and crucially, the defendant knew that their client was young and naive in the world of business and was happy for them to manage him and believed they would treat him fairly.

The biased agreements in favour of the defendant would be set aside as being voidable due to undue influence on Gilbert when he entered into them. He was entitled to have the copyright in, and the master tapes of, his recordings returned to him. But the defendant was allowed a *quantum meruit* for the work undertaken in establishing and promoting Gilbert. The court recognised that before the parties met, Gilbert had had no success as an artiste and had similarly had no success after they had parted company. His success was due to the defendant. Not only was the defendant entitled to a reasonable sum for the work undertaken, it was also entitled to a profit as the justice of the case demanded it.

There was, of course, a distinction between the *quantum meruit* awarded in *Boardman v Phipps* and that awarded in this case. In *Boardman v Phipps*, it was accepted that the fiduciaries were morally blameless for the course of action that they had undertaken. Conversely, in *O'Sullivan v Management Agency and Music Ltd*, it was felt that the defendant was morally guilty of ensuring that Gilbert entered into such biased contracts. The Court of Appeal did not believe this mattered in awarding a *quantum meruit*. The whole situation had to be taken into account as opposed to

---

46 *O'Sullivan v Management Agency and Music Ltd* [1985] QB 428.

moral blameworthiness. That situation showed that the defendant was instrumental in generating Gilbert's success and should be entitled to appropriate recompense.

This fiduciary duty has recently been discussed in *Imageview Management Ltd v Jack*,[47] a case which concerned an individual and his agent.

Making connections

Imageview Management Ltd v Jack concerned a principal and his agent. The relationship between these two characters is fiduciary in nature. The law of agency essentially provides that the principal instructs the agent to make a contract between him (the principal) and a third party. So the agent is not actually a party to the contract. An everyday example is where a person sells his house. Typically, he will instruct an estate agent to find a buyer and negotiate the sale. But the actual contract to sell the house is, of course, made between the seller and the eventual buyer. The agent is not party to that contract.

Kelvin Jack was a footballer who was Trinidad and Tobago's international goalkeeper. He engaged the claimant to negotiate a contract for him to play for Dundee United. The agreement between Kelvin and the claimant was that Kelvin would pay the claimant 10 per cent of his monthly salary provided that the claimant successfully negotiated a contract for him to play with a UK club. The claimant duly arranged a contract between Dundee United and Kelvin began to honour the fee due to the claimant.

As a non-EU national, Kelvin needed a work permit to play for Dundee United. Unbeknownst to him, the claimant agreed with Dundee United that it would arrange for a work permit for him, provided Dundee United paid the claimant £3,000. There was a large profit element for the claimant company in arranging the work permit: the trial judge found that the actual value of the work done by the claimant to obtain the work permit was £750.

Approximately one year after he began playing for Dundee United, Kelvin discovered the arrangement the claimant had entered into concerning the work permit. He stopped paying the claimant its fee. He claimed that he and the claimant were in a fiduciary relationship with each other and that by negotiating the secret arrangement to obtain the work permit, the fiduciary had caused its duty to Kelvin and his own personal interest to conflict.

In delivering the leading judgment of the Court of Appeal, Jacob LJ set out with considerable clarity what the fiduciary duty meant to an agent:

> An agent's own personal interests come entirely second to the interest of his client. If you undertake to act for a man you must act 100%, body and soul, for him. You must act as if you were him. You must not allow your own interest to get in the way without telling him. An undisclosed but realistic possibility of a conflict of interest is a breach of your duty of good faith to your client.[48]

The same words generally encapsulate the duty of a trustee towards their beneficiary, with the exception that the beneficiary could only consent to a trustee's disclosure of a conflict of duty and interest if the beneficiary was of full age and mentally capable of consenting.

The claimant had breached his duty to Kelvin with its own self-interest. The duty the claimant owed was to negotiate the best agreement it could for Kelvin to play professional

---

47 *Imageview Management Ltd v Jack* [2009] Bus LR 1034.
48 Ibid at 1037.

football in the UK. But its own interests meant that it was biased in favour of Dundee United as it was only this club that had agreed to pay £3,000 for it to obtain a work permit for Kelvin. When it had breached its fiduciary duty to Kelvin, he was entitled to stop paying the claimant its fee due under his agreement with it. He was also entitled to recover the fees he had already paid in their entirety. As Jacob LJ explained, the reason for this was punitive and was rooted in deterring the agent from breaching its fiduciary duty:

> The policy reason runs as follows. We are here concerned not with merely damages . . . but with what the remedy should be when the agent has betrayed the trust reposed in him – notions of equity and conscience are brought into play. Necessarily such a betrayal may not come to light. If all the agent has to pay if and when he is found out are damages the temptation to betray the trust reposed in him is all the greater.[49]

Jacob LJ rejected the claimant's argument that it was entitled to at least a reasonable sum for the work undertaken in obtaining Kelvin's work permit. He placed restrictions on the discretion that the court enjoys to award a *quantum meruit*. It was one to be exercised 'sparingly'.[50] If it was to be exercised at all, it should not be exercised in a case like this which was one of 'surreptitious dealing'[51] by the fiduciary.

The case has reinforced that fiduciaries will only be entitled to a *quantum meruit* where their duty to their principal and their own self-interest has come into conflict, but which has not damaged the principal's interests, such as in *Boardman v Phipps*. In *Imageview Management Ltd v Jack*, the fiduciary's decision to negotiate a contract with Dundee United was influenced by the side arrangement over the £3,000. This damaged Kelvin's interests as he did not obtain the benefit of his fiduciary negotiating what was necessarily the best contract available to him with any other football club. The fiduciary's view was tainted by its own interests in securing a 'bonus' of £3,000. The fiduciary, therefore, was not entitled to any reward in the form of a *quantum meruit* for obtaining the work permit.

Of course, the issue of whether a fiduciary's duty to his principal and his self-interest conflict, depends on the circumstances of each case. If there is no conflict on the facts, the fiduciary duty is not breached and no liability attaches to the fiduciary. Alternatively, if the beneficiary's consent to a conflict of duty and interest is freely given, the fiduciary will not be liable. Both of these principles can be illustrated by the decision in the Australian case of *Queensland Mines Ltd v Hudson*.[52]

Here, the managing director of the claimant company had two licences issued to him for mining exploration. He had obtained those licences due to the strength of the claimant company's resources and reputation. The company itself had no funds with which the licences could be implemented.

The managing director made a profit as a result of the licences being issued to him. The claimant company claimed against him for breach of fiduciary duty and for an account of the profits that he had made.

The Privy Council said that he was not liable to account for the profits made. He had made the profit due to his original position in the claimant company, but he had fully advised the company of his intention to make use of the licences. The company had consented to his use of them.

---

49 Ibid at 1048.
50 Ibid at 1050.
51 Ibid at 1049.
52 *Queensland Mines Ltd v Hudson* (1978) 18 ALR 1.

The effect of the decision of the Privy Council was to hold that there was no 'real sensible possibility'[53] of conflict between his duty to the company and his self-interest.

> ### ❖ ANALYSING THE LAW
>
> *Queensland Mines* does not necessarily fit easily with *Regal (Hastings) Ltd v Gulliver*. In the latter case, the House of Lords held that the only way the company could have consented was for its shareholders to approve the transaction in a general meeting. Yet in *Queensland Mines*, the mining company was able to consent not through undertaking this procedure but simply by the far less formal procedure of the Managing Director advising it of his intentions and the company not objecting.
>
> Read both cases. Do you think the decision in *Queensland Mines* is consistent with *Regal (Hastings) Ltd v Gulliver*?

Summary of this fiduciary duty

Decisions such as that reached in *Queensland Mines Ltd v Hudson* appear to be rare. In most cases, the fiduciary's duty to his principal and his self-interest will conflict, as he will usually have been given a personal opportunity due to being in a fiduciary relationship with his principal. Equity remains suspicious about fiduciaries benefiting from their principals. The fiduciary is in a potentially stronger position now than in *Keech v Sandford*. Whilst the fiduciary *prima facie* is liable to the principal for breach of this fiduciary duty, cases such as *Boardman v Phipps* illustrate that, provided the fiduciary has been open with the principal about his dealings, he will be able to claim a *quantum meruit* for work he had undertaken. Such an award can be 'liberal' and should be made on the basis of the 'justice' of the case, according to the Court of Appeal decision in *O'Sullivan v Management Agency and Music Ltd*. If the fiduciary has not, however, been open and transparent about his dealings, the risks for him are greater, as he will be held to be a constructive trustee for the personal profit he has made and, as *Imageview Management Ltd v Jack* shows, he will not be entitled to a reasonable sum for the work he has undertaken.

It may be that the courts are moving to adopting a softer line towards fiduciaries. In *Murad v Al-Suraj*,[54] both Arden and Jonathan Parker LJJ felt that the Supreme Court needed to re-examine this whole line of cases and suggested that in the future, this strict rule as to conflict of duty and self-interest might be relaxed, at least where the trustee had acted openly, in good faith and believing he was acting in the beneficiary's best interests. Of course, due to the doctrine of precedent, such a movement could only be made by the Supreme Court.

Not act for his personal benefit or for the benefit of a third party without the consent of the beneficiaries

This fiduciary duty is known as the 'fair-dealing' rule. It was set out by Megarry V-C in *Tito v Waddell (No. 2)*[55] as follows:

---

53 Per Lord Upjohn in *Boardman v Phipps* [1967] 2 AC 46.
54 *Murad v Al-Suraj* [2005] EWCA Civ 959.
55 *Tito v Waddell (No.2)* [1977] Ch 106.

The fair-dealing rule is (again putting it very shortly) that if a trustee purchases the beneficial interest of any of his beneficiaries, the transaction is not voidable *ex debito justitiae*, but can be set aside by the beneficiary unless the trustee can show that he has taken no advantage of his position and has made full disclosure to the beneficiary, and that the transaction is fair and honest.[56]

This is different from the self-dealing rule. The self-dealing rule guards against where the trustee is both selling and buying trust property. Such a contract can make no sense as effectively the same person is both seller and buyer.

The fair-dealing rule, on the other hand, guards against contracts where the trustee only buys the beneficiary's interest in the trust property. The beneficiary has, being of full age and mental capacity, consented to the transaction occurring. Best practice must be for the beneficiary to obtain independent legal advice before entering into the contract. Such a contract will be allowed to stand, providing the trustee has been open and honest with the beneficiary and can show that the contract is 'fair and honest' – for example, that the trustee is purchasing the interest for a fair sum, as opposed to a discounted sum because he is taking advantage of his position as trustee.

The rule exists, once again, to protect beneficiaries and to ensure that the trustee is showing absolute loyalty to the trust instead of himself. A trustee may be tempted to offer less than the beneficiary's interest in the trust property is worth. The trustee may know the true value, but seek to 'undercut' this whilst the beneficiary is entirely ignorant of the worth of his interest. Thus contracts made by a trustee to purchase the beneficial interest are voidable at the beneficiary's instance, if one of the criteria for their validity set out by Megarry V-C is not satisfied.

In addition to these fiduciary duties, the trustee must also observe his non-fiduciary duties when managing the trust. He also enjoys a number of powers. These are considered in the next chapter.

Points to Review

You have seen:

- how trustees are appointed to the trust and how they might retire or be removed from it;
- the different duties and powers that trustees possess; and
- the fiduciary duties of trustees and the potentially harsh consequences that follow for the trustees if any of these duties are breached by the trustees, however inadvertently. The trustee will normally be made a constructive trustee of any profit he makes, even if the trust itself has suffered no loss. It will be interesting to see in the future if the Supreme Court chooses to relax this harsh rule.

Making connections

This chapter considered the appointment and termination of trusteeship together with the most important duties that trustees find themselves subject to – fiduciary ones. Ultimately, you should understand that a breach of a fiduciary duty is something which is to be avoided at all costs. Fiduciary duties are red lines over which trustees must not cross.

---

56 Ibid at 241.

If a fiduciary duty is breached, the trustee will be made a constructive trustee of the personal profit he has made, for the beneficiaries' benefit. Constructive trusts are discussed in Chapter 3.

Chapter 9 continues looking at obligations imposed upon and discretions that trustees enjoy, in the form of their non-fiduciary duties and powers. These have already been introduced in this chapter.

Useful Things to Read

The best reading is contained in the primary sources listed below. It is always good to consider the decisions of the courts themselves as this will lead to a deeper understanding of the issues involved. A few secondary sources are also listed, which you may wish to read to gain additional insights into the areas considered in this chapter.

Primary sources

Boardman v Phipps [1967] 2 AC 46.
Bray v Ford [1896] AC 44.
Holder v Holder [1968] Ch 353.
Imageview Management Ltd v Jack [2009] Bus LR 1034.
Kane v Radley-Kane [1999] Ch 274.
Queensland Mines Ltd v Hudson (1978) ALR 1.
Regal (Hastings) v Gulliver [1967] 2 AC 134.
Tito v Waddell (No. 2) [1977] Ch 106.
Williams v Barton [1927] 2 Ch 9.

Trustee Act 2000, s 29.

Secondary sources

Matthew Conaglen, 'The nature and function of fiduciary loyalty' (2005) LQR 121 (Jul) 452–480. This article considers what 'fiduciary' means and looks at the relationship between fiduciary and non-fiduciary duties.

Matthew Conaglen, 'A re-appraisal of the fiduciary self-dealing and fair-dealing rules' (2006) CLJ 65(2) 366–396. This considers the relationship between the two fiduciary rules and suggests that the fair-dealing rule is an example of the broader fiduciary principle that a fiduciary's duty to the trust and his self-interest must not conflict.

Andrew D Hicks, 'The remedial principle of *Keech v Sandford* reconsidered' (2010) CLJ 69(2) 287–320. This article considers the extent to which *Keech v Sandford* gives rise to the principle that a constructive trust arises against a fiduciary if the fiduciary has made a gain at the expense of the beneficiary. It argues that the imposition of such a trust was largely as a result of nineteenth century case law.

Jonathan Hilliard, 'The flexibility of fiduciary doctrine in trust law: How far does it stretch in practice?' (2009) Tru LI 23(3), 119–129. This article looks at how the orthodox notion that the trustee must always act in the beneficiary's best interests may fall into conflict with other more modern issues such as a settlor's wishes and the practical operation of a pension trust.

Alastair Hudson, *Equity & Trusts* (7th edn, Routledge-Cavendish, 2012) ch 8.

Law Commission, Fiduciary *Duties and Regulatory Rules: A Summary* (Law Com No. 124, 1992). This Consultation Paper contains a useful review of the fiduciary duties of trustees.

Mohammed Ramjohn, *Text, Cases and Materials on Equity and Trusts* (4th edn, Routledge-Cavendish, 2008) ch 18.

Chapter 9

Trustees' Non-Fiduciary Duties and Powers

Chapter 8 introduced the trustee: How a trustee may be appointed and how their trusteeship may be ended. This chapter builds upon Chapter 8 and moves forward to address a trustee's non-fiduciary duties. It also considers the powers that a trustee enjoys in administering the trust.

As You Read

Look out for the following:

- the types of non-fiduciary duties that a trustee is subject to;
- the types of power that a trustee enjoys; and
- the standard of care and skill that a trustee should use when exercising his duties and powers.

Fiduciary Duties, Non-Fiduciary Duties and Powers

As was seen in Chapter 8, a trustee is a type of fiduciary who is subject to a number of duties of both a fiduciary and non-fiduciary nature. The trustee also possesses a number of powers. As a reminder, these duties and powers are set out in the table in Figure 9.1.

Non-Fiduciary Duties

Breach of a non-fiduciary duty generally means that the trustee will be liable to pay equitable compensation to the trust for the loss it has sustained. Of course, the trustee will only be liable

FIDUCIARY DUTIES	NON-FIDUCIARY DUTIES	POWERS
To act in good faith	Various duties upon appointment as a trustee including collecting in the trust assets and becoming familiar with the terms of the trust	To invest the trust property
Not to make a profit from the trust	To act unanimously and personally in administering the trust	To maintain infant beneficiaries
Not to put himself in a position where his duty to the trust and his self-interest conflict	To account to the beneficiaries with information about the trust	To advance capital to beneficiaries
Not to act for his own benefit or any third party's benefit without the beneficiaries' consent	To distribute the property when the trust comes to an end	

Figure 9.1 Table of Fiduciary duties, non-fiduciary duties and powers.

to pay compensation providing a true loss can be shown[1] to have been sustained by the trust and the trustee's liability for such loss has not been successfully excluded or limited by a trustee exemption clause. Both of these issues are considered further in Chapter 12.

Duties upon appointment as a trustee

The trustee is subject to various duties when he is appointed to be a trustee. These duties were outlined by Kekewich J in *Hallows v Lloyd*.[2] He said that the trustees must:

- ascertain what the trust property is;
- ascertain the terms of the trust which they are required to administer; and
- read the trust documents to see what, if any, incumbrances affect the trust.

Kekewich J's comments are logical. The trustee's duties should, as a matter of basic principle, include understanding the terms of the trust which he is bound to administer. This will include making himself familiar with the beneficiaries and the terms of the trust and seeing what, if any, specific duties the settlor has placed upon him and what powers he enjoys. The trustee must also ascertain what incumbrances (obligations) bind the trust so that he can comply with them.

The trustee must own an interest in the trust property if he is to administer the trust. The settlor must, consequently, constitute the trust.[3] Provided a deed has been used to appoint him, s 40 of the Trustee Act 1925 provides that the trust property will be vested in the trustee automatically upon his appointment.

The additional duty of the trustee to collect in the trust assets if he is not appointed by deed – forcefully if necessary – was spelt out by the Court of Appeal in *Re Brogden*.[4]

The facts concerned trusts established by John Brogden. He left £10,000 in his will to each of his two daughters and one of his sons. During his life, he worked in partnership with his three sons in a colliery business. After his death, one of his daughters, Mary Jane Billing, wanted her share of the money to be appropriated to her benefit under the trust. The trustee was reluctant to do so as to do so would have resulted in the trustee obtaining the money from the business which Mr Brogden's three sons continued to run. In correspondence with Mary, the trustee thought to press for the money would have put him 'in a very unpleasant position with your brothers'. Ultimately, the colliery business became insolvent. The issue for the Court of Appeal was what, if any, liability was to be borne by the trustee for not pressing for the money to be transferred to the trust.

Cotton LJ believed that the trustee's duty was to demand the payment of the money due to the trust and, if the money was not paid by the business, to take 'reasonable means'[5] to enforce the payment. The trustee should have acted far more forcefully than he did. If needed, he should have taken legal action against the business to recover the money for the trust. His action fell far short of this. He did not demand the payment due and was willing to enter into negotiations with the partnership over what types of assets the business would give to the trust to satisfy the debt owed to the trust. Consequently, the trustee was personally responsible for the loss to the trust fund. Only if the trustee could show that the trust would not have

1   See the discussion of *Nestle v National Westminster Bank* [1993] 1 WLR 1260 in Chapter 12.
2   *Hallows v Lloyd* (1888) LR 39 Ch D 686.
3   As considered in Chapter 7.
4   *Re Brogden* (1888) LR 38 Ch D 546.
5   Ibid at 564.

recovered the money from the business could he be excused from liability. The trustee could not show that here.

The case illustrates that the duty of the trustee upon taking office is to secure the trust assets, taking legal action if necessary. It also shows the serious consequence for the trustee if such assets are not secured: the trustee will have to make good the loss to the trust from his own personal assets. Fry LJ described the trustee's duty as 'the duty – the dominant duty, the guiding duty – of recovering, securing, and duly applying the trust fund'.[6]

Breach of the duty does not depend on the trustee acting with bad faith or dishonestly. On the contrary, the Court of Appeal accepted that the trustee had behaved honourably throughout. That was irrelevant, however. The task for the trustee was to collect in the trust assets which he had failed to do.

Duty to act unanimously and personally

At common law, the trustee was obliged to administer the trust personally. In the case of more than one trustee, this means that all of the trustees have to become involved in the administration of the trust. As Cross J pointed out in *Re Lucking's Will Trusts*,[7] a passive trustee will be responsible for decisions which cause loss to the trust fund if he simply allows an active co-trustee to make decisions on his own. There is, therefore, a disincentive for a trustee to stand by and let his fellow trustees make decisions in administering the trust.

The liability of two or more trustees is joint and several.[8]

Glossary: Joint and several liability

Joint and several liability can only apply where two or more people are acting together. 'Joint' means that they are together responsible for their actions. 'Several', however, means their liability can attach just to one of them. For example, if two trustees breached a trust, it would be open to a beneficiary to take legal action against them both – for they are both jointly liable for the breach – or just one of them to recover the entire loss sustained by the trust.

Exceptions can occur when trustees do not have to act unanimously. One such exception concerns small charitable trusts (with an income of less than £10,000 in the previous financial year) where two-thirds of their trustees may decide under s 268 of the Charities Act 2011 to exercise a range of powers, for example, to transfer trust property to another charitable trust.

The duty to act personally was founded on the Latin maxim *delegates non potest delegare* – the person to whom something has been delegated cannot himself then delegate his task. The logic behind it is self-explanatory: the settlor has deliberately chosen someone to administer his trust and had he wanted the trustee to delegate their functions to another person, the settlor would have chosen that second person himself. This duty could be altered in the terms of the trust deed if the settlor so wished. But the duty of personal service had an exception, as Viscount Radcliffe explained in *Pilkington v IRC*,[9] '[t]he law is not that trustees cannot delegate: it is that trustees cannot delegate unless they have authority to do so'.[10]

---

6 Ibid at 571.
7 *Re Lucking's Will Trusts* [1968] 1 WLR 866.
8 See, for example, *Fry v Tapson* (1885) LR 28 Ch D 268, considered below at pp 234–235.
9 *Pilkington v IRC* [1964] AC 612.
10 Ibid at 639.

As trusts became ever more complex to manage and the types of investment grew wider in scope, trustees began to delegate their functions more and more, whilst remaining in overall charge of the trust.

The functions that a trustee may delegate

Trustees now enjoy a wide ability to delegate their powers. This ability is set out in Part IV of the Trustee Act 2000.

The Trustee Act 2000 greatly enhanced the trustee's ability to delegate their functions. In non-charitable trusts, s 11(2) provides that a trustee may delegate any of their functions apart from what may be termed their 'core' duties. The functions that a trustee cannot delegate are those related to:

(a)   whether and how the assets of the trust may be distributed;
(b)   whether and how any payments owed by the trust should come out of capital or income funds;
(c)   any power to appoint a new trustee; and
(d)   any power that the trustee otherwise enjoys to delegate one of their functions.

The people to whom a trustee may delegate functions

Trustees may appoint agents, nominees and custodians to whom they may delegate their functions.

❖ EXPLAINING THE LAW

Suppose Scott declares a trust appointing Thomas as his trustee. The trust property is £100,000. Thomas has no knowledge of investment opportunities that may exist and realises he needs some assistance in deciding what type of investments to make.

Thomas can appoint an agent to advise him what type of investment to make. An obvious example might be that if he decided that he wanted to invest in shares, he might appoint a stockbroker to advise him which companies were performing well and worthy of investment. He might instruct the stockbroker to buy shares suitable for the trust. If the stockbroker is appointed as an agent, the actual contract for the purchase of the shares is made between the trustee and the company selling the shares. The agent is not part of the transaction.

A nominee is a slightly different concept. A nominee is someone in whose name property might be registered, but who is not the true owner. Thomas might appoint a nominee if he wished to keep an investment secret from the outside world. Alternatively, nominees are often used to purchase shares in a speedy manner. It is quicker for the nominee to buy the shares in its name rather than advising the trustee to purchase shares for the trust and then waiting for that transaction to take place.

A custodian receives assets for safe-keeping. A trustee might decide to place trust assets into the hands of a custodian where they will remain until the trustee collects them. Custodians are often used by charities for them to retain the legal title to a charity's property whilst the trustees administer the trust.

Under s 12 of the Trustee Act 2000, the trustees may appoint one of themselves to be an agent for the trust. A beneficiary cannot, however, be appointed as an agent.[11] The trustees have the capacity to decide the terms of the agent's appointment.[12] Special rules exist under s 15 for agents appointed to exercise asset management functions. These include that the agreement under which such an agent is appointed must be in writing[13] and the trustees must prepare a written policy statement guiding the agent as to how the trust assets should be managed.[14] This statement must be kept under constant review.[15]

A nominee may be appointed by the trustees under s16 of the Trustee Act 2000. Such appointments must be in writing[16] and can be in relation to any of the trust's assets, except for settled land.

Trustees may also appoint a custodian of the trust's assets under s 17 of the Trustee Act 2000. Such appointment must again be in writing.[17] A custodian is defined in s 17(2) as:

> For the purposes of this Act a person is a custodian in relation to assets if he undertakes the safe appointment of the assets or of any documents or records concerning the assets.

Under s 19 of the Trustee Act 2000, nominees and custodians must either be people who carry on businesses as professional nominees, or custodians, or a corporate body, which is controlled by the trustees. Provided this condition is met, agents, nominees and custodians can all be one and the same person.[18] The trustees may decide the terms of appointment of any nominee or custodian.[19]

Steps that trustees must take when delegating their functions

(a) Choose prudently

Whoever the trustees choose, the trustees must exercise their choice prudently, as illustrated by Fry v Tapson.[20] If they do not, they are liable for his errors.

Two trustees were appointed by the will of John Dunn to invest trust monies either by lending the money as mortgages over property in Tasmania or Great Britain or by investing the money in shares in public companies in the UK. The trustees decided to invest £5,000 by advancing it over a property in Liverpool. The money was to be secured by a mortgage, which was to earn the trust interest at 4.5 per cent. The solicitor of the trustees recommended a surveyor to value the property and the trustees accepted that recommendation. The problem was that the surveyor was based in London and there was no evidence that he even went to Liverpool to value the house. It was valued at £7,000–£8,000 and the mortgage was duly entered into.

The borrower failed to repay the mortgage and went bankrupt. Developments had taken place adjacent to the house which meant that its value had fallen and was worth less than the amount due under the mortgage (this is known as 'negative equity' although this has nothing to do with the courts of equity). One of the beneficiaries brought an action against the trustees

---

11 Trustee Act 2000, s 11(3).
12 Ibid s 14(1).
13 Ibid s 15(1).
14 Ibid s 15(2), (4).
15 Ibid s 22(2).
16 Ibid s 16(2).
17 Ibid s 17(3).
18 Trustee Act 2000, s 19 (6), (7).
19 Trustee Act 2000, s 20.
20 Fry v Tapson (1885) LR 28 ChD 268.

for breach of trust. Evidence showed that the house, even when the mortgage was created, was worth barely enough to cover the amount advanced.

Kay J described the appointment of a London surveyor to value a property in Liverpool as a 'most incautious act'.[21] He had no local knowledge of either that particular house, or the general property market in Liverpool. His report was written to generate interest in the house. Kay J acknowledged that, if an agent was properly employed by a trustee, the trustee would not be responsible for the agent's faults. But the agent was not properly employed here. He was employed 'out of the ordinary scope of his business'[22] as he was not familiar with the Liverpool property market. By failing to choose their agent prudently, the trustees were liable for his faults.

(b) Review performance

If an agent, nominee or custodian is appointed, the trustees' task does not end upon that appointment. Section 22 of the Trustee Act 2000 makes it clear that the trustees must keep the appointment under constant review. Trustees must, if necessary, consider whether to intervene in the appointment and exercise any power that they may have.[23] Section 22(4) specifies that an intervention may take the form of the trustees giving directions to their agent, nominee or custodian or even going so far as to revoke the appointment entirely. What is clear is that, once appointed, the trustees cannot sit back and let their appointee run the trust in their place. This was shown in Re Lucking's Will Trust.[24]

Here, a trust was set up which consisted of a majority shareholding in Stephen Lucking Ltd, a small business which had a factory in Chester. Profits in the business were falling. The trustee (who was also a director of the company) appointed Mr Peter Dewar to be a director and the new manager of the business. The company had a bank account on which cheques could be drawn, but the cheques needed the signature of two directors. A practice developed whereby the trustee would sign blank cheques and send them to Peter for him to complete the amounts and also sign them. Peter lived in Scotland and had considerable commuting expenses, which he settled using the 'blank cheque system' of payment. Peter then borrowed money from the company without the trustee's knowledge, simply recording the borrowing as a 'loan to a director'. Whilst the trustee accepted Peter's explanation for this, again the loan was facilitated using the blank cheque payment method. Over a few years, Peter's indebtedness to the company increased to over £15,800. Peter went bankrupt, owing the company this money.

One of the beneficiaries brought an action against the trustee for failing to supervise Peter. She alleged that she had been caused a loss because the company had itself suffered a loss which could have been distributed to her as effectively a shareholder in the company.

Cross J held that the trustee was liable for breach of trust for part of the loss suffered by the trust. The trustee was not liable for breach of trust simply by signing blank cheques, even though such action was described by Cross J as inherently 'notoriously dangerous'.[25] Further, the trustee was not liable for the period of time that he had no reason to suspect Peter was abusing the confidence that the trustee had placed in him. This changed, however, when Peter began withdrawing excessive amounts from the company, in addition to his salary and expenses. At that point, the trustee should have noticed that Peter was abusing his position. The trustee would only have seen this if he had kept a closer eye on Peter's dealings. Failure to do so meant that the trustee was liable for that loss sustained by the trust fund.

---

21 Ibid at 279.
22 Ibid at 280.
23 Trustee Act 2000, s 22(1).
24 Re Lucking's Will Trust [1968] 1 WLR 866.
25 Ibid at 876.

Duty to account to the beneficiaries with relevant information about the trust

It might be assumed that, because the beneficiaries have an interest in the trust property, they are entitled to be kept fully and entirely up-to-date with accurate information about the trust. For example, beneficiaries might wish to know how the trust property is being invested, how those investments are performing and to what extent any of their number has enjoyed any of the trust property.

Over the last century, the courts have narrowed the circumstances when beneficiaries are entitled to see information about the trust.

In *O'Rourke v Darbishire*,[26] the House of Lords gave beneficiaries a wide entitlement to see information concerning the trust. The facts concerned a disputed winding up of the estate of Sir Joseph Whitworth. The claimant's case was that he was entitled to part of the estate of Sir Joseph. To pursue his claim successfully, he needed to have sight of certain documents.

Lord Wrenbury agreed with the decisions of the Court of Appeal and the High Court in the case in that a beneficiary had a proprietary right to see trust documents, explaining, '[t]he beneficiary is entitled to see all trust documents because they are trust documents and because he is a beneficiary. They are in this sense his own'.[27]

A beneficiary did not need to take court action to enjoy this right. It was a proprietary right he enjoyed.

Lord Wrenbury said the beneficiary's right was not to be confused with the legal process of discovery (now called 'disclosure'). In a civil action, this is the stage of legal proceedings where each party reveals to the other relevant documents which either help or hinder their case.[28] The beneficiary did not enjoy his right under this process as discovery was, and disclosure remains, the right to see another party's documents. The beneficiary's right was a proprietary one which he enjoyed as a beneficiary. It was entirely separate to this process.

On the facts of the case, the claimant was not a beneficiary and had, therefore, to establish an entitlement to see the disputed documents through the process of discovery. The claimant was partly successful in obtaining an order to see certain documents. What is important is that beneficiaries were recognised to have a proprietary right to have sight of all trust documents.

This issue was considered again by the Court of Appeal in *Re Londonderry's Settlement*[29] where its members curtailed a beneficiary's right to see documents relating to the trust.

The facts concerned a discretionary trust of shares in Londonderry Collieries Ltd declared by the Seventh Marquess of Londonderry in 1934. The trustees, together with people referred to as 'appointers', were to decide who was to benefit from the defined class from the capital and income of the trust fund. One of the settlor's daughters, Lady Helen Walsh, was a member of the class.

In 1962, the trustees decided to distribute the capital and thus bring the trust to an end. Lady Helen wanted more money than she had been given by the trustees. She asked the trustees to supply her with various documents but the trustees supplied only copies of documents detailing people whom they had chosen to benefit from the trust together with the trust's annual accounts. Lady Helen's motive in seeking these documents was to scrutinise the trustees' reasons for preferring other beneficiaries over her. The trustees, to prevent family discord, decided not to supply any further documents detailing either the agendas or minutes of their meetings, or their correspondence with the appointers and other beneficiaries. The trustees

26 *O'Rourke v Darbishire* [1920] AC 581.
27 Ibid at 626.
28 Civil Procedure Rules 1998, r 31.
29 *Re Londonderry's Settlement* [1965] Ch 918.

brought an action for directions to the court, asking which documents they were bound to supply to Lady Helen.

In giving the leading judgment of the Court of Appeal, Harman LJ reminded the court that the trustees had never been under a duty to disclose to beneficiaries their reasons for reaching a decision over which they enjoyed a discretion. The reasoning behind this ensured trustees had some freedom to make decisions without their motives being called into question. If, however, trustees volunteered their reasons, whether or not they were sound could be questioned by the court.[30]

Harman LJ, with whom Danckwerts LJ agreed, thought that the observations of the House of Lords in O'Rourke v Darbishire over the right that a beneficiary had to inspect 'trust documents' were too general and provided little assistance to a beneficiary's request to see specific documents. Harman LJ held that the minutes of the trustees' meetings and the agendas prepared for such meetings were not documents that the beneficiary could inspect, because an inspection would immediately reveal the trustees' motives and the reasons for their decisions. He did not believe that these documents could be described as 'trust documents'. Even if they could, however, the beneficiary could not see them, because the principle that protected trustees' deliberations on a matter of exercising their discretion could override the competing principle that the beneficiary was entitled to see all trust documents. The correspondence between the trustees, appointers and beneficiaries were not documents which a beneficiary enjoyed a right to inspect.

Salmon LJ agreed that as long as the trustees exercised their discretion honestly, their reasons for the exercise of that discretion could not be challenged. There was thus no point in disclosing trustees' reasons to the beneficiaries – even if the reasons were disclosed, they were not open to challenge. Challenging trustees' reasons would mean that trustees' decisions would become impossible to make if they felt that such decisions were always open to be criticised in court.

Salmon LJ laid down the characteristics of 'trust documents':

> Trust documents do . . . have these characteristics in common: (1) they are documents in the possession of the trustees as trustees; (2) they contain information about the trust which the beneficiaries are entitled to know; (3) the beneficiaries have a proprietary interest in the documents and, accordingly, are entitled to see them.[31]

He said that if any part of a document contained information which the beneficiaries were not entitled to know – such as trustees' reasons for making a decision – then the document would not be one that the beneficiaries were entitled to see.

As well as providing information about what constituted a trust document, the decision in this case also placed limits on what beneficiaries were entitled to see. In particular, beneficiaries were not entitled to see the reasons for trustees' decisions. This was either because, in Harman LJ's view, non-disclosure of such reasons trumped the beneficiaries' right to see the trust document or because the document containing the reasons was not a 'trust document' as defined by Salmon LJ.

The matter was addressed again in *Schmidt v Rosewood Trust Ltd*[32] where a new approach to the issue of disclosure was given by the Privy Council.

---

30 These principles were originally stated by Lord Truro LC in *Re Beloved Wilkes's Charity* (1851) 3 Mac & G 440.
31 *Re Londonderry's Settlement* [1965] Ch 918 at 938.
32 *Schmidt v Rosewood Trust Ltd* [2003] 2 AC 709.

The facts concerned two discretionary trusts, co-set up by Vitali Schmidt, under the jurisdiction of the Isle of Man. His son, Vadim, as administrator for his father's estate, brought an action to obtain accounts of the trusts and other information from the trustee, the defendant. As administrator for his father's estate, the trustee had paid Vadim $14.6 million which the trustee said was his entitlement under the trusts. Vadim's case was that his father had been entitled to a larger share of the total of $105 million that constituted the trust fund. He wanted access to certain documents to assist his claim. The defendant's defence, *inter alia*, was that neither Vitali nor Vadim were beneficiaries under either trust, but were mere objects of a power. As such, neither of them had any entitlement to see trust documents.

In giving the opinion of the board, Lord Walker did not think that beneficiaries had an absolute proprietary right to see trust documents. Instead:

> the more principled and correct approach is to regard the right to seek disclosure of trust documents as one aspect of the court's inherent jurisdiction to supervise, and if necessary to intervene in, the administration of trusts.[33]

An applicant did not need a beneficial interest as such in the trust property to avail himself of such a right as '[t]he object of a discretion (including a mere power) may also be entitled to protection from a court of equity'.[34] Such protection would depend on the court's discretion to intervene in the administration of a trust.

In exercising that discretion, Lord Walker said that there were three areas which the court would have to consider:

(a) whether a beneficiary (or other applicant, such as an object under a power) should be assisted by the court;

(b) the types of documents which should be disclosed to the applicant and whether they should be disclosed in an edited or unedited form; and

(c) whether any safeguards should be imposed to restrict the use of the disclosed documents (e.g. by stating that the documents could only be inspected at a solicitor's offices).

The tide in favour of beneficiaries had turned since *O'Rourke v Darbishire* as Lord Walker stated:

> the recent cases also confirm . . . that no beneficiary . . . has any entitlement as of right to disclosure of anything which can plausibly be described as a trust document. Especially when there are issues as to personal or commercial confidentiality, the court may have to balance the competing interests of different beneficiaries, the trustees themselves, and third parties. Disclosure may have to be limited and safeguards may have to be put in place.[35]

On the facts, Vadim's case was remitted to the High Court in the Isle of Man for determination as to whether he could seek disclosure of documents related to the trust. Lord Walker thought that Vadim's claims were potentially sound and was therefore entitled to the disclosure that he sought.

---

33 Ibid at 729.
34 Ibid.
35 Ibid at 734.

❖ ANALYSING THE LAW

Lord Walker thought that the three judgments of the Court of Appeal in *Re Londonderry's Settlement* were not easy to reconcile. Harman and Danckwerts LJJ had treated the beneficiary's right to see trust documents as a qualified right, which could be overridden by the competing principle that a trustee's reasons should be kept confidential. Salmon LJ had preferred to try to define what could and could not amount to a 'trust document'.

Do you think there is any discernible common thread running through these separate judgments?

Is a wish letter to be treated differently from other documents?

This question concerned the High Court in the more recent case of *Breakspear v Ackland*.[36]

The facts concerned three potential beneficiaries' application for a wish letter to be disclosed to them.

Glossary: A wish letter

A 'wish letter' – or, sometimes, a 'letter of wishes' – is a document in which a settlor expresses a desire to the trustees to use their powers in a particular way.

Perhaps the most common use for a wish letter is with a discretionary trust. This is where the settlor initially establishes the trust for the benefit of a defined class. That class might be fairly large. The settlor might then attempt to narrow down the field in the class by expressing a wish to his trustees that certain people in the class be chosen as beneficiaries.

Wish letters are not binding on trustees. Yet often, out of courtesy, the trustees will take into account the people the settlor has set out in his wish letter.

Briggs J recognised that the use of a wish letter had two competing interests behind it. On the one hand, a wish letter was a useful device whereby a settlor could communicate sensitive and secret information to his trustees. It was therefore useful if such letters could be seen to be confidential and not subject to disclosure to beneficiaries. On the other hand, as in this case, the sight of a wish letter would often give the potential beneficiaries a solid idea of whether they were likely to benefit from the trust and would therefore prove invaluable to them in planning their lives and those of their children and dependants. Such competing interests had to be balanced by the court.

Briggs J referred to what he described as the '*Londonderry* principle':

the process of the exercise of discretionary dispositive powers by trustees is inherently confidential, and that this confidentiality exists for the benefit of beneficiaries rather than merely for the protection of the trustees.[37]

---

36 *Breakspear v Ackland* [2009] Ch 32.
37 Ibid at 42.

He did not believe the decisions in *Re Londonderry's Settlement* and *Schmidt v Rosewood Trust Ltd* conflicted. The cases were not on all fours with each other. *Re Londonderry's Settlement* concerned documents that had a confidential nature about them. *Schmidt v Rosewood Trust Ltd* did not. The issue in that case was whether the applicant was entitled to see the documents, not whether the documents themselves were confidential or not.

After a thorough review of English, Australian and Channel Islands authorities, Briggs J held that the conclusion nowadays was not that the beneficiaries enjoyed any proprietary right to see trust documents but instead any request for the disclosure of a document possessed by the trustees was a request to the court to exercise its discretion. Bound by precedent, he followed the *Londonderry* principle. He also agreed with the reasoning behind it – that beneficiaries might in fact be protected by not having certain documents disclosed to them. Documents passing between a trustee and a settlor over which beneficiary should be chosen to benefit from a discretionary trust might, for example, reveal that one particular beneficiary was suffering from a life-threatening illness. Trustees had to have the security that their enquiries as to such matters could be kept confidential.

A wish letter in a family trust was written 'for the sole purpose of serving and facilitating an inherently confidential process'.[38] It was therefore appropriate that such a document should, *prima facie*, be seen to be confidential as between the settlor and trustees and not be disclosed to the beneficiaries. This confidence could be voluntarily overridden by the trustees but Briggs J thought that the trustees should only disclose a wish letter if 'disclosure is in the sound administration of the trust, and the discharge of their powers and discretions'.[39]

Briggs J gave guidance for how trustees should manage a beneficiary's request to them to disclose a wish letter in relation to family discretionary trusts. The trustees are obliged to consider whether they should exercise their discretion to allow the beneficiary sight of the document. The trustees may simply answer 'yes' or 'no' to the beneficiary's request and do not have to provide reasons for their decision. Providing reasons is, in some ways, more dangerous for the trustees, as the court can consider whether their reasons are honest.

The trustees may seek the court's assistance as to whether they should disclose the wish letter. In such a case, the court itself had to have full disclosure of the letter. If disclosure was ordered, Briggs J thought that the safeguards mentioned by Lord Walker in *Schmidt v Rosewood Trust Ltd* could be employed. Briggs J thought that, as a matter of policy, the courts were not biased towards disclosure.

On the facts, Briggs J held that the wish letter had to be disclosed. That was due to the trustees' intention to seek the court's later sanction to their proposed distribution scheme of the trust fund. At that later stage, the contents of the wish letter would be relevant to the proposed distribution and the potential beneficiaries had to be permitted to comment on the scheme. All disclosure of the wish letter would do at this stage would be to give that information to the potential beneficiaries at an earlier stage. Their right to comment on the proposed distribution scheme outweighed any family disharmony that might be suffered due to the disclosure of the wish letter.

Summary of the duty to account

The decision in *Breakspear v Ackland* is an interesting one. Aside from precedent considerations, Briggs J made it clear that he would have followed *Re Londonderry's Settlement* in any event, over *Schmidt v Rosewood Trust*. It seems that he followed the views of Harman and Danckwerts LJJ in *Re Londonderry's Settlement* and it is their views that he termed 'the *Londonderry* principle'. In general, it

---

38 Ibid at 52.
39 Ibid at 53.

seems clear that the beneficiaries no longer enjoy a proprietary right to see any trust document that they might wish to see. Certain documents which contain trustees' reasons or other confidential information may be protected from disclosure. The trustees themselves may always override this by deciding voluntarily to disclose the document. If not, the actual (or potential, in the case of a discretionary trust) beneficiary may ask the court to order disclosure. The *Londonderry* principle – that trustees exercising their discretion to dispose of the trust fund is a confidential process and can override a beneficiary's desire to see a document – remains good law. The court must balance the beneficiaries' desire to see confidential documents with the need to allow trustees the ability to make decisions without fear of being impeached. If a document was ordered to be disclosed, then the safeguards suggested in *Schmidt v Rosewood Trust Ltd* could be employed.

Duty to distribute the trust fund

When the trust comes to an end, perhaps because the beneficiary has fulfilled the contingency, or a life tenant has died to be succeeded by the remainderman, the duty of the trustees is to pay the fund to the beneficiaries.

The trustees must ensure that they pay the money to the correct beneficiaries. This did not occur in *Eaves v Hickson*[40] albeit the trustees were perhaps more unfortunate than deliberately neglectful or dishonest.

Mary Babinton left realty to her two trustees on trust to be divided into two halves: one half was for John Knibb's children and the other for the children of William Knibb. The trustees sold the property. William Knibb sent the trustees a marriage certificate, in which he claimed to have been married in 1826. He also sent in his children's baptismal certificates, with dates following that year. In fact, the marriage took place in 1836, but the marriage certificate had been forged. William's children were all illegitimate. The trustees, acting in good faith and relying on the marriage certificate, paid out the money to William's children. The children of John Knibb discovered the marriage certificate was a forgery and brought an action for the money which had been wrongfully paid out of the trust fund to be replaced.

The Master of the Rolls held that the fund had to be replaced. Although he believed that it was a 'very hard case on the trustees',[41] ultimately they had paid the money out wrongly. The loss had to be borne by the person who had paid out the money. On the facts, the court strived to ameliorate the position to the innocent trustees. The court ordered the children who had benefited from the money to repay it with interest, with any shortfall being made up by William Knibb, who must have known that the marriage certificate had been forged. If any further shortfall remained, the trustees had to make it good.

Normally, it will be apparent when the trust has come to an end because either a beneficiary will have clearly fulfilled a contingency or the life tenant will have died. The court has power, however, to order the trustees to distribute the trust fund. An order to distribute the trust fund was made by the High Court, in unusual circumstances, in *Re Green's Will Trusts*.[42]

The facts concerned the will of Evelyne Green and her only son, Barry. Barry was a tail gunner in a bomber aircraft that left RAF Linton-on-Ouse in January 1943 on a mission to Berlin. Barry was never heard of again. Later in 1943, Evelyne saw a photograph of a man in a Swiss magazine whom she believed to be Barry. Both the Red Cross and the government could not confirm this to her and believed the photograph to be dubious. Evelyne wound up her

---

40 *Eaves v Hickson* (1861) 30 Beav 136.
41 Ibid at 141.
42 *Re Green's Will Trusts* [1985] 3 All ER 455.

son's estate in 1948 but she continued to believe that he was alive. When writing her will in 1972, she left her estate to Barry. She gave him until 1 January 2020 to come forward to claim it. If he failed to do so, then after that date the money was to go to establishing a foundation to treat deprived animals. One of the issues for the court was whether Evelyne's estate should be distributed to the foundation or whether it should remain in trust pending Barry coming forward to claim it.

Nourse J held that Barry must have been presumed to have died on the night of the bombing raid, given that nothing further had been seen or heard of any of the crew members of that mission. An order would be made that the trustees must distribute the trust fund in favour of the charitable foundation that Evelyne had established in her will.

Nourse J made what is known as a *Benjamin* order. This originates from the case of *Re Benjamin*,[43] in which the testator left his residuary estate in his will on trust for his 13 children. One of his sons had last been seen 10 months before the testator died in Aix-la-Chapelle, France, allegedly making his way to London. Nothing had been seen or heard of the son since that time. The High Court made an order permitting the trustees of the testator's will to distribute the estate of the testator as though the son had predeceased his father. This meant that the estate would be distributed amongst the other 12 children. Joyce J said the burden of proof of establishing that the son had survived his father was on those claiming under the son. They had failed to satisfy this burden.

Nourse J described a *Benjamin* order as one that:

> does not vary or destroy beneficial interests. It merely enables trust property to be distributed in accordance with the practical probabilities, and it must be open to the court to take a view of those probabilities entirely different from that entertained by the testator.[44]

As to whether further time should elapse before the trustees should distribute the fund, Nourse J said that the test to be applied was:

> whether in all the circumstances the trustees ought to be allowed to distribute and the beneficiaries to enjoy their apparent interests now rather than later.[45]

The case illustrates that a court can order the trust fund to be distributed, by making use of a *Benjamin* order. Such an order is a useful way of administering trusts which might otherwise, subject to the perpetuity period, remain in suspense for potentially a long period of time. It enables the trustees to carry on their trusteeship by distributing the trust property.

A statutory mechanism exists in s 27 of the Trustee Act 1925 for the trustees to distribute trust property to beneficiaries of whom they have notice. This section provides that trustees can place an announcement in the *London Gazette* and in a newspaper local to the area connected to the trust giving notice that they intend to distribute the trust fund to all those beneficiaries of whom they have notice. The announcements must set out a period (not less than two months) in which beneficiaries can notify the trustees of their claim to the trust fund. If any genuine claims are made during that time period, those 'new' beneficiaries will obviously benefit from the trust. If, on the other hand, the trustees receive

---

43 *Re Benjamin* [1902] 1 Ch 723.
44 *Re Green's Will Trusts* [1985] 3 All ER 455 at 462.
45 Ibid at 463.

no claims, they can simply distribute the trust fund to all those beneficiaries of whom they have notice.

Making connections

Reflect now on why certainty of object is vital to form a valid trust. The key principle of certainty of object was that beneficiaries had to be at least ascertainable. Hopefully, they will all have been ascertained by the trustees before the trust fund is distributed but if not, provided they are ascertainable, the trustees may benefit from either a *Benjamin* order or the mechanism in s 27 of the Trustee Act 1925 to distribute the trust fund.

If you have forgotten about certainty of objects, now might be a good time to refresh your memory of that part of Chapter 5.

As well as these non-fiduciary duties, which trustees must undertake, they also enjoy various powers, which they may or may not use at their discretion.

Trustees' Powers

Trustees enjoy three key powers:

- a power to invest the trust property;
- a power to maintain beneficiaries; and
- a power to advance capital to the beneficiaries before they become entitled to it.

Making connections

A certain type of power has already been discussed in Chapter 2: the power of appointment. This is a power that a donee/trustee has to choose who will benefit from the donor or settlor's generosity. The powers considered here are of a different type: they are concerned with managing the trust as opposed to selecting who will benefit from it.

The key concept of any power, however, is that there is no obligation on the recipient to use it. The trustee always has the choice whether to use it or not. Failing to comply with a duty is more serious as a duty carries with it an obligation to do or not do an act.

A trustee cannot, however, refuse to consider whether to exercise a power. Such a refusal would undoubtedly be a breach of one of the core fiduciary duties to act in good faith in the beneficiaries' best interests.

A power to invest the trust property

This is probably the most important of the trustees' powers. If the central concept of a trust is to administer property on behalf of another, it is logical that administering that property will mean investing it to secure a return in either capital or income or both forms.

Somewhat surprisingly, it was not until the Trustee Act 2000 came into force that trustees were permitted to make a wide range of investments. The Trustee Investment Acts 1961 had limited the types of investments that trustees could invest in to low-risk securities, such as government bonds and shares in public limited companies with a solid history of producing good profits. The purpose was to reduce risk to beneficiaries, but restricting trustees' investment choices meant that beneficiaries suffered as the low-risk securities tended to produce low returns.

❖ APPLYING THE LAW

Under the Trustee Investments Act 1961, trustees were encouraged to invest in UK Government bonds (also called 'gilts'). These remain today one of the safest forms of investment. They work by a purchaser effectively lending the government the purchase price of the gilt for usually a fixed period of time, say five years. When that fixed time expires, the amount of the gilt purchase price is repaid by the government, together with interest.

Many trusts will continue to invest a certain proportion of their wealth into gilts because they are considered to be a secure form of investment. It is highly unlikely that the UK Government will not repay the purchase price of the gilt to the investor. As they are low-risk, they tend to have low rates of return and the interest paid on them is not very high. It makes comparatively little sense for trustees to invest huge amounts, when slightly riskier investments could produce a better rate of return.

Fortunately, s 3 of the Trustee Act 2000 widened a trustee's investment powers considerably. Section 3(1) provides that:

> Subject to the provisions of this Part, a trustee may make any kind of investment that he could make if he were absolutely entitled to the assets of the trust.

This is known as the trustees' 'general power of investment'.[46] The general power applies to trusts created before or after the Trustee Act 2000[47] and dramatically simplifies the modern-day investment rules for trustees.

Section 3 of the Trustee Act 2000 gives the trustee very wide powers of investment. The restrictions of safe investments imposed by the Trustee Investments Act 1961 are consigned to history. Nowadays, trustees will wish to spread their risk when investing and do not wish to invest in just one or two types of investment.[48] Investments might be in various types of property, providing the trust with both secure and riskier types of investment. A typical trust might therefore invest in some or all of the following:

- *Bank accounts.* Investing the money in a bank account should be a low-risk form of investment. Care should be taken as the UK Treasury will only (presently) guarantee to reimburse up to £85,000 invested in each financial institution. The return on the investment will be interest that the bank pays on the investment. There will be no capital growth on the investment. As such, unless the trust is for a very short duration, depositing large amounts of the trust fund in a bank account is probably not a sound investment strategy. This type of investment is useful if the trustees wish to access the money quickly and constantly, perhaps in fulfilling a decision they may have taken to use the trust fund to maintain an infant beneficiary under s 32 of the Trustee Act 1925;
- *Gilts.* Although these tend to have a low rate of return, they are perhaps the most secure form of investment possible and therefore the risk to the trust fund of losing money is low;

---

46 Trustee Act 2000, s 3(2).
47 Ibid s 7(1).
48 Diversification may be more appropriate for a large trust fund than a small fund: *Cowan v Scargill* [1985] Ch 270 at 289.

● *Shares.* If a company makes a profit, it can declare that part of the profit is returned to each shareholder. This is known as a 'dividend' and is the income that shareholders receive from their investment in the company. If the company makes profits consistently, its shares will be in demand from other investors, so the capital value of the shares should rise. Shares in public limited companies (especially those in the largest 100 publicly quoted companies on the FTSE index) are generally low-risk,[49] but again, produce a comparatively low rate of return in that dividends paid tend to be low as do the capital value increases of the shares. Shares in private limited companies in the UK or abroad are riskier, but might produce higher rates of return for the trust, as occurred in *Boardman v Phipps*.[50]

Investing in shares tends to be undertaken over a long period, say for a minimum of 10 years, so that fluctuations in a company's fortunes can be ironed out over time. Trustees should therefore only invest in shares if the trust will last for at least such a period of time;

● *Land.* Section 3(3) of the Trustee Act 2000 states that the 'general power of investment does not permit a trustee to make investments in land other than in loans secured on land'. It then refers the reader to section 8 of the Act. Section 8 specifically states that trustees may acquire either freehold or leasehold land in the UK for any of the following purposes:

– for an investment;
– to enable the beneficiary to occupy the land; or
– for any other reason.

Section 8(3) makes it clear that the trustee enjoys the powers of a person who owns the land absolutely.

'Land' as such is not defined in the Trustee Act 2000. The non-binding Explanatory Notes to the Act refer the reader to Schedule 1 to the Interpretation Act 1978.[51] This states that 'land' includes:

> building and other structures, land covered with water, and any estate, interest, easement, servitude, or right in or over land.

Unless land is acquired for a beneficiary to live on, the most popular form of investment for a trust fund will be for 'loans secured on land' – in other words, a mortgage. The trust is therefore permitted to advance money to a borrower so that the borrower can buy the land and then repay the mortgage to the trust. This will result in income generation for the trust, as the loan will usually be repaid with interest.

When making an investment, trustees must have regard to what s 4(1) of the Trustee Act 2000 describes as the 'standard investment criteria'. These are set out in s 4(3) as:

(a) the suitability to the trust of investments of the same kind as any particular investment proposed to be made or retained and of that particular investment as an investment of that kind; and

(b) the need for diversification of investments of the trust, in so far as is appropriate to the circumstances of the trust.

---

49 Albeit no investment in any company, however large, can be seen to be risk-free, especially as the worldwide financial crisis, which has prevailed since 2008, has resulted in many companies becoming insolvent.
50 *Boardman v Phipps* [1967] 2 AC 46.
51 At n. 22.

The aims of the criteria are to make the trustees consider explicitly whether the particular type of investment under consideration is appropriate for this particular trust and for the trustees to spread the risk of their investments. They are obliged to keep their investments under review in accordance with the criteria under s 4(2). They should aim to balance investments which produce income generation and those which produce capital growth.[52] In that way, they are generating a return for both life tenants and remaindermen beneficiaries.

To apply these principles, trustees should prepare a statement of investment setting out their investment guidelines before they make investments.

The trustees failed to comply with s 4(2) in *Jeffery v Gretton*.[53] Here a house in Cowes, Isle of Wight, was left by Paula Beken on a trust declared in her will to benefit Keith Beken for life with remainder to her son and his two children. The house was potentially worth a substantial amount but was in a run-down condition. After Paula died in 2001, her will was varied by terminating Keith's life interest and the house being vested in the three other beneficiaries.

The trustees set about repairing the house themselves. The repairs needed were substantial and took approximately six years to complete. The house was eventually sold in 2008. One of the three beneficiaries brought an action for breach of trust against the trustees. Part of the claim was that the trustees had failed to keep the investment under the trust under review. Had they done so, the beneficiary claimed that the house would have been sold shortly after Paula had died. Instead, the house had been retained for six years and the trust had been deprived of income from it being rented out whilst the repairs dragged on.

The High Court held that, on the facts, there was no loss to the trust fund due to the trustees' actions of retaining the house for such a long period of time but that was largely due to luck: 'it is a case of a thoughtless breach of trust that happens to have turned out well'.[54] But the trustees had been guilty of breaching s 4(2). They had not taken proper advice on the implications of their repairing the property themselves and, as such, they were in breach of their duty to keep the investment under review.

Under s 5 of the Trustee Act 2000, before investing and when reviewing the investments, the trustees must obtain and consider 'proper advice' as to whether the investment meets the standard investment criteria. 'Proper advice' is defined as coming from a person whom the trustees reasonably believe is suitably qualified to give it, due to the advisor's 'ability in and practical experience of financial and other matters relating to the proposed investment'.[55] The only exception to obtaining and considering such advice is if the trustees reasonably believe that 'in all the circumstances it is unnecessary or inappropriate to do so'.[56] The Explanatory Notes suggest that an example of such an occasion could be if the proposed investment is small in value, so that any cost incurred in obtaining professional advice would be disproportionate to the benefit gained in doing so.[57]

---

52 Trustee Act 2000, Explanatory Notes, n. 23.
53 *Jeffery v Gretton* [2011] WTLR 809.
54 Ibid at para. 84 *per* Judge Leslie Blohm QC.
55 Trustee Act 2000, s 5(4).
56 Ibid, s 5(3).
57 Ibid, Explanatory Notes, n. 26.

❖ **EXPLAINING THE LAW**

Suppose that Scott creates a trust of £1 million, appointing Thomas as his trustee.

The trust fund is comparatively large and Thomas understands the need for diversification of the investments. Thomas has decided that part of the trust fund should be invested in paintings by old masters, part in land and part in gilts. As a financial adviser himself, Thomas would probably not wish to take separate advice about the investment in gilts. He would, however, need to take proper advice for the other investments. A surveyor with knowledge of the local area would be someone capable of giving proper advice for the investment concerning land. An antiques expert in art would be appropriate for giving advice for the paintings.

Before the Trustee Act 2000 was enacted, it was usual for settlors to give wide express powers of investment to their trustees, due to the restrictions imposed upon them by the Trustee Investment Act 1961. Settlors may still give such powers to their trustees if they wish. Given the wide wording of s 3(1) of the Trustee Act 2000, such express powers are probably unnecessary today. If, however, an express power of investment is given, it is in addition to the general power of investment under s 3.[58]

From the Explanatory Notes to the Trustee Act 2000, it appears that trustees may now take ethical considerations into account when deciding the types of investment to make. Previously, it had appeared that such consideration had been frowned on by the courts, as *Cowan v Scargill*[59] demonstrates.

The facts concerned a pension scheme established by the National Coal Board (NCB) to provide retirement benefits to mineworkers. The scheme had approximately £200 million to invest each year. The scheme was managed by 10 trustees: five were appointed by the NCB and the remainder by the National Union of Mineworkers (NUM).

A plan of investment was proposed by which some of the annual fund was to be invested in overseas investments and oil and gas. The five trustees appointed by the NUM refused to adopt the plan as it was against Union policy. Deadlock ensued between the trustees, with those appointed by the NCB wishing to press ahead with the investments. Those trustees sought directions from the High Court over whether the investments could go ahead.

Megarry V-C held that they could. He said the main duty of the trustees in terms of wielding their powers was to use them 'in the best interests of the present and future beneficiaries of the trust, holding the scales impartially between different classes of beneficiaries'.[60] The interests of the beneficiaries had to come first, before those of the trustees. As Megarry V-C said, the beneficiaries' interests usually meant:

When the purpose of the trust is to provide financial benefits for the beneficiaries, as is usually the case, the best interests of the beneficiaries are normally their best *financial* interests.[61]

---

58 Trustee Act 2000, s 6(1).
59 *Cowan v Scargill* [1985] Ch 270.
60 Ibid at 287.
61 Ibid (emphasis added).

In deciding whether to invest, trustees had to set aside their 'own personal interests and views'[62] and press ahead with the investment, if it would make the best financial return for the beneficiaries. Megarry V-C held that the proposed investments by the NCB were in the best financial interests of the beneficiaries of the trust.

Megarry V-C did conceive of a 'very rare'[63] exception whereby an investment might not be made for ethical considerations. He gave the example of a trust where all the beneficiaries were adults who had strong moral views against alcohol, tobacco and 'popular entertainment'. In such a case, he thought that it might not be for those beneficiaries' benefit for their trust to make investments in such industries, even though they would generate larger returns than in other industries. The key concept was that the investment had to be made for the beneficiaries' benefit. Whilst that normally meant their financial benefit, the ethical benefit of a particular investment not being made could outweigh their financial benefit, but only on very limited occasions when it appeared that *all* of the beneficiaries would not wish the investment to go ahead.

The concept of benefit was considered again by the High Court in *Harries v The Church Commissioners for England*.[64]

Here, Richard Harries, Bishop of Oxford together with two colleagues, brought an action to determine the extent to which the defendants should have regard to promoting the Christian faith and ethics through their investment policies. The claimants' concern was that the defendants were too focused on realising the best financial returns on their investments, rather than giving weight to religious and ethical considerations when investing Church of England funds. The facts were slightly different from *Cowan v Scargill* as they concerned a charitable trust as opposed to a pension fund.

Nicholls V-C held that charitable trustees had to try to obtain 'the maximum return, whether by way of income or capital growth, which is consistent with commercial prudence'.[65] The reason for this was pragmatic: '[m]ost charities need money; and the more of it there is available, the more the trustees can seek to accomplish'.[66]

Once again, therefore, trustees had to set aside questions of ethical consideration as the best interests of the charity meant they should make investments which gave the best return, taking into account diversification of investment and the need to balance income generation and capital growth.

Making investments on the basis of ethical principles was a difficult task for trustees to undertake. Nicholls V-C pointed out that often there was no definitive right or wrong answer to many moral questions. Trustees might take into account beneficiaries' moral objections against particular investments, but only if they were satisfied that not making particular investments would not result in serious financial disadvantage to the charity.

On the facts, the defendants did have an ethical investment policy. For example, investments were not permitted in companies whose main business was in arms dealing, alcohol or tobacco. Their policy excluded approximately 13 per cent of listed UK companies. If the claimants' more restrictive ethical considerations were accepted, an additional 24 per cent of UK listed companies would join the list of banned investments. Such a policy would lead to less diversification of investments. The defendants' existing investment policy was sufficiently sound that it did not need to be disturbed.

---

62 Ibid.
63 Ibid at 288.
64 *Harries v The Church Commissioners for England* [1992] 1 WLR 1241.
65 Ibid at 1246.
66 Ibid.

In summary, the trustees' power of investment is to invest the trust funds for the benefit of the beneficiaries, balancing the needs of income generation for life tenants with capital growth for the remaindermen. The beneficiaries' benefit will almost always mean their financial benefit. On occasion, financial benefit may be set aside where adult beneficiaries are all opposed to a particular investment or in the case of a charity, as Nicholls V-C suggested in *Harries v The Church Commissioners of England*, where a particular type of investment would conflict with the charity's aims, such as where a charity for the relief of cancer does not wish to invest in a tobacco company. Ethical considerations may play a greater part in future investment strategies, as the Explanatory Notes to the Trustee Act 2000 state that ethical considerations may be taken into account as part of the standard investment criteria under s 4(3).[67]

Power to maintain a beneficiary

The settlor may grant the trustees an express power to maintain a beneficiary in the trust document itself.

In the absence of such an express power, there is also a statutory power to maintain infant beneficiaries contained in s 31 of the Trustee Act 1925. This power only arises providing that there are no prior interests to that of the infant beneficiary whom the trustees seek to maintain.[68]

Section 31(1) provides that the trustees may pay money to the parent or guardian of the infant beneficiary for their 'maintenance, education or benefit'.[69] This money must be generated by the income from the investments. This means that the infant beneficiary must be entitled to the income from the investment. When a beneficiary will be entitled to the income from the trust fund is set out in Figure 9.2; this is when he either has a vested interest in the property, or alternatively, has a contingent interest which, according to s31(3), 'carries the intermediate income of the property'.

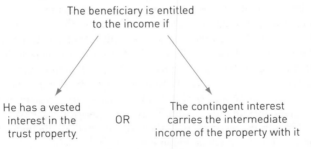

Figure 9.2 When a beneficiary is entitled to income from a gift.

The general principle is that those beneficiaries with a vested interest are entitled to the income from the trust property. They have no condition left to fulfil other than attain the age (18, nowadays) in which they may acquire the trust property absolutely. The issue is more controversial when concerned with contingent interests, which is where the beneficiary must fulfil a specific condition (for example, becoming a solicitor) before they are entitled to the trust property. The beneficiary might never meet the contingency so, at first glance, it is difficult to see why they should be entitled to the income from the trust property in the meantime.

---

67 Trustee Act 2000, Explanatory Notes, n. 23.
68 Trustee Act 1925, s 31(1).
69 Ibid, s 31(1)(i).

The basic principle, then, is that only a beneficiary who enjoys a vested interest or a limited version of a contingent interest which carries with it the intermediate income (essentially, the interest generated by the money when it is invested) in the trust property may be maintained by the trustees from the income it generates.

If the trust is created by the settlor, *inter vivos*, the contingent interest will generally carry the intermediate income with it – in other words, the beneficiary will generally be entitled to enjoy the income from the trust property and the power exists, therefore, for the trustees to use it to maintain him.

The position if the trust is created in the testator's will is more complicated. Statute provides that specific property – either realty or personalty – left to a beneficiary on trust will carry the intermediate income[70] but a contingent gift of money (a legacy) will generally not unless it falls into one of the following categories:

(a) If the legacy is made by a parent or a person standing in the position of a parent (in *loco parentis*) to the beneficiary under s 31(3) of the Trustee Act 1925 the legacy is expressly said to carry the income with it;

(b) If the testator has shown an intention to maintain the beneficiary elsewhere, as occurred in *Re Churchill*.[71] This case concerned the will of Louisa Churchill. She left £200 to her grand-nephew, Charles Plaskett, contingent upon him attaining 21 years of age. She gave a specific direction to her trustees that they could use the money to maintain him. The trustees sought directions from the High Court asking if interest was payable to Charles on his legacy.

Warrington J stated the general rule that the beneficiary should not become entitled to interest on the money until he attained a vested interest which in his case was when he attained 21. He acknowledged that there was an exception which allowed an infant to be maintained by interest payable on a contingent interest if the testator had shown an intention to maintain the beneficiary 'as part of the testator's bounty'.[72] Louisa's specific declaration that she permitted her trustees to maintain Charles demonstrated that she had showed an intention to maintain him and that the legacy should carry the interest which could also be used to maintain him as well as the actual gift itself; or

(c) If the testator has set the legacy aside specifically for the beneficiary, then it will carry the intermediate income with it. This occurred in *Re Medlock*.[73] Here a testator left a legacy of £750 to his trustees on trust for the benefit of his grandchildren, providing they attained 21. If they did not, the money was to fall into his residuary estate, which he left to his wife for life. The court held that as the £750 was specifically set aside for the benefit of the grandchildren in the testator's will, they were entitled to the interest from the money. That gift carried the intermediate income with it.

Providing the beneficiary enjoys either a vested or a contingent interest, which carries the intermediate income with it, the trustees may use the income from the trust property to maintain him. The trustees can decide to pay some or all of the income generated by the trust property. Section 31(1) provides that, in deciding whether or not to pay the money for the maintenance, education or benefit of the beneficiary, the trustees must take into account:

---

70 Law of Property Act 1925, section 175 (1).
71 *Re Churchill* [1909] 2 Ch 431.
72 Ibid at 433.
73 *Re Medlock* (1886) 55 LJ Ch 738.

- the beneficiary's age;
- the beneficiary's requirements;
- the circumstances of the case;
- what (if any) other income is available to maintain, educate or benefit the beneficiary; and
- where there is other income available, unless it has been used entirely in the beneficiary's maintenance, education or other benefit, or the court directs, only a proportion of the trust fund should be used to maintain the beneficiary. The logic behind this appears to be to preserve the income from the trust fund wherever possible and to rely on other funds to maintain the beneficiary first.

If, by the time the beneficiary reaches 18, he does not have a vested interest in the trust property, the trustees must then pay the income from the property to the beneficiary until he either attains a vested interest or dies.

The power to maintain an infant beneficiary under s 31 only gives the trustees a right to maintain the beneficiary. They are not obliged to do so. Under s 31(2), if the trustees do not use the income that the beneficiary is entitled to from the trust property for his maintenance, then that income should generally be accumulated (rolled up). The general position is that the accumulated income should be added to the capital of the trust fund. If, however, the infant beneficiary already has a vested interest during his infancy or upon attaining the age of 18 or marrying under that age becomes absolutely entitled to the trust property, the trustees will not add the accumulated income into the capital of the trust fund but must pay that income directly to the beneficiary.

A power to advance capital to the beneficiaries before they become entitled to it

Again, a trust document may contain an express power to advance capital to the beneficiaries before they become entitled to it. If not, s 32 of the Trustee Act 1925 contains a power for the trustees to advance capital to any beneficiary who is entitled to the capital interest in the trust property. This includes beneficiaries who enjoy either an absolute or contingent interest. The ability under this section is not limited to just infant beneficiaries, as under s 31.

The power is to apply capital money for the 'advancement or benefit' of a beneficiary. 'Advancement' used to mean using money to establish a beneficiary in an 'early period of life'.[74] Viscount Radcliffe, in Pilkington v IRC,[75] identified that such advancements in the nineteenth century might have been used to purchase an apprenticeship for the beneficiary or an army commission. Lloyd v Cocker[76] demonstrated that an advancement could be used to fund a dowry for a woman who was in the process of getting married. The key to all of these advancements was that they established 'some step in life of permanent significance'.[77]

'Benefit' always appears to have had a wider meaning than advancement. More recently, it has been held to have a very wide meaning with few restrictions imposed upon it, as Pilkington v IRC[78] shows.

The case concerned the will of William Pilkington. He provided that his residuary estate should be held on trust in equal shares for his nephews and nieces, living at his death who

---

74 Per Malins V-C in Re Kershaw's Trusts (1868) LR 6 Eq 322 at 323.
75 Pilkington v IRC [1964] AC 612 at 634.
76 Lloyd v Cocker (1870) 27 Beav 645.
77 Per Viscount Radcliffe in Pilkington v IRC [1964] AC 612 at 634.
78 Pilkington v IRC [1964] AC 612.

should attain 21 or marry under that age. Each nephew or niece was only to have a life interest, with the remainder interests being settled on such of their children as they chose with a default trust imposed for the nephews' or nieces' own children who attained 21 or married under that age if they failed to make a choice. At best, therefore, the great-nephews and nieces had a contingent reversionary interest in William's trust fund.

The trustees wished to make an advancement to one of William's great-nieces, Penelope (who was only five years old), to set up a further trust in her favour. The reason behind the advancement was to save on death duties which would have been due if the trust property had come to her after her father's death. The advancement was planned to be made by taking a large sum (£7,600) out of the trust under William's will and placing it on a new trust in favour of Penelope. The Inland Revenue objected to the advancement as they believed it amounted to a completely new trust, something that was not within the scope of s 32 of the Trustee Act 1925.

Viscount Radcliffe thought that the combined meaning of 'advancement or benefit' was very wide. He said that the phrase 'means any use of the money which will improve the material situation of the beneficiary'.[79] Section 32 was drafted in very wide terms, so much so that Viscount Radcliffe had not been able to find 'anything which in terms or by implication restricts the width of the manner or purpose of advancement.'[80] It was not relevant that a new trust was being established by the advancement in the case itself, in favour of Penelope and her own children. As long as the beneficiary (Penelope) benefited, it was of no consequence that other people (her own children) might also obtain an incidental benefit from the advancement occurring.

The majority in the Court of Appeal had thought that the beneficiary had to obtain a benefit personal to him or herself if s 32 was to be used successfully. Viscount Radcliffe disagreed with this. He thought that asking trustees only to advance capital if a personal need of the beneficiary justified it was imposing an almost impossible task. As he said, this was a fine distinction to draw:

> What distinguishes a personal need from any other need to which the trustees in their discretion think it right to attend in the beneficiary's interest?[81]

On the facts, the trustees could have made the advancement under s 32, but the terms of the new settlement infringed the rule as to remoteness of vesting.

❖ ANALYSING THE LAW

Consider the meaning of 'benefit' in *Pilkington v IRC*. Now turn to Chapter 10 and consider the meaning of 'benefit' under the Variation of Trusts Act 1958 as interpreted in decisions such as *Re Weston's Settlements*. Do you think there is a common thread in these decisions?

The inherent problem with exercising the power of advancement under s 32 is that the capital funds of the trust are depleted. It is no doubt with this in mind that there are three safeguards embodied in s 32:

---

79 Ibid at 635.
80 Ibid at 636.
81 Ibid at 640.

(a)   the trustees can only advance up to one half of the vested or presumptive share that the beneficiary may be entitled to;

(b)   if the beneficiary does become entitled to a share in the trust property (for example, because he fulfils the contingency) the advancement that he has already received must be taken into account when calculating the remaining share of the trust property due to him. This is sometimes called 'hotchpot'; and

(c)   no advancement may be made without the prior written consent of any life tenant who may exist. To give valid consent, the life tenant must be 18 years of age or over. This safeguard has been described as the 'eternal check'[82] on the system of advancement.

❖ EXPLAINING THE LAW

Suppose Scott sets up an *inter vivos* trust appointing Thomas as his trustee with £10,000 to Ulrika (currently 45 years old) for life, remainder to Vikas provided he becomes a barrister and attains 30 years of age. Vikas, currently 23, needs an advancement from the trust fund to purchase his barrister's wig and gown to receive his rights of audience.

Thomas might decide to make use of the power of advancement under s 32. The power of advancement is all about balance. Enabling him to achieve his ambition to become a barrister is arguably both an advancement to him and a benefit. But using the money will deplete the capital available to earn interest to pay to Ulrika. If Thomas is minded to use the power to advance capital to him, he will first need to obtain Ulrika's written consent. The total sum advanced cannot be more than half of Vikas' eventual share of the trust fund (£5,000) and it must be taken into account when he finally receives the absolute interest in the trust property.

Duty of Care and Skill Required of a Trustee

When exercising his duties and powers a trustee is bound to exercise them with a particular standard of care and skill.

The first case in which the trustee's duty of care was discussed was *Speight v Gaunt*.[83]

The case concerned the misappropriation of money from a trust fund by a broker, Richard Cooke. Isaac Gaunt was a trustee of the trust created by the will of John Speight. The adult beneficiaries of the trust agreed with the trustee that £15,000 should be invested in local authority bonds. Mr Gaunt mentioned using his own broker to buy the bonds, but the adult beneficiaries preferred him to use their own broker, Mr Cooke. Mr Cooke produced a note to Mr Gaunt, showing that he had committed himself to buy the bonds and that he required the money to complete the transaction. Mr Gaunt duly gave him the money. However, instead of using the money to buy the bonds, Mr Cooke kept it for himself. Mr Cooke was declared bankrupt. The adult beneficiaries brought an action against Mr Gaunt, alleging breach of trust. They wanted him to repay the monies lost to the trust fund.

Jessel MR set out the general standard of skill and care that a trustee should adopt:

---

82 Per Viscount Radcliffe in *Pilkington v IRC* [1964] AC 612 at 641.
83 *Speight v Gaunt* (1883) LR 22 ChD 727.

> a trustee ought to conduct the business of the trust in the same manner that an ordinary prudent man of business would conduct his own, and that beyond that there is no liability or obligation on the trustee.[84]

He stressed that a trustee should not be subjected to any higher standard of skill and care than anyone else:

> In other words, a trustee is not bound because he is a trustee to conduct business in other than the ordinary and usual way in which similar business is conducted by mankind in transactions of their own. It never could be reasonable to make a trustee adopt further and better precautions than an ordinary prudent man of business would adopt, or to conduct the business in any other way.[85]

The policy reason for this was straightforward: '[i]f it were otherwise, no one would be a trustee at all. He is not paid for it.'[86]

Given that the office of trustee was voluntary and unpaid, it would be unfair to expect a trustee to adopt a higher duty of care and skill when administering the trust than that which an 'ordinary prudent man of business' conducted his own affairs. Any higher duty of care imposed upon a trustee would result in individuals not agreeing to be trustees.

On the facts of the case, Mr Gaunt was not liable for the loss occasioned to the trust. He had acted as an ordinary prudent man of business throughout the transaction. It was entirely reasonable to invest in local authority bonds and to purchase them on the stock market. Purchasing them on the stock market necessitated using a broker, whom he had been instructed to use by the adult beneficiaries. Handing over the money for the broker to complete the purchase of the bonds was again entirely normal and reasonable. It could not be said that, in choosing the broker, investing in the bonds or handing over the money, Mr Gaunt had acted unlike an ordinary prudent man of business.

The 'ordinary prudent man of business' test was refined by the Court of Appeal in Re Whiteley.[87] The facts concerned trustees who invested money in investments that caused a loss to the trust fund. The trustees lent £3,000 to a borrower to buy a brickworks and secured the loan by a mortgage, with interest at 5 per cent. A further £2,000 was lent to purchase four houses, again secured by a mortgage with interest at 5 per cent. Both borrowers went bankrupt before the money was repaid. The value of the brickworks and the houses was insufficient to repay the money lent.

On the facts, the Court of Appeal thought that the investment in trade premises, such as in the brickworks, was too risky an investment and trust money should never have been used. The trustees were liable for the loss sustained. The investment in houses was, however, a proper investment to make and the trustees were not liable for the loss sustained in that investment.

Cotton LJ believed that the 'ordinary prudent man of business' test propounded in Speight v Gaunt could be explained as that a trustee must behave as a 'reasonably cautious man'.[88] When administering the trust, however, the trustees had to have regard to all beneficiaries, whether their interests were in possession or in remainder.

---

84 Ibid at 739.
85 Ibid at 739–740.
86 Ibid at 740.
87 Re Whiteley (1886) LR 33 Ch D 347,
88 Ibid at 350.

The trustee was not to be deemed to have any specialist knowledge and he 'must be dealt with as an ordinary man of ordinary intelligence'.[89] It was proper, instead, for a trustee to take advice from a specialist in the subject matter which concerned the investment. Yet this advice could not overrule the duty of a trustee to act as a reasonably cautious man. A surveyor had advised the trustees that £3,000 could safely be lent against the brickworks, but Cotton LJ said that a reasonably cautious man would still not have made that particular investment due to the risks involved. Much of the overall valuation of the property was dependent on the value of the buildings, plant and machinery, which were only of any worth if brickmaking continued on the site. When the business became insolvent and the brickmaking could not be continued, only the land remained of any real value and even that was less than the £3,000 advanced. A reasonably cautious man would have been aware of these risks and would have taken them into account when deciding whether or not to make the investment.

Lindley LJ clarified Jessel MR's 'ordinary prudent man of business' test by explaining that it must be taken into account that the trustee is investing funds belonging to others:

> The duty of a trustee is not to take such care only as a prudent man would take if he had only himself to consider; the duty rather is to take such care as an ordinary prudent man would take if he were minded to make an investment for the benefit of other people for whom he felt morally bound to provide.[90]

This does not mean to say that the trustee must avoid every possible risk involved in any venture; as Bacon V-C spelt out in Re Godfrey,[91] '[p]rudent businessmen in their dealings incur risk. That may happen and must happen in almost all human affairs'.[92]

As such, the trustee should exercise more caution when investing funds than a prudent man of business would exercise if investing his own money for his own benefit. Whilst still being prudent, the ordinary man of business might be prepared to take higher risks when investing his own money if only he was to benefit from it. The trustee should be conscious of investing others' money so that any risks taken are comparatively low. As Brightman J said in Barlett v Barclays Bank Trustee Co Ltd (Nos 1 & 2),[93] '[t]he distinction is between a prudent degree of risk on the one hand, and hazard on the other'. The latter must be avoided.

In nineteenth-century decisions, the courts were conscious of balancing two perhaps competing interests: the need to protect the beneficiaries by ensuring that trustees thought about the decisions they took, especially concerning investing the trust property whilst, on the other hand, not imposing too great a burden on trustees, many of whom were family members who acted as trustees on a voluntary basis with no particular skill or knowledge of how a trustee should act. As the twentieth century progressed, however, the concept of the professional trustee grew. More and more trusts came to be administered not by well-meaning amateurs but instead by professional individuals and organisations who had specialist skills and knowledge. These professional trustees charged the trust fund for their services.

It would appear incongruous if those professional trustees were subject to the same standard of care and skill as individuals who possessed no specialist skills and knowledge. Indeed, Harman J reached this conclusion in Re Waterman's Will Trusts.[94]

---

89 Ibid at 351.
90 Ibid at 355.
91 Re Godfrey (1883) 23 ChD 483.
92 Ibid at 493.
93 Barlett v Barclays Bank Trustee Co Ltd (Nos 1 and 2) [1980] 2 WLR 430 at 441.
94 Re Waterman's Will Trusts [1952] 2 All ER 1054.

Here, Lloyds Bank Ltd was the professional trustee of the trust created by Edith Waterman in her will. In *obiter* comments, Harman J distinguished between trustees who undertook their duties voluntarily and those who were paid and professional and non-professional trustees:

> I do not forget that a paid trustee is expected to exercise a higher standard of diligence and knowledge than an unpaid trustee, and that a bank which advertises itself largely in the public Press as taking charge of administrations is under a special duty.[95]

Harman J felt that such a special duty in the case of a large organisation would include making available parts of the organisation knowledgeable about the administration of trusts, rather than simply offering the services of the local branch manager to manage the trust.

This higher standard of care due from a professional trustee was spelt out categorically by Brightman J in *Bartlett & Barclays Bank Trust Co Ltd (Nos 1 & 2)*.[96]

The case concerned a trust set up by Sir Herbert Bartlett of the shares in a property investment company called Bartlett Trust Ltd. The company was originally formed to manage freehold and leasehold properties. The company would manage these properties profitably and account to its shareholders for the profits made. The trustee was the defendant.

The company wanted to invest in more risky types of property transactions, originally to fund death duties. This resulted in the company becoming involved in a development opposite the Central Criminal Court in London, which it named the 'Old Bailey Scheme'. It formed a joint venture company with another partner company to press ahead with the development. The transaction involved the joint venture company purchasing freehold and leasehold properties, which were owned by 20 different people, and redeveloping the whole site into office accommodation. The trustee's consent for this was not sought by the company and the Bank never enquired about the Scheme. The Old Bailey Scheme itself was, as Brightman J described it, 'imprudent and hazardous and wholly unsuitable for a trust'[97] as the government of the time wished to discourage office use in the centre of London. In addition, the Scheme would only work if all of the owners of the properties agreed to sell.

In fact, planning permission was never obtained for the redevelopment of the site of the Old Bailey Scheme. The shares in Bartlett Trust Ltd's parent company were sold at a considerable loss and this caused a knock-on loss to the trust fund.

The beneficiaries of the trust brought an action against Barclays Bank Trust Company Ltd arguing that it was guilty of a breach of trust by permitting the company to engage in the speculative business of property development. Their argument was that the bank, as trustee, could and should have stopped such a risky adventure going ahead. It was argued that the bank should make good to the trust the loss sustained.

Brightman J held that if the bank was a non-specialist trustee, its duty was to act as a prudent man of business would have done. Such a man would have taken necessary measures to ensure his investment was safe. He could, for example, take action to replace the board of directors of the company if he learned of such a speculative venture as this company proposed. What was key was to ensure that the trustee, as a prudent man, received such constant information that would enable him to control the trust in the interest of the beneficiaries.

---

95 Ibid at 1055.
96 *Bartlett & Barclays Bank Trust Co Ltd (Nos 1 and 2)* [1980] 2 WLR 430.
97 Ibid at 444.

Arguably, the bank failed to meet this requirement, as it simply waited for details of the company's annual report to be sent and made no further enquiries as to the Old Bailey Scheme.

The bank was, of course, a specialist trustee which levied a charge to administer the trust. Brightman J thought that a different standard of care was to be expected from such a trustee:

> I am of the opinion that a higher duty of care is plainly due from someone like a trust corporation which carries on a specialised business of trust management.[98]

He explained his reason for this view:

> A trust corporation holds itself out in its advertising literature as being above ordinary mortals. With a specialist staff of trained trust officers and managers, with ready access to financial information and professional advice, dealing with and solving trust problems day after day, the trust corporation holds itself out, and rightly, as capable of providing an expertise which it would be unrealistic to expect and unjust to demand from the ordinary prudent man or woman who accepts, probably unpaid and sometimes reluctantly from a sense of family duty, the burdens of a trusteeship.[99]

Brightman J held that the bank could and should have done more to prevent the Old Bailey Scheme from going ahead. All it did was to attend the company's annual general meetings and read the company's annual financial statements. It should have been more proactive in finding out what the company's plans were, as it had enough information to ask questions of the company's intentions. The Bank failed to act both according to the standard of a non-specialist trustee (as a prudent man of business) and to the higher standard of a professional trustee. It was liable for the loss that the trust suffered and would have to make recompense for that loss.

Section 1 of the Trustee Act 2000 seeks to codify these decisions on the standard of care to be expected from a trustee in the particular situations listed in Schedule 1. The section imposes an objective standard on all trustees, by stating that they must exercise 'reasonable' care and skill. That is to be read in the light of the guidance given in *Speight v Gaunt* and *ReWhiteley*.

Professional trustees are subjected to the higher standard of care in s 1 as interpreted in the light of *Bartlett v Barclays Bank Trust Co Ltd (Nos 1 and 2)*. This can either be because the professional trustee personally has specialist skill and knowledge, or because he is a member of a business or profession and it is reasonable to expect that he has a specialist skill or knowledge in administering a trust. There is, however, a strong subjective element in s 1; the court has to take into account the trustee's personal skills and knowledge when determining the standard of care and skill to which the trustee should adhere.

Section 1 of the Trustee Act 2000 sets out the standard of skill and care that a trustee must adopt when undertaking certain duties and in s 1(1), has arguably widened the gap between the professional and lay trustee:

(1)   Whenever the duty under this subsection applies to a trustee, he must exercise such care and skill as is reasonable in the circumstances, having regard in particular –

---

98 Ibid at 443.
99 Ibid.

(a) to any special knowledge of experience that he has or holds himself out as having, and

(b) if he acts as trustee in the course of a business or profession, to any special knowledge or experience that it is reasonable to expect of a person acting in the course of that kind of business or profession.

(2) In this Act the duty under subsection (1) is called 'the duty of care'.

Section 2 of the Trustee Act 2000 provides that the circumstances when the duty of care in s 1 applies are set out in Sched 1 to the Act, which provides that the duty of care will apply whenever a trustee:

(a) Invests the trust fund or reviews the investments of the trust fund;

(b) acquires land;

(c) appoints an agent, nominee or custodian or reviews their performance or arrangements they have entered into on the trust's behalf;

(d) compounds the trust's liabilities under s 15 of the Trustee Act 1925. (Section 15 of the Trustee Act 1925 gives a trustee powers to settle debts or accept property for money owed to the trust even though the trust may not receive the full amount it is strictly owed);

(e) insures trust property; and

(f) ascertains an up-to-date valuation of the trust property, under ss 22(1) and (3) of the Trustee Act 1925.

As is apparent, the duty of care in s 1 therefore applies to all of the major actions that a trustee might be expected to undertake. Investing the trust fund, reviewing the trust fund, appointing an agent, coming to arrangements with regard to monies the trust owes, insuring trust property and obtaining valuations of the trust's property are the key activities that a trustee will undertake. It is appropriate that the statutory duty of care applies in these situations. The existing common law duty of care appropriate to the trustee will continue to apply to the exercise of all of the other duties and powers a trustee possesses.

❖ EXPLAINING THE LAW

Scott establishes two *inter vivos* trusts. In the first trust, he chooses Thomas, his brother, to be his trustee, as Scott knows that he is of an honourable character. Thomas is a plumber. Thomas would be subject to the objective standard of care in s 1 of the Trustee Act 2000 when he undertakes those acts mentioned in Sched 1.

In Scott's second trust, he appoints Abigail & Co, his solicitors, to be the trustee. Abigail & Co successfully defended Scott against a driving offence. The firm's practice is solely in criminal law. Nonetheless, a higher standard of care is due from the firm under s 1(1)(b) Trustee Act 2000, as it is a member of a profession of which it is reasonable to expect its members to have specialist skill and knowledge in the administration of a trust.

Points to Review

You have seen:

- how trustees are subject to a number of non-fiduciary duties but enjoy a number of powers in their administration of the trust;
- how the courts and statutes, particularly the Trustee Act 2000, have sought to control the trustees' exercise of their duties and powers to the extent that fairly rigid requirements now exist in relation to both duties and powers; and
- how the standard of care and skill by which the trustees must use their duties and powers has evolved over the years to take account of greater numbers of professional trustees administering trusts. The standard of care and skill depends on the trustee's status and a higher standard is expected of a paid, professional trustee than the traditional lay individual who has volunteered to be a trustee of a family trust.

Making connections

This chapter should be read in conjunction with Chapter 8, where a trustee's fiduciary duties are considered, to gain a thorough understanding of the obligations that a trustee finds himself under.

If a trustee breaches any of his obligations or fails to exercise a power correctly, it is possible that a beneficiary will wish to take action against him for breach of trust. Over the years, professional trustees have sought to guard against such actions by imposing express exemption clauses in the trust instrument, either excluding or limiting their liability. The action for breach of trust together with the use and control of trustee exemption clauses is considered in Chapter 12.

 Useful Things to Read

The best reading is contained in the primary sources listed below. It is always good to consider the decisions of the courts themselves as this will lead to a deeper understanding of the issues involved. A few secondary sources are also listed, which you may wish to read to gain additional insights into the areas considered in this chapter.

Primary sources

Bartlett v Barclays Bank Trust Co Ltd (Nos 1 & 2) [1980] 2 WLR 430.
Breakspear v Ackland [2009] Ch 32.
Cowan v Scargill [1985] Ch 270.
Hallows v Lloyd (1888) LR 39 ChD 686.
Harries v Church Commissioners for England [1992] 1 WLR 1241.
O'Rourke v Darbishire [1920] AC 581.
Pilkington v IRC [1964] AC 612.
Re Brogden (1888) LR 38 ChD 546.
Re Green's Will Trusts [1985] 3 All ER 455.
Re Londonderry's Settlement [1965] Ch 918.
Re Whiteley (1886) LR 33 ChD 347.
Schmidt v Rosewood Trust Ltd [2003] AC 709.
Speight v Gaunt (1883) LR 22 ChD 727.

Trustee Act 2000, ss 1, 2, 3, 4, 5, 8, 27, 31, 32 and Sched 1.

Secondary sources

Cedric Bell, 'Some reflections on choosing trustees' (1988) TL & P 2(3) 86–88. This article reflects on choosing trustees based on a research project.

Michael Gibbon, 'Beneficiaries' information rights' (2011) T &T 17(1) 27–33. This article contains a useful review of the decisions of *Breakspear v Ackland* and *Schmidt v Rosewood Trust Ltd.*

Alastair Hudson, *Equity & Trusts* (7th edn, Routledge-Cavendish, 2012) chs 8, 9 and 10.

Mohamed Ramjohn, *Text, Cases and Materials on Equity and Trusts* (4th edn, Routledge-Cavendish, 2008) ch 19.

K Senior, 'Trustees' powers and duties' (Part 1) (2001) NLJ 151 (6966) 25. This article, together with the next one, contains a useful summary of trustees' powers and duties and considers the implications of the enactment of the Trustee Act 2000.

K Senior, 'Trustees' powers and duties' (Part 2) (2001) NLJ 151 (6968) 84, 105.

Chapter 10

Variation of a Trust and Setting a Trust Aside

The next topics concern whether it is possible to change a trust after it has been established and, secondly, when a trust can be set aside by the court even if, at first glance, it appears to have been validly created. This chapter builds upon the creation and operation of express trusts.

As You Read

Look out for the following issues:

- the common law and statutory authorities which permit a trust to be varied;
- the Variation of Trusts Act 1958, which is the main statutory authority, which enables the court to approve proposed variations of trust in certain situations; and
- when a trust may be set aside if it has been set up to defeat or defraud a settlor's creditors.

Variation of a Trust

Background

It has been shown that there are a number of requirements to establish a valid trust. To set up a workable trust, the settlor must:

(a) fulfil any formality requirements if the type of property to be left on trust requires it[1] (for example, a trust of land must be evidenced in writing and signed by someone able to declare the trust under s 53(1)(b) of the Law of Property Act 1925);

(b) comply with the three certainties: intention, subject matter and object;[2]

(c) comply with the beneficiary principle;[3]

(d) adhere to the rules against perpetuity;[4] and

(e) constitute the trust.[5]

These rules generally exist to provide some protection for the trustee. The first four criteria – relating to declaring the trust – ensure that it must be absolutely clear that a trust has been created, spell out categorically what it is that the trustee is supposed to administer and in whose favour the trustee must manage the trust. Constituting the trust ensures that the trustee can manage the trust property by transferring the legal title in the property to him.

If, however, the settlor has jumped through all of the hoops required in creating a trust, it might be thought that varying the trust would be very strange to him as he will have spent a lot of time and trouble setting up the trust and perhaps would not want those arrangements disturbed by their being subsequently altered.

---

1   See Chapter 4.
2   See Chapter 5.
3   See Chapter 6.
4   See companion website.
5   See Chapter 7.

Key Learning Point

The basic rule here is that, once established, it is not possible to vary a trust. This was explained by Lord Evershed MR in *Re Downshire Settled Estates*:[6]

> The general rule ... is that the court will give effect, as it requires the trustees themselves to do, to the intentions of a settlor as expressed in the trust instrument, and *has not arrogated to itself any overriding power to disregard or rewrite the trusts*.[7]

Yet equity has always permitted a trust to be varied in certain circumstances. Originally, equity's jurisdiction to alter a trust was used to deal with property or the management of it for children or mentally disabled individuals.[8]

Trusts nowadays tend to be established as a method of saving tax. Each year, however, the Finance Act following the government's Budget makes changes to the taxation system. Consequently, an original tax-efficient trust that may have been established may have become less tax efficient than it was at the time the trust was set up. The beneficiaries might, therefore, wish to vary the trust to minimise their liability to tax.

❖ APPLYING THE LAW

Varying a trust to avoid tax can result in large savings to the beneficiaries. Such a variation occurred in *Re Norfolk's Will Trusts; Norfolk v Howard*[9] in which the sixteenth Duke of Norfolk successfully applied to the High Court to vary the trusts set up by his father. As a result of the court approving the variation, the beneficiaries of the revised trust enjoyed an additional £550,000 that would otherwise have been payable in taxation.

The court does not act as a slave to HM Revenue & Customs and is not predisposed to prevent variations of trust occurring just because their purpose is to avoid tax. In fact, the contrary is true, according to Lord Evershed MR in *Re Downshire Settled Estates*, in that it is:

> not an objection to the sanction by the court of any proposed scheme in relation to trust property that its object or effect is or may be to reduce liability for tax.[10]

It is important to note, however, that a trust may only be varied when permitted and saving tax does not have to be a prerequisite to a successful application to vary a trust. The crucial issue is when it is permitted to vary a trust.

---

6 *Re Downshire Settled Estates* [1953] Ch 218.
7 Ibid at 234 (emphasis added).
8 See, for example, *Earl of Winchelsea v Norcliffe* (1680–1687) 1 Vern 403.
9 *Re Norfolk's Will Trusts; Norfolk v Howard* (1966) TLR 22 March.
10 *Re Downshire Settled Estates* [1953] Ch 218 at 233.

Circumstances When a Trust Can Be Varied Today

A trust may be varied using one of three main methods. Before the intricacies of each method are examined, a table setting out the main parts of those methods is set out in Figure 10.1. These methods only apply if there is not an express power to vary the trust contained in the

Main methods of varying a trust	Requirements	Consequences of the variation
The rule in *Saunders v Vautier*	All beneficiaries must be: 1. *sui juris* (at least 18 years old and have mental capacity); and 2. entitled (collectively) to an absolute interest in the trust property.	The trust is brought to an end.
The court's inherent jurisdiction	The jurisdiction may only be applied for one of the following grounds: 1. conversion; 2. emergency; 3. maintenance; or 4. compromise.	This depends on which ground has been applied by the court: 1. conversion: this converts some/all of the trust property from realty to personalty or vice versa; 2. emergency: the trust can be varied due to an event unforeseen by the settlor; 3. maintenance: the trust is varied so that a beneficiary who is an infant child of the settlor may benefit from the income of the trust; 4. compromise: the trust is varied to resolve a genuine dispute between the beneficiaries.
The Variation of Trusts Act 1958	The category of beneficiary on whose behalf the application is made must fall into one of the following: 1. one who is under 18 years old or who lacks mental capacity; 2. a potential beneficiary under a discretionary trust; 3. an unborn beneficiary; or 4. a beneficiary who might enjoy their interest under a discretionary trust should a protective trust come to an end.	The variation may be: 1. substantive: the court is able to approve any scheme proposed to vary or revoke a trust; and/or 2. administrative: the court may approve any scheme which will enlarge the trustees' powers in varying or administering trust property.

Figure 10.1 The main methods of varying a trust.

trust document for, if such a power exists, obviously it makes more sense to take advantage of that power.

Each of these methods must be examined in turn.

Varying a trust with the consent of all adult beneficiaries

If they act together, all adult beneficiaries are entitled to vary the trust provided that they all collectively enjoy an absolute interest in the trust property. They must all enjoy mental capacity. The result of a group of adult beneficiaries owning the entire equitable interest collectively is that the trustees hold the trust property on a bare trust. The ability of the beneficiaries to vary the trust comes from the decision in *Saunders v Vautier*,[11] which gives rise to what is sometimes known as 'the rule in *Saunders v Vautier*'.

Here, a testator left shares in the East India Company worth £2,000 on trust for the benefit of his great-nephew, Daniel Wright Vautier. There was a direction in the testator's will that the income from the shares had to be accumulated (reinvested) into the capital until Daniel reached 25 years old. At that point, the capital of the shares, together with all of the accumulated income, was to be transferred to him. The testator died when Daniel was still a child.

In March 1841, Daniel attained 21 years old, then the age of majority. He applied to the Court of Chancery to have the whole fund (both the value of the shares and the accumulated income) transferred to him, four years earlier than that envisaged by the creation of the trust.

Lord Langdale MR agreed that the whole fund should be transferred to Daniel. He said that:

> the legatee, if he has an absolute indefeasible interest in the legacy, is not bound to wait until the expiration of that period, but may require payment the moment he is competent to give a valid discharge.[12]

The moment when Daniel could give a valid discharge – or receipt – for the money was when he reached the age of majority.

The decision in the case turned on the fact that Daniel had an absolute interest in the trust property. The other residuary legatees argued that he had a contingent interest, an interest which he could only enjoy provided he reached the age of 25. The court rejected this argument. It seems it was on the basis that the testator had merely directed the income to be accumulated. He had actually given Daniel a vested interest in the shares but simply directed the income to be accumulated for his maintenance.

The decision in the case shows that beneficiaries who enjoy an absolute vested interest in the trust property may call for it to be transferred to them. In a sense, it is an example of a trust being varied but it is a rough-and-ready variation as it simply brings the trust to an end. As the trust was, in any event, a bare trust only, it is not a particularly significant step for the adult beneficiary to call for the trust property to be transferred to themselves.

The principle from *Saunders v Vautier* still stands but now applies to beneficiaries at a younger age. As a result of s 1 of the Family Law Reform Act 1969 being enacted, the age of majority was lowered in English law to 18 years of age from 21. That means that if a beneficiary reaches the age of 18 and enjoys an absolute vested interest in trust property, he can compel the trustee to transfer the trust property to himself. That transfer will mark the end of the trust. The *ratio*

---

11 *Saunders v Vautier* (1841) 4 Beav 115; 49 ER 282.
12 Ibid at 116.

decidendi of the case also applies where there are a number of adult beneficiaries who collectively all enjoy the equitable interest in the trust property, provided they all have mental capacity.

Varying a trust under the court's inherent jurisdiction

As You Read

This area is concerned with when the court has an inherent right to sanction a variation of trust on behalf of infants, those unborn or mentally incapable beneficiaries as those categories of people cannot give their own consent. Beneficiaries who are 18 years or over and mentally capable must continue to give their own consent and the court cannot override such beneficiaries' wishes.

As will be seen, the extent of the court's inherent jurisdiction to vary a trust is very limited and it could be questioned whether such a jurisdiction even exists at all.

The difficulty with the rule in *Saunders v Vautier* is that it is of very limited application. It only applies to beneficiaries who:

● are all adults and who are mentally capable ('*sui juris*');
● all have an absolute, vested interest in the trust property; and
● have no other desire than to end the trust by transferring the legal interest in the trust property to themselves.

Before the decision of the House of Lords in *Chapman v Chapman*,[13] the courts also thought that they enjoyed a much wider discretion to vary a trust if asked to do so, as part of an inherent jurisdiction that the Court of Chancery originally enjoyed. Quite how wide their discretion lay depended on the views of the individual judges.

The relatively wide view of the Court of Appeal

In *Re Downshire Settled Estates*, Lord Evershed MR, with whom Romer LJ agreed, whilst not wishing to impose 'undue fetters'[14] on the court's discretion, thought that the court actually enjoyed only a limited inherent discretion (as a successor to the Court of Chancery) to vary a trust. This limited discretion enjoyed by the court was to enable the court to give the trustees such additional administrative powers as were necessary for the trustees to deal with the trust property if an 'emergency' arose. Such administrative powers had to be used for the benefit of 'everyone interested'[15] under the trust. An 'emergency' was defined to mean something that the settlor had not planned for when setting up the trust as opposed to involving notions of extreme urgency in the need to vary the trust. It also had to be for everyone's benefit that the court granted the trustees additional administrative powers.

Lord Evershed MR quoted from the example given in the judgment of a different Romer LJ in *Re New*[16] of the emergency situation under consideration. In that case, Romer LJ gave the

---

13 *Chapman v Chapman* [1954] AC 429.
14 *Re Downshire Settled Estates* [1953] Ch 218 at 232.
15 Ibid at 235.
16 *Re New* [1901] 2 Ch 534.

example of a testator creating a trust in his will giving a direction to his trustees to sell some of the trust property at a particular point in time. When that time arrived, the market for the property had fallen, which meant that complying with the testator's wishes in selling the property would create a loss to the estate. He said that in such a situation, the court would authorise a power to be given to the trustees to postpone the sale of the property until a later date. Such an event was an 'emergency' because it was unforeseen by the settlor when establishing the trust. The court was able to intervene to grant further administrative powers to the trustee.

In *Re Downshire Settled Estates*, Lord Evershed MR said a wider exception existed where the beneficiaries were either infants or mentally incapable. In those situations, the court was able to step in more generally to vary the trust. This was because the beneficiaries were not adults and not, therefore, in a position to act together, so as to enjoy the benefit of the rule in *Saunders v Vautier*. In acting in this situation, the court would be permitting the variation of the interests of the infants or mentally incapable beneficiaries. Those who were adults and mentally capable would need to give their own consent. This was known as 'compromising' the claims of the infant or mentally incapable beneficiaries, which really meant the court was acceding to a bargain that the *sui juris* beneficiaries had put forward. The word 'compromise' was to be given a wide meaning and was not to be limited to settling disputed claims.

The third judge in the case, Denning LJ, took a typically more robust position as to when the court should be able to exercise its inherent jurisdiction. He believed that the Court of Chancery had enjoyed a jurisdiction to sanction any acts done by trustees for the benefit of either infant or mentally incapable beneficiaries provided the court was satisfied that the variation was indeed for their benefit. Given that, acting together, beneficiaries who were *sui juris* could agree to a variation of trust themselves, Denning LJ's views would have given the court a wide discretion to vary a trust in the case of infant or mentally incapable beneficiaries: the variation simply had to be for their benefit.

The narrower view of the House of Lords

The decision of the House of Lords in *Chapman v Chapman* (handed down within 16 months of the Court of Appeal's decision in *Re Downshire Settled Estates*) placed strict limits on when a court could sanction the variation of a trust.

The facts concerned trusts established by Sir Robert and Lady Chapman for the benefit of their grandchildren. The trusts contained substantial sums of money for their benefit, with the effect that upon the settlors' deaths, a large sum (approximately £30,000) would be due to the Inland Revenue in the form of death duties. A scheme was proposed by the adult beneficiaries and trustees under which money would be taken from the established trusts and transferred to new trusts which would omit the provisions that gave rise to the tax being charged. The court's consent was needed on behalf of the infant beneficiaries.

The House of Lords refused to approve the scheme on the basis that the court enjoyed no jurisdiction to give authority to such a variation of trust on behalf of the infant beneficiaries. The House of Lords adopted a firm stance against the court having any jurisdiction to vary a trust and thought that any such ability the court did enjoy was by way of exception rather than the norm.

The most detailed opinion was delivered by Lord Morton. He believed that previous case law of when the court had sanctioned variations of trust under its inherent jurisdiction could be grouped together under four heads:

(a)   the 'conversion' jurisdiction;
(b)   the 'emergency' jurisdiction;

(c) the maintenance jurisdiction; and
(d) the compromise jurisdiction.

The 'conversion' jurisdiction

This jurisdiction concerns the ability of the court to sanction a variation of trust in converting the nature of the property to which an infant or mentally incapable beneficiary is entitled. For example, a trust might wish to be varied so as to allow the infant's interest in personalty to be invested in realty.[17] Lord Morton believed that the court had always enjoyed an inherent jurisdiction to sanction such variations of trust. Such a jurisdiction was uncontroversial and would continue to be permitted.

The 'emergency' jurisdiction

Lord Morton believed that the court did enjoy a jurisdiction to sanction a trust being varied on behalf of those beneficiaries who were incapable of giving their own consent but such jurisdiction was of an extremely limited nature.

He quoted with approval the comments delivered by Romer LJ in *Re New*. The facts of that case concerned three separate trusts set up by shareholders in the Wollaton Colliery Company Ltd for the benefit of their children. The originally priced £100 shares left on the trusts had increased substantially in value to be worth £175 each. The shareholders of the company wanted to reorganise the company so that, effectively, each of the shares would be split into smaller shares. Shares worth a smaller amount could be bought and sold more easily as they would appeal to more investors. This would be achieved by the creation of a new company and the exchange of the original shares for shares in the new company. All of the shareholders of the company were keen for the scheme to go ahead, as were the trustees of the trusts. The problem was that some of the beneficiaries were not *sui juris* and could not give their own consent to the variation of the trust. The court's consent would be needed if the scheme was to go ahead.

❖ APPLYING THE LAW

> Even today, certain companies' share prices increase dramatically beyond initial expectations when the shares are first issued. The best example nowadays is probably that of Apple, whose shares initially traded at $22 but were worth over $600 each in early 2012.

In giving the judgment of the Court of Appeal, Romer LJ began by stating the general rule that the court has no jurisdiction to sanction any acts that the trustees wish to undertake which are not permitted by the terms of the trust. However, the court could sanction acts which had to be done by trustees in an 'emergency'. An emergency was one which:

> may reasonably be supposed to be one not foreseen or anticipated by the author of the trust, where the trustees are embarrassed by the emergency that has arisen and the duty cast upon them to do what is best for the estate, and the consent of all the beneficiaries cannot be obtained by reason of some of them not being *sui juris* or in existence . . .[18]

---

17 See Chapter 4 (pp. 85–86) for examples of different types of personalty and realty.
18 Ibid.

But the court would exercise its jurisdiction with 'great caution'[19] and

> will not be justified in sanctioning every act desired by trustees and beneficiaries merely because it may appear beneficial to the estate . . . each case brought before the Court must be considered and dealt with according to its special circumstances.[20]

On the facts of the case, the proposed variations of each of the three trusts were permitted.

The decision of the Court of Appeal in Re Tollemache[21] (in which Romer LJ again sat) just two years later set out limits of the emergency jurisdiction considered in Re New. Cozens-Hardy LJ described the decision in Re New as 'the high-water mark of the exercise by the court of its extraordinary jurisdiction in relation to trusts'.[22] Vaughan Williams LJ said that the court could only exercise its emergency jurisdiction to sanction a variation of trust if the emergency had to be dealt with 'at once'.[23]

Lord Morton approved the comments of Romer LJ in Re New and the decision of the Court of Appeal in Re Tollemache as setting limits on the extent of the emergency jurisdiction. He summed up[24] the jurisdiction as being there to 'salvage' trust property rather than do anything more proactive in the management of a trust.

The maintenance jurisdiction

This concerns the court's ability to provide for children of the settlor. If a trust has been created which directs the income from it to be accumulated into the capital, prima facie, any children of the settlor would not be provided for on a day-to-day basis from the trust fund. The court has assumed that such a settlor would not have desired their children to be destitute and so has sanctioned the maintenance of such children.

Lord Morton regarded this ability to provide maintenance as a limited exception to the principle that the court had no jurisdiction to vary a trust. He quoted, with approval, Farwell J in Re Walker:[25]

> I decline to accept any suggestion that the court has an inherent jurisdiction to alter a man's will because it thinks it beneficial. It seems to me that is quite impossible.

Lord Morton believed Farwell J's words were 'equally true in the case of a settlement'.[26]

The facts of Re Walker concerned a trust established by Sir James Walker in his will of 1882 in which he left a considerable amount of land in Yorkshire on trust for the life of his son and, in turn, each of his sons. The trust contained a direction that £500 per year should be used from the income of the land to maintain any infant beneficiary. This maintenance was to include the upkeep of the house, Sand Hutton Hall, in which each beneficiary was directed to reside. An infant beneficiary, the great-grandson of Sir James, brought an action to vary the trust so that £4,000 might be used from the income each year for his maintenance and education, arguing that £500 per year was insufficient to maintain such a vast residence as Sand Hutton Hall.

---

19 Ibid.
20 Ibid.
21 Re Tollemache [1903] 1 Ch 955.
22 Ibid at 956.
23 Ibid.
24 Chapman v Chapman [1954] AC 429 at 455.
25 Re Walker [1901] 1 Ch 879 at 885.
26 Chapman v Chapman [1954] AC 429 at 462.

Although wary of altering Sir James' will, Farwell J sanctioned the variation of the trust in this manner. The judge found that the will contained a 'paramount intention'[27] by Sir James that Sand Hutton Hall should be kept in good repair, but he had made no specific provision for maintaining the house. In addition, he found the will contained a separate allowance of £500 per year for an infant beneficiary's personal maintenance, which could take the form of meeting the costs of the child's education. As Sir James had not forbidden a larger sum being spent on the maintenance and education of an infant beneficiary when more was needed than he had provided for in the trust, the trust could be varied to reflect Sir James' intentions that the property and the infant beneficiary both be maintained appropriately.

Re Walker is a good illustration of the court exercising a jurisdiction to sanction the variation of a trust to maintain an infant beneficiary by providing a suitable place for him to live. But as the comments of Farwell J make clear, as supported by Lord Morton in Chapman v Chapman, the court's ability to vary the trust in this manner is clearly limited. The court must find an intention of the settlor to maintain a beneficiary and, in that sense, the court is not really approving a dramatic variation of a trust. In Re Walker, the settlor had always made provision for the infant beneficiary; all that was in issue was the appropriate amount that should be apportioned to this maintenance.

Even if a settlor has made no specific provision to maintain an infant beneficiary in the trust, the jurisdiction here appears to be limited to trusts concerning the settlor's family, according to Pearson J in Re Collins.[28] It may be that this jurisdiction could be extended slightly although the prospects of that occurring are small. It is perhaps only a small step for the court to sanction the maintenance of a person that the settlor would have naturally maintained during their life.

❖ ANALYSING THE LAW

Does Re Collins reflect modern day lives? Should the court's jurisdiction be extended to maintain other children for whom, perhaps, the settlor has assumed responsibility during his life? For example, if the settlor has made his infant godchild a beneficiary under a trust in his will, should the court nowadays be permitted to vary that trust to maintain the child?

The compromise jurisdiction

Lord Morton acknowledged that there were 'many'[29] reported cases in which the Court of Chancery and the High Court had approved compromises in relation to infants or unborn children. This did not mean that the court enjoyed an unlimited jurisdiction to vary a trust, however, by compromising beneficiaries' claims to the trust. Trusts which were potentially to benefit infants and unborn children were, at that stage, 'ex hypothesi, still in doubt and unascertained'[30] because their interests had not yet been ascertained. The problem arose when interests were ascertained:

---

27 Re Walker [1901] 1 Ch 879 at 886.
28 Re Collins (1886) 32 ChD 229.
29 Chapman v Chapman [1954] AC 429 at 457.
30 Ibid.

> If, however, there is no doubt as to the beneficial interests, the court is, to my mind, exceeding its jurisdiction if it sanctions a scheme for their alteration, whether the scheme is called a 'compromise in the broader sense' or an 'arrangement' or is given any other name.[31]

Lord Morton thought that the views of the members of the Court of Appeal on the ability of the court to approve compromises in *Re Downshire Settled Estates* were too wide. The court did not have any jurisdiction to approve contrived 'compromises' between beneficiaries.

Lord Simonds LC made it clear in his speech that the court's jurisdiction to sanction a compromise meant that the court could only make a decision in the event of a genuine dispute of a beneficiary's rights. A practice had grown up in the first half of the twentieth century in which High Court judges would, in chambers, approve variations to trusts on behalf of infants or unborn children. Disputes had often been manufactured by the parties to the trust as this was the only way to obtain the court's sanction to a variation of the original trust. Lord Simonds LC disapproved of such a procedure as frequently it had simply been assumed that the High Court had jurisdiction to make such orders varying beneficial interests in this manner. As such hearings were in chambers, they were not subject to the transparency and scrutiny that decisions in open court enjoy. Lord Simonds LC believed that the only time the compromise jurisdiction should be used by the courts was in the case of a real dispute over beneficial rights and where the court's consent was sought on behalf of infants or unborn children. In doing so, Lord Simonds LC disagreed with the comments of the majority of the Court of Appeal in *Re Downshire Settled Estates* that the word 'compromise' could be interpreted widely, to authorise the imposition of a fresh bargained agreement between the adult beneficiaries and trustees concerning all of the beneficiaries' interests.

Summary of the court's inherent jurisdiction to vary a trust

Following *Chapman v Chapman*, the court only had authority to sanction a variation of a trust in four strictly limited situations. These were in situations of conversion, emergency, maintenance and genuine compromise.

The difficulty with this conclusion was that it limited the court's ability to sanction the variation of a trust on behalf of a beneficiary who was not *sui juris*. In doing so, it put an end to the practice of High Court judges in chambers approving such applications to vary a trust on a relatively informal basis.

As a result of the decision in *Chapman v Chapman*, the Variation of Trusts Act 1958 was enacted.

Variation of a trust under statute

Variation of Trusts Act 1958

This statute is the main method nowadays by which trusts are varied. The long title to the Variation of Trusts Act 1958 expressly confirmed that the purpose behind its enactment was to remedy the restrictive decision in *Chapman v Chapman* as to when a trust could be varied:

---

31 Ibid at 461.

> An Act to extend the jurisdiction of courts of law to vary trusts in the interests of beneficiaries and sanction dealings with trust property.

The Act thus sought to restore the courts' ability to vary trusts to the relatively informal operation that had been carried out by judges pre-*Chapman*.

Section 1 of the Act gives the High Court[32] two powers: (i) substantive and (ii) administrative:

(a) the substantive power is that the court may 'approve . . . any arrangement' proposed by any person to vary or revoke a trust; and

(b) the administrative power permits the court to approve an arrangement which seeks to enlarge the trustees' powers in varying or administering the trust property.

'Arrangement' was described by Lord Evershed MR in *Re Steed's Will Trusts*[33] as having a very wide meaning which would include 'any proposal which any person may put forward for varying or revoking the trusts'.[34]

Taken together, the powers enable the court to sanction a wide range of variations of trust.

But the powers are curtailed because the court is not able to sanction arrangements for any variation of trust under s 1. The court can only give its sanction for a variation, revocation or enlargement of the trustees' powers if it is doing so on behalf of a category of person who falls into one of the four categories listed in s 1(1). Those categories are:

(a) a beneficiary who is incapable of giving their own consent because they lack capacity (i.e. they are under 18 years of age or are mentally incapable);

(b) a potential beneficiary who may become entitled to an interest under a trust in the future. Such potential beneficiaries merely enjoy a hope (or *spes*) of being chosen to be a beneficiary and enjoy the trust property. The court may consent on behalf of such a person. If they have been chosen by the trustees to be an actual beneficiary, then the court can no longer consent on their behalf;

(c) an unborn beneficiary; and

(d) a person who may enjoy an interest under a discretionary trust but one which arises because there is a protective trust in operation and the principal beneficiary under the protective trust has not yet determined their trust. Once again, the discretionary beneficiary may or may not actually receive the trust property in the future, depending on whether the protective trust is determined.

Key Learning Point

The key point is that the High Court may only give its permission for a variation or revocation of a trust on behalf of a person who falls into one of the categories listed in (a)–(d). There is no jurisdiction for the High Court to consent on behalf of any other category of person.

---

32 Variation of Trusts Act 1958, s 1(3).
33 *Re Steed's Will Trusts* [1960] Ch 407.
34 Ibid at 419.

Glossary: Protective trust

A protective trust in the 1958 Act is defined by reference to Trustee Act 1925, s 33. This defines a protective trust as one where income is invested for the life of a beneficiary. That beneficiary is then known as the 'principal beneficiary'. The nature of a protective trust is paternalistic in that it seeks to prevent the beneficiary from gaining access to anything other than income from the trust. If the beneficiary seeks to take any action to gain any more than the income, the trust will immediately determine.

At the point of the protective trust determining, a discretionary trust comes into existence. The trustees enjoy a discretion to pay the income to a group which includes the principal beneficiary and their spouse or partner and issue or, if there is no spouse, partner or issue, those people who would be entitled to the beneficiary's property on his dying intestate. Whilst the beneficiary might still enjoy some of the income under the trust, he may not now enjoy any as a result of the discretionary trust coming into existence and the trust property, instead of being solely his own, may now be distributed between a group of people.

The nature of a protective trust is, therefore, to protect a beneficiary against dissipating the trust property. If he simply accepts the income from the trust, he will be entitled to that for his lifetime or any other period the settlor may have stated in the trust. But if he tries to vary the trust so as to enjoy the capital as well, a discretionary trust comes into existence under which the income from the trust property may be shared between a wider group.

❖ EXPLAINING THE LAW

Suppose Scott creates a trust and appoints Thomas as his trustee. The trust provides that £100,000 is left on trust for the benefit of Ulrika for life remainder to Vikas. Ulrika is 25 years old but Vikas is only five years of age. Scott dies the following day.

Ulrika decides that she would like a little more freedom with the trust money but she does not wish to deprive Vikas of his fair share. She proposes that the trust be varied so that they both become absolutely entitled to £50,000 each.

The High Court could give its consent on behalf of Vikas as he falls within category (a) of s 1(1). Vikas is not able to give his own consent to the proposed variation as he lacks capacity due to being an infant.

If, however, Vikas was 18 years of age or older and enjoys mental capacity, there is no jurisdiction for the High Court to consent on his behalf. Ulrika would need to seek his own consent, under the rule in *Saunders v Vautier*. The trust would then end and both of them would enjoy their shares. If Vikas refused to give his consent, then the trust would have to continue.

The final criterion under s 1 is that for the court to approve any arrangement brought before it on behalf of those categories of people listed in (a)–(c) it must be shown that such an arrangement is for that person's benefit. The requirement to demonstrate that it is for a person's benefit does not apply to the court giving its consent on behalf of those individuals falling into category (d).

'Benefit'...

The requirement that the variation or revocation of the trust or enlargement of the trustees' powers be for the 'benefit' of the person on whose behalf the court consents under paragraphs (a)–(c) of s 1(1) is a real one and not one to which the court simply pays lip-service, as was shown in *Re Weston's Settlements*.[35]

The facts concerned two trusts set up in 1964 by Stanley Weston, one for each of his two sons and their respective future children. The trust property was shares in a public company. In 1965, Capital Gains Tax was introduced by the Government which would have resulted in a heavy taxation liability when the shares were sold. However, tax could be avoided if the majority of the trustees and all of the beneficiaries were not resident in the UK. To save tax, Stanley and his family moved to Jersey.

❖ APPLYING THE LAW

Located just 14 miles off the coast of northern France, Jersey is a 'peculiar' of the English Crown. Originally owned by William of Normandy (later William the Conqueror), the island allied itself to King John of England in 1215 as opposed to being ruled by France. Loyal to the English Crown since, it has its own separate legal system which has its roots more in Norman-French law than that of the English legal system. Its residents enjoy lower taxation than their English counterparts, which means that it remains an attractive jurisdiction to this day for the establishment and management of trusts.

Stanley brought an application to bring the two trusts under the control of Jersey's legal system and for the trust property to be transferred to trustees resident in Jersey. This was really an application to revoke the original trusts, made under English law, and reconstitute them under Jersey law. The elder son gave his consent for the trust to be revoked in this manner. The younger son was an infant and so lacked capacity to give his own consent. The High Court was asked to give its consent on his behalf under s 1(1)(a) of the 1958 Act. As the trusts were originally established for the benefit of the two sons' own children, permission was also sought for the High Court to approve the revocation of the trusts for these unborn children too, under s 1(1)(c).

The High Court refused to give its permission to revoke the trusts in this manner and the Court of Appeal agreed with its decision.

Giving the leading judgment in the Court of Appeal, Lord Denning MR pointed out that the 1958 Act gave the courts no guidance as to when a variation or revocation of a trust should be sanctioned under it. In making a decision over whether to agree to a variation or revocation of a trust, he said that two propositions were clear. The first emphasised that any consent given by the court to vary or revoke a trust had to be for the individual's benefit, '[i]n exercising its discretion, the function of the court is to protect those who cannot protect themselves. It must do what is truly for their benefit'.[36]

The second proposition was that it was an acceptable benefit to be the avoidance of taxation. As Harman LJ put it, the court's function was not to be 'the watch-dog of the Inland Revenue'.[37]

---

35 *Re Weston's Settlements* [1969] 1 Ch 223.
36 Ibid at 245.
37 Ibid at 246.

Lord Denning MR defined 'benefit' widely. Whilst 'benefit' could mean financial benefit to infants or unborn beneficiaries in saving tax through a variation of a trust, it also concerned social and educational benefits of the proposed variation, which had to be considered too:

> There are many things in life more worth while than money. One of these things is to be brought up in this our England, which is still 'the envy of less happier lands'.[38]

When considering 'benefit' in terms of the children and unborn children's social and educational upbringing, Lord Denning MR did not believe it was for their benefit to be 'uprooted from England and transported to another country simply to avoid tax'.[39] On the facts, the family had lived in Jersey for only three months before they made the application to revoke the trusts and to bring them under Jersey law. There was no evidence to say that the family would remain in Jersey for any length of time. Lord Denning MR did not think it was right to encourage the revocation of the trust as to do so would effectively sanction the uprooting of children on an on-going basis to different jurisdictions depending on which legal system offered the most attractive taxation regime. Such continuous moving could not be considered to be for the children's 'benefit'. Whilst taxation avoidance was lawful:

> [t]he Court of Chancery should not encourage or support it – it should not give its approval to it – if by doing so would imperil the true welfare of the children, already born or yet to be born.[40]

The case illustrates that avoiding paying tax can be a valid benefit for which the court will sanction a variation or revocation of trust. But such a benefit must be weighed up against the other disadvantages of the proposed variation. Social or educational disadvantages connected to the proposed variation or revocation can outweigh the taxation benefits.

Less than a year after the decision in Re Weston's Settlements, however, the High Court did sanction the revocation of a trust under English law and the re-establishing of it in Jersey in Re Windeatt's Will Trusts,[41] but the differing facts meant the court could take a different view on 'benefit'.

The testator, Thomas Windeatt, wrote his will in 1951 in which he declared a trust leaving the income in the trust property to be paid to his wife during her lifetime with remainder to their daughter Mary and her children. Thomas and his wife had always lived in England. Mary lived in Jersey with her husband and children. After the death of her parents, to save tax, Mary brought an application seeking the same revocation of the trust as in Re Weston's Settlements – that new trustees (residents of Jersey) be appointed to administer the trust and that the trust be re-established in Jersey.

Pennycuick J approved the application made to revoke the trusts under English law and to re-establish them in Jersey. He believed the facts before him enabled him to distinguish Re Weston's Settlements easily. Unlike in Re Weston's Settlements where the family had moved to Jersey shortly before the application to the court to revoke the trust, in the present case Mary and her husband had lived in Jersey for 19 years. Their permanent home was in Jersey. Their children had been born on the island. Following Re Seale's Marriage Settlement,[42] an order would be made revoking the trust under English law and permitting it to be transferred to Jersey's jurisdiction.

---

38 Ibid at 245.
39 Ibid at 245.
40 Ibid.
41 Re Windeatt's Will Trusts [1969] 1 WLR 692.
42 Re Seale's Marriage Settlement [1961] Ch 574.

Pennycuick J did not consider 'benefit' in any detail in his short judgment but it must be clear that he felt that the benefits to be saved in reduced taxation in moving the trust to Jersey did not come into conflict with the children's social or educational benefits. There was no suggestion that the family was seeking to move the trust purely for taxation advantages. It made sense that the trust should be administered in Jersey given that the family's life was there. The taxation savings were a benefit but, unlike in *Re Weston's Settlements*, there were no adverse social or educational consequences to varying the trust which conflicted with the benefit of avoiding tax.

The concept of 'benefit' was examined more broadly by Megarry J in *Re Holt's Settlement*.[43] Here, Alfred Holt declared a trust of £15,000 from which income was directed to be paid to his daughter, Patricia, for life with remainder to her children that should attain 21 years of age. Patricia had three infant children at the time she made the application to the High Court to vary the trust. The original money had been invested in company shares which had grown to be worth £320,000. In order to save tax, Patricia wanted to give half of her life interest to her children but to postpone the children's entitlement in their capital interests until they reached 30 years of age. Her reasoning behind increasing the age before their entitlements became vested in them was to prevent them from being entitled to substantial sums of money at the comparatively young age of 21. The variation was to be carried out by revoking the trust declared by Alfred and establishing a new trust. Patricia needed the High Court's consent to the variation on behalf of her current children and any future children she might have had.

Megarry J recognised that the children might be subject to a financial detriment by having the age at which the property was to vest in them postponed by nine years. Yet against that could be weighed up the advantages of the general proposal: the savings of tax were substantial and the children would also enjoy additional money when their interests did vest as Patricia was surrendering half of her life interest to them. Such benefits here were overwhelming and the High Court would give its consent on behalf of the children and any future unborn children.

In terms of 'benefit', Megarry J believed that, '[t]he word "benefit" in the proviso to section 1 (1) is, I think, plainly not confined to financial benefit, but may extend to moral or social benefit . . .'[44]

In terms of approving the arrangement for unborn children, Megarry J held that the court should be prepared to authorise the variation on their behalf if such arrangement was one in which there was at least likely to be some benefit to them. Only where it could be said that there would be no benefit accruing to an unborn child from the variation should the court not give its consent.

On the other hand, even if it can be shown that a proposed variation will benefit one particular beneficiary under the trust, it is not always the case that the court will order the variation to take place if the proposal is not for the benefit of other beneficiaries. This was shown in *Re Steed's Will Trusts*.[45]

Joshua Steed declared two trusts in favour of his sister, Gladys, in his will in which he left a farm with approximately 50 acres of land and £4,000 for her life with remainder to whoever she might appoint either in her lifetime or by her will. Joshua made it clear that the trust was to be of a protective nature in that whilst Gladys could be entitled to the capital in the farm, the trustees had to bear in mind that they had to retain sufficient funds to support her during

---

43 *Re Holt's Settlement* [1967] 1 Ch 100.
44 Ibid at 121.
45 *Re Steed's Will Trusts* [1960] Ch 407.

her life. Joshua was concerned that one of their brothers would seek, to paraphrase Lord Evershed MR, to 'sponge'[46] off Gladys if she was given the property absolutely.

After Joshua's death, the trustees wanted to sell the farm. They were concerned that the farm would cost too much to keep in good repair. Gladys, however, instituted proceedings to restrain them from selling the farm. She also put forward an application to vary the trust under the 1958 Act.

Her proposal was that she should be entitled to the farm absolutely. She sought to appoint herself as the remainder beneficiary and her arrangement under the Act was for the court to recognise and sanction that appointment. The trustees resisted the proposal.

The court's approval to the arrangement was needed before it could go ahead. Gladys came within s 1(1)(d) of the Act, being entitled to the trust property under a protective trust. In addition, the language of the trust created by Joshua was of a discretionary nature which could include a future husband that Gladys might marry. In theory, she could have married and appointed her future husband as the remainder beneficiary under Joshua's trust. The potential of this occurring meant that the court would also need to give its consent to the variation under s 1(1)(b) of the Act.

Lord Evershed MR believed that the court could not just consider the arrangement from Gladys' point of view, even though she was the only beneficiary in existence at the present time. The court also had to consider the position from the point of view of all potential beneficiaries which, on the facts, would include any future husband that she might marry. In deciding whether to give its consent on behalf of a person who could not give their own consent, the court had 'to look at the scheme as a whole and, when it does so, to consider, as surely it must, what really was the intention of the benefactor.'[47]

Upjohn LJ put the court's duty under the Act in a similar way:

> this court is not confined to the narrow duty of inquiring into the effect of a proposed scheme upon those *on whose behalf approval by the court is sought*. The court must be satisfied that the scheme, looked at as a whole, is proper to be sanctioned by the court.[48]

The court could not, in this case, blindly follow Gladys' wishes. The court had to take a wider view of the proposal and give or withhold its consent on behalf of those people who could not give their own consent under the 1958 Act. In doing this, the court would take into account the wishes of the proposer of the arrangement, together with the wishes of the trustees but ultimately the court would revert to the reasons why the settlor established the original trust. Here Joshua was concerned that Gladys would feel pressurised by another individual to divest herself of some of the money under the trust if she was entitled to it absolutely. Such a consequence had to be resisted, even if Gladys herself felt that a variation of the trust in this manner was to her own personal benefit. It was not her benefit that was in issue (as s 1(1)(d) prevented the court from assessing whether the variation was to her benefit or not) but the potential benefit to a future husband.

Re Steed's Will Trusts was distinguished by the Court of Appeal in *Goulding v James*[49] where it was held that the testator's intentions were not to have great weight applied to them when the court decided whether to permit the variation to go ahead. Here Violet Froud created a trust

---

46 Ibid at 415.
47 Ibid at 421.
48 Ibid at 422 (emphasis added).
49 *Goulding v James* [1997] 2 All ER 239.

in her will, leaving a life interest in her residuary estate to her daughter, June with remainder to her grandson, Marcus, provided Marcus reached 40 years old. After Violet's death, June and Marcus wished to vary the trust, giving them both a 45 per cent share in the absolute interest in the residuary estate with the final 10 per cent share to be left to Marcus's children. The application to vary the trust was made under s 1(1)(c) of the Act on behalf of Marcus's future children.

Unusually, at first instance, Laddie J refused to sanction the variation. Relying on *Re Steed's Will Trusts*, he took into account Violet's wishes when setting up the original trust. Violet had only given June a life interest in the trust property because she did not trust her son-in-law. She also thought that Marcus needed time to settle down in life, so chose a fairly old contingency age (40) for him to receive his share.

On appeal, the Court of Appeal approved the proposed variation. *Re Steed's Will Trusts* could be distinguished. *Re Steed's Will Trusts* concerned an application primarily under s 1(1)(d) where the court had no opportunity to assess whether the variation was for the benefit of the person on whose behalf it consented. The arrangement in the present case was proposed under s 1(1)(c). This meant that the court had to weigh up whether the proposed variation was for the benefit of Marcus's children or not. The court was specifically charged with this task under the Act. It was not charged with the task of assessing whether the variation was for the settlor's benefit. As the variation was plainly for the benefit of Marcus's children, it could go ahead.

Goulding v James shows that the settlor's intentions therefore carry very little (if any) weight to an application to vary a trust made under s 1(a)–(c). The court approves the variation for the person on whose behalf the application is made and the settlor's intentions should usually be disregarded. Mummery LJ in *Goulding v James* made it clear that *Re Steed's Will Trusts* was an application under s 1(1)(d) of the Act, where the court could take into account the settlor's original intentions as it is not directed to assess whether the variation is for the proposed beneficiary's benefit.

Section 1(1)(b)

Section 1(1)(b) was considered specifically in *Knocker v Youle*[50] and given a very narrow interpretation by the High Court.

Charles Knocker established a trust in favour of his daughter, Augusta, for life with remainder to such persons as she should appoint in her will. If she failed to appoint any further beneficiary, the trust fund would pass to her brother. Then, if he failed to choose beneficiaries, the fund would pass to her mother for her life with the remainder interest to her four sisters and their issue. The issue were effectively Augusta's 17 cousins. Due to the fact that there were so many of them, some of whom lived in Australia, none were made party to the proposed variation to the trust. Instead it was argued that the High Court could vary the trust using its powers under s 1(1)(b) as these were persons who 'may become entitled' to an interest in the trust.

Warner J refused to sanction the variation of the trust. He held that the cousins were not people who 'may become entitled' to the trust fund. They already enjoyed an interest under the trust, albeit a contingent one. Of course, their interest was subject to neither Augusta nor her brother appointing any other beneficiaries of their share but that did not matter: the legal reality was that the cousins enjoyed an interest in the trust fund and the court had no jurisdiction to consent on their behalf under s 1(1)(b).

The decision in this case is probably right. The court should not be in a position to override the consent required from adults who are *sui juris* whose consent is simply difficult to obtain.

---

50 *Knocker v Youle* [1986] 1 WLR 934.

Perpetuities and variations under the 1958 Act

In *Re Holt's Settlement*, Megarry J also dealt with the question of perpetuities in his judgment and answered the question of when the perpetuity period should commence in a variation. Was the perpetuity period to commence from the original declaration of trust or from the time the variation was sanctioned by the court? He believed the period should commence from when the variation was sanctioned by the court as that was when the new 'instrument' effecting the variation would take effect. This has the effect that a variation today of, say, a declaration of trust entered into in 2001 would now be able to enjoy an almost certainly longer perpetuity period (of 125 years) than that which the original declaration of trust contained.[51]

Substance v form under the 1958 Act: the substratum guideline

In *Re Holt's Settlement*, Megarry J had no issue with how the variation was effected. He believed that a complete revocation of the current trust and the drafting of a new trust could amount to a variation under the Act. He felt that this was merely a question of form. Varying the trust by a revocation and the drafting of an entirely new trust deed would be as valid as varying the trust by merely altering some of the words in the original trust document.

Whilst equity is not concerned about the form the variation takes it is, of course, concerned to see that the substance of the original trust is not affected by the variation. If the substance of the original trust is affected by the proposed variation, the court will not sanction such a variation to go ahead, as is shown by *Re T's Settlement Trusts*.[52]

The facts concerned a trust being held for two infants. Their interests would vest when they reached 21. The relevant infant was due to reach 21 in November 1963. In June 1963, her mother applied to the court to vary the trust. Her view was that her daughter was 'alarmingly immature and irresponsible as regards money'[53] and would not be able to manage such a large sum. Her proposal was that her daughter's share should be transferred to new trustees for it to be held on protective trusts.

Wilberforce J refused to consent to the variation as proposed. He thought that he did not have any jurisdiction to do so under the 1958 Act as the proposal went too far beyond a variation and was an entirely new resettlement. In most cases where a proposal was made to vary a trust so close in time to the infant beneficiary reaching adulthood, he would expect the infant's views to be taken into account so that she could decide for herself whether to consent to such a variation.

The notion that the 1958 Act does not permit a wholly new resettlement to take place but merely a variation of the existing trust was summed up by Megarry J in *Re Ball's Settlement Trusts*[54] as follows:

> If an arrangement changes the whole *substratum* of the trust, then it may well be that it cannot be regarded merely as varying that trust. But if an arrangement, while leaving the *substratum*, effectuates the purpose of the original trust by other means, it may still be possible to regard that arrangement as merely varying the original trusts, even though the means employed are wholly different and even though the form is completely changed.[55]

---

51 Most declarations of trust entered into before the Perpetuity and Accumulations Act 2009 would have made use of the fixed perpetuity period of up to 80 years under the Perpetuity and Accumulations Act 1964.

52 *Re T's Settlement Trusts* [1964] Ch 158.

53 Ibid at 160 per Wilberforce J.

54 *Re Ball's Settlement Trusts* [1968] 1 WLR 899.

55 Ibid at 905.

The court, thought Megarry J, should exercise a wide jurisdiction to give consent on behalf of those individuals listed in s 1(1)(a)–(d). The court was merely giving consent which those people could not give and, in that regard, 'the power of the court to give that assent should be assimilated to the wide powers which the ascertained adults have'.[56]

The facts concerned a trust which gave a life interest to the settlor and a power for him to appoint the trust fund to each of his two sons or their wives or their children, providing that not more than half of the trust fund could be appointed to either family. The proposed variation was simply to split the trust fund into two equal shares. Each share was to be held on trust for each son for their lives, remainder to their children.

Megarry J approved the proposal. He believed that the *substratum* of the original trust remained in the variation. The new trusts still gave half of the trust fund to each son and his family. The variation was not being used to take a beneficiary's interest from them, as occurred in *Re T's Settlement Trusts*.

❖ ANALYSING THE LAW

It is essential to understand that a variation of a trust will not be permitted if it changes the fundamental basis, or *substratum*, of it.

But the cases illustrate that the '*substratum* test' has been set at a high level. As you have seen, variations of trust have been sanctioned where the beneficial interest vesting in beneficiaries has been delayed and even where some beneficiaries have the potential to lose out from their original entitlement.

Perhaps the underlying rationale of the cases where such variations have been permitted is to enable trustees to retain a certain amount of discretion and room to manoeuvre when administering the trust. So variations have been permitted when administering the trust would otherwise result in adverse taxation consequences which the settlor did not intend. But where proposals overstep the mark in terms of surpassing manoeuvring room and extending into altering the settlor's original intentions (as to who should benefit, for example) the *substratum* test would mean that the court would not give its sanction.

Summary of the Variation of Trusts Act 1958

The usual procedure for a proposed variation to occur is for an adult beneficiary to make an application to the High Court for approval to the variation. The key requirements are:

(a)   the arrangement has to benefit the person(s) on whose behalf the court is being asked to consent (unless the person comes within s 1(1)(d)). 'Benefit' under the Act may be financial but the court will consider the matter in the round, taking into account social and moral factors too. In reality, the court looks at the whole proposal to decide if there is a benefit for the beneficiary on whose behalf the court is being asked to consent, weighing up the advantages and disadvantages of the proposal; and

---

56 Ibid.

(b) the underlying basis of the trust – the *substratum* – must not be affected by the proposed variation.

The Variation of Trusts Act 1958 is the main statutory source that allows for the most wide-ranging variations and revocations of trust to occur. The following statutes permit trusts to be varied but only in specific circumstances.

Trustee Act 1925, s 57

Section 57 of the Trustee Act 1925 permits trustees or beneficiaries[57] to seek the court's consent to vary a trust by granting the trustees a power either to acquire or dispose of trust property. Its enactment was intended to supplement the 'emergency' inherent jurisdiction of the court to vary a trust if the court did not believe that an emergency (as defined under its inherent jurisdiction) had arisen.

The step-by-step requirements of s 57 were given by Evershed MR in *Re Downshire Settled Estates*:[58]

> the section envisages, on analysis: (i) an act unauthorized by a trust instrument, (ii) to be effected by the trustees thereof, (iii) in the management or administration of trust property, (iv) which the court will empower them to perform, (v) if in its opinion the act is expedient.[59]

The purpose behind s 57 is to widen trustees' powers of management or administration when such a power has not been included in the original trust instrument by the settlor. 'Management or administration' means 'the managerial supervision and control of trust property on behalf of beneficiaries'.[60] The reference in the section to 'management or administration' does not allow the court to grant the trustees a power to alter the extent of beneficial interests under the trust.

The court may grant the power subject to such terms as it thinks fit and may direct how costs be paid as between the capital and income of the trust. 'Expedient' in the legislation means that the power requested must be in the interests of the trust as a whole.

Section 57 was recently considered in *NBPF Pension Trustees Ltd v Warnock-Smith*,[61] where the High Court concluded that the ability of the court to grant the trustees a power under the section could not be used if it would affect the substance of the beneficial interests under the trust.

Key Learning Point

The Variation of Trusts Act 1958 is much wider in scope than s 57 of the Trustee Act 1925. The 1958 Act enables much more fundamental variations to the trust to occur such as varying the beneficial entitlements under the original trust, as occurred in *Re Holt's Settlement*. Section 57 of the Trustee Act 1925 is designed to be used to grant trustees power to making administrative changes to the trust.

---

57 Trustee Act 1925, s 57(3).
58 *Re Downshire Settled Estates* [1953] Ch 218.
59 Ibid at 244.
60 Ibid at 247 per Evershed MR.
61 *NBPF Pension Trustees Ltd v Warnock-Smith* [2008] EWHC 455 (Ch).

The facts concerned the distribution of surplus money in two pension schemes. The trustees had over £350 million to distribute to members of the schemes. Most of the money was distributed, but the trustees had been obliged to set up reserve funds for beneficiaries they could not successfully trace. The original idea was that if any untraced beneficiaries came forward at a later stage, they would be paid the amounts due to them from the reserve funds. Approximately £22 million remained in the reserve funds and five years after establishing the reserve funds, the trustees wanted to wind the schemes up completely and distribute the money held in the reserve funds. The matter fell within s 57 due to taxation reasons: in distributing the money, the trustees would have been making taxable payments and such payments were not allowed on the terms of the original schemes. The trustees thus needed to be granted a power of management or administration to distribute the trust property that had not been granted to them when the original schemes were established.

Floyd J recognised the court's ability to grant a power of management or administration of the trust property to the trustees 'but not where it would affect the substance of the beneficial trusts themselves'.[62] On the facts, however, he believed that a power could be granted to the trustees to make the taxable payments they desired and to wind up the schemes. He thought the powers desired were 'practical ones aimed at getting some money to particular classes of recipient who are otherwise fully entitled to receive benefits under the scheme'.[63] The trustees sought only a specific and not a general power to achieve that aim. The power sought was 'merely a variation in the mechanism for getting that money to its intended recipient, and does not disturb the underlying interests [of the trust]'.[64]

The trustees also wanted the ability to purchase an insurance policy to protect them from claims for breaching their duty as trustees, perhaps, for example, for wrongly paying beneficiaries who were not entitled to benefit from the schemes or for not paying those who were actually entitled. Floyd J held that the purchase of such insurance was probably within the terms of the schemes as drafted but if he was wrong about that, he authorised it under s 57.

In granting this power, he emphasised that powers granted by the court under s 57 had to be for the benefit, not just of the trustees but for the trust as a whole.

Emphasis had been placed on the trust as a whole benefiting in the earlier case of *Re Craven's Estate, Lloyd's Bank Ltd v Cockburn (No. 2)*,[65] where Farwell J had said:

> the word 'expedient' quite clearly must mean expedient for the trust as a whole. It cannot mean that however expedient it may be for one beneficiary if it is inexpedient from a broad view of other beneficiaries concerned the court ought to sanction the transaction. In order that the matter may be one which is in the opinion of the court expedient, it must be expedient for the trust as a whole.[66]

In *Re Earl of Strafford, Dec'd, Royal Bank of Scotland Ltd v Byng*,[67] Buckley LJ emphasised that, when considering the interests of the beneficiaries, the court must balance their competing interests between them in as fair a manner as possible:

> 'Expedient for the trust as a whole' must mean, it seems to me, the same as 'expedient in the interests of all beneficiaries under the trust', provided that it be kept in

---

62 Ibid at para. 27.
63 Ibid at para. 28.
64 Ibid.
65 *Re Craven's Estate, Lloyd's Bank Ltd v Cockburn (No. 2)* [1937] Ch 431.
66 Ibid at 436.
67 *Earl of Strafford, Dec'd, Royal Bank of Scotland Ltd v Byng* [1980] 1 Ch 28.

mind that in considering the interests of the beneficiaries collectively, trustees must take into account the effect of what is proposed upon the several individual interests of the beneficiaries and hold the scale fairly between them.[68]

In *NBPF Pension Trustees Ltd*, Floyd J held that the entire trusts would benefit from an insurance policy as it would meet any claims for breach of duty instead of the trust fund itself.

It was not, however, for the benefit of the trust as a whole to purchase a second type of insurance policy to meet claims of any unknown beneficiaries coming forward. Such individuals were excluded from the terms of the schemes in any event and hence could have no grounds for bringing any claim. An insurance policy to guard against any claims would be superfluous and, consequently, a waste of the trust fund's assets in purchasing such a policy.

Section 57 cannot be used if to do so would change the beneficial interests under the trust. An application under s 57 may be successful, however, if it can be shown that changing the beneficial interests is an incidental consequence of the granting of the additional administrative power, as was shown in *Southgate v Sutton*.[69]

The facts concerned an application to divide a trust fund into two parts: one part was to be for beneficiaries in the United Kingdom and the other was to be held on trust for beneficiaries in the United States of America (known as the 'Southgate beneficiaries'). There was no express provision in the trust instrument permitting the trust to be divided in such a manner. An application was made to the court requesting such a power be granted to the trustees to do so under s 57. At first instance, Mann J refused the application. He felt that allowing the application would change the beneficial interests in the trust as the beneficiaries would be divided into two distinct groups, the Southgate beneficiaries and the UK beneficiaries, with each group being entitled to their own fund.

In giving the judgment of the Court of Appeal, Mummery LJ said[70] that the court should take a 'cautious' approach to applications made to it under s 57. Yet the application to split the trust into two could be granted under s 57. He did not believe that the purpose of the application was to alter the beneficial interests of the trust. The purpose was to save taxation being paid, primarily in the United States. This was expedient for the trust as a whole. Any impact on the beneficial interests being altered was an incidental consequence of the trust being partitioned. Where this was the case, the additional administrative powers needed for dividing the trust could be granted under s 57.

Trustee Act 1925, s 53

Section 53 of the Trustee Act 1925 contains another bespoke provision enabling the court to vary a trust. The section applies only to infants who are beneficiaries under a trust. The court is given the ability to appoint a person to sell trust property or sell shares or receive dividends from shares for the 'maintenance, education or benefit' of the infant beneficiary.

Essentially, the aim of s 53 is to grant a power to raise money for the infant beneficiary's benefit by appointing an individual either to sell trust property or secure income from shares owned by the trust.

It is doubtful whether many modern-day applications are made to the court under s 53 given the usual wide powers drafted expressly in modern trust deeds which were not available when s 53 was originally enacted.

---

68 Ibid at 45.
69 *Southgate v Sutton* [2011] EWCA Civ 637.
70 Ibid at para. 36.

Inheritance (Provision for Family and Dependants) Act 1975

The Inheritance (Provision for Family and Dependants) Act 1975 gives certain categories of individual a right to claim against the estate of a deceased person if it can be shown that the claimant was maintained by the deceased immediately prior to their death and that the will and/or law of intestacy fails to make 'reasonable financial provision'[71] for the claimant.

Section 2(1)(f) of the Act specifically enables the court to make an order varying a particular type of trust in the claimant's favour. The type of trust that the court may vary is a marriage settlement (a trust made at the time two individuals get married) made in favour of the deceased or the deceased and his spouse.

To benefit from a variation of the trust in their favour, the claimant must be:

(a)   the surviving spouse;
(b)   a child of the marriage; or
(c)   a person who was treated as a child of the marriage by the deceased.

If the claimant is successful, the court may vary the marriage settlement of the deceased in order to provide reasonable financial provision for the claimant.

Setting a Trust Aside

The previous part of this chapter considered how an existing trust might be varied. A more fundamental question must now be addressed: When can an otherwise perfectly formed trust be set aside? Initially, this may appear to be an odd thought: If a settlor has correctly declared a trust and constituted it, why should it be set aside at all? The main reason is bound up in public policy, as the facts of Re Butterworth[72] demonstrate.

Charles Butterworth was a baker who owned his own business in Manchester. He owned several houses. In 1878, he entered into a trust in which he placed the houses and some of his other property on trust with his wife and children as beneficiaries. At the same time as declaring the trust, he decided to expand his business by purchasing a grocer's business. He owned the grocery business for only eight months when he sold it, not having managed to make a profit from it. He sold the business for the same price as he had bought it. Just over two years later, he filed a petition for bankruptcy. His trustee in bankruptcy sought to have access to the houses that had been placed on trust for Charles' wife and children. He wanted the trust declared to be non-binding on him as being able to sell the houses would raise a large amount of money which could be used to pay Charles' creditors.

Glossary: Trustee in bankruptcy

A trustee in bankruptcy's main task is to administer a bankrupt's estate to settle the debts of their creditors. This type of trustee is akin to a personal representative of a deceased individual in that they gather in as many assets as possible, realise their value and then distribute the fund to the creditors.

---

71 Inheritance (Provision for Family and Dependants) Act 1975, s 1.
72 Re Butterworth (1881–81) LR 19 ChD 588.

Charles sought to hide behind the declaration of trust. His argument was that he was not bankrupt at the time he made the declaration of trust, therefore it ought to stand. That would mean that his wife and children would own the equitable interests in the houses and he, of course, would still be able to continue living in one of the houses with them, whilst his creditors would receive nothing. The difficulty he had was that he was not, in fact, able to pay his debts when he first entered into the declaration of trust.

The Court of Appeal set aside the declaration of trust. Jessel MR said:

> a man is not entitled to go into a hazardous business, and immediately before doing so settle all his property voluntarily, the object being this: 'If I succeed in business, I make a fortune for myself. If I fail, I leave my creditors unpaid. They will bear the loss'.[73]

The settlor could not have it both ways: he could not place his property into the hands of someone else by using the mechanism of a trust and yet still benefit from that property if his business failed. The trust was essentially a sham:[74] there was no real intent to benefit his wife and children; merely instead to put his property beyond his creditors' reach where he might still enjoy it. The declaration of trust was void although it is probably the case nowadays that such a declaration of trust would be voidable.[75]

Re Butterworth was not the first decision in the area, but is a useful case for clearly illustrating the policy behind the law. The law in this area has now been enshrined into the Insolvency Act 1986. Two sections of the Act are relevant: ss 339 and 423.

Insolvency Act 1986, s 339

Section 339 of the Insolvency Act 1986 applies to an individual who has (i) entered into a transaction with anyone at an 'undervalue' and (ii) within a certain time period. 'Undervalue' is defined in s 339(3) as:

(a)   making a gift to a recipient or receiving no consideration from the recipient for property given to him;

(b)   entering into a transaction with a recipient the consideration for which is marriage or a civil partnership; or

(c)   entering into a transaction with a recipient where the consideration given by the recipient is significantly less than the value of the transaction itself.

The relevant time period is generally five years before the petition for bankruptcy is presented. However, transactions entered into between two and five years before the petition for bankruptcy is presented will be immune unless the debtor was insolvent at the time or became insolvent due to entering into the transaction. Being insolvent generally means being unable to pay debts as they fall due.

---

73 Ibid at 598.
74 I.e. a document purporting to be one thing on its face, yet seeking to achieve another.
75 *British Eagle International Airlines Ltd v Compagnie Nationale Air France* [1975] 1 WLR 758, HL.

❖ **EXPLAINING THE LAW**

Suppose Scott owns a house solely by himself and wishes to go into business.

Scott may decide to declare a trust in which he gives the property to his fiancée, for her to hold on trust for both of them. The consideration may be the parties' forthcoming marriage.

Such a trust would be liable to be set aside by Scott's trustee in bankruptcy if Scott was to receive a petition for his bankruptcy within two years of declaring the trust. The marriage cannot be good consideration for the transaction. Effectively, Scott is divesting himself of a valuable asset which could have been used to pay his creditors if he goes bankrupt.

The declaration of trust would be valid after two years had passed since it was entered into unless Scott was either insolvent at the time he declared the trust or became insolvent as a result of it.

The 'long-stop' date under s 339 is five years, after which all transactions entered into at an undervalue are immune from being attacked, even if Scott was insolvent at the time of the transaction or it caused his insolvency.

If a transaction has been entered into at an undervalue within the relevant time period, the trustee in bankruptcy can apply to the court to make an order under s 339(2) to restore 'the position to what it would have been if that individual had not entered into that transaction'. Effectively, this means that any declaration of trust may be set aside so that the individual once again owns the property that he tried to divest himself of in the declaration of trust. The property would then become part of the bankrupt's assets which the trustee would seek for himself. Alternatively, under s 342(1)(a), the court may order the property to be transferred directly to the trustee in bankruptcy.

Insolvency Act 1986, s 423

To bring a successful action under s 339 of the Insolvency Act 1986, the trustee in bankruptcy must show that the bankrupt either was insolvent at the time he entered into the relevant transaction at an undervalue, or became insolvent as a consequence of it. There is no requirement that dishonesty has to be found on the bankrupt's part (for example, he may have been following the advice of a professional).

Section 423 again applies where an individual enters into a transaction at an undervalue as defined in s 339. The court may, once again, make an order restoring the individual to his pre-undervalue transaction. Under this section, however, the court can only make such an order one if either requirements of s 423(3) are satisfied. They are that:

(a)   the transaction was entered into specifically to put assets beyond the reach of a creditor who was making or had the possibility of making a claim against the individual; or

(b)   the court is satisfied that the interests of a creditor were prejudiced by the transaction at an undervalue being entered into.

Section 424 sets out who may bring an action under s 423. If the debtor has already been adjudged bankrupt or is a company in the process of being wound up, the trustee in bankruptcy or liquidator respectively may apply to the court. Only with the court's permission may a victim of the debtor bring an action. In any other case, s 424 (1)(c) provides that it is only a victim of the debtor who can bring a claim.

Taken together, the provisions of ss 339 and 423 provide useful tools to ensure that trustees in bankruptcy may set aside declarations of trust if the declaration has been entered into essentially for an illegal reason: to place the individual's assets beyond the reach of his creditors. A comparison table highlighting key differences between the two sections can be found at Figure 10.2.

	Section 339	Section 423
Aim of section when applied to the law of trusts	To recover property which would otherwise be subject to a validly entered into declaration of trust.	As section 339.
Application	Only to individuals who have become bankrupt.	To individuals and companies.
Condition on bringing an action	The transaction must be at an 'undervalue' as defined. The action is governed by time: it must be brought generally within 5 years before the petition for bankruptcy is presented BUT action cannot be taken against transactions entered into 2–5 years before the petition for bankruptcy is presented unless the bankrupt was insolvent at the time of the declaration of trust or became insolvent due to entering into it. Insolvency is presumed if the declaration of trust is entered into with the bankrupt's spouse or a close relative (brother, sister, uncle, aunt, nephew or niece amongst others).	The transaction must be at an 'undervalue' as defined. The action looks at the purpose for which the transaction was entered into. To be attacked the declaration of trust must have been entered into for the purpose of putting assets beyond the reach of creditors OR for the purpose of prejudicing the interests of a person who is making the claim.
Claimant	The trustee in bankruptcy.	If adjudged bankrupt already, the trustee in bankruptcy or if a company in liquidation, the liquidator. The victim of the declaration of trust can only bring an action at this stage with the court's permission. If not adjudged bankrupt, only the victim can bring an action.
Main outcome if claim is successful	The parties can be restored to the pre-declaration of trust position.	As section 339.
Consequences for an innocent party of an action under either section	A *bona fide* purchaser of the property for value without notice cannot be attacked.	As section 339.

Figure 10.2 Comparison of ss 339 and 423 Insolvency Act 1986.

Points to Review

You have seen:

- the general rule is that a trust, if properly formed, is sacrosanct and will not be varied or altered by the court;
- a trust can be varied but only in exceptional circumstances by the court's inherent jurisdiction and in particular circumstances by various statutes. The Variation of Trusts Act 1958 is of the most general application but that only applies where the court is consenting because a particular type of beneficiary under the trust cannot give their own consent; and
- that a trust can be set aside if it has been entered into for an illegal reason, such as to put the individual's assets beyond the reach of his creditors. Specific sections of the Insolvency Act 1986 have codified the ability of a trustee in bankruptcy to have access to the individual's property that they believed they were securing by means of a trust.

Making connections

Varying and setting aside a trust are essentially two stand-alone topics that are necessary for you to understand if you are to gain a rounded knowledge and appreciation of how trusts operate in practice, as well as in theory.

 Useful Things to Read

The best reading is contained in the primary sources listed below. It is always good to consider the decisions of the courts themselves as this will lead to a deeper understanding of the issues involved. A few secondary sources are also listed, which you may wish to read to gain additional insights into the areas considered in this chapter.

Primary sources
Chapman v Chapman [1954] AC 429.
Re Holt's Settlement [1967] 1 Ch 100.
Re Steed's Will Trusts [1960] Ch 407.
Re Weston's Settlements [1969] 1 Ch 223.
Re Windeatt's Will Trusts [1969] 1 WLR 692.
Southgate v Sutton [2011] EWCA Civ 637.

Insolvency Act 1986, ss 339 and 423.
Trustee Act 1925, ss 53 and 57.
Variation of Trusts Act 1958.

Secondary sources
Robert Blower, 'The limits of section 57 Trustee Act 1925 after *Sutton v England*' (2012) T & T 18(1), 11–16 (note). This article examines the decision of the Court of Appeal in *Southgate v Sutton*.
Alastair Hudson, *Equity & Trusts* (7th edn, Routledge-Cavendish, 2012) ch 10.

Peter Luxton, 'Variation of trusts: Settlors' intentions and the consent principle in *Saunders v Vautier*' (1997) MLR 60(5) 719–726 (note). This article considers the decision in *Goulding v James*.

Peter Luxton, 'An unascertainable problem in variation of trusts' (1986) NLJ 136 (6279) 1057–1058. This article discusses the decision in *Knocker v Youle*.

Mohamed Ramjohn, *Text, Cases and Materials on Equity and Trusts* (4th edn, Routledge-Cavendish, 2008) ch 20.

Chapter 11

Secret Trusts, Half-Secret Trusts and Mutual Wills

Chapter Contents

In this chapter, you consider the topic of secret trusts and the related area of mutual wills. The connecting link between the two topics is that the details of both are based on an agreement which is not necessarily apparent from the documentation. Secret trusts are so called because a testator has made a secret agreement with a trustee that they will hold property on trust for an undisclosed beneficiary after the testator's death. Mutual wills are where two people make identical wills and each binds the other to the same undisclosed agreement where their property will go after their deaths.

As You Read

Look out for the following key points:

- the definition of a secret trust, a half-secret trust and how they differ from each other;
- the rationale underpinning the court's enforcement of secret and half-secret trusts; and
- the concept of mutual wills and the notion that they are based on an agreement formed between the testators that the survivor should not alter their will after the first one of them has died.

Secret Trusts and Half-Secret Trusts

Definition

A secret trust is a trust of which there is, *prima facie*, no evidence of its existence in a testator's will. The secret trust is probably an example of an express trust although there is debate (both judicial and academic) about whether it might be a constructive trust. It appears, on a reading of the relevant clause in the will, that property has simply been given to the recipient and that they are both the legal and beneficial owner of it. Unbeknown to readers of the will, however, the recipient is not the beneficial owner of it. Instead, he will have been asked by the testator (obviously before the testator's death) to hold the property on trust for the real beneficiary. In that manner, a trust will be formed of the property after the testator dies. The recipient will own the legal title and the 'real' beneficiary will enjoy the equitable interest. A trust will have been formed by the testator but its existence will be kept secret from the world at large. Sometimes these trusts are known as 'fully' secret trusts, in part to differentiate them from 'half'-secret trusts.

A half-secret trust is similar to a fully secret trust. The difference is that whilst there is absolutely no clue in the testator's will that a fully secret trust has been formed, there is a giveaway that the testator has declared a half-secret trust. A half-secret trust gives an indication that the property is subject to a trust by using the words 'on trust' or similar. What remains secret are the terms of the trust. Consequently, a reader of a will where a half-secret trust has been declared knows that the recipient is a trustee but does not know who the true beneficiary is or any other terms of the trust.

Both types of secret trust are illustrated using the now-familiar diagram in Figure 11.1.

Background: Scandal in the law of trusts!

Fully and half-secret trusts appear in wills. Section 9 of the Wills Act 1837 provides that no will can be valid unless it is in writing, signed by the testator and witnessed by at least two witnesses present at the same time.[1] After the testator has died, the will usually becomes a

---

1   The most obvious exception to this is that members of the armed forces may make oral wills if they are on 'actual military service' or, in the case of a mariner, 'at sea' under the Wills (Soldiers and Sailors) Act 1918.

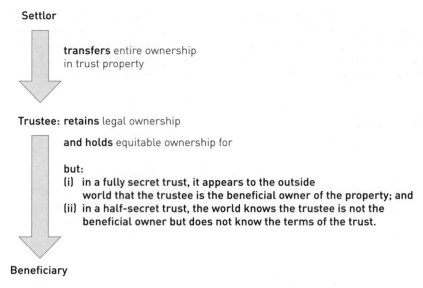

Settlor

transfers entire ownership in trust property

Trustee: retains legal ownership

and holds equitable ownership for

but:
(i) **in a fully secret trust, it appears to the outside world that the trustee is the beneficial owner of the property; and**
(ii) **in a half-secret trust, the world knows the trustee is not the beneficial owner but does not know the terms of the trust.**

Beneficiary

Figure 11.1 The secret trust.

public document, which any member of the public may inspect. This means that the contents of a testator's will become available for the world at large to read.

As will become clear, a number of the early cases on secret trusts revolved around a testator wishing to make provision in his will for his mistress and/or illegitimate offspring. Leaving property as a gift or declaring a trust in the will would have meant that the testator's wife and family would have immediately become aware of the existence of the testator's mistress and illegitimate children. Thus testators began to use the mechanism of a secret trust to conceal the true beneficiary of their generosity in their will. The testator would commonly provide the detail of the trust in a separate document to their will or even sometimes in oral instructions to the trustee. The latter is sometimes referred to as 'parol evidence'.

The difficulty with the terms of secret trusts being contained in parol evidence is, however, that they run contrary to the principle of transparency and openness enshrined in s 9 of the Wills Act 1837 that all terms of a will should be in writing and that the will usually becomes a document available to the public for their inspection after the testator's death. It is this conflict that the courts have wrestled with from the nineteenth century when wills containing secret trusts first became prevalent.[2]

Fully Secret Trusts

Requirements

The requirements for the validity of a fully secret trust were set out by Brightman J in *Ottaway v Norman*.[3] He said that it must be shown that:

---

2 Although the first reported case of a secret trust was actually much earlier in 1688: see *Crook v Brooking* (1688) 2 Vern 50; 23 ER 643.
3 *Ottaway v Norman* [1972] Ch 698.

(a)   the testator intended to impose an obligation on the recipient of the property that the
      recipient should hold the property on trust for the 'true' beneficiary;
(b)   the testator communicated that intention to the recipient; and
(c)   the recipient accepted the testator's intention. The recipient's acceptance of that
      obligation could be either express or implied by acquiescence.

First requirement: An intention to impose an obligation on the recipient that the property should be held on trust for the true beneficiary

The facts of *Ottaway v Norman* showed that all three requirements for a valid trust were met. The facts are summarised in Figure 11.2.

Figure 11.2 Ottaway v Norman.

Harry Ottaway wrote his will in 1960, in which he left his bungalow in Cambridgeshire together with its contents to his partner, Miss Eva Hodges, with whom he had lived for nearly 30 years. Harry died in 1963. Eva died five years later, having left the bungalow and the contents to the defendant, Mr Basil Norman. Harry's son, William Ottaway, brought an action claiming a declaration that the house and its contents were rightfully his. The legal basis of his action was that his father had told Eva on a number of occasions that he wanted the bungalow and its contents to go to William on her death. Eva was to have the property for her life but thereafter it should go to William. William said that Eva had accepted this obligation by never disagreeing with Harry's intention. Eva's first will had indeed contained a provision leaving the bungalow and its contents to William. She made a later will in 1967, however, leaving the bungalow and the contents to Basil. The difficulty for William (as with all claimants alleging the existence of a secret trust) was that it appeared on the face of Eva's will that Basil was the true and rightful recipient of the bungalow and its contents. William's action was, therefore, based on the existence of a secret trust founded on the conversations between Harry and Eva.

Having heard the evidence, Brightman J found that Harry had established a secret trust in William's favour. Harry had intended that Eva give the bungalow and its contents to William after her death, he had communicated that intention to her and that she had accepted that intention.

Brightman J also made other important points concerning secret trusts:

(a) he felt that it made no difference to the existence of a secret trust as to how the recipient was to carry out the testator's wish. In other words, it did not matter whether the recipient was to carry out the trust through leaving property by will to the true beneficiary, as was Harry's intention here, or if the property was to be left to the true beneficiary by means of an *inter vivos* gift; and

(b) it was not necessary for the establishment of a fully secret trust to show that the recipient had been guilty of committing a deliberate wrong in denying the existence of the trust. There was no evidence that Eva had purposefully sought to defraud William of his entitlement. She simply made an alternate will due to a friendship she had formed with Basil after Harry's death.

William's second claim for money which his father had left Eva, allegedly for her use during her lifetime and thereafter for William, failed. Brightman J was prepared to accept, without deciding as such, that in theory a secret trust could be created of property for the recipient to use during her lifetime with remainder of it being left to the true beneficiary. He thought that such a trust would be suspensory in effect during the recipient's life and would activate itself on her death. But such a trust could not be established on the evidence. It failed the test for certainty of subject matter as it was not clear quite how much money was supposed to be left for William after Eva's death and to fulfil such certainty, Eva would have had to keep an amount separate from her own money during her lifetime. Such unascertainable amounts infringed the principle of certainty of subject matter and could not create a valid trust. Whilst it is possible to have a secret trust of an asset that would inevitably be wasted by the recipient, the settlor must make the precise subject matter of the trust categorically clear.

Making connections

Remember from Chapter 5 that all express trusts must fulfil the three certainties: of intention, subject matter and object. Certainty of subject matter requires that it must always be clear what the nature and extent of the trust property is. If this is not clear, the trust will fail.

The facts of *Ottaway v Norman* demonstrated that the testator possessed an intention to subject the recipient to an obligation in favour of the true beneficiary. The other criteria to form a valid trust of communicating that intention to the recipient and the recipient accepting that obligation are no less important. All three criteria must be present for a secret trust to be established.

Ultimately, though, a secret trust is a type of express trust and the requirements needed to form a valid express trust must all be fulfilled. Specifically the three certainties must be satisfied for, as Megarry V-C said in *Re Snowden*:[4]

The more uncertain the terms of the obligation, the more likely it is to be a moral obligation rather than a trust: many a moral obligation is far too indefinite to be enforceable as a trust.

This *dictum* is a salutory reminder that all secret trusts must comply with the necessary ingredients to declare an express trust.

---

4   *Re Snowden* [1979] Ch 528 at 534.

Second requirement: The testator must communicate his intention to the recipient

The testator must clearly place the recipient of their property under a binding obligation to hold that property on trust for the true beneficiary. There must be no doubt that the testator communicates their instructions to the trustee. The controversial issue is when such communication must occur.

It seems not to matter whether the testator communicates his intention to the trustee either before or after he makes his will. This was spelt out by Lord Warrington of Clyffe in *Blackwell v Blackwell*[5] when he said, 'it is immaterial whether the trust is communicated and accepted before or after the execution of the will'.[6]

Arguably, it is tidier if the testator can communicate his intention to establish a secret trust with the recipient of that information as trustee before he executes his will. In that way, the testator can be sure, when signing his will, that he has a trustee in place. But it seems that, alternatively, the testator can communicate his intention to create a secret trust after he has executed his will. The reason given by Lord Warrington for this was that, in the worst case scenario, if the testator communicates his intention after he has executed his will and the trustee declines to accept the terms of the trust and administer it, the option always remains open to the testator to write another will, disposing of his property in a different manner or by a secret trust with a different trustee.

What seems to be clear, however, is that the testator must communicate his intention to the trustee during his lifetime and that communication must include the terms of the trust in it. The testator cannot communicate the terms of the trust to the trustee after his (the testator's) death, as occurred in *Re Boyes*.[7]

George Boyes wrote his will in London in June 1880. On the face of the document, he left everything to his solicitor, Mr Carritt, absolutely. George died two years later, in Ghent (Belgium). Mr Carritt's evidence was that during the writing of the will, George had made it clear to him that he was not to take the property absolutely, but was instead to hold the property on trust, the terms of which George would make clear in a letter which he would send to Mr Carritt when he arrived in Europe. Mr Carritt said that he accepted the trusteeship.

No letter was ever sent to Mr Carritt but after George's death, two near-identical letters were found in his personal belongings. Both letters said that his property was to be held on trust by Mr Carritt for George's mistress, Nell Brown. The issue for the High Court was whether this secret trust had been validly declared.

Kay J held that the trust had not been validly declared. There had been no valid communication of its terms – specifically, who the objects of the trust were – during the lifetime of the testator. What the testator had done in writing the two letters was effectively to leave further wills, or codicils (documents which amend part of a will), which did not comply with the requirements of s 9 of the Wills Act 1837. Such a trust could not be allowed to be valid as it would go against the policy of s 9 which required all wills and codicils to be validly witnessed. There was no trust in favour of Nell in the case. Instead, Mr Carritt held George's property on trust for George's next-of-kin, as if he had died intestate.

---

5   *Blackwell v Blackwell* [1929] AC 318.
6   Ibid at 341.
7   *Re Boyes* (1884) LR 26 ChD 531.

Glossary: Codicil

A codicil is a supplementary document that amends a will. It must comply with the requirements of s 9 of the Wills Act 1837. Codicils were useful in pre-word processor days, as they enabled a testator to amend his will quickly without the need to rewrite the entire will. They are used much less often nowadays as it is often just as quick to amend the will on a computer and reprint the entire document.

Can the terms of the secret trust be constructively communicated by the testator to the trustee?

In Re Keen,[8] the issue was whether valid communication had taken place during the testator's lifetime by a trustee being in possession of an envelope sealed by the testator which contained details of the terms of the trust.

The facts concerned the will of Harry Keen. He wrote his will in 1932, leaving £10,000 on trust to his trustees, on terms which were to be notified by him to his trustees during his lifetime. No mention of the beneficiary's details were contained in the will. Mr Keen, however, had written a separate memorandum, in which he had set out the details of the beneficiary – a lady whom he knew. He handed the memorandum, which was in a sealed envelope, to one of his trustees. The trustee only opened the envelope after Mr Keen's death. The issue for the court was whether Mr Keen had successfully created a valid secret trust. (In fact, this was a case concerning a half-secret trust as Mr Keen had made it apparent from his will that the £10,000 was being left on trust.)

Both the High Court and the Court of Appeal held that there was no valid secret trust, but they did so for different reasons.

In the High Court, Farwell J held that Mr Keen had failed to notify the trustees of the intended beneficiary of the trust during his lifetime, as he had promised to do in the clause in his will. Leaving a note which was read only after his death did not constitute notifying the trustees of the beneficiary during his lifetime. No trust of the money could be established. As the trust failed, the money had to fall into Mr Keen's residuary estate.

In the Court of Appeal, Lord Wright MR thought that Farwell J's view of Mr Keen's failure to notify the trustees of the intended beneficiary during his lifetime took a far too narrow view of what 'notifying' meant. He said that by holding the beneficiary's details in a sealed envelope, the trustees had the 'means of knowledge available [to administer the trust] when it became necessary and proper to open the envelope'.[9] He gave a vivid example for which his judgment is famous: '[t]o take a parallel, a ship which sails under sealed orders, is sailing under orders though the exact terms are not ascertained by the captain till later.'[10]

It could not be disputed that the ship sailing under sealed orders had been validly despatched and, in the same manner, the trust could still be successfully administered by the trustee when the time came to do so.

But Mr Keen's trust still failed. The primary reason was that while he had 'notified' the trustee of his chosen beneficiary, the means of his notification contravened s 9 of the Wills Act 1837. The notification by Mr Keen was not correctly drafted according to the requirements of s 9 and neither was it witnessed. He had merely left a letter which, whilst signed by him, had not been witnessed. Mr Keen was not at liberty effectively to reserve to himself a power to circumvent the requirements of s 9, which his letter did.

---

8 Re Keen [1937] Ch 236.
9 Ibid at 242–243.
10 Ibid at 242.

In addition, any trust which Mr Keen sought to declare had to be consistent with the actual clause in his will in which he promised to declare the trusts. The clause in his will spoke about a notification that he proposed to give to the trustees in the future. In fact, he had prepared the letter well before he had written his will. The details of the beneficiary in the letter, therefore, were not consistent with what he had described in his will.

Communication of the terms of the trust to the trustees can occur either before or after the will is written, but they must be consistent with the precise wording of the will.

Does the testator have to communicate his intention to *all* of his trustees, or will just some of them suffice? The answers to this question were summarised by Farwell J in *Re Stead*:[11]

(a) If the testator makes a fully secret trust by giving property to two trustees to hold as tenants in common but only one promised to hold the property on trust, the other trustee is not bound by the trust and can take their share of the property absolutely; and

(b) If the testator makes a fully secret trust by giving the property to two trustees to hold as joint tenants, whether both trustees are bound by the trust depends on whether the fully secret trust was made in response to a prior promise by the trustees to administer the trust:

- if yes, both trustees will be bound to administer the trust; but
- if no, only the trustee making the promise is bound to administer the trust. The other trustee may take his share of the property beneficially for himself.

Third requirement: The trustee must accept their obligation to administer the trust

As with any express trust, the trustee must accept their trusteeship. If it cannot be shown that they have accepted their trusteeship, there will be no trust. Acceptance of trustee obligations can be either express or implied. Implied acceptance, according to Lord Westbury in *McCormick v Grogan*,[12] may be 'by any mode of action which the disponee knows must give to the testator the impression and belief that he fully assents to the request'.

An example of trustees not accepting their obligations was shown in *Wallgrave v Tebbs*.[13] The facts concerned the will of William Coles who by his will made in 1850, left £12,000 to Messrs Tebbs and Martin together with freehold lands and houses in Chelsea and Kensington, London. The will seemed to leave the property to Messrs Tebbs and Martin absolutely. After Mr Coles' death, however, it was claimed that it was not Mr Coles' intention that they should enjoy the property themselves, but instead that they should hold it on trust for charitable purposes. Their reply to that was they had never had any such communication with Mr Coles. They said that they had understood from Mr Coles' solicitor who prepared the will that he had left them the property because he knew one of them personally and the other by reputation as being interested in religious and charitable causes. Mr Coles simply presumed that if he left them money they would use it for such purposes. In addition, Mr Coles had set out his thoughts on this basis in a letter written by Mr Coles' solicitor to Messrs Tebbs and Martin but Mr Coles had never signed it.

They said that they were sympathetic to Mr Coles' wishes but denied that there was a formal trust of the property in existence for such purposes. Their view was that Mr Coles had

---

11 *Re Stead* [1900] 1 Ch 237.
12 *McCormick v Grogan* (1869–70) LR 4 HL 82 at 97.
13 *Wallgrave v Tebbs* (1855) 2 K & J 313; 69 ER 800.

not communicated his views to them before his death and they had not accepted the alleged trust.

The Vice-Chancellor, Sir W Page Wood, accepted that Messrs Tebbs and Martin knew nothing about Mr Coles' wishes until after his death. No communication of the terms of the trust had occurred by Mr Coles and no acceptance of that trust had similarly taken place. Both ingredients were needed if a trust was to be found. No trust was established and Messrs Tebbs and Martin took the property for themselves absolutely.

This decision must surely be right because the office of trusteeship is onerous. It is not equitable if it is enforced upon someone who has known nothing about the prospect of becoming a trustee until after the testator's death, when it is too late to object to it. A trustee must agree to their role voluntarily. Messrs Tebbs and Martin were denied that opportunity and it was right that no trust was created.

Can the property be increased in a secret trust?

This issue was addressed by the Court of Appeal in *Re Colin Cooper*.[14] Colin Cooper wrote a will, leaving £5,000 on a half-secret trust. His trustees accepted the trust. He then went on a big-game shooting holiday to South Africa, but contracted a fatal illness. Shortly before his death, he wrote another will, puporting to increase the amount left on trust to £10,000. His trustees did not know about this increase, so were never given the chance to accept their new obligation.

The Court of Appeal held that the increase was void. The key ingredients for a valid secret trust of communication to the trustees and agreement by them to administer the trust were only made in relation to the initial £5,000. The trustees had only ever been given the chance of agreeing to administer a trust for £5,000. A trust for double the sum needed their consent.

Sir Wilfred Green MR, *obiter*, thought that no consent from the trustees would be needed if:

(a) the testator increased the sum to be left on trust by such a small amount ('*de minimis*') that the increase would really make no difference to the trustees administering the trust; or

(b) if the testator in fact left a lower amount to the trustees to administer than he had set out in his trust. Their consent to the greater amount would, by definition, mean that they had agreed to administer a trust up to that sum.

Although the decision concerned a half-secret trust, the judgment of the Court of Appeal was not limited to these types of secret trust and so can apply equally to fully secret trusts.

The rationale underpinning why secret trusts are enforced: Fraud vs the 'dehors' the will theories

The cases thus far have shown a desire by testators to set up a trust by using a separate document to convey its terms to the trustees. Sometimes the testator might instead wish to communicate the terms of the trust to the trustees orally as opposed to in writing. But whether the communication is oral or written, the difficulty is the same: unless there is a written

---

14 *Re Colin Cooper* [1939] Ch 811.

document, signed by the testator and duly witnessed by at least two witnesses, s 9 of the Wills Act 1837 will not have have been fulfilled. The *prima facie* conclusion from this is that any trust which is set out by the testator orally or in a document which does not comply with s 9 is that it cannot be valid. And yet, as has been shown in *Ottaway v Norman*, such trusts are valid. The reason why equity will recognise such a trust was first explained by the House of Lords in *McCormick v Grogan*.[15]

The facts concerned the will of Abraham Craig. He contracted cholera and, on his death-bed, sent for his friend, Mr Grogan, the defendant. He explained to Mr Grogan that he had left all of his property to him. Mr Grogan was to find his will in a desk with a letter with it. Mr Craig never asked for agreement from Mr Grogan to the letter or its contents.

After Mr Craig's death, Mr Grogan found the will and the letter. The letter contained a long list of friends and relatives to whom Mr Craig wanted his money to be left. It contained the following words towards the end:

> I do not wish you to act strictly as to the foregoing instructions, but leave it entirely to your own good judgment to do as you think I would if living, and as the parties are deserving, and as it is not my wish that you should say anything about this document there cannot be any fault found with you by any of the parties should you not act in strict accordance with it.

Mr Grogan made a number of payments to some of the individuals named in the letter. But he declined to make a payment to others, one of whom was the claimant in the case. James McCormick brought an action claiming that Mr Craig had established a trust in his letter and that, as such, Mr Grogan was obliged to pay him the £10 per year for the rest of his life that Mr Craig had awarded him.

The Irish court of first instance declared that the letter did give rise to a trust binding on Mr Grogan. The Court of Appeal in Chancery in Ireland reversed that decision. Mr McCormick appealed to the House of Lords. The House of Lords held that there was no trust on the facts of the case. All Mr Craig had done was to leave a guide for Mr Grogan as to what he should do with the property. The very words used by Mr Craig, giving Mr Grogan freedom and discretion over the choice of the ultimate recipients of the property, showed that he was not imposing any form of obligation on Mr Grogan to distribute the property to particular individuals or a class of them.

What is interesting, though, is that the House of Lords discussed the rationale underpinning secret trusts. Lord Westbury explained that a court of equity would enforce a secret trust due to the maxim that equity would not allow a statute to be used as an instrument of fraud. If a trustee denied that a trust existed simply because the testator had not complied with the requirements of s 9 of the Wills Act 1837, equity would intervene to recognise the trust.

Making connections

The rationale underpinning the recognition of secret trusts as explained in *McCormick v Grogan* is the maxim that equity will not allow a statute to be used as an instrument of fraud. An executor cannot, therefore, hide behind the Wills Act 1837 and refuse to recognise a secret trust, that he voluntarily accepted to administer, before the testator died. Such a response

---

15 *McCormick v Grogan* (1869–70) LR 4 HL 82.

would be to rely on the strict letter of the Wills Act 1837 to the detriment of the testator's true intentions for their property. Equity will not permit this to occur.

This maxim also underpins equity's recognition of an oral declaration of a trust of land which is *prima facie* contrary to the requirements of s 53(1)(b) of the Law of Property Act 1925, as shown in *Rouchefoucauld v Boustead*.[16] See Chapter 4 where this topic is discussed.

However, to intervene, equity had to be absolutely certain that the trustee was committing a fraud. A 'malus animus' (bad mind) had to be proved 'by the clearest and most indisputable evidence'.[17] No presumption of fraud could be led but only direct evidence of fraud on the part of the trustee would be accepted by the court. This fraud would have to be that the trustee 'knew that the testator . . . was beguiled and deceived by his conduct'.[18]

If such fraud could be proven, the court would recognise the secret trust, even though its terms were not set out in a document that would comply with s 9 of the Wills Act 1837. Equity would impose a trust on the conscience of the trustee to ensure that they administered the trust that they had agreed to administer. The constructive trust would be the vehicle used for achieving the testator's true intentions.

In recognising the secret trust, equity was not, according to Lord Westbury, setting aside an Act of Parliament. Instead, it super-imposed upon the person who was appointed an executor under that Act an additional 'personal obligation, because he applies the Act as an instrument for accomplishing a fraud'.[19]

On the facts, there was no evidence that Mr Grogan had committed a fraud. He was merely attempting to do his best to administer the property left to him by his friend.

If, however, equity recognises a secret trust due to its maxim that it will not permit a statute to be used as an instrument of fraud, the logical question that arises is why it does recognise the very terms of the trust that the testator set out. Surely recognising the secret trust is equity doing far more than it really needs to do. If equity is merely concerned to prevent the Wills Act 1837 from being used as an instrument of fraud, it could achieve that objective by imposing a resulting trust on the trustee, obliging the trustee to hold the property not for his own benefit but on trust for the testator's estate. It is, at first glance, odd that equity goes further in imposing a constructive trust which gives effect to the very terms of the trust that ultimately circumvent the requirements of an Act of Parliament.

In *Re Snowden*, Megarry V-C explained that the law had moved on from the justification given by the House of Lords for the existence of secret trusts in *McCormick v Grogan*. In this way, he supported the *dictum* of Brightman J in *Ottaway v Norman* that fraud was not a prerequisite to establish a secret trust. Megarry V-C felt that fraud was relevant to secret trusts in two ways:

(a)   fraud explained the historical development of secret trusts as they were recognised originally as a method of preventing fraud from occurring by trustees denying a trust's existence. But he said that that did not mean that fraud was nowadays an essential prerequisite for a secret trust to exist; and

(b)   fraud did indeed occur on the facts of some cases.

Megarry V-C explained Lord Westbury's words that equity would need absolutely categorical evidence of fraud existing before intervening to recognise a secret trust. He said Lord Westbury had only intended such high evidence to be needed where the trustee was indeed acting

16   *Rouchefoucauld v Boustead* [1897] 1 Ch 196.
17   Ibid at 97 per Lord Westbury.
18   Ibid at 98.
19   Ibid at 97.

fraudulently. If the trustee was not acting fraudulently, then such a high standard of proof was not needed against him. All that was needed was the normal, civil standard of proof which was that the secret trust had to be proved on the balance of probabilities. It was on those alleging that a secret trust had been created that the burden of proof lay.

There was, in fact, no evidence of fraud occurring on the facts of Re Snowden. There, Ethel Snowden made her will in January 1973, six days before her death. She left everything to her brother. The evidence was that she had entrusted him to deal with the property for her after her death. Surviving her were a number of her relatives, some of whom claimed that she had established a secret trust in her oral instructions to her brother.

In reaching a conclusion that there was no secret trust imposed upon her brother, Megarry V-C quoted with approval comments from Christian LJ in the Court of Appeal in Ireland in McCormick v Grogan[20] that:

> The real question is, what did he [the testator] intend should be the *sanction?* Was it to be the authority of a court of justice, or the conscience of the devisee?

It was only if the sanction was a court of law that a trust would be imposed.

In Megarry V-C's view, all the testatrix intended on the facts was that her brother's conscience should guide him as to what he should do with her property. She never intended him to face any sanction from a court. No secret trust had been established and, accordingly, the property belonged to her brother absolutely.

Both *Ottaway v Norman* and *Re Snowden* decided that no evidence of fraud was needed in the modern world to establish a secret trust. If fraud is alleged, then Lord Westbury's comments in *McCormick v Grogan* continue to apply: that clear, indisputable evidence of it is needed. But it seems that fraud, although the historical basis for equity recognising a secret trust, is not needed to establish one in modern times. As such, it must be questioned if it can still be considered to be the underpinning rationale of secret trusts. It seems the more modern justification of a secret trust being recognised – given that fraud is not an essential prerequisite – is that a secret trust is simply an example of an *inter vivos* trust created by a testator. Provided the testator has fulfilled the requirements as to a valid declaration, the trust is constituted on his death and the trust will be upheld. Fraud seems the historical justification for secret trusts but, in truth, secret trusts are probably no more than examples of normal express trusts nowadays.

The more modern view, therefore, is that the testator actually creates an express trust whilst he is alive. This *inter vivos* trust is entirely separate from the testator's will. It is sometimes said to be *dehors* the will, or outside it. This more modern theory helps explain that the Wills Act 1837 has no application to the trust at all because the trust is not made by the testator's will but entirely separate to it.

Why does it matter whether the basis of a secret trust is fraud or *dehors* the will? It only really matters if the subject matter of the secret trust is land. Remember that all trusts of land must be evidenced in writing and signed by someone able to declare the trust.[21] If the basis of the trust is fraud, *McCormick v Grogan* said that equity will enforce the trust by imposing a constructive trust on the trustee. A constructive trust need not be evidenced in writing.[22] But if the basis of a secret trust is *dehors* the will and it is merely an example of equity recognising

---

20 *McCormick v Grogan* (1867) 1 IR Eq 313 at 328.
21 Law of Property Act 1925, s 53(1)(b). See Chapter 4 for a full discussion.
22 Law of Property Act 1925, s 53(2).

an express trust, then express trusts of land need to be evidenced in writing (and signed) to be valid under s 53(1)(b) of the Law of Property Act 1925. If a secret trust really is simply an express trust, it seems that equity is overlooking this statutory requirement.

Secret trusts: A modern application

It might be thought that secret trusts are a product of history and of a time when men desired to leave their property to mistresses and children whose existence they wanted to be kept confidential. But a secret trust was claimed to exist in the much more recent case of *Davies v The Commissioners for Her Majesty's Revenue & Customs*,[23] which illustrates the application of the topic to tax saving.

Mrs Rhona Goodman had died in 2006. Her estate was valued at approximately £164,000. It included the lease of the flat in which she lived together with a portfolio of shares in BP. The Inland Revenue claimed that inheritance tax was chargeable on the value of Mrs Goodman's estate.

Mrs Goodman's two daughters, who were the executrices and beneficiaries under her will, denied that any inheritance tax was due. They based their argument on a combination of Sched 6, para 2 to the Inheritance Tax Act 1984, ss 5(2) and 22(i)(c) of the Finance Act 1914 and the proviso to s 14 of the Finance Act 1914. In combination, these statutory provisions provided that no tax would be due when one party to a marriage died if its predecessor, estate duty, had been paid when the other party to the marriage died. Mrs Goodman's husband had died in 1969 and estate duty had indeed been paid on the value of his estate.

To take advantage of this opportunity to save tax, Mrs Goodman's daughters also had to show that Mrs Goodman's property was held by her on trust and she did not have the right to dispose of it freely herself. They said that the property left by their father was always held by their mother on a secret trust and they were the residuary beneficiaries of it. The Inland Revenue's response was that there was never any evidence to support the existence of a trust of their father's property. They argued that Mrs Goodman was never under any obligation to leave the property that he left to her to their daughters. They also argued that the alleged trust lacked certainty of subject matter, given that it was impossible to say how much of the father's property had been left on the alleged trust.

The First-Tier Tribunal Judge found that there was no evidence to establish a secret trust. Mrs Goodchild had wished to benefit her daughters on her death but this fell a long way short of her being subject to a binding obligation from her husband to use certain property in particular ways, it being clear that the property then had to be passed on to their children.

Whilst the case suggests that secret trusts are, in theory, not confined to the years of the nineteenth and early twentieth centuries and instances of men wishing to benefit their mistresses, it is a salutory reminder that there must always be cogent evidence of a secret trust before the court will recognise one. This is, of course, vital in the case of a fully secret trust as it will always contradict the terms of a testator's will who, at first glance, appears to leave property to the recipient absolutely.

Summary of fully secret trusts

The courts seem wary of recognising secret trusts in the modern environment. The words of Viscount Sumner in *Blackwell v Blackwell*[24] seem as relevant today as when he first delivered them:

---

23 *Davies v The Commissioners for Her Majesty's Revenue & Customs* [2009] UKFTT 138 (TC).
24 *Blackwell v Blackwell* [1929] AC 318 at 333.

'[i]t is a grave thing to affirm a doctrine that violates the prescriptions of a statute and especially such a statute as the Wills Act.'

It is true that the courts have moved away from basing the doctrine on fraud but the three criteria set out by Brightman J in *Ottaway v Norman* are still required before a secret trust can be established. The concept of a secret trust is based upon an agreement that was communicated to the trustee and which was accepted by the trustee, either expressly or by conduct, before the testator's death. Whilst the courts have, in *Re Snowden*, relaxed the standard of proof required to establish a secret trust to that based on the balance of probabilities, it is suggested that it will always be a difficult task to establish such a trust. This is because the evidence of a secret trust is outside the testator's will which must remain the best evidence available of the testator's intentions after his death.

Nowadays, secret trusts are probably examples of *inter vivos* trusts. As such, if a court is persuaded that one is established, it must comply with all of the requirements needed to declare a valid trust, especially the elements of the three certainties. The theoretical basis of a fully secret trust means that, despite the problem with trusts of land, the *dehors* the will theory explaining the courts' recognition of the trust probably carries more weight than the fraud theory.

Half-Secret Trusts

A fully secret trust is a trust based on an agreement between the testator and the trustee but whose very existence is not revealed in the testator's will. A half-secret trust is still based on an agreement between the testator and the trustee but there is a clue as to its existence in the testator's will, for the testator makes it clear that he leaves property to the recipient on trust. The actual terms of the trust are kept secret from wider view.

An example of a half-secret trust has already been discussed in the case of *Re Keen*, where Mr Keen had made it clear in his will that the £10,000 was being left on trust. His mistress beneficiary's details were set out in a separate letter which was, of course, separate from the will.

The establishment of a half-secret trust was first recognised by the House of Lords in *Blackwell v Blackwell*.[25]

The facts concerned the will of John Blackwell, who left £12,000 on trust in his will to five trustees so that they should use the money 'for the purposes indicated by me to them'. There was a power to pay over two-thirds of the money 'to such person or persons indicated by me to them' but if this occurred, the remaining £4,000 was to be paid to Mr Blackwell's residuary estate. Mr Blackwell wrote a separate document stating that the 'person or persons indicated' were his mistress and his illegitimate son. After his death, his wife and legitimate son brought an action against the trustees, claiming that there was no valid trust of the original £12,000. The House of Lords held that there was a trust and that the separate document could be used as evidence to establish it, despite the fact that it did not comply with s 9 of the Wills Act 1837.

Lord Buckmaster discussed the rationale of fraud underlying a fully secret trust and was of the view that the same rationale could support the existence of a half-secret trust. Preventing the trustee from fraudulently claiming the beneficial interest in the trust property for his own purposes was the reason why a fully secret trust was recognised. The same principle could apply for the recognition of a half-secret trust. If the trustee failed to administer a half-secret trust, the true beneficiary, as well as the testator, would still be defrauded by his actions. Lord

---

25 *Blackwell v Blackwell* [1929] AC 318.

Buckmaster almost sought to sum up the rationale underpinning secret trusts as a whole by using language that would today be thought of as being similar to the language of estoppel:[26]

> It is, I think, more accurate to say that a testator having been induced to make a gift on trust in his will in reliance on the clear promise that such trust will be executed in favour of certain named persons, the trustee is not at liberty to suppress the evidence of the trust and thus destroy the whole object of its creation, in fraud of the beneficiaries.[27]

Viscount Sumner did not see any conflict between the court's recognition of any secret trust and the requirements of the Wills Act 1837. Equity's general jurisdiction would act on a trustee's conscience to ensure that he honoured the terms of the trust. This equitable jurisdiction could run alongside the written will. Equity did not need to concern itself with the majority of wills and only needed to intervene to enforce the trust if the trustee refused to honour it: '[equity] makes him do what the will in itself has nothing to do with'.[28] Section 9 of the Wills Act 1837 set out merely the form that a will had to take but was silent over how the law of trusts could apply to a trust created in a will. A testator could not, however, reserve to himself a power in his will to set up a trust at some point in the future. Such a provision would fall foul of s 9. A testator could communicate the terms of the trust to the trustee and, provided the trustee accepted that obligation, a secret trust would be established. Such an event would enable the law of trusts to intervene and recognise the trust.

Viscount Sumner was of the view that a half-secret trust should be recognised by equity as much as a fully secret trust:

> In both cases the testator's wishes are incompletely expressed in his will. Why should equity, over a mere matter of words, give effect to them in one case and frustrate them in the other?[29]

Blackwell v Blackwell was the first case in which it was decided that a half-secret trust could be as valid as a fully secret trust. It also determined for the first time that *personal* fraud of the trustees was not necessary to establish any secret trust. The trustees in the case were not claiming the beneficial interest in the trust property as their own. Rather, by not recognising the trust, the court would have been sanctioning a fraud on the beneficiaries whom the testator intended to benefit and such fraud would also be on the testator himself.

Requirements

In *Blackwell v Blackwell*, the House of Lords made no distinction between the requirements for a half-secret trust and those for a fully secret trust: '[t]he necessary elements, on which the question turns, are intention, communication and acquiescence.'[30]

There does, however, appear to be a distinction in terms of timing and when the trustee must have accepted their obligation from the testator. In the case of a fully secret trust, the communication to and acceptance by the trustee of their obligations could occur either before

---

26 See Chapter 17.
27 Ibid at 329.
28 Ibid at 335.
29 Ibid.
30 Ibid at 334 per Viscount Sumner.

or after the testator made his will. The reasoning behind this was that if the trustee chose not to administer the trust, the testator always had the freedom to write a further will containing different requirements.

It seems that for a half-secret trust to be valid, the trustee must accept his obligations before the testator makes his will. This can be demonstrated by the facts of *Re Keen*. In that case, Mr Keen had left a letter in a sealed envelope which the trustee only read after Mr Keen's death. The Court of Appeal held that such action circumvented the requirements of s 9 of the Wills Act 1837, as effectively, Mr Keen was trying to reserve to himself a power to avoid compliance with the statutory formalities in creating a will by leaving an unsigned addendum (addition) to his will.

This same conclusion was reached again in *Re Bateman's Will Trusts*[31] by the High Court. John Bateman wrote his will in 1924 in which he directed his trustees to pay the income arising from £24,000 to 'such persons and in such proportions' as he intended to set out in a sealed letter. After his death, the trustees did act upon a sealed letter written by Mr Bateman. Amongst the issues for the court to decide was whether Mr Bateman had successfully created a valid trust. It would be a half-secret trust as it was clear from the wording of his will that the trustees were not to retain the beneficial interest in the money for themselves but were to pay it to other recipients.

Pennycuick V-C held that the trust was invalid. Following *Re Keen*, he held that Mr Bateman had referred in his will to a future sealed letter. He had, therefore, attempted to reserve to himself a power to dispose of his property at a future date by an instrument which did not comply with the formalities of s 9 of the Wills Act 1837. Such letter was void and the trust invalid.

Whilst the courts seem united on the premise that it is not possible to create a half-secret trust by reference to a future document, the fact that it is possible to create a fully secret trust by reference to the same type of document is interesting. Perhaps the distinction is down to the concept of the trustee accepting the obligation to administer the trust. In the case of a fully secret trust, if the testator asks the trustee to administer the trust subsequent to writing his will, the trustee still retains complete freedom of choice over whether or not to accept the responsibility. If he declines the obligation, the testator may write a new will. But in the case of a half-secret trust, where the testator states that he will reveal his instructions in a future piece of correspondence, he is effectively obliging the trustee to administer the trust and removing his freedom of choice over whether to be a trustee at all.

❖ ANALYSING THE LAW

Do you think the distinction over future correspondence as to the terms of a trust is merited? Would the law practically be disadvantaged if it was permitted to create half-secret trusts in the same manner as fully secret trusts? And might there be any advantages in simplifying the law in this manner?

---

31 *Re Bateman's Will Trusts* [1970] 1 WLR 1463.

Summary of fully and half-secret trusts

The following points can be made:

(a)   The successful creation of either a fully or half-secret trust depends on:

   (i)   intention by the testator to subject the trustee to an obligation to hold property on trust for a beneficiary;

   (ii)   'true' communication of that intention by the testator to the trustee; and

   (iii) acceptance of that obligation by the trustee.

(b)   The original theoretical justification for both trusts was fraud. Due to its maxim, equity would not allow the Wills Act 1837 to be used as an instrument of fraud and for the trustee to hide behind it and deny that a trust existed. It seems that that theory has given way nowadays to the *dehors* theory: that a secret trust is merely an example of an *inter vivos* express trust, created outside the will. The Wills Act 1837 is thus irrelevant to its creation. However, the requirement of a trust of land needing to be evidenced in writing under s 53(1)(b) of the Law of Property Act 1925 undermines this theory.

(c)   If fraud remains the basis of a secret trust, a constructive trust is implied on a trustee to administer the trust. This can work for trusts of land too as a constructive trust of land does not have to be evidenced in writing (by virtue of s 53(2) of the Law of Property Act 1925).

Mutual Wills

As has been seen, a secret trust arises where a testator reaches an agreement with another person that that person will not, as appears from the testator's will, be entitled beneficially to property seemingly left to him but will instead hold that property on trust for a third-party beneficiary. The terms of the secret trust are outside of the will. The existence of a secret trust depends, however, on an agreement being reached between the testator and the trustee.

The doctrine of mutual wills similarly depends on the notion of agreement. This time, however, the agreement reached is between two people who have agreed between themselves that they will leave their property to each other initially and thereafter to the same beneficiaries. The agreement impliedly confirms that after the death of one, the survivor will honour the agreement by not making a fresh will, distributing their property to other recipients. In consequence of that agreement, they both make wills in identical – or very similar – forms at the same time as each other. If this is the case, the doctrine of mutual wills applies.

Key Learning Point

The consequences of the doctrine of mutual wills applying means that after the first testator's death, the surviving testator will not be permitted to alter their will under the agreement reached with the first testator. Equity will recognise the agreement reached between both testators and hold that, on the death of the first testator, the survivor becomes bound by a constructive trust and is obliged to hold property on trust for those beneficiaries that the two testators had jointly agreed would benefit.

Requirements

The requirements of mutual wills were set out by Nourse J in Re Cleaver:[32]

(a)   there must be a 'definite agreement' between the two testators as to whom they were to leave their property. The agreement had to 'impose on the donee a legally binding obligation to deal with the property in the particular way';[33]

(b)   the evidence to establish the agreement must be 'clear and satisfactory'.[34] The standard of proof needed to establish such an agreement was the usual civil standard of on the balance of probabilities an agreement was made;

(c)   crucially, relying on the decision of the Privy Council in Gray v Perpetual Trustee Co Ltd,[35] it was not enough to show that the two wills were made at the same time as each other and that their terms were similar in order for the doctrine of mutual wills to apply. Those two factors were merely a 'relevant circumstance to take into account'[36] and the 'whole of the evidence had to be looked at' to establish if, in fact, the testators intended that they wanted the doctrine of mutual wills to apply to them. The agreement had to be more than the two testators would make wills: it had to be that they would not revoke them.

Nourse J also reviewed the link between secret trusts and mutual wills. His view was that underpinning both doctrines was equity's willingness to intervene with a constructive trust on the person who denied that a valid agreement existed to deal with property in a particular way. As equity used a trust to enforce an agreement, the certainties of subject matter and of object in particular had to be absolutely settled from the agreement between the two testators. It had to be clear, therefore, what property was being left on trust and who the ultimate beneficiaries were.

The facts of Re Cleaver give a useful illustration of when the doctrine of mutual wills would apply. Arthur Cleaver Sr married Flora Cleaver in 1967. They wrote several near-identical wills, the last one being in 1974. They left everything to each other initially. In Arthur's will, if Flora did not survive him, he directed that his residuary estate be divided into three equal shares, each share being left to one of his three children from his earlier marriage. Importantly, one of those children, Martha, was only to have a life interest in her share with remainder to the other two children equally. Flora's will was nearly the same except that if Arthur predeceased her, she left legacies to her two nieces before dividing her estate into the same three parts.

After Arthur's death, Flora made a new will in 1977. In breach of the agreement she had made with Arthur, she left her residuary estate to Martha and her husband absolutely.

Nourse J held that the doctrine of mutual wills applied to the wills written by Arthur and Flora. He found that they made an agreement which they intended should impose 'mutual legal obligations'[37] on each of them as to how their property was to be disposed. The agreement was that Arthur would leave his estate to her if, in return, she would leave hers to his children. The 1974 wills reflected that agreement, not the 1977 will.

Further comments on the nature of the agreement underpinning the doctrine of mutual wills were added by Morritt J in Re Dale.[38] Morritt J confirmed that the doctrine did not just apply to where two testators had initially left their property to each other, as had occurred in Re Cleaver.

---

32 Re Cleaver [1981] 1 WLR 939.
33 Ibid at 947.
34 Ibid.
35 Gray v Perpetual Trustee Co Ltd [1928] AC 391.
36 Re Cleaver [1981] 1 WLR 939 at 945.
37 Ibid at 948.
38 Re Dale [1994] Ch 31.

In *Re Dale*, Norman and Monica Dale wrote identical wills on 5 September 1988 in which they left all of their property to their son and daughter in equal shares. After Norman's death, Monica wrote a new will in which she left £300 to their daughter but the remainder of all of her property to their son. After her death, her daughter brought an action claiming that the new will was of no effect and that the doctrine of mutual wills applied. A preliminary issue was whether the doctrine of mutual wills could apply to the facts of the case. In all previous cases where the doctrine had applied, the survivor of the two testators had initially left property to the other. It was argued, on the son's behalf, that the surviving testator had to receive such a benefit for the doctrine of mutual wills to apply; that the receiving of such a benefit constituted the consideration upon which the contract to make mutual wills was based.

Morritt J held that the doctrine of mutual wills did not depend on showing mutual benefit between the two testators. It was not a prerequisite that each had to leave the other their property first. The doctrine simply depended on there being a contract between the two testators. Such a contract had to be supported by consideration, as with all contracts not made by deed. Sufficient consideration could be found on an executory basis by the first testator promising not to revoke his will whilst alive and, secondly, on an executed basis by the first testator not, in fact, revoking his will whilst alive.

Morritt J deduced that the foundation of the doctrine of mutual wills was originally the prevention of fraud. It would be a fraud on the deceased testator if the surviving testator was allowed to revoke their mutually agreed will and leave the property to beneficiaries other than those agreed between them. It was a fraud on the deceased testator not to uphold the mutual will and it made no difference to the committal of that fraud whether the surviving testator had benefited from the estate of the deceased testator.

In *Re Goodchild, Dec'd*,[39] the Court of Appeal stressed that not only did an agreement have to be found between the testators, but that there also had to be a mutual intention found not to alter the wills after they had been made.

The facts concerned the wills of Dennis and Joan Goodchild. Each will left their property to the other, but if the other did not survive for 28 days after the first's death, each residuary estate was left to their son, Gary. After Joan's death, Dennis married Enid. He made a new will, in which he revoked his previous will and left everything to Enid.

Dennis died in 1993. Gary brought an action claiming that the doctrine of mutual wills applied and that Enid held his parents' residuary estate on constructive trust for him. This action was dismissed by Carnwath J and Gary appealed to the Court of Appeal.

Leggatt LJ set out the reason why the court was concerned to find an agreement between the testators as a prerequisite before holding that the doctrine of mutual wills applied:

> the reason why, if mutual wills are to take effect, an agreement is necessary, is that without it the property of the second testator is not bound . . .[40]

Leggatt LJ said a 'key feature' of mutual wills was:

> the irrevocability of the mutual intentions. Not only must they be binding when made, but the testators must have undertaken, and so must be bound, not to change their intentions after the death of the first testator.[41]

---

39 *Re Goodchild, Dec'd* [1997] 1 WLR 1216.
40 Ibid at 1224.
41 Ibid at 1225 (emphasis added).

Finding such mutual intentions went beyond two testators leaving their estates to each other and thereafter to a chosen beneficiary. Such a plan did not carry with it a notion that it would be irrevocable. It had to be evidenced that the testators intended not to change their minds after the death of the first testator. For this, Leggatt LJ said:

> The test must always be, suppose that during the lifetime of the surviving testator the intended beneficiary did something which the survivor regarded as unpardonable, would he or she be free not to leave the combined estate to him? The answer must be that the survivor is so entitled unless the testators agreed otherwise when they executed their wills. Hence the need for a clear agreement.[42]

On the facts, the doctrine of mutual wills did not apply. Dennis and Joan undoubtedly wanted Gary to inherit their residuary estates. But that was not sufficient to subject Enid to a constructive trust of the property in Gary's favour because that was not enough to prevent Dennis from writing a new will. What was required was 'a mutual intention that both wills should remain unaltered and that the survivor should be bound to leave the combined estates to the son'.[43]

Joan felt the arrangement was irrevocable but Dennis did not. They did not share a mutual intention to leave the property to Gary.

The case illustrates that it is not any agreement that will be sufficient to prove that the doctrine of mutual wills applies. The agreement must not only comply with the requirements set out in *Re Cleaver*, but also it must be made under an intention, shared by both parties, that the arrangement is irrevocable. Dennis thought that he had merely a moral obligation not to revoke his will but such obligation was not sufficient to establish that the doctrine applied.

Mutual wills v two identical wills

As has been seen, there is a difference between two wills which are subject to the doctrine of mutual wills and two wills that two testators make and are merely identical to one another. The key difference, of course, is that where mutual wills have been made, there is little point in the surviving testator altering their will due to the contract that they formed with the deceased testator. Equity will ensure that the agreed property is held by the surviving testator on constructive trust for the agreed beneficiaries.

It will not, it is suggested, often be the case that two individuals wish to make mutual wills and effectively surrender their freedom of testamentary disposition by doing so. If, however, two individuals do wish to make mutual wills, it is best practice for each will to state expressly that they are mutual wills, as well as being in the same form as each other. An express statement is the best possible evidence of a mutual intention that the testators intended to invoke the doctrine of mutual wills.

Revocation of mutual wills

Given what has been discussed, it might be thought that, provided the elements needed to establish mutual wills are found, it is impossible to revoke mutual wills. Whilst this is true after the first testator's death, it is not the case whilst both testators remain alive. During the testators' lifetimes, either one may revoke their mutual will, providing they give notice to the other.

---

42 Ibid.
43 Ibid at 1225–6.

It is, of course, impossible to revoke a mutual will after the death of the first testator as at that point, the surviving testator will be subject to a constructive trust to hold the property for the agreed beneficiaries.

This was made clear in the case which was the basis of the doctrine of mutual wills in English law, *Dufour v Pereira*,[44] where Lord Camden LC said[45] a mutual will:

> might have been revoked by both jointly; it might have been revoked separately, provided the party intending it had given notice to the other of such revocation. But I cannot be of opinion, that either of them, could, during their joint lives, do it secretly; or that after the death of either, it could be done by the survivor by another will.

❖ EXPLAINING THE LAW

Suppose two testators make mutual wills. Whilst they are both alive, one desires to alter their will. They give notice of that wish to the other. The other refuses to give consent.

Freedom of testamentary disposition states that the one desiring to alter their will can do so. Lord Camden LC's words also suggest that the agreement that the testators would write mutual wills can be broken.

But, in a sense, there is little point in breaking an agreement to make mutual wills if the other testator does not agree to it. If one testator materially alters their will, such alteration will not have any effect: *Re Hobley*.[46]

In this case, Mr and Mrs Hobley made mutual wills in favour of each other in 1975. They left their house to Mr Blythe, if one of them had predeceased the other. After making his will, Mr Hobley executed a codicil revoking the gift of the house to Mr Blythe. There was no evidence that Mrs Hobley knew of this act by her husband.

After his death, Mrs Hobley executed a further will which was different from the 1975 will. The issue for the High Court was whether this will was valid or whether a constructive trust had been imposed on her executors by the doctrine of mutual wills affecting the earlier wills.

Judge Charles Aldous QC held that Mrs Hobley's later will was valid, due to the unilateral alteration made to the earlier mutual will by Mr Hobley. That alteration was sufficient to prevent the constructive trust arising.

The court found that any unilateral alteration without the consent of the other testator would prevent a constructive trust arising. The court could not try to embark on an exercise in discovering whether the alteration really mattered to the surviving testator. Such evidence would be difficult to ascertain, as in usual cases involving mutual wills, both testators have died before litigation results.

Testators should, therefore, think carefully before making mutual wills and just as carefully before trying to alter them.

---

44 *Dufour v Pereira* (1769) 1 Dick 419; 21 ER 332.
45 Ibid at 420.
46 *Re Hobley* (1997) Times, 16 June.

Mutual wills and the constructive trust

If it is found that two testators intended to execute mutual wills, equity forces the survivor to honour the agreement made with the deceased testator by means of the constructive trust. The constructive trust arises from the moment the first testator dies: *Re Hagger*.[47]

The facts concerned a document called the 'joint will' of John and Emma Hagger, written in 1902. The document stated that after the first of them had died, the income from their properties was to be paid to the survivor for life. After the survivor's death, the estate was to be split between several named individuals.

Emma died in 1904. The income from their properties was paid to John for his life. In 1921, John made another will in which he left his estate to people who were not mentioned in the earlier joint will. By the time John died in 1928, three of the original beneficiaries, one of whom was Eleanor Palmer, under the joint will had themselves died. The issues for the court were (i) whether all of the property owned by John at the date of his death was to be left on the trusts declared in the joint will and (ii) who should receive the property left to Eleanor Palmer, as she had predeceased John. The argument was that her personal representatives were not entitled to it as her share lapsed on her death.

Clauson J held that a trust came into existence at the moment Emma died. At that stage, John became a trustee of the property in favour of the trusts declared in the will. John himself had no beneficial title to the property, other than the life interest in his favour. Consequently, Eleanor's personal representatives were entitled to receive her share as it had not lapsed on her death. The trust had been constituted on Emma's death.

The difficulty with holding that there is a constructive trust is that, in a case such as *Re Hagger*, John was entitled only to a life interest in the property during his lifetime. It is an interesting question as to precisely what and how much property is caught by the imposition of the constructive trust. In *Re Hagger*, the testators had regarded their property as jointly acquired by their joint efforts, so it was apt that the constructive trust covered all of the property left in the joint will. In other mutual wills, it must be best practice for testators to define precisely the property which they intend should be subject to the constructive trust. If no definition of property is given, it appears that the property will consist of the whole of the property owned by both testators, according to Lord Camden LC in *Dufour v Pereira*:[48] '[t]he property of both is put into a common fund, and every devise is the joint devise of both.'

The Australian decision of *Birmingham v Renfrew*[49] considered the extent to which the surviving testator could use the property if all of it had been subjected to a constructive trust by the mutual wills.

The facts concerned Joseph and Grace Russell. Grace had inherited a substantial amount of property from an uncle. Joseph had no property of his own. They came to an agreement in which, in their wills, Grace would leave the entire property to Joseph and in turn, he would leave it on his death to certain of her relatives. (The alternative would have been simply for Grace to leave Joseph a life interest in the property with the remainder interest to her relatives but such option was not pursued by her.) Both of them made wills to that effect. Grace died before Joseph, whereupon he made a different will under which he appointed different beneficiaries, leaving his former wife's relatives with little or no property. The trial judge recognised the agreement formed by Joseph and Grace to the extent that a trust was recognised as being imposed over their property in favour of her relatives. Joseph's relatives appealed to the High Court of Australia. Their appeal was dismissed.

---

47   *Re Hagger* [1930] 2 Ch 190.
48   *Dufour v Pereira* (1769) 1 Dick 419; 21 ER 332 (fuller report located in *Hargrave's Juridical Arguments* (1799), vol ii pp 306–312).
49   *Birmingham v Renfrew* (1937) 57 CLR 666.

The case is known for the interesting comments of Dixon J who considered the extent to which the surviving testator could make use of the property subject to the trust during his lifetime. He considered the trust to be 'floating'[50] in nature. This floating trust enabled the survivor to deal with the property as he wished during his lifetime but ensured that the property would always be subject to the agreed trusts on the survivor's death. This occurred because the 'floating obligation, suspended, so to speak, during the lifetime of the survivor can descend upon the assets at his death and crystallize into a trust'.[51]

The survivor could use the property as he wished during his lifetime and even convert realty into personalty if he so desired. He could spend money raised by the sale of the property but only to a point: Dixon J held that the survivor was not permitted to dispose of the property so that the intentions of the agreement made between the two testators would be defeated.

Dixon J also held that it was irrelevant that the two testators had not written down the terms of their agreement before they wrote their mutual wills, even though part of the property concerned land. The argument before him was that as the testators were creating a trust of land, they should have had to comply with the equivalent of s 53(1)(b) of the Law of Property Act 1925. This did not matter, as the contract formed by the testators was to operate not on any specific property, such as land, but on whatever assets the testatrix had at her death. In any event, the maxim underpinning the doctrine of mutual wills was that equity would not permit a statute to be used as an instrument of fraud. It was not possible for Joseph's relatives to argue that the writing requirements of the equivalent of s 53(1)(b) had not been fulfilled as, had that argument been accepted, they would have been using those requirements to commit a fraud on both the testatrix and the original beneficiaries.

The analysis led by Dixon J in *Birmingham v Renfrew* of the notion of a floating trust over all of the property of the trust was accepted by the English courts in the decision of Nourse J in *Re Cleaver*.

The issue of the extent of the property subject to a constructive trust was considered recently by the Court of Appeal in *Olins v Walters*.[52]

The case concerned the wills of Harold and Freda Walters. Freda died in 2006. As Mummery LJ put it in giving the leading judgment, the 'novel aspect'[53] about the case was that Harold was still alive at the time of the litigation and thus could give first-hand evidence about the alleged agreement. He denied that he and Freda had ever made such an agreement that would subject them both to the doctrine of mutual wills.

Harold and Freda had made wills in 1988. Ten years later, they made codicils to their wills. These were drawn up by one of their grandsons, Andrew, who was a solicitor. Each codicil confirmed that it was supplementary to their earlier wills, which had been intended to be 'mutual testamentary dispositions'. In a letter to his grandparents, Andrew explained the doctrine of mutual wills to them. He recorded that they wanted their wills to be mutual so that Freda would not be pressured into changing her will by their family should Harold predecease her.

By the time Freda died, Harold and Andrew's relationship had deteriorated. Harold denied wishing to make a mutual will and said he could not recall the meeting in which he had instructed Andrew to draft the codicils or the agreement to make the wills mutual. Andrew began proceedings for a declaration that Freda's codicil took effect as a valid mutual will. At first instance, Norris J held that there was a contract to make mutual wills between Harold and Freda. Harold appealed to the Court of Appeal. His appeal was unanimously dismissed.

---

50 Ibid at 689.
51 Ibid.
52 *Olins v Walters* [2009] Ch 212.
53 Ibid at 216.

Norris J had held that, as a matter of construction of the codicil, it was only Freda's property that was subject to the constructive trust. He did not regard the issue of Harold's estate as requiring determination. Harold submitted on appeal that this showed that there was little evidence as to the terms of the contract which was alleged to have been formed between him and Freda. He said that without evidence as to the terms of the contract, it was not appropriate to decide that the wills were mutual.

The Court of Appeal disagreed. Mummery LJ said that all that was required to establish the doctrine of mutual wills was evidence of the intentions of Harold and Freda. This gave rise to a trust which became binding on Harold when Freda died. The operation of the trust was not postponed to take effect from Harold's death.

There was no need to search for the exact terms of the contract on which the mutual wills were based. Mummery LJ said that disputes as to the actual operation of the trust normally hinged on the construction of the agreement formed between the two testators. Such differences could be resolved informally between beneficiaries of sound mind and full age. If the beneficiaries lacked capacity, or could not agree, any dispute could be resolved by the court as and when necessary.

Olins v Walters shows that the court will take a pragmatic approach to the issue of the terms of the contract underpinning the constructive trust. The court will not seach exhaustively for all of its terms which will usually be a time-consuming exercise as normally both testators will have died before litigation reaches the court. Instead, the court will intervene only when required to answer specific questions that the beneficiaries have been unable to resolve for themselves. Prevention, however, remains better than cure and careful drafting of the subject matter of the trust which forms the agreement underpinning the mutual wills must remain the order of the day.

Mutual wills – the future

In general terms, it is suggested that mutual wills are a bad idea. Whilst they do prevent a surviving testator from being pressured into altering their will, they effectively tie up that survivor to an agreement formed perhaps many years previously in different circumstances to leave property to particular beneficiaries. For young couples in particular, mutual wills should be regarded with caution. The death of one of them at a young age will prohibit the survivor from altering their testamentary intentions with their property even though they may have subsequently formed a new life with a different individual. Indeed, Mummery LJ gave cautionary guidance in Olins v Walters:

> The likelihood is that in future even fewer people will opt for such an arrangement and even more will be warned against the risks involved.[54]

The courts have indicated a wish not to try to define the extent of the property subject to a mutual will but rather, in Olins v Walters, to retain a watching brief over the administration of the deceased's estate. Birmingham v Renfrew confirms that the surviving testator has freedom to use the property but such use is curtailed in that the property cannot be sold off in swathes such as would defeat the intentions of the deceased testator to leave it to particular beneficiaries.

---

54 Olins v Walters [2009] Ch 212 at 215.

Points to Review

You have seen:

- how secret trusts and mutual wills are based on the concept of agreement that takes effect outside of a testator's will;
- that both secret trusts and mutual wills were based on the doctrine of fraud. Equity's desire to prevent fraud continues to underpin mutual wills but the doctrine of secret trusts has moved away from fraud. Secret trusts now simply appear to be an example of equity's enforcement of a validly created trust; and
- how, once made, it is a breach of the original agreement for one testator to revoke the mutual will unilaterally without the consent of the other testator and that revocation of the agreement after the first testator's death is impossible, as equity will recognise a constructive trust of the property.

Making connections

The mechanism for enforcing mutual wills is that of a constructive trust. Constructive trusts are discussed in Chapter 3. You should turn to that chapter to refresh your memory on that topic.

Secret trusts and mutual wills also involve parol evidence being allowed to prove their existence. Depending on the type of property being left on trust, in theory this runs contrary to statutory requirements such as s 53(1)(b) of the Law of Property Act 1925 which requires all trusts of land to be evidenced in writing. Equity will not, however, allow a statute to be used to commit a fraud and in this context, will not permit someone to invoke a statute in order to deprive a rightful beneficiary of their property. The topic of formalities being required in relation to a trust being properly formed and equity's views on a statute not being used as an instrument of fraud are discussed in Chapter 4.

 Useful Things to Read

The best reading is contained in the primary sources listed below. It is always good to consider the decisions of the courts themselves as this will lead to a deeper understanding of the issues involved. A few secondary sources are also listed, which you may wish to read to gain additional insights into the areas considered in this chapter.

Primary sources

Birmingham v Renfrew (1937) 57 CLR 666.
Blackwell v Blackwell [1929] AC 318.
McCormick v Grogan (1869–70) LR 4 HL 82.
Olins v Walters [2009] Ch 212.
Ottaway v Norman [1972] Ch 698.
Re Bateman's WT [1970] 1 WLR 1463.
Re Cleaver [1981] 1 WLR 939.
Re Dale [1994] Ch 31
Re Goodchild [1997] 1 WLR 1216.
Re Hagger [1930] 2 Ch 190.
Re Keen [1937] Ch 236.
Re Snowden [1979] Ch 528.

Secondary sources

Alastair Hudson, *Equity & Trusts* (7th edn, Routledge-Cavendish, 2012) ch 6.

Ruth Hughes, 'Mutual wills' (2011) PCB 3, 131–136. This article compares the constructive trust to proprietary estoppel in the context of mutual wills.

Diana Lincaid, 'The tangled web: The relationship between a secret trust and the will' (2000) Conv Sep/Oct 420–443. This article considers aspects of secret trusts in more depth and is a logical next step having read this chapter. It addresses such issues as the ability of the secret trustee to witness the will, whether the will is revocable and what would occur if the secret trustee and/or beneficiary died before the testator.

Mark Pawlowski and James Brown, 'Constituting a secret trust by estoppel' (2004) Conv Sept/Oct 388–398. This considers a topic additional to this chapter which is whether a secret trust can be constituted by an estoppel if the testator seeks to alter his will at a later stage. The article considers whether the beneficiary can already argue that the secret trust has been constituted before the testator changes his mind.

Mohamed Ramjohn, *Text, Cases and Materials on Equity and Trusts* (4th edn, Routledge-Cavendish, 2008) ch 12.

David Wilde, 'Secret and semi-secret trusts: Justifying the distinctions between the two' (1995) Conv Sept/Oct 366–378. This article argues that there are valid distinctions between a fully and a half-secret trust which do justify the courts treating them differently.

Chapter 12

Remedies for Breach of Trust Against Trustees

As shown in Chapters 8 and 9, being a trustee is an onerous responsibility and is subject to numerous duties, of both a fiduciary and non-fiduciary nature. Breach of one of these duties is something that a trustee should obviously guard against. This chapter is the first of two to consider a beneficiary's remedies for breaches of trust. It focuses on the remedies the beneficiary might pursue against the trustee whilst Chapter 13 considers the remedies the beneficiary might use to recover lost trust property and personal remedies against non-trustees.

As You Read

As you read this chapter, look out for the following key issues:

- what a breach of trust is, when a trustee is liable, the extent of a trustee's liability and how the beneficiary must show that he has suffered loss in order to take successful action against a trustee;
- how a trustee may rely on an exemption clause to exclude his liability for breach of trust; and
- the defences and mitigating circumstances that a trustee may rely on in an action taken against him for breach of trust.

Breach of Trust

A trustee is subject to a number of duties, of both a fiduciary and non-fiduciary nature.[1] A breach of trust will have occurred when 'the trustees made decisions which they should not have made or failed to make decisions which they should have made'.[2]

In *Nestle v National Westminster Bank plc*[3] Staughton LJ recognised that it may be difficult to prove that either a trustee had made a decision when he should not have done so, or failed to make a decision when he should have done so. The difficulty of proving either event, however, was not a reason to absolve a beneficiary from proving it.

❖ EXPLAINING THE LAW

Suppose Scott sets up a trust in his will, settling £100,000 on trust for the benefit of Vikas during his life with remainder to Ulrika. He appoints Thomas as his trustee.

An animal lover all his life, Scott sets out in a term of the trust that Thomas must not invest any money into organisations that test medicines on animals.

Whilst administering the trust, Thomas becomes aware that shares in MedicalResearch plc are increasing in value. This is a company that uses animals in medical research. He therefore decides to purchase a large amount for the benefit of the trust.

Suppose after purchasing the shares in MedicalResearch plc, the shares then fall significantly in value. The beneficiaries might decide to take action against Thomas in order to recover their loss.

---

1   See Chapter 9 at Figure 9.1 (p 230).
2   *Nestle v National Westminster Bank plc* [1993] 1 WLR 1260 per Staughton LJ at 1276.
3   *Nestle v National Westminster Bank plc* [1993] 1 WLR 1260.

In purchasing the shares, Thomas *prima facie* committed a breach of trust. It was a term of the trust that he must not invest in such a company. The beneficiaries may sue him for breach of trust to recover the loss to the trust fund.

Who is liable for a breach of trust?

If only a sole trustee exists, clearly that trustee must be liable for every breach of trust that he commits. If there are two or more trustees, the general rule remains that only the trustee who has committed the breach of trust will be liable for it. However, all of the trustees may be liable for any breach of trust that occurs, even if it was only committed by one of them, in the following circumstances:

(a) if one trustee leaves a matter to a co-trustee without enquiring as to what has happened and a breach of trust occurs. For example, in *Hale v Adams*,[4] trust property was sold and the money received by only one of the trustees. The money was then lost by that trustee. The trustee who did not receive the money made no enquiry of the receiving trustee about what had happened to the sale proceeds. The court held that both trustees were liable for breach of trust. Effectively, both trustees had received trust property when the property was sold and even the 'innocent' trustee should be responsible for its loss;

(b) if one trustee is aware of a breach of trust by a co-trustee and does nothing to remedy it (*Styles v Guy*[5]); or

(c) if a trustee allows the trust funds to remain in the sole control of a co-trustee. In *English v Willats*,[6] trust property was sold but the sale proceeds were paid only to one of two trustees. The non-receiving trustee was held liable to make good the loss to the trust fund.

A further example of one trustee allowing a co-trustee to manage the trust fund by themselves occurred in *Bahin v Hughes*.[7]

The facts concerned a trust established in the will of Robert Hughes. He settled £2,000 on trust for the money to be held for the benefit of his wife for her lifetime and afterwards for his children. The trustees were Eliza Hughes, Mr and Mrs James Burden and Mr Edward Edwards.

Eliza managed the trust on a daily basis. She advised the beneficiary and the other trustees that a good investment would be for the money to be lent by way of mortgage over eight houses in Wood Green, Middlesex. It transpired, however, that all of the properties over which the money was lent were leasehold. At that time, the types of investments in which trust funds could be placed were curtailed and the terms of the trust did not allow investment in leasehold properties.

The leasehold houses were not sufficiently valuable to be used as security for the money lent by way of the mortgage and so the trust fund suffered a loss. The beneficiaries brought an action for breach of trust against all of the trustees, on the basis that the trustees should never have invested in an unauthorised investment. Mr Edwards felt that he should not be liable for the loss suffered by the trust, as the decision to invest was taken only by Eliza Hughes. He therefore claimed an indemnity from her for any money he had to pay to the trust fund.

---

4 *Hale v Adams* (1873) 21 WR 400.
5 *Styles v Guy* (1849) 1 Mac. & G. 422; 41 ER 1328.
6 *English v Willats* (1831) 1 LJ Ch 84.
7 *Bahin v Hughes* (1886) LR 31 ChD 390.

The two questions for the court were (i) was Mr Edwards liable for the breach of trust and (ii) could he claim an indemnity from the acting trustee, Eliza Hughes?

The Court of Appeal held that Mr Edwards was responsible for the breach of trust. The court took the view that the trust was entitled to look to the trustees to repay the loss. As a trustee, Mr Edwards could not be treated any differently from any of the other trustees. As regards the position between the trustees and the beneficiaries, all of the trustees were responsible for the loss.

The position between the trustees themselves was more difficult. The court concluded that Mr Edwards should not be entitled to an indemnity from Eliza Hughes. The court felt that, even though Eliza had made the investment, Mr Edwards was just as much at fault for the loss occasioned to the trust fund as she was. He had done nothing to enquire about the investment, let alone prevent it, until six months after the mortgages had been entered into.

Bahin v Hughes confirms that the courts view who is liable for a breach of trust from the beneficiaries' standpoint. The beneficiaries are the innocent parties if a breach of trust has occurred. They should be permitted the greatest possible number of opportunities to take action against to restore the trust fund to its pre-breach position. In that regard, the liability of trustees is joint and several: the beneficiaries may sue either all of the trustees or any of them individually for their loss.

With regard to indemnities between trustees, the decision confirms that, prima facie, a trustee is not liable to indemnify another trustee against loss which the first trustee may have caused. That remains the general principle. That is because all trustees are equally responsible for administering the trust. If one mismanages the trust so that loss is caused, it is probable such mismanagement has only occurred because other trustees have allowed it to happen through their inactivity. For a trustee, therefore, inactivity is just as much a risk as taking incorrect positive action.

The issue of a 'guilty' trustee indemnifying an innocent trustee for breach of trust that the former has committed has moved on since *Bahin v Hughes*. Section 1 of the Civil Liability (Contribution) Act 1978 gives a general right to a person who is jointly and severally liable to receive a contribution (as opposed to complete indemnity) from the guilty party. The contribution that the guilty party is to make to the innocent party is to be adjudged on a 'just and equitable' basis by the court.[8] The court may decide, however, that such contribution could amount to a 'complete indemnity'.[9]

❖ EXPLAINING THE LAW

Suppose that Mr Edwards claimed a contribution from Eliza Hughes towards the compensation he had to pay to the trust fund. If the facts of *Bahin v Hughes* were repeated nowadays, it would be open to the court to decide that Mr Edwards should receive a contribution from Eliza to represent the breach of trust that she committed. The Act does not alter who the beneficiaries may sue so the beneficiaries would retain the right to sue both Eliza and Mr Edwards jointly or simply one of them.

The court might order Eliza to make a contribution to Mr Edwards for the compensation he has had to pay to the trust fund, on the basis that the investment in the leasehold properties was effectively all Eliza's doing.

---

8   Civil Liability (Contribution) Act 1978, s 2(1).
9   Ibid at s 2(2).

But there is nothing in the Act to compel the court to order that one trustee makes a contribution to the other. Remember that on the facts of *Bahin v Hughes*, the court decided that Mr Edwards was as guilty of the breach of trust as Eliza Hughes. If that remained the decision of the court, Eliza would not have to contribute to the sum Mr Edwards would have to pay to the trust fund. The 1978 Act merely gives the court more flexibility to apportion the loss between the trustees; it does not compel the court to do so.

A trustee is not always liable for breach of trust . . .

For a trustee to be liable for breach of trust, it must be shown that the trust fund has suffered loss. A true loss must be shown to have occurred from the actual decisions that the trustee took. It is not enough to demonstrate that the trust fund might possibly have increased more in value had the trustee taken different decisions, as *Nestle v National Westminster Bank plc*[10] demonstrates.

The case concerned a trust established by William Nestle in his will. William died in 1922, but established a trust benefiting his family. The defendant was the trustee. In 1986, the claimant, William's granddaughter, Edith Nestle, became the beneficiary entitled to the remainder interest under the trust. At that point in time, the trust fund was worth £269,203. The claimant alleged, however, that the trust fund should have been worth over £1 million had the defendant not committed various breaches of trust. She claimed that the trustee had breached the trust by failing to act with proper care and skill. In particular, she alleged that the trustee had failed to keep the investments under review, had misinterpreted its investment powers under the terms of the original trust and the Trustee Investments Act 1961 and had failed to keep an appropriate balance between the capital and income interests. Accordingly, the claimant claimed compensation for the difference between what the fund was actually worth and what she alleged it should have been worth.

The trustee was, of course, subject to the duty originally set out by Lindley LJ in *Re Whiteley*:[11]

to take such care as an ordinary prudent man would take if he were minded to make an investment for the benefit of other people for whom he felt morally bound to provide.

The trustee was also bound to balance the interests of both the life tenants and the claimant as the remainderman.[12] Professional trustees, such as the defendant, were subject to a higher duty of care and skill than a lay trustee, as they charged for their time and skill in administering the trust.[13]

All three Lords Justices in the Court of Appeal did not believe that the trustee had showered itself with glory in the administration of this particular trust. The trustee had misinterpreted its original power of investment in the trust. It believed that it could only invest the trust funds in a limited range of companies but, on a true construction of its powers, it could in fact have invested the funds in any type of company. As the trustee had very wide powers of investment specifically granted to it in the trust instrument, the restrictions on investments

---

10 *Nestle v National Westminster Bank plc* [1993] 1 WLR 1260.
11 *Re Whiteley* (1886) 33 Ch D 347 at 355.
12 *Re Whiteley* (1886) 33 Ch D 347. See Chapter 9 (pp 254–255) for a full discussion.
13 *Bartlett v Barclays Bank Trust Co Ltd (Nos 1 and 2)* [1980] Ch 515. See Chapter 9 at p 255.

introduced by the Trustee Investments Act 1961 did not apply. Overall, Dillon LJ thought it 'inexcusable'[14] that the trustee had not sought legal advice over what it could invest in. Staughton LJ put it in these black-and-white terms:

> Trustees are not allowed to make mistakes in law; they should take legal advice, and if they are still left in doubt they can apply to the court for a ruling.[15]

Both Lords Justices also thought the bank failed to review the investments regularly.

However, the trustee's failings were not enough to make the bank liable to pay compensation. The question for the court to decide was:

> whether the onus remains on the [claimant] to prove loss for which fair compensation should be paid, or whether it is enough for her to claim compensation for loss of a chance . . . that she would have been better off if the equities had been properly diversified.[16]

All three members of the Court of Appeal held that the claimant had to prove that she had suffered actual loss. The difficulty was that the claimant could offer no proof that the trust fund had suffered any loss. 'Loss' would be occasioned, according to Leggatt LJ, where the trust fund failed to make a gain less than that which would have been made by a prudent businessman investing the trust fund. No evidence could be led which showed that the bank had caused such a loss.

All that the claimant could show was that, with the benefit of hindsight, other investments the bank may have made would have given her (as remainderman) a better return. That was not sufficient. Staughton LJ confirmed that hindsight could not be used against a trustee to show that the trustee could perhaps have produced a greater return for the trust fund than actually occurred, 'the trustees' performance must not be judged with hindsight: after the event even a fool is wise, as a poet said nearly 3,000 years ago'.[17]

It also had to be recognised that investment policies naturally changed over a period of time, to deal with issues brought about by wider economic views. Investing in shares, for example, had been seen to be particularly risky in the 1920s and 30s and it was not appropriate to look back and criticise the trustees for their choice of investments with today's values in mind, where investing in shares is considered to be much less adventurous.

The decision in the case is perhaps best summarised by the words of Leggatt LJ, that '[a] breach of duty will not be actionable, and therefore will be immaterial, if it does not cause loss'.[18]

Monetary Remedies Available for Breach of Trust

Background to monetary awards

Traditionally, equity saw no role for itself in awarding damages: that was the function of the common law. Equity's role was to provide a remedy which would actually enforce equitable obligations themselves. Hence the courts of equity developed their own peculiar remedies, such as decrees of specific performance and injunction. The remedy of specific performance enables

---

14 *Nestle v National Westminster Bank plc* [1993] 1 WLR 1260 at 1265.
15 Ibid at 1275.
16 Ibid at 1269 per Dillon LJ.
17 Ibid at 1276.
18 Ibid at 1283.

a party to compel another party to adhere to the terms of a contract. An injunction usually prevents a party from committing an act. These remedies are considered in depth in Chapter 17.

With these specific remedies in mind, equity's original preference for a remedy against a trustee who had committed a breach of trust was to order the trustee to restore the actual property to the fund.[19] If the trustee was not able to restore the specific property to the trust fund, the trustee could, instead, pay a monetary sum to the value of the loss the fund suffered.[20] This evolved into a second right of requiring the trustee to pay equitable compensation to the individual beneficiary.

Strict common law issues of causation, foreseeability of loss and remoteness of damage do not readily apply to equitable compensation. All there has to be in equity is, according to Lord Browne-Wilkinson in *Target Holdings Ltd v Redferns (A Firm)*,[21]

> some causal connection between the breach of trust and the loss to the trust estate for which compensation is recoverable, viz. the fact that the loss would not have occurred but for the breach.

'Compensation': Restoration v equitable compensation

Traditionally, equity made a distinction between the two remedies of restoring the trust property and equitable compensation. The terminology can be confusing. Both remedies are examples of compensation in the broadest sense of making good a party's loss. 'Restoration' refers to equity holding the trustee to account to the trust fund for a loss that he has caused to the trust. The remedy is for the trustee to restore to the trust fund either the property that he has caused to be taken from it, or a monetary payment instead. The trust fund must be restored to its full value as long as the trust subsists. 'Equitable compensation' refers to compensation payable by the trustee to a beneficiary instead of to the trust fund and is usually payable after the trust has come to an end.

Key Learning Point

The right to equitable compensation is the right for the beneficiaries to sue the trustee personally for loss that he has caused to the trust fund.

By contrast, restoration of the trust property is a right that the beneficiaries enjoy against the trust property itself. It is said to be a right *in rem*: a right 'in the thing itself'.

The liability of the trustee to restore the trust fund and/or pay equitable compensation was discussed by the House of Lords in *Target Holdings Ltd v Redferns (A Firm)*.[22]

The facts concerned a commercial property transaction of two plots of land in Birmingham. Mirage Properties Ltd agreed to sell the plots to Crowngate Developments Ltd. The purchase was not straightforward and went via a series of other companies, with the price increasing in stages at each step in the transaction.

---

19 According to Viscount Haldane LC in *Nocton v Lord Ashburton* [1914] AC 932 at 952, 958.
20 *Caffrey v Darby* (1801) 6 Ves 488; 31 ER 1159.
21 *Target Holdings Ltd v Redferns (A Firm)* [1996] AC 421 at 434.
22 *Target Holdings Ltd v Redferns (A Firm)* [1996] AC 421.

The defendants were the solicitors acting for Crowngate, as well as the claimant (it is entirely usual for the same firm of solicitors to act for both buyer and lender in such a transaction). The claimants were the lenders for the purchase of the land, who were fully aware of all of the companies involved in the property transaction.

The claimant sent the loan money to the defendants in readiness for the purchase of the land to occur. Redferns had the implied authority of the claimant to pay the money across to Crowngate when it purchased the property.

The problem was that Redferns paid the loan money away too early: before the purchase of the land was completed. This was a breach of trust. Redferns admitted this but argued that the claimant did have a mortgage – secured by a legal charge – over the two properties in Birmingham. In this sense, therefore, the claimant had attained what it originally wanted to attain from the transaction: its money had been lent and secured by way of a legal charge.

Crowngate became insolvent and so was unable to repay the loan lent to it by the claimant. As mortgagee, the claimant could – and did – sell the two plots of land, but only for £500,000. It therefore sought to recover its £1.2 million loss from the defendant.

The claimant argued that when Redferns paid out the mortgage money in breach of trust, they were liable to restore the trust fund in the sum of the whole of the money that they paid out. The claimant further argued that the common law principles of causation did not apply and that it made no difference that the claimant had achieved its objective in securing a mortgage over the land.

The actual litigation in the case concerned the claimant's application for summary judgment against the defendant.

Glossary: Summary judgment

Summary judgment is where judgment is given against a party because it is categorically clear that the party has committed a wrong, such as a breach of contract or breach of trust. There is consequently no need for a full trial to determine the issue.

At first instance, Warner J thought that the claimant had a very good claim for summary judgment for the breach of trust, but nonetheless gave the defendant permission to defend the action on the condition they deposited £1 million in court. The defendant appealed against his refusal to give them unconditional permission to defend the claim.

By a majority, the Court of Appeal dismissed Redferns' appeal. Giving the leading judgment, Peter Gibson LJ held that, in general, the liability of a trustee for breach of trust was not to pay damages but instead the correct measure of liability was either:

(a)   to restore the trust fund to the value of what had been lost. This was to be the entire amount of the fund's loss such that the fund would be reconstituted with the total amount it had in it immediately before the breach of trust occurred; or

(b)   pay the beneficiary equitable compensation for his loss. The beneficiary was to be returned to the position he was in but for the breach of trust. Thus causation was itself broadly relevant but the common law rules of causation were not relevant.

On the facts, the Court of Appeal held that as money had been paid by a trustee to a third party stranger, there was an immediate loss to the trust fund which could only be remedied by the trustee restoring the same amount to the fund. The court gave judgment to the claimant for £1.49 million less the £500,000 that the claimant had made when it sold the land as mortgagee. Peter Gibson LJ felt that equity could be sufficiently flexible to take into account the amount the claimant had made when it subsequently sold the land, after the breach of trust had occurred. Redferns appealed to the House of Lords.

Lord Browne-Wilkinson delivered the only substantive opinion of the House of Lords. He stated that the principles underlying the common law's award of damages and equity's award of compensation were two-fold and were the same: (i) the defendant's act must cause the damage and (ii) the claimant had to be put back into the position he would have been in had the damage not been committed. It had to be shown that the defendant was at fault for causing the claimant's loss. If no loss could be shown, the beneficiary would enjoy no right to recompense.

Lord Browne-Wilkinson rejected the first conclusion reached by the majority of the Court of Appeal that, in a case such as this where the commercial purpose of the transaction had come to an end, the whole of the trust fund should be restored if a breach of trust had occurred. When Redferns paid the money, the commercial purpose of the transaction came to an end. From that point on, there was no obligation to force Redferns to reconstitute the entire trust fund. Such an obligation would lead to over-compensation for the beneficiary, for the whole £1.7 million would need to be reconstituted by Redferns, despite the fact that the claimant's loss was 'only' £1.2 million as it had successfully sold the land for £500,000.

The trustee's liability to restore the trust fund by reconstituting it was only appropriate in the case of a traditional family trust, where the fund was held for multiple beneficiaries (such as to A for life, remainder to B) and they all had to benefit from being compensated. Restoration of the entire loss reflected that all beneficiaries needed to be compensated for the breach of trust. It was inappropriate in a modern, commercial use of the trust where the trust had come to an end and where there was only one beneficiary. Restoration of the trust fund was not the appropriate remedy here.

❖ ANALYSING THE LAW

Do you think Lord Browne-Wilkinson's decision in *Target Holdings Ltd v Redferns (A Firm)* is compelling? Look back to Chapter 2 and the uses to which trusts are put in today's world. Could restoration of the trust fund not be appropriate in some modern, commercial trusts?

As regards the Court of Appeal's second argument of paying compensation to a beneficiary, Lord Browne-Wilkinson did not agree that 'one "stops the clock" at the date the moneys are paid away'[23] when assessing the measure of compensation. He acknowledged that as soon as a trustee commits a breach of trust causing loss to the trust fund, the beneficiary has a right of action against him. But that did not mean that the measure of equitable compensation due to the beneficiary was also fixed at that point in time. Instead, the amount of compensation was to be measured at the later date of the trial. It was at that later point that an amount could be awarded which would put the estate or beneficiary back into the position they were in before the breach was committed. Lord Browne-Wilkinson quoted with approval from the judgment of McLachlin J in the decision of the Supreme Court of Canada in *Canson Enterprises Ltd v Boughton & Co*:[24]

---

23 Ibid at 437.
24 *Canson Enterprises Ltd v Boughton & Co* (1991) 85 DLR (4th) 129.

The basis of compensation at equity, by contrast, is the restoration of the actual value of the thing lost through the breach. The foreseeable value of the items is not in issue. As a result, the losses are to be assessed as at the time of trial, using the full benefit of hindsight.

Taking this into account, at this stage, Redferns were entitled to defend the claim against the claimant. It could not be proven, without a full trial into the issue, that the claimant had actually suffered any loss as a result of Redferns' actions. The claimant had lent the money and had ultimately secured it by way of a legal charge. However, Lord Browne-Wilkinson ended his opinion by saying *obiter* that whilst this was the strict result, it was probable at trial that the claimant would be able to show a causal link between Redferns' breach of trust and the claimant's loss. If this was the case, then the claimant's remedy would be equitable compensation of £1.2 million: the loss of £1.7 million less the value of the land of £500,000 which the claimant had recovered when it sold the two plots. Such an amount was the amount of loss at the date of the trial, as opposed to the loss of £1.7 million when the breach of trust occurred.

Summary

'Compensation' in the broadest sense in equity consists of two rights that the trust enjoys: the trustee may be liable to account to the trust fund for the loss suffered or, alternatively, may have to pay equitable compensation to the beneficiaries personally.

The trustee's liability to restore the loss to the trust fund he has caused it was said by Lord Browne-Wilkinson in *Target Holdings Ltd v Redferns (A Firm)* to be the beneficiary's 'only right'[25] of monetary remedy against a trustee in the case of a traditional trust where the trusts were still subsisting. When a traditional trust comes to an end, the beneficiary is not usually entitled to have the trust fund restored. There is no need, as the beneficiary becomes absolutely entitled to the trust property. As such, he is instead entitled to equitable compensation should the trustee have breached the trust.

Equitable compensation is a personal right of action against the trustee to compensate the beneficiary for the breach of trust he has caused. It must be shown that the trustee caused the loss but the detailed common law requirements on causation do not apply. In more modern trust examples where the trust has arisen – and since ended – due to the commercial nature of a transaction, the decision in *Target Holdings Ltd v Redferns (A Firm)* suggests the courts are more inclined to award equitable compensation against the trustee rather than order him to restore the trust fund. Equitable compensation will be assessed as the loss to the trust fund at the date of trial, taking into account any reduction in the loss that may have occurred.

Making connections

The measure of compensation for breach of trust is interesting. An express trust is formed on the broad notion of a contract between the settlor and the trustee that the equitable interest should be held on trust for the beneficiary. But the measure of compensation is based more upon tortious principles than contractual ones. When paying damages to a beneficiary, the measure is said to be returning the beneficiary to the position he would have been in but for the breach of trust. This is similar to how damages in tort are assessed: they are based on returning the innocent party to the position he was in before the tort was committed against him.

---

25 *Target Holdings Ltd v Redferns (A Firm)* [1996] AC 421 at 434.

Awarding equitable compensation on tortious principles is logical. It has to be correct that the beneficiary is returned, insofar as money can do so, to the position he was in before the breach of trust occurred.

Restoration v equitable compensation: A strategic choice

Assuming actions for either restoration or equitable compensation are available, the beneficiary should bear in mind the following principles as to whether to pursue an action in rem for restoration of the trust property or personally against the trustee for equitable compensation:

(a) As equitable compensation is a personal right of action against the trustee, it is only worth pursuing such a remedy if the trustee is solvent. If the trustee is insolvent, whilst the wronged beneficiary may still sue the trustee, he will simply wait with the rest of the trustee's creditors before he is paid and will receive no preferential treatment as a beneficiary of a trust. On the other hand, as restoration of the trust property is a right in rem against the property itself, this will enable the beneficiary to claim the actual property of the trust or a sum of money representing it. If the trustee has gone insolvent, this means that the beneficiary will effectively sidestep the queue of the trustee's other creditors by pursuing the trust property itself.

(b) Restoration of the trust fund will usually be appropriate if the trustee is in breach of a fiduciary duty.[26] For example, making a secret profit will mean that the trustee holds that gain on constructive trust for the benefit of the actual trust. The profits must be restored to the trust.

(c) Equitable compensation is normally appropriate for breach of a non-fiduciary duty.[27] For instance, if the trustee has failed to account to the beneficiaries with information about the trust, it would be hard to see how the trustee could be liable to restore anything to the trust. The more appropriate – and only – action in such circumstance would be for the trustee to pay equitable compensation to the trust.

Where the two remedies are available, the trust must choose between restoration and equitable compensation

It is normally the case that action cannot be taken against the trustee for both the restoration of the trust fund as well as equitable compensation. The two remedies are alternatives to each other.[28] This was made clear by the decision of the Privy Council in *Tang Man Sit v Capacious Investments Ltd*.[29]

The facts concerned 22 houses built, as a joint venture, by Mr Tang and Capacious Investments Ltd in Kam Tin, Yuen Long, New Territories. Mr Tang owned the land on which they were built and Capacious provided the finance for their construction. The houses were finished in 1981. There was an agreement between the two parties that 16 of the houses would be transferred by Mr Tang to Capacious but this never happened. Instead, as the houses were empty, Mr Tang proceeded to let all 16 of them out as homes for the elderly. Capacious did not know of these lettings. The houses were over-occupied and deteriorated in value, as they were

---

26 See Chapter 8.
27 See Chapter 9.
28 The policy reason underlying this is the general one that a claimant should not be able to recover twice for the same claim.
29 *Tang Man Sit v Capacious Investments Ltd* [1996] AC 514.

not kept in good repair. Capacious therefore brought an action against Mr Tang for, *inter alia*, a declaration that it was entitled to the equitable interest in the houses from when the agreement to transfer them was entered into, an account of the secret profit made by Mr Tang by letting the properties out and compensation for breach of trust.

What Capacious was claiming was that it wanted both the secret profit made by Mr Tang to be restored to the trust fund and equitable compensation for the breach of trust that Mr Tang had committed by letting the properties out without its knowledge or permission. Capacious argued that it was entitled to compensation for breach of trust because had Mr Tang not breached the trust in failing to transfer the properties to them and letting the properties out, Capacious could itself have let the properties. The Court of Appeal of Hong Kong held that Capacious was not entitled to both remedies. They were alternatives. Capacious had accepted the account of secret profits (HK $1.8 million) and was now precluded from also claiming compensation for breach of trust. But Capacious was able to claim an additional amount of HK $11 million compensation representing the diminution in value of the properties. Both parties appealed to the Privy Council.

Delivering the opinion of the Judicial Board, Lord Nicholls agreed with counsel for Mr Tang that there was a difference between restoration of the trust fund by an account of a secret profit and an award of compensation. Restoration of the trust fund by an account of the secret profit was where a party chose to accept however much money the guilty party had made for the secret use of the trust property. Compensation for breach of trust would, on the other hand, equal the amount the claimant himself would have made for the same period had he been able to use the property himself. Lord Nicholls described the two remedies as 'alternative, not cumulative'.[30]

The facts of this particular case were different from normal, however. The trial judge had ordered that Mr Tang deliver both an account of his secret profit and pay compensation for breach of trust. The judge had not required, as he should have done, Capacious to choose which remedy it wanted. When Mr Tang therefore duly handed over the HK $1.8 million as an account of his secret profit, it could not be said that in accepting that sum, Capacious chose that as their remedy as they were ignorant of their need to make a choice. It would be unfair on Capacious if they were now said to have accepted that sum as their remedy in the case, given that the award for compensation was much larger.

The Privy Council held that an account of a secret profit and compensation for breach of trust were alternative remedies. It was only on the particular circumstances of this case, caused by the trial judge's error in awarding both to Capacious, that Capacious was held to be entitled to both.

Exclusion of Liability for Breach of Trust

If a trustee would otherwise be *prima facie* liable for breach of trust, it would not be unnatural for him to seek to protect himself in some way.

An exemption clause may either exclude entirely, or otherwise restrict, a trustee's liability for breach of his duties in carrying out the trust. The clause may exclude or restrict liability for breach of a fiduciary or non-fiduciary duty. Such clauses are usually included in trust deeds where professional trustees are appointed to administer the trust. At first glance, it appears that the inclusion of an exemption clause by a professional trustee results in the trustee having the best of both worlds: charging for their time and skill in administering the trust, whilst at the

---

30 Ibid at 520.

same time stating that they are not to be liable, or that their liability will be limited, if they breach the trust. On the other hand, the ability of a trustee to benefit from an exemption clause helps to make the role of trustee more attractive and generate competition in the market of professional trusteeship.[31]

The leading case on the subject is the decision of the Court of Appeal in *Armitage v Nurse*.[32] Paula Armitage enjoyed an interest under a trust of a piece of land and £30,000. She brought an action for breach of trust against the trustees for failing to prioritise her interests as a beneficiary over interests of other members of her family, who were not beneficiaries under the particular trust. Her allegation was that this breach of trust resulted in her suffering loss.

The trustees sought to rely on an exemption clause in clause 15 of the trust deed, which stated that no liability would attach to them unless it was 'caused by [the trustees'] own actual fraud'.

In giving the only substantive judgment of the court, Millett LJ held that the meaning of the words of the exemption clause was that it absolved the trustees from liability provided they had not acted dishonestly. The trustee, relying on clause 15, could be excluded from liability for breach of his duties, 'no matter how indolent, imprudent, lacking in diligence, negligent or wilful he may have been, so long as he has not acted dishonestly'.[33] Millett LJ did not believe that the trustee had acted dishonestly, but was guilty of gross (serious) negligence. The next issue for the court was, therefore, whether it was permissible in English law for a trustee to rely on an exemption clause excluding liability for gross negligence.

Making connections

In your studies of contract law, you have probably considered that it is not possible for liability to be excluded for a fraudulent misrepresentation. Fraudulent misrepresentations are those that are essentially made dishonestly. The judgment of Millett LJ in *Armitage v Nurse* that a trustee cannot exclude liability for being dishonest is a related concept: both involve attempts to exclude dishonesty which, as a matter of policy, should not be permitted or encouraged.

Millett LJ did not believe that any previous English or Scottish decision had decided as a matter of policy that a trustee could not rely on an exemption clause which would absolve his responsibility for gross negligence. Clause 15 would be given effect, therefore, to absolve the trustees of responsibility 'for all loss or damage to the trust estate except loss or damage caused by their own dishonesty'.[34] As Paula did not go so far as to allege that the trustees had been dishonest, the clause was sufficient to absolve them for liability for the loss to the trust fund.

The case established that there was no reason in terms of public policy why a clearly worded exemption clause could not exclude or restrict liability for trustees at least as far as negligence was concerned. Millett LJ believed that a clause which went further and sought to exclude the trustees' liability for fraud or dishonesty would not be effective and it would mean that the deed did not effectively create a trust:

> The duty of the trustees to perform the trusts honestly and in good faith for the benefit of the beneficiaries is the minimum necessary to give substance to the trusts . . .[35]

---

31 Law Commission, *Trustee Exemption Clauses* (Law Com No. 301) Cmnd 6874, 2006, para. 1.16.
32 *Armitage v Nurse* [1998] Ch 241.
33 Ibid at 251.
34 Ibid at 256.
35 Ibid at 253–254.

Millett LJ did provide a warning in *obiter* comments about the use of trustee exemption clauses:

> the view is widely held that these clauses have gone too far, and that trustees who charge for their services and who, as professional men, would not dream of excluding liability for ordinary professional negligence should not be able to rely on a trustee exemption clause excluding liability for gross negligence.[36]

He did, however, believe that for such clauses to be denied effect was a step that only Parliament could take.

The issue of the extent to which trustee exemption clauses should be permitted has been considered twice by the Law Commission in recent years.[37] In making its final recommendations for reform, the Law Commission took into account the responses to its earlier Consultation Paper which included:

(a) general unease about the use of trustee exemption clauses, especially if the settlor was unaware of the clause in the trust deed or its meaning;

(b) the idea that, ultimately, it should be the settlor's decision whether or not to include an exemption clause for the trustee's benefit rather than that decision being imposed upon the settlor by Parliament; and

(c) that the Commission's notion that instead of relying on an exemption clause, trustees should insure against being sued for breach of duty may be difficult to implement in practice due to the possible unavailability or high cost of such insurance.

As a result, the Law Commission recommended what might be considered at first glance to be something of a 'light-touch' idea of regulation. Its key recommendation[38] was that the settlor should be made aware of 'the meaning and effect' of any exemption clause that the trustee wished to be included in the trust deed. This would only take the form of a rule of practice. This means that a breach of the rule would be enforced not through the courts but through the trustee's or trust draftsman's professional body. Being subject to the possibility of receiving a sanction from a professional body was thought to be sufficient impetus for the professional draftsman to make a settlor aware of an exemption clause.

❖ APPLYING THE LAW

The Society of Trust and Estate Practitioners (STEP) had, by the time of the Law Commission's final report, already adopted its own rule obliging its members to draw a settlor's attention to a trustee exemption clause.

The rule applies where a STEP member either 'prepares, or causes to be prepared' a trust or will which (i) contains a charging clause or gives the STEP member a financial interest in the trusteeship and (ii) contains a trustee exemption clause.

---

36 Ibid at 256.
37 Law Commission, *Trustee Exemption Clauses* (Consultation Paper No. 171, 2003) and Law Commission, *Trustee Exemption Clauses* (Law Com No. 301, 2006).
38 Law Commission, *Trustee Exemption Clauses* (Law Com No. 301, 2006) paras 7.1–7.4.

> The rule provides that STEP members are obliged to ensure that they use 'reasonable endeavours' to advise the settlor of the existence of the exemption clause and that the STEP member has 'reasonable grounds' for believing the settlor 'has given his full and informed acceptance' to the clause before he signed the trust deed.

In a statement given by the Ministry of Justice on 14 September 2010, the government accepted the Law Commission's recommendations in its final report.

Such regulation of exemption clauses is to be welcomed. Sanction by a professional body for not advising the settlor of the meaning and effect of an exemption clause should act as a sufficient deterrent against breach of the rule. The issue is whether the Law Commission and the government should have gone further in perhaps recommending the abolition of trustee exemption clauses altogether. It must be asked whether a settlor really has any practical choice but to agree to an exclusion clause if he wants his trust to make use of the skills that the appointment of a professional trustee brings. Pragmatically, due to the divergence of views in its consultation exercise, any stronger recommendation would have been impossible for the Law Commission to make. No doubt this is an area likely to see further change in future as trustees may attempt to use exemption clauses of wider application, albeit with the settlor's alleged blessing.

Defences and Mitigating Circumstances for Breach of Trust

Once it has been established that a trustee has committed a breach of trust that has resulted in a loss being occasioned to the trust fund, the trustee is *prima facie* liable either to restore that loss to the fund or to pay equitable compensation to the affected beneficiary.

The trustee may, however, be able to take advantage of one or more of the following defences that may be open to him, depending on the facts of the case:

(a) the rule in *Re Hastings-Bass*[39] (although that rule has been severely curtailed by the decision of the Court of Appeal in *Futter v Futter*[40]);
(b) indemnity by a co-trustee;
(c) indemnity if the breach of trust is committed by a solicitor-trustee;
(d) indemnity if the breach of trust is committed by a beneficiary-trustee;
(e) participation by or consent of a beneficiary in the breach of trust;
(f) release by the beneficiary;
(g) impounding the interest of a beneficiary;
(h) the Trustee Act 1925, s 61;
(i) the Limitation Act 1980, s 21; or
(j) the doctrine of laches.

Each of these must now be considered.

The (curtailed) rule in *Re Hastings-Bass*

In 1974, the Court of Appeal decided in *Re Hastings-Bass* that trustees could enjoy a second bite at the cherry if they had made a decision that subsequently turned out to have the

---

39 *Re Hastings-Bass* [1975] Ch 25.
40 *Futter v Futter* [2011] 3 WLR 19.

consequences which they were originally intending to avoid. The relevant parties in *Re Hastings-Bass* are illustrated in Figure 12.1.

Figure 12.1 Re Hastings-Bass.

The case concerned a trust that had been established in 1947. The trust property was originally to be held on a protected life interest for Captain Peter Hastings-Bass and after his death for such of his sons as he should appoint. Captain Hastings-Bass had four children and he appointed his son William to benefit from the trust. After the appointment had occurred, the trustees (using their power under s32 of the Trustee Act 1925) transferred £50,000 from the trust to a second trust that had been set up for William's benefit. This was done to save the estate duty payable on Captain Hastings-Bass' death. The problem with this course of action was that the new trust infringed the rules against perpetuity, according to the later decision of the House of Lords in *Re Pilkington's Will Trusts*[41] (because William was not a 'life in being' at the date the 1947 trust had been created).

The Inland Revenue argued that, as the rules against perpetuity had been infringed, the £50,000 remained in the original 1947 trust. The trustees argued that, although the rules against perpetuity had, unwittingly, been infringed, a valid life interest in the £50,000 in William's favour had still been created. Thus no estate duty was due as the beneficial interest had still been assigned from Captain Hastings-Bass to William.

The Court of Appeal held that no estate duty was due to be paid. The trustees had advanced the money to William's second trust using their powers under s 32 of the Trustee Act 1925. Such an advancement could still take effect as, in itself, it did not infringe the rules against perpetuity. The advancement was free-standing and was not touched by the rules against perpetuity. The trustees' exercise of their discretion under s 32 was valid and the advancement of the money to William was effective.

The Court of Appeal laid down that the court should not generally interfere with the exercise of a trustee's discretion, even if the exercise of that discretion did not have the full effect that the trustee intended, as had occurred here. The only times the court should interfere was when:

> (1) what he [the trustee] has achieved is unauthorised by the power conferred upon him, or (2) it is clear that he would not have acted as he did (a) had he not taken into account considerations which he should not have taken into account, or (b) had he not failed to take into account considerations which he ought to have taken into account.[42]

The decision of the Court of Appeal in the case was, of course, designed to address the particular issue that had been presented to the court: William's second trust had failed but the question was whether the power of advancement exercised by the trustees under s 32 of the Trustee Act 1925 could still be valid. The court held it could.

The problem was that subsequent decisions took the *dictum* of Buckley LJ and applied it as the *ratio decidendi* of the case. Buckley LJ's words were used to justify that the court would

---

41 *Re Pilkington's Will Trusts* [1964] AC 612.
42 Ibid at 41 per Buckley LJ.

not interfere with the exercise of a trustee's discretion unless the trustee had accomplished something he plainly could not or:

(a)   he had taken into account matters he should not have taken into account; or
(b)   he had failed to take into account matters he should have considered.

The turning of Buckley LJ's words into ratio was achieved in the decision of Warner J in Mettoy Pension Trustees Ltd v Evans[43] where he described Buckley LJ's dictum as 'a principle which may be labelled "the rule in Hastings-Bass" '.[44] The 'principle' was set out by Lloyd LJ (in the High Court) in Sieff v Fox[45] as:

> Where trustees act under a discretion given to them by the terms of the trust, in circumstances in which they are free to decide whether or not to exercise that discretion, the court will interfere with their action if it is clear they would not have acted as they did had they not failed to take into account considerations which they ought to have taken into account, or taken into account considerations which they ought not to have taken into account.

What the 'rule' in Hastings-Bass meant was that if the trustees' decision had unintended consequences – such as it subsequently gave rise to a large charge to taxation – the trustees could apply to the court to have their decision set aside on the basis that they had failed to take into account matters they should have done or had taken into account factors they should have ignored. For trustees, the 'rule', as developed, was effectively a 'get out of jail free' card. No cases after Hastings-Bass went to the Court of Appeal or higher as trustees were content to take advantage of the 'rule' as interpreted in Mettoy Pension Trustees Ltd v Evans. HM Revenue & Customs did not take issue with the 'rule' for many years even though invariably the application of it meant that their tax revenue declined a little.

The 'rule' has, however, been reviewed and heavily curtailed by the recent decision of the Court of Appeal in Futter v Futter[46] which was the first case since Hastings-Bass itself in which HM Revenue & Customs intervened.

The facts concerned two trusts established for the benefit of Mark Futter, his wife and their children. The trusts were offshore. When money is moved back into UK jurisdiction, a taxation charge will normally arise. These trusts were expected to be subject to a high charge to capital gains tax (CGT) when the money was brought back into the UK.

The trustees, therefore, attempted a pre-emptive strike by, in the case of the first trust, enlarging Mark's life interest so that he became entitled to the whole trust absolutely. In relation to the second trust, the trustees exercised their power of advancement under s 32 of the Trustee Act 1925 by appointing £12,000 to each of Mark's three children. Mark and his children would, prima facie, be liable to pay CGT, but the intention was to offset their gains by losses they incurred by selling other property.

Unfortunately, their solicitors made an error. Section 2(4) of the Taxation of Chargeable Gains Act 1992 provides that losses cannot be offset against gains made in such circumstances. The result was that a large gain was made and a high amount of CGT was due. The trustees therefore instituted proceedings seeking a declaration that their transactions were void, relying on a part of the Hastings-Bass 'rule' – namely, that they had failed to take into account considerations

43   Mettoy Pension Trustees Ltd v Evans [1990] 1 WLR 1587.
44   Ibid at 1624.
45   Sieff v Fox [2005] 1 WLR 3811 at 3847.
46   Futter v Futter [2011] 3 WLR 19.

which they should have taken into account and so the court should interfere with their decision and declare the transactions void.

In delivering the leading judgment of the Court of Appeal, Lloyd LJ held that the *ratio* of *Hastings-Bass* was limited to the particular circumstances that the court had had to consider in that former case. The *ratio* was that, when considering exercising their powers of advancement, trustees had to consider whether any sub-trust created by it did operate to benefit the person receiving the advancement. Just because the other intended consequences had not happened (such as effective creation of a whole new trust in *Hastings-Bass*) did not mean that the advancement could not take effect to the recipient in its own right. The exercise by the trustees of their power of advancement would still be good. As Lloyd LJ pointed out,[47] the issue for the court to decide in *Hastings-Bass* was narrow: it was merely concerned with whether a true advancement had occurred or not. Any wider words used by Buckley LJ could not, therefore, be considered to be part of the *ratio*.

Lloyd LJ felt that subsequent cases (in particular *Mettoy Pension Trustees Ltd v Evans*) had focused too much on the more general words of Buckley LJ in *Hastings-Bass* and had considered those words to be the 'principle' arising from the case. The Court of Appeal overruled *Mettoy Pension Trustees Ltd v Evans* and sought to state the limitations of when the original rule in *Hastings-Bass* might be used.

According to Lloyd LJ, the correct principle was that:

(a)   The trustees' failure to take into account (a) something they should have considered or, alternatively, (b) taken something into account that they should not have done rendered their acts voidable, not void. This meant that in future only beneficiaries would have standing to challenge the trustees' decisions as opposed to trustees wishing to have a 'second bite of the cherry' by setting their earlier decision aside.

(b)   Beneficiaries could only show that the trustees' actions were voidable if they could show that the trustees had breached their fiduciary duties to the trust.

(c)   It would be a breach of a fiduciary duty for trustees to fail to take into account a relevant matter (such as failing to consider an adverse taxation consequence as a result of the trustees' decisions).

(d)   If the trustees obtained and followed professional advice on the issue, the trustees would not be in breach of their fiduciary duties. If there was no breach of fiduciary duties, the beneficiaries would have no claim against the trustees for breach of trust. The trustees' actions would not, therefore, be voidable and capable of being set aside. They would have to stand.

❖ ANALYSING THE LAW

Curiously, Lloyd LJ recognised that there would be a distinction between the trustee who sought and followed professional advice and the one who simply blundered on by himself. Where professional advice was sought and followed, there was to be no breach of fiduciary duty and, therefore, no right of action against the trustee to have the decision set aside. But where no advice was sought, that might be a breach of fiduciary duty and an action might occur against the trustee for breach of fiduciary duty, leading to the trustee's decision being set aside.

Do you think this is necessarily logical?

---

47 Ibid at 40.

Applying the 'correct principle' to the facts of the case, the issue for the Court of Appeal was whether the trustees failed to have regard to the relevant taxation consequences of their decisions and whether that could constitute a breach of fiduciary duty on their part.

The Court of Appeal held that the taxation consequences of their decisions were relevant factors for the court to take into account but that the trustees had sought and followed professional legal advice before making the advancements to the beneficiaries. It could not be said that there was a breach of fiduciary duty by the trustees. They had acted on proper advice. The real problem lay not with the trustees but in that the advice was incorrect.

The decision of the Court of Appeal in Futter v Futter has both legal and pragmatic consequences. Legally, it essentially reverses the enlargement of the Hastings-Bass principle as developed in Mettoy Pension Trustees Ltd v Evans and takes it back to the original position in Hastings-Bass itself. Trustees may not now seek to set aside decisions they have taken on the basis that they failed to take into account a relevant matter, or took into account an irrelevant matter when they made the original decision, unless it can be shown that they committed a breach of a fiduciary duty. This will not be possible if the trustees obtained and followed professional advice.

Pragmatically, trustees under the Hastings-Bass rule as interpreted in Mettoy Pension Trustees Ltd v Evans enjoyed a 'get out of jail free' card. They could set aside their decisions if they subsequently turned out to be wrong. That will no longer be the case, unless it can be demonstrated that they breached their fiduciary duties when reaching the decision. Beneficiaries are not, however, deprived of a remedy by the decision in Futter v Futter. Instead, their remedy now will normally be to sue the trustees for negligence in place of breach of trust.[48]

Indemnity by a co-trustee

As already mentioned,[49] s 1 of the Civil Liability (Contribution) Act 1978 provides that an 'innocent' party may receive a contribution from a 'guilty' party for the loss that the guilty party has caused. This means that if an innocent trustee is obliged to restore the trust fund or pay equitable compensation, he may claim a contribution from the guilty trustee who has actually caused the loss to the trust fund. If both trustees are equally guilty of the breach of trust, the contribution will usually be for half of the loss sustained by the trust if one trustee has been obliged to restore the entire loss to the trust fund.

Whether one trustee is bound to offer a complete indemnity to the other will depend on 'what is just, as between the two, and this depends on what they have respectively done' according to Lindley LJ in Chillingworth v Chambers.[50]

But the awarding of such an indemnity will, it is suggested, rarely be appropriate.[51] In Bahin v Hughes,[52] Fry LJ thought the courts should be 'very jealous' of holding one trustee generally liable to indemnify another due to the risk of the trustees concentrating more on arguing between themselves over who is liable to the trust rather than focussing on undertaking their duties. In Bahin v Hughes,[53] Cotton LJ gave the example of one trustee effectively stealing money from the trust for his own personal use. In such a situation, the guilty trustee would be liable to indemnify the other trustee should the innocent one have to restore the loss to the trust fund. Whilst refusing to set down any limits of when an indemnity would be ordered against

---

48 Permission to appeal was granted by the Supreme Court (Lords Walker, Collins and Clarke) on 1 August 2011 (UKSC 2011/0089).
49 See above at p 319.
50 Chillingworth v Chambers [1896] 1 Ch 685 at 696.
51 See Lindley LJ in Chillingworth v Chambers [1896] 1 Ch 685 at 696.
52 Bahin v Hughes (1886) LR 31 Ch D 390 at 398.
53 Bahin v Hughes (1886) LR 31 Ch D 390.

a guilty trustee, the Court of Appeal in that case thought that it was only appropriate where a guilty trustee obtained a personal benefit from the breach of trust or, where there was a relationship between the trustees which justified the court in holding that the guilty trustee was solely responsible for the breach of trust. One such relationship is where one of the trustees is a solicitor.

Indemnity if the breach of trust is committed by a solicitor-trustee

If one of the trustees is a solicitor and the other trustees rely on the solicitor's advice, the solicitor-trustee may be liable to indemnify the other trustees should they be sued for breach of trust. This was established in Lockhart v Reilly.[54]

The indemnity owed by the solicitor-trustee is based on the notion that the other trustees have followed the solicitor's advice but the advice was negligent. As a matter of policy, it is probably right that lay trustees would follow the advice of such a professional trustee and should, if that advice turns out to be wrong and causes the trust loss, be indemnified if they are sued for that loss.

Indemnity if the breach of trust is committed by a beneficiary-trustee

The general position is that a trustee who is also a beneficiary will be liable to indemnify the other trustee for loss occasioned to the trust. Moreover, the indemnity must be for the extent of the beneficiary's interest in the trust property and not just for the extent of the gain the trustee-beneficiary has received: Chillingworth v Chambers.[55]

In this case, the claimant and defendant were the trustees of the will of John Wilson. He left money on trust for the benefit of his wife for life and thereafter for his five children in equal shares. The trust contained a power to invest by way of granting mortgages over leasehold property. The claimant was also the husband of one of John's daughters.

During the administration of the trust, the two trustees decided to lend £8,650 to a builder who was constructing eight leasehold houses. In 1881, the claimant became beneficially entitled to a share in John's trust as his wife (one of John's daughters) died. In 1883, the claimant brought an action for the removal of the defendant as a trustee. The action failed but the court ordered accounts to be drawn up in relation to the trust. During this process, the eight mortgages were sold on but there was a deficit of £1,580. The court ordered that both trustees were equally liable for that loss to the trust fund. The loss was actually made good from the money that the claimant was now beneficially entitled to. The issue for the Court of Appeal was whether the claimant could claim an indemnity from the defendant. The claimant alleged that the defendant had previously made loans to the builder but had not been repaid. He said that the defendant had induced him to advance the trust money to the builder so that the builder could repay the defendant's personal loans. The claimant's case was that the defendant effectively held the trust money himself and that he should, therefore, bear all of the loss that the fund had sustained.

The Court of Appeal did not accept that there had been a breach of trust in lending the money to the builder. The builder was merely obliged to repay the money lent, as any contract for a loan would entail. As no breach of trust had occurred by the defendant, there was no obligation on him to indemnify the claimant.

---

54 *Lockhart v Reilly* (1857) 1 De G & J 464; 44 ER 803.
55 *Chillingworth v Chambers* [1896] 1 Ch 685.

The decision backfired on the claimant. The Court of Appeal held that the claimant was entitled to no indemnity from the defendant. As Lindley LJ explained:

> If I request a person to deal with my property in a particular way, and loss ensues, I cannot justly throw that loss on him. Whatever our liabilities may be to other people, still, as between him and me, the loss clearly ought to fall on me.[56]

Moreover, the Court of Appeal decided that it was the claimant who had to bear the loss. The loss was not to be limited to the benefit the claimant had received but the indemnity the claimant had to provide was to the extent of his share of the beneficial interest in the trust property.

Participation by or consent of a beneficiary in the breach of trust

If a beneficiary himself is party to, or consents in, a breach of trust committed by a trustee, the trustee is not liable to make good the breach of trust. To consent to a breach of trust, the beneficiary must:

(a)   be aged 18 or older and have mental capacity;
(b)   freely consent to the breach of trust having occurred; and
(c)   have the necessary knowledge required of the breach having happened to consent to it.

It is the third requirement – the type and extent of knowledge that the beneficiary must possess – that the courts have considered in most detail.

The issue was considered by Wilberforce J in Re Pauling's Settlement Trusts.[57] The facts concerned alleged breaches of trust that Coutts & Co had made when administering a trust set up in 1919 by two parents for their lives with remainder to their four children. The family had always lived beyond their means. A considerable number of advancements were made by the trustee to the two eldest children, Francis and George; some of the money advanced was used for the benefit of the family as a whole by, for example, purchasing a home in the Isle of Man and paying off the family's overdraft. The allegation against the trustee was that it had breached its duty of balancing the interests of the life tenants (the parents, who had the overdraft liability) and the remaindermen (the children, whose capital interest was being advanced to pay off the overdraft). The children claimed that the trustee should repay the amounts it had advanced in breach of trust.

Wilberforce J held that the advancement to purchase the house in the Isle of Man was a breach of trust as the property had been placed into the parents' names without Francis' and George's consent. Other advances that were placed into the parents' bank account to pay off their overdraft also constituted a breach of trust as advancing money for such a reason was not a solid exercise of the trustee's fiduciary power of advancement.

But despite these prima facie breaches of trust, Wilberforce J then said he had to consider whether he could hold the trustee liable for them. He thought not. He held that the court's duty was to:

> consider all the circumstances in which the concurrence of the [beneficiary] was given with a view to seeing whether it is fair and equitable that, having given his concurrence, he should afterwards turn round and sue the trustees . . .[58]

---

56   Ibid at 699.
57   Re Pauling's Settlement Trusts [1962] 1 WLR 86.
58   Ibid at 108.

In terms of the knowledge that the beneficiary had to possess when giving his consent to a breach of trust occurring, Wilberforce J held that it was not necessary for the beneficiary to know that he was agreeing to a breach of trust. All that was needed was that the beneficiary had to understand fully what he was agreeing to. There was no requirement that the beneficiary should benefit personally from the breach of trust.

On the facts, it was held that the trustee had to replace the money advanced used to purchase the home in the Isle of Man as such advancement had occurred in breach of trust without Francis' and George's independent consent. The trustee was not liable to restore to the trust the other sums advanced as Francis and George had known about them, were both aged over 21 and had given their free consent to them.

Release by the beneficiaries

The decision in Re Pauling's Settlement Trusts shows that it is possible for a beneficiary to consent to a breach of trust and if that occurs, the beneficiary cannot then take action against the trustee to recover sums lost as a result of that breach.

The facts of Re Pauling's Settlement Trusts showed the beneficiary consenting to the breach of trust as it occurred. It may be that the beneficiary is initially unaware of the breach of trust but becomes aware of it after it has happened. In such a situation it is, in some circumstances, open to the beneficiaries to give their consent to the breach of trust after the event. Such consent would operate to release the trustee from liability from the breach of trust.

In order to release the trustee from a breach of trust, the beneficiaries must all act together and must all be over 18 years of age and be mentally capable. They must also have knowledge of all of the facts of the breach of trust.

A trustee might wish to be formally released by beneficiaries for any potential breaches of trust he may have committed if he wishes to retire as a trustee. Any trustee retiring will usually continue to be liable for any breaches of trust he may have committed whilst a trustee, so beneficiaries should, it is suggested, be reluctant to grant such release.

Impounding the interest of a beneficiary

Impounding the interest of a beneficiary originally applied only if that beneficiary was also a trustee who had committed a breach of trust.

If a trustee-beneficiary had committed a breach of trust, his interest was liable to be impounded by the court. That meant that he was not entitled to enjoy his beneficial interest until he rectified the breach of trust. His interest, then, was taken as a type of insurance policy for the other beneficiaries: if the trustee made good his breach of trust, he was entitled to enjoy the interest; if not, he forfeited it. The court remains entitled to impound the trustee's beneficial interest under its inherent jurisdiction as a successor to the Court of Chancery.[59] The ability to impound a beneficial interest was widened by s 62 of the Trustee Act 1925. Section 62(1) provides:

> Where a trustee commits a breach of trust at the instigation or request or with the consent in writing of a beneficiary, the court may, if it thinks fit, make such order as to the court seems just, for impounding all or any part of the interest of the beneficiary in the trust estate by way of indemnity to the trustee or persons claiming through him.

---

59 See Chapter 1 (pp 7–10) for a discussion about the Court of Chancery and its origins.

Section 62 applies to any beneficial interest, where the beneficiary has asked the trustee to breach the trust. The power to impound under the section means there is now an effective sanction against any beneficiary who requests or consents to a breach of trust. But the court has a wide discretion over whether to order the impounding of the beneficiary's interest. If such an order is made, the beneficiary will be deprived of their equitable interest in order that it can be used to make good the loss to the trustee arising from the breach of trust. Before ordering the impounding of the beneficiary's interest, the court must be satisfied that the beneficiary knew all of the facts surrounding the breach of trust but the beneficiary need not be aware that a breach of trust would arise.[60]

Trustee Act 1925, s 61

Section 61 of the Trustee Act 1925 provides a statutory defence that a trustee may use. The section provides that the court has a discretion to excuse a trustee 'either wholly or partly' from liability for the breach of trust if the trustee 'has acted honestly and reasonably and ought fairly to be excused for the breach of trust'.

Section 61 is often pleaded as a defence by a trustee who is *prima facie* liable for a breach of trust but the fairly stringent requirements of the section mean that it is rarely successful. It is often the twin requirements that the trustee must have acted both (i) honestly and (ii) reasonably that will prevent the court from exercising its discretion to relieve the trustee from liability. For example, in *Re Pauling's Settlement Trusts*, as part of their defence, Coutts & Co pleaded that they should be absolved from liability under s 61. Wilberforce J was quite prepared to accept that the bank had acted entirely honestly in advancing the money to the children but the bank's actions were not reasonable in advancing the money where the breaches of trust were found. His judgment also makes clear that s 61 contains a third separate requirement if it is to be used successfully: liability ought fairly to be excused by the court. This third requirement will always be a value judgment on the facts of the case and Wilberforce J did not think it was right that the bank should have been excused from liability on the facts of this particular case.

Commenting on virtually identical New Zealand provisions to s 61[61] in the High Court of Wanganui in *Berube v Gudsell*,[62] McGechan J confirmed that the onus of proof of establishing this defence lay on the trustees. His view was that the court should be slow to allow a trustee to claim this defence:

> the court granting relief, and thus depriving a beneficiary of redress, should act cautiously. A cavalier attitude to trust administration should not be encouraged.

Limitation Act 1980, s 21

Section 21 of the Limitation Act 1980 provides a general defence that a trustee who has committed a breach of trust may be able to rely on. It provides,[63] generally, that an action for a breach of trust must be commenced against the trustee within six years from when the breach occurred. There are exceptions to this six-year time limit:

---

60 *Re Somerset* [1894] 1 Ch 231 at 274 per A L Smith LJ.
61 Trustee Act 1956, s 73.
62 *Berube v Gudsell* [2008] WTLR 2008–16.
63 Limitation Act 1980, s 21(3).

(a) Where the beneficiary is entitled to a future interest under the trust, the time limit commences not from the breach of trust but from when the beneficiary's interest falls into their possession.

(b) No time limitation is prescribed for taking action for a fraudulent breach of trust or, alternatively, to recover trust property (or its proceeds) from a trustee where that property or proceeds remain in his possession.

It is equity's doctrine of laches that governs when a beneficiary may take action against a trustee who has committed a fraudulent breach of trust or who has taken trust property and retains it (or its proceeds).

The doctrine of laches

Laches is the doctrine of equity that prevents equity intervening and providing a remedy to a beneficiary after more than a reasonable time period has passed since the cause of action originally arose. It is based on the equitable maxim that 'delay defeats equities'. The policy behind the doctrine is that as time passes, it is unfair that litigation may be brought against parties as (i) it is often more difficult to prove allegations the longer the time has passed and (ii) even if the party has a solid case against a trustee, it is probably right that at some point in time, the trustee is allowed to move on notwithstanding the wrong he may have committed against the trust. The nature of the doctrine of laches was discussed by the House of Lords in Fisher v Brooker.[64]

The facts of the case concerned what the trial judge, Blackburne J, described as a song which verged on having acquired 'cult status'.[65] The claim in the action concerned the copyright to the song 'A Whiter Shade of Pale', a song which is renowned for its introductory organ solo. The song was sung by the group Procul Harum. The main body of the music was composed by Gary Brooker, but the famous eight-bar organ solo at the start, together with the organ melody underpinning the song, was added by another member of Procul Harum, Matthew Fisher.

Matthew Fisher did not, for a long time, force the issue about who owned the copyright in the song, which had made a considerable amount of money for Mr Brooker and their record label. During 2005, however, he wrote to Mr Fisher and the group's music label, claiming a share of the copyright in the music and wanting a share of the royalties stretching back over six years before he made his claim. Mr Fisher recognised that he could not claim for royalties arising any further back in time due to the Limitation Act 1980. Blackburne J awarded Mr Fisher a 40 per cent share in the copyright of the music. Mr Brooker appealed to the Court of Appeal, which decided that his delay in pursuing his claim prevented him from being awarded a share in the musical copyright. It was against this decision, inter alia, that Mr Fisher appealed to the House of Lords.

The House of Lords allowed the claimant's appeal and restored the declaration given by the trial judge awarding Mr Fisher a 40 per cent share in the music. In giving the main substantive opinion of the House, Lord Neuberger thought that 'some sort of detrimental reliance is usually an essential ingredient of laches'.[66] There was none on the facts suffered by Mr Brooker.

---

64 Fisher v Brooker [2009] 1 WLR 1764.
65 Fisher v Brooker [2007] FSR 255.
66 Fisher v Brooker [2009] 1 WLR 1764 at 1781.

Lord Neuberger also pointed out that laches could only bar an equitable remedy, whilst here the claimant's claim was based on a statutory claim: a declaration under the Copyright, Designs and Patents Act 1988. The doctrine of laches did not apply to the facts in the case, as the claimant was not claiming an equitable remedy. Lord Neuberger quoted[67] the requirements set down by Lord Selborne LC in *Lindsay Petroleum Co v Hurd* for laches to apply. The court had to consider:

> the length of the delay and the nature of the acts done during the interval, which might affect either party, and cause a balance of justice or injustice in taking the one course or the other, so far as relates to the remedy.[68]

Mr Brooker could not show any acts undertaken from when the song was written to 2005 which might have affected him adversely. Even if he could have shown such acts, Lord Neuberger was of the view that the benefit Mr Brooker obtained from Mr Fisher's delay in bringing proceedings would outweigh any prejudice.

Fisher v Brooker therefore shows that the doctrine of laches is only applicable when an equitable remedy is being sought; it will not enable a defendant to allege delay for every claim a claimant makes. It might be used as a defence by a trustee charged with a breach of trust (as the remedy sought would normally be equitable compensation or a restoration of the trust property) but if it is to be used successfully, the trustee would normally have to show that he has suffered detrimental reliance on the beneficiary's delay in bringing an action against him. The court must also be satisfied that the balance of justice requires the doctrine to be used.

Points to Review

You have seen:

- what a breach of trust is and that a trustee, if liable, is liable to restore the trust property to the trust or pay equitable compensation to the beneficiaries;
- that a trustee may rely on an exemption clause to limit or restrict his liability for breach of trust; and
- that a trustee may rely on a number of defences and other mitigating circumstances when charged with a breach of trust.

Making connections

This chapter has considered the remedies that may be taken against a trustee personally for breach of trust. The risk inherent with those remedies is that it may, for instance, not be worthwhile for a beneficiary to pursue them as they depend on the trustee being sufficiently solvent to remedy the breach of trust.

The beneficiary may, as an additional or alternative remedy, wish to take action to recover the trust property if it has been transferred into another party's hands. Another option for the beneficiary might be to take action against any assistance that the trustee may have had in breaching the trust. These remedies are considered in Chapter 13.

---

67 Ibid.
68 *Lindsay Petroleum Co v Hurd* (1874) LR 5 PC 221 at 239–240.

Useful Things to Read

The best reading is contained in the primary sources listed below. It is always good to consider the decisions of the courts themselves as this will lead to a deeper understanding of the issues involved. A few secondary sources are also listed, which you may wish to read to gain additional insights into the areas considered in this chapter.

Primary sources
Armitage v Nurse [1998] Ch 241.
Chillingworth v Chambers [1896] 1 Ch 685.
Fisher v Brooker [2009] 1 WLR 1764.
Futter v Futter [2011] 3 WLR 19.
Re Hastings-Bass [1975] Ch 25.
Tang Man Sit v Capacious Investments Ltd [1996] AC 514.
Target Holdings Ltd v Redferns (A Firm) [1996] AC 421.

Limitation Act 1980, s 21.
Trustee Act 1925, ss 61 and 62.

Secondary sources
Jon Baker and Euan Lawson, '*Fisher v Brooker*: "Whiter Shade of Pale" organist Matthew Fisher wins case in House of Lords – but with a sting in the tail' (2009) Ent LR 20(8), 296–299. A discussion of laches, estoppel and acquiescence in the context of claiming for music royalties.
Judith Bray, 'Sink or swim? The future for the rule in *Re Hastings-Bass*'. (2012) T & T 18(2) 96–115. This article considers the decision in *Futter v Futter* and discusses whether the rule in *Re Hastings-Bass* should be upheld or overruled.
Alastair Hudson, *Equity & Trusts* (7th edn, Routledge-Cavendish, 2012) ch 18.
Law Commission, *Trustee Exemption Clauses* (Consultation Paper No. 171, 2003). This document contains a useful summary of the law relating to exemption clauses together with the Law Commission's reform proposals.
Law Commission, *Trustee Exemption Clauses* (Law Com No. 301, 2006). This document sets out the Law Commission's recommendations for reform of the area relating to exemption clauses and explains the reasons for their recommendations.
Mohamed Ramjohn, *Text, Cases and Materials on Equity and Trusts* (4th edn, Routledge-Cavendish, 2008) ch 21.

Chapter 13

Tracing and Actions Against Strangers to the Trust

This chapter considers two subjects, both connected to remedies: (i) the process of tracing and (ii) personal remedies against strangers to the trust. Tracing is the ability to follow property into another's hands. Personal remedies against a stranger to the trust continues the study of personal actions against individuals who have assisted in the commission of a breach of trust by the trustee. This latter subject builds upon personal actions against the trustee himself discussed in Chapter 12.

As You Read

Look out for the following issues:

- what tracing is, what it involves and why it might be more advantageous for a beneficiary to pursue on some occasions as an alternative to a personal action against the trustee;
- how tracing leads to different remedies at common law and in equity. At common law, tracing may give rise to an action for money had and received; in equity, it renders the recipient of the property liable to account for it as a constructive trustee; and
- how equity might enable a claim to be taken against anyone helping a trustee in committing a breach of trust, or for receiving trust property.

Tracing

Chapter 12 considered how a beneficiary might pursue a trustee personally for a breach of trust. On occasion, even if a trustee would otherwise be found liable for a breach of trust, it may not be worthwhile for the beneficiary to bring an action against him. If, for instance, the trustee has been made bankrupt, the beneficiary is in no stronger a position than the rest of the trustee's creditors who are owed by him. The beneficiary will simply have to wait his turn in the queue of general creditors. Alternatively, if the trustee has breached the terms of the trust and has then disappeared, any action against him personally will be all but impossible to commence.

Fortunately, another process is available. It is a proprietary action. This means that it is a right *in rem* in that it attaches itself to the property itself that has been misused. It is known as 'tracing'.

Tracing may occur at common law or in equity. Common law tracing involves the trustee pursuing the legal title to property which has found its way into the wrong hands. Equitable tracing offers someone who has benefited from a fiduciary relationship (for example, a beneficiary) the ability to follow the equitable interest in property which has been misappropriated.[1]

As tracing is a proprietary claim, the claim is not against the recipient of the property personally but instead against the actual property. So, for example, this means that in the event of the trustee's bankruptcy, the beneficiary is able to circumvent the trustee's other creditors by claiming that the trust property itself should be returned to the trust and should not be available as part of the trustee's personal assets to be distributed to his general creditors.

'Tracing' was defined by Millett LJ in *Boscawen v Bajwa*.[2] To Millett LJ, tracing was neither a remedy nor a claim in its own right. It was, instead, a process. This process could be pursued not just against a wrongdoer but anyone who had knowingly assisted in a breach of trust or who had received the property, knowing that it was really trust property. 'Tracing', said Millett LJ, was:

---

1 Tracing is not limited to recovering trust property as such and is available to anyone who has the benefit of a fiduciary relationship, provided the conditions for tracing are satisfied. See Chapter 8 for the definition of a 'fiduciary'.
2 *Boscawen v Bajwa* [1996] 1 WLR 328.

the process by which the plaintiff traces what has happened to his property, identifies the persons who have handled or received it, and justifies his claim that the
money which they handled or received (and, if necessary, which they still retain) can
properly be regarded as representing his property.[3]

What can be shown from this definition is that tracing is where the claimant follows his property and brings a claim to have it – or its value – returned to the trust. It does not matter how
many people have handled the property provided that, generally, the trust property remains
identifiable. The claim to the property is 'based on the retention by him of a[n] . . . interest in
the property which the defendant handled or received.'[4]

A successful tracing claim does not depend on proving that the defendant has been
enriched by the claimant's property. Tracing is not dependent on principles of the law on
unjust enrichment[5] being met. It can be illustrated diagrammatically in the following example.

❖ EXPLAINING THE LAW

Thomas is a trustee administering a trust on behalf of Ulrika, the beneficiary. Thomas
commits a breach of trust by selling trust property to Roberta and then disappears with
the proceeds of sale. Roberta sells the trust property to Peter who, in turn, sells it to
Quentin. Each of the purchasers is aware that the property is trust property.

Thomas → Roberta → Peter → Quentin

↑

Ulrika

Ulrika may, in theory, bring an action against Thomas personally for breach of the trust.
But such an action would be difficult as he has disappeared. Instead, Ulrika's better claim
would be against Quentin. She would seek to trace the trust property into Quentin's hands.

Tracing may be undertaken against the wrongdoer or anyone who has knowingly acquired
an interest in the trust property or knowingly assisted in the breach of trust. In *Boscawen v Bajwa*,
Millett LJ identified three defences that a defendant subjected to a tracing process may put
forward:

- the tracing exercise is not valid because, in reality, the claimant has no claim against the
property;
- the defendant is a *bona fide* purchaser of the property without notice of the trust and therefore takes the property free from the trust; and/or
- the defendant has innocently changed his position since he acquired the trust property.[6]

---

3   Ibid at 334.
4   Ibid per Lord Millett LJ.
5   See comments of Lord Millett in *Foskett v McKeown* [2001] 1 AC 102 at 129.
6   This defence was first recognised in English law in *Lipkin Gorman v Karpnale Ltd* [1991] 2 AC 548. See the discussion of this case on
pp 353–355. It is available to an action of tracing at common law although it was said *obiter* in that decision that it could be
available to a claim of tracing in equity.

If none of these defences succeed, the claimant is entitled to a remedy. What the remedy is depends on whether the claimant traces at common law or in equity.

At common law, the remedy that tracing leads to is restitutionary. It is for money had and received. The money that the defendant has received must be returned by him to the claimant. Nowadays, this remedy that the claimant enjoys is subject to the defendant successfully arguing that he has innocently changed his position as a result of the money being given to him, or that he acted in good faith and provided full consideration for the money.[7]

If tracing is pursued in equity, the main remedy that the claimant enjoys is a personal one against the recipient of the property. That would entail the recipient paying equitable compensation to the beneficiary or restoring the trust fund to the value it was worth before the breach of trust occurred.

The claimant may wish to have the trust property returned to him. Thus he may pursue a proprietary remedy against the property itself, or what it has subsequently turned into if the recipient of it has used it in some way. To do so, he must prove that the property is still in the defendant's hands. If this can be shown, the court may order that the defendant holds the property on constructive trust for the claimant and further compel the defendant to transfer it to him. If the defendant has, however, used the trust property in some way, other proprietary remedies may be open to the claimant to pursue. In *Boscawen v Bajwa*, Millett LJ gave the example of where trust property had been used to improve a building. The beneficiary may ask the court for a charge over the building to the amount by which the building has increased in value.

Key Learning Point

Tracing is merely the road along which a claimant must travel to seek his remedy. It is not the remedy in itself. The remedy awarded depends if the claimant traces at common law or in equity.

At common law, tracing leads to a claim for money had and received by the defendant. The defendant must return the money he has received – or what remains of it.

In equity, the remedy is normally equitable compensation or, alternatively, a declaration that the defendant holds the money on constructive trust for the claimant and must return it to him.

In both cases, the claimant may generally enjoy an 'uplift' if the money has been successfully used by the defendant to generate further money.

Tracing v Following

Tracing is different from following. As Lord Millett said in *Foskett v McKeown*, '[f]ollowing is the process of following the same asset as it moves from hand to hand'.[8] In contrast, '[t]racing is the process of identifying a new asset *as the substitute* for the old'.[9]

---

7   See *Lipkin Gorman v Karpnale Ltd* [1991] 2 AC 548.
8   *Foskett v McKeown* [2001] 1 AC 102 at 127.
9   Ibid (emphasis added).

The recent decision in *Sinclair Investments (UK) Ltd v Versailles Trade Finance Ltd (in administrative receivership)*[10] gave the Court of Appeal the opportunity to comment generally on tracing and in particular on (i) when a proprietary interest arises and (ii) what would constitute sufficient notice to defeat a *bona fide* purchaser's claim that he bought without notice in good faith.

The facts concerned a fraudulent investment scheme. Versailles Group plc owned the defendant trading company. The main shareholder of Versailles Group plc was Mr Carl Cushnie. Versailles Group plc sought investments from both individuals and banks. Their money would be given to another company, Trading Partners Ltd, again controlled by Mr Cushnie, who would buy goods and resell them. Any money not used to buy goods was to be placed in a bank account. The investors would receive a share of the profits on the goods bought and resold. The defendant company managed the workings of Trading Partners Ltd.

In fact, the money received by Trading Partners Ltd was passed to the defendant company but it was not used as agreed. Instead, it was used to pay the profits to the investors, stolen by Mr Cushnie (to buy a house in Kensington, London, for nearly £10 million) or sent to other companies controlled by Mr Cushnie. Effectively, Mr Cushnie was using the investors' funds simply to circulate around between the other investors, himself and his other companies. The purpose of such circulation was to inflate (falsely) the value of the defendant's turnover. Mr Cushnie eventually floated the company and it was listed on the London Stock Exchange. He sold some of his shares for nearly £29 million and distributed the proceeds to various parties including effectively himself and various banks who had advanced loans to him.

Eventually, in 2000, Versailles Group plc collapsed as the scale of the fraud (involving hundreds of millions of pounds) became clear. The traders were owed nearly £23 million. The banks were owed £70.5 million. The claimant in the action was one of the traders that were owed money.

The claimant brought two claims. The first is relevant here: that it was entitled to the proceeds of the shares that Mr Cushnie had sold and which proceeds had subsequently been distributed to, *inter alia*, various banks. The claimant's case was that Mr Cushnie held the proceeds on constructive trust for it. This claim was based on Mr Cushnie, as a director, owing fiduciary duties to Trading Partners Ltd not to make a secret profit and not to misuse funds.[11] Breach of these duties resulted in a £29 million gain for Mr Cushnie. The claimant said that it was entitled to trace its money through these shares to the eventual recipients (the banks).

Delivering the only substantive judgment of the Court of Appeal, Lord Neuberger MR held tracing required the party to show that he had owned an interest in property which could then be followed. A 'consistent line'[12] of previous Court of Appeal decisions had stated that a beneficiary of a fiduciary's duties could not claim a proprietary interest in property unless the beneficiary had originally enjoyed an equitable interest in that property. If the beneficiary had owned no interest in the property, his remedy was limited to equitable compensation for breach of fiduciary duty.

Mr Cushnie had not acquired the shares in Versailles Group plc with any money that had originally been owned by Trading Partners Ltd. The claim for the profits of £29 million that Mr Cushnie gained was based on the transaction in which that profit was made. That gave rise to a duty to pay equitable compensation only. As Trading Partners Ltd had not provided the money to purchase the shares originally, there could be no tracing of any of their property to be done through to the eventual profit Mr Cushnie made.

---

10 *Sinclair Investments (UK) Ltd v Versailles Trade Finance Ltd (in administrative receivership)* [2011] Bus LR 1126.
11 See Chapter 8 for a detailed discussion of these (and other) fiduciary duties.
12 *Sinclair Investments (UK) Ltd v Versailles Trade Finance Ltd (in administrative receivership)* [2011] Bus LR 1126 at 1150.

In reaching this conclusion, Lord Neuberger MR disagreed with the Privy Council's earlier decision in *Attorney-General for Hong Kong v Reid*.[13] Mr Reid was a solicitor who worked as the Acting Director of Public Prosecutions in Hong Kong. He accepted substantial bribes for not prosecuting certain individuals. He purchased three properties in New Zealand with the bribes. The Crown brought an action claiming the value of those properties, which were worth HK $12.4 million. The properties had increased in value from when Mr Reid had originally purchased them. The Privy Council held that the claimant could trace the bribe into the properties.

The Privy Council decided that a recipient of a bribe held the legal title in that bribe, but that equity would insist that the recipient of the bribe should hold the bribe on trust for the person to whom his fiduciary duties were owed. In this case, that was the Government of Hong Kong. It could not be the provider of the bribe as he had committed a criminal act in offering the bribe. If the bribe was used and increased in value, the beneficiary had to be entitled to that gain as well as the original bribe, to prevent the 'guilty' individual from benefiting from breach of his fiduciary duties.

Lord Neuberger MR doubted that the reasoning of the Privy Council was correct in that case. The decision was odd in that the Government of Hong Kong was held to be entitled to recover both the bribe and its gain even though it had never enjoyed an equitable interest in the money used in the bribe. It had never had any proprietary interest in the original money which had, as a bribe, been paid to the corrupt employee by a third party.

Lord Neuberger MR thought that where the beneficiary did not have any equitable interest in property, he could not pursue a proprietary claim. His claim was limited to that of equitable compensation for the breach of fiduciary duty that the fiduciary had committed by conducting the transaction. This conclusion reflected many earlier Court of Appeal cases.[14]

Making connections

In delivering his judgment, Lord Neuberger MR reminded the court of the doctrine of precedent. There had been a number of Court of Appeal decisions over the previous 95 years deciding that tracing could only occur if the tracing party could show that he had previously owned an interest in the property. Then a Privy Council decision in *Attorney-General for Hong Kong v Reid* had decided that such Court of Appeal cases were wrongly decided.

Lord Neuberger MR believed that the Court of Appeal must follow its own previous decisions in preference to one of the Privy Council. This had been decided earlier in *Young v Bristol Aeroplane Company Ltd*.[15] It was, if necessary, to be left to the Supreme Court to overrule a Court of Appeal decision if it felt it was wrong, not for the Court of Appeal effectively to do that itself by following a Privy Council decision in preference to its own.

Whilst Lord Neuberger MR was not stating anything radical, the effect of his words is perhaps radical, for it involved the rejection of a principle decided by Law Lords sitting as the Privy Council just 17 years previously.

Lord Neuberger MR hesitantly thought that the actual result in *Attorney-General for Hong Kong v Reid* might be justified on a policy ground, presumably that a corrupt employee in receipt of a

---

13 *Attorney-General for Hong Kong v Reid* [1994] 1 AC 324.
14 Such as the key decisions in *Lister v Stubbs* (1890) 45 ChD 1 (where the Court of Appeal there contained arguably three of the greatest judges in Cotton, Lindley and Bowen LJJ) and *Metropolitan Bank v Heiron* (1880) 5 Ex D 319.
15 *Young v Bristol Aeroplane Company Ltd* [1946] AC 163.

bribe should not be allowed to keep the bribe or any profit generated by its use. But the reasoning underpinning the employer acquiring that profit was suspect. It did not depend on tracing. He thought that if the beneficiary, as the employer in *Attorney-General for Hong Kong v Reid*, was to benefit from the gain made by the fiduciary (the employee), that should be reflected by an increase in the award of equitable compensation, as opposed to holding that tracing could occur without the beneficiary enjoying a proprietary interest in the original trust property. This last point was entirely new as it seems to have been rejected in the earlier leading Court of Appeal decision in *Lister v Stubbs*.[16]

Bona fide purchaser for value without notice

In a purely *obiter* part of his judgment, Lord Neuberger MR addressed the type of notice required for a *bona fide* purchaser for value of assets to take free of an interest. The banks' alternative argument was that, when they received the proceeds from the shares sold by Mr Cushnie in partial discharge of their loans, they received it as a *bona fide* purchaser for value without notice of the Trading Partners' equitable claim to the money. Strictly this part of the judgment was unnecessary, as Lord Neuberger MR had already decided that there was no tracing claim. But if there was, he considered whether the banks would have had a good defence, based on whether they had notice of Trading Partners' interest. This depended on what 'notice' constituted. It meant whether the banks knew, or should be taken to have known, of the relevant facts surrounding their repayments by Mr Cushnie. But it also revolved around whether the banks should have been taken to know the *relevant legal consequences* of accepting the money in partial discharge of their loans (i.e. if they knew that the money was paid to them under suspicious circumstances, should then they be taken to have known that the money was probably owned by another party and susceptible to a tracing claim).

Lord Neuberger MR did not believe it was right automatically to say that the banks either knew or should have known of the legal consequences of accepting the money from Mr Cushnie. He said the question was whether:

> a reasonable person with their attributes (i.e. those of a responsible large bank with the benefit of highly experienced insolvency practitioners as their appointed administrative receivers) should either have appreciated that a proprietary claim probably existed or should have made inquiries or sought advice, which would have revealed the probable existence of such a claim.[17]

Lord Neuberger MR held that the trial judge had been right to conclude that the banks were *bona fide* purchasers for value and took the money without notice of Trading Partners' claim. In terms of the facts, it had subsequently been made clear that the transactions made by the group of companies were fraudulent, but that was not apparent at the time the banks accepted the money from Mr Cushnie. As those facts were not clear at the time, it could not be said that the banks should have appreciated the potential legal consequence that the money paid by Mr Cushnie might have been owned by Trading Partners Ltd.

Tracing may occur at common law or in equity.

---

16 *Lister v Stubbs* (1890) 45 ChD 1.
17 *Sinclair Investments (UK) Ltd v Versailles Trade Finance Ltd (in administrative receivership)* [2011] Bus LR 1126 at 1155.

Tracing at Common Law

Tracing at common law involves following the legal interest in the trust property into another's hands and claiming that it, or the property it has subsequently become, should be returned to the trust. As it is the legal interest in trust property that is being traced, action will normally be taken by the trustee. Millett LJ has described there being 'no merit in having distinct and different tracing rules at law and in equity'[18] but be that as it may, it seems that different rules do exist. The ability to trace the legal interest of trust property at common law is curtailed more than the right to trace the beneficial interest of the trust property in equity.

The ability to trace at common law

The right to trace trust property at common law is said to arise from the decision in *Taylor v Plumer*.[19] The decision in that case was given by the Court of King's Bench (a common law court) and so it was, for many years, assumed that the common law therefore gave its own right to trace trust property. It has subsequently been accepted by Millett LJ[20] in the Court of Appeal's decision of *Trustee of the Property of F C Jones & Sons (A Firm) v Jones*, that the Court of King's Bench was actually applying equitable principles. Millett LJ's view was that equity was following the law, as per its maxim, but the law happened not to be declared until much later.

The facts concerned the instruction by the defendant to a Mr Walsh, a stockbroker, to purchase Exchequer bills on his behalf. The defendant gave him £22,200 to effect the purchase. Mr Walsh spent £6,500 on the purchase of Exchequer bills. But then he had a different plan, for his own personal gain. He was insolvent. He planned to use the remainder of the money in the purchase of American government bonds and gold bullion. He duly did so, but not before he had exchanged some of the defendant's money for a banker's draft which he then used to buy the gold bullion. He then proceeded to Falmouth, where he was due to board a ship to begin a new life in America.

The defendant heard about Mr Walsh's plan and managed to send a police officer to intercept him. Mr Walsh surrendered the bullion and the American bonds.

The case came about because Mr Walsh had been made bankrupt. His trustee in bankruptcy brought an action at common law, seeking the court's decision on whether he was entitled to some or all of the American bonds and bullion. His claim was that they were owned by Mr Walsh and, upon his bankruptcy, passed to the trustee in bankruptcy. The defendant argued that the bonds and bullion were rightfully his, as they had been bought with his money.

Lord Ellenborough CJ held that the defendant was entitled to retain the bonds and bullion as his own property. The property given to Mr Walsh had been subject to a trust in favour of the defendant and the trust still stood. It made no difference that the original money that the defendant had given Mr Walsh had changed its composition into American government bonds and bullion for as Lord Ellenborough said:

> if the property in its original state and form was covered with a trust in favour of the principal, no change of that state and form can divest it of such trust.[21]

---

18 In *Trustee of the Property of F C Jones & Sons (A Firm) v Jones* [1997] Ch 159 at 169.
19 *Taylor v Plumer* (1815) 3 M & S 562; 105 ER 721.
20 Based on an article by Lionel Smith, 'Tracing in *Taylor v Plumer*: Equity in the Court of King's Bench' [1995] LMCLQ 240.
21 *Taylor v Plumer* (1815) 3 M & S 562 at 574.

Tracing was available to trace the legal interest in the defendant's money into the subsequent property – the bonds and bullion – that the trustee (Mr Walsh) had purchased with it.

Tracing depended, however, on there being a clear link between the original trust property and what that property had been turned into. Here there was a clear link: it was clear that the bonds and bullion were only purchased with the defendant's money and so the money had been turned into those bonds and bullion.

Where, however, it was not possible to show such a link between the original trust property and what that property had turned into, tracing would not be available. Such an occasion would be where the trust property was turned into money and the money was then mixed with other money. Lord Ellenborough CJ said this gave rise to a 'difficulty of fact and not of law'[22] in that it was then simply not possible to say which of the mixed money was the original trust property. All that would remain would be 'an undivided and undistinguishable mass of current money'.[23] Tracing original trust property which had been mixed with other money would need to wait for the development of the later equitable rules on tracing.

Key Learning Point

The common law will, therefore, permit tracing to occur provided that the trust property remains clearly identifiable. It is not the case that the common law will not permit money to be traced, merely that the money must have been kept separate from any other money.

Money was kept separate in *Banque Belge pour L'Etranger v Hambrouck*.[24]

The facts concerned a company called A M Pelabon which had its bank account with the claimant bank. The company's chief assistant accountant, Mr Hambrouck, fraudulently forged a number of the company's cheques and made them payable to himself. He paid the cheques in and, over a period of two years, appropriated £6,680 from the company to himself in this manner. He then wrote cheques to his mistress, Mademoiselle Spanoghe. She paid the cheques into her personal bank account. By the time the fraud was discovered, £315 remained in her account. The claimant bank brought an action for the recovery of that sum. They wished to trace the legal title of the money and reclaim it. The trial judge found the claimant could trace the money. Mlle Spanoghe appealed, claiming that because the money had passed through two bank accounts before it reached her, it was not possible to identify the money which she received as the claimant's original money.

Two Lords Justices in the Court of Appeal rejected the proposition that tracing could not occur at common law. Atkin LJ pointed out that the only restriction on tracing money identified in *Taylor v Plumer* was where the trust money could no longer be ascertained. Equity had summoned up the courage since that case[25] to go further and hold that tracing could occur in equity where trust money had been mixed with other money and it was difficult to identify the original trust money. Yet here there was no difficulty in identifying the original trust money. The same money belonging to A M Pelabon had been paid into Mr Hambrouck's personal account. There had never been any other money in his bank account. He withdrew cheques on that account to pay them to his mistress. She paid them into her personal account

---

22 Ibid at 575.
23 Ibid.
24 *Banque Belge pour L'Etranger v Hambrouck* [1921] 1 KB 321.
25 In *Re Hallett's Estate* (1879–80) LR 13 Ch D 696, considered below at p 358.

and again, there was never any other money in that account. The money in Mlle Spanoghe's account could, clearly, be ascertained as trust money. The process of tracing could thus be undertaken. The remedy in the case was for the claimant to have a claim for money had and received against Mlle Spanoghe.

Not all of the judges in the Court of Appeal reached the same conclusion, illustrating that tracing at common law remains a difficult concept. Scrutton LJ thought that tracing at common law was not possible on the facts, as the money had probably changed its identity when Mr Hambrouck paid it into his own bank account. Scrutton LJ thought that tracing was permitted in equity on the facts of the case.

That tracing at common law remains separate and distinct from tracing in equity and that it can only occur provided the original trust property remains ascertainable was emphasised by the Court of Appeal in *Trustee of the Property of F C Jones & Sons (A Firm) v Jones*.[26]

The facts concerned speculation in potato futures. A firm of potato growers was in financial difficulties. One of the partners of the firm gave his wife, the defendant, a cheque for £11,700 drawn on the firm's account. She used the money to speculate on the London potato futures market. She was very successful at this and the original money grew into a sum of £50,760 which she paid into a deposit account that she had opened. The Official Receiver demanded the money, saying that the original sum had been released by the partnership in breach of trust to her as it had been released to her after the partnership was effectively bankrupt. The Official Receiver's argument was that it was not the partnership's money to release to the defendant as it became his when the partnership became bankrupt. As a proprietary action, the Official Receiver wished to trace the original sum into what it had turned into, thus ensuring a large 'uplift' if the whole successful investment could be traced.

All three Lords Justices in the Court of Appeal held that the defendant had no legal or equitable title to the money. The defendant held no ownership in the original money at all. The legal title was vested in the Official Receiver when the firm committed an act of bankruptcy. As such, its only claim was to trace the legal title in the original money into the profit which had been made. The £11,700 had not been mixed with any other money during the transactions and it was clearly traceable at common law. The Official Receiver could follow the £11,700 from the hands of the defendant into the broker who invested the money on the London potato futures market and from the profit generated there back to the account into which that profit had been paid.

The Court of Appeal held that the Official Receiver was entitled to all of the profit made by the defendant. That was due to the nature of the claim. The Official Receiver's claim was a chose in action and it constituted the right not to claim merely the original amount but also the balance, whether or not that represented a profit or loss.

Tracing was the process which gave the Official Receiver the ability to follow the legal title in the original sum to the profit made. Nourse LJ pointed out that the remedy granted to the Official Receiver was that it had a right to claim for money had and received.

If the ability to ascertain the trust property has been lost, tracing will not be permitted at common law. This was emphasised in *Agip (Africa) Ltd v Jackson*.[27]

Agip (Africa) Ltd was part of the larger Italian oil giant, Agip SPA. It held permits to drill for oil in Tunisia. It also had a bank account at the Banque du Sud in Tunis. Its chief accountant, Mr Zdiri, fraudulently altered payment orders signed by directors of the claimant (the payment

26 *Trustee of the Property of F C Jones & Sons (A Firm) v Jones* [1997] Ch 159.
27 *Agip (Africa) Ltd v Jackson* [1991] Ch 547.

orders were instructions to the claimant's bank to pay a certain recipient) to make payments to different recipients instead. The different recipients were companies controlled by the defendants. This fraud occurred over many years, but between March 1983 and when the fraud was discovered in January 1985, $10.5 million was fraudulently taken by this method. The action in the case concerned the ability of the claimant to recover nearly $519,000 – the final payment before the fraud was discovered – from the defendant.

The companies controlled by the defendants were shell companies which did not trade. They seem to have been established simply for receiving, and then distributing, the money fraudulently received from the claimant. The companies each had a bank account with Lloyds Bank in London. The procedure of transferring the money from the claimant to the companies is set out in Figure 13.1 below.

Step 1: Payment order (authorising a genuine payment to be made) is signed by an authorised signatory of Agip (Africa) Ltd.

Step 2: Payment order is then, unbeknownst to Agip (Africa) Ltd, altered so that the recipient's details are changed to a company controlled by the defendants.

Step 3: The payment order is taken to the Banque du Sud, Tunis.

Step 4: The Banque du Sud acts on the payment order: it orders the transfer of money to the recipient company's account at Lloyds Bank, London.

Step 5: Lloyds Bank credits each company's account with the amount stated on the payment order and uses its own funds to do so.

Step 6: At the same time as instructing Lloyds Bank to credit the company's account, Banque du Sud instructs Citibank in New York to debit its account with Citibank and to transfer the same amount as was on the payment order to Lloyds Bank, to reimburse Lloyds for the money it had used in crediting the company's account.

Figure 13.1 The steps in *Agip (Africa) Ltd v Jackson*.

In giving the substantive judgment of the Court of Appeal, Fox LJ pointed out that tracing at common law did not depend on the existence of a fiduciary relationship. Liability depended simply on the fact of the defendant receiving the claimant's money. As tracing at common law hinged upon receipt, it was irrelevant that the defendant had not retained the money. It also did not matter whether the defendant had acted honestly or not.

But what was essential for tracing to occur at common law was that the money had to be clearly identified in the defendant's hands. This was not the case here. The money had been mixed in the New York clearing system. The original payment order had been taken into the Banque du Sud. That bank then instructed Lloyds Bank to credit the companies' accounts. Lloyds Bank duly did so, but because of the time difference between the US and the UK, it would be some time later that Lloyds Bank would be reimbursed the amount by which it had credited the companies' accounts. Lloyds Bank therefore paid the companies with its own money – money that was different from that original payment order taken into the Banque du Sud. That payment order was mixed into the New York clearing system and then came out later from the clearing system to reimburse Lloyds Bank. The original money and the money which found its way to the companies controlled by the defendants was not the same. Consequently, tracing at common law could not be established.

The claimant did, however, successfully argue that tracing could be permitted in equity.[28]

The remedy at common law if tracing is successful

The remedy at common law is restitutionary in nature. It is that the claimant may bring an action against the defendant for money had and received. This is founded on principles of unjust enrichment. The defendant, through the misuse of the claimant's money, has unjustly enriched himself at the claimant's expense and should return the money to the claimant.

Such remedy was awarded by the Court of Appeal against Mrs Jones in *Trustee of F C Jones & Sons (A Firm) v Jones* where it was held that the claimant could claim the additional money that had been made with the original investment. That was due to the nature of the claim the claimant enjoyed. The claimant's chose in action could be taken against the balance left in the account, whether that was greater or lesser than the original investment. As Lord Goff explained in *Lipkin Gorman v Karpnale Ltd*:[29]

> 'tracing' or 'following' property into its product involves a decision by the owner of the original property to assert his title to the product in place of his original property.

The claim for money had and received has existed for centuries. It is based upon a simple premise: the principle that the defendant cannot, in good conscience, retain the money he has received.[30] Money had and received is a personal claim against the defendant.

In *Lipkin Gorman v Karpnale Ltd*,[31] the House of Lords held that two defences might apply to such a claim. These are either that the defendant has acted in good faith and for valuable consideration – or is, in other words, a *bona fide* purchaser of a legal estate for value without notice (the so-called 'equity's darling') – or where the defendant has innocently changed his position.

The facts concerned the activities of Mr Norman Cass, who was a partner in the claimant firm of solicitors. Unbeknownst to his other partners, he was a compulsive gambler and, between March and November 1980, he helped himself to over £323,000 from the firm's client account (he was later to repay approximately £100,000 of this sum). He went to the defendant's Playboy Club, in London, whereupon he converted the money to gambling chips, which he used to place bets. Some bets he won but ultimately the net amount of his losses amounted to nearly £151,000 which, on a different way of looking at the matter, were the winnings that the Club enjoyed from his custom. Mr Cass absconded but was brought to trial and convicted of theft. His firm, however, was anxious to recover the money he had misappropriated from its client account. The firm brought proceedings against the Club's owners for money had and received in respect of the net amount stolen by Mr Cass from the client account: nearly £223,000. To arrive at this remedy, the firm sought to trace the money from their client account via Mr Cass to the Club's owners.

The first issue for the House of Lords to resolve was who had legal title to the money taken from the firm's client account. The firm needed to show that it had legal title, so it could trace that title into the hands of the defendants, the Club's owners. The defendants argued that legal title to the money passed to Mr Cass immediately when it was withdrawn from the account as he had no authority from the rest of the partners to withdraw it.

---

28 See p 356 in this chapter for further discussion.
29 *Lipkin Gorman v Karpnale Ltd* [1991] 2 AC 548 at 573.
30 See the judgment of Lord Mansfield in *Clarke v Shee & Johnson* (1774) 1 Cowp 197; 98 ER 1041.
31 *Lipkin Gorman v Karpnale Ltd* [1991] 2 AC 548.

Lord Goff was of the opinion that the firm did have legal title in the money. Before Mr Cass withdrew the money, the relationship between the bank and the firm was that of debtor and creditor: the bank owed a debt to the firm. This was a chose in action. The firm could have taken action at any point, if necessary, against the bank to enforce that chose in action. Due to this, the firm must have enjoyed legal ownership to the chose in action and hence to the money it represented. As the firm owned the legal title to the money, it could trace this money through Mr Cass to the defendants.

The defendants advanced two arguments as part of their defence:

(a) they maintained that when Mr Cass exchanged the money for their chips, they provided valuable consideration for his money. If he had received valuable consideration for the money, they owed the claimant nothing; and

(b) they said that a claim for money had and received could be denied by the court on broad grounds if the court felt that it would be unjust or unfair to order the defendants to repay the money to the claimant. Specifically, on the facts, the defendants argued that they had innocently changed their position as a result of receiving the money and it would be unfair to order them to repay it to the claimant.

The first argument was accepted by a majority of the Court of Appeal but rejected by the House of Lords. Lord Goff explained that s 18 of the Gaming Act 1845 rendered contracts for gaming or wagering void in English law. As such, there was no contract between the Club and Mr Cass. The Club had provided no consideration to Mr Cass in the form of a chance of winning. If Mr Cass' bet was unsuccessful, the Club's promise to him was only to pay him if his bet won and so was of no effect. If his bet won, due to the Gaming Act, Mr Cass would have no legal right to call for his winnings to be paid to him and in paying the winnings, the Club was making a gift of them to him.

As to the second argument, Lord Goff denied that the court had 'carte blanche'[32] to reject claims for money had and received simply on the basis that it might be unjust or unfair to the defendants. He said the claim could only succeed if the defendants had been unjustly enriched. Such a claim did not depend on any wrongdoing by the defendants to the claimant.

Lord Goff thought that a general defence of innocent change of position should be recognised in English law. This principle had already been recognised in other common law jurisdictions, such as the United States, Canada and New Zealand. The defence would be applicable where:

> an innocent defendant's position is so changed that he will suffer an injustice if called upon to repay or to repay in full, the injustice of requiring him to repay outweighs the injustice of denying the plaintiff restitution.[33]

Lord Goff was, however, unwilling to limit the defence to specific situations and preferred that it should be developed on a case-by-case basis. He did, however, confirm that the defence would not be available where a defendant had changed his position in bad faith, such as where the defendant had dissipated the claimant's money knowing that doing so was wrong. He stated the defence as being open

---

32 Ibid at 578.
33 Ibid at 579.

to a person whose position has so changed that it would be inequitable in all the circumstances to require him to make restitution, or alternatively to make restitution in full.[34]

The fact that a defendant has just spent the money that he has been given would not, however, make the defence available to the defendant. The money might have been paid away in the 'ordinary course of things',[35] which would not invoke the defence.

Applied to the facts, Lord Goff believed that the defendants should prima facie be liable in an action for money had and received for the amount of money that Mr Cass had taken to the Club less the amount the Club had paid him in winnings. That meant that the claimant could recover approximately £151,000. In respect of the remainder of the original £323,000 that Mr Cass had originally taken to the Club, the Club had innocently changed its position.

As can be seen, the defence of change of position is related to a broader balancing act as to whether it is fairer that either the claimant or defendant should lose out. In cases such as Lipkin Gorman v Karpnale Ltd, the court was involved in a difficult balancing act, given that both claimant and defendant were innocent parties of Mr Cass' deception. In the end, the claimant did not recover all its losses but neither did the defendant have to pay out more than it had taken from Mr Cass. Such a decision, according to Lord Goff, 'may not be entirely logical, but it is just'.[36]

Tracing in Equity

In Agip (Africa) Ltd v Jackson,[37] Fox LJ explained the main difference between tracing at common law and in equity:

> Both common law and equity accepted the right of the true owner to trace his property into the hands of others while it was in an identifiable form. The common law treated property as identified if it had not been mixed with other property. Equity, on the other hand, will follow money into a mixed fund and charge the fund.[38]

In this sense, therefore, equity offered greater scope to the process of tracing. The common law, as shown on the facts of Agip (Africa) Ltd v Jackson, would not permit tracing if the property had been mixed, which often occurred in a bank account. The property no longer remained clearly identifiable. This was summed up in a memorable dictum by Atkin LJ in Banque Belge pour L'Etranger v Hambrouck:[39]

> But if in 1815 [in Taylor v Plumer] the common law halted outside the bankers' door, by 1879 equity had had the courage to lift the latch, walk in and examine the books: In re Hallett's Estate.

Whilst tracing in equity offers a clear advantage over tracing at common law – in that tracing into mixed funds can occur – it also comes with an additional requirement that must be

---

34 Ibid at 580.
35 Ibid.
36 Ibid at 583.
37 Agip (Africa) Ltd v Jackson [1991] Ch 547.
38 Ibid at 566.
39 Banque Belge pour L'Etranger v Hambrouck [1921] 1 KB 321 at 335.

satisfied. It is that there has to be a fiduciary relationship which enables the claim in equity to arise. Equity enables the claimant to trace the beneficial interest in the property and to do that, the claimant must show that a fiduciary relationship exists under which he is entitled to an equitable interest in the property.

Equity allowed tracing to occur on the facts in *Agip (Africa) Ltd v Jackson*. There was a fiduciary relationship between Agip (Africa) Ltd and its chief accountant, Mr Zdiri. Such a relationship enabled the equitable interest in the money to be traced through the bank clearing system in New York, even though it was mixed there with other money.

In a typical trustee-beneficiary relationship, the fiduciary nature of the relationship is obvious between the parties. But it is this fiduciary relationship which gives rise to the equitable interest in the trust property being held for the beneficiary and enables the beneficiary to trace that trust property into another's hands.

It is possible to use equity to trace into unmixed funds. This is where the equitable interest in the money had been kept clearly separate from other money. In such a situation, equity adheres to its maxim that it follows the law. The same result will be reached as if tracing had occurred at common law, which is that tracing will be permitted albeit this time it is the tracing of the equitable, as opposed to legal, interest.

It is really where money has been mixed that equity came into its own with regard to tracing.

Tracing in mixed funds: two innocent parties

Where money has been mixed with other money and there is some remaining in the bank account but it is insufficient to meet the demands of two or more creditors, the general rule is that the money that has been paid in first has been withdrawn first. This principle comes from *Clayton's Case*.[40] It is sometimes known as 'first in, first out'.

❖ EXPLAINING THE LAW

Suppose Francesca receives £500 from Anna on Monday and the same amount from Bernard on Tuesday. Francesca pays both amounts into the same bank account. On Wednesday, Francesca pays £500 to Clare.

The rule in *Clayton's Case* deals with the £500 remaining in the account after the payment to Clare has been made. The rule states that the remaining money belongs to Bernard in equity: 'first in, first out'. Anna's money was paid in first and is therefore deemed to be withdrawn first when Francesca pays Clare on Wednesday. Bernard's money remains untouched.

As can be shown, the rule of *Clayton's Case* is merely a rule of convenience. It is essentially a rule of chance: Anna loses out simply because her money is deemed to be used first.

---

40 *Clayton's Case* (1816) 1 Mer 529; 35 ER 781.

The facts of *Clayton's Case* concerned whether a deceased former partner's estate could be liable for a debt incurred before the partner died. It was a case which involved the consideration and discussion of principles of partnership and banking law, as the partnership in question ran a banking business.

The principle in *Clayton's Case* was accepted as applying to fiduciaries in *Re Hallett's Estate*.[41] Jessel MR described the principle as a 'convenient rule'[42] but one which was effectively only a presumption, which would apply subject to particular evidence being led to the contrary. So 'first in, first out' could be disapplied if it could be proven on the facts of the case that it should not apply, as occurred in *Re Hallett's Estate* itself.[43]

The principle from *Clayton's Case* was applied in *Re Stenning*.[44] Mr Stenning was a solicitor who paid both his clients' and his own money into the same bank account that he held at the Bank of England. When he died, his estate was insolvent and he owed more money than he had in the account. Mrs Sydney Smith was one of his clients. She claimed £448 from the account. Her claim, along with those of Mr Stenning's other clients, was that Mr Stenning held their money on trust for them. The trust should operate to 'ring fence' their money so that they would be paid before Mr Stenning's general creditors.

Mr Stenning had paid in Mrs Smith's money – £448 – to the account in March 1890. By the end of August 1890, he had subsequently deposited other sums of money, belonging to his other clients, but had also withdrawn significant sums. His account had always been in credit for more than the money Mrs Smith claimed but not by enough money to repay all of his clients. Mr Stenning died on 1 November 1890.

North J held that Mrs Smith had no claim to the money she had paid Mr Stenning, despite his account being in credit for more than her claim. The actual decision in the case was that there was, on the facts, no trust of the money created, but that there was simply a loan of the money from Mrs Smith to Mr Stenning. However, as *obiter dicta*, North J thought that the money left in the account could not, on the principle coming from *Clayton's Case* and *Re Hallett's Estate*, belong to Mrs Smith. After Mr Stenning had paid her money into the account, he had paid in other clients' money. He had then withdrawn money. On the 'first in, first out' principle, the withdrawals that he had made had made use of Mrs Smith's money first, as it was the first to be paid in to the account. As such, she had no claim against the money remaining in the account, as her money had been used first.

Tracing in mixed funds: Where the trustee mixes his own money with a beneficiary's

In this scenario, there are not two innocent parties: the trustee has mixed his own money with that of the beneficiary. If the principle in *Clayton's Case* was to apply, then it would simply be down to mere chance as to which party would lose out. For example, suppose a trustee paid in £500 of a beneficiary's money to his own bank account and added £500 of his own money. He then spends £500. The rule in *Clayton's Case* would state that the trustee spent the beneficiary's money first, leaving his own money untouched. Such a result would be unjust. It would enable the trustee to use another's money for his own purposes with no effective sanction for the beneficiary, except for pursuing a personal remedy against the trustee.

---

41 *Re Hallett's Estate* (1879–80) LR 13 ChD 696.
42 Ibid at 728.
43 See p 358.
44 *Re Stenning* [1895] 2 Ch 433.

The rule in *Clayton's Case* does not apply to the situation where a trustee mixes trust money with his own money. The trustee's personal money is deemed to be spent first. This was established in *Re Hallett's Estate*.[45]

Mr Hallett was a solicitor and a trustee of some Russian bonds belonging to a Mrs Cotterill. Without her permission, he sold the bonds and placed the proceeds into his own personal bank account, in so doing, mixing Mrs Cotterill's money with his own. He then withdrew money from the account, using the money for his own purposes. After his death, the account was in credit, with more money in it than represented the proceeds of sale from Mrs Cotterill's bonds, but if *Clayton's Case* was applied to the facts, it would result in Mr Hallett having spent Mrs Cotterill's money before his own.

The Court of Appeal held that, in such a case, the principle in *Clayton's Case* could not apply. The trustee had to be deemed to have withdrawn the money which he had a right to withdraw first, before he touched any other money. That would mean that he withdrew his own money first, before a beneficiary's. Jessel MR gave the following example to explain his decision:

> The simplest case put is the mingling of trust moneys in a bag with money of the trustee's own. Suppose he has a hundred sovereigns in a bag, and he adds to them another hundred sovereigns of his own, so that they are commingled in such a way that they cannot be distinguished, and the next day he draws out for his own purposes £100, is it tolerable for anybody to allege that what he drew out was the first £100, the trust money, and that he misappropriated it, and left his own £100 in the bag? It is obvious *he must have taken away that which he had a right to take away*, his own £100.[46]

Clayton's Case was a presumption which could only apply unless there was evidence led to the contrary against it. Such was a case where money was mixed between an innocent party and a non-innocent party, namely a fiduciary who had committed a breach of trust.

In *Sinclair Investments (UK) Ltd v Versailles Trade Finance Ltd (in administrative receivership)*,[47] the defendant fiduciary argued that once money was mixed with that owned by the defendant, it became so unclear which money was which that tracing was not possible. It was impossible to tell which money was that of the claimant's. The defendant argued that all of the money had simply disappeared into a 'black hole' or 'maelstrom'.

In delivering the only substantive judgment in the Court of Appeal, Lord Neuberger MR rejected that argument. He said he accepted the general contention that for tracing to be successful, there had to be a 'clear link'[48] between the claimant's property and the resulting asset into which the claimant claims the money has been put. He continued:

> However, I do not see why this should mean that a proprietary claim is lost simply because the defaulting fiduciary, while still holding much of the money, has acted particularly dishonestly or cunningly by creating a maelstrom.[49]

---

45 *Re Hallett's Estate* (1879–80) LR 13 ChD 696.
46 Ibid at 727 (emphasis added).
47 *Sinclair Investments (UK) Ltd v Versailles Trade Finance Ltd (in administrative receivership)* [2011] Bus LR 1126.
48 Ibid at 1160.
49 Ibid.

Moreover, in such a situation where the fiduciary has mixed trust money with his own, 'the onus should be on the fiduciary to establish that part, and what part, of the mixed fund is his property'.[50]

Once the claimant had shown that its money had been mixed by the defendant with its own, the burden of proof switched to the defendant to show that – on the balance of probabilities – the money in the account was not the claimant's.

It is thus not open to a fiduciary to claim that the beneficiary's money has simply been 'swallowed up' by his own money in the same account so that the ability to trace has been lost. The fiduciary is under an onus to prove that the mixed money is not trust money.

Tracing in mixed funds: Where a trustee purchases property with mixed funds

Suppose a trustee, having mixed trust money with his own, decides to purchase property with the mixed funds. If Re Hallett's Estate applied to this position, it would result in the purchased property being owned by the trustee himself (because by the decision in that case, the trustee would be deemed to spend his own money first). This would be a surprising conclusion as it would provide an opportunity for trustees to breach trusts quite easily with the knowledge that tracing could not occur.

The High Court in Re Oatway[51] held that in such a position, the beneficiary may successfully trace his money into the purchased property.

As can be seen, the facts of a number of these cases give solicitors a poor reputation! Mr Oatway was a solicitor who was trustee of a trust. In breach of trust, he advanced £3,000 to his co-trustee in return for security in the form of a mortgage. The mortgage was redeemed, to the amount of £7,000, which Mr Oatway paid into his own account.

From that account, Mr Oatway bought shares for £2,137 in the Oceana Company. They were sold for £2,474. Mr Oatway died insolvent. The co-trustee brought an action, arguing that the sum of £2,474 should be held for the trust. The problem with this argument was that Mr Oatway's account had been in credit to the sum of £6,635 when the shares were purchased. It was, therefore, alleged that Mr Oatway bought the shares with his own money, following Re Hallett's Estate.

Joyce J held that the shares belonged to the trust. He said that (i) if money was withdrawn by a trustee and invested by him and (ii) the remainder of the balance in the bank account had been spent by the trustee, then (iii) the trust could trace its money into the investment. The investment was trust property.

To the argument that Mr Oatway's account was in credit when the shares were purchased and were therefore purchased with his own money, Joyce J held that Mr Oatway had never been entitled to withdraw the purchase money for the shares from the account before the trust money had properly been reinstated. The trust money had first priority in the account and that should have been repaid to the trust initially. Only after that was done could Mr Oatway have purchased property. As this was never done, the property purchased by Mr Oatway belonged to the trust.

---

50 Ibid.
51 Re Oatway [1903] 2 Ch 356.

❖ ANALYSING THE LAW

It is of some academic debate as to whether *Re Oatway* conflicts with, or follows, *Re Hallett's Estate*. *Re Hallett's Estate* established that the trustee had to spend money to which he had a right before trust money. If applied to *Re Oatway*, that would result in the Oceana shares being held for the trustee personally. Yet the decision in *Re Oatway* was that the property bought by the trustee belonged to the trust. On one level, this seems to be a triumph of pragmatism over jurisprudence. On another, however, it is possible to see *Re Oatway* as following *Re Hallett's Estate*. The policy behind both decisions is the same: to give the innocent beneficiary the right to trace their equitable interests into what remains of their original property.

Do you think that *Re Oatway* follows or contradicts *Re Hallett's Estate*?

Tracing in equity: The remedy

If it is possible to trace mixed money in equity, the beneficiary is entitled to a remedy. The remedies were set out by Jessel MR in *Re Hallett's Estate*.[52]

If no mixing of the beneficiary's money with other money has occurred, equity's remedy is to offer the beneficiary the choice of either the property itself (that is, what the trust property has turned into) or to have a charge over the property to the value of the trust money spent in acquiring the property.

If the beneficiary's money has been mixed with other money, Jessel MR believed that the beneficiary could only have a charge (or 'lien') over the property to the extent of the amount of trust money spent in acquiring the property. The beneficiary could not have the property itself, because the property had not been purchased with only trust money. This was considered further by the House of Lords in *Foskett v McKeown*.[53]

The facts initially concerned a scheme for the development of land in the Algarve, Portugal. Purchasers gave a total of £2.6 million to Timothy Murphy for the money to be used to build and develop a resort. Mr Murphy bought a life assurance policy and, in breach of trust, used £20,440 to pay two premiums for it. The policy paid £1 million when Mr Murphy died. The property development scheme in the Algarve was not carried out. Accordingly, the purchasers sought to trace their money into the life assurance proceeds. They wanted their remedy to be the whole of the £1 million paid out by the life assurance company. The problem with this argument was that as the purchasers' money had been mixed with Mr Murphy's own money, the dictum from Jessel MR in *Re Hallett's Estate* provided that the purchasers could only have a charge over the proceeds to the extent of the amount spent in acquiring the policy. Thus the purchasers' claim would be limited to £20,440.

Lord Millett described the action as a 'textbook example of tracing through mixed substitutions'.[54] There was an express trust under which Mr Murphy held the purchasers' money in a bank account. He mixed the money with his own money and bought an insurance policy. The purchasers' original money could be traced through to the eventual proceeds from that policy, which were paid to Mr Murphy's children.

---

52 *Re Hallett's Estate* (1879–80) LR 13 ChD 696 at 709.
53 *Foskett v McKeown* [2001] 1 AC 102.
54 Ibid at 126.

Lord Millett thought that there was no justification for limiting the beneficiary's right to a charge over an asset if that asset had been bought using trust money mixed with the trustee's own funds. He said:

> Where a trustee wrongfully uses trust money to provide part of the cost of acquiring an asset, the beneficiary is entitled *at his option* either to claim a proportionate share of the asset or to enforce a lien upon it to secure his personal claim against the trustee for the amount of the misapplied money.[55]

It made no difference if the trust money was initially mixed with the trustee's own money and an asset was then purchased or if, as on the facts of the case, the asset was bought over a period of time with the payments being made, on a sequential basis, from trust money and then the trustee's own money.

Mr Murphy's children could not claim that they were innocent of any wrongdoing in this case as a successful defence. As Lord Millett pointed out, the children were volunteers of Mr Murphy and they could stand in no better position than him, as they derived title to the money from him.

Prima facie the whole of the insurance proceeds were trust property as the policy had been bought partly with trust money. But Lord Millett said that in the case of money, it may be possible to have a *pro rata* division of the proceeds of the policy between the wrongdoer (or his children, in this case) and the beneficiaries.

The proceeds of the policy (£1 million) could be divided between the children and the purchasers in proportion to the contributions they had each contributed to the premiums of the policy. This was because the 'policy' in this case did not represent the strict contract of insurance between Mr Murphy and the insurance company. Instead it represented the chose in action that Mr Murphy enjoyed against the company in return for paying the insurance premiums. The purchasers were able to trace their money through the payment of the insurance premiums to the proceeds paid out by the insurance company. The purchasers' beneficial interest arose as soon as Mr Murphy used their money to pay the insurance premium. They attained a share in the chose in action that he enjoyed against the insurance company because their money was partly used in acquiring that chose in action. The purchasers were entitled to the same proportion of the insurance proceeds as Mr Murphy had used in acquiring his chose in action against the insurance company. They were not to be limited to a lien over the proceeds, as Jessel MR had suggested in *Re Hallett's Estate*.

The decision of the House of Lords was of benefit to the purchasers for they were able to claim a much larger share of the proceeds than in fact they had (unknowingly) contributed to the premiums. This was due to their ability to trace their money not only into the premiums but further into the proceeds from the policy. In addition, in stating that their remedy was not limited merely to a lien over their share of the proceeds, the House of Lords provided an effective, immediate, remedy for the purchasers.

Summary flowchart

The essential elements of tracing are summarised in the flowchart below.

---

55 Ibid at 131.

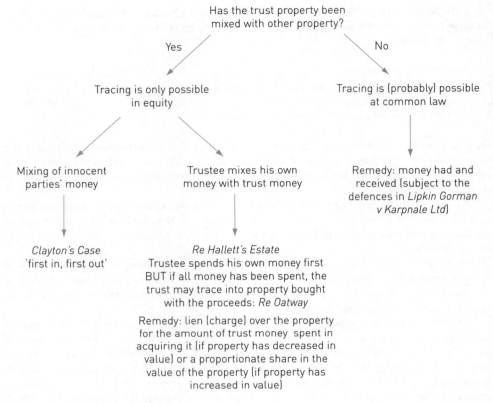

Figure 13.2 Tracing flowchart.

Actions Against Strangers to the Trust

The discussion of tracing considered the ability to follow trust property and reclaim it from a recipient of it. Tracing at common law involved the trustee tracing the legal title; tracing in equity concerned a beneficiary, or someone else in a fiduciary relationship, tracing the beneficial title.

Another category of claim also exists if someone has not breached the trust themselves but has either assisted in the breach of trust or simply received trust property. These are claims against so called 'strangers' to the trust. There are two actions that equity permits:

(a)   a claim of 'accessory liability' (formerly 'knowing assistance[56]'); and
(b)   a claim of 'recipient liability' (formerly 'knowing receipt'[57]).

These claims are personal actions against the strangers to the trust. Both claims originate from a dictum of Lord Selborne LC in *Barnes v Addy*[58] as quoted by Lord Nicholls in *Royal Brunei Airlines v Tan:*[59]

---

56 Before the decision of the Privy Council in *Royal Brunei Airlines v Tan* [1995] 2 AC 378.
57 Ibid.
58 *Barnes v Addy* (1874) LR 9 Ch App 244 at 251–252.
59 *Royal Brunei Airlines v Tan* [1995] 2 AC 378 at 382.

[The responsibility of a trustee] may no doubt be extended in equity to others who are not properly trustees, if they are found . . . actually participating in any fraudulent conduct of the trustee to the injury of the [beneficiary]. But . . . strangers are not to be made constructive trustees merely because they act as the agents of trustees in transactions within their legal powers, transactions, perhaps of which a court of equity may disapprove, unless those agents receive and become chargeable with some part of the trust property, or unless they assist with knowledge in a dishonest and fraudulent design on the part of the trustees.

Key Learning Point

Accessory liability, then, is assisting in a breach of trust. Accessory liability can only arise when there has been a breach of trust and the accessory has actual knowledge of that breach. It is fault-based and depends on the accessory knowing that he has behaved dishonestly in assisting in the commission of a breach of trust.

Recipient liability occurs where a stranger to the trust receives trust property (or its proceeds which have been traced) or deals with it for his own use and benefit. This is a restitutionary-based claim and is not dependent on fault on the part of the stranger.

❖ EXPLAINING THE LAW

An example of how accessory or recipient liability can arise may be explained using the facts of *Agip (Africa) Ltd v Jackson*.

The claimant was defrauded out of millions of dollars by its chief accountant, Mr Zdiri. The money passed into Lloyds Bank in London and from there it went into the accounts of a number of companies, all of which seemed to be formed simply for the purpose of accepting the money. The three defendants in the case were the partners and an employee of Jackson & Co, a firm of accountants in the Isle of Man, who set up the companies on the instructions of a French client.

Agip's claim was made against the three defendants for both recipient and accessory liability. Such claims were needed as it was not the defendants personally who received the money from the claimant but companies set up by them. The defendants were, consequently, strangers to the trust.

The claim for recipient liability failed at first instance, as the defendants had not received trust property personally. The claim for accessory liability was upheld at the Court of Appeal; the defendants had assisted, knowingly, in a fraudulent design.

Accessory liability

Accessory liability is a subject with which the highest courts have grappled over the last twenty years. As Fox LJ said in *Agip (Africa) Ltd v Jackson*,[60] a person will be liable for accessory liability where he 'knowingly' assists in a 'fraudulent design' on the trustee's part, even though he does not personally receive trust property.

As You Read

Accessory liability depends on the assistor to the breach of trust being dishonest. The courts have, over the last 20 years, grappled with (i) what 'dishonest' should mean in this context and (ii) what it is that the assistor has to 'know' about being dishonest. Look out for these two issues as you read this part of the chapter.

The first recent case where this was considered was *Royal Brunei Airlines v Tan*.[61]

The Privy Council's first attempt to define 'dishonesty' . . .

Royal Brunei Airlines entered into an agreement with Borneo Leisure Travel ('BLT') to act as its agent for selling passenger and cargo transportation on its aircraft. Mr Tan was the managing director and main shareholder in BLT. BLT was obliged to account to the airline for all sales it made and, in return, was paid a commission. The sales money was to be held by BLT on trust for the airline, in a separate account. In fact, BLT paid money that it received from customers into its general bank account and, instead of paying the money to the airline, used some of the money for its own purposes, in breach of trust.

BLT breached the contract with the airline in failing to pay money to it. The airline terminated the contract and began an action to recover the money due. BLT went insolvent. The airline's action was therefore against Mr Tan personally. The allegation was that Mr Tan had been guilty of accessory liability. He had assisted BLT in breaching the trust with the airline. The issue for the Privy Council was whether BLT had had a 'dishonest and fraudulent design' as it was only if this was the case and Mr Tan had known about it that he could be considered guilty of accessory liability.

In delivery the opinion of the Privy Council, Lord Nicholls lamented that the formulation given by Lord Selborne in *Barnes v Addy* had been applied so rigidly by the courts. He said that in the case of a breach of trust, a trustee would always be liable, unless excused either by an exemption clause or by the courts. The issue of a trustee's liability did not, therefore, depend on the trustee being dishonest or fraudulent. Rather, it was the person accused of accessory liability that had to be shown knowing that in assisting a breach of trust, he was acting dishonestly and fraudulently. It should be the accessory's state of mind that was in issue, not that of the trustee. It was the case that a trustee whom the accessory was assisting would, in fact, usually be dishonest but the real test was whether the *accessory* was dishonest or not.

Lord Nicholls defined 'dishonesty' as 'not acting as an honest person would in the circumstances'.[62] He said it was an 'objective standard'.[63] As such, individuals could not set their own standards of what was honest and what was not. It involved an assessment of 'what a person actually knew at the time'.[64] The honest person would be 'expected to attain the standard

---

60 *Agip (Africa) Ltd v Jackson* [1991] Ch 547 at 567.
61 *Royal Brunei Airlines v Tan* [1995] 2 AC 378.
62 Ibid at 389.
63 Ibid.
64 Ibid.

which would be observed by an honest person placed in those circumstances'.[65] The court would, however, have regard to the 'personal attributes' of the person, 'such as his experience and intelligence and the reason why he acted as he did'.[66]

The question was whether a person dishonestly assisted in a breach of trust, not whether he 'knowingly' assisted in a breach of trust. Asking whether the breach was committed 'knowingly' involved questions of the type of knowledge required; the issue was simpler phrased as one of whether the person acted dishonestly or not.

On the facts, Mr Tan had acted dishonestly in helping with the breach of trust committed by BLT in using money for its own purposes instead of paying it straight to the airline. Mr Tan had known that the money should not have been used in that way.

The objective standard of dishonesty set out in *Royal Brunei Airlines v Tan* was revisited by the House of Lords in *Twinsectra Ltd v Yardley*.[67]

The House of Lords' attempt to define 'dishonesty' . . .

The facts concerned a loan from Twinsectra Ltd for the purposes of enabling Mr Yardley to purchase land. In breach of the trust that existed between Twinsectra Ltd and the solicitor receiving the loan money (Mr Sims), Mr Sims transferred the money to Mr Leach. Part of the money was in fact used to buy property but a substantial amount, over £357,000, was not. Twinsectra brought proceedings to recover that sum. Their claim against Mr Leach was that he had dishonestly assisted the breach of trust committed by Mr Sims in releasing the money early to him.

The majority in the House of Lords thought that Mr Leach was not guilty of dishonesty. Lord Hoffman thought that dishonesty required:

> more than knowledge of the facts which make the conduct wrongful. [Dishonesty requires] a dishonest state of mind, that is to say, consciousness that one is transgressing ordinary standards of honest behaviour.[68]

Mr Leach had 'buried his head in the sand' according to Lord Hoffman.[69] He thought that the loan money was at the free disposal of Mr Yardley. Such behaviour may have been misguided, but it did not constitute dishonesty.

Lord Hutton, with whom the other Lords in the majority agreed, thought that Lord Nicholls in *Royal Brunei Airlines v Tan* had not defined 'dishonesty' as having entirely objective connotations to it. If he had, he would not have seen it necessary to have regard to the accessory's personal experience and intelligence. Lord Hutton thought that Lord Nicholls had intended to define dishonesty as including knowledge by the accessory that he knew that what he was doing was dishonest, 'dishonesty requires knowledge by the defendant that what he was doing would be regarded as dishonest by honest people . . . .'[70]

This, therefore, introduced a subjective element into the test for dishonesty and aligned it more closely to the test for dishonesty in criminal law, as developed by Lord Lane CJ in *R v Ghosh*.[71] Lord Hutton pointed out, however, that an accessory could not escape liability

---

65 Ibid at 390.
66 Ibid at 391.
67 *Twinsectra Ltd v Yardley* [2002] 2 AC 164. See Chapter 7 (p 199) for a detailed discussion of the facts of this case.
68 Ibid at 170.
69 Ibid.
70 Ibid at 174.
71 *R v Ghosh* [1982] QB 1053.

simply by arguing that he did not believe his actions to be dishonest if he knew that they would 'offend the normally accepted standards of honest conduct'.[72]

In his dissenting speech, Lord Millett argued that the test for dishonesty in criminal law focused on the defendant's state of mind. Yet dishonesty in civil matters had previously focused on the defendant's outward conduct instead. Dishonesty came from the defendant's wrongdoing, not what was in his mind. He did not believe that Lord Nicholls in *Royal Brunei Airlines v Tan* had brought in a test of dishonesty equivalent to the criminal standard, requiring an assessment of the defendant's state of mind. He thought Lord Nicholls' test for dishonesty focused solely on the defendant's conduct. His state of mind was thus irrelevant. It was of no consequence that the defendant had not thought about what he was doing and that he had given no consideration as to whether he was acting honestly or not. Lord Millett thought that considering the accessory's state of mind had no place in a civil action. *Mens rea* was a part of criminal law, not civil. Outward wrongdoing was sufficient to constitute dishonesty.

The two divergent views of Lord Nicholls' opinion in *Royal Brunei Airlines v Tan* were not helpful. Lord Millett's dissenting speech is carefully crafted and logically argued. On the other hand, the views of the majority perhaps pragmatically achieved the more palatable result on the facts of the case.

Lord Nicholls' words as interpreted in *Twinsectra Ltd v Yardley* were reviewed again by the Privy Council in *Barlow Clowes International Ltd (in liquidation) v Eurotrust International Ltd*.[73]

The Privy Council's second attempt at 'dishonesty' . . .

The case concerned an investment scheme set up by Barlow Clowes International Ltd, which was run by Peter Clowes. He purported to offer high rates of return in an investment scheme. Investors deposited a total of £140 million with the company, but most of the money was used by Mr Clowes personally, to fund his own business ventures and extravagant lifestyle. In 1988, the investment scheme collapsed. Mr Clowes was convicted and imprisoned. Some of the £140 million was paid away through a company called International Trust Corporation ('ITC'), which acted through its two directors. ITC, controlled by a Mr Henwood, made several payments to businesses controlled by Mr Clowes. The liquidator of Barlow Clowes International Ltd brought proceedings alleging that ITC and Mr Henwood dishonestly assisted Mr Clowes in the breach of trust by misusing investors' money. Mr Henwood was found not guilty of dishonestly assisting in the breach of trust on appeal in the Isle of Man. The liquidator of Barlow Clowes appealed against that decision to the Privy Council.

In delivering the opinion of the Privy Council, Lord Hoffman confirmed that the trial judge had summarised the law correctly. She had referred to *Royal Brunei Airlines v Tan* and had said that dishonesty required a dishonest state of mind by the person assisting in the breach of trust. That could occur either through knowing that the transaction was not honest or being suspicious that the transaction is not honest coupled with a 'conscious decision'[74] not to make enquiries about the transaction which would confirm it to be dishonest. Lord Hoffman said:

> Although a dishonest state of mind is a subjective mental state, the standard by which the law determines whether it is dishonest is objective. If by ordinary standards a defendant's mental state would be characterised as dishonest, it is irrelevant that the defendant judges by different standards.[75]

---

72 *Twinsectra Ltd v Yardley* [2002] 2 AC 164 at 174.
73 *Barlow Clowes International Ltd (in liquidation) v Eurotrust International Ltd* [2006] 1 WLR 1476.
74 Ibid at 1479.
75 Ibid at 1479–1480.

Mr Henwood argued that he could not be characterised as dishonest. His defence was that he felt himself obliged to carry out Mr Clowes' instructions. He never gave any conscious thought as to whether the money he was being instructed to invest belonged to Mr Clowes or was really money belonging to other investors who believed their money was being invested in other securities. He relied on part of Lord Hutton's speech in *Twinsectra Ltd v Yardley* where Lord Hutton had said that dishonesty required that 'the defendant must himself appreciate that what he was doing was dishonest by the standards of honest and reasonable men'[76] and that 'dishonesty requires knowledge by the defendant that what he was doing would be regarded as dishonest by honest people . . .'[77]

Lord Hoffman acknowledged that there might have been 'an element of ambiguity'[78] in Lord Hutton's remarks in *Twinsectra* but what Lord Hutton meant in the decision was that the defendant's

> knowledge of the transaction had to be such as to render his participation contrary to normally acceptable standards of honest conduct. It did not require that he should have had reflections about what those normally acceptable standards were.[79]

Mr Henwood's knowledge was, on the facts, contrary to normally acceptable standards of honest conduct. His knowledge of Mr Clowes and his companies meant that he was at least suspicious about where Mr Clowes' money came from. But Mr Henwood chose not to investigate further. That was contrary to normally acceptable standards of honest conduct. No additional requirement existed that Mr Henwood had to reflect upon what normally accepted standards of honest conduct were.

Two years later, the Court of Appeal in *Abu Rahman v Abacha*[80] believed that the decision of the Privy Council in *Barlow Clowes* represented a correct statement of the law of dishonesty in England.

Lord Hoffman's opinion in *Barlow Clowes International Ltd (in liquidation) v Eurotrust International Ltd* maintained that Lord Hutton's speech in *Twinsectra* followed the test of dishonesty set out in *Royal Brunei Airlines v Tan*. It is hard to see how it did. The test set out in *Royal Brunei Airlines v Tan* seems to have been objective with some elements of subjectivity included in it. The majority in *Twinsectra* suggested that it was not possible to have a purely objective test of whether a person's state of mind was dishonest or not – by definition, when considering a person's state of mind, what he subjectively believed had to creep in somewhere. The decision in *Barlow Clowes* sought to prevent *Twinsectra* being taken to its logical conclusion which was to argue that the subjective element meant that the defendant had to have consciously considered whether his conduct was dishonest. Had that argument been accepted, it would have raised the threshold for the test of dishonesty to a high level to be satisfied. The rejection of this argument in *Barlow Clowes* was probably right but it was undoubtedly wrong to say that the majority in *Twinsectra* followed the test laid down in *Royal Brunei Airlines v Tan*.

The Court of Appeal's attempt at 'dishonesty': *Barlow Clowes* applied

This issue of dishonesty has been revisited recently by the Court of Appeal in *Starglade Properties Ltd v Nash*.[81]

---

76 *Twinsectra Ltd v Yardley* [2002] 2 AC 164 at 174.
77 Ibid.
78 *Barlow Clowes International Ltd (in liquidation) v Eurotrust International Ltd* [2006] 1 WLR 1476 at 1481.
79 Ibid.
80 *Abu Rahman v Abacha* [2007] 1 Lloyd's Rep 115.
81 *Starglade Properties Ltd v Nash* [2010] EWCA Civ 1314.

Roland Nash was the sole director and shareholder of Larkstore Ltd. It developed houses on a site in Hythe, Kent, relying on a report into the suitability of the land prepared by Technotrade Ltd. Unfortunately, a landslip happened and the houses were damaged. The house owners sued Larkstore. Larkstore, in turn, wanted to sue Technotrade Ltd, but their report was prepared for the previous owners of the site, the claimant company. So the claimant, Larkstore and Mr Nash entered into an arrangement whereby the claimant would transfer its contractual rights to Larkstore, in return for which Larkstore would hold any successful litigation proceeds on trust for itself and the claimant in equal shares. Larkstore went insolvent, after its claim had been settled by Technotrade. In breach of trust, Larkstore distributed the money to its other creditors, the majority of which had a connection to Mr Nash. The claimant sued Mr Nash for dishonestly assisting in the breach of trust.

At first instance, the trial judge found that Mr Nash had deliberately preferred to pay other creditors over the claimant. In doing so, he did not find that Mr Nash was dishonest largely on the basis that Mr Nash did not know that he was acting unlawfully in doing so. He had sought – and obtained – rather vague advice from his solicitors and thought he was justified in paying his other creditors before the claimant. In doing so, he was not acting dishonestly.

Giving the leading judgment of the Court of Appeal, the Chancellor said that:

> There is a single standard of honesty objectively determined by the court. That standard is applied to specific conduct of a specific individual possessing the knowledge and qualities he actually enjoyed.[82]

The standard of honesty was the 'ordinary standard of honest behaviour'.[83]

The Chancellor found that in making the payments to other creditors, Mr Nash's aim was to frustrate the claimant in claiming its share of the litigation proceeds. Deliberately removing assets of a company which was insolvent so as to defeat a creditor's claim was dishonest because it did not accord with the 'ordinary standards of honest commercial behaviour'.[84] An experienced businessman such as Mr Nash could not have thought otherwise, even though he did not know the precise legal position concerning the payment of creditors in general.

Rather intriguingly, Leveson LJ expressed a:

> note of concern if the concept of dishonesty for the purposes of civil liability differed to any marked extent from the concept of dishonesty as understood in the criminal law.[85]

In *Royal Brunei Airlines v Tan*, Lord Nicholls had rejected an inter-lining of the same test for dishonesty in both the criminal and civil law. Lord Millett also thought the same in his dissenting speech in *Twinsectra*. Yet the majority in *Twinsectra* effectively thought that the same standard should apply across both criminal and civil law, before the Privy Council in *Barlow Clowes* reinterpreted the decision in *Twinsectra*. In *Starglade Properties Ltd v Nash*, Leveson LJ thought that the Court of Appeal (Criminal Division) should consider again the test for dishonesty in criminal law.

---

82 Ibid at para 25.
83 Ibid at para 32.
84 Ibid at para 39.
85 Ibid at para 42.

❖ **ANALYSING THE LAW**

Apart from simplifying the law, it must be asked why it is felt that the test for dishonesty should be the same in criminal and civil law. Do you think the reasons given by Lord Millett in *Twinsectra* remain valid as to why different tests apply?

Case	Test
Royal Brunei Airlines v Tan (Privy Council)	Lord Nicholls: an objective test: 'not acting as an honest person would in the circumstances' but the court would take into account the 'personal attributes' of the accessory, including his experience, intelligence and the reasoning behind his actions.
Twinsectra v Yardley (House of Lords)	The majority, led by Lords Hoffman and Hutton: dishonesty had a subjective element to it. The accessory had to know that his actions would be regarded as dishonest by honest people. Lord Millett: dishonesty in civil cases was an objective and purely factual test. There should be no enquiries made into the accessory's state of mind, as in criminal law.
Barlow Clowes International Ltd (in liquidation) v Eurotrust International Ltd (Privy Council)	Lord Hoffman: A dishonest state of mind was subjective to the accessory but that is judged by ordinary, objective standards. There was thus no requirement that the defendant should have asked himself whether he was acting dishonestly. Dishonesty could occur in two situations, either: (i) if the accessory knew that the transaction was not honest; or (ii) if the accessory suspected that the transaction was not honest and took a conscious decision not to enquire into it.
Abu Rahman v Abacha (Court of Appeal)	The decision in *Barlow Clowes* states the correct test for dishonesty for accessory liability.
Starglade Properties Ltd v Nash (Court of Appeal)	Seems to apply the *Barlow Clowes* test but emphasises elements of the *Tan* test. Dishonesty is to be judged objectively but with regard to the 'specific conduct' of the particular accessory with his 'knowledge and qualities'.

Figure 13.3 Summary of the test for dishonesty in accessory liability cases.

Recipient liability

The requirements for recipient liability to be established were set out by Hoffman LJ in *El Ajou v Dollar Land Holdings plc*[86] as being that the claimant had to show that:

(a) his property had been disposed of in breach of fiduciary duty;
(b) the property could be traced to the defendant and shown to be the claimant's; and
(c) the defendant had to have knowledge that the property he received was 'traceable to a breach of fiduciary duty'.

If the defendant does have knowledge that the property he received was traceable to a breach of fiduciary duty, he will be subject to a constructive trust to account for that property.

Again, the issue of what the defendant had to know has been considered by the courts. In *Twinsectra*, Lord Millett said that the defendant did not need actual knowledge that a breach of trust had been committed. Lord Millett opined that constructive knowledge – that he should have known of the breach of trust – was sufficient and such knowledge may not itself even be necessary to a successful claim for recipient liability. If this is correct, recipient liability depends simply on a fact: did the defendant receive or apply the trust money for his own use?

The nature of the knowledge that the defendant has to have in order to be liable to a claim for recipient liability was explored in more depth by the Court of Appeal in *BCCI (Overseas) Ltd v Akindele*.[87]

The facts concerned the fraudulent activities of employees of the claimant company. They arranged for a subsidiary company of the claimant, Credit and Investment Co (Overseas) Ltd, to enter into a loan agreement with a Nigerian businessman, Chief Labode Onadimaki Akindele. The loan agreement was entered into to give a false impression that certain loans were performing normally. Entering into the loan agreement was a breach of the employees' fiduciary duties to their employer. The agreement involved the defendant paying $10 million in return for shares in the claimant and contained a promise that the shares would be sold and the defendant would receive an agreed return on his investment. This duly happened and the defendant received $16.679 million when the shares were sold in 1988. Three years later, the claimant became insolvent. The liquidator of the claimant alleged that the defendant was liable to account as a constructive trustee for the profit he had made on the basis that he had dishonestly assisted in the breach of trust, or had received the profit knowing that the employees had committed breaches of trust (recipient liability). The defendant's dishonesty was said to be based on his knowing that the loan agreement was artificial and the high rate of return he was to expect.

The trial judge, Carnworth J, held that the test for accessory and recipient liability was the same and that it required that the defendant's dishonesty be proved. However, he held that the claimant had failed to satisfy the test that the defendant had been dishonest. The claimant appealed.

The Court of Appeal held that the test for accessory liability was not the same as for recipient liability. Accessory liability depended on proving the defendant's dishonesty; recipient liability did not. The trial judge had found that the defendant was not dishonest and so could not be guilty of accessory liability to the breach of trust.

For recipient liability, however, the test was different. It depended on the answer to two questions:

---

86 *El Ajou v Dollar Land Holdings plc* [1994] 2 All ER 685 at 700.
87 *BCCI (Overseas) Ltd v Akindele* [2001] Ch 437.

(a)   What did the defendant have to know?

(b)   Did the defendant have to have acted dishonestly?

The Court of Appeal held the answer to the second question was that there was no requirement that the defendant had to have acted dishonestly albeit, in practice, it was often the case that the defendant would have been dishonest. In this way, proving recipient liability is easier as there is no higher requirement to show that the defendant had to have acted dishonestly.

In terms of what the defendant had to know, Nourse LJ said that the test to be applied was 'that the recipient's state of knowledge should be such as to make it unconscionable for him to retain the benefit of the receipt.'

The traditional classification of knowledge into actual (what the recipient knew) and constructive (what he should have known) served little purpose. The court had to ask if instead it was conscionable, based on the defendant's state of knowledge, that he should retain the proceeds of the property.

On the facts it was not unconscionable that the defendant should retain the proceeds of the property. He had simply sold his shares on the basis of rumours that he had heard about the dealings of BCCI. He had simply made a commercial decision to sell his shares.

There is an alternative way to consider recipient liability. Lord Millett described the nature of recipient liability in *Twinsectra Ltd v Yardley*[88] as being based on the defendant simply receiving money. There was no requirement that the defendant should be at fault. He said that a claim for recipient liability was a restitutionary one.

In *Twinsectra*, Lord Millett left open the possibility that, as the claim was essentially restitutionary based, the change of position defence[89] may be available to a defendant.

In *BCCI (Overseas) Ltd v Akindele*, Nourse LJ, with whom Ward and Sedley LJJ agreed, preferred not to adopt that restitutionary analysis of a claim for recipient liability. He thought that such an approach would, of course, result in the recipient being strictly liable for the receipt of property, subject only to relying successfully on the change of position defence. He pointed out that, on the facts of the case before him, it seemed harsh that the burden of proof should switch to the defendant to escape liability only by showing that he had innocently changed his position when liability would arise simply due to the internal workings of a company that the defendant would know nothing about.

At present, it seems that recipient liability is based on tracing the claimant's property to the defendant. If it would be unconscionable for the defendant to retain the benefit of the property, he will be made a constructive trustee of it. That is equity applying to govern the position. It will be interesting to see if future decisions of the higher courts retain this approach, or pursue Lord Millett's restitutionary-based approach.

Points to Review

You have seen:

- that both common law and equity give an owner of property the ability to trace that property into another person's hands and to reclaim it, or its proceeds;
- that tracing is a process and not the final remedy. Tracing at common law involves tracing the legal estate in the property and returning it to the legal owner. Tracing in equity

---

88 *Twinsectra Ltd v Yardley* [2002] 2 AC 164 at 194.

89 As enunciated in *Lipkin Gorman v Karpnale Ltd* [1991] 2 AC 548.

(where the beneficial interest is followed) is more flexible, as it is possible to follow property where it has been mixed with other property; and

● tracing is the process to eventual remedies against strangers who have dealt with trust property, through accessory or recipient liability. Accessory liability depends on proving the dishonesty of the recipient; recipient liability depends on showing that it would be unconscionable for the defendant to retain the proceeds of the property.

Making connections

This chapter has considered the key process of tracing and how that leads to remedies against people who have received or assisted in a breach of trust. It forms part of the general area of remedies for a breach of trust and so should be read in conjunction with personal remedies that may be pursued against the trustee in Chapter 12.

As the eventual remedy that tracing leads to is a constructive trust, you are advised to re-read Chapter 3, which deals with how a constructive trust operates.

 Useful Things to Read

The best reading is contained in the primary sources listed below. It is always good to consider the decisions of the courts themselves, as this will lead to a deeper understanding of the issues involved. A few secondary sources are also listed, which you may wish to read to gain additional insights into the areas considered in this chapter.

Primary sources

Banque Belge pour L'Etranger v Hambrouck [1921] 1 KB 321.
Barlow Clowes International Ltd (in liquidation) v Eurotrust International Ltd [2006] 1 WLR 1476.
BCCI (Overseas) Ltd v Akindele [2001] Ch 437.
Boscawen v Bajwa [1996] 1 WLR 328.
Foscett v McKeown [2001] 1 AC 102.
Lipkin Gorman v Karpnale Ltd [1991] 2 AC 548.
Royal Brunei Airlines v Tan [1995] 2 AC 378.
Sinclair Investments (UK) Ltd v Versailles Trade Finance Ltd (in administrative receivership) [2011] Bus LR 1126.
Starglade Properties Ltd v Nash [2010] EWCA Civ 1314.
Twinsectra Ltd v Yardley [2002] 2 AC 164.

Secondary sources

Matthew Conaglen, 'Difficulties with tracing backwards' (2011) LQR 127 (Jul) 432. This considers so-called 'backwards' tracing, which appears to have occurred on the facts of *Foskett v McKeown* but which the English courts seem reluctant to recognise. The article suggests that the arguments prohibiting backwards tracing contain weaknesses.

David Hayton, 'The extent of equitable remedies: Privy Council versus Court of Appeal' (2012) 33(6) Comp Law 161–164. This considers the judgment of the Court of Appeal in *Sinclair Investments (UK) Ltd v Versailles Trade Finance Ltd (In Administration)* and whether it was right for the court to follow one of its own judgments which had not been followed by the Privy Council in *Attorney-General for Hong Kong v Reid*.

Alastair Hudson, *Equity & Trusts* (7th edn, Routledge-Cavendish, 2012) chs 19 and 20.

Charles Mitchell, 'Dishonest assistance, knowing receipt and the law of limitation' (2008) Conv 3, 226–237. A good overview of the two actions that can be brought against a third party for participating in a breach of trust: accessory and recipient liability.

Mark Pawlowski, 'Tracing into improvements, debts and overdrawn accounts' (2011) 17(5) T & T 411–414. This looks at the extent to which money can be traced in equity which has been used by an innocent volunteer to make improvements to property, pay off a debt or make a payment into an overdrawn bank account.

Mohamed Ramjohn, *Text, Cases and Materials on Equity & Trusts* (4th edn, Routledge-Cavendish, 2008) pp 575–612 and ch 11.

Lionel Smith, 'Tracing in *Taylor v Plumer*: Equity in the Court of King's Bench' [1995] LMCLQ 240–268. A detailed review of the first key decision involving tracing: *Taylor v Plumer*.

Chapter 14

Trusts of the Family Home

This chapter concerns equity's treatment of the family home and when one party may claim that they are entitled to a share in that home because they are the beneficiary of a trust even though they do not also own the legal estate. This is a modern application of the law of trusts. This chapter therefore builds upon your knowledge of resulting and constructive trusts, which are discussed in Chapter 3. You are advised to re-read Chapter 3 if you are unfamiliar with such trusts before progressing to the rest of this chapter.

As You Read

Look out for the following matters:

- that this area can be broken down into two broad questions: can a trust be established and, if so, what shares are the parties to be treated as owning in equity? and
- that equity traditionally used the resulting trust to establish and quantify the shares owned by the parties but over the last 15 years, there has been a shift in emphasis to make more use of the constructive trust.

The Typical Scenario

The typical scenario involves a home being bought in one of the party's sole names following which, at some later point, the parties' relationship breaks down. At that stage, to claim a beneficial share in the property, the non-owning party of the legal estate must rely on equity to intervene: their claim is based on the argument that their partner held the legal estate on trust for the two of them together. The non-owning party's position may be summed up in Figure 14.1.

An unmarried couple

↓

share a property together

↓

but the legal estate is registered in one of their names only

↓

the relationship breaks down

↓

who owns the equitable interest?

Figure 14.1 The argument for a trust of the family home.

The establishment and quantification of an interest in the family home by using the law of trusts applies nowadays only to unmarried couples. From 1973, the Matrimonial Causes Act has given the court a wide discretion to make a property adjustment order (which will alter a couple's beneficial interest in their home) on a divorce, provided the couple were married on or after the date the Act came into force.[1] No such power exists for the court when an unmarried couple's relationship ends and whether the non-legally owning party may claim a beneficial interest in the family home is regulated by the law of trusts.

The relationship with the rules of formality

As discussed in Chapter 4, s 53(1)(b) of the Law of Property Act 1925 provides that any declaration of a trust concerning land must be evidenced in writing and signed by a person who is able to declare the trust. The usual difficulty in dealing with an unmarried couple's rights to their home is that they will not have fulfilled the requirements of s 53(1)(b) when they purchased the property. *Prima facie*, it appears therefore that there can be no valid declaration of trust and the legal owner must also be the sole beneficial owner.

Fortunately, s 53(2) of the Law of Property Act 1925 comes to the rescue of the non-legal owner. If the non-legal owner can establish a resulting or constructive trust in their favour, s 53(2) proves that such trusts need not be evidenced in writing.

Case law pre-*Lloyds Bank v Rosset*

The leading case on this area of law today is the 1990 decision of the House of Lords in *Lloyds Bank v Rosset*.[2] To understand that decision, however, it is important to consider certain key decisions of the superior courts before then. The first occasion in modern times that the House of Lords had to consider a claim for a beneficial interest under a trust of a family home where the legal title had been vested solely in one party's name was *Pettitt v Pettitt*.[3]

Harold Pettitt and his wife, Hilda, were married[4] in 1952. They lived in a house which they had built themselves, called 'Tinker's Cottage', in Bexhill-on-Sea, Sussex. They had been able to fund the building of the property by selling their only previous matrimonial home, which had been given to Hilda by her grandmother. Tinker's Cottage was bought in Hilda's name only. Their relationship broke down and Hilda moved out of the house.

Harold applied for a declaration from the court that he had an equitable interest in Tinker's Cottage. His claim was based on the fact that he had undertaken work on Tinker's Cottage which had enhanced its market value by, he estimated, £1,000. He said that s 17 of the Married Women's Property Act 1882 gave the court the discretion to override and vary any existing rights in property and to regulate the parties' equitable ownership in whatever way the court thought fit.

The County Court registrar and the Court of Appeal both agreed that Harold had an equitable interest in the property. They agreed that his equitable interest was worth £300. Hilda appealed to the House of Lords.

The House of Lords held that Harold had no equitable interest in the cottage. Their Lordships held that s 17 of the Married Women's Property Act 1882 should be narrowly construed. It could not have been Parliament's intention to give a judge *carte blanche* to vary parties' existing property rights. Such would create uncertainty in the law. Parties' equitable rights had to be settled by means of established principles of trusts law. Unfortunately, the members of the House of Lords could not agree on one uniform set of established principles.

---

1   Similar provisions exist for civil partnerships: Civil Partnership Act 2004, s 66(2).
2   *Lloyds Bank plc v Rosset* [1991] 1 AC 107.
3   *Pettitt v Pettitt* [1970] AC 777.
4   Although Mr and Mrs Pettitt were married, this case remains a key case on the law of trusts regulating parties' beneficial interests in real property as the case occurred before the enactment of the Matrimonial Causes Act 1973.

Lord Reid said that traditionally the issue had been divided into a non-owning party making (i) a contribution to the purchase price and (ii) an improvement to the property after it had been bought. Contributions to the purchase price would normally give rise to an equitable interest. Improvements carried out after the property had been purchased would not, unless an agreement had been made between the parties that the improvements would create an equitable interest.

On the facts, he was not willing to hold that Harold had acquired an interest in Tinker's Cottage. The improvements he had carried out were too temporary in nature to acquire an equitable interest in the property. The improvements essentially had to be of either a capital or recurring nature to lead to the acquisition of an equitable interest.

Lord Upjohn held that the equitable ownership of property had to depend on the agreement of the parties at the time they acquired the property. That meant looking at the conveyance (or 'transfer' document nowadays) under which the parties bought the property. If the transfer spelt out who was to own the equitable interest, that was the end of the matter, unless fraud or mistake could be found.

If the transfer was silent as to equitable ownership, Lord Upjohn thought that the court might be able to 'draw an inference as to their intentions [as to equitable ownership] from their conduct'.[5] Such conduct could only be at the time the property was acquired and not afterwards. If no such evidence was forthcoming, the court could apply legal presumptions:

(a)   if the legal title to the property was vested in one party's name only, that party will also own all of the equitable interest, even if the property was to be used for the benefit of both parties during their marriage;

(b)   if the legal title was vested in two parties' joint names, both parties would own the equitable interest. *Prima facie*, those parties would hold the equitable interest as joint tenants (hence equally) but normally this would not be the case. Usually, the doctrine of the resulting trust would apply which would mean that both parties held the equitable interest in proportion to their contributions to the purchase price; but

(c)   if both parties had contributed towards the purchase price, whether or not the legal title was vested in their joint names or solely in one party's name, their intention was that they intended to be joint equitable owners, due to the application of the resulting trust presumption.

As can be seen, Lord Upjohn relied heavily on the notion of the resulting trust.

Lord Upjohn rejected the notion that property could be bought by one person but owned as a 'family asset' which would give rise, due to it being acquired for use by the family, to other members of the family acquiring an equitable interest in that property. English law did not recognise 'family assets'. Equitable interests should not be accidentally created in favour of spouses because property was allegedly intended to be used as a family asset. More was needed than this to create an equitable interest in property: what was needed was an agreement between the spouses that they would share the equitable ownership.

Here there was no agreement that Harold and Hilda should share the property between them. Nor could one be inferred by their conduct at the time the land for Tinker's Cottage was purchased.

---

5   Ibid at 813.

Pettitt v Pettitt was considered by the House of Lords just over a year later in *Gissing v Gissing*.[6]

Raymond Gissing married Violet in 1935. In 1951, Raymond bought a home for them in Orpington, Kent. The majority of the purchase price of nearly £2,700 was paid by a mortgage and a loan from Raymond's employer. Raymond paid the small balance due and the legal costs. The legal title to the house was transferred to him alone. During their time living in the house, Raymond paid the mortgage. Violet spent £200 on furniture and remedial work on their lawn. In 1961, the parties' relationship broke down and Raymond left the matrimonial home. Violet applied to the court for a declaration that she had an equitable interest in the house. Her claim was on the basis that her indirect contributions to the property should be reflected in a half-share of the house. She effectively said that it was due to her contributions that Raymond was able to work and be paid a sufficient sum to purchase the property intially and then pay the mortgage instalments.

The trial judge held that Violet had no equitable interest in the property. By majority, the Court of Appeal reversed this decision. Raymond appealed to the House of Lords. The House of Lords restored the trial judge's decision and held that the equitable interest in the house belonged solely to Raymond.

Lord Diplock (who had also been in *Pettitt v Pettitt*) explained that the principle behind the recognition of an equitable interest by a non-legal owner was that the law of trusts was seeking to give effect to an implied trust created by the parties:

> in connection with the acquisition by the trustee of a legal estate in land, whenever the trustee *has so conducted himself* that it would be inequitable to allow him to deny to the [beneficiary] a beneficial interest in the land acquired.[7]

Such a trust would be recognised because the court could infer – based on the evidence – that there was a common intention by the parties to share the property in equity. Lord Diplock accepted that he had probably been wrong in *Pettitt v Pettitt* to say that a trust could be imputed (imposed) onto the situation. The trust could be inferred by one of two methods:

(a) where the parties had come to an express agreement to share the equitable interest. The express agreement had to contain an obligation on the non-legal owning spouse to act on it by contributing to the purchase price of the property, or paying the instalments under the mortgage. If there was no such obligation on the spouse, she would be a volunteer and equity would, of course, not assist a volunteer; or

(b) where the conduct of the legal owner had induced the non-legal owner to act to her detriment in the belief that she would obtain an equitable interest in the property.

If a wife used part of her earnings to pay joint household bills that otherwise the husband would have to pay, which enabled him to pay the mortgage instalments, that would be corroborative of a common intention to share the equitable ownership of the property.

In terms of valuing a contribution to the purchase price, the resulting trust mechanism could be used: the non-legal owner would therefore be entitled to a share in the property in proportion to the amount originally contributed towards its purchase or subsequently paid in mortgage instalments. Both contributions went towards acquiring the property itself and therefore entitled the contributor to a share in it.

---

6   *Gissing v Gissing* [1971] AC 886.
7   Ibid at 905 (emphasis added).

If, however, the court could not find a common intention between the parties to share the equitable ownership of the property, the court could not award her a share just because she made contributions to the household expenses. All such contributions showed – without a common intention to share the property – was a common intention to share in the property's expenses. On the facts, Violet had simply provided money for chattels for the family's use. That could not give rise to a common intention to share the equitable interest in the freehold of the house. Those contributions did not go so far as to enable Raymond to meet the mortgage expenses by relieving him of other financial burdens.

Summary of *Pettitt v Pettitt* and *Gissing v Gissing*

In both *Pettitt v Pettitt* and *Gissing v Gissing*, members of the House of Lords laid down a fairly narrow test for recognising that a non-legal owning spouse should be entitled to an equitable interest in the property. The key is that there had to be a common intention, possessed by the parties, that they should share the property in equity. In turn, that common intention could be evidenced by an agreement or by detrimental reliance by the non-legally owning party.

Developments by Lord Denning MR . . .

At first glance, a more generous result appears to have been reached for the non-legally owning spouse by Lord Denning MR in the Court of Appeal's decision in *Eves v Eves*.[8]

Janet Eves met Stuart Eves when she was 19. They moved into a house together in Romford, Essex. They were not married, although Janet changed her surname to Stuart's. The house was bought solely by Stuart – partly by the proceeds of his former home and partly by a mortgage in his name alone. Stuart told Janet that he would have put the legal title into their joint names but he could not as Janet was under 21. He later admitted this was a lie and that he never intended the property to be in their joint names.

After moving in, Janet did a lot of heavy work to the property by, for example, breaking up concrete using a 14lb sledgehammer and helping to construct a new shed. She and Stuart had two children. Then, four years after meeting, Stuart told Janet that he intended to marry another woman, Gloria. Janet applied for a share of the property, even though the legal title was solely owned by Stuart. The Court of Appeal unanimously held that Stuart held the property on trust for himself and Janet, but the members of the court did so for different reasons.

Lord Denning MR quoted Lord Diplock in *Gissing v Gissing*, focusing on Lord Diplock's assertion that an implied trust could be imposed 'whenever the trustee has so conducted himself that it would be inequitable to allow him to deny [the beneficiary] a beneficial interest'. He said the imposition of a constructive trust to the facts in the case before him showed that '[e]quity is not past the age of child bearing'[9] to help a claimant such as Janet. He also quoted[10] his own earlier judgment in *Cooke v Head*[11] that:

> whenever two parties by their joint efforts acquire property to be used for their joint benefit, the courts may impose or impute a constructive or resulting trust.

---

8 *Eves v Eves* [1975] 1 WLR 1338.
9 Ibid at 1341.
10 Ibid.
11 *Cooke v Head* [1972] 1 WLR 518 at 520.

Lord Denning MR felt that the house had been acquired by both Janet and Stuart. Stuart had contributed financially. Janet had contributed by non-financial means. Both, however, had contributed with the shared intention that it should be their joint property. Lord Denning MR felt that his conduct meant that Stuart had effectively declared a trust of the property for them both as equitable owners. Janet was to be awarded a quarter share of the house.

The difficulty with Lord Denning MR's judgment is not in the result that was reached, but in that it seems to recognise the concept of a 'family asset' rejected by Lord Upjohn in *Pettitt v Pettitt*. In addition, Lord Denning MR sought to go further than a constructive trust had gone previously. Prior to this case, constructive trusts had been recognised by the courts as arising from particular facts; Denning wanted to go further by imposing – or imputing – a constructive trust on particular facts, effectively as a measure of doing justice between the parties. This was part of his greater scheme to develop the remedial constructive trust in English law which would have used the constructive trust as a proactive remedy, as opposed to it being used reactively to recognise a party's legitimate claim.[12] The imputation of a constructive trust had been rejected by the majority in *Pettitt v Pettitt* and by its only proponent in that case, Lord Diplock, in *Gissing v Gissing*.

Brightman J (with whom Browne LJ agreed) was of the same view that Janet should be awarded a quarter share of the house, but for more conventional reasons than Lord Denning MR. He focused on Stuart's lie that he would have put the legal title into their joint names but could not as Janet was under 21. He said that such lie gave a 'clear inference'[13] that she was intended to have an interest in the property. That could be seen to be agreement to share the property. Brightman J said that, without more, that agreement would be a voluntary declaration of trust. Equity would not help Janet as she would be a volunteer. But there was more here: the agreement was that Janet would gain a share in the property provided she contributed in labour towards the acquisition of the house. There was little reason to suppose that Janet would have undertaken such heavy work in the property unless she was to acquire an equitable interest.

Brightman J and Browne LJ's reasoning was more consistent with the jurisprudence expressed by the House of Lords in *Pettitt v Pettitt* and *Gissing v Gissing*. Stuart and Janet could be said to have made an agreement that she would be entitled to a beneficial share of the property. She acted (significantly) to her detriment on that agreement. Lord Denning MR was, not for the first time, seeking to develop equity on the principled basis of justice in the case, whilst giving little time to certainty. This sounds attractive but it might, for instance, be difficult to judge in successive cases whether property had been acquired by two people for their joint benefit. It is far preferable to find either an agreement between the parties or particular conduct by the legal owner to recognise that a trust should be inferred between the parties. In that way, each case may be evidence-led, instead of being subject to judicial whim.

❖ ANALYSING THE LAW

Do you think there was really an agreement between Janet and Stuart Eves to share their house in equity? Was there, in fact, *no* agreement as he had deliberately set out *not* to be a joint legal owner with her? Do you find the majority's view in the Court of Appeal convincing?

---

12 For a fuller discussion on the remedial constructive trust, see Chapter 3 (pp 76–78).
13 *Eves v Eves* [1975] 1 WLR 1338 at 1344.

It was partly due to Lord Denning MR's attempt to develop equity to recognise jointly acquired property that led to the House of Lords restating when a trust might be imputed in the key decision in *Lloyds Bank v Rosset*.[14]

The Leading Case Today: *Lloyds Bank v Rosset*

A farmhouse in Thanet, Kent was purchased by Mr Rosset and he was registered as the sole legal owner. The house was bought partly with the aid of a mortgage from Lloyds Bank. After his marriage to his wife broke down, the bank claimed possession of the property to pay off his overdraft. Mrs Rosset resisted the claim. She argued that her husband held the property on trust for them both in equity. The trial judge and the Court of Appeal held that Mr Rosset held the property on trust for them both, but that her interest could not override the bank's mortgage as it was created after the bank's mortgage had been entered into.

Mrs Rosset's claim was that she and her husband had expressly agreed that the property was to be jointly owned and that, acting to her detriment, she had made a significant contribution towards acquiring the property by supervising extensive renovation works to make the farmhouse inhabitable.

In giving the only substantive opinion of the House of Lords, Lord Bridge drew a distinction between (i) sharing occupation and (ii) sharing the ownership of the asset of the matrimonial home. The former would be quite natural in a relationship. But it could not 'throw any light'[15] upon the latter, which was quite a separate issue.

Lord Bridge held that Mrs Rosset's conduct was not of a type that could give rise to the acquisition of an equitable interest in the property. She had merely helped out with the renovation works. Those were entirely natural acts for a spouse to undertake when a dilapidated house had been purchased. The actions were not sufficient detrimental conduct which could support any arrangement that she should be entitled to an equitable interest in the property.

Lord Bridge held that it was a constructive trust that the non-legally owning party sought to establish. He also recognised that guidance needed to be given as to when that trust could be recognised in this type of situation. He said it could arise on either one of two occasions:

(a) When there is – prior to acquiring the property or exceptionally afterwards – an agreement between the parties that they would share the equitable interest in it. That could only be based on express discussions. But those discussions could be 'imperfectly remembered'[16] and their terms 'imprecise'.[17] In addition, the claiming partner would have to show that they acted to their detriment or 'signficantly'[18] altered their position to create a constructive trust or a claim in proprietary estoppel. There was no evidence of such an agreement between the parties on the facts of the case itself; or

(b) when there is no evidence of any express agreement, a constructive trust could be acknowledged by the court based on the parties' common intention to share the property. In this scenario, Lord Bridge said that only 'direct contributions' to the purchase price of the property – initially when the property was bought or later by paying mortgage instalments – would be acceptable as the common intention relied

---

14 *Lloyds Bank v Rosset* [1991] 1 AC 107.
15 Ibid at 130 per Lord Bridge.
16 Ibid at 132.
17 Ibid.
18 Ibid.

upon by the non-legally owning party. Mrs Rosset made no such direct contributions towards the purchase price of the property.

Lord Bridge said that both *Pettitt v Pettitt* and *Gissing v Gissing* were examples of his second category of constructive trust. He approved of *Eves v Eves*[19] as an example of a constructive trust falling in the first category.

Whilst Lord Bridge's first type of constructive trust is clear, it must be questioned as to how appropriate it is to infer a trust on an alleged express agreement between two parties who probably gave little thought to sharing the beneficial interest in their home at a time when their relationship was new. As Waite J said in *Hammond v Mitchell*:[20]

> the tenderest exchanges of a common law courtship may assume an unforeseen significance many years later when they are brought under equity's microscope and subjected to an analysis under which many thousands of pounds of value may be liable to turn on fine questions as to whether the relevant words were spoken in earnest or in dalliance and with or without representational intent.

Lord Bridge distinguished between the type of detrimental conduct needed by a claimant in both cases. The detrimental conduct needed to establish a constructive trust in his first category was less than that needed in his second category. Janet Eves, for example, had been able to establish a trust in her favour due to the heavy DIY work she had undertaken. That was because she could demonstrate that there had existed an express agreement for her and Stuart to share the property beneficially. Her heavy DIY work would not have been sufficient conduct to establish a constructive trust of the second category, in the absence of any express agreement. She would have needed to show direct financial contribution to the acquisition of the property, either initially, or by making mortgage instalment payments.

Key Learning Point

A *constructive* trust of the home can only be acquired by one of two methods:

(a) express agreement + some detrimental reliance. This will now be referred to as a '*Rosset* category 1 trust'; or

(b) the parties' conduct but such conduct can only be making (a) direct contributions to the purchase price of the property or (b) mortgage payments. This will now be referred to as a '*Rosset* category 2 trust'.

This issue has recently returned to the Supreme Court in *Jones v Kernott*.[21] The facts of *Jones v Kernott* concerned the right approach that the court should take when quantifying beneficial ownership when the parties had not done so for themselves when they purchased the property. Unfortunately, very little was said about the establishment of the trust and the decision in *Lloyds Bank v Rosset* was not mentioned at all. *Rosset* remains the leading authority as

---

19 Along with *Grant v Edwards* [1986] Ch 638.
20 *Hammond v Mitchell* [1991] 1 WLR 1127 at 1139.
21 *Jones v Kernott* [2011] UKSC 53. The facts of this case are considered at p. 399.

to when a trust of the family home may be established and it is now time to turn to when the courts have held that such a trust has been created.

Examples of *Rosset* category 1 trusts

In his opinion in *Lloyds Bank v Rosset*, Lord Bridge expressly approved[22] the earlier cases of *Eves v Eves* and *Grant v Edwards* as examples of where a trust would be recognised by the courts in his first category: where the parties made an express agreement to share the beneficial interest and it had been acted upon by the non-legal owner to their detriment. These are sometimes referred to as the 'excuse' cases: where the court found an intention to share the equitable interest because the legal owner used a fairly flimsy excuse not to put the legal title into joint names.

The 'excuse' cases . . .

Eves v Eves has already been considered. There the legal interest in the house was owned by Stuart at law, but Janet was able to show that he held it on trust for them both in equity. This was based on his promise to her that they would both have owned the legal interest were she not under 21. In *Lloyds Bank v Rosset*, Lord Bridge viewed that promise as a clear indication by Stuart to Janet that the house would be owned by them jointly. Janet had acted to her detriment on that promise by undertaking the significant renovation works to the property.

Not dissimilar circumstances arose in *Grant v Edwards*. Linda Grant met George Edwards in the late 1960s and they moved in with each other. Both of their previous marriages had broken down and each was in the process of obtaining a divorce from their former spouses. They decided to purchase a house together in London, but the legal interest was registered in the name of George with his brother, Arthur. This was done so that Arthur's income could be taken into account in obtaining a mortgage to purchase the house. George told Linda that she should not own the house as that would prejudice any settlement she was to obtain from her former husband in their divorce proceedings. This was a lie. George never had any intention of ensuring that Linda also became an owner of the house. After they had moved in together, Linda made contributions towards the general household expenses and to the raising of the children.

The Court of Appeal held that there was a common intention to share the property beneficially. This could be inferred from the excuse given by George to Linda as to why the legal interest in the property would not be registered in their joint names. Nourse LJ said that George only used the excuse that putting the house into their joint names would prejudice Linda's divorce settlement for the very reason that he had an intention that they should share the ownership of it. Linda had acted to her detriment on the agreement that they had reached by making significant contributions to the household expenses and bringing up the children. Her contributions enabled George to make the mortgage payments.

Nourse LJ questioned the type of conduct that was needed by the non-owning party to establish an equitable interest under this category of trust. He said it had to be, 'conduct on which the woman could not reasonably have been expected to embark unless she was to have an interest in the house'.[23]

That meant that there was a certain basic 'level' of conduct that a non-legally owning party would have to show before the court could infer a constructive trust in their favour. There had

---

22 *Lloyds Bank v Rosset* [1991] 1 AC 107 at 133.
23 *Grant v Edwards* [1986] Ch 638 at 648.

to be some connection between the conduct they undertook and the point that they only under-took it because they expected to acquire an equitable interest in the property. Janet wielding a 14lb sledgehammer in *Eves v Eves* was an example cited by Nourse LJ: she only undertook such work because it could objectively be said that she intended to acquire an equitable interest in the property. On the other hand, Nourse LJ said that merely moving in with the legal owner would not amount to conduct required to establish an equitable interest: the law was 'not so cynical as to infer that a woman will only go to live with a man to whom she is not married if she understands that she is to have an interest in their home'.[24]

It is suggested that it is hard to disagree with the eventual decisions of the Court of Appeal in both *Eves v Eves* and *Grant v Edwards*. Both non-legally owning spouses had been misled by their partners and both had made significant contributions to their households. On first principles, it might be thought of as 'fair' that both Janet Eves and Linda Grant should be seen to enjoy equitable interests in their houses. But, it is also suggested that it is hard to see evidence of direct agreements between them and their respective partners to share their properties beneficially.[25] In both cases, the Court of Appeal found evidence of agreement on the basis that their partners misled them only because they realised that they intended to share the property. Yet it is equally plausible to argue that there was no evidence of an agreement to share the properties at all: that was the reason why the excuses were given to Janet and Linda. *Hammond v Mitchell*,[26] however, is one of the very few examples of cases in this area that does show evidence of a clear agreement to share the equitable ownership of the property.

A clear agreement case . . .

Tom Hammond met Vicky Mitchell in 1977. They moved into a bungalow in Essex together in 1979. The legal title to the property was registered in Tom's sole name. He was in the process of obtaining a divorce, but whilst they were looking at the bungalow before buying it, he said to Vicky, '[d]on't worry about the future because when we are married it will be half yours anyway and I'll always look after you'.[27]

In fact, the parties never did marry although Tom did obtain a divorce from his wife. Throughout their relationship, he developed his business of buying and selling household goods with her support. She would, for example, place advertisements, sell goods on his behalf and act as his secretary. His business expanded to buying a business in Spain and both Tom, Vicky and their children went to live in Spain for two years, during which she helped out running the Spanish business. A house in Valencia was bought, again with Tom as the sole legal owner. Their relationship finally broke down in 1989. Vicky brought a claim for a beneficial interest in the bungalow and the house in Spain.

Waite J held that there was an agreement between the two parties to share the Essex bungalow beneficially. There was an express discussion on the ownership of it, which culmi-nated in Tom's promise to look after Vicky and that they would each be entitled to a half share of the property. She had relied on that by helping out with Tom's speculative business ventures, which might have resulted in the bungalow having to be sold to pay debts incurred in those ventures had they not turned out successfully. That was ample detrimental reliance to establish a share in the property.

Waite J did not find, however, that there had ever been any agreement to share the benefi-cial ownership of the Spanish property. As Vicky had not contributed to the initial deposit or

---

24 Ibid.
25 As recognised by Mustill LJ in *Grant v Edwards* [1986] Ch 638 at 653.
26 *Hammond v Mitchell* [1991] 1 WLR 1127.
27 Ibid at 1131.

mortgage payments for that house, she was not able to show a trust should be inferred in her favour in terms of Lord Bridge's second category of constructive trust in Lloyds Bank v Rosset.

The Essex bungalow had been expanded over the years of their relationship as Tom had purchased adjoining fields. Was there an intention that she should be a beneficial owner of those fields too, or was that intention limited to the purchase of the initial property? Waite J said that in every such case it would be a 'question of fact and degree'[28] whether the trust was to be extended to additional property. That had to be determined by 'a review of the whole course of dealing between the parties'.[29] On the facts, he found that the parties' intention was that it was the bungalow, as it became enlarged by the additional land, which was to be shared beneficially, as the entire property was to be subject to the same agreement that it should be shared beneficially.

Time for assessing detrimental reliance in a *Rosset* category 1 trust

In Lloyds Bank v Rosset, Lord Bridge had made it clear that the amount of detrimental reliance that the non-legally owning party had to show for this category of trust was quite small. In Levi v Levi,[30] the High Court believed, however, that although little detrimental reliance was needed, whether or not there was reliance had to be assessed at the end of the conduct relied upon, not at the start.

The facts concerned the purchase of a council house. Mrs Hakak had left her interest in her council house to her son, Isaac. After her death, he purchased it with the aid of a mortgage but also by using £4,267 from the half share of his mother's estate which rightfully belonged to his sister, Sherone. She seemingly accepted this arrangement, because she was willing to lend him a further sum of £5,000 if he wished. In the event, this offer of a loan was not taken up by Isaac.

Isaac repaid the £4,267 to Sherone. He later sold the property for £385,000. Sherone argued that Isaac had held the beneficial interest on trust for both of them, based on an agreement reached between them. She argued that her willingness to advance a loan to Isaac was evidence of her detrimental reliance on that agreement.

The judge, Geoffrey Vos QC, held that whether something constituted detrimental reliance had to turn on the facts of each case. A loan could be used as evidence of detrimental reliance here as Sherone was not to be repaid her money until the property was sold which was an event over which she had no control. The loan had never been taken up by Isaac. The detrimental reliance had to be judged at the end of the conduct in issue, not at the start. That meant the court had to take account of all of the facts surrounding the alleged conduct. It was crucial here that the loan was never taken up by Isaac and so, despite its offer by Sherone, there was no detrimental reliance by her on the agreement to share the property beneficially.

Rosset category 1 trusts: The agreement must be shared between the parties

If this type of trust is to be successfully established, it must be based on a common intention that is shared between the parties. As Steyn LJ put it in Springette v Defoe,[31] 'trust law does not allow property rights to be affected by telepathy'. It is not enough that each party may have even had the same thoughts as to beneficial ownership as the other party: those thoughts must have been communicated between them so that an agreement to share is reached.

Statements made by the legally-owning party must not be taken out of context when compared to other evidence available. In James v Thomas,[32] Sharon James argued that Peter

---

28 Ibid at 1137.
29 Ibid.
30 *Levi v Levi* [2008] 2 P & CR DG1.
31 *Springette v Defoe* (1993) 65 P & CR 1.
32 *James v Thomas* [2007] EWCA Civ 1212.

Thomas' promise that 'this will benefit us both' meant that the improvements they carried out together on their home was sufficient to establish a trust in her favour. Sir John Chadwick pointed out that the court could not ignore other compelling evidence against the establishing of that trust, such as Peter being evasive and unwilling to transfer the property into their joint names when she specifically raised it with him.

In *Grant v Edwards*, Nourse LJ described this first category of trust as being 'rarer'[33] than the second category.[34] That is because if the non-owning party has made payments towards the purchase of the property, either through the initial deposit or mortgage instalments, those actions can be used to establish both the existence of a common intention to share the beneficial interest in the property and provide the evidence to show that the claimant has acted upon it to establish their constructive trust. The number of cases in the first category may well be fewer as it is not usual for parties to make an express agreement that they will share the beneficial ownership in their new home. When setting up a new home together, parties are much more concerned with the day-to-day practicalities of their relationship and do not usually have conversations about sharing the beneficial interest in the property.

Examples of *Rosset* category 2 trusts

To establish a trust of Lord Bridge's second category, there is no evidence of express agreement between the parties to share the property beneficially, coupled with detrimental reliance. Instead, the non-legally owning party must establish a common intention to share the property by conduct. Sir Peter Gibson spelt out the requirements of this second type of *Rosset* trust in *Morris v Morris*[35] as:

> the court should be satisfied that the relevant parties each had the intention, commu-
> nicated to each other, that, notwithstanding the paper title in [one party] and notwith-
> standing the absence of any writing, there should be a disposal of a beneficial
> interest in land to the claimant.

Lord Bridge in *Rosset* said that the only type of conduct that would be acceptable would be direct contributions by the non-legally owning party to the purchase price of the property, paying either the initial deposit or the mortgage.

❖ ANALYSING THE LAW

Lord Bridge was clear in *Rosset* that only 'direct contributions' towards the purchase price of the property would be enough to establish a category 2 trust. He referred to both categories of trust as constructive trusts.

Do you think, however, that the category 2 trust was, at least when recognised by Lord Bridge, essentially an example of a resulting trust? If so, why?

---

33 *Grant v Edwards* [1986] Ch 638 at 647.
34 Although in his later judgment in *Stokes v Anderson* [1991] 1 FLR 391, Nourse LJ thought he might have been wrong in saying these *Rosset* category 1 cases were rarer than the second category.
35 *Morris v Morris* [2008] EWCA Civ 257 at [19].

The bar for this second type of trust is higher than the first, because the court must go on clear evidence that the parties intended to share the ownership of the property, not just occupation of it or sharing their lives together. That is why it is only monetary contributions made directly towards the purchase price that will count here.

The House of Lords had held that the non-owning spouse had not established a trust through her non-monetary contributions to the household in both *Pettitt v Pettitt* and *Gissing v Gissing*. These cases were applied by the Court of Appeal in *Burns v Burns*.[36]

Patrick Burns met Valerie Burns in 1961 and two years later, a house was purchased which was legally owned by Patrick only. The majority of the purchase price was raised by a mortgage in his sole name. He also paid the balance of the price. There were never any discussions between the parties as to the ownership of the property. They split up in 1980, at which point Valerie claimed a share of the equitable interest.

During their relationship, Valerie made no payments towards the mortgage. She did not contribute towards the household expenses to relieve Patrick from doing so so that he could pay the mortgage although she did meet some household bills and bought some furniture.

The Court of Appeal held that Valerie had failed to establish a trust in her favour of the second type set out by Lord Bridge in *Rosset*, based on conduct. For this second type of trust to arise, '[w]hat is needed . . . is evidence of a payment or payments by the plaintiff which it can be inferred was referable to the acquisition of the house'.[37]

Paying bills and buying furniture was not connected to acquiring an interest in the property by common intention. Neither were undertaking domestic household tasks or raising the children. In the absence of any agreement to share the property beneficially, there was no conduct upon which Valerie could rely to establish a trust in her favour.

Cases have shown that the courts are prepared to take a relatively wide view of contributions which may show evidence of conduct upon which this type of trust may be based. In *Springette v Defoe*, Mr Defoe moved in to Miss Springette's council house and, as a result of Miss Springette being a council tenant for many years, she was able to purchase the property with the benefit of a 41 per cent discount from the sale price. Steyn LJ held that such discount could be seen to be a 'direct contribution'[38] by Miss Springette towards the purchase price. Although the property was registered in their joint names, she was held to be entitled to a larger share in the equitable interest of 75 per cent which represented her greater overall contribution to the purchase price of the property.[39]

In *Le Foe v Le Foe*,[40] Mr Le Foe initially paid the mortgage after their home was purchased, but his wife used money which she had inherited to pay off a lump sum from the mortgage debt. She then used the house as bed and breakfast premises which provided an income which was used to pay the mortgage instalments. The High Court held that such contributions could be used as evidence that Mrs Le Foe was entitled to a share in the equitable interest in the property.

A share of a wedding gift was held to be a direct contribution to the purchase price in *Midland Bank plc v Cooke*.[41] Mr Cooke purchased a house in Abbotsley, Cambridgeshire on 1 July 1971 in his sole name. The purchase price was £8,500. Of that, nearly £6,500 was

---

36 *Burns v Burns* [1984] Ch 317.
37 Ibid at 329 per Fox LJ.
38 Ibid at 8.
39 The exact method of quantification of the parties' shares in this case (based on a resulting trust) must now be treated with caution following the decision of the House of Lords in *Stack v Dowden*. The case remains authority, however, for contributions being slightly wider than 'pure' monetary ones either to the initial deposit or mortgage instalments.
40 *Le Foe v Le Foe* [2001] 2 FLR 970.
41 *Midland Bank plc v Cooke* (1995) 27 HLR 733.

provided by way of mortgage. Mr Cooke's parents gave £1,100 to the couple as a wedding gift and Mr Cooke provided the remainder of the money himself. Mrs Cooke made no payments to the mortgage during their relationship. In 1987, Midland Bank plc brought proceedings against them both, seeking repayment of its mortgage over the house. Mrs Cooke claimed, *inter alia*, a one-half share in the equitable interest in the house. There had been no agreement between them as to the equitable ownership of the property.

The Court of Appeal held that the wedding gift was a gift to both Mr and Mrs Cooke jointly and that it was appropriate to treat it as a contribution towards the purchase price of the property.

All of these decisions, however, concerned contributions made by a party to the purchase price of the property which fell squarely within Lord Bridge's dictum in *Rosset*. All of the contributions were concerned with financing the purchase of the property, either initially or through mortgage payments.

Indirect contributions: Are they enough to establish a *Rosset* second category trust?

The orthodox position is that only direct payments towards the purchase price of the property – whether at the time the property was bought or subsequently through paying mortgage instalments – are sufficient to establish a common intention trust based on the parties' conduct alone. That was what Lord Bridge had made clear in *Rosset*. Indirect contributions (such as, for example, raising a family so that a partner can earn money to meet mortgage repayments) are not, according to *Rosset*, capable of establishing a category 2 trust.

Somewhat ironically, the same indirect contributions have been seen to support the establishment of a *Rosset* category 1 trust. For example, Janet's contributions towards the renovation of the home in *Eves v Eves* amounted to sufficient detrimental reliance to support her claim to be entitled to a common intention trust based on an agreement between the parties. But this is because the law has distinguished between indirect contributions in terms of the two types of *Rosset* trusts. Less overall contribution is required for a *Rosset* category 1 trust because that is founded on an agreement. All the claimant needs to show is that they acted on that agreement. Much more is needed in a *Rosset* category 2 trust because the claimant is asking the court to draw the inference that they had a common intention to share the property beneficially. Lord Bridge in *Rosset* thought it right to set the bar higher, and accept only direct contributions to the purchase price, when establishing a *Rosset* category 2 trust.

In *Stack v Dowden*,[42] however, two members of the House of Lords thought that the law should go further in recognising different types of contributions which could show a common intention to create a trust of the family home. The case concerned the quantification of an equitable interest, not its establishment as the home had been registered in both parties' joint names, so the discussion of this decision which follows is of remarks made *obiter* by members of the House of Lords.

Lord Walker said that the crucial question in the establishment of a trust was whether the court had to find a 'real bargain between the parties or whether it can (in the absence of any sufficient evidence as to their real intentions) infer or impute a bargain'.[43] Lord Diplock in *Pettitt v Pettitt* had talked about the court imputing a trust but the other members of the House of Lords in that case generally talked about inferring one. One year later, in *Gissing v Gissing*, Lord Diplock accepted that he had been in the minority with this view and that a trust was to be

---

42 *Stack v Dowden* [2007] 2 AC 432.
43 Ibid at 442.

inferred based on the parties' conduct, not imposed (or imputed) upon the parties by the courts.

Lord Walker felt that Lord Bridge's second category of trust occurred because the court inferred the agreement between the parties. He felt that Lord Bridge had been too restrictive in holding that his second category of trust could only arise on making direct contributions to the purchase price of the property.

Lord Walker believed that the law should be developed to take more into account than just a party's direct contributions towards the cost of acquiring a property in terms of Lord Bridge's second category of constructive trust. He said the law should take:

> a wide view of what is capable of counting as a contribution towards the acquisition of a residence, while remaining sceptical of the value of alleged improvements that are really insignicant . . .[44]

Baroness Hale held that the law had 'indeed moved on in response to changing social and economic conditions'[45] from the dictum of Lord Bridge in Lloyds Bank v Rosset. She agreed with the Law Commission[46] that Lord Bridge might have set 'the hurdle rather too high'[47] in terms of the establishment of his second category of trust. But she felt no need to add further comments on the establishment of a constructive trust given that that issue was not before her.

In making these comments, Lord Walker and Baroness Hale were trying to steer the establishment of a Rosset category 2 trust into the arena of a 'true' constructive trust, rather than a disguised resulting trust being based solely on the premise that the paying party retained the equitable interest in the property for his sole benefit.

Baroness Hale went further when she delivered the opinion of the Privy Council in Abbott v Abbott[48] when she said:

> The law has indeed moved on since [Lloyds Bank v Rosset]. The parties' whole course of conduct in relation to the property must be taken into account in determining their shared intentions as to its ownership.[49]

It seems, however, that two decisions of the Court of Appeal since Stack v Dowden and Abbott v Abbott have shown no inclination to widen the types of contribution which may be used to establish a trust of Lord Bridge's second category.

James v Thomas[50] was the first decision of the Court of Appeal, delivered just seven months after Stack v Dowden. Peter Thomas had purchased a property near Whitchurch, Shropshire in 1985. Four years later, he met Sharon James. She moved in with him until their relationship ended in 2004. Peter ran his own building business and Sharon helped him with that, undertaking heavy manual work such as laying concrete and fetching materials. Both of them also carried out renovation works on the property. Sharon wanted a declaration that Peter held the property on trust for both of them.

---

44 Ibid at 448.
45 Ibid at 455.
46 Law Commission, *Sharing Homes, A Discussion Paper* (Law Com No. 278, 2002).
47 *Stack v Dowden* [2007] 2 AC 432 at 456.
48 *Abbott v Abbott* [2007] UKPC 53.
49 Ibid at [19].
50 *James v Thomas* [2007] EWCA Civ 1212.

The Court of Appeal held that Sharon had not established that Peter held the property on trust for them both. Her contributions to the business were just that: they did not establish that she had made contributions towards acquiring an interest in their home.

In delivering the only substantive judgment of the court, Sir John Chadwick believed that:

> in the absence of an express post-acquisition agreement, a court will be slow to infer from conduct alone that parties intended to vary existing beneficial interests established at the time of acquisition.[51]

The beneficial interest in the property was owned initially by Peter. Sharon was not able to show that her conduct in helping with the business or in renovating the property meant that she was entitled to a share in the property.

The Court of Appeal applied *Rosset* strictly: the contributions Sharon made were neither to the acquisition of the property initially (which was impossible on the facts) nor through the payment of the mortgage. As such, she was entitled to no interest in the property.

❖ ANALYSING THE LAW

Do you think in *James v Thomas* that the Court of Appeal should have acted on the comments of Lord Walker and Baroness Hale in *Stack v Dowden* and accepted a wider definition of the contributions that could establish a *Rosset* category 2 trust?

For instance, suppose you had moved into your partner's house and had undertaken the works that Sharon had. Would you expect your endeavours to be acknowledged by an interest in the property or would you be content to have no interest at all?

It might, however, be argued that it was entirely appropriate for the Court of Appeal to apply *Rosset* strictly on the facts of *James v Thomas*. Sharon James had moved into a house which had been in Peter's family for decades, made no contribution towards it and the work she had undertaken was to enhance the value of their business and lifestyle.

However, the Court of Appeal also declined to follow the comments of Lord Walker and Baroness Hale in a second case decided within a year of *Stack v Dowden*: *Morris v Morris*.[52]

The facts revolved around a farming business and a farm named Ty Canol Farm, situated in Caerphilly, Wales. The farm had been owned by generations of Richard Morris' family. Catherine met Richard in the early 1990s and they began to live together shortly afterwards. To begin with, she helped out in the farming business and then, from 1997 onwards, she started a riding school at the farm. Their relationship broke down in 2004. Richard's mother died a year later and left the farm to her grandchildren. Catherine began proceedings claiming a beneficial interest in the farm, arguing that the grandchildren held it on trust for her as a beneficiary. She based her claim on a *Rosset* second category trust: that she could establish a beneficial interest based on conduct.

At trial, Wyn Williams J held that Catherine was entitled to a beneficial share in the property based on conduct alone. He said that there was a common intention based on the parties' conduct that she should have an equitable interest. This could be evidenced from

---

51 Ibid at [24].
52 *Morris v Morris* [2008] EWCA Civ 257.

Catherine paying towards the construction of the riding school equipment, her business lending a large sum of money to the farm and, lastly, by her working free of charge for the farming business in the early years of her relationship with Richard. The judge awarded her a 25 per cent share of the farm. Richard appealed to the Court of Appeal.

Giving the leading judgment, Sir Peter Gibson quoted with approval[53] the comments of Sir John Chadwick in *James v Thomas* (quoted above) that the court will be slow to infer a common intention trust based on conduct alone. It may be thought that Sir Peter Gibson was limiting his approval to cases with similar facts to the one before him and *James v Thomas*, both cases in which the legal ownership of the property had been acquired many years before another party sought to establish an equitable interest in it. Sir Peter Gibson then reinforced his general point by emphasising that 'a common intention constructive trust based only on conduct will only be found in exceptional circumstances'.[54] He did not limit those comments to the case before him.

The Court of Appeal held that Catherine had no beneficial interest in the farm. Her evidence led to the conclusion that she had played an integral role in the business, not that she had expected to receive a beneficial interest in the farm itself. The money that she had paid towards the construction of the riding school equipment directly benefited her. It was her business that had lent the large sum of money to the farm and not her in a personal capacity.

It depends what view is taken over the two Court of Appeal decisions in *James v Thomas* and *Morris v Morris* as to whether the courts are likely to recognise other, indirect, contributions as being able to establish a trust of the family home. Both cases were unusual in that they concerned properties owned by one party for some time before the non-legally owning party sought to establish a beneficial interest. They were not 'classic' cases of both parties moving in together and buying their first home at the same time. Pragmatically, perhaps, the Court of Appeal was predisposed to find against both claimants in the two cases due to this. In turn, it is easy to see why the courts will be slow to infer a common intention trust based on conduct alone when it involves a significant change to the equitable ownership which has been established for many years by the time the claimant moves in. However, none of comments made limiting the recognition of such trusts are specifically restricted to just the cases in which they were made – they are all rather generalised, sweeping statements that the court will hesitate before recognising the *Rosset* second category of constructive trust. The door may still be open to future courts to take up the offer made by Lord Walker and Baroness Hale in *Stack v Dowden* to recognise other contributions to establish a trust but the subsequent comments in the two Court of Appeal decisions seem to leave that door open only for the Supreme Court.

Quantification of the Equitable Interest

If a trust can be established, the second issue for the court to decide is the amount of the equitable interest to which the beneficiary should entitled. The methods of quantifying the beneficial interest depend if the trust which has been found is a *Rosset* category 1 or 2.

Quantification of *Rosset* category 1 trusts

Rosset category 1 trusts are based upon the parties coming to an agreement to share the beneficial interest in the property. As such, *prima facie*, that agreement should be analysed to ascertain

---

53 Ibid at para.19. May LJ made similar comments at para. 36, as did Pill LJ at para. 45.
54 Ibid at para. 23.

if the parties went further than simply deciding to share the equitable interest and actually agreed the proportions in which they were to share the property. If they did, the court will recognise the shares that the parties intended each should have.[55] If additional land has been added to the original property, it is a question of fact and degree in each case for the court to ascertain if the trust should also bind that additional land: *Hammond v Mitchell*.[56]

In his opinion in *Rosset*, however, Lord Bridge was prepared to accept trusts as falling into this category even though their exact terms may be 'imprecise' and 'imperfectly remembered' by the parties.[57] It will probably be the case on many (if not most) occasions that the parties' agreement simply did not extend to quantifying their equitable interests. In this event, it seems that the court may take a 'broad brush'[58] approach to quantifying the parties' equitable interests: *Drake v Whipp*.[59]

Mrs Drake and Mr Whipp decided to buy a barn together. The barn was purchased in Mr Whipp's sole name in 1988. The purchase price was just over £61,000 and Mrs Drake contributed £25,000 with Mr Whipp providing the remainder. Extensive works were needed to convert the barn into a home. The works cost roughly £130,000 of which Mrs Drake paid £13,000 with Mr Whipp paying for the remainder. Both undertook renovation works themselves with Mr Whipp contributing 70 per cent and Mrs Drake 30 per cent of the overall man hours spent on the project. They shared a joint bank account and both of them had paid employment. Their salaries were paid into the joint account. Mrs Drake met the food and household bills. In 1992, Mrs Drake left the barn and sought a declaration that Mr Whipp held the property on trust for them both.

The trial judge found that a *Rosset* category 1 trust was established by Mrs Drake. He awarded Mrs Drake a 19.4 per cent share in the barn, based on a resulting trust. The resulting trust carried with it a presumption that the parties would share in the property in the proportions to which they had contributed to its acquisition.

Peter Gibson LJ held that the trial judge was wrong to hold that there was a resulting trust in Mrs Drake's favour. Rather, she had established a constructive trust. In constructive trust cases, 'the court can adopt a broad brush approach to determining the parties' respective shares'.[60] The court had to consider 'the parties' entire course of conduct together'.[61] This meant that not only would the court take into account the direct contributions both parties had made to the purchase price, but also indirect contributions such as:

(a)   they contributed their labour to the conversion works in a 70:30 ratio in favour of Mr Whipp;

(b)   they had a joint bank account from which the cost of the conversion works was paid but Mr Whipp's salary going into the account was always considerably more than Mrs Drake's; and

(c)   that Mrs Drake paid for the food for them both and the housekeeping money.

Applying this 'broad brush' approach and taking into account their direct and indirect contributions to the cost of acquiring the property, the right share for Mrs Drake was one-third of the overall beneficial interest.

---

55 Per Browne-Wilkinson V-C in *Grant v Edwards* [1986] Ch 638 at 657.
56 *Hammond v Mitchell* [1991] 1 WLR 1127.
57 *Lloyds Bank v Rosset* [1991] 1 AC 107 at 132.
58 *Drake v Whipp* (1996) 28 HLR 531 at 536 per Peter Gibson LJ.
59 *Drake v Whipp* (1996) 28 HLR 531.
60 Ibid at 536.
61 Ibid at 537.

It is clear, then, that when an agreement and detrimental reliance leads to the creation of a constructive trust but where the parties have not themselves quantified their shares, the court has a wide discretion over how a party's share should be calculated, taking into account the parties' entire conduct.

Quantification of *Rosset* category 2 trusts

The *Rosset* category 2 trust is created where the conduct undertaken by the parties shows evidence of a common intention to create a trust. Originally, that trust was seen to be a resulting trust which brought with it the relevant presumptions that apply to resulting trusts.[62] Lord Upjohn explained it thus in *Pettitt v Pettitt*:

> in the absence of evidence to the contrary if . . . the purchase money has been provided by two or more persons the property is held for those persons in proportion to the purchase money that they have provided.[63]

The courts were not prepared to value a party's non-monetary contributions, as Dillon LJ explained in *Walker v Hall*:[64]

> Equally it is not open to this court to "top up" [the non-legally owning party's] share, beyond which it would be on the basis of her financial contribution, on some broad notion of what would be fair simply because the house was bought as the family home . . .

The resulting trust approach continued in *Springette v Defoe*,[65] where both parties were the legal owners, albeit Dillon LJ held that the resulting trust approach could take into account parties' indirect contributions towards the acquisition of the property when quantifying equitable interests.

The courts began to move away from the resulting trust approach to quantification of the equitable interest in *Midland Bank plc v Cooke*.[66] There the Court of Appeal had to decide specifically how to quantify Mrs Cooke's interest in the property. Her *Rosset* category 2 trust had been recognised through her contribution of her half of the wedding present from Mr Cooke's parents. Waite LJ thought that the answer was not as straightforward as awarding her an interest based on a resulting trust approach. Instead:

> the duty of the judge is to undertake a survey of the whole course of dealing between the parties relevant to their ownership and occupation of the property and their sharing of its burdens and advantages.[67]

The court was not just to have regard to the direct contributions which had been needed to establish this type of trust initially. Instead the court 'will take into consideration *all conduct* which throws light on the question what shares were intended'.[68]

---

62 See Chapter 3.
63 *Pettitt v Pettitt* [1970] AC 777 at 814.
64 *Walker v Hall* [1984] FLR 126 at 134.
65 *Springette v Defoe* (1993) 65 P & CR 1.
66 *Midland Bank plc v Cooke* (1995) 27 HLR 733.
67 Ibid at 745.
68 Ibid (emphasis added).

Only if the search for any such conduct proved fruitless would the equitable maxim 'equity is equality' apply and the parties would hold their beneficial interests in equal shares.

The decision in Midland Bank plc v Cooke was that the parties owned the equitable interest in the house in equal shares. This was not because the court relied on the equitable maxim. It was because the evidence of the parties' conduct so informed the court. Indirect contributions could be taken into account: the parties had shared their lives equally. They were both responsible for repaying loans which they had taken out, they both brought up their children and Mr Cooke ploughed money into improving the family home, whilst Mrs Cooke contributed labour in undertaking those improvements.

Midland Bank plc v Cooke shows the Court of Appeal recognising the quantification of the second type of Rosset trust on constructive trust lines. Such an approach gives the court much more flexibility to quantify parties' shares than an approach based on a resulting trust tied into its legal presumptions. It also meant the court could take into account indirect, later contributions by both parties into valuing their equitable shares.

The different, more flexible, approach to quantification of this type of trust was developed further by Chadwick LJ in Oxley v Hiscock.[69]

Allan Hiscock and Elayne Oxley purchased a property in Hartley, Kent, in 1991. The purchase price of £127,000 was paid by three methods: (i) a mortgage of £30,000; (ii) Allan contributing £35,500 from his savings; and (iii) by the proceeds of their former home of £61,500. Their former home had been owned by Elayne alone as a council tenant. That former home had been bought five years earlier for £45,200. Of that sum, by being a council tenant, she had secured a 'discount' of £20,000 and Allan had paid the remaining money. That effectively meant that when they purchased their second home in 1991, Allan had contributed the original £25,200 plus an additional £35,500. The legal title to the second home was registered solely in Allan's name.

The parties separated in 2001 and Elayne sought a declaration that Allan held the property on trust for them in equal shares in equity.

The trial judge found that there was a common intention, based on the parties' conduct, to share the equitable interest in the property. She awarded them equal shares. Both of them had evidenced an intention to share the benefit and burdens of the house equally and both should be entitled to the same amount when the property was sold. Allan appealed. The basis of his appeal was that their values in the property should be decided on a resulting trust approach. He said that Elayne's contribution to the purchase of the property was roughly 22 per cent (taking into account his contributions and that the mortgage, as with the property, was registered solely in his name so he had the sole responsibility of repaying it) and that she should only receive that amount from its value when it was sold.

The Court of Appeal held that Allan should be entitled to 60 per cent of the property and Elayne to the remaining 40 per cent. But it was the reasoning of Chadwick LJ's judgment that makes the decision interesting.

Chadwick LJ held that whilst direct contributions towards the purchase price could give rise to a Rosset category 2 constructive trust, that did not necessarily mean that the parties' shares had to be held on the same proportions as their contributions. No longer were parties' shares in a property to be quantified on a strict resulting trust basis. Chadwick LJ thought that the law had moved on in this area from when Grant v Edwards had been decided and expressed doubt that the resulting trust approach was the correct one in Springette v Defoe.

---

69 Oxley v Hiscock [2005] Fam 211.

Chadwick LJ thought that the approach of Peter Gibson LJ in *Drake v Whipp* was the correct one for valuing a beneficial interest in the property. The constructive trust, rather than the resulting trust, was the correct approach to be adopted. Once the court accepted that, the resulting trust, with its legal presumptions, could be dispensed with and the more flexible approach of the constructive trust proceeded with. The task of the court was then, according to Chadwick LJ, that each party, 'is entitled to that share which the *court considers fair* having regard to the whole course of dealings between them in relation to the property'.[70]

The 'whole course of dealings' applied not just to the money which the parties contributed towards the acquisition of the property, as on a resulting trust approach. As the constructive trust was the correct vehicle to use for quantification, indirect contributions made after the property was acquired could also be taken into account when valuing each party's share, so that the valuation would include:

> the arrangements which they make from time to time in order to meet the outgoings (for example, mortgage contributions, council tax and utilities, repairs, insurance and housekeeping) which have to be met if they are to live in the property as their home.[71]

Interestingly, Chadwick LJ agreed with the reasoning of Sir Nicolas Browne-Wilkinson V-C in *Grant v Edwards* that the relationship between the constructive trust and that of proprietary estoppel was now so close that there should be 'no difference in outcome, in cases of this nature'[72] between whether the decision was made on either basis. There is, however, a difference in outcome in terms of the remedy that each doctrine provides. Proprietary estoppel gives the minimum remedy required to do justice between the parties.[73] A constructive trust, however, based on the parties' inferred intentions, seeks to reflect those intentions that the parties had in terms of sharing their property. As such, it will not seek purposely to award one party the minimum required to do justice between them.

The judgment of Chadwick LJ came to be reviewed, and approved, by the majority of the House of Lords in *Stack v Dowden*.[74]

Somewhat unusually, the case involved a property being legally owned by both partners, but they had not set out the proportions in which they wanted to hold their beneficial interests. Barry Stack and Dehra Dowden met in 1975, but they did not start living together until 1983. They eventually bought a property in London in 1993 with Dehra making a greater financial contribution towards its purchase. She contributed roughly half of the purchase price from her savings and the sale proceeds of their former home (which had been registered in her sole name). The other half of the purchase price was made up of a mortgage which, as with the property itself, was in their joint names. Barry paid the mortgage instalments as they arose, but they both paid off the capital of the mortgage, with Dehra again contributing more than Barry. They always maintained separate bank accounts and throughout their time together, Dehra always earned far in excess from her employment than Barry did from his.

They separated in 2002. Barry brought an action for the property to be sold and a declaration that he should be entitled to half of the sale proceeds. The trial judge duly made such an order. The Court of Appeal adjusted their ownership proportions of the property to 65 per cent

---

70 *Oxley v Hiscock* [2005] Fam 211 at 246 (emphasis added).
71 Ibid.
72 Ibid at 247.
73 See Chapter 17, pp 481–482.
74 *Stack v Dowden* [2007] 2 AC 432.

in Dehra's favour with the remainder for Barry. Barry appealed to the House of Lords, seeking the trial judge's original Order to be restored. The House of Lords unanimously dismissed his appeal but their reasoning for doing so differed between the majority of the Law Lords and Lord Neuberger.

Lord Walker expressed disquiet that judges in previous decisions had freely interchanged the nomenclature between constructive and resulting trusts. The two were different. With the resulting trust came legal presumptions – for example, the presumption that a beneficiary's value in the property is limited to the same proportion as their initial direct contribution to the purchase of the property. A constructive trust had no similar legal presumptions. Lord Walker thought that the resulting trust was not the appropriate vehicle to use to classify parties' interests in the matrimonial home, unless it was updated to take into account all significant contributions made by each party.

Baroness Hale, with whose reasoning the other Law Lords (except Lord Neuberger) agreed, delivered the most detailed opinion. She said that where the legal ownership in a residential property had been vested in joint names, the presumption was that the equitable ownership would also be held in equal shares.[75] Similarly, if the legal ownership was vested in one person's name only, the presumption would be that the equitable interest would be too. These presumptions reflected the maxim that equity follows the law. If the presumptions were to be displaced, the onus was on the person arguing that they did intend their equitable shares to be different from their legal shares to prove that. But, in doing that, she said that '[m]any more factors than financial contributions may be relevant to divining the parties' true intentions'.[76] Amongst other factors, she said the court could take into account:

(a)   any discussions or advice the parties had when they bought the property;
(b)   the reasons why the legal ownership of the property was placed in their joint names;
(c)   the purpose for which the home was bought;
(d)   the nature of the parties' relationship;
(e)   whether they both had a responsibility to provide a home for their children;
(f)   how the purchase of the property was financed;
(g)   how the parties dealt with their finances; and
(h)   how the parties paid the household expenses.

In addition, Baroness Hale said that the parties' intentions may have altered since the property was originally purchased. She gave express approval for contributions to be taken into account which were made after the property had been purchased – such contributions being, for example, an 'extension or substantial improvement'[77] to the property. However, Baroness Hale did place a *caveat* on her comments for joint legal owners by saying that, 'cases in which the joint legal owners are to be taken to have intended that their beneficial interests should be different from their legal interests will be very unusual'.[78]

All of these factors would be taken into account when deciding to what share of the property each party was entitled. That share would be adjudged on the basis of what, following Chadwick LJ's judgment in *Oxley v Hiscock*, was deemed to be 'fair'.

---

75   This presumption was held not to have been displaced in *Fowler v Barron* [2008] EWCA Civ 377. The Court of Appeal held that a home registered in joint names was held by the two parties in equal shares in equity due to their shared lives reinforcing that intention to share the property.
76   Ibid at 459.
77   Ibid.
78   Ibid.

The context of the case itself showed, however, that the presumption for joint beneficial ownership could be displaced even though they were joint legal owners. They had only put their last home into their joint names at law. Everything else throughout their relationship had been kept entirely separate. They effectively lived financially separate lives. The only inference to be drawn, as Dehra never denied, was that Barry was to have some interest in their last home. The House of Lords agreed that his fair share should be 35 per cent.

Whilst agreeing with both the result in the present case and that in *Oxley v Hiscock*, Lord Neuberger delivered a judgment urging caution before refashioning the law over the quantification of trusts. He believed that such changes should only be effected by Parliament, after due consultation with the public. He thought that the courts should continue to apply quantification principles based on the principles of a resulting trust, which would have arrived at the same solution in both the present case and in *Oxley v Hiscock*. As such, there was no need to make different rules to deal with the ownership of residential and commercial property: the resulting trust approach could address both.

Lord Neuberger was 'unhappy'[79] with the approach to quantification of a party's interest based on a constructive trust through the doctine of what is 'fair'. He thought that fairness was not the appropriate test of quantifying a party's beneficial interest in a property. It was too imprecise a term. It also involved the court imputing an intention to the parties rather than inferring one from their evidence. He distinguished between inference and imputations:

> An inferred intention is one which is objectively deduced to be the subjective actual intention of the parties, in the light of their actions and statements. An imputed intention is one which is attributed to the parties, even though no such actual intention can be deduced from their actions and statements, and even though they had no such intention.

He also thought that Chadwick LJ's 'whole course of dealing' was too imprecise, as it focused too much on the parties' lifestyle as opposed to contributions that should be taken into account to quantify a beneficial interest in their home. 'Whole course of dealing', thought Lord Neuberger, would be relevant only to establishing the parties' background – not the sharing of their equitable interests. He said:

> To say that factors such as a long relationship, children, a joint bank account and sharing daily outgoings of themselves are enough, or even of potential central importance, appears to me not merely wrong in principle, but a recipe for uncertainty, subjectivity, and a long and expensive examination of facts.[80]

❖ ANALYSING THE LAW

Consider the different approaches of Baroness Hale and Lord Neuberger to quantifying the equitable interest in *Stack v Dowden*. Which do you think is to be preferred and why?

---

79 Ibid at 476.
80 Ibid at 477.

The speeches of the majority, on the one hand, and Lord Neuberger, on the other, reveal a fundamental difference over the methodology of quantifying an equitable interest in the property. The majority, led by Baroness Hale, favoured the flexible nature of a constructive trust in valuing an equitable interest in a residential property. Lord Neuberger, ultimately for reasons of certainty, preferred a resulting trust approach, based on monetary contributions.

The decision of the majority in Stack v Dowden was limited to the quantification of the equitable interest in a domestic property. The Court of Appeal in Laskar v Laskar[81] held that the resulting trust approach to quantification should be applied to a property bought as an investment.

Rini Laskar and her mother, Zubera Laskar, bought Zubera's council house from Welwyn Hatfield Council in 1998. The purchase price was £79,500. Zubera enjoyed the right to purchase it from the local authority but could not afford to buy it by herself so it was agreed between them that they would both buy it, with the aid of a mortgage and roughly equal personal contributions from each of them (£3,400 by Rini). The legal interest in the property was registered in their joint names. They made no mention of the equitable ownership of the house. After the property was purchased, it was let out to tenants, whose rent was paid to Zubera who, in turn, used it to meet the mortgage payments. In 2003, the parties had a serious disagreement and Rini sought to realise her investment in the property. The trial judge awarded her a 4.28 per cent interest in the property, founded on her monetary contributions to the overall purchase price. Rini appealed to the Court of Appeal.

Lord Neuberger gave the only substantive judgment of the Court of Appeal. He was able to distinguish the decision in Stack v Dowden. He said that the parties in the case before him had no intention of sharing the property as a domestic dwelling.[82] The constructive trust approach to quantification of the beneficial interest as developed in Stack should not, therefore, apply to this case where the property was purchased for a commercial investment purpose. Rather, their beneficial shares should be valued on a resulting trust basis based on their contributions to the purchase price. Based on those contributions – and particularly given that the mortgage was in their joint names and so they were jointly responsible for paying it – Rini was entitled to a 33 per cent share of the property in equity. Despite his reservations in Stack over the concept of fairness, Lord Neuberger was prepared to ask, as a supplementary question, whether that share produced a 'fair' result for the parties. He thought it was fair on the facts.

The latest Supreme Court pronouncement on quantification: Jones v Kernott

Ms Jones met Mr Kernott in 1980. They bought a house in their joint names in 1985. One-fifth of the purchase price was met by the proceeds from the sale of Ms Jones' former home. Ms Jones met the mortgage instalments, but Mr Kernott helped to build an extension which increased the value of the property by 50 per cent.

In 1993, the parties separated and Mr Kernott moved out of the house. He made no more contributions to the property. Two years later, the parties cashed in an endowment policy and

---

81 Laskar v Laskar [2008] 1 WLR 2695.

82 Lord Neuberger did affirm the decision of the Leeds County Court in Adekunle v Ritchie [2007] 2 P & CR DG 20 in holding that Stack v Dowden was not confined to parties in a sexual relationship with each other. In Adekunle v Ritchie, it was held that Stack v Dowden could apply to a property bought by a mother and son, but it was purchased to provide a home for them.

split the proceeds between them. Mr Kernott used his share to purchase a new home for himself. In 2006, Mr Kernott began proceedings to claim a share in the former matrimonial home, still occupied by Ms Jones and their children. The Court of Appeal decided that they owned the home as tenants in common in equal shares.

On appeal, the Supreme Court disagreed and restored the trial judge's decision: Ms Jones was entitled to an 88 per cent share of the property and Mr Kernott to the remaining 12 per cent. The decision in *Stack v Dowden* was followed.

Lord Walker and Lady Hale SCJJ gave the leading, joint judgment. In terms of where the legal title to the family home had been vested in joint names but where there had been no declaration of beneficial ownership, the presumption would be, following *Stack v Dowden*, that the parties intended to create a joint tenancy in equity. This also reflected modern family life where two parties usually contributed in equal shares to their relationship and where both were invariably responsible for meeting mortgage payments. Their Lordships rejected the notion that the resulting trust was the appropriate medium for quantifying the equitable interest any more. The resulting trust presumption of one party buying a property and putting it in joint names at law but equity presuming that that paying party was the (larger) equitable owner was outdated and no longer reflected the partnership approach of modern family life.

In *Jones v Kernott*, Lord Walker and Lady Hale SCJJ thought that the constructive trust should be used to quantify parties' equitable interests. Their common intention had to be inferred from the evidence. The resulting trust would only be appropriate in two cases:

(a)   where the two parties who owned the home were also business partners; or
(b)   where it was impossible to infer the amount of their shares based on their common intention.

In these two cases, a resulting trust could be imputed to the parties. If these two situations did not apply, the mechanism of the constructive trust should be used to award the parties a 'fair' share each in the home.

Lord Walker and Lady Hale SCJJ laid down the following principles at the end of their joint opinion. These would apply to where the legal title to the property had been placed in joint names:

(a)   equity followed the law, which meant that the equitable ownership should, *prima facie*, also be equal;
(b)   the presumption in (a) could be displaced by evidence to the contrary by showing that the parties had a different common intention to own the beneficial interest in the property either at the time they purchased it or at a later stage;
(c)   the parties' common intention had to be proved objectively by considering their conduct;
(d)   if the parties did not intend to share the property as joint tenants in equity either when it was purchased or later, each party should be awarded a 'fair' share in the property, following *Oxley v Hiscock*; and
(e)   each case turned on its own facts. Financial and other contributions could all be relevant in determining a party's share.

In the case of a single legal owner where the common intention did not show their shares, the court was to proceed by following principles (d) and (e).

Summary

How is a trust of the family home established?	Lloyds Bank v Rosset	Category 1: through agreement and detrimental reliance; or Category 2: through the parties' conduct: a common intention to share the property beneficially
If established, how is the non-legally owning party's interest in the family home quantified?	Category 1: Drake v Whipp	Step 1: Consider the agreement reached between the parties. Only if the agreement is silent as to the beneficial shares do you proceed to step 2; Step 2: The court will adopt a 'broad brush' approach, valuing the equitable interest on the basis of the parties' contributions to their relationship. This approach uses the constructive trust as its basis.
	Category 2: Stack v Dowden (as reiterated in Jones v Kernott)	Holistic approach: the court takes into account the whole course of the parties' relationship from when they agreed to purchase the property to the break-down of their relationship. This approach uses the constructive trust as its basis.
Are there any exceptions to the quantification principles above?	Laskar v Laskar	Exception 1: property acquired on a commercial basis as an investment. The resulting trust approach should still govern quantification of the parties' interests.
	Jones v Kernott	Exception 2: for residential property where there is no evidence for the court to base its valuation of the parties' interests on, the resulting trust approach will remain appropriate.

Figure 14.2 Summary of trusts of the family home.

Points to Review

You have seen:

- how the issue of whether a constructive trust of the family home arises remains to be determined by applying the ratio of Lloyds Bank v Rosset. The issue is whether the parties showed a common intention to share the beneficial interest of the property. That intention can be established by an agreement together with detrimental reliance on it by the non-legally owning party. Such reliance may take a variety of forms and need not be too extensive. Alternatively, the common intention to share the beneficial interest can be shown by the parties' conduct but, despite the comments of Lord Walker and Baroness Hale in *Stack v Dowden*, that conduct can only constitute direct payments to the purchase price of the property, through making a contribution either to the deposit or the mortgage payments;

- if a trust of the family home is established, then *Rosset* category 1 trusts are valued primarily by considering the agreement made between the parties and seeing whether the parties agreed the shares in which they were to hold the property. If the agreement does not reveal such information, the court may take a 'broad brush'[83] approach to quantification; and

- *Rosset* category 2 trusts are now generally to be quantified on what is a 'fair' result for both parties, taking into account their 'whole course of dealing'[84] as reflected in the factors laid down by Baroness Hale in *Stack v Dowden*. This enables the court to take a flexible approach in quantifying beneficial interests. The resulting trust approach remains on only two occasions: (i) for a commercial property or (ii) where the court has no evidence as to the parties' intentions to value their interests using a flexible, constructive trust-based approach.

Making connections

This chapter considered the area of the application of established implied trusts to what will normally be an individual's single biggest investment of their lifetime: their home. As you have seen, this involved a discussion and application of constructive and resulting trusts. The principles behind these trusts, together with a full explanation of them, are discussed in Chapter 3. These trusts are implied trusts and, as has been shown, usually these trusts are not written down despite being trusts of land. They therefore enjoy 'immunity' under s 53(2) of the Law of Property Act 1925 from the formality requirements relating to trusts of land found in s 53(1)(b) of the Law of Property Act 1925. These statutory requirements are discussed further in Chapter 4.

 Useful Things to Read

The best reading is contained in the primary sources listed below. It is always good to consider the decisions of the courts themselves, as this will lead to a deeper understanding of the issues involved. A few secondary sources are also listed, which you may wish to read to gain additional insights into the areas considered in this chapter.

Primary sources
Eves v Eves [1975] 1 WLR 1338.
Jones v Kernott [2011] UKSC 53.
Laskar v Laskar [2008] 1 WLR 2695.
Lloyds Bank v Rosset [1991] 1 AC 107.
Oxley v Hiscock [2005] Fam 211.
Stack v Dowden [2007] 2 AC 432.

---

83 See *Drake v Whipp* (1996) 28 HLR 531 at 536 per Peter Gibson LJ.
84 See *Oxley v Hiscock* [2005] Fam 211 at 246 per Chadwick LJ.

Secondary sources

Simon Gardner and Katharine Davidson, 'The Supreme Court on family homes' [2012] LQR 178–183. An article which considers the theory of awarding an equal equitable interest in the family home where it is in joint names at law and which also looks at the role of imputing an intention in this area of law.

Robert H George, 'Cohabitants' property rights: When is fair fair?' [2012] CLJ 39–42 (note). A short article reviewing *Jones v Kernott* and *Stack v Dowden*.

Sarah Greer and Mark Pawlowski, 'Constructive trusts and the home maker' [2010] Denning LJ 35–49. This article discusses the extent to which Lord Bridge's requirement of a financial contribution to establish a *Rosset* category 2 constructive trust remains good law in the light of *Stack v Dowden*.

Alastair Hudson, *Equity and Trusts* (7th edn, Routledge-Cavendish, 2012) chs 15 and 17.

Law Commission, *Sharing Homes, A Discussion Paper* (Law Com No. 278, 2002). This is the Law Commission paper which played such an important role in Baroness Hale's opinion in *Stack v Dowden*.

John Mee, '*Jones v Kernott*: inferring and imputing in Essex' [2012] 2 Conv 167–180 (note). This article considers *Jones v Kernott* and examines areas which continue to remain uncertain even after this judgment.

Mohamed Ramjohn, *Text, Cases and Materials on Equity and Trusts* (4th edn, Routledge-Cavendish, 2008) ch 10.

Juanita Roche, '*Kernott, Stack* and *Oxley* made simple: A practitioner's view' [2011] 2 Conv 123–139. Written with practitioners in mind, this article considers the various tests to ascertain the share of a beneficial interest in the family home from the three most important cases in recent years.

Chapter 15

Charities

This chapter considers an application of the law of trusts to a concept that has existed from at least the seventeenth century: charity. It is suggested that most people would believe that charities exist with the broadest purpose of doing good in society. This chapter looks at how charities exist in law and illustrates how charities in law are not limited to the everyday examples (such as the RSPCA or Cancer Research UK) with which you may be familiar.

As You Read

Look out for the following key issues:

- how charities are administered and the advantages of having charitable status; and
- the three essential requirements that an organisation must possess to be defined as a charity under the Charities Act 2011. These are that the organisation must:
  - have a charitable purpose (as defined under s 3(1) of the Act);
  - be shown to benefit the public (as required under s 2(1)(b) of the Act); and
  - be wholly and exclusively charitable.

Background

The first example of Parliament recognising what was, at the time, a charity, was set out in the Preamble to the Statute of Charitable Uses Act 1601 (sometimes colloquially known as the 'Statute of Elizabeth'). This Preamble contained a list of what was, in Elizabethan times, seen to be charitable although, as Lord Macnaghten pointed out in *The Commissioners for Special Purposes of the Income Tax v Pemsel*,[1] the courts had recognised that charities could exist long before the 1601 Act. The courts used the Preamble to recognise those organisations or gifts as having charitable status if they either fell within the list contained in it, or fell within the 'spirit and intendment' of that list.

Making connections

You should remember from your studies of the English legal system that it is, of course, not usual for the Preamble of an Act to have such a prominent role as the one to the Statute of Charitable Uses 1601 enjoyed. The Preamble to an Act usually has no legal status and is usually an explanation of why the Act was enacted. But not only did the courts define whether an organisation or gift had charitable status by considering whether it fell within the definition in the Preamble, they also asked whether organisations or gifts of a similar nature to those set out in the Preamble could have charitable status.

Perhaps even more surprising is that the Preamble has been repealed (by the Charities Act 1960) and yet it is still referred to in the most modern of legislation: see s 1(3) of the Charities Act 2006.

Nowadays whether something enjoys charitable status is governed by the requirements of the Charities Act 2011. Section 2(1) sets out that, to enjoy charitable status, two requirements must be satisfied: (i) there must be a charitable purpose permitted by law; and (ii) there must be an element of benefit to the public in the work the organisation will undertake.

---

1 *The Commissioners for Special Purposes of the Income Tax v Pemsel* [1891] AC 531 at 581 (the actual purpose of the 1601 legislation was to give new powers to control and reform abuses which had appeared in relation to charities).

Charity Administration

Charities are an important part of today's society. There are, as of 2012, over 161,000 charities registered with the Charity Commission.[2] As will be shown, not all charities have to be registered with the Charity Commission, so the total number of charities will be even higher.

The advantages of enjoying charitable status

There are several advantages of having charitable status, the most important being (i) taxation and (ii) legal.

Taxation

Generally, any income received by individuals or companies in England and Wales is subject to taxation. The rates of tax may change in the annual Budget delivered by the Chancellor of the Exchequer. For example, if you are in paid employment and earn over £8,105[3] you will have to pay tax on that income. Similarly, if you own shares and the company declares a dividend, that will result in income being paid to you, which again will be taxed.

Charities enjoy substantial tax relief on income they receive, provided that income is used for charitable purposes. For example, if a charity holds land which it rents out (such as, for instance, the National Trust), no tax will be payable on the income, provided it is only used for charitable purposes. Likewise, a charity's income from money it may hold in a bank account is not subject to tax. Charities may also receive dividends from any company shares they own free from income tax.

> ### ❖ EXPLAINING THE LAW
>
> Have you ever been asked to 'gift aid' a donation to a charity? Gift aid enables a charity to reclaim basic rate tax that a taxpayer making the donation will have paid on their income.
>
> For example, suppose Scott goes to a National Trust property and there is a £5 entrance charge. He may be asked if he wishes to take advantage of the 'gift aid' scheme. It costs Scott no additional money. The entrance fee is then treated as a donation upon which the National Trust can reclaim the basic rate of tax (currently 20 per cent) that Scott will have been charged when he earned his salary. That means that the National Trust may reclaim a further 20 per cent (£1.25) from HM Revenue & Customs.

Charities enjoy other taxation exemptions and reliefs too. For example, the charity will not be charged capital gains tax (CGT) on any gains it makes, provided that the monetary gain is used for charitable purposes. When buying land, the charity will be able to purchase it free of stamp duty land tax (SDLT). If it has premises, the charity will pay lower business rates than a non-charitable organisation.

All of these reliefs and exemptions from taxation make charitable status attractive for an organisation or gift.

---

2   See www.charity-commission.gov.uk, last accessed 16 January 2012.
3   In the tax year 2012–2013.

Legal advantages

Charities may exist under one of several different legal structures. For example, a charity may take the form of:

(a)   *A company limited by guarantee.* This is where a limited company is formed to manage the charity and directors are appointed to run it. The company's liability is limited by a guarantee provided by those individuals establishing it. No shares in the company are issued.

(b)   *An unincorporated association.* This is a club or society where its members hold property on the basis of a contract between themselves (see Chapter 6 for further discussion).

(c)   *An express trust.*

It is the concept of establishing a charity by an express trust that is of the most interest here and, generally, the discussion in this chapter will now proceed as though an express trust has been chosen as the medium to establish a charity.

As you know, express trusts have to be both declared and constituted.[4] Charities are, however, allowed to deviate from several of the usual requirements needed to declare an express trust:

(a)   To a certain extent, charitable trusts can deviate from the usual rules of certainty required when a trust is established.[5] Usually there must be certainty of intention, subject matter and object when an express trust is established. Certainty of intention and certainty of object do not need to be complied with as rigidly in a charitable trust, because defined individuals are not intended to benefit from the trust: the trust is instead being established to benefit a purpose. Instead of specifying precisely who will benefit from the charitable trust, it is possible to state that the charity will exist for one or more of the general charitable purposes set out in s 3 of the Charities Act 2011.

Having said that, however, there are limits as to how far the rules of certainty can be disapplied, as shown in *Chichester Diocesan Fund & Board of Finance (Incorporated) v Simpson.*[6]

In his will, Caleb Diplock left his residuary estate (approximately £250,000) to 'such charitable institution or institutions or any other charitable or benevolent object or objects in England' as his executors should choose. The executors asked the court whether such a gift was valid as a charitable one or whether it was void for uncertainty. By a bare majority, the House of Lords held that it was void for uncertainty.

The key focus for the House of Lords was on the phrase 'charitable or benevolent'. These words were seen by the majority to be disjunctive (not connected to each other). If necessary, the court could administer a trust for a charitable purpose, as the court could decide what a charitable purpose is in law. But the court could not administer a trust for a benevolent purpose. A benevolent purpose might be wider or narrower than a charitable purpose: it was impossible to say. By the use of the key word 'or' in his will, Mr Diplock had not demonstrated sufficient intention to benefit only a charitable object.

A different decision had been reached by the High Court in *Re Best.*[7] The decision illustrates how vital the use of the word 'and' can be instead of 'or'.

Thomas Best left his residuary estate to the Lord Mayor of Birmingham to be used for 'charitable and benevolent' purposes in the city of Birmingham and the wider counties

---

4   See Chapter 4 for an overview of these requirements and Chapters 4–7 for a detailed discussion.
5   See Chapter 5.
6   *Chichester Diocesan Fund & Board of Finance (Incorporated) v Simpson* [1944] AC 341.
7   *Re Best* [1904] 2 Ch 354.

in the Midlands. Farwell J held that the gift was a valid charitable gift. Mr Best had clearly stated an intention that his estate should only go to charities and he had simply limited those charities who could benefit by stating that they also had to have a benevolent purpose.

What is clear, therefore, is that certainty of intention must still be present in a charitable trust in that the settlor must show a clear intention to benefit a charity. The precise objects – as to which particular type of charity may benefit – may be dispensed with, as long as the court can construe an intention to benefit a charitable purpose as now defined in the Charities Act 2011;

(b)   Generally speaking, English law discourages the use of purpose trusts.[8] Yet charities are, by their very nature, examples of trusts established for a purpose as opposed to benefiting an individual. English law not only permits this, but actively encourages it, through the taxation reliefs and exemptions discussed. The rather cynical reason for this is that if the law stuck rigidly to its beliefs in that all trusts must benefit an individual, an increased burden would result on the government to take the place of providing all of the good works currently undertaken by charities which would result in an increased taxation burden to society in general;

(c)   The beneficiary principle[9] need not be met. Beneficiaries generally have a dual role: they not only enjoy the trust property but they also act as 'enforcers' of the trust against the trustee. They ensure the trustee administers the trust for their benefit and not his own. The beneficiary principle is, however, dispensed with in the case of a charitable trust. Bespoke enforcers of each charitable trust are not required because it is the Charity Commission's role to take enforcement action[10] against the charity trustees if they breach the terms of the trust; and

(d)   Charitable trusts need not comply with the Rules against Perpetuity.[11] Section 4 of the Perpetuity and Accumulations Act 2009 provides that the only perpetuity period permitted for trusts is a fixed period of 125 years. Broadly, this means that the property of the trust must vest in the beneficiaries within that time to prevent the trust being void. Charities do not suffer from such a requirement and may exist in perpetuity. For example, Thomas Barnardo started his work in 1867 and his charity still exists today.

The Charity Commission

The Charity Commission was formed by the Charities Act 2006.[12] Prior to that Act, the Charity Commissioners[13] had exercised the same roles as the Commission.

The Charity Commission has two main roles.[14] The first is to keep a list of 'registered' charities. In doing this, it must decide whether charitable status can be granted to the organisation. The Charity Commission must base its decision on the definition of 'charity' in s 1 of the Charities Act 2011 and case law both prior to, and since, the enactment of that Act.

---

8   See Chapter 6.
9   Ibid.
10 Any litigation is conducted by the Attorney-General as representative of the Crown.
11 See the companion website for a full discussion of the rules against perpetuity. See also Lord Macnaghten in *The Commissioners for Special Purposes of the Income Tax v Pemsel* [1891] AC 531 at 580–581.
12 Charities Act 2006, s 6, amending Charities Act 1993, s 1. This corporate body is now recognised under the Charities Act 2011, s 13.
13 The office of Charity Commissioner was abolished by the Charities Act 2006, s 6(3) and their functions, property, rights and liabilities transferred to the Charity Commission (Charities Act 2006, s 6(4)).
14 For a list of all its functions, see Charities Act 2011, s 15.

The Charity Commission's second function is to police charities. This means, to give just two examples, that it is responsible for ensuring that (a) a charity makes an annual return demonstrating its public benefit, and (b) that the trustees of the charity are administering the charity's property correctly towards the aims of the charity and for the benefit of the public.

The Charity Commission's two main functions are summarised in Figure 15.1.

Charity Commission

Maintains list of registered charities

Polices charities' trustees

Figure 15.1 The Charity Commission's two main functions.

Certain charities cannot have 'registered' status with the Charity Commission.[15] These include those charities:

(a)   with an annual income of less than £5,000. Many local charities will fall into this category;

(b)   known as 'excepted' charities providing that they have an annual income of £100,000 or less. Excepted charities are those which remain regulated by the Charity Commission but may not be registered unless their annual income exceeds £100,000. Excepted charities are so called because they are excepted from registration either by an order made by the Charity Commission or specific legislation. Such charities would, for instance, include Scout and Girl Guide groups; and

(c)   known as 'exempt' charities. Exempt charities fall into two groups: those with a principal regulator and those without. Those with a principal regulator are regulated not by the Commission but by that regulator,[16] which has usually been appointed by Parliament. Housing Associations often fall into this category.[17] The regulator also ensures that the charity complies with its obligations under the Charities Act 2011 so there is no need for the Charity Commission to provide a second layer of regulation. Some exempt charities have no principal regulator,[18] but these charities' status is now being changed to 'excepted'. This means that the Charity Commission will regulate all of this group but only those with an annual income exceeding £100,000 will have to register with the Charity Commission.

The Charity Commission will, therefore, regulate the vast majority of charities. In turn, the vast majority of charities will be registered.

On a day-to-day basis, however, it is the charity's trustees who manage the trust property and administer the trust, just as in the case of any express trust. Under s 34(3)(a) of the Trustee Act 1925, there is no limit to the number of trustees of a charitable trust where the

---

15 See Charities Act 2011, s 30.

16 Ibid s 26.

17 Not all housing associations will be charitable. For example, in *Helena Partnerships Ltd v Revenue & Customs Commissioners* [2012] EWCA Civ 569, the Court of Appeal held that a housing association which also offered accommodation to people who were not in poverty was not charitable.

18 For example, the British Museum in London is governed by its own statute (the British Museum Act 1963) and is answerable directly to the Attorney-General.

trust property includes land, unlike that of a non-charitable trust where the maximum number is limited to four.[19]

Definition of a Charity

Key Learning Point

There are three main requirements to be a charity in law:

(a) the trust must be for a charitable purpose;

(b) the trust must be for the public benefit, either as a whole or a sufficiently large section of it such that it can be seen to be benefiting the public; and

(c) the purposes of the trust must be wholly and exclusively charitable.

'Charity' in law is not defined in any popular sense. As Lord Simonds said in relation to its derived term 'charitable' in *Chichester Diocesan Fund & Board of Finance (Incorporated) v Simpson*,[20] 'it is a term of art with a technical meaning'. That 'technical meaning' is today to be found in s 1 of the Charities Act 2011, which provides that a charity:

(a) is established for charitable purposes only, and

(b) falls to be subject to the control of the High Court in the exercise of its jurisdiction with respect to charities.

Section 2 states that a charitable purpose must be one falling within s 3(1) and be one which benefits the public. Section 3(1) sets out a list of 13 charitable purposes which are illustrated in Figure 15.2.

Charitable purpose
(a) poverty
(b) education
(c) religion
(d) health
(e) citizenship
(f) arts, culture, heritage or science
(g) amateur sport
(h) human rights
(i) environmental protection
(j) youth, age, ill-health, disability, financial hardship
(k) animal welfare
(l) armed forces and civilian services
(m) other previously recognised charitable purposes or charitable purposes similar to those in the list or previously recognised

Figure 15.2 Charitable purposes under s 3(1) of the Charities Act 2011.

---

19 Trustee Act 1925, s 34(2).
20 *Chichester Diocesan Fund & Board of Finance (Incorporated) v Simpson* [1944] AC 341 at 368.

Section 2(1) of the Charities Act 2011 sets out categorically that not only must there be a charitable purpose, but that any organisation wishing to claim charitable status must also be for the benefit of the public. The enactment of this requirement and the earlier Charities Act 2006 was the first time that this public benefit requirement was enshrined in legislation.

The Charities Act 2006 was not the first time that 'charitable purpose' was defined in law. The first recognition of what a charitable purpose could be was in the Preamble to the Statute of Charitable Uses 1601, but it was effectively the opinion of Lord Macnaghten in *The Commissioners for Special Purposes of the Income Tax v Pemsel*[21] which provided a more modern definition of the phrase by summarising those charitable purposes under four main heads; this definition lasted until the Charities Act 2006.

The facts of the case concerned land left on trust in 1813 for the Moravian Church. One-half of the profits made from the land were instructed by the settlor to be used to maintain and support missionary work in other nations in order to convert people to Christianity. Relief from income tax for profits made from land owned for charitable purposes had been enacted under the Income Tax Act 1842.

Until 1886, the Inland Revenue had duly refunded income tax that the Church had paid on the profits it made from the land. In that year, however, the Revenue refused, claiming that the lands were not held on trust for 'charitable purposes'. The Revenue's view was that 'charitable purposes' revolved around how 'charity' would be defined in popular meaning which, in turn, meant solely the relief of poverty. That was the only sense in which most people would define 'charity'. There was, the Revenue argued, no charitable purpose here as it was not necessarily the case that the money made from the land was to be used to relieve poverty.

By a majority, the House of Lords held that the phrase 'charitable purpose' was not restricted solely to the relief of poverty; instead the phrase had to be given its much wider legal meaning. The land was used for charitable purposes, so the relief from income tax should be reinstated by the Inland Revenue.

The case is known for the decision of Lord Macnaghten. He explained that the Court of Chancery:

> has always regarded with peculiar favour those trusts of a public nature which, according to the doctrine of the Court derived from the piety of early times, are considered to be charitable.[22]

Later, the Statute of Charitable Uses 1601 was enacted to deal with abuses of charities. In order to do so, the Preamble to that Act had contained a definition of charitable purpose. This definition was 'so varied and comprehensive that it became the practice of the court to refer to it as a sort of index or chart'.[23] Successive courts viewed the list as a not exhaustive definition of what a charitable purpose could be; according to Lord Cranworth LC in *University of London v Yarrow*,[24] those charitable purposes in the Preamble were 'not to be taken as the only objects of charity but are given as instances'. In turn, that meant that the courts saw purposes

---

21 *The Commissioners for Special Purposes of the Income Tax v Pemsel* [1891] AC 531.
22 Ibid at 580 per Lord Macnaghten.
23 Ibid at 581.
24 *University of London v Yarrow* 1 De G & J 72 at 79; 44 Eng Rep 649 1557–1865.

which were similar to those listed in the Preamble as deserving of charitable status. As Chitty J put it in *Re Foveaux*:[25]

> Institutions whose objects are analogous to those mentioned in the statute are admitted to be charities; and, again, institutions which are analogous to those already admitted by reported decisions are held to be charities.

This approach effectively continues to this day as s 3(1)(m)(ii) of the Charities Act 2011 gives the court the ability to recognise as charitable anything which is either 'analogous to, or within the spirit of' any of the main charitable purposes listed in s 3(1) of the Act.

❖ ANALYSING THE LAW

Think about the phrase 'analogous to, or within the spirit of' any of the main charitable purposes listed in s 3(1) of the Charities Act 2011.

Suppose a celebrity chef opens a cookery school. He charges a fee for each participant to attend and learn from him. Could he claim that it is analogous to, or within the spirit of, the advancement of education and so claim charitable status for this activity?

Could the grower of a plantation of genetically modified crops claim that it is analagous to, or within the spirit of, advancing science?

It is questions such as these that the courts have had to wrestle with over centuries to decide whether to grant charitable status. These conundrums are set to continue due to the need to retain flexibility in the courts' approach of being able to grant charitable status to purposes similar to those which already enjoy such status.

Lord Macnaghten set out his definition of the charity:

> 'Charity' in its legal sense comprises four principal divisions: trusts for the relief of poverty; trusts for the advancement of education; trusts for the advancement of religion; and trusts for other purposes beneficial to the community, not falling under any of the preceding heads.[26]

This definition was described by Wilberforce J in *Re Hopkins' Will Trusts* as 'the accepted classification into four groups of the miscellany found in the Statute of Elizabeth'.[27]

Lord Macnaghten's summary of charity lasted until the Charities Act 2006 was enacted to consolidate the earlier Charities Act 1993 and other Acts relating to charity law. However, the first three heads of charity under s 3(1) of the Charities Act 2011 are practically the same as those enunciated by Lord Macnaghten. His final head has, arguably, been split up by the Act into the remaining ten heads listed in that subsection which perhaps give the definition of charity a more contemporary flavour. Those modern charitable purposes must now be examined.

---

25 *Re Foveaux* [1895] 2 Ch 501 at 504.
26 *The Commissioners for Special Purposes of the Income Tax v Pemsel* [1891] AC 531 at 583.
27 *Re Hopkins' Will Trusts* [1965] Ch 669 at 678.

The statutory definitions of 'charity' and 'charitable purpose' enacted for the first time in the 2006 Act were probably overdue. The Preamble was, by that stage, over 400 years old and its acknowledgement of charitable purposes reflected those prevalent in the time of Elizabeth I. The courts, by recognising further purposes as charitable by whether that new purpose was analogous to those listed in the Preamble, had created case law which was, at times, inconsistent. The new statutory definition of charity, including modern-day charitable purposes, was at least an attempt to bring charity law up-to-date and into the twenty-first century.

First Requirement of Charitable Status: There Must Be a Charitable Purpose

Each charitable purpose will be examined in the same order as it appears in s 3(1) of the Charities Act 2011.

The prevention or relief of poverty

The Preamble to the Statute of Charitable Uses 1601 referred to the relief of the aged, impotent (disabled) or poor.

In his opinion in *The Commissioners for Special Purposes of the Income Tax v Pemsel*, Lord Macnaghten showed that relieving poverty was essentially the only meaning the Victorians gave to charity. Lord Macnaghten argued persuasively that a charitable purpose could have other meanings, which he then defined.

Until the 2006 Act, this charitable head was concerned merely with relieving poverty. This head suggested any charity would have to demonstrate that it *reacted* to poverty by seeking to ameliorate it. The 2006 Act retained this definition, but also added to it by providing that charities under this head could, for the avoidance of doubt, act proactively. This charitable purpose would also include preventing poverty and not just relieving it. The 2011 Act retains this definition.

Do you think that the words of the 2006 Act changed this charitable purpose substantively? Is there, in practical terms, a great deal of difference between the prevention or relief of poverty? It is surely unlikely that the Charity Commissioners before the 2006 Act was enacted would have refused to register a charity which sought merely to prevent, as opposed to relieve, poverty.

In *Attorney-General v Charity Commission for England and Wales*,[28] Warren J thought that there could, in theory, be a difference between preventing and relieving poverty. He gave

---

28 *Attorney-General v Charity Commission for England and Wales* [2012] WTLR 977.

the example of a charity providing money management advice as being one that could exist solely to prevent poverty. Yet, practically, in most cases charities will have objects that are for both the prevention and relief of poverty.

If a charity's purpose must be the 'prevention or relief' of poverty, what is meant by 'poverty'?

'Poverty' was defined by Evershed MR in *Re Coulthurst*.[29] John Coulthurst declared a discretionary trust of £20,000 in his will and directed that his trustee should pay an allowance to any widows and orphaned children of either officers or ex-officers of Coutts & Co as the trustees thought were 'most deserving of assistance', according to their financial circumstances.

The Court of Appeal held that the trust was charitable, as it existed to relieve poverty. It did not matter that the trust did not precisely spell out that its objective was to relieve poverty. The court would look at the purpose of the trust as a whole and, if its aim was to relieve poverty, that would be sufficient to ensure that it could attain charitable status under this head. The decision may thus be seen as an application of the maxim that equity looks to the substance of the testator's aim and not to the precise form of the words he chose to use.

Evershed MR went on to define 'poverty':

poverty does not mean destitution; it is a word of wide and somewhat indefinite import; it may not unfairly be paraphrased for present purposes as meaning persons who have to 'go short' in the ordinary acceptation of that term, due regard being had to their status in life, and so forth.[30]

The very nature of this trust suggested that its aim was to relieve poverty. It only benefited widows and orphaned children who were 'most deserving of [financial] assistance'.

The notion that poverty is a relative concept may be shown by considering the facts of *Re de Carteret*.[31]

Here, the Right Reverend Frederick de Carteret, formerly the Bishop of Jamaica, declared a trust in his will of £7,000 which was to be invested and the income generated by it to be used to pay an annuity of £40 each to widows or spinsters living in England with a preference for those widows who had young dependent children. But the trust had a condition placed on it: to receive this annual sum, the widows or spinsters had to have an annual income of between £80 and £120. This level of minimum income meant, of course, that the potential recipients of the money were perhaps not poor by the standards of the 1930s. Again, the issue was whether such a trust could be valid as a charitable trust for, if not, it would be void as infringing the rules against perpetuity.

Maugham J held the trust was charitable. He stressed that poverty did not mean absolute destitution. A trust could be held to be charitable for the relief of poverty if its aim was to relieve people of limited means who were obliged to incur expenses as part of their 'duties as citizens'.[32] He said that, effectively, the widows had to have young dependent children to receive the annuity.

Whilst this decision affirms that poverty does not mean absolute destitution, it is suggested that it is, in some ways, a strange decision for the court to reach. Maugham J effectively

---

29 *Re Coulthurst* [1951] Ch 661.
30 Ibid at 666.
31 *Re de Carteret* [1933] Ch 103.
32 Ibid at 114.

reinterpreted the trust. The testator had placed a preference on widows with dependent children to benefit from the gift, but there was no compulsion on the trustees to distribute the money solely to these individuals. It may well be that the testator intended that widows without dependent children or spinsters could have benefited from his generosity. These two groups would not have had to incur the type of expenses in raising their children to which Maugham J referred as justifying his decision. His only way around this was to restrict the trust set up by the testator to widows with dependent children; it must be questioned whether restricting the testator's trust truly reflected the testator's wishes.

Whilst these decisions illustrate that the trust does not have to mention 'poverty' expressly to be considered charitable under this head, trusts are not usually charitable unless they are restricted to benefiting those who are poor. Where anyone can benefit from the trust, it will probably not be held to be charitable, as Re Sanders' Will Trusts[33] illustrates.

William Sanders created a discretionary trust over one-third of his residuary estate in his will so that his trustee could provide housing for the 'working classes and their families' who lived in the area of Pembroke Dock, Wales.

Harman J held that the trust was not charitable. It could not fall under this charitable head because it was not restricted to those people who were poor. As he put it, '[a]lthough a man might be a member of the working class and poor, the first does not at all connote the second'.[34] 'Working classes' had no connection to the concept of poverty.

The decision could be distinguished from the earlier cases of Re de Carteret and Re Coulthurst. Both of those decisions concerned widows and/or orphaned children, where poverty could, apparently, be readily inferred. Mr Sanders' trust was simply for the 'working classes', which were 'merely men working in the docks and their families'.[35]

The decision in Re Sanders' Will Trusts was, however, distinguished by Megarry V-C on not dissimilar facts in Re Niyazi's Will Trusts.[36]

Mehmet Niyazi was originally a Turkish Cypriot. He left his £15,000 residuary estate on trust for the construction of a 'working mens hostel' (sic) in Famagusta, Cyprus. The issue was whether such trust could be charitable, considering the earlier decision of Harman J in Re Sanders' Will Trusts.

Whilst acknowledging that the case was 'desperately near the borderline',[37] Megarry V-C held that the trust was charitable. 'Working men' impliedly contained within its definition a reference to lower incomes. The use of the word 'hostel' was key to distinguishing the decision from Re Sanders' Will Trusts. A hostel connoted a form of basic accommodation that only those who were poor would use, especially when prefixed by the phrase 'working mens'. Re Sanders' Will Trusts referred to 'dwellings' where those who were better off financially could live; the better off would be unlikely to benefit from the hostel in this trust.

Megarry V-C thought that he should take into account the comparatively small amount of money left by the testator for the project. Such a sum was unlikely to build the hostel by itself or, if it did, it would be a very modest one. In the latter case, only the poor would wish to live in it. Second, he thought that where a trust was to benefit a particular area, he should take the conditions in that area into account. He thought that:

a trust to erect a hostel in a slum or in an area of acute housing need may have to be construed differently from a trust to erect a hostel in an area of housing affluence or

---

33 Re Sanders' Will Trusts [1954] Ch 265.
34 Ibid at 270.
35 Ibid at 272.
36 Re Niyazi's Will Trusts [1978] 1 WLR 910.
37 Ibid at 915.

plenty. Where there is a grave housing shortage, it is plain that the poor are likely to suffer more than the prosperous . . .[38]

❖ ANALYSING THE LAW

Re Sanders' Will Trusts and *Re Niyazi's Will Trusts* seem to give different decisions on what is meant by 'working' classes. Do you think the decisions can be reconciled? If so, how?

Charitable trusts for the relief of poverty used not to be required to show that they benefited either the public as a whole or a section of it.[39] This was confirmed by the Court of Appeal in *Re Scarisbrick*.[40] Neither is it a requirement that a charitable trust be perpetual in nature, even though the majority of them are.

Dame Bertha Scarisbrick left the remainder interest in half of her residuary estate (some £6,000) to be paid to her relatives who were in 'needy circumstances'. The issue for the Court of Appeal was whether this could be construed as for the relief of poverty and thus be charitable. The difficulty with this phraseology was that it did not carry with it any objective standard of poverty and it did not limit the trustees to relieving the poverty of the relatives.

Evershed MR held that 'needy circumstances' could mean poverty. He pointed out that poverty was not an 'absolute standard'[41] and the recipients falling into such category had to be chosen. Those choosing had to do so honestly and the power of choice was a fiduciary discretion, so it had to be exercised in good faith.

Charitable status could be given even though it was the relatives of the testatrix whose poverty was being relieved. As will be discussed,[42] public benefit must generally be demonstrated by a charity. A trust in favour of poor relations was an exception to this principle. Additionally, there was no requirement that the trust had to be perpetual in nature. Charitable trusts often were but if the trust fund was exhausted by making donations to those relatives in need, that did not mean to say that the trust was not charitable.

The issue of what is meant by relieving poverty needs to be addressed. Relieving poverty will, of course, often be undertaken by handing out monetary gifts, as demonstrated in a number of cases considered so far. Yet this is not the only way in which poverty can be relieved, as shown in *Joseph Rowntree Memorial Trust Housing Association Ltd v Attorney-General*.[43]

The claimant desired to build small flats or bungalows which it would then lease out to elderly people on a long lease in return for the person making a capital payment. Each resident would pay 70 per cent of the cost of the property; the remaining amount would be paid by a housing association grant. The properties were effectively what is known as 'sheltered accommodation' where a warden is also present to liaise with the elderly residents as and when required.

The Charity Commissioners argued that such a scheme was not charitable. They said that any benefits were provided by contract with the owners of the dwellings, not by way of outright gift, which was needed to relieve poverty and which gift could not be withdrawn,

---

38 Ibid at 916.
39 Although see the views of Warren J in *Attorney-General v Charity Commission for England and Wales*, discussed at pp 430–431.
40 *Re Scarisbrick* [1951] Ch 622.
41 Ibid at 635.
42 See the discussion of public benefit beginning at p 428.
43 *Joseph Rowntree Memorial Trust Housing Association Ltd v Attorney-General* [1983] Ch 159.

even if the people ceased to meet the qualifying criteria. Second, the scheme benefited private individuals as opposed to a class. Third, they also said that such a scheme could not be charitable, as it would result in the people making a profit on their dwellings as the amount of their investment rose with general property prices.

Peter Gibson J held that the scheme was charitable.

It was not necessary under the Preamble to the Statute of Charitable Uses that beneficiaries should have to prove that they were aged, impotent and poor. Those words had to be read disjunctively. It was enough that beneficiaries fell into one of those three categories. He defined 'relief' as meaning:

> the persons in question have a *need attributable to their condition* as aged, impotent or poor persons which requires alleviating and which those persons could not alleviate, or would find difficulty in alleviating, themselves from their own resources.[44]

Peter Gibson J therefore considered that the *need* of the recipients had to have a causal connection to the generosity of the trust in order for their need to be relieved. On the facts, the recipients' needs were due to their being elderly which could be relieved by the provision of housing accommodation. Such a trust could be considered charitable. The fact that the elderly people received their accommodation under a contract as opposed to pure gift was irrelevant to whether the trust could be charitable.

The scheme was for the benefit of a class of people: it was for the benefit of the class of people who were aged who had particular accommodation needs. Nor did it matter that the residents might receive a profit should the value of their properties increase: this was an incidental benefit to the charitable purpose as opposed to the main objective of the scheme. As such it was of no consequence. In addition, it was not as though the residents profited at the scheme's expense.

Relief of poverty does not, therefore, entail simply handing out money to recipients. It can entail providing any relief to a condition caused by poverty.

The advancement of education

The Preamble to the Statute of Charitable Uses 1601 referred to charitable uses at the time being 'Schools of Learning, Free Schools and Scholars in Universities' as well as for the 'Education and Preferment of Orphans'.

These original purposes continue to be charitable today. Most universities have charitable status as do some private schools.

❖ APPLYING THE LAW

The issue of whether independent schools should have charitable status and therefore enjoy tax reliefs and exemptions has long troubled politicians.

Guidance given by the Charity Commission in 2008 provided that to continue to receive charitable status, independent schools had to demonstrate that they benefited the public.

---

44 Ibid at 171 (emphasis added).

> Such benefit could, for example, mean that they formed partnerships with state schools to share learning resources with them, or perhaps opened their sporting facilities to the local community at weekends.
>
> A recent decision[45] of the Upper Tribunal has, however, cast doubt on whether the Charity Commission can force independent schools to demonstrate such a level of public benefit. The Charity Commission is currently rewriting its guidelines as to what level of public benefit private schools must show to enjoy charitable status.

To be seen to be charitable under this head, the key feature seems to be that the organisation must demonstrate that it is involved in the development of knowledge. This is why universities and schools may enjoy charitable status, as well as institutions such as zoos and museums[46] and even the Boy Scouts.[47] All are involved with the generation and dissipation of knowledge.

Given the restrictive nature of the list of charitable purposes in the Preamble, a number of previous cases featured attempts by parties to try to show that their purpose fell under this particular charitable head. The usual attempt was for the party to demonstrate that there was the development of knowledge involved in their purpose and hence it could be seen to be for the advancement of education.

Games . . .

An example of this occurred in *Re Mariette*.[48] Edgar Mariette left a legacy of £1,000 in his will to the Aldenham School for the construction of Eton fives courts or squash courts. The issue for the High Court was whether such a gift was charitable, or whether it was void as for infringing the rules against perpetuity.

Eve J held that he had to consider not only the gift itself, but also the recipient of the gift, which was itself a charitable institution. The object of the school was to educate boys between 10 and 19 years old. The gift to the school could be seen as advancing that charitable purpose:

> No one of sense could be found to suggest that between those ages any boy can be properly educated unless at least as much attention is given to the development of his body as is given to the development of his mind.[49]

Providing games for the pupils was as much a part of advancing their education as undertaking classroom-based studies. It made no difference that the testator had spelt out specifically the precise purpose for which the legacy should be used.

Re Mariette was applied by the House of Lords in *Inland Revenue Commissioners v McMullen*.[50]

Here, the Football Association decided to declare a trust called 'The Football Association Youth Trust'. The purpose of the trust was said to be the 'furtherance of education' in schools and universities by encouraging pupils and students to play football. The Inland Revenue disputed that such a trust could have charitable status.

---

45 *The Independent Schools Council v The Charity Commission for England and Wales* [2011] UKUT 421 (TCC). See further discussion at pp 433–434.
46 Some of these charitable institutions will now, almost certainly, fall into other heads under the 2011 Act. For example, museums and zoos may also be considered to be for the 'advancement of the arts, culture, heritage or science' under s 3(1)(f).
47 *Re Webber* [1954] 1 WLR 1500.
48 *Re Mariette* [1915] 2 Ch 284.
49 Ibid at 288.
50 *Inland Revenue Commissioners v McMullen* [1980] 2 WLR 416.

The House of Lords held that the trust was charitable. Lord Hailsham LC expressly approved the decision of Eve J in Re Mariette, a decision which he found 'stimulating and instructive'.[51] Even though the facts in Re Mariette concerned a gift left to a particular institution, the decision could be applied in a wider context as on the present facts where money was being left to schools and universities in general. Lord Hailsham LC believed that education could be seen to be a balanced process of 'instruction, training and practice'[52] which should not be confined to the classroom or lecture theatre but also to playing fields.

Lord Hailsham also pointed out that 'education' was not a concept fixed at any particular point in time but which varied as time went on. This would mean, for example, that what was seen not to be educational 100 years ago might well be seen to be educational now.

What was important in the decision in the case was that the trust was established to benefit pupils and students at schools and universities.

A prize fund for a game which may generally be seen to be of a more educational character – chess – was held to be charitable in Re Dupree's Deed Trusts.[53] Vaisey J felt that the facts were 'a little near the line'[54] and remarked that '[o]ne feels, perhaps, that one is on a rather slippery slope. If chess, why not draughts?'[55]

Unless, however, the game is educational in itself, or there is a link to an educational establishment, a trust purely for sporting or games could not be charitable, as Re Nottage[56] demonstrates.

Here, George Nottage left £2,000 to the Yacht Raching Association of Great Britain for them to hold on trust to invest the money and to use its proceeds to establish an annual competition with the prize of 'The Nottage Cup' for the best yacht of each season. His will stated that the purpose behind the establishment of the competition was to encourage the sport of yacht racing. The issue was whether this could be a valid bequest. If it was to avoid infringing the rules of perpetuity, it had to be charitable.

Both Kekewich J, at first instance, and all of the members of the Court of Appeal held that the gift was not charitable. As Lindley LJ put it rather succinctly, '[i]t is a prize for a mere game'.[57]

The decision in Re Nottage demonstrates that sport in itself was not charitable where there was no link to it being educational or, as was argued in the case itself, where it could not be said to be a for a purpose beneficial to the community. The decision in the case would probably be different now. Section 3(1)(g) of the Charities Act 2011 provides that a charitable purpose can be the 'advancement of amateur sport'. This is considered in more depth below.[58]

Research . . .

Trusts for the purpose of research can be charitable under this head providing, again, that there can be shown to be some link to education as opposed to conducting research for its own sake. This appears to be the conclusion from the decisions of the High Court in Re Hopkins' Will Trusts[59] and Re Shaw.[60]

In Re Hopkins' Will Trusts, Evelyn Hopkins left one-third of her residuary estate to the Francis Bacon Society Inc to be held on trust by it and used for the purpose of finding the original

51 Ibid at 17.
52 Ibid at 18.
53 Re Dupree's Deed Trusts [1945] Ch 16.
54 Ibid at 20.
55 Ibid.
56 Re Nottage [1895] 2 Ch 649.
57 Ibid at 655.
58 See pp 423–424.
59 Re Hopkins' Will Trusts [1965] Ch 669.
60 Re Shaw [1957] 1 WLR 729.

manuscripts of those Shakespearean plays that some people believe were written by Francis Bacon. The society itself was charitable, but the issue was whether the trust was in its favour, or whether it was void for perpetuity.

Wilberforce J held that the trust was charitable. Searching, finding and researching into the original manuscripts of the Shakespearean plays would be of great value to both history and literature.

In contrast, Harman J held that a trust to conduct research into a new alphabet was not charitable in *Re Shaw*.[61]

George Bernard Shaw established a trust of his residuary estate in his will and directed his trustees to hold the money on trust to conduct research into how practical a new, 40-letter alphabet would be. He also instructed his trustees to translate his play *Androcles and the Lion* into the new alphabet's form and to use the translation to promote the new alphabet's use.

Harman J held that the trusts were not charitable. He said that, to be charitable, a trust for the promotion of research had to be 'combined with teaching or education'.[62] There was no teaching or education involved in this trust. It was merely to enable research to be undertaken into whether a new alphabet would save time and then to promote that new alphabet, by way of propaganda, to the public. Such purposes could not be charitable. Neither could the research fall into Lord Macnaghten's fourth head of being beneficial to the community. Advertising and promoting a new alphabet could not be seen to benefit the community, who might prefer to remain with the usual English alphabet.

In *Re Hopkins' Will Trusts*, Wilberforce J considered the view of Harman J that charitable trusts for the advancement of education had to have some link with teaching or education. He did not feel that was necessarily the case. Academic research could be seen to be charitable even though the researcher was not linked either to the teaching profession or an educational establishment.

Wilberforce J said that research could be charitable under this head, or if it could otherwise be seen to be for the benefit of the community. 'Education' had to be given a wide meaning. This meant the research could be:

> of educational value to the researcher or must be so directed as to lead to something which will pass into the store of educational material, or so as to improve the sum of communicable knowledge in an area which education may cover.[63]

Naturally, there had to be some public benefit to this research as he held that private research, the results of which were made known only to the members of a society, would not be charitable.

Alternatively, he said that research could be charitable if it fell under Lord Macnaghten's fourth charitable head – for the benefit of the community. In this case, 'beneficial' would be given a wide interpretation, to mean not just of material benefit (Wilberforce J gave the example of medical research giving a material benefit to the community as a whole) but also of intellectual or artistic benefit to the community.

These two decisions can be reconciled in that a trust for genuine research, improving knowledge with dissemination to show a public benefit, can be seen to be charitable either under this head, or for a purpose beneficial to the community (perhaps now under s 3(1)(f) of the Charities Act 2011 – a purpose which is for the advancement of the arts, culture,

---

61 Ibid.
62 Ibid at 737.
63 Ibid at 680.

heritage or science). On the other hand, a trust for research conducted to promote one's own subjective point of view, as opposed to increasing knowledge objectively, will not be seen to be charitable.

Music . . .

A society formed to advance choral singing in London was held to be charitable under this head in *Royal Choral Society v Commissioners of Inland Revenue*.[64] The society argued that its objectives were charitable: to provide choral concerts in the Royal Albert Hall, London and to encourage choral singing generally.

The Court of Appeal held that the society was charitable under this head. Providing music educated the listener. Lord Greene MR said he did not accept the view that 'education' had to be defined as narrowly as teaching when considering 'aesthetic education'.[65] The society, he thought, had been established for educational purposes because it was of the utmost relevance that the 'education of artistic taste is one of the most important things in the development of a civilised human being'.[66] Improving artistic taste of the general public was just as educational, he thought, as lecturing or teaching. The fact that entertainment was a by-product of the society was not important – its overall objective was to educate.

The advancement of religion

At first glance, perhaps oddly, the advancement of religion never featured as a charitable use within the Preamble. It was mentioned by Lord Macnaghten as his third charitable head in *Pemsel* and has been enshrined in s 3(1)(c) of the Charities Act 2011.

Section 3(2)(a) of the Charities Act 2011 provides guidance as to what is meant by 'religion'. It states that a religion may involve believing in more than one god. It also states that a religion may involve not believing in a god at all.

Established religions such as Christianity, Judaism and Islam[67] are all encompassed within the term 'religion' and so trusts to benefit such religions can be charitable in nature, provided public benefit is also demonstrated either by the religion or by the trust. The provision that religion may involve believing in more than one god would now specifically mean that trusts in favour of such religions as Hinduism and Shintoism could also be charitable.

The fact that 'religion' can now include a religion which does not involve believing in any god would suggest that the decision of the High Court in *Re South Place Ethical Society*[68] would be decided differently today.

The trustees of the South Place Ethical Society held its property on trust, the stated objective of the society being 'the study and dissemination of ethical principles and the cultivation of a rational religious sentiment'. The society's members were agnostics, who held meetings on Sundays at which the public could attend. Their beliefs involved, according to Dillon J, 'the belief in the excellence of truth, love and beauty but not belief in anything supernatural'.[69] The trustees sought a declaration that their objects were charitable.

Dillon J held that the objects of the trust were not charitable under the advancement of religion head. To Dillon J, 'two of the essential attributes of religion are faith and worship; faith

---

64 *Royal Choral Society v Commissioners of Inland Revenue* [1943] 2 All ER 101.
65 Ibid at 105.
66 Ibid.
67 See the dictum of Lord Parker in *Bowman v Secular Society Ltd* [1917] AC 406 at 449 that 'a trust for the purpose of any kind of monotheistic theism would be a good charitable trust'.
68 *Re South Place Ethical Society* [1980] 1 WLR 1565.
69 Ibid at 1569.

in a god and worship of that god'.[70] The society did not believe in a god and did not worship that god. Dillon J held, however, that the society's objects could be seen to be charitable under Lord Macnaghten's fourth head – that they were beneficial to the community.

Following the enactment of the Charities Act 2006, the objects of the society would undoubtedly be classed as religious. The definition in s 3(2)(a) of the 2011 Act widens out 'religion' considerably.

A more difficult issue remains with whether Scientology would be considered a religion.

❖ EXPLAINING THE LAW

Scientology involves a belief in the writings of an American named L Ron Hubbard. This involves the notion that everyone was placed on earth by aliens. Devotees of this faith include a number of celebrities such as Tom Cruise and John Travolta.

Traditionally, the English courts have not viewed Scientology as a religion.[71] This was largely due to the view of the courts, set out by Dillon J in *Re South Place Ethical Society*, that religion had to involve believing in a god. The cases on Scientology were all decided before the Charities Act 2011 was enacted, however, so it might be that a different conclusion would now be reached.

Support for Scientology being seen to be a religion for taxation purposes can be gained from the decision of the High Court of Australia in *Church of New Faith v Commissioner of Pay-Roll Tax (Victoria)*.[72] There the Church of New Faith followed the writings of L Ron Hubbard and its followers were Scientologists. The High Court of Australia held that the beliefs and practices of the church did fall into the definition of 'religion'. The High Court thought that religion should not be confined to those religions which believed in a god.

Having said this, even if Scientology was held to fall within the definition of 'religion' set out in the Charities Act 2011, it is suggested that it is unlikely it would be held to be charitable in England and Wales. This is because the second requirement of having charitable status – that of benefiting the public – is not satisfied by Scientology. Its practices benefit its members alone and it is, perhaps, more akin to a private club or society which benefits only its members rather than the general public.

The advancement of health or the saving of lives

The Preamble contained reference only to the 'Maintenance of Sick and Maimed Soldiers and Mariners'.

The 2011 Act contains a much wider definition, not limiting this head to those servicemen mentioned in the Preamble. Section 3(2)(b) refers to this head including 'the prevention or relief of sickness, disease or human suffering'. It seems that a charitable purpose could be the advancement of mental, as well as physical, health. For instance, Mind would be an example of a charity for the promotion of mental health in England and Wales that could now fall under this head.

---

70 Ibid at 1572.
71 See, for example, *Church of Scientology v Kaufman* [1973] RPC 635.
72 *Church of New Faith v Commissioner of Pay-Roll Tax (Victoria)* (1986) 154 CLR 120.

The advancement of health or the saving of lives was a new separate charitable head under the 2006 Act, but this purpose was seen as charitable under case law decided before the Act. In *Re North Devon and West Somerset Relief Fund Trusts*,[73] a trust to help save lives was recognised as charitable by Wynn-Parry J.

On 15 August 1952, torrential rain poured down over North Devon and West Somerset, causing severe flooding. An appeal was made by the Lord Lieutenants of both Devon and Somerset for donations to be made to a fund to be used to help both the inhabitants of the counties and visitors who had been affected by the rain. One issue for the High Court was whether this trust could be held to be charitable.

Wynn-Parry J held that it was. Its objective was to provide financial assistance to those who had been affected by the floods. It was designed to help those who had suffered and its aim was to help save lives.

Whilst the Preamble spoke specifically of maintaining sick and maimed servicemen, in truth this charitable head has probably always existed but as part of the more general relief of poverty purpose. In *McGovern v Attorney-General*,[74] Slade J accepted the analysis that poverty itself was probably merely a species of a more general charitable head which included the 'relief of suffering and distress in all the various forms enumerated'.[75] If this is right, the addition of this specific head in the 2006 Act (re-enacted in the 2011 Act) adds little to pre-existing charity law.

The advancement of citizenship or community development

The Preamble took a pragmatic approach to what might nowadays be referred to as 'community development'. It referred to charitable purposes being the 'Repair of Bridges, Ports, Havens, Causeways, Churches, Sea-banks and Highways'.

Section 3(2)(c)(i) states that this charitable head would continue to include physical projects by describing 'rural or urban regeneration' as falling within section 3(1)(e).

It is not necessary for the advancement of citizenship or community development to consist of building or repair works to community structures. Section 3(2)(c)(ii) states that this head would also include 'the promotion of civic responsibility, volunteering, the voluntary sector or the effectiveness or efficiency of charities'.

The notion that rewarding the community could consist of something other than physical construction was shown in *Re Mellody*.[76] There money was left on trust to provide an annual treat to schoolchildren in Turton. Eve J held that the trust could be seen to be charitable on two grounds: (i) for the advancement of education, and (ii) for the benefit of the community. The schoolchildren were a 'large and important section'[77] of the community who might be benefited by, for example, being taken out of their school and shown the countryside.

A more modern example of a trust which was to benefit the community was considered by the High Court in *Re Harding*.[78]

Sister Joseph Harding made a will in which she left all of her property to the 'Diocese of Westminster to hold in trust for the black community of Hackney, Haringey, Islington and Tower Hamlets'. Sister Joseph made no provision of what she expected the Diocese of

---

73 *Re North Devon and West Somerset Relief Fund Trusts* [1953] 1 WLR 1260.
74 *McGovern v Attorney-General* [1982] Ch 321.
75 Ibid at 333.
76 *Re Mellody* [1918] 1 Ch 228.
77 Ibid at 231.
78 *Re Harding* [2008] Ch 235.

Westminster to do with her property so that the black community of those London areas would benefit, but it appears it was intended for that community's general development.

Lewison J held that the trust was valid as a charitable trust. It did not matter that Sister Joseph had not set out precisely how she expected the Diocese to apply the property.

Both decisions concerned charitable trusts benefiting large sections of the community so it would appear that, to fall under this charitable head, the trust need not seek to advance the entire community.

The advancement of the arts, culture, heritage or science

Many of the decisions already considered as falling into Lord Macnaghten's fourth charitable head as being for the benefit of the community would now most likely be held to be charitable under this particular head. Cases that have already been considered which would now fall into this category include the provision of choral music to the public in *Royal Choral Society v Inland Revenue Commissioners* and also research in *Re Hopkins' Will Trusts*. The research into the true author of the Shakespearean plays would now be seen to be for the advancement of the arts, culture and/or heritage.

There are many organisations with charitable status that would now fall under this charitable head. These could include museums, libraries and galleries, all of which exist to promote any or all of the parts of this charitable head.

The advancement of amateur sport

It will be remembered that before the Charities Act 2006 was enacted, sport itself was not a charitable purpose.[79] Sport could only be charitable if it was linked in some way to another charitable head, such as education or for the benefit of the community.

The Charities Act 2006 marked a shift in thinking that had occurred since *Re Nottage*. Perhaps concerned to promote exercise and physical activity, the advancement of amateur sport is now a charitable head in its own right and there is no need to show any link with any other charitable purpose.

In guidance produced in April 2003, however, the Charity Commission[80] had already confirmed that playing sport in its own right with no link to education could be charitable. Its guidance was based on the fact that the playing of sport could fall into Lord Macnaghten's fourth head, so that playing sport as part of the community could be seen to be charitable. The guidance focuses on the need for the sport to be healthy. 'Healthy' is defined to mean 'those sports which, if practised with reasonable frequency, will tend to make the participant healthier, that is, fitter and less susceptible to disease'.[81] In turn, 'fitness' could be met by the sport helping to increase 'stamina, strength and suppleness'[82] albeit that only one of those three criteria is required for a sport to be recognised as advancing fitness. Having said that, in a note at the front of the guidance, the Commission does accept that the promotion of health does not just have to be the promotion of physical health, but can also include the promotion of mental skill. The provision for chess in *Re Dupree's Deed Trusts*[83] might, if decided today, be seen to be charitable under this head.

---

79 *Re Nottage* [1895] 2 Ch 649.
80 Charity Commission, *The Review of the Register of Charities, Charitable Status and Sport*, April 2003.
81 Ibid at 9.
82 Ibid.
83 *Re Dupree's Deed Trusts* [1945] Ch 16.

The Charity Commission provided a list of some sports which it did not feel met its definition of 'healthy'. These included angling, pool, snooker and any form of motor sport.

Dangerous sports will not generally be seen to be charitable, as the Commission's view is that their danger outweighs any health benefits the sport may generate. If the dangers can be reduced, it may be that the Commission would recognise the sport as charitable, for it would then be focusing primarily on promoting health rather than being dangerous. It seems that risks must be reduced severely, however. The Commission gives the example[84] of amateur boxing and suggests that if risks were mitigated to an 'absolute minimum', it would consider recognising such a club for the promotion of that sport as charitable.

The Commission's guidelines state that they are being revised to take into account this charitable head. Although issued before the enactment of the 2006 Act, the guidelines in some ways pre-empted it. Section 3(2)(d) confirms that 'sport' in s 3(1)(g) means 'sports or games which promote health by involving physical or mental skill or exertion'. The Commission's suggestions of those sports which would not be charitable must almost certainly continue to be correct, due to the statutory requirements in the Act itself of the requirements needed for sports to be charitable.

The advancement of human rights, conflict resolution or reconciliation or the promotion of religious or racial harmony or equality and diversity

This, together with the next charitable head in s 3(1) of the 2011 Act, may arguably be seen to be the two most contemporary charitable purposes set out in the Act.

It will now be seen to be charitable to undertake any or all of these purposes set out in this paragraph, but a settlor must take care to ensure that his charitable purpose is not political in any way. A trust for a political purpose cannot be charitable. This was set out by Slade J in *McGovern v Attorney-General*.[85]

The facts concerned a trust established in 1977 by Amnesty International.

❖ EXPLAINING THE LAW

Amnesty International itself was formed in 1961 with the purpose of ensuring that every country in the world observed the United Nations' Universal Declaration of Human Rights. Specifically, Amnesty International was – and is – concerned about political prisoners: people who might be summarily arrested and held without trial and perhaps even executed in countries simply for holding political beliefs. Amnesty International seeks the abolition of such practices, by working for political prisoners to be released, helping their families and generally seeking to persuade public opinion throughout the world that such practices should be abolished.

Amnesty International never considered itself to be charitable, but it received advice that some of its purposes could be. It therefore decided to filter out what it considered to be its charitable purposes into a Declaration of Trust. The trust document said that the trustees were to hold money on trust for the following purposes:

---

84 Ibid at 24.
85 *McGovern v Attorney-General* [1982] Ch 321.

(a)   the relief of certain categories of 'needy persons' (e.g. political prisoners or their relatives or dependants);

(b)   to try to secure the release of political prisoners;

(c)   to procure the abolition of torture or inhuman or degrading treatment;

(d)   to research into human rights; and

(e)   to disseminate the reserach undertaken into human rights.

The Charity Commissioners' view was that the trust was not charitable as its objects were not 'exclusively charitable'. The only purpose likely to be charitable was (a). The remainder were not charitable as they were of a political nature.

Slade J referred to the two decisions of the House of Lords in Bowman v Secular Society Ltd[86] and National Anti-Vivisection Society v Inland Revenue Commissioners.[87] Both decisions had held that trusts for political purposes could not be charitable. The purposes both involved procuring a change of the law in England. Slade J explained that there were two reasons why such a trust could not be charitable: (i) there will not usually be any evidence available to the court to decide if the change in the law is for the benefit of the public or not, and (ii) even if there is evidence, it is for Parliament (and not the court) to decide if a change in the law is needed and to modify the law as required.

The same reasons could be made for a trust to procure the law being changed in a foreign country. A further reason, based on public policy, existed in the case of such a trust – such a trust might have an adverse impact on relations between the UK and that foreign country.

A trust for political purposes could not, therefore, be charitable. But Slade J did not just feel that political purposes involved procuring a change of law in this country or abroad. Political purposes could also entail trying to reverse government policy or change administrative decisions of governmental authorities. Political purposes could also involve furthering the interests of a political party.[88]

Trusts seeking to advance any of these purposes as their main objective would also not be charitable. The reasons were exactly the same: the court could not assess if these purposes were of any benefit to the public and in promoting such trusts as charitable, the court would be encroaching on the government's role.

The main purposes of Amnesty International's trust deed were political. Each of the objectives listed above (with the exception of (a)) sought to bring pressure to bear on governments to reverse their policy on each particular matter. As each of the purposes could not be separated from one another, the entire trust was political and not charitable.

This does not mean that any tainting of a trust with some degree of political purpose will render the trust non-charitable. The focus is on the main objective of the trust. If any of the trust's main objectives are political in nature, the trust cannot be charitable. But if a political objective of the trust is subsidiary to an otherwise charitable main purpose, the trust can still be charitable. Similarly, a trust could still be charitable if it set about achieving its charitable purpose by campaigning for a change in the law: the campaigning would be subsidiary to achieving its charitable objective.

McGovern v Attorney-General was, of course, decided prior to the implementation of the new charitable purposes in the 2006 Act. In Hanchett-Stamford v Attorney-General,[89] the issue arose as to whether, by the specific enacting of new, more diverse, charitable heads in the 2006 Act, some

86 Bowman v Secular Society Ltd [1917] AC 406.
87 National Anti-Vivisection Society v Inland Revenue Commissioners [1948] AC 31.
88 See Re Hopkinson [1949] 1 All ER 346.
89 Hanchett-Stamford v Attorney-General [2009] Ch 173.

arguably with political overtones in them, it could be said that the Act had impliedly consented to political purposes now being deemed to be charitable.

The facts in *Hanchett-Stamford* concerned an application for an unincorporated association to be recognised as charitable under s 2(2)(k) of the Charities Act 2006 (now s 3(1)(k) of the Charities Act 2011) but the decision concerning political purposes is relevant to any trust or organisation claiming charitable status.

Mrs Hanchett-Stamford was the last surviving member of the Performing and Captive Animals Defence League, an unincorporated association originally formed in 1914 in order to prevent the use of animals performing in circuses or in films. The Inland Revenue's view was that the League's main purpose was to try to change the law in the UK, so it could not be charitable.

The league had had many members, particularly during the 1960s, but slowly membership had declined to where the claimant was the only member. She was elderly and lived in a nursing home. The league, however, still had assets worth over £2 million and she wanted to transfer them to another charity promoting animal welfare under the doctrine of *cy-près*.[90] To transfer the entire amount, she needed the league to be recognised as having charitable status.

Lewison J held that the league was not charitable when it was originally established, as its main purpose was to change the law to ban performing animals. Such a purpose was political in nature.

Lewison J rejected the view that the Charities Act 2006 had changed the law to permit trusts with political objectives to be regarded as charitable. It was, he said, a 'fundamental principle'[91] that if at least one of the objectives of the trust was political, it could not be charitable. As the last surviving member of this non-charitable unincorporated association, the assets belonged to Mrs Hanchett-Stamford absolutely and not on any charitable trust.

It is, therefore, possible to establish a charitable trust with the objective of advancing any or all of the purposes listed under s 3(1)(h). Yet as neither the Charities Act 2006 nor its 2011 successor have altered the key rule that a charity's main purpose must not be political, it is suggested that perhaps more care needs to be taken under this head than any other that that rule is not infringed.

The advancement of environmental protection or improvement

This is, again, a reflection of modern concerns to protect the environment. There are a number of well-known charitable organisations which would now be seen to fall under this head, such as Friends of the Earth.

The relief of those in need by reason of youth, age, ill-health, disability, financial hardship or other disadvantage

As discussed, in *McGovern v Attorney-General*,[92] Slade J accepted the proposition that the 'relief of suffering and distress' had always formed part of the charitable head of the relief of poverty.[93] There are many organisations which may fall under this specific head today (for example, youth clubs and well-known organisations such as Help the Aged). Section 3(2)(e) states that 'relief' under this head may include the provision of care or accommodation to those categories of person described.

---

90 See Chapter 16 for a discussion of this doctrine.
91 *Hanchett-Stamford v Attorney-General* [2009] Ch 173 at 181.
92 *McGovern v Attorney-General* [1982] Ch 321.
93 Ibid at 333.

It must be asked if this charitable head was specifically needed in the Act at all. Almost all of the other heads under s 3(1) either added to, or clarified, pre-existing charitable purposes. Given that purposes considered charitable before the Act was enacted will continue to be charitable[94] and the comments of Slade J in *McGovern v Attorney-General*, it is doubtful that this head adds anything except, perhaps, for the addition of 'other disadvantage'. It is unclear what this phrase would encompass although any charitable object would need to be analogous to the other definitions in this paragraph.

The advancement of animal welfare

The advancement of animal welfare has long been seen to be charitable. The reasoning behind this was discussed in *Re Wedgwood*.[95]

Frances Wedgwood made a will in which she appeared to leave her residuary estate to Cecil Wedgwood absolutely. Evidence arose, however, that she had actually declared a fully secret trust in which she had appointed Cecil her trustee to hold the property on trust for the benefit and protection of animals. The Court of Appeal held that there was, in fact, a secret trust. Following earlier authorities,[96] it held that a trust for the benefit and protection of animals could be said to be charitable.

Swinfen Eady LJ explained that the trust would fall under Lord Macnaghten's fourth head in *Pemsel*, as one being for the benefit of the community. The trust could:

> stimulate humane and generous sentiments in man towards the lower animals, and by these means promote feelings of humanity and morality generally, repress brutality, and thus elevate the human race.[97]

In *Hanchett-Stamford v Attorney-General*,[98] Lewison J did not think that the enactment of a bespoke charitable head, in what is now s 3(1)(k) for the advancement of animal welfare, had made any substantial change in the law.[99]

The promotion of the efficiency of the armed forces of the Crown, or of the efficiency of the police, fire and rescue services or ambulance services

This paragraph concerns both the military and civilian services and 'rescue services' would undoubtedly include particular services which are not mentioned specifically under the head, such as the coastguard. The Preamble mentioned only military services and then only the 'Maintenance of Sick and Maimed Soldiers and Mariners'. The promotion of the efficiency of the armed forces and civilian forces was, however, recognised by subsequent decisions as being within the spirit and intendment of the Preamble.[100]

Quite what 'efficiency' means in this paragraph is open to debate. 'Efficiency' usually entails reducing something in terms of time or cost. So could, for example, a trust receive charitable status if it was established to produce nuclear weapons as those would, on a rather

---

94 Charities Act 2011, s 3(1)(m)(i).
95 *Re Wedgwood* [1915] 1 Ch 113.
96 For example, *University of London v Yarrow* 1 De G & J 72; *Tatham v Drummond* (1864) 4 D J & S 484.
97 *Re Wedgwood* [1915] 1 Ch 113 at 122.
98 *Hanchett-Stamford v Attorney-General* [2009] Ch 173.
99 Ibid at 181.
100 See Lord Normand in *Inland Revenue Commissioners v City of Glasgow Police Athletic Association* [1953] AC 380 at 391.

Machievellian analysis, be more efficient for the armed forces to use than conventional weapons? It would be rather surprising if this was the case. Perhaps, therefore, 'efficiency' in terms of the armed forces would have to be restricted to their administrative operations.

Other purposes

Paragraph (m) provides three further categories of recognised charitable purpose:

(a)   any previously existing purpose declared charitable by statute or case law which does not fall within paragraphs (a)–(l);[101]

(b)   any purpose that may reasonably be seen to be 'analogous to, or within the spirit of' any of the above 12 purposes;[102] and

(c)   any purpose that may reasonably be seen to be 'analogous to, or within the spirit of' any previously recognised charitable purpose.[103]

The overall aim of these provisions is that the law will continue to recognise as charitable any previous charitable purpose or any purpose of a similar nature to it. This means that pre-existing case law deciding charitable purposes as being within the spirit and intendment of the Preamble will continue to be good and may continue to be followed.

Second Requirement of Charitable Status: There Must Be Public Benefit

Section 2(1)(b) of the Charities Act 2011 provides that the charity must benefit the public. 'Public benefit' carries with it the meaning that has evolved in case law decided before the Act was enacted.[104]

This second requirement of charitable status is just as important as the first: the charitable trust must benefit the public or a sufficiently large section of it so that it can be said that the public is benefiting. As Dillon J put it in Re South Place Ethical Society:[105]

> One of the requirements of a charity is that there should be some element of public benefit in the sense that it must not be merely a members' club or devoted to the self-improvement of its own members.

In Hanchett-Stanford v Attorney-General, Lewison J recognised that public benefit could be direct or indirect. Direct public benefit is where there is a clear benefit to the public by the use to which the trust property is put. Indirect public benefit exists where the public will not directly benefit from the trust property, but where it can be showed that the public will benefit simply by virtue of the trust being created. In the case of trusts against animal cruelty, for example, the public benefit is indirect: the trust property is not being used to benefit the public, but the public benefits spiritually from knowing that animals will be better treated.

---

101 Charities Act 2011, s 3(1) (m) (i).
102 Ibid, s 3(1) (m) (ii).
103 Ibid, s 3(1) (m) (iii).
104 Charities Act 2011, s 4(3).
105 Re South Place Ethical Society [1980] 1 WLR 1565 at 1570.

The 'personal nexus' test: *Oppenheim v Tobacco Securities Trust Co Ltd*[106]

Mr and Mrs Phillips created a trust in 1930 under which they granted a remainder interest[107] in certain property to Tobacco Securities Trust Co Ltd. The income from it was to be used to educate the children of employees, or ex-employees, of British American Tobacco Ltd, or any of its subsidiary companies. The issue was whether the trust was valid. As in so many other cases, it could only validly take effect as a charitable trust, as it would otherwise infringe the rules against perpetuity.

By a majority, the House of Lords held that the trust was not charitable because it did not benefit the public. It undoubtedly had a charitable purpose to it – to advance education – but that was not enough in itself to make the trust charitable. It also had to benefit the public.

In giving the leading speech of the majority, Lord Simonds emphasised that, to be charitable, the trust had to benefit either the community as a whole, or a section of it. 'Section of the community' had two parts to it, both of which had to be satisfied:

(a)   that the number of possible beneficiaries could not be 'numerically negligible';[108] and

(b)   that the attribute that distinguished the section of the community from the community as a whole could not be a quality which rested on their relationship to a particular individual. In other words, there could be no personal nexus – or connection – which linked all of those in the section of the community with a particular individual.

On the facts, the number of possible children who could benefit from the trust was not numerically negligible. There were over 110,000 current employees of the companies mentioned in the trust deed so the number of their children (together with the children of the ex-employees) who could benefit from the trust must have been far higher. But the trust fell down on Lord Simonds' second requirement. Those benefiting from the trust could only benefit because their parents worked at one of a few companies. All of the beneficiaries had to have that connection between them to be eligible to benefit from the trust. As such, they could not constitute either the community itself (where everyone would have to benefit) or a section of it.

Dissenting, Lord Macdermott would have held that the trust was valid. He thought that, as the trust was for a charitable purpose and did benefit a large number of beneficiaries, there should be an assumption that the trust was charitable unless evidence was led to the contrary. He pointed out that he thought the requirement that there must be no personal nexus between the beneficiaries was illogical and would lead to different results on substantially similar facts. One of his examples was a trust set up to benefit coal miners. Such a trust could be valid if the miners had no connection to one another. Yet when the coal mines were nationalised after World War II, the miners would have had a connection to each other as they were then all employed by the National Coal Board. It was odd that a trust could be valid prior to, but not after, the nationalisation of the coal industry.

Despite the (valid) doubts expressed by Lord Macdermott, the views of the majority do, of course, represent the law and the majority decision was applied by the Court of Appeal in *Inland Revenue Commissioners v Educational Grants Association Ltd*.[109] What was interesting about the latter case was that not all of the beneficiaries shared the same connection.

---

106 *Oppenheim v Tobacco Securities Trust Ltd* [1951] AC 297.
107 For a discussion of what a remainder interest is, see Chapter 2, Figure 2.5.
108 *Oppenheim v Tobacco Securities Trust Ltd* [1951] AC 297 at 306.
109 *Inland Revenue Commissioners v Educational Grants Association Ltd* [1967] Ch 993.

John Ryan was a director of Metal Box Co Ltd. He was interested in education and helping out individuals who had difficulty in educating their children at private schools, colleges or universities, if they did not receive a grant from their local authority. He persuaded his company to set up the Educational Grants Association Ltd which would pay scholarships to such students. Metal Box Co Ltd would fund the Association. This money was held on trust by the Association for the benefit of the children. The aim of the Association was to provide grants primarily for the children of the employees of Metal Box Co Ltd. The Association claimed it administered a charitable trust; the Inland Revenue argued to the contrary.

The Association had not just benefited children whose parents worked for the Metal Box Co Ltd, but that had been its main aim and those children were the main recipients of the grants. In most years, at least 85 per cent of the grants had gone to such children with only the remaining 15 per cent going to other organisations or individuals. The lowest number of grants that had gone to the children whose parents were employed by Metal Box Co Ltd was 76 per cent – and that only occurred in one year.

Applying *Oppenheim*, the Court of Appeal held that the money applied for the children whose parents worked for Metal Box Co Ltd was not charitable. There was a personal nexus between those children: they could only benefit from the trust because their parents worked for the company. That was a private characteristic and did not provide evidence that the trust for them was of a public nature. It could not be said to benefit the public and was not, therefore, charitable.

Is the public benefit requirement different in trusts for the prevention or relief of poverty?

In *Oppenheim*, the House of Lords acknowledged that charities for the relief of poverty had historically been treated differently from other charities. The issue was whether such charities did have to show public benefit or not. Previous case law was split on this issue. In *Oppenheim*, Lord Simonds did not agree or disagree with previous decisions in that regard: he merely accepted that they were a separate category.

Section 4(2) of the Charities Act 2011 makes no exception that trusts for the relief or prevention of poverty need not be for public benefit; on the contrary, s 4(1) provides that all purposes within s 3(1) must benefit the public if they are to be regarded as charitable. These sections of the 2011 Act repeated earlier sections of the Charities Act 2006.

The issue of whether the Charities Act 2006 had introduced a new requirement that trusts for the prevention or relief of poverty now had to demonstrate that they benefited the public was considered by the Upper Tribunal (Tax and Chancery Chamber) in *Attorney-General v Charity Commission for England and Wales*.[110] In giving the judgment of the Tribunal, Warren J thought that public benefit generally could be broken down into two categories:

(a) 'the nature of the purpose itself must be such as to be a benefit to the community';[111] and

(b) 'those who may benefit from the carrying out of the purpose must be sufficiently numerous'.[112]

To have charitable status, the trust would have to show that it fell within either (or both) categories within his definition. But Warren J felt that trusts for the relief of poverty had all

---

110 *Attorney-General v Charity Commission for England and Wales* [2012] WTLR 977.
111 Ibid at 30.
112 Ibid at 33.

satisfied the first category of public benefit and it was not the case previously that trusts for the relief of poverty had not benefited the public. The express requirement in s 4(1), that all charities must now benefit the public, had not altered the pre-Act law substantively because all trusts for the relief of poverty could be said in the past to have benefited the public in the sense Warren J defined it in his first category.

If Warren J is correct, it therefore seems that trusts for the prevention or relief of poverty are not treated any differently from any other charitable trust in that they are required to show that they do benefit the public. This is no change from the pre-Act position. But it is suggested that in the vast majority of trusts concerning poverty, it will be fairly straightforward for them to show that they do benefit the public when viewed in the light of Warren J's two categories.

'Section of the community'

It was recognised in *Oppenheim* that a trust did not have to benefit the entire community to satisfy the public benefit requirement. Instead, the trust need only satisfy a section of the community.

It is clear, however, that a section of the community cannot be unduly restricted by the trust so that a 'class within a class'[113] is created. This was decided by the House of Lords in *Inland Revenue Commissioners v Baddeley*,[114] because the public, as such, is not truly benefiting from the trust; instead the trust is conferring a benefit on a group of private individuals.

Two pieces of land in Essex were conveyed to the trustees of the Newtown Trust. There was a church on the first piece of land and recreational grounds on the second. The trusts on which the trustees were to hold the land were for current (or those likely to become) members of the Methodist Church in West Ham and Leyton. The trustees claimed that they should pay a lower than normal amount of stamp duty on the conveyances as they said the trusts on which they held the land were charitable.

The majority of the House of Lords disagreed. They held that there was no charitable purpose to the trusts as they were too vaguely defined to fall into any of the *Pemsel*-defined charitable purposes. In *obiter* comments, Viscount Simonds went further. He held that in confining the enjoyment of the lands to Methodists in those areas of Essex, the trust created a class within a class. That was not the same as saying that the entire community, or even a section of it, could benefit from the trust, which was required to be charitable. It could not be considered to benefit the public if its benefit was expressly restricted to a particular group within the community. It would be a different matter if the benefit of the trust was, in fact, open to the community and only a few chose to benefit from it. What mattered was that the trust specifically restricted the benefit of the land to members of the community who had to meet a particular criterion.

Whether a class within a class had been created arose more recently on the facts of *Re Harding*.[115] A trust was established to benefit members of the black community in certain London boroughs. Making use of s 34 of the Race Relations Act 1976, Lewison J removed the requirement that only black people could benefit from the trust. This meant that no class within a class had been created by the testatrix when drafting the trust and it could, therefore, take effect as a charitable trust.

---

113 Per Viscount Simonds in *Inland Revenue Commissioners v Baddeley* [1955] AC 572.
114 *Inland Revenue Commissioners v Baddeley* [1955] AC 572.
115 *Re Harding* [2008] Ch 235.

Public benefit and trusts for the advancement of religion

Thus far, the remarks on public benefit are apt to apply to all charitable heads. But it seems that trusts for the advancement of religion may have slightly different requirements of public benefit which are wider than in the case of the other charitable heads.

Clearly, it will be for the benefit of the public, in the sense of either the whole community or a section of it, if money is held on trust for religious purposes which invite attendees. But it appears that there may be public benefit even though members of the community do not attend a religious building. In *Neville Estates Ltd v Madden*,[116] Cross J held that a trust for members of a synagogue in Catford could be charitable. Even though the membership of the synagogue was restricted to Jewish persons who conformed to particular rituals, the trust could be seen to have public benefit by members of the synagogue mixing with and disseminating their religious knowledge and beliefs into the wider community.

Cross J was able to distinguish *Baddeley* on the basis that no charitable purpose had been found by the House of Lords for the trust in that case as the purposes for which the lands were to be held were too vaguely defined. He held that there was a charitable purpose in the present case: the advancement of religion.

The Charity Commission's guidance on public benefit

Section 4 of the Charities Act 2006 obliged the Charity Commission to consult on, and thereafter issue, guidance on what may constitute public benefit.[117] Under s 14(2), the Commission is obliged to 'promote awareness and understanding of the operation' of the public benefit requirement needed to attain charitable status.

In January 2008, the Charity Commission published its guidance[118] on public benefit. It contains two key principles:[119]

(a)   a charity has to have an 'identifiable benefit or benefits'; and
(b)   that benefit 'must be to the public, or a section of the public'.

There must be an identifiable benefit or benefits

Within each key principle, there are a number of what the Commission labels 'important factors' to consider to test if each key principle is met. For the first key principle, these are:

(a)   the benefit(s) must be clear;
(b)   there must be a connection between the benefit(s) and the purpose(s) of the charity; and
(c)   the benefit(s) must be balanced against any harm that the charity may cause.[120]

In terms of (a), the Charity Commission recognises that some charitable purposes will invariably have clear benefits to them. For example, when the National Trust opens a property to the public, it is undoubtedly a benefit that the public learns first-hand about the heritage of the property and the people who lived there. Where the public benefit is not immediately obvious,

---

116   *Neville Estates Ltd v Madden* [1962] Ch 832.
117   The Charity Commission remains obliged to continue to issue guidance on what may constitute public benefit under s 17(1) of the Charities Act 2011.
118   The Charity Commission, *Charities and Public Benefit* (January 2008, amended December 2011).
119   Ibid at C3.
120   Ibid at E1.

the guidance states that the benefits that the charity gives should generally be 'capable of being recognised, identified, defined or described'.[121]

For (b), the benefits the charity gives must be related to its charitable aim. One cannot use an accidental benefit generated by the charity in support of a proposition that the charity generally benefits the public. The Commission gives the example[122] of the charitable aim to preserve a historic building. The trustees might decide to generate further income by providing a skating rink in the winter months. But they could not claim that the health benefits of people using the skating rink are related to the aim of the charity, which is to preserve the building. The health benefits have no connection to the aim of the charity.

Important factor (c) is about balance. Incidental, and minimal, harm caused by a charity's aim must be balanced against the public benefit from pursuing the aim. If the harm caused is minimal, it is unlikely that the charity will not be held to benefit the public. The Commission gives the example[123] of a charitable aim to provide motorised transport for people with a disability. It could be said that such transport harms the environment but such harm would be outweighed by the benefit of providing the transport.

The benefit must be to the public, or a section of the public

The Commission originally listed[124] four important factors for this principle:

(a) the beneficiaries must be 'appropriate to the aims';
(b) if the benefit is to a section of the public, the chance to benefit cannot be restricted by (i) 'geographical or other restrictions' or (ii) the 'ability to pay any fees charged';
(c) those in poverty could not be excluded from the chance to benefit from the charity; and
(d) any private benefits generated by the charity had to be incidental to the public benefits.

Under important factor (a) the Commission recognises that the beneficiaries may only be a section of the public if the aim of the charity is only to benefit a proportion of people. The Commission effectively reiterates the decision in *Inland Revenue Commissioners v Baddeley* that a charity's aims cannot be restricted to benefiting such a small section of the public that it effectively means that the public is not benefiting at all.

Under important factor (b), the Commission states that any restrictions on who may benefit must be 'legitimate, proportionate, rational and justifiable' in relation to the aims of the charity.[125] The general principle must be that as many people as possible benefit from the charity's aims. Geographical restrictions may have a part to play in, say, a village hall which is intended to benefit those inhabitants of a village. But such a charity would be expected to be open to all those living in the village as opposed to a select few.

As originally drafted, important factor (b) contained a second guideline: that the opportunity to benefit could not be 'unreasonably restricted by the ability to pay any fees charged'. This (together with guideline (c)) is in the process of being revised extensively by the Commission following the decision of the Upper Tribunal (Tax and Chancery Chamber) in *The Independent Schools Council v The Charity Commission for England and Wales*.[126] The Independent Schools Council applied for these guidelines to be quashed. The Upper Tribunal held that these parts

---

121 Ibid at E2.
122 Ibid at E3.
123 Ibid at E4.
124 Ibid at F1.
125 Ibid at F3.
126 *The Independent Schools Council v The Charity Commission for England and Wales* [2011] UKUT 421 (TCC).

of this guidance were wrong, with the consequence that the Commission will shortly be consulting on new guidelines with the aim of publishing final guidelines in summer 2012.

In terms of independent, fee-charging schools, the Upper Tribunal held that there would be no public benefit unless the school provided some benefit for those people who were not paying its fees. But the Upper Tribunal said that, provided a minimum threshold of public benefit was provided, it was a decision for the trustees of the school, not the Charity Commission, to decide how those benefits should be provided.

In interim guidance issued since the decision of the Upper Tribunal was given, the Commission has given some examples[127] of how fee-charging schools could provide such benefit. These include offering financial assistance for a number of places at the school, sharing facilities with state school pupils, or engaging in a teacher-exchange programme with a state school.

Other fee-paying charities also need to demonstrate their public benefit and not restrict their benefit to those members of society who can afford to pay their fees. Museums, for example, could offer concessionary tickets to those who are financially disadvantaged. Theatres could give free drama workshops for students. A private hospital could offer treatment at a reduced rate for those unable to afford its full fees.

Guideline 2(d) states that any private benefits received must be incidental to those public benefits generated by the charity. The Commission is concerned not with reasonable private benefits that beneficiaries of the charity may receive. It is also not concerned with benefits that non-beneficiaries may receive, again as long as they are subsidiary to the charity's aim. It gives the example[128] of local businesses benefiting from a charity's regeneration project in a particular area. That would be a purely incidental private benefit of the charity's public work.

The Commission here is concerned about private benefits that only its trustees can receive or, alternatively, that its members can receive if the charity effectively takes the form of a members' club. Such benefits cannot be reconciled with the general principle that the charity must benefit the public.

Third Requirement of Charitable Status: The Objects Must Be Exclusively Charitable

This requirement means that, as a general principle, the trust must exist only for charitable reasons. Thus it is said that the trust's objects (or aims) must be 'exclusively charitable'.

The leading case on this third requirement of charitable status is the decision of the House of Lords in *Inland Revenue Commissioners v City of Glasgow Police Athletic Association*.[129]

Here the Police Athletic Association existed to provide sporting and recreational facilities for the officers (and ex-officers) of the City of Glasgow Police department.

The House of Lords held that the Association had a charitable purpose: it existed to promote the efficiency of the police. But it also had a non-charitable purpose, which was to provide sporting facilities for its members. It could not be charitable to provide facilities to a group of people who were not the public or a section of it. Effectively, the Association was a private club, as only serving or former police officers could join it. The issue was whether this non-charitable purpose could be incidental to its charitable purpose.

---

127 The Charity Commission, *Upper Tribunal's decision on public benefit and fee-charging charities: Questions and answers and interim advice for charity trustees.*
128 The Charity Commission, *Charities and Public Benefit* at F12.
129 *Inland Revenue Commissioners v City of Glasgow Police Athletic Association* [1953] AC 380.

The House of Lords held it could not. The private benefits, that of making use of the sporting and recreational facilities, were 'essential' to the members. As Lord Normand put it:

> The private advantage of members is a purpose for which the assocation is established and it therefore cannot be said that this is an association established for a public charitable purpose only.[130]

It is only if the non-charitable purpose is incidental to the charitable purpose that the trust can still be seen to be charitable. This was shown in *London Hospital Medical College v Inland Revenue Commissioners*.[131]

The objects of the London Hospital Clubs Union were to promote 'social, cultural and athletic activities' and 'to add to the comfort and enjoyment of the students'. The Union considered itself part of, and controlled by, the London Hospital Medical College. The Inland Revenue thought that the Union could not be seen to be charitable as its purposes were not exclusively charitable and instead it was a club which existed simply for the benefit of its members.

Brightman J recognised that a club existing for its members' benefit only could not be seen to be charitable. Here, however, the Union existed to further the educational purposes of the College. That was its main purpose. Any personal benefits that the individual members of the Union attained as members were incidental to the main charitable purpose for which it existed.

As Brightman J said, it will be a question of fact whether the trust has one or more purpose and whether that purpose is, or is not, charitable. Provided the trust's main purpose is charitable and any other purpose is incidental to it, and it benefits the public, the trust will be held to be charitable.

As can be seen, there is a strong connection between this third requirement to be a charity and the Charity Commission's guideline that private benefits must be incidental to the public benefit generated by the charity. It is probably still the case, however, that the two requirements remain distinct.

Points to Review

You have seen:

- how charities are administered on a day-to-day basis by their trustees but that the Charity Commission exists in part to oversee that the trustees act properly;
- the taxation and legal advantages of having charitable status;
- that to be charitable, a trust must exist for a charitable purpose, benefit the public and its objects (or aims) must be exclusively charitable;
- that charitable purposes have not stood still since the Preamble to the Statute of Charitable Uses 1601. From the time the Preamble was written, the courts would interpret purposes which were within the 'spirit and intendment' of the Preamble to be charitable. In turn, purposes which were similar to those interpreted by the courts as charitable would also be seen to be charitable. That approach continues under the Charities Act 2011. As such, the law of charities is not fixed in time to the age of Elizabeth I but is constantly changing and evolving, reflecting society's needs and demands as to what should be seen to be charitable; and

---

130 Ibid at 396.
131 *London Hospital Medical College v Inland Revenue Commissioners* [1976] 1 WLR 613.

- that the requirement that the charity must exist not just for the few but for the many has been strengthened by the provisions of the Charities Act 2011 and the guidance issued by the Charity Commission. Charities must exist to benefit the public or a not numerically negligible section of the public. Those beneficiaries cannot just benefit from the charity because of some personal connection with the settlor of the trust.

Making connections

This chapter has considered the law of charities. It discussed how charities exist and often break the rules against perpetuities because they may last for an indefinite period of time. Please see the chapter on the Rules against Perpetuities on the companion website. Charities may also be established with less certainty in their aims than other express trusts. If you are unsure about the certainties involved in the creation of an express trust, please see Chapter 5. Charities also breach the beneficiary principle in that there is no human beneficiary to enforce the trust against the trustees. The beneficiary principle is discussed in Chapter 6.

If an express trust fails, the normal 'default' position is that a resulting trust will be implied so that the trust property jumps back to the settlor. If a charitable trust fails, a cy-près scheme can be implied so that another charity benefits from the trust property. Cy-près schemes are considered in Chapter 16.

 Useful Things to Read

The best reading is contained in the primary sources listed below. It is always good to consider the decisions of the courts themselves as this will lead to a deeper understanding of the issues involved. A few secondary sources are also listed, which you may wish to read to gain additional insights into the areas considered in this chapter.

Primary sources
Attorney-General v Charity Commission for England and Wales [2012] WTLR 977
Hanchett-Stamford v Attorney-General [2009] Ch 173
Inland Revenue Commissioners v City of Glasgow Police Athletic Association [1953] AC 380
McGovern v Attorney-General [1982] Ch 321
Oppenheim v Tobacco Securities Trust Ltd [1951] AC 297
The Commissioners for Special Purposes of the Income Tax v Pemsel [1891] AC 531

Secondary sources
The Charity Commission, 'Charities and Public Benefit' (January 2008, amended December 2011) http://www.charity-commission.gov.uk/Charity_requirements_guidance/Charity_essentials/Public_benefit/Public_benefit.aspx. This contains the Charity Commission's original (and interim) advice on the requirements of public benefit that charities must demonstrate.
Alison Dunn, 'The governance of philanthropy and the burden of regulating charitable foundations.' (2011) 2 Conv 114–128. This article looks at the extent to which administrative burdens act as a disincentive to charities and actually discourage charitable giving.
Alastair Hudson, *Equity & Trusts* (7th edn, Routledge-Cavendish, 2012) ch. 25
Andreas Rahmatian, 'The continued relevance of the "poor relations" and the "poor employees" cases under the Charities Act 2006.' (2009) 1 Conv 12–20. This

considers whether the abolition of the presumption of public benefit in the Charities Act 2006 affected the 'poor relations' and 'poor employees' line of cases. This article should be read in conjunction with the decision in *Attorney-General v Charity Commission for England and Wales*.

Mohamed Ramjohn, *Text, Cases and Materials on Equity & Trusts* (4th edn, Routledge-Cavendish, 2008) chs 14–16.

Brian Sloan, 'Public schools for public benefit?' (2012) CLJ 71 (1) 45–47 (case comment). This article considers the judgment of the Upper Tribunal in *R (on the application of Independent Schools Council) v Charity Commission for England and Wales* on how the public benefit test applies to independent schools.

Mary Synge, 'Poverty: an essential element in charity after all?' (2011) CLJ 70(3) 649–668. This article looks at whether the Charity Commission made a mistake in concluding that a school that failed to operate for the public benefit and failed to provide opportunities for those in poverty could not be charitable.

Chapter 16

Cy-près

This chapter builds upon the discussion of charities in Chapter 15 and specifically looks at the doctrine of cy-près. This is a doctrine which can apply when a charitable gift fails. The doctrine broadly operates to enable the property in the gift to be transferred to another charity with similar objects.

As You Read

Look out for the following issues:

- how the doctrine of cy-près may be defined;
- how, if it applies, cy-près ensures that the charitable gift will not revert to the donor on a resulting trust; and
- how the provisions of the Charities Act 2011 give the doctrine of cy-près a wider application than that under the common law.

Definition of *Cy-près*

Cy-près means 'as near as possible'. The general principle is that if a charitable gift has failed because it cannot be carried out by the trustees of the testator's will exactly according to his wishes, the trustees may make an application to the Charity Commission[1] to apply the gift to another charity whose objects are, as near as possible, to that charity whom the donor intended to benefit. In this way, it may be said that as much charitable good as possible in the circumstances will still come from the donor's gift as the donor intended.

The application of cy-près to the gift means that a resulting trust[2] of that property to the donor's estate is disapplied.

Cy-près will not apply in every situation where a charity fails. It will only apply if the donor of the gift showed a general charitable intention in giving his gift or establishing his charitable trust.

If the charitable gift has not failed, cy-près has no application. There are three occasions when it has been held that the gift has not failed. These are where:

(a)   the charity continues in another form;
(b)   there is a gift for the purposes of an unincorporated assocation;[3] or
(c)   the charitable institution has been described incorrectly.

These exceptions to when cy-près may be used will be considered first.

Glossary – testator/testatrix

These terms are used throughout this chapter. A testator is a male who has written his will; a testatrix a female who has done the same.

---

1   Originally it was the Court of Chancery which authorised cy-près schemes, but the Charitable Trusts Act 1860 s 2 permitted the Charity Commissioners to do so.
2   See Chapter 3.
3   See Chapter 6, pp 164–171.

Exceptions to *Cy-près*

The charity continues in another form

If the charity continues in another form, the charitable gift will not have failed. This occurred in *Re Faraker*.[4]

Mrs Faraker left £200 in her will to 'Mrs Bailey's Charity Rotherhithe'. There was no charity by that name in Rotherhithe, but there was a similarly named 'Hannah Bayly's Charity'. The latter charity had been established originally to benefit poor widows in Rotherhithe. Some six years before Mrs Faraker's death, Hannah Bayly's Charity had been merged with 13 other charities in the Rotherhithe area and the combined charity's object was to aid the poor in that area. It was admitted that Mrs Faraker had meant to leave the money to Hannah Bayly's Charity, but the issue for the court was whether the gift had lapsed when that charity had merged with the others.

The Court of Appeal held that the gift had not lapsed. Hannah Bayly's Charity was not, said Cozens-Hardy MR, extinct. All that had happened was that its objects had changed. These objects had changed lawfully as a scheme to merge the charity with the 13 others had been approved by the Charity Commissioners. Mrs Faraker did not give her money to a particular charity; she gave it to a charity which was simply identified by a particular name. The gift to the charity had not failed at all. It was only if the charity had failed by, for example, there ceasing to be any poor widows in Rotherhithe, that the doctrine of cy-près could apply.

There is a gift for the purposes of an unincorporated association

A gift left for the purposes of an unincorporated association will not be subject to the cy-près doctrine as long as those purposes continue. This occurred in *Re Finger's Will Trusts*.[5]

Georgia Finger divided her residuary estate in her will into 11 equal parts and left them to charitable insitutions. Amongst the recipients were the National Radium Commission and the National Council for Maternity and Child Welfare. Both of these organisations no longer existed by the time of her death. Her executors sought directions as to whom the sums left to those two bodies should be paid.

The National Radium Commission was an unincorporated association which was charitable. Appoving the *obiter* comments of Buckley J in *Re Vernon's Will Trusts*,[6] Goff J held that a gift to an unincorporated charity could be seen to be a purpose trust whose purpose would not fail but could be carried on by another charitable insitution because the original gift was to further particular purposes. This was subject to two provisos. First, if the testatrix's intention was to benefit a particular institution which had ceased to exist at the date of her death, the gift could not take effect as a purpose trust. It had to be established that the testatrix wanted to benefit the purpose in general, as opposed to the particular institution. Second, the charitable purpose still had to exist now even though the particular institution to whom the gift was left had disappeared.

The gift to the National Council for Maternity and Child Welfare failed because this body was incorporated. Goff J held that this meant the testatrix's intention was to benefit that particular institution and not charitable purposes in general. When that institution ceased to exist, the gift had to fail.

---

4   *Re Faraker* [1912] 2 Ch 488.
5   *Re Finger's Will Trusts* [1972] Ch 286.
6   *Re Vernon's Will Trusts* [1972] Ch 300.

As the gift had failed, Goff J considered whether he could find a general charitable intention by the testatrix. He held that she did have a general charitable intention by leaving the whole of her residuary estate to charitable institutions. Consequently, the doctrine of cy-près could apply to the gift for the National Council for Maternity and Child Welfare. A scheme was proposed to pay that gift to the National Association for Maternal and Child Welfare, which Goff J approved.

The charitable institution has been described incorrectly

If the donor incorrectly describes the recipient institution but it is clear that the donor intended to benefit only that particular organisation, the gift can still take effect to that organisation under a scheme. This can be shown by the decision of Megarry V-C in *Re Spence*.[7]

Beatrice Spence left half of her residuary estate in her will for the benefit of the patients at 'The Blind Home, Scott Street, Keighley'. No such exact institution existed. There was, however, a Keighley and District Association for the Blind which had existed for decades. It had a blind home at 31 Scott Street, Keighley. Megarry V-C quickly held that the actual home was the same as that described by Miss Spence in her will and it should benefit.

More difficult was the subsequent issue of whether the money could only be used for the home at Scott Street, Keighley or whether it had to be put towards the charity's general funds, as the charity also ran another home in Bingley. Megarry V-C held that Miss Spence's intention was that only the patients at the particular home in Keighley should benefit from her gift. As this was not quite how she had described her intention in her will, he ordered that a scheme should be made under which the gift could be paid for the benefit of the patients at the home owned by Keighley and District Association for the Blind at Scott Street, Keighley.

Cy-près was not relevant to this part of her residuary estate as the gift had not failed as such.

If none of these exceptions are valid and the gift has failed because the recipient no longer exists, *prima facie*, the gift will return to the donor's estate on a resulting trust. If, however, it can be said that the donor displayed a general charitable intention in their gift, a cy-près scheme will be ordered by the court so that the gift may instead be transferred to another recipient and not returned to the donor's estate.

Cy-près and General Charitable Intention

General charitable intention must be shown before a gift can be transferred to another recipient. A proposed transfer of the gift to another recipient is called a 'scheme'. In *Re Lysaght*,[8] Buckley J defined general charitable intention as:

> a paramount intention on the part of the donor to effect *some charitable purpose which the court can find a method of putting into operation*, notwithstanding that it is impracticable to give effect to some direction by the donor which is not an essential part of his true intention – not, that is to say, part of his paramount intention.[9]

If a general charitable intention can be found, another charitable recipient can receive the gift provided their charitable objects are broadly the same as the original recipient intended by the testator.

---

7 *Re Spence* [1979] Ch 483.
8 *Re Lysaght* [1966] Ch 191.
9 Ibid at 202 (emphasis added).

❖ **EXPLAINING THE LAW**

Suppose Scott leaves £100,000 in his will for the advancement of education at Derbyshire School. Derbyshire School closed before Scott's death but after he wrote his will.

The gift would be charitable as it is for the advancement of education under s 3(1)(b) of the Charities Act 2011 and it is for the public benefit.

As the school has closed, the gift cannot be administered by Scott's trustees in the manner anticipated by Scott. Whether the gift can be applied *cy-près* to another similar institution depends on whether Scott displayed a general charitable intention in his will.

If it could be shown that Scott intended to benefit educational charity in general, then the gift could be applied *cy-près* to another institution. If, on the other hand, it was only Derbyshire School that Scott intended to benefit, no *cy-près* scheme can be ordered as Scott did not display a general charitable intention.

Buckley J's words show that the court draws a distinction between where the testator includes an essential provision in his gift that the entire gift depends upon for it to be administered. In such a case, no general charitable intention can be shown and the gift cannot be applied *cy-près* if it fails. Such would be the case in the example above if the court concluded that the only way of effecting the gift would be the now-impossible task of paying the money to Derbyshire School because Scott had intended that *only* that school should benefit from his generosity. In contrast, if the testator merely indicates how he would like the gift to be administered, he does display a general charitable intention because the precise means of how the gift should be applied are not essential to the gift being administered. In such a case, the gift can be applied *cy-près*.

Buckley J also emphasised that general charitable intention did not mean that the testator could only leave an original gift which benefited either 'charity' in the most general terms or one particular head of charity again in general terms. 'General' is used in contrast to a particular set of instructions being given so that the gift can only be administered in a certain way. Provided no set of instructions was given by the testator, it can usually be said that he had a general charitable intention.

General charitable intention can be demonstrated by the donor or under the provisions of s 62 of the Charities Act 2011.

General charitable intention by the donor

Key Learning Point

General charitable intention must be considered in two situations: (i) subsequent failure and (ii) initial failure.

Subsequent failure occurs when the gift fails after the testator has died but before his estate (property) is distributed. This is, of course, usually a comparatively short period of time.

Initial failure covers a much wider timescale. It occurs where the recipient of the gift had ceased to exist at the date of the testator's death but was still in existence when the testator wrote his will.

Subsequent failure

'Subsequent failure' is so called because the gift fails subsequent to the testator's death, but before his estate is distributed by his personal representatives. If this occurs, the gift can readily be applied for an alternative charitable institution. The phrase 'subsequent failure' was used by Kay LJ in describing how the gift had failed after the testator's death in Re Slevin.[10]

In the case, a gift was left in a will of £200 'to the Orphanage of St Dominic's, Newcastle-on-Tyne'. The orphanage closed after the testator's death, but before his estate was distributed. The issue for the Court of Appeal was whether the gift could be applied cy-près to another charity, or whether it would fall back to the estate as a resulting trust as the object had ceased to exist.

In giving the judgment of the Court of Appeal, Kay LJ compared the position to that of an individual who had been left a legacy under a will and who had died after the testator but before the money was given to him. The money would belong to the individual from the point of the testator's death. Such money would not fall back into the estate under a resulting trust.

The same principle could be applied to an institution. The institution became the equitable owner of the £200 at the date Mr Slevin died. When the orphanage ceased to exist, its property had to be administered by the Crown whose task was to apply it for a similar charitable purpose as that undertaken by the orphanage.

Re Slevin was followed by Romer J in Re King,[11] which considered the issue of a surplus of money remaining after the charitable purpose of the gift had been fulfilled.

Here the testatrix left her entire estate on trust to provide a stained glass window in the church in Irchester for certain members of her family and herself. There was approximately £300 remaining of her residuary estate after the cost of providing the window had been deducted from it. The executors sought directions as to whether the entire gift was charitable or not and if it was, whether the surplus could be applied cy-près in providing a further stained glass window in the church. The next-of-kin (who, if successful, would have received the surplus) argued that a general charitable intention on the testatrix's behalf had to be found if the surplus was to be applied cy-près and that simply leaving a gift to make and install a stained glass window showed no general charitable intention.

Romer J had no doubt that the gift was charitable. He also held that the surplus could be applied cy-près for a second window in the church. He referred to Re Slevin and held that the decision in that case was authority for a more general principle that if a gift was left for a charitable purpose which was otherwise well provided for without the gift, the gift would be applied cy-près. He thought that was the case here.

It must be questioned whether the principle in Re Slevin is necessarily as wide as propounded by Romer J in Re King. The institution had ceased to exist after the testator's death in Re Slevin but this was largely irrelevant as it had already had the gift given to it at the point of the testator's death. Clearly, the church in Re King had not ceased to exist after the date of the testatrix's death but the gift had still been given to it at the date of her death. A perhaps narrower interpretation

---

10 Re Slevin [1891] 2 Ch 236.
11 Re King [1923] 1 Ch 243.

needs to be applied to *Re Slevin* than that propounded in *Re King*. It is suggested that all the principle in *Re Slevin* consists of is that once property is given to an institution, the institution may keep it (because equitable ownership has passed) and if the institution then ceases to exist, it may be applied as a *cy-près* scheme for the purposes of a similar charitable organisation.

Initial failure

Initial failure occurs when the recipient institution had ceased to exist before the testator's death. If it can be shown that the testator intended to benefit charity generally in his will, another charitable organisation can receive the gift under a *cy-près* scheme. If, on the other hand, no general charitable intention can be shown, the gift will simply return to the testator's estate under a resulting trust.

Some of the case law under this heading is difficult to reconcile with other decided cases. In all cases, however, the court is attempting to decide whether the testator showed a general charitable intention or simply a specific desire to benefit one particular charity. If the latter and the institution has ceased to exist after the testator's death, no *cy-près* scheme can be permitted.

Instances where general charitable intention has been found . . .

The decision of the Court of Appeal in *Biscoe v Jackson*[12] is one of the earliest which shows this distinction between a general purpose and a particular recipient.

Joseph Jackson left £10,000 in his will to his trustees to establish a soup kitchen and cottage hospital in Shoreditch, London. Unfortunately, no land could be found in Shoreditch to establish either the hospital or soup kitchen. The issue was whether a *cy-près* scheme could be ordered to vary the gift.

The Court of Appeal held that the testator had shown a general charitable intention by his gift. Cotton LJ explained that the testator had shown a general intention to benefit the poor and sick of Shoreditch. The testator had simply pointed out how he wished the gift to be effected: by the creation of a soup kitchen and hospital.

If, therefore, the testator has shown a charitable intention with simply a desire as to how that should be carried out and it is impossible to accede to the testator's desire, a *cy-près* scheme can alter the mechanism suggested by the testator to implement his gift for a similar charitable purpose.

Such general charitable intention was shown again in *Re Roberts*.[13] Jane Roberts left her residuary estate on trust to be split into six equal parts and then to be applied to six named charities. One part was to be applied to the 'Sheffield Boys Working Home (Western Bank, Sheffield)'. The home had been closed and sold some 16 years before the testatrix died, but after she had made her will. The money held by the trustees of the home mainly went to the Sheffield Town Trust to create a fund called the 'Sheffield Boys Working Home Fund' with a request that the income from it should be used to benefit boys' organisations in the city. A small balance was retained by the two trustees of the home.

Wilberforce J held that the courts had gone 'very far'[14] in cases to avoid reaching the conclusion that a gift to a charity had lapsed. He held that the trust of the home still continued, as the trustees had retained a small amount of money to meet expenses after the home itself was sold. *Re Faraker* had decided that the Charity Commissioners had no general power to bring a charitable trust to an end; Wilberforce J held that neither did the particular trustees on the exact terms of this trust. Consequently, the trust of the home still existed.

---

12 *Biscoe v Jackson* (1887) LR 35 Ch D 460.
13 *Re Roberts* [1963] 1 WLR 406.
14 Ibid at 412.

He said that despite the precise wording of the gift leaving money for the home, the gift was actually for the purposes of the institution as opposed to the home itself. He cited the decision of the Court of Appeal in Re Lucas,[15] which had held that it was always a question of construction of the testator's words in his will as to whether the gift was for the purposes of a specific institution or whether general charitable intention had been shown. On the facts, he thought that the testatrix had shown an intention to benefit a charitable purpose, not just its physical building.

As the testatrix had intended to benefit the charity in general as opposed to its physical building and as the trust continued to exist, the funds could be administered by a cy-près scheme.

The issue here is always whether the testator intended to benefit charity in general or a particular institution. A gift to several charities and one non-charitable organisation may suggest in itself that the testator had a general charitable intention. Megarry V-C referred to this as 'charity by association' in Re Spence.[16] It can be illustrated by the contrasting decisions in Re Satterthwaite's Will Trusts[17] and Re Jenkins' Will Trusts.[18]

In Re Satterthwaite's Will Trusts, Phyllis Sattherthwaite wrote her will in which she left all of her residuary estate to animals, claiming that she hated the human race. She asked her bank manager to prepare for her a list of animal charities and he did so by referring to the London telephone directory. She divided her residuary estate into nine equal parts and left each part to what she thought was an animal charity. One of the 'charities' was the London Animal Hospital. This was not a charity at all, but a private veterinary practice. Mr Rich, the owner of the London Animal Hospital, claimed the share of the money.

The Court of Appeal held that the testatrix's aim was to benefit a purpose as opposed to any individual. Harman and Russell LJJ thought that due to the other recipients of the testatrix's residuary estate being charitable in nature, a general charitable intention could be inferred. A cy-près scheme would be ordered so that another similar charity could benefit.

Russell LJ offered an additional explanation. He thought that if a name under which a person was working was descriptive, as Mr Rich's London Animal Hospital, any testamentary gift should be taken not as an intention to benefit either the particular business or its owner but instead a charitable purpose, because it would appear to the outside world as though the business was charitable. The difficulty with this analysis is how it can be reconciled with the testatrix's intention. It is, perhaps, stretching the point to suggest she showed a general charitable intention by specifically naming a recipient which constituted a mere example of the type of charity she wished to benefit.

This decision may be contrasted with Re Jenkins' Will Trusts. Here, Frances Jenkins left her residuary estate to be divided into seven equal parts. One part was to be given to the British Union for the Abolition of Vivisection for them to use to obtain an Act of Parliament to abolish animal testing. This was not a charitable purpose as abolishing vivisection was a political aim.[19] The issue was whether this gift could be applied cy-près as the other six gifts were charitable.

Buckley J held that the gift could not be applied cy-près. Simply because other charitable gifts had been left by the testatrix did not mean that this particular one was also charitable. As he put it, '[i]f you meet seven men with black hair and one with red hair you are not entitled

---

15 Re Lucas [1948] Ch 424.
16 Re Spence [1979] Ch 483 at 494.
17 Re Satterthwaite's Will Trusts [1966] 1 WLR 277.
18 Re Jenkins' Will Trusts [1966] Ch 249.
19 See Chapter 15 at pp 424–426.

to say that here are eight men with black hair'.[20] The testatrix had not shown a general charitable intention simply by leaving other gifts for charitable purposes.

It is hard to reconcile *Re Jenkins' Will Trusts* with *Re Satterthwaite*. The latter was decided only 12 days before the former and the decision of the Court of Appeal in *Re Satterthwaite* does not appear to have been cited to Buckley J in *Re Jenkins' Will Trusts*.

❖ ANALYSING THE LAW

Re Satterthwaite's Will Trusts suggests that it is relevant to consider the other bequests that the testator made in his will as they must throw light upon the testator's general intention. *Re Jenkins' Will Trusts* questions how other gifts can be relevant to the one specific gift in question.

Which decision do you think takes the correct approach – and why?

Instances where no general charitable intention has been found . . .

In *Re Spence*, Miss Spence left the other half of her residuary estate for the benefit of the patients at 'the Old Folks' Home at Hillworth Lodge, Keighley'. Hillworth Lodge had been closed down as a home for aged persons after Miss Spence had executed her will, but before she died. The Home had not been run as, or by, a charity.

Megarry V-C held that the gift itself was for charitable purposes but that, as it could not be given when Miss Spence died, the gift would fail unless a general charitable intention could be found on her part. He could not find a general charitable intention. He said that it would be difficult to find a general charitable intention where there was only one other gift the court had to consider: in *Re Satterthwaite's Will Trusts*[21] a general charitable intention had been found partly because the testatrix had left eight other charitable gifts. There was more evidence of a general charitable intention the greater the number of other clearly charitable gifts were left.

Megarry V-C compared gifts which had been left to particular institutions and those left to particular purposes, both of which existed at the time the testator made the will but had ceased by the time the testator had died. The court was reluctant to sieve out of a gift to a particular institution an intention to benefit charity generally. The same was true for a gift left for a particular purpose, as in this instance. It could clearly be said that Miss Spence intented to benefit the aged persons at Hillworth Lodge, Keighley. It would be something of a leap to say that she had a general charitable intention. As such, no cy-près scheme was ordered and this part of her residuary estate passed as on intestacy.

If the testator takes care in his will to describe a particular recipient, the court will find it difficult to construe a general charitable intention if the institution then ceases to exist before the testator dies, as was shown by the decision of the High Court in *Re Harwood*.[22]

The testatrix left £200 to 'the Wisbech Peace Society, Cambridge'. The society had ceased to exist before she died. The issue was whether the testatrix had demonstrated any general charitable intent as she had left a list of other charitable societies in her will who should benefit from legacies.

---

20 Ibid at 256.
21 *Re Satterthwaite's Will Trusts* [1966] 1 WLR 277.
22 *Re Harwood* [1936] Ch 285.

Farwell J held that a *cy-près* scheme for the gift could not be ordered. He held that where the testatrix had 'gone out of her way to identify the object of her bounty',[23] there was no room to imply a general charitable intent from her gift. She intended to benefit the Wisbech Peace Society and that was all.

On the other hand, her other legacy to the 'Peace Society of Belfast' could be applied *cy-près*. This society had never existed. Farwell J held that the testatrix intended to benefit any society which promoted peace in Belfast. She thus demonstrated a general charitable intention and so her gift could be applied *cy-près*.

The consequences of *cy-près* applying

If a general charitable intention is found to exist and *cy-près* is, therefore, applicable, the court (or the Charity Commission) will authorise a scheme to ensure that, in most cases, a charitable recipient with similar charitable objects receives the charitable gift.

It is not always the case, however, that the recipient of the gift has to be a different organisation from that intended by the testator if the recipient does still exist. This occurred in *Re Lysaght*[24] where the gift failed largely for administrative reasons. *Cy-près* may, after all, apply where it is impossible to carry the testator's gift into effect as desired by the testator.

The facts in *Re Lysaght* concerned Rosalind Lysaght's purported gift to the Royal College of Surgeons to establish scholarships for students to study medicine. Her gift had a number of conditions attached to it. The contentious one was in clause 11(D) that any recipient of a scholarship could not be either Jewish or Roman Catholic. The gift failed because the Royal College of Surgeons declined to accept it on such terms.

Buckley J held that the overall purpose of the testatrix was to establish medical scholarships through the Royal College of Surgeons. This purpose evidenced a general charitable intention on her part. The criteria she included, of which those in clause 11(D) were part, did not detract from this intention: they were merely there to administer the gift.

Normally, a trustee could not modify the terms of a trust: the trustee's task was to administer it only and if he did not wish to do so, his normal course of action would be to step down from the office of trusteeship to be replaced by a trustee who will administer the trust. But here the testatrix had made it clear that her scholarships could only be administered by the Royal College of Surgeons.

Buckley J held that her insistence that scholarship recipients must not be Jewish or Catholic would have defeated the testatrix's paramount intention that the gift be administered by the Royal College of Surgeons. It would have destroyed the trust. Hence he held that the court would order a *cy-près* scheme under which the gift could still be given to the Royal College without the conditions as to religion attached to it.

The *cy-près* scheme will, therefore, be used flexibly by the court to deal with a charitable gift that cannot be carried into operation precisely according to the testator's instructions.

A summary of the doctrine of *cy-près* can be found at Figure 16.1.

---

23 Ibid at 287.
24 *Re Lysaght* [1966] Ch 191.

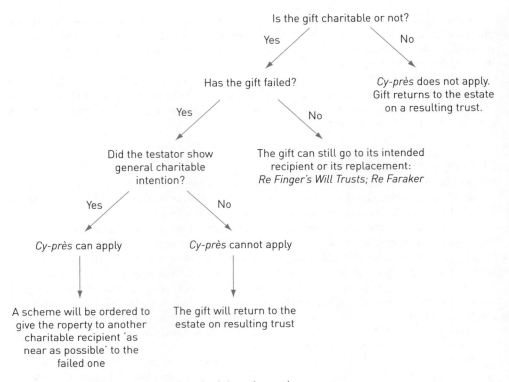

Figure 16.1 Summary of the main principles of *cy-près*.

Charities Act 2011, s 62

Section 62 of the Charities Act 2011 has widened out when a cy-près scheme may be permitted. Before the first predecessor of this section was enacted,[25] it used to be the case that a cy-près scheme would only be permitted if it was absolutely impossible or impracticable to carry out the testator's intention. A cy-près scheme could not be put into effect just because it was thought that using the money in a different way would be a better use of the testator's gift. This principle was illustrated in *Re Weir Hospital*.[26]

Benjamin Weir left two houses for the purposes of converting them into a dispensary or cottage hospital for the benefit of the residents of Streatham. He also left his residuary estate (£100,000) to maintain the dispensary or hospital. The trustees of the trust initially used one house as a dispensary, but then suggested a cy-près scheme to the Charity Commissioners under which the other house would be used as a nurses' home and the majority of the residuary estate would be used to enlarge the general hospital which was located outside the parish of Streatham.

The Charity Commissioners approved the cy-près scheme, but the Court of Appeal held that it was *ultra vires* (outside) the main purposes of the testator's will and had to be discharged. A cottage hospital could still be established using the testator's houses and his money used to maintain it. The Charity Commissioners, who themselves had suggested the scheme to the trustees, merely considered it more desirable to benefit the general hospital. Cy-près was not applicable in such circumstances. As Cozens-Hardy MR put it, 'there can be no question of

25 Charities Act 1960, s 13.
26 *Re Weir Hospital* [1910] 2 Ch 124.

cy-près until it is clearly established that the directions of the testator cannot be carried into effect'.[27]

It was neither for the court nor the Charity Commissioners to weigh up the advantages or disadvantages of the testator's charitable gift. If at least one purpose intended by the testator remained, his gift had to be administered for that purpose. A cy-près scheme could not be used to disregard the testator's intentions unless those intentions simply could not be carried out.

Section 62 of the Charities Act 2011 widens out when cy-près may be applied.[28] Section 62(1) provides the following five alternate circumstances where, although the testator's intended use of the gift might not have failed entirely, the doctrine of cy-près may nonetheless still be applied. These are where 'the original purposes of a charitable gift can be altered':

(a) where the original purposes, in whole or in part –

    (i)   have been as far as may be fulfilled; or
    (ii) cannot be carried out, or not according to the directions given and to the spirit of the gift,

(b) where the original purposes provide a use for part only of the property available by virtue of the gift,

(c) where (i) the property available by virtue of the gift, and (ii) other property applicable for similar purposes, can more effectively be used in conjunction, and to that end can suitably, regard being had to the appropriate considerations, be made applicable to common purposes,

(d) where the original purposes were laid down by reference to (i) an area which then was but has since ceased to be a unit for some other purpose, or (ii) a class of persons or to an area which has for any reason since ceased to be suitable, regard being had to the appropriate considerations, or to be practical in administering the gift, or

(e) where the original purposes, in whole or in part, have, since they were laid down –

    (i)   been adequately provided for by other means, or
    (ii)   ceased, as being useless or harmful to the community or for other reasons, to be in law charitable, or
    (iii) ceased in any other way to provide a suitable and effective method of using the property available by virtue of the gift, regard being had to the appropriate considerations.

Each of these circumstances must be considered. As a preliminary point, however, s 62 cannot be used as a method of altering administrative arrangements in a charitable gift. Its objective is to enable the court to apply the gift for similar charitable purposes as the testator intended, as Re JW Laing Trust[29] illustrates.

John Laing established a trust under which he left what became a considerable sum of money (approximately £24 million) to trustees to distribute to Christian evangelical causes. The trust was established with a provision which required the capital sum to be distributed within ten years of the settlor's death. After his death, the trustees sought the court's approval to remove this stipulation either under the equivalent of s 62(1)(e)(iii) or the court's inherent jurisdiction.

Peter Gibson J held that the 'original purposes' of the gift within the meaning of s 62 meant those 'for which the property given is applicable'.[30] 'Purposes' did not include

---

27 Ibid at 132.
28 An identical provision giving the court the power to use the cy-près doctrine was first enacted in s 13 of the Charities Act 1960.
29 Re JW Laing Trust [1984] Ch 143.
30 Ibid at 150.

administrative directions on the trustees as to when the distribution of the property had to occur. The direction that the property had to be distributed within a certain time was concerned with how the property was to be distributed – not for what purpose. As such, it was an administrative provision that could not be altered by s 62.[31]

Section 62(2) sets out that the 'appropriate considerations' in paragraphs (c), (d)(ii) and (e)(iii) refer to two distinct matters: (i) the 'spirit of the gift' and (ii) social and economic circumstances prevailing at the time the scheme is proposed. Neither matters were new to the Charites Act 2011. That regard must be had to the 'spirit of the gift' was mentioned in the Charities Act 1960[32] and the explicit need to take into account social and economic factors was first enacted in the Charities Act 2006, s 15.

As You Read

As you read the following part of this chapter, considering paragraphs (c), (d)(ii) and (e)(iii) of s 62, ask yourself whether the courts were perhaps already taking into account social and economic factors when they came to approve the various cy-près schemes even before this requirement was mentioned explicitly by s 15 of the Charities Act 2006.

Where the original purposes have been carried out or cannot be carried out

An example of the identical predecessor to s 62(1)(a)(ii) was considered in Re Lepton's Charity,[33] where the High Court discussed the meaning of the phrase 'spirit of the gift'.

Joseph Lepton wrote his will in 1715 and provided that his land in Pudsey, Yorkshire, should be left to his trustees to pay a Protestant dissenting minister the annual sum of £3 and to distribute any other profits from the land to the poor and aged in Pudsey. Mr Lepton died the following year, when the annual income from his land was £5.

By 1968, the annual income from the trust had increased to £791. The trustees brought an action asking whether the testator's direction that an annual sum of £3 be paid to the minister was really a charitable gift of £3 per annum or three-fifths of the annual income of the land. The trustees also wanted a scheme approved whereby £100 per annum would be paid to the only Protestant dissenting meeting place in Pudsey, the Congregational chapel. They brought their action under the previous identical provisions to s 62(1)(a)(ii) and s 62(1)(e) (iii).

Pennycuick V-C considered the meaning of the phrase 'spirit of the gift' in paragraphs (a) (ii) and (e)(iii) meant 'the basic intention underlying the gift'.[34] That intention could be ascertained from the terms of the testator's will and any admissible evidence. He also thought that paragraph (e)(iii) simply expanded upon paragraph (a)(ii) and was not distinct from it.

The phrase 'the original purposes of a charitable gift' applied to the trusts as a whole and not to each of the recipients – the minister and the poor – separately. That was because the testator had left one sum of money to be divided between two recipients. He had effectively left only one gift. The question for the court was whether the original purposes could not be carried out in relation to the basic intention of the testator underlying the gift or whether, in

---

31 Peter Gibson J did, however, hold that the court could remove the condition as to distribution in the exercise of its inherent jurisdiction.
32 Charities Act 1960, s 13.
33 Re Lepton's Charity [1972] Ch 276.
34 Ibid at 285.

the language of paragraph (e)(iii), the gift 'ceased to provide a suitable and effective method of using the property'.[35]

Pennycuick V-C held that the testator's intention was to split one amount of money so that the minister would get a 'modest but not negligible sum'. When the testator's gift took effect in the will, the minister would receive a three-fifths share of the money. As Pennycuick V-C put it, the testator's 'intention is plainly defeated when in the conditions of today the minister takes a derisory £3 out of a total of £791'.

He thought that the conditions for cy-près to operate had been satisfied. £100 was a reasonable amount for the minister to receive at the time of the decision and a scheme would be ordered to that effect. The poor and aged of Pudsey would continue to receive the rest of the annual income.

The decision of Pennycuick V-C is interesting in amalgamating paragraphs (a)(ii) and (e) (iii). It is suggested that the paragraphs are not necessarily the same. Paragraph (a)(ii) seems to suggest that the original purposes of the gift cannot be carried out from the very beginning of the gift taking effect. Paragraph (e)(iii), on the other hand, talks about the purposes ceasing, which suggests that they have been at least capable of being carried out but they are no longer capable of being carried out. If this is right, the facts of Re Lepton's Charity suggest that the cy-près scheme should more properly have been ordered under paragraph (e)(iii). It is, admittedly, true that on the facts of Re Lepton's Charity this was probably a distinction without a difference.

If the original purposes provided for a use for part only of the property

Here, the whole property has been given as a charitable gift but the testator has only provided a use for part of it. It makes logical sense for a scheme to be ordered, perhaps to enlarge the charitable purpose to cover the whole gift.

Where the property and other property can be used more effectively together

Again, a scheme can be ordered here, where it makes sense to mix the property left by the testator with other property. The recipient charity can only benefit more from such an approach being adopted.

Where the original purposes were set out by reference to an area or a class of people which have ceased to be suitable

The meaning of this paragraph was considered by the High Court in Peggs v Lamb.[36]

Various pieces of land had been used since time immemorial (1189) for the benefit of freemen and their widows in Huntingdon. The Charity Commissioners had recognised the gift of the land as a charity. However, by 1991, the number of freemen had reduced to such an extent, and the value of the income from the land increased to such an extent for those few freemen, that the Charity Commissioners doubted that the gift of the land could still be seen to be charitable. Various parts of the land had been sold for housing development. Too much benefit was being paid to too few people, regardless of their need: for example, in

---

35 This question was formulated by Pennycuick V-C at 285.
36 Peggs v Lamb [1994] Ch 172.

1900, 34 freemen received about £17 each, but in 1990, each freeman received £31,750. The Charity Commissioners suggested that the trustees of the trust apply for a cy-près scheme that the income should only be paid to freemen of Huntingdon in need and the surplus to the poor and sick of the borough.

Morritt J held that the trust of the land was a charitable trust:[37] the land was originally a gift for the benefit of all of the freemen and the widows of Huntingdon. He followed Pennycuick V-C's definition of 'spirit of the gift' in Re Lepton's Charity and held that the original purposes of the gift were general charitable purposes for freemen and their widows in Huntingdon.

A scheme for the gift could be ordered under paragraph (d). When the land was first assumed given to the trust, freemen constituted a large section of society. The declaration of a trust to benefit such freemen was practicable at the time. But the importance and number of freemen had declined over the centuries.

Morritt J held that the spirit – or original intention – of the gift was to benefit the borough of Huntingdon. He held that it would be consistent with that intention to enlarge the beneficiaries of the gift to the entire inhabitants of the borough. The original class of persons was now unsuitable to benefit from the trust so a scheme could be ordered under paragraph (d) in favour of a new class. That new class was still within the spirit of the original gift.

Where the original purposes of the charitable gift have ceased

This paragraph consists of three parts:

(a)   where the original purpose is now being provided for by other means;
(b)   where the original purpose has ceased as being 'useless or harmful to the community';
      and
(c)   where the original purpose has ceased 'in any other way' to be a 'suitable and effective method' of using the property for the intended gift.

As already noted, Pennycuick V-C in Re Lepton's Charity was of the view that (iii) was merely an expansion of the right contained in paragraph (a)(ii).

The application of paragraph (e)(iii) was considered by the Court of Appeal in Varsani v Jesani.[38]

The facts of the case concerned the religious followers of the Swaminarayan faith as taught by its founder in the UK, Shree Muktajivandasji Swaminarayan. A charitable trust had been declared in 1967 of property for the faith which mainly consisted of a temple in London. The followers of the faith had split into two groups in 1985, with the minority group refusing to accept the authority of the then leader of the faith. The two groups were also divided on which group should continue to use the temple. Both groups wanted the court to resolve which group could use the temple.

The Court of Appeal commented on the applicability of s 13 of the Charities Act 1993 (the immediate and near identical predecessor to s 62). The enactment of this section had replaced the previous case law, exemplified in decisions such as Re Weir Hospital, which decided that cy-près could only apply if performing the charitable gift was impossible or impractical. There was no need for the court to decide if it was impossible or impractical for the gift to be performed.

---

37 He relied on the decision of the House of Lords in Goodman v Mayor of Saltash 7 App Cas 633.
38 Versani v Jesani [1999] Ch 219.

Section 13 of the Charities Act 1993 widened out the applicability of cy-près. On the facts, the test now was to be found in paragraph (e)(iii): had the original purpose of the gift ceased to provide a suitable and effective use of the property, regard being had to the spirit of the gift?

Both Morritt and Chadwick LJJ commented on the phrase 'the spirit of the gift'. Morritt LJ said it was only used in certain paragraphs of s 13 – these were paragraphs where the court had to make a 'value judgment'.[39] He said it meant the court had to have regard to 'the basic intention underlying the gift or the substance of the gift rather than the form of words used to express it or conditions imposed to effect it'.[40]

The 'spirit of the gift' also referred to when the gift was originally given, not at the stage of litigation. The court sought to ascertain the spirit in which the donor gave the gift. That could generally be ascertained from the trust document and other evidence of the circumstances in which the gift was made.

The purposes of the gift when it was given was to promote the Swaminarayan faith through Muktajivandasji's teachings and worship in a temple in London. Until the group split, those purposes were a suitable and effective method of using the temple as a place of worship. Now the groups could no longer worship together and so the temple could no longer be used to pursue the original purposes. The court did enjoy jurisdiction to make a cy-près scheme under paragraph (e)(iii).

Charities Act 2011, s 63

Section 63 of the Charities Act 2011 specifically deals with the application of cy-près to a charitable gift given by an anonymous donor or by a donor who has executed a document disclaiming the return of the gift in the event of the gift failing. The purpose of s 63 is that surplus money arising from when a charity fails may be applied cy-près without the need to seek the original donor's consent.

❖ EXPLAINING THE LAW

An anonymous donor under s 63 of the Charities Act 2011 would include a person who contributes to a charity through a collecting tin in a street or who buys a lottery ticket to support the good cause.

The application of s 63 is not restricted to such persons, however. It also applies to people who cannot be identified or found after making a charitable gift to a charity which has then failed or simply fulfilled its purpose. It additionally applies to those people who, despite being identifiable, have expressly stated that they do not want their gift returned to them if the charity fails.

If money remains after the purpose has failed or been fulfilled, the trustees may make a cy-près scheme to deal with the money raised.

---

39 Ibid at 234.
40 Ibid.

In all cases, before a cy-près scheme can be made by the charity trustees, the trustees must show that the gifts originally belonged to the donors. For people who have made their gift through a collecting box or via a 'lottery, competition, entertainment, sale or similar money-raising activity', s 64(1) states that such property will be 'conclusively presumed' to belong to the donors who cannot be identified. Similarly, if the donor has executed a disclaimer specifically stating that they do not want their gift returned if the charity fails, the property can be taken as belonging to them when they made the gift.[41] There is no need for the charity's trustees to seek those donors out. In all other cases,[42] the trustees must show that they have tried to trace the donors and that the donors cannot be identified or found, according to s 63(1)(a). The advertisements must be in a format and for a content prescribed in regulations made by the Charity Commission.[43] Providing no donors come forward within that time period, their gifts can be applied cy-près.

Section 65 of the Charities Act 2011 provides that the donor can request the return of his gift instead of it being given cy-près to another charity if his original charity fulfils its purpose or otherwise fails. To do so, the original gift must have been given for 'specific charitable purposes' and the charity must have made it clear originally that it would apply the gift cy-près if its original, specific charitable purpose failed.[44]

If the charity's purposes fail and the trustees do offer the donor the return of his gift but he refuses it or cannot be found, he is treated as though he has executed a disclaimer of the gift under s 65(6).

Points to Review

You have seen:

- that when a charitable gift fails, the doctrine of cy-près may apply which will enable an alternative charity which is 'as near as possible' to the recipient of the original gift to benefit from that gift. This contrasts with a non-charitable trust where the gift will usually go back to the settlor on a resulting trust basis;
- for cy-près to be applicable, the testator must have held a general charitable intention to benefit charity. This is particularly important if the gift has failed initially; and
- that it used to be the case that it must be impossible or impractical to apply the gift for the original charity for cy-près to be applied. This impossibility or impracticability has been widened out by the circumstances in s 62 of the Charities Act 2011 which now defines when cy-près may apply.

Making connections

Cy-près is concerned with when a charitable gift fails. It is important to understand when a gift will be classed as charitable and when not. This is discussed in Chapter 15.

---

41 Charities Act 2011, s 63(1)(b).
42 Unless the Charity Commission orders that it is unreasonable either in relation to the (small) amounts involved or in relation to the time lapse since the gifts were given, for such advertisements to be made: s 64(2).
43 Charities Act 2011, s 66(4),(6).
44 Ibid, s 65(1).

Useful Things to Read

The best reading is contained in the primary sources listed below. It is always good to consider the decisions of the courts themselves as this will lead to a deeper understanding of the issues involved. A few secondary sources are also listed, which you may wish to read to gain additional insights into the areas considered in this chapter.

Primary sources
Re Lysaght [1966] Ch 191.
Re Satterthwaite's Will Trusts [1966] 1 WLR 277.
Re Jenkins' Will Trusts [1966] Ch 249.
Varsani v Jesani [1999] Ch 219.

Charities Act 2011, ss 62–65.

Secondary sources
Elise Bennett Histed, 'Finally barring the entail?' (2000) LQR 445–473. An article of interest to those who enjoy legal history as it considers the history of the cy-près doctrine and the notion of barring the entail, a concept which may have been touched upon in your studies of land law.
Jonathan Garton, 'Justifying the *cy-près* doctrine' (2007) Tru. L.I. 134–149. An interesting article which discusses how the *cy-près* doctrine has been justified in case law.
Alastair Hudson, *Equity & Trusts* (7th edn, Routledge-Cavendish, 2012) ch 25.9.
John Picton, '*Kings v Bultitude* – a gift lost to charity' [2011] 1 Conv 69–74 (note). This article examines the decision of the High Court in the recent case of *Kings v Bultitude* [2010] EWHC 1795 (Ch) that a charitable gift to an independent church which had ceased to exist after the testator's death could not be saved by the *cy-près* doctrine. The article asks whether the gift could, in fact, have been saved.
Mohamed Ramjohn, *Text, Cases and Materials on Equity & Trusts* (4th edn, Routledge-Cavendish, 2008) ch 17.
Paul Ridout, 'Settling the tab' (2011) T.E.L & T.J. 127 (Jun), 14–17. This article considers the judgment of the court in *White v Williams (No. 2)* [2011] EWHC 494 (Ch) concerning the transfer of a place of worship from one charitable trust to another. It looks at how to prepare a *cy-près* scheme from a practitioner's point of view.

Chapter 17

Equitable Remedies and Proprietary Estoppel

Chapter Contents

This chapter concerns two topics: the general remedies that equity offers to the legal system together with the proactive remedy that particularly concerns the recovery of land or shares: proprietary estoppel. You may have studied the topic of equitable remedies in contract law so, hopefully, this chapter should act as something of a reminder to you about these principles.

As You Read

Look out for the following issues:

- the nature of the general remedies that equity offers and how they each achieve a different objective;
- the ingredients required to establish a successful claim in proprietary estoppel; and
- the flexibility of proprietary estoppel in offering a range of remedies should a claimant establish a successful cause of action.

Equitable Remedies

The common law offered a 'rough and ready' remedy for a successful claimant: damages. This remedy continues to this day so that, for example, a claimant suing for breach of contract will be awarded damages with the aim of placing him in the position he should have been in had the contract been honoured and not breached.[1] The common law remedy of damages is, of course, good for providing compensation to right a wrong, but it is a poor remedy to try to pre-empt a wrong from initially occurring.

Equity developed a number of different remedies which are designed to be proactive instead of reactive, as damages at common law. Moreover, equitable remedies attempt to give the claimant a more tailored remedy than common law damages. As Lord Selbourne LC put it in *Wilson v Northampton & Banbury Junction Railway Company*,[2] equitable remedies exist 'to do more perfect and complete justice' than common law damages.

Equitable remedies are only available at the court's discretion and to claim an equitable remedy, the claimant must show that common law damages will not be an adequate remedy in their own right. Equity, of course, also developed its own version of damages, called equitable compensation, but this has been discussed in Chapter 12 and will not be considered further here.

The remedies equity offers are illustrated in Figure 17.1 (overleaf).

Each of these remedies must be considered.

Injunction

There are five main types of injunction: prohibitory, mandatory, *quia timet*, search orders and freezing orders. All can be awarded on an interim or a permanent basis.

An interim (formerly 'interlocutory') injunction is awarded before the main trial of the claim occurs and, as such, is of a temporary nature. If an interim injunction is to be granted, the court will require an undertaking from the claimant that (i) he will pay the defendant damages if it turns out at trial that the claimant had no basis to restrain the defendant by way

---

1   *Robinson v Harman* (1848) 1 Exch 850; 154 ER 363.
2   *Wilson v Northampton & Banbury Junction Railway Company* (1874) LR 9 Ch App 279 at 284.

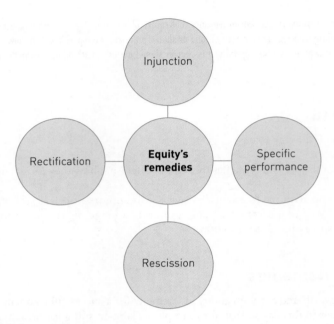

Figure 17.1 Equity's remedies.

of an injunction and (ii) as a result of the injunction being granted, the defendant has suffered loss. In *American Cyanamid Co v Ethicon Ltd*,[3] Lord Diplock said the court was always trying to balance two competing interests in awarding an interim injunction:

(a) the protection the claimant needed and which would not be compensated adequately by the award of damages at a later trial; and

(b) the fact that granting an interim injunction deprived the defendant of being able to exercise his legal rights (by, say, continuing to trade in a particular product) which would not be adequately compensated by the claimant's undertaking to pay him damages if the defendant were to be successful at trial.

A permanent injunction, as the name suggests, is of a permanent nature and is awarded to a successful claimant after a trial of the claim.

An injunction is used to enforce a legal or equitable right. As Lord Denning MR said in *Mareva Compania Naviera SA v International Bulkcarriers SA; The Mareva*,[4] '[t]he court will not grant an injunction to protect a person who has no legal or equitable right whatever'.

Prohibitory injunction

A prohibitory injunction is designed to prevent a party from undertaking an action. This type of injunction was considered by Lord Diplock in *American Cyanamid Co v Ethicon Ltd*.[5] The case concerned a patent.

3   *American Cyanamid Co v Ethicon Ltd* [1975] AC 396.
4   *Mareva Compania Naviera SA v International Bulkcarriers SA; The Mareva* [1980] 1 All ER 213 at 214.
5   *American Cyanamid Co v Ethicon Ltd* [1975] AC 396.

Glossary – A patent

A patent is a term from the law relating to intellectual property. If you hold a patent, you enjoy a period of time in which you have the monopoly over your invention. No-one else may compete directly with you and market a copy of your hopefully lucrative invention.

The claimant company had the benefit of a patent over a type of surgical suture. The defendant company was in the process of launching a competitor suture into the British market. The claimant sought an interim injunction preventing it from doing so, claiming that the defendant's suture infringed its patent. The High Court awarded the injunction, but the Court of Appeal reversed it, holding that the claimant's patent had not been infringed. The claimant appealed to the House of Lords. The House of Lords granted the injunction.

The only substantive opinion was delivered by Lord Diplock. He said that in deciding to grant an interim injunction, the court had to be satisfied that 'the claim is not frivolous or vexatious, in other words, that there is a serious question to be tried'.[6] The court should go no further than this: in particular, the court's task was not to try to decide which party would succeed at trial as this involved relying on untested witness statements.

Provided the court was satisfied that there was a 'serious question to be tried', the court then had to consider whether the 'balance of convenience'[7] meant that the injunction should be granted or refused. Lord Diplock set out the following two principles:

(a)   if it seemed that the claimant would succeed at trial but damages would compensate him adequately, the injunction should be refused; but

(b)   if damages would not be an adequate remedy, but it seemed likely that the defendant would succeed at trial and be adequately compensated by the claimant's undertaking to pay him damages, the court should normally grant the injunction.

The key to these principles is whether damages would be an adequate remedy for the claimant at trial. If damages are an adequate remedy, no injunction should be awarded. Conversely, if they are not, the injunction should be granted.

If the court was in doubt as to whether damages were an adequate remedy, the 'balance of convenience' test applied. One party was, of course, always liable to suffer disadvantages from an interim injunction being granted. The extent of the disadvantages suffered were a 'significant factor'[8] in deciding where the balance of convenience lay over whether or not to grant the injunction. The court could, provided the parties' arguments over the extent of their disadvantages were equal, take into account how strong each of their arguments were in each party's witness statements. But the court was to go no further than this and, particularly, was not conduct a trial of the action.

The trial judge had taken into account such factors that the defendant's sutures were not yet in the UK market and they had no ongoing business that an interim injunction would prevent from continuing. This meant that the granting of an injunction against the defendant would not mean factories closing and a workforce being denied employment. The claimant was in the process of establishing a growing market in the UK of this particular type of suture. Had the defendant been able to market its product before the trial of the action to ascertain if the patent had been infringed, the claimant's opportunity to take a share of that market would

---

6   Ibid at 407.
7   Ibid at 408.
8   Ibid at 409.

have been stunted. These factors indicated that, on the balance of convenience, the trial judge's injunction should be restored.

Although the case concerned an interim injunction, many of Lord Diplock's views may apply equally to a permanent injunction. The key test must surely be the same for both types of prohibitory injunction: Are damages a remedy that will adequately compensate the claimant? If not, the injunction should be granted; if they are, the injunction should be refused.

❖ APPLYING THE LAW

The injunction, especially the prohibitory injunction, has been much in the news recently, due to the rise of the so-called 'super-injunction'. The grant of such an injunction is usually requested by well-known celebrities to prevent the press from publishing stories about them. The injunctions have been termed 'super-injunctions' because the court has, on occasions, restricted the press from reporting which celebrity has been granted an injunction and the subject-matter of the injunction. Well-known celebrities who have had super injunctions granted in their favour include the footballer Ryan Giggs and the TV personality Jeremy Clarkson.

The danger with super-injunctions is, of course, that they infringe the free reporting of legal news stories and, due to the fact that a claimant must give an undertaking to pay damages, are restricted to the wealthy who can afford to give such an undertaking.

Do you think that the super-injunction is really an example of a 'sledge-hammer to crack a nut'?

Mandatory injunction

A mandatory injunction compels performance of an obligation. A comparison between prohibitory and mandatory injunctions, together with interim and final injunctions, was made by Megarry J in *Shepherd Homes Ltd v Sandham*.[9]

The claimant had built a large number of houses in Caerphilly, South Wales. The estate was laid out in an 'open plan' style, which meant that each house owner had covenanted not to construct a fence, or any other erection, in front of the building line of each house. The problem was that Welsh mountain sheep and horses began to graze in the gardens of the properties. The defendant constructed a fence to prevent this occurring. The claimant sought an injunction to compel the defendant to remove the fence. The injunction sought was of a mandatory nature because it would have forced the defendant to comply with the obligation he had entered into not to construct a fence.

Megarry J refused to grant the injunction. This was largely due to the fact that the claimant had delayed for four months after issuing his claim before seeking the interim injunction it required. This suggested that even the claimant thought that the matter was not of an urgent nature.

Megarry J distinguished between prohibitory and mandatory injunctions. The latter were harder to obtain. The very nature of a mandatory injunction meant that it was used to correct what had happened in the past, so inflicting an additional cost on a defendant in having to take

---

9 *Shepherd Homes Ltd v Sandham* [1971] Ch 340.

steps to undo his previous actions. A prohibitory injunction looked to the future: it sought to prevent future conduct from occurring and so imposed no cost onto a defendant to undo actions he had previously undertaken.

There were also theoretical differences between mandatory and prohibitory injunctions. A mandatory injunction obliged a defendant to carry out positive steps; a prohibitory injunction was an order to refrain from continuing an activity.

Megarry J said that in deciding whether or not to grant a mandatory injunction, the court would assess whether granting the injunction produced a 'fair result'.[10] The court would take into account how trivial the damage was to the claimant seeking the injunction, the detriment granting it would have on the defendant, as well as the benefit the claimant would gain from having the injunction granted. The general principle was that it was far harder to obtain a mandatory than a prohibitory injunction.

Further differences could be made between interim and final injunctions. Megarry J made the following points about an interim injunction:

(a)   an interim injunction 'for a mandatory injunction was one of the rarest cases that occurred';[11]

(b)   the case 'had to be unusually strong and clear before a mandatory injunction will be granted'.[12] That was because the court had to take into account that the injunction may not be awarded following a full trial of the claimant's claim;

(c)   before granting the interim mandatory injunction, the court had to 'feel a high degree of assurance that at trial it will appear that the injunction was rightly granted';[13] and

(d)   if an interim mandatory injunction was granted, it would not usually be extended at trial, as by then the defendant will have been ordered to take a particular step which, by the stage of trial, he should have normally taken. In contrast, a prohibitory injunction would usually be continued at trial for there would still be a purpose in preventing the defendant from continuing with his behaviour.

An injunction will not be granted where its effect would be to grant an order of specific performance if the court could not validly grant that order of specific performance. For example, specific performance will not be ordered to enforce a contract for personal services,[14] as was shown in *Page One Records Ltd v Britton*.[15]

Here a pop group called 'The Troggs' engaged the claimant as their manager. Approximately two years later, the group sought to dismiss the claimant as their manager and appoint another manager in its place. The group's argument was that the manager had breached its fiduciary duties to the group. The claimant applied for a mandatory injunction to compel the group to honour the contract between them (and, therefore, to prevent the group from using the services of the other manager) which was to last for a further three years.

Stamp J refused to grant the injunction. His judgment shows a lack of general sympathy with the group. In fact, the group had not demonstrated even a prima facie case that the manager had breached its contract. It was, in fact, likely that the claimant would have a successful claim for damages against the group for wrongfully terminating the contract between them. But that did not mean that the claimant could also claim a mandatory injunction.

---

10 Ibid, quoting Buckley J in *Charrington v Simons & Co Ltd* [1970] 1 WLR 725.
11 Ibid at 348.
12 Ibid at 349.
13 Ibid at 351.
14 See pp 468–469.
15 *Page One Records Ltd v Britton* [1968] 1 WLR 157.

Stamp J held that he could not grant an injunction where its effect would be to grant an order for specific performance of the contract if the particular contract could not be subjected to an order for specific performance. To grant such an injunction here would have that consequence. A contract for personal services cannot be subject to an order for specific performance, as it is tantamount to forcing a party to work for another which is akin to slavery. Granting a mandatory injunction here would have the same consequence: it would force the manager to work for the group.

The comments by Megarry J in *Shepherd Homes Ltd v Sandham*, together with the decision in *Page One Records Ltd v Britton*, provide a useful analysis of the court's approach to mandatory and prohibitory injunctions. A mandatory injunction seems to be a rarely sighted creature, mostly due to the fact that its very nature imposes on the defendant a cost of undoing actions that he has already taken. The court is, in addition, wary of granting interim mandatory injunctions when the defendant may well succeed at trial of defending the claim for the injunction. It is unfair to compel a defendant to incur the additional costs of undoing his actions when he may successfully defend such a claim at trial.

Quia timet injunction

This Latin phrase means 'because he fears'. This type of injunction is granted because the claimant can show that he fears that the defendant will take a particular course of action. An injunction to this effect was upheld by the Supreme Court in *Secretary of State for the Environment, Food & Rural Affairs v Meier*.[16]

The defendants were travellers who occupied part of Hethfelton Wood, Dorset. The wood belonged to the Forestry Commission. The Forestry Commission sought a possession order to repossess the wood from the travellers, together with an injunction preventing them from returning to the wood to occupy it again.

The Supreme Court upheld the decision of the majority in the Court of Appeal to grant the injunction against the travellers returning to the wood. As Lord Neuberger MR put it:

> where a trespass to the claimant's property is threatened, and particularly where a trespass is being committed, and has been committed in the past, by the defendant, an injunction to restrain the threatened trespass would, in the absence of good reasons to the contrary, appear to be appropriate.[17]

The court, thought Lord Neuberger MR, was not bound not to grant the injunction simply because it believed that the injunction was unlikely to be enforced if it was breached. It was, he said, likely in this case that the two usual methods of enforcing the breach of an injunction – the seizing of the defendant's property and/or the imprisonment of the defendant – were unlikely to happen here. That is because the defendants were unlikely to have significant assets and given that a number of defendants had young dependent children, imprisonment could be seen to be disproportionate to the breaking of the injunction. Nonetheless, this did not mean that the injunction had to be refused. The court could still take the view that the defendants would be more likely to refrain from further trespasses if the injunction was granted. The injunction might, in any event, act as a deterrent to the defendant from trespassing onto the claimant's land as they might be afraid of being imprisoned if they breached the injunction.

Of course, the problem with this injunction was that it was likely that the court would not know the identities of some of the trespassers. This caused no difficulty for the Supreme Court.

---

16 *Secretary of State for the Environment, Food & Rural Affairs v Meier* [2009] 1 WLR 2780.
17 Ibid at [79].

Lord Rodger, in particular, disagreed with the earlier view of Wilson J in *Secretary of State for the Environment, Food & Rural Affairs v Drury*[18] that the injunction would be 'useless' as you could not ask the court to imprison a 'probably changing group of not easily identifiable travellers'. There was no evidence here that an injunction against a potentially changing group would fail to work. It could be effectively served upon them, by being displayed in the wood, for example, so they would know about it.

Search orders (formerly *Anton Piller* orders)

This type of injunction enables a claimant to enter a defendant's premises and search for documents if the claimant believes the defendant might destroy the documents before trial. This type of injunction was recognised by the Court of Appeal in *Anton Piller KG v Manufacturing Processes Ltd*.[19]

The claimant was a German company who manufactured computer components. The defendant was their English agent. It transpired that the defendant intended to disclose confidential information to two competitors of the claimant. The claimant sought an interim injunction to prevent this from occurring. They also sought an order permitting them to enter into the defendant's premises, search for incriminating documents that they feared the defendant would destroy before trial and seize such material. The Court of Appeal granted the injunction and granted permission for the claimant to enter the defendant's premises.

Lord Denning MR pointed out that the court's order might look like a 'search warrant in disguise',[20] but was at pains to explain that no court could grant an order which permitted a person to force their way into another's premises without the latter's consent. Instead, the order allowed the claimant to enter into the defendant's premises. The defendant could refuse to give his permission to such an entry or could challenge the validity of the court order. If the order had been validly granted, the defendant risked being held in contempt of court for failing to comply with it.

Safeguards had to be applied when the claimant executed the court's order. When serving the order on the defendant, the claimant had to be accompanied by his solicitor who, as an officer of the court, could ensure that the order was correctly executed. The defendant should be given the chance to consider the order and to take legal advice upon it. If the defendant refused permission to allow the claimant to enter his premises, the claimant could not force his way in.

Such an order as was granted in the case should only be made, according to Ormrod LJ, when three criteria are satisfied:

> First, there must be an extremely strong *prima facie* case. Secondly, the damage, potential or actual, must be very serious for the applicant. Thirdly, there must be clear evidence that the defendants have in their possession incriminating documents or things, and that there is a real possibility that they may destroy such material before any application *inter partes* can be made.[21]

The *Anton Piller* order, then, is a temporary order requested by one party without notice to the other, to enter their premises, search for incriminating documents and seize them before the actual trial of the action occurs.

---

18 *Secretary of State for the Environment, Food & Rural Affairs v Drury* [2004] 1 WLR 1906 at 1912.
19 *Anton Piller KG v Manufacturing Processes Ltd* [1976] Ch 55.
20 Ibid at 60.
21 Ibid at 62.

The essence of the *Anton Piller* order is now embodied in s 7 of the Civil Procedure Act 1997. The High Court may make an order permitting a party to enter into premises for the purposes of searching for evidence or to make a copy, photograph, sample or other record of such evidence.[22] Whilst this is a statutory right enjoyed by claimants, it appears to leave the original *Anton Piller* order untouched.

Freezing orders (formerly *Mareva* injunctions)

Freezing orders are designed to prevent a party from dealing with his assets so as to prevent the other party from claiming them. As such, this is a type of interim injunction. It is granted to the claimant to prevent the defendant from dissipating his assets before the trial of the action can be heard. It is designed to stop the defendant from frustrating the litigation that the claimant is about to pursue.

The leading case remains the decision of the Court of Appeal in *Mareva Compania Naviera SA v International Bulkcarriers SA; The Mareva*.[23]

The facts concerned the charter of a ship, *The Mareva*. The claimant owners chartered it to the defendants. The defendants themselves sub-chartered it to the President of India. The President duly paid the charter fee to the defendants. The defendants, in turn, paid some of their charter fee but not all of it. The claimant claimed the unpaid part of the charter fee ($30,800) together with damages for wrongful repudiation of the contract. The defendant had retained a sizeable sum in its bank in London and the claimant sought an interim injunction preventing the defendant from disposing of that money.

Lord Denning MR held that the court had a very wide right to grant an injunction. This included applying for an interim injunction to force the defendant to retain money even though the claimant had not established that he was actually entitled to the money at trial. Lord Denning MR explained the injunction as follows:

> If it appears that the debt is due and owing, and there is a danger that the debtor may dispose of his assets so as to defeat it before judgment, the court has jurisdiction in a proper case to grant an [interim] judgment so as to prevent him disposing of those assets.[24]

This was a 'proper case' for the injunction to be granted. The charterers had their money in a bank and they could have moved it to another country at any point, making it highly unlikely that, in practical terms, the owners would be able to recover the money owed to them. The injunction would be granted until a full trial of the claimant's claim took place.

Since the Civil Procedure Rules 1998 came into effect, *Mareva* injunctions have been known as 'freezing orders'. Rule 25.1(f) of the Civil Procedure Rules 1998 specifically provides that the court may now make a freezing order which has the effect of:

(a) restraining a party from removing from the jurisdiction assets located there; or
(b) restraining a party from dealing with any assets whether located within the jurisdiction or not.

This rule makes it clear that such an order can apply to assets even if they are not located within the jurisdiction. The extension of a *Mareva* injunction to assets located outside of the

---

22 Civil Procedure Act 1997 s 7(4).
23 *Mareva Compania Naviera SA v International Bulkcarriers SA; The Mareva* [1980] 1 All ER 213.
24 Ibid at 215.

jurisdiction of the court[25] was confirmed by the Court of Appeal in *Derby & Co Ltd v Weldon* (*Nos 3 and 4*).[26] There the Court of Appeal held that it was not a prerequisite to the granting of a *Mareva* injunction that the defendant had to have assets within the jurisdiction.

The claimant alleged that the defendant had defrauded it in dealings in the cocoa market. At first instance, Sir Nicholas Browne-Wilkinson V-C had granted a worldwide *Mareva* injunction against a Luxembourg-based company defendant, but had refused to grant such an injunction against a Panamanian defendant. Neither company had any assets within the jurisdiction of the court. But Browne-Wilkinson VC believed that a *Mareva* injunction could ultimately be enforced under the European Convention on Jurisdiction and the Enforcement of Judgments in Civil and Commercial Matters[27] against the Luxembourg company, but there was no effective enforcement mechanism against the Panamanian company.

Lord Donaldson MR held that a *Mareva* injunction could be granted against foreign defendants and should be granted against both foreign defendants in this case. In deciding whether to grant a *Mareva* injunction, whether or not that injunction could be enforced abroad was not the primary consideration for the court. The essential point was that if a defendant refused to honour the *Mareva* injunction, he could be denied the right to defend the claimant's claim at trial. This in itself was an effective enforcement mechanism against a defendant. Neither was it relevant that a defendant may have no assets. A *Mareva* injunction operated *in personam* against the defendant personally, so it was appropriate that it could be made against the defendant wherever he was in the world.

A freezing order may now, therefore, be made against a defendant who has assets located anywhere in the world. Indeed, the order would also seemingly apply against a defendant who appears to have no assets (although, if the claimant knows this, it is difficult to see why the claimant would seek the injunction initially).

Guidance as to when the court should permit a worldwide freezing order to be enforced was given by the Court of Appeal in *Dadourian Group International Inc v Simms*[28] (these are known as the *Dadourian* guidelines). In delivering the judgment of the court, Arden LJ thought that there were eight guidelines that the court should take into account. These are:

(i)   the granting of permission to enforce a worldwide freezing order should be 'just and convenient'[29] to ensure the worldwide freezing order is effective. In addition, it must be oppressive to the parties in the English proceedings or to third parties who might be joined into proceedings abroad;

(ii)   the court needs to consider all relevant circumstances and options;

(iii)   the court should balance the claimant's interests with those of the other parties to the proceedings, including any party likely to be joined in the foreign proceedings;

(iv)   the court should normally withhold its permission if the claimant would obtain a better remedy in the foreign court than in England;

(v)   the claimant's evidence in support of his application should contain all necessary information to enable the court to make an 'informed'[30] decision. This would, for example, include evidence as to the law and practice of the foreign court;

(vi)   the standard of proof required was that the claimant must show that there was a 'real prospect'[31] of assets existing within the foreign court's jurisdiction;

---

25 i.e. outside England and Wales.
26 *Derby & Co Ltd v Weldon* (*Nos 3 and 4*) [1990] Ch 65.
27 This convention was incorporated into English law under the Civil Jurisdiction and Judgments Act 1982.
28 *Dadourian Group International Inc v Simms* (*Practice Note*) [2006] 1 WLR 2499.
29 Ibid at 2502 per Arden LJ.
30 Ibid.
31 Ibid.

(vii) there usually had to be a risk that the assets might be dissipated; and

(viii) usually the claimant should notify the defendant that he intended to seek the enforcement of the worldwide freezing order but in urgent cases, this could be omitted. In such a case, the defendant should be allowed the 'earliest practicable opportunity'[32] to have the matter reconsidered by the court.

These guidelines were not, as Arden LJ made clear at the end of her judgment, an exhaustive list. The court should consider any other issue which needed consideration in an individual case.

Specific performance

Specific performance is an order of the court to one party to a contract that it must adhere to the terms of a contract. An order for specific performance will be rarely granted, as normally damages at common law will be an adequate remedy in the event that the contract is breached. The claimant must show that damages are not an adequate remedy to invoke equity's jurisdiction to grant an order for specific performance. To do that, the claimant usually has to show that the contract concerns unique property, where the payment of damages cannot adequately compensate the claimant for the defendant's breach of contract.

As a general rule, an order for specific performance will not be granted if the court's constant supervision is required in monitoring whether the order is implemented by the defendant: Co-operative Insurance Society Ltd v Argyll Stores (Holdings) Ltd.[33]

The defendant traded as 'Safeway' and had a supermarket in the Hillsborough Shopping Centre, Sheffield. The claimant was its landlord. The 35-year lease provided that the defendant would keep the supermarket open. Safeway operated the leading store in the shopping centre to which customers would be drawn. It was essential that the store continued to trade so that the landlord could attractively market the remaining units in the shopping centre to other potential business tenants. Unfortunately, the supermarket was loss-making, so the defendant decided to close it. The claimant applied for an order for specific performance, claiming that damages for the defendant's breach of the lease would not be an adequate remedy. The Court of Appeal granted the order for specific performance, but this was reversed unanimously by the House of Lords.

Lord Hoffman confirmed that it had been the usual practice of the courts not to grant an order for specific performance (or a mandatory injunction) compelling a party to continue to run their business because such an order would require the court's constant supervision. This would take the form of the claimant often coming to the court seeking the court's further punishment of the defendant for breaching the order of specific performance. The only weapon of punishment open to the court would be to treat the defendant as being guilty of contempt of court. This sanction by the court was not, perhaps, appropriate for a corporate defendant who would have to waste time and money in running their business (at a loss) simply to comply with a court order.

In addition, the loss that the defendant incurs in continuing to run the business may be far greater than the detriment the claimant would suffer through the defendant breaching his contract with the claimant. The aim of the law of contract was not to punish the defendant in his wrong-doing but to give the claimant adequate (but no more) compensation for his loss. Requiring the defendant to continue to run a loss-making business was punishing him whilst not essentially compensating the claimant.

---

32 Ibid.
33 Co-operative Insurance Society Ltd v Argyll Stores (Holdings) Ltd [1998] AC 1.

Lord Hoffman held that an order for specific performance should not be granted if it required a defendant to continue an activity over a period of time. On the other hand, it could be granted where it required the defendant to achieve a one-off objective. Specific performance had been ordered, for example, in relation to a tenant's repairing covenants in a lease[34] because the court just had to satisfy itself that the work had been carried out.

Lord Hoffman described the remedy of specific performance as being an 'exceptional remedy'.[35] Certain types of contract can be considered where specific performance will, and will not, usually be granted. They are contracts concerning:

(a)   the sale of land;
(b)   the sale of chattels;
(c)   the sale of shares; and
(d)   employment obligations.

The sale of land

The breach of a contract for the sale of land[36] will normally merit an order for specific performance being granted for it. Such a contract is made in English law when both parties exchange their own part of the contract. After that point, the contract is *prima facie* specifically enforceable if one party should breach the contract by refusing to sell the land to the other.

The rationale behind this is that all land is seen as unique. No amount of damages can adequately compensate a claimant if the defendant refuses to sell the land to him for the claimant cannot go and buy another identical piece of land on the open market.

The sale of chattels

A contract for the sale of chattels will be subject to an order for specific performance if the chattel is unique so that damages are not an adequate remedy for the buyer if the seller subsequently decides not to sell his property. This was decided in *Falcke v Gray*.[37]

Mr Falcke rented a house from Mrs Gray. It was a term of the contract that, at the end of the tenancy, Mr Falcke should have the opportunity to purchase two china jars for the total sum of £40. Mrs Gray was ignorant of their true value, but Mr Falcke was a dealer in such curiosities. Before the lease ended, Mrs Gray sold the jars to a third party for £200. Mr Falcke sought an order for specific performance of that contractual obligation, with the aim of securing the delivery from the third party of the jars.

The Vice-Chancellor confirmed that a court of equity would give an order for specific performance for a contract for the sale of chattels on the same basis as any other contract: if damages at common law were an adequate remedy, the claimant must be content with such a remedy. If damages were not an adequate remedy, the court of equity could order that the contract be specifically performed. Damages were an adequate remedy if the buyer could go into the market and purchase comparable items; if he could not, damages were not an adequate remedy. Here the contract was for the purchase of 'articles of unusual beauty, rarity and distinction'[38] so damages were not an adequate remedy for non-performance of the contract.

An order for specific performance would normally have been granted in the case, as the items were unique. On the facts, the order was refused as the claimant had not offered a fair price and in doing so, could not claim the assistance of a court of equity. After all, according to the

---

34   See, for instance, *Jeune v Queens Cross Properties Ltd* [1974] Ch 97.
35   *Co-operative Insurance Society Ltd v Argyll Stores (Holdings) Ltd* [1998] AC 1 at 11.
36   For an example of this occurring, see *Penn v Lord Baltimore* (1750) 1 Ves Sen 444; 27 ER 1132.
37   *Falcke v Gray* (1859) 4 Drew 651; 62 ER 250.
38   Ibid at 658 per the Vice-Chancellor, Sir R T Kindersley.

equitable maxim,[39] he who seeks equity must do equity. The claimant had not acted equitably in deliberately offering a non-competitive price and so specific performance was refused.

Section 52 of the Sale of Goods Act 1979 now contains a specific statutory provision enabling the court to grant an order of specific performance for specific or ascertained goods. Section 52(3) provides that the order may be 'unconditional, or on such terms and conditions as to damages, payment of the price and otherwise as seem just to the court'. The section probably adds little to the pre-existing law on specific performance for the sale of specific or ascertained goods.

The sale of shares

In a contract for the sale of shares, whether an order for specific performance is likely to be awarded depends on whether damages would be an appropriate remedy. Again, this follows a similar principle to that already considered: if the shares are unique in nature, an order for specific performance is likely to be granted, as damages would not be an adequate remedy.

Shares in private limited companies are usually seen to be unique in nature. If the company is private, its shares are not freely traded on a stock market. This means that damages are not an adequate remedy should a contract for the sale of such shares be breached by the seller. As the shares are not available for sale on the open market, the buyer cannot use any damages awarded to purchase alternative shares.[40]

In contrast, shares in a public limited company are traded on the open market. This means that if a seller of a contract for the sale of such shares breaches the contract, damages are an adequate remedy for the buyer as the buyer can freely purchase alternative shares instead.

Employment obligations

Employment contracts are not usually subject to an order for specific performance. Section 236 of the Trade Union and Labour Relations (Consolidation) Act 1992 provides categorically that the court cannot make an order of specific performance or grant an injunction if its effect is to 'compel an employee to do any work or attend at any place for the doing of any work'. Consequently, if an employee breaches his employment contract, the usual remedy for the employer is that of common law damages.

There are two reasons why contracts of employment are not susceptible to an order for specific performance or injunction. The first is that the court usually views an order that a party perform his employment obligations towards his employer as tantamount to slavery. As Fry LJ explained in *De Francesco v Barnum*:[41]

> I have a strong impression and strong feeling that it is not in the interests of mankind that the rule of specific performance should be extended to forcing people to maintain permanent and continuous relations which they are unwilling to maintain. I think the courts are bound to be jealous in case they should turn contracts of service into contracts of slavery . . .

The second reason is more pragmatic: that it is difficult, if not impossible, for the court to judge whether an employee would be upholding any order for specific performance or injunction made against him, as Megarry J explained in *C H Giles & Co Ltd v Morris*:[42]

---

39 See Chapter 1, pp 17–18.
40 See *Duncuft v Albrecht* (1841) 12 Sim 189; 59 ER 1104 (specific shares in a private railway company).
41 *De Francesco v Barnum* [1886–90] All ER Rep 414 at 418.
42 *C H Giles & Co Ltd v Morris* [1972] 1 WLR 307.

If a singer contracts to sing, there could no doubt be proceedings for committal if, ordered to sing, the singer remained obstinately dumb. But if instead the singer sang flat, or sharp, or too fast, or too slowly, or too loudly, or too quietly, or resorted to a dozen of the manifestations of temperament traditionally associated with some singers, the threat of committal would reveal itself as a most unsatisfactory weapon: for who could say whether the imperfections of performance were natural or self-induced? To make an order with such possibilities of evasion would be vain; and so the order will not be made.[43]

The facts of the case concerned a contract for the sale of shares in a company called Invincible Policies Ltd to the claimant company. Invincible owned a subsidiary company, Trafalgar Insurance Co Ltd. A term of the contract was that Mr C Giles would be appointed as both the Managing Director of Invincible and as a director of Trafalgar. The entire share sale contract was eventually subject to an agreed order of specific performance made between the claimant and defendants. But the defendants then refused to appoint Mr Giles to be the director of both companies. Their defence was that an order for specific performance for a contract of employment had been granted by the judge and such an order should not have been made. The question for Megarry J was whether the presence of the employment clause in the overall contract prevented the court from making an order of specific performance for the whole share sale agreement.

Megarry J drew a distinction between ordering specific performance of a contract for personal services and for the overall contract for the sale of shares. Specific performance could be ordered for the contract as a whole, even though it could not be ordered for a particular provision of the agreement, because it related to personal services. The personal services element was simply one element of the overall contract and the balance lay in ordering specific performance of the entire agreement.

Rescission

Rescission is an equitable remedy which enables both parties to a contract to be restored to their pre-contract positions in the event that one party commits a repudiatory breach of contract. It is most often applied in cases where there has been a misrepresentation made by one party to the other before the contract was entered into or the contract was entered into as a result of duress or undue influence by the other party.

In order to rescind the contract, the general principle is that the claimant must make it clear to the defendant that he intends to rescind the contract or, if that is not possible, he must do some overt act to make his intention to rescind plain.[44]

Rescission may apply providing none of the bars to rescission themselves apply. The bars to rescission are:

(a)   affirmation;
(b)   laches;
(c)   where *restitutio in integrum* is impossible; or
(d)   where a *bona fide* purchaser of a legal estate for value without notice acquires an interest in the property.

---

43 Ibid at 318.
44 See, for example, *Car & Universal Finance Co Ltd v Caldwell* [1961] 1 QB 525.

Affirmation

The contract cannot be rescinded if the innocent party has affirmed it. Affirmation may be express or implied. Express affirmation occurs where the innocent party confirms categorically that he wishes to continue with the contract, notwithstanding the repudiatory breach that has been committed. Implied affirmation occurs where the innocent party does some act showing that he intends to continue with the contract, as occurred in Long v Lloyd.[45]

Stanley Long bought a second-hand lorry from the defendant. The defendant had described the lorry as being in 'exceptional condition' and also that it was 'in first-class condition'. These descriptions were found to be innocent misrepresentations. Two days after the contract of sale had been concluded, the lorry needed a replacement part. The defendant agreed to pay half of the costs of the part. The following day, the lorry broke down again, following which the claimant sought to rescind the contract of sale.

The Court of Appeal held that the claimant had lost his right to rescind the contract. His right to rescind was impliedly lost when the claimant, knowing the condition of the lorry after it had been repaired the first time, then used it again afterwards. Pearce LJ held that that second occasion amounted to a 'final acceptance'[46] of the lorry 'for better or for worse'.

Laches

This is equity's doctrine of delay. Where a party seeks an equitable remedy he must bring his action without undue delay. If he delays unduly in bringing his claim, he will not be entitled to an equitable remedy. This doctrine is discussed further in Chapter 12.[47]

Where *restitutio in integrum* is impossible

For rescission to be awarded to a claimant, it must be possible to restore both parties to their pre-contractual positions. That is known as *restitutio in integrum*. If it is not possible to restore both parties to substantially their pre-contractual positions, the claimant will not be able to rescind his contract.

❖ EXPLAINING THE LAW

Suppose Scott buys a truffle, after being told by Terry that the truffle is a fine Italian one. On eating it, Scott discovers that it is not an Italian truffle at all, but has in fact been dug up in Derbyshire.

Terry's misrepresentation would make the contract with Scott voidable. Scott would normally be entitled to rescind the contract. But here, as Scott has eaten the truffle, it is impossible to place both parties into their pre-contractual positions. As such, rescission cannot be awarded and Scott will have to be content to claim damages at common law (or under the Misrepresentation Act 1967) for Terry's misrepresentation.

---

45 Long v Lloyd [1958] 1 WLR 753.
46 Ibid at 761.
47 See Chapter 12, pp 339–340.

Where a *bona fide* purchaser of a legal estate for value without notice acquires an interest in the property

If an honest purchaser for value acquires a legal estate in the property which is the subject matter of the contract and does so before the claimant exercises his chance to rescind the contract, the claimant cannot claim to rescind the contract any longer. His claim is defeated by that of the *bona fide* purchaser, who is also known by the somewhat romantic name of 'equity's darling'.

Rectification

Rectification is an equitable remedy which allows mistakes in documents to be corrected by the court. The typical case is that involving a mutual misunderstanding – where the parties are at cross-purposes with each other in forming the written contract.

The nature of an order for rectification was originally set out by James V-C in *Mackenzie v Coulson*[48] where he said:

> Courts of Equity do not rectify contracts; they may and do rectify instruments purporting to have been made in pursuance of the terms of contracts. But it is always necessary for a plaintiff to show that there was an actual concluded contract antecedent to the instrument which is sought to be rectified; and that such contract is inaccurately represented in the instrument.[49]

The claimant had, therefore, to show that the written document did not accurately reflect the actual contract made between the parties before the written document was entered into.

This requirement of showing that there had to be a prior contract agreed between the parties was considered by the Court of Appeal in *Joscelyne v Nissen*.[50] There a father agreed to transfer his business to his daughter, in return for which she would pay him a pension and certain household expenses, such as his gas and electricity bills. The actual written contract failed to mention the household bills specifically and the daughter stopped paying them when the parties argued with each other. The father sought rectification of the written agreement. The daughter argued that rectification was not possible as there had been no 'concluded contract antecedent' before the written agreement entered into between them.

Russell LJ held that there was a 'strong burden of proof'[51] on the party seeking rectification of the contract, but that it was not a prerequisite to rectification that an actual concluded contract needed to be proven before the written contract could be rectified. It would be sufficient that one party was able to show some form of 'outward expression of accord'[52] without going so far as to prove that a definitive contract existed before the written agreement was entered into.

This 'strong burden of proof' was qualified by Brightman LJ in *Thomas Bates Ltd v Wyndham's (Lingerie) Ltd*.[53] He held that the standard of proof that the claimant had to show was the normal civil one of the balance of probabilities. But he pointed out that, in reality, what the claimant was trying to do was to prove that a written contract was mistakenly drafted. As such, a high

---

48 *Mackenzie v Coulson* (1869) LR 8 Eq 368.
49 Ibid at 375.
50 *Joscelyne v Nissen* [1970] 2 QB 86.
51 Ibid at 98.
52 Ibid.
53 *Thomas Bates Ltd v Wyndham's (Lingerie) Ltd* [1981] 1 WLR 505.

evidential requirement of 'convincing proof'[54] from the claimant was set by the courts to counteract the contradictory written contract.

The courts have also considered rectification in the event of a unilateral (one-sided) mistake. Rectification will be rarely ordered. As Slade LJ explained in *Agip SpA v Navigazione Alta Italia SpA (The Nai Genova)*:[55]

> in the absence of estoppel, fraud, undue influence or a fiduciary relationship between the parties, the authorities do not in any circumstances permit the rectification of a contract on the grounds of unilateral mistake, unless the defendant had actual knowledge of the existence of the relevant mistaken belief at the time when the mistaken plaintiff signed the contract.[56]

This is because the consequences of an order of rectification are very serious for the non-mistaken party. The order would amend the contract, probably to their disadvantage, when they had no awareness that there was ever anything amiss with the written contract.

To obtain an order for rectification for unilateral mistake, the claimant must show that the defendant knew of the mistake when entering into the written agreement. In *Commission for the New Towns v Cooper (Great Britain Ltd)*,[57] Stuart-Smith LJ reiterated that actual knowledge of the mistake was required. But this could also include the defendant shutting its eyes to the obvious or wilfully or recklessly omitting to do what an honest and reasonable person would have done. Only then would an order rectifying the agreement be made.

In *George Wimpey UK Ltd v V I Construction Ltd*,[58] George Wimpey UK Ltd entered into an agreement with V I Construction Ltd to buy a plot of land for £2,650,000. The claimant was to develop the land and build 231 flats on it. Added to the purchase price was to be a further sum if the claimant sold flats with 'enhancements': for example, the higher up in the block the flats were built, the higher the price they commanded. In turn, that would mean that V I Construction Ltd would receive a further overall payment from George Wimpey UK Ltd after the flats had all been sold. Unfortunately, the written contract between the parties failed to take into account the enhancements, to George Wimpey's disadvantage. The company therefore sought rectification of the contract, on the basis of its unilateral mistake about which, it argued, the defendant must have known. George Wimpey said that the defendant had acted unconscionably in not pointing out the mistake to them.

The Court of Appeal refused to order rectification. George Wimpey had failed to show convincingly that the defendants had either shut their eyes to an obvious error in failing to include the enhancements in the contract price or had wilfully and recklessly failed to make such enquiries as an honest and reasonable man would make. Far more convincing proof was needed for rectification to be ordered than the defendant simply acting unconscionably.

Summary of equitable remedies

A discussion of the range of equitable remedies shows that each of them is only awarded in exceptional circumstances, when an award of damages at common law would not adequately compensate the claimant. Each equitable remedy has its own hurdles over which a successful claimant must jump to secure success.

---

54 Ibid at 521.
55 *Agip SpA v Navigazione Alta Italia SpA (The Nai Genova)* [1984] 1 Lloyd's Rep 353.
56 Ibid at 365.
57 *Commission for the New Towns v Cooper (Great Britain Ltd)* [1995] Ch 259.
58 *George Wimpey UK Ltd v V I Construction Ltd* [2005] EWCA 77.

Proprietary Estoppel

Proprietary estoppel is an equitable cause of action that enables a claimant to claim an interest in property. It was described by Lord Scott in *Cobbe v Yeoman's Row Management Ltd*[59] as:

> [a]n 'estoppel' bars the object of it from asserting some fact or facts, or, sometimes, something that is a mixture of fact and law, that stands in the way of some right claimed by the person entitled to the benefit of the estoppel. The estoppel becomes a 'proprietary' estoppel – a sub-species of promissory estoppel – if the right claimed is a proprietary right, usually a right to or over land but, in principle, equally available in relation to chattels or choses in action.

Making connections

You may recall promissory estoppel from your studies of contract law. That doctrine was developed by Denning J in his landmark decision in *Central London Property Trust Ltd v High Trees House Ltd*.[60] It enables a defendant to keep a claimant to his promise not to collect a full debt due to him from the defendant, in certain circumstances.

As such, promissory estoppel is reactive in nature. Birkett LJ described it as a 'shield and not a sword' in *Combe v Combe*.[61] Proprietary estoppel, on the other hand, is proactive in nature. It enables a claimant to claim an interest in property which, as Lord Scott states, is normally land.

As Lord Walker pointed out in *Thorner v Major*,[62] promissory estoppel is based on the existing legal relationship between the parties. Proprietary estoppel, on the other hand, need not be based on a legal relationship at all: it is instead based on property owned by the defendant.

The relationship between the two types of estoppel: Promissory and proprietary

Promissory estoppel is sometimes called 'estoppel by representation' whereas proprietary estoppel is sometimes known as 'estoppel by acquiescence'. The notion underpinning proprietary estoppel is that the defendant has stood idly by whilst the claimant has undertaken some action which is inconsistent with his strict legal rights in relation to property. The defendant has acquiesced in the claimant undertaking such action but then refuses to recognise the claimant's claim for an interest in the property. The defendant can be estopped (through his acquiescence) from denying the claimant a claim to the property. When the claim of proprietary estoppel was originally recognised by the courts in the nineteenth century,[63] it was as a response to the defendant defrauding the claimant of the right or interest in the property he had acquired by his actions. The basis of the claim is that the defendant cannot now defeat the claimant's interest in property which he had previously encouraged the claimant to acquire.

Several judges believe that proprietary estoppel is a species of promissory estoppel. Lord Scott certainly thought so in *Cobbe v Yeoman's Row Management Ltd* as did Oliver J in *Taylors Fashions Ltd v Liverpool Victoria Trustees Co Ltd*.[64] This view is based on the notion that all estoppels are based on

---

59 *Cobbe v Yeoman's Row Management Ltd* [2008] 1 WLR 1752 at 1761.
60 *Central London Property Trust Ltd v High Trees House Ltd* [1947] KB 130. See the discussion of this decision in Chapter 1 at pp 11–13.
61 *Combe v Combe* [1951] 2 KB 215.
62 *Thorner v Major* [2009] 1 WLR 776.
63 Proprietary estoppel was first recognised in the dissenting speech of Lord Kingsdown in *Ramsden v Dyson* (1866) LR 1 HL 129.
64 *Taylors Fashions Ltd v Liverpool Victoria Trustees Co Ltd* [1982] QB 133 at 150.

a promise not to enforce strict legal rights. Other members of the judiciary believe that estoppel itself may be divided into two parts: promissory and proprietary. This was probably the view of Lord Walker in *Thorner v Major*[65] and was certainly the analysis led by Lord Denning MR in *Crabb v Arun District Council*.[66] The latter believed that estoppel as a concept was based on broad principles of equity mitigating the effects of the common law. Promissory estoppel did not give rise to a cause of action but proprietary estoppel does.

The requirements to establish proprietary estoppel

These were confirmed by Lord Walker in *Thorner v Major*[67] as being three-fold:

> a representation or assurance made to the claimant; reliance on it by the claimant; and detriment to the claimant in consequence of his (reasonable) reliance.

However, Robert Walker LJ (as he then was) in the earlier Court of Appeal decision in *Gillett v Holt*[68] had recognised that it was often not possible to break these requirements down into 'watertight compartments'.[69] He said that 'the quality of the relevant assurances may influence the issue of reliance, that reliance and detriment are often intertwined' and that '[i]n the end the court must look at the matter in the round'.[70]

As You Read

Be aware that the inherent difficulty with any type of estoppel is that it is an example of an equitable principle varying strict legal rights (which have often been written down) between the parties. In the case of proprietary estoppel, that variation is particularly powerful as it means that a claimant can acquire an interest in property. As will be shown, such a dramatic consequence has not dissuaded the courts from recognising a claimant's claim in proprietary estoppel and the higher courts have dealt with a number of cases since the turn of the millennium.

Each of three elements to establish a claim in proprietary estoppel must be considered.

A representation

Given Lord Walker's requirements for a claim in proprietary estoppel to arise, one might consider that a specific, defined representation was needed as the first ingredient for a successful claim. Naturally, a specific representation will always assist a claimant, but case law shows that it is normally difficult to pin-point when a precise representation was made to the claimant. The cases here may be broken down into two broad groups: where words are used to encourage the claimant to believe he will acquire a proprietary interest and where no such words are used.

The defendant's assurance must concern specific property owned by him.[71] Yet the doctrine of proprietary estoppel will not be restricted to cases where the defendant has defined precisely

---

65 *Thorner v Major* [2009] 1 WLR 776.
66 *Crabb v Arun District Council* [1976] Ch 179 at 187.
67 *Thorner v Major* [2009] 1 WLR 776 at 786.
68 *Gillett v Holt* [2001] Ch 210.
69 Ibid at 225.
70 Ibid.
71 Per Lord Walker in *Thorner v Major* [2009] 1 WLR 776 at 795.

the extent of the property to which his assurance relates, as Lord Neuberger explained in *Thorner v Major*:

> it would represent a regrettable and substantial emasculation of . . . proprietary estoppel if it were artificially fettered so as to require the precise extent of the property the subject of the alleged estoppel to be strictly defined in every case.[72]

Indeed, it was held by the High Court in *Re Basham*[73] that a proprietary estoppel could arise for an individual's entire residuary estate. However, the decision in this case was described in *MacDonald v Frost*[74] as having to be treated with the 'utmost caution'[75] and in the latter case, the High Court thought that it was inconsistent with the views expressed by the House of Lords in *Thorner v Major* that the property generally had to be precisely defined.

Words . . .

If a claim in proprietary estoppel is to be based on words, those words cannot be too general to the extent that it is impossible to say that the defendant ever made the claimant any promise with regard to specific property. This is illustrated by *Lissimore v Downing*.[76]

Here, Kenneth Downing (a successful rock star with Judas Priest) commenced a relationship with Sarah Lissimore. During the course of that relationship, he drove her to the edge of his country estate in Shropshire and said 'I bet you never thought all of this would be yours in a million years'. At times during their relationship, he also used phrases such as she 'did not need to worry her pretty little head about money' and repeatedly referred to her as the 'Lady of the Manor'. When the parties split up, she brought a claim in proprietary estoppel against him, claiming a share of the property.

The High Court held that she had not established any entitlement to a claim. The words used by the rock star were simply too general to found a claim in proprietary estoppel. It was impossible to say from those words that he ever intended that she should have a share in any specific property. The words referred to both parties enjoying the property together, not sharing the equitable interest of it.

This case may be contrasted with the decision of the Court of Appeal in *Gillett v Holt*.[77]

Mr Holt met Mr Gillett in 1952 when Mr Gillett was only 12 years old. Mr Holt was a farmer. The two men got on very well, to the extent that their close friendship lasted some 40 years. Mr Gillett gradually took on more day-to-day responsibility at Mr Holt's farm, to the point where Mr Holt retired from farming and was content to leave running the business to Mr Gillett. On seven occasions, Mr Holt explained to Mr Gillett that he would be entitled to the farming business, together with the farmhouse, when Mr Holt died.

In 1992, Mr Holt met a Mr Wood, whom he liked. Mr Holt liked Mr Wood. His friendship with Mr Gillett began to deteriorate and, three years later, Mr Gillett was sacked by Mr Holt from the farming business. Mr Holt also made a will, making Mr Wood the main beneficiary and leaving nothing at all to Mr Gillett. Mr Gillett brought a claim in proprietary estoppel against Mr Holt.

At first instance, Carnworth J held that he could not find an irrevocable promise by Mr Holt to Mr Gilllett that the latter would inherit the farming business. Carnworth J thought

---

72 *Thorner v Major* [2009] 1 WLR 776 at 804.
73 *Re Basham* [1986] 1 WLR 1498.
74 *MacDonald v Frost* [2009] EWHC 2276 (Ch).
75 Ibid per Geraldine Andrews QC at para. 19.
76 *Lissimore v Downing* [2003] 2 FLR 308.
77 *Gillett v Holt* [2001] Ch 210.

that such an irrevocable promise was essential for Mr Gillett to establish a claim. Mr Gillett was successful in his appeal to the Court of Appeal.

In giving the main judgment of the court, Robert Walker LJ held that it did not have to find an irrevocable promise on the part of the defendant as an initial step. The court merely had to find a promise made by the defendant. The claimant's detrimental reliance on that promise then turned the promise into being irrevocable.

There were numerous examples of the types of promise required for Mr Gillett to establish a successful claim here. The assurances made by Mr Holt were repeated a number of times, usually before many witnesses. The assurances were also unambiguous. Moreover, as Robert Walker LJ put it, the assurances 'were intended to be relied on, and were in fact relied on'.[78]

Representations over a number of years were also the subject of *Jennings v Rice*.[79] Here the representations were perhaps not as explicit as in *Gillett v Holt*.

Mrs Royle lived in Shapwick, Somerset. She died a childless widow. After the death of her husband, she met Mr Jennings and initially employed him to tend her garden. Over a period of nearly 30 years, his duties increased as Mrs Royle became more incapacitated. He started to run errands for her and eventually, after a burglary at her home, she persuaded him to sleep overnight at the property to act as a quasi-security guard for her. Mr Jennings did this latter task for nearly three years, until Mrs Royle's death in 1997.

For the vast majority of their relationship, Mrs Royle paid Mr Jennings no wage at all. Instead she said words to the effect that 'he would be all right' and that 'this will all be yours one day'.

At first instance, the trial judge found that Mr Jennings had established a claim in proprietary estoppel and that he should be awarded £200,000 to satisfy the equity (the claim) that had arisen in his favour. The trial judge held that such assurances by Mrs Royle were sufficient to satisfy the first requirement of raising a proprietary estoppel. This finding was undisturbed by the Court of Appeal.

Making connections

It is, at first glance, odd that virtually the same words were used in both *Lissimore v Downing* and *Jennings v Rice* but with entirely different results: no claim was established in the former case, but was in the latter. This, it is suggested, exemplifies the principle that the court considers a claim of proprietary estoppel 'in the round'.[80] It is true that the words used by the defendant are important, but they cannot be judged solely on their own. They must be viewed in the context of the facts of the case to ascertain whether the defendant did create an expectation in the claimant's mind that he would be entitled to a share in the defendant's property. The claimant's expectation can be evidenced by whether he subsequently relied on the defendant's words to his detriment. As will be shown, no reliance occurred in *Lissimore v Downing* whilst there was substantial reliance in *Jennings v Rice*.

This is all part of the same notion that equity always considers words in the context in which they are used. This has been demonstrated, for instance, in terms of certainty of intention in forming an express trust (see Chapter 5).

The recent decision of the House of Lords in *Thorner v Major*[81] illustrates that the court will take into account the peculiarities of the parties to determine if an assurance has been made.

---

78 Ibid at 228.
79 *Jennings v Rice* [2003] 1 P & CR 8.
80 Per Robert Walker LJ in *Gillett v Holt* [2001] Ch 210 at 215.
81 *Thorner v Major* [2009] 1 WLR 776.

This was a case in which words were spoken, but to say that they were unclear is an understatement. The House of Lords held that a combination of words and the defendant's conduct could constitute the requisite assurances on which the claimant could rely.

The facts concerned two members of the Thorner family, Peter and David. Peter was a farmer of land in Cheddar, Somerset. In 1976, David began to help him with the farming business. He did so for 29 years, without being paid. As the years passed, David's responsibilities increased. Peter was described by the trial judge as being 'a man of few words'[82] and, in addition, had a habit of not talking about the subject matter directly in a conversation.

A key event occurred in 1990 when Peter gave David the bonus notice on two life assurance policies and said to him 'That's for my death duties'. The trial judge found that, in so doing, Peter had indicated to David that he would be his successor to the farm. David understood the remark to mean that he would inherit the farm on Peter's death. As a consequence of this comment, David did not pursue other farming opportunities which may have benefited him more, but continued to work for Peter. Peter later died intestate and David brought a claim in proprietary estoppel for the farm, together with various assets of the farming business.

The trial judge held that David's claim in proprietary estoppel should succeed, but the Court of Appeal reversed this decision. Lloyd LJ held that an assurance had to be 'clear and equivocal'[83] in order to establish a claim in proprietary estoppel. David appealed to the House of Lords.

The House of Lords agreed that David's appeal must succeed. Lord Walker said that the necessary assurance did not have to be clear and unequivocal, but that it had to be 'clear enough'.[84] He quoted (with approval) Hoffman LJ's exposition of such a test in *Walton v Walton*[85] that:

> The promise must be unambiguous and must appear to have been intended to be taken seriously. Taken in its context, it must have been a promise which one might reasonably expect to be relied upon by the person to whom it was made.

Peter's assurances were intended to be taken seriously by David and were to be relied upon by him. As such they were clear enough. Lord Rodger emphasised[86] that the test was not whether the words were clear enough to an outsider, but to the person to whom they were addressed. It was David who had to form a reasonable view that the words used by Peter amounted to an assurance that he would receive the farm on Peter's death.

It is the point that the court will take into account the parties' backgrounds when considering the nature of the assurance that may explain the otherwise contradictory decision of the House of Lords in *Cobbe v Yeoman's Row Management Ltd*,[87] a case decided just eight months before *Thorner v Major* but in which a different conclusion was reached as to whether there was an assurance and, seemingly, on the requirements for a valid assurance in proprietary estoppel.

Mr Cobbe negotiated with Yeoman's Row Management Ltd to apply for (and obtain) planning permission to convert a block of flats into townhouses. Provided planning permission was obtained, Yeoman's Row was to sell the land to Mr Cobbe for £12 million. Mr Cobbe was then to develop the townhouses, whereupon any proceeds of the sales over an agreed amount

---

82 Quoted by Lloyd LJ in the Court of Appeal's decision in the case [2008] EWCA Civ 732 at [31].
83 Ibid at [54].
84 *Thorner v Major* [2009] 1 WLR 776 at 794.
85 *Walton v Walton* [1994] CA Transcript No. 479 at [16].
86 *Thorner v Major* [2009] 1 WLR 776 at 786.
87 *Cobbe v Yeoman's Row Management Ltd* [2008] 1 WLR 1752.

were to be split equally between the parties. This agreement was not recorded in writing. Mr Cobbe obtained planning permission, having spent time and money in so doing. At that point, Yeoman's Row wanted to renegotiate the agreement. It wanted £20 million as payment upfront, together with a higher share of the proceeds from the sale of the townhouses. Mr Cobbe brought a claim in proprietary estoppel, claiming the company was estopped from denying its agreement with him.

Etherton J and the Court of Appeal held that Mr Cobbe's claim in proprietary estoppel was made out. The House of Lords allowed the defendant's appeal.

Lord Scott held that any right Mr Cobbe had could 'be described as neither based on an estoppel nor as proprietary in character'.[88] The fatal problem for Mr Cobbe was that no final agreement was ever reached between the parties. The parties knew that the oral deal that they had reached was always subject to a final, written contract being concluded. There was nothing that the defendant was estopped from denying. In addition, he had no proprietary interest to protect as he was not able to make out that the defendant owned the property on trust for him.

Lord Scott expressly rejected the views of the Court of Appeal and Etherton J that a remedy in proprietary estoppel could be granted simply on the unconscionable conduct of the defendant. He said:

> To treat a 'proprietary estoppel equity' as requiring neither a proprietary claim by the claimant nor an estoppel against the defendant but simply unconscionable behaviour is, in my respectful opinion, a recipe for confusion.[89]

Lord Walker made the same point in starker terms:

> [proprietary estoppel] is not a sort of joker or wild card to be used whenever the court disapproves of the conduct of a litigant . . .'[90]

Mr Cobbe had to show that he had received an assurance from the defendant to be entitled to a certain interest in land. He could not. All he could show was that, if and when he obtained planning permission, the parties would then negotiate a formal contract for the development of the land. Until that point, he had no interest in the land at all. Whilst Lord Scott agreed[91] with the Court of Appeal and Etherton J that such conduct by the defendant was unconscionable, that was not enough to found a claim in proprietary estoppel.

At first glance, it is perhaps difficult to reconcile the decision in *Cobbe* with that in *Thorner v Major*. In the former, the House of Lords appears to be insisting quite strictly on fairly rigid requirements to establish a claim in proprietary estoppel; it seems in the latter that a fairly loose statement from one party to the other sufficed. Yet it is suggested that the cases can be reconciled, on the basis that the court considers the issue 'in the round', taking into account the parties' attributes. In *Cobbe*, the House of Lords appreciated that both claimant and defendant were experienced commercial negotiators who would have been well aware that their initial oral deal was not a binding agreement justifying the intervention of the equity in terms of proprietary estoppel. In *Thorner v Major*, it was important that the defendant would have known that the claimant would have understood his fairly oblique assurances. An assurance is always required as a key ingredient to establish a proprietary estoppel, but the court will consider that

---

88 Ibid at 1761.
89 Ibid at 1762.
90 Ibid at 1775.
91 Ibid at 1768.

assurance in the light of the parties' backgrounds and personal attributes. Certainly this was how Lord Neuberger understood the matter in *Thorner v Major*:

> it is sufficient for the person invoking the estoppel to establish that *he* reasonably understood the statement or action to be an assurance on which he could rely.[92]

No words . . .

On occasions, no words – or no clear words – pass between defendant and claimant on which the claimant can found a claim. But he must still identify an assurance that the defendant has given him, relating to the defendant's property.

An example of an assurance arising from conduct occurred in *Crabb v Arun District Council*.[93]

The facts involved a disputed right of access to a piece of land near Bognor Regis. A piece of land was divided into two smaller pieces and a right of access reserved onto a new road from the northern piece. The southern piece would have been effectively landlocked without a similar right of access to the new road. The new road was on land owned by the defendant. At a site meeting, the claimant and defendant reached an agreement in principle that the claimant could have access to the new road directly from the southern piece of land. The trial judge found as a fact that there was no definitive assurance spoken by the defendant to that effect but, nonetheless, the parties proceeded as though a right of access had been granted. The defendant constructed a fence along the boundary between their road and the southern piece of land but left a gap for the right of access for the claimant and initially installed a pair of gates across that right of access. Unfortunately, the parties had a disagreement, resulting in the defendant dismantling the gates and erecting a fence across the right of access. This left the southern piece of land with no access to it.

The claimant brought an action in proprietary estoppel. There was no specific verbal or written assurance he could point to so instead his action was based on the defendant's conduct of leaving a gap and constructing the gates as recognition of a right of access in the claimant's favour.

In the Court of Appeal, Lord Denning MR explained that proprietary estoppel did not require the claimant to go so far as to show that he had entered into a contract with the defendant. The claimant had simply to rely on the defendant's words or conduct. Here the defendant's conduct could raise an estoppel in the claimant's favour. The construction of the gates led the claimant to believe that he was entitled to enjoy a right of access to the new road.

Reliance

It is not enough for the claimant to show that the defendant made an assurance to him that he would have an interest in specific property. In addition, the claimant must rely on that representation, to his detriment. It is the detrimental reliance that turns an initially revocable promise into an irrevocable assurance. The reliance must be reasonable but in *Thorner v Major*, Lord Neuberger thought that it would be 'rare'[94] for the court to decide that no estoppel arose because the defendant could not reasonably have expected the claimant to rely on his assurance.

---

92 *Thorner v Major* [2009] 1 WLR 776 at 801 (emphasis added).
93 *Crabb v Arun District Council* [1976] Ch 179.
94 *Thorner v Major* [2009] 1 WLR 776 at 799.

Reliance was considered by Robert Walker LJ in *Gillett v Holt*. He said that this meant that there had to be a 'sufficient link'[95] between the assurance given by the defendant and the detriment suffered by the claimant. The link was straightforward. It could be said to be akin to offer and acceptance in contract where the defendant had used words to encourage the claimant to believe he would have an interest in his property. If no words were used, the link could be provided by the defendant otherwise encouraging the claimant to spend money on the property.

Detriment

The claimant must act to his detriment in relying on the assurance. This suggests that the claimant must go beyond what would normally be expected in the relationship between the parties.[96]

Robert Walker LJ defined detriment as follows in *Gillett v Holt*:

> it is not a narrow or technical concept. The detriment need not consist of the expenditure of money or other quantifiable financial detriment, so long as it is something substantial. The requirement must be approached as part of a broad inquiry as to whether repudiation of an assurance is or is not unconscionable in all the circumstances.[97]

The detriment must be causally connected to the assurance. The time for judging whether detrimental reliance has occurred is at the point where the defendant tries to go back on his assurance. Robert Walker LJ explained that whether or not the detriment is substantial enough 'is to be tested by whether it would be unjust or inequitable to allow the assurance to be disregarded'.[98]

Clear cases of detrimental reliance have emerged from some cases. In *Inwards v Baker*,[99] the Court of Appeal held that it occurred when a son built a new bungalow on land owned by his father, after being encouraged to do so by a verbal assurance by his father that he could construct a property on it.

A similar decision was reached in *Pascoe v Turner*.[100] Here, Samuel Pascoe began an affair with another woman but told his current partner, Ms Turner, that a house in Tuckingmill, Cornwall, together with its contents, was hers. The Court of Appeal held that her actions of continuing to live in the house, spending money on redecorating and making substantial improvements to it, were evidence of detrimental reliance on her part.

These cases were evidence of short-term detrimental reliance and the spending of money as a result of assurances being made. Longer-term detrimental reliance can also be illustrated in *Gillett v Holt*.[101] The facts of this case also show that the spending of considerable time can also be seen to be detrimental reliance.

In *Gillett v Holt*, Robert Walker LJ held that detrimental reliance could, of course, only come after the assurance made to the claimant. Anything done beforehand could only be by way of (useful) background. But detriment could clearly be found by looking at the cumulative effect of the claimant's actions. Mr Gillett spent considerable sums on the farmhouse, believing that he

---

95 *Gillett v Holt* [2001] Ch 210 at 230.
96 As explained by Judge Norris QC in *Lissimore v Downing* [2003] EWHC B1 (Ch) at para. [21].
97 *Gillett v Holt* [2001] Ch 210 at 232.
98 Ibid.
99 *Inwards v Baker* [1965] 2 QB 29.
100 *Pascoe v Turner* [1979] 1 WLR 431.
101 See also the facts of *Jennings v Rice* for a similar proposition (above at p 470).

would acquire it on Mr Holt's death. He effectively provided Mr Holt with a family for 30 years, after he married and had children of his own, all of whom continued to have a close relationship with Mr Holt. Both Mr and Mrs Gillett worked for Mr Holt for this long period of time, spurning opportunities to earn a better living elsewhere and failing to plan for their futures, precisely because they believed they would be entitled to a proprietary interest in Mr Holt's property. There was more than adequate evidence of detrimental reliance over a long period of time.

The short-term spending of time appears generally not to amount to detrimental reliance, probably because it is not seen to be sufficiently substantial. For example, Mrs Rosset's alternative claim in Lloyds Bank plc v Rosset[102] was that she was entitled to a share of the house based on proprietary estoppel. Her evidence of detrimental reliance – supervising builders undertaking renovation works – was rejected by the House of Lords. It simply was not substantial enough.

Neither was detrimental reliance found on the facts in Lissimore v Downing. Miss Lissimore argued that she gave up her employment only because she had been promised an interest in Mr Downing's property. Yet this was not done on the strength of an assurance from Mr Downing that he would provide for her forever, but because she disliked her job. She also argued that she had undertaken gardening works as well as helping to manage the estate and the accounts. None of this was evidence of detrimental reliance on an assurance to share the property beneficially. It simply evidenced the parties sharing a relationship. Viewed against the other evidence of Mr Downing's reluctance to part with a share in his £2 million estate, it could not be argued in the round that any claim in proprietary estoppel had been made out.

Remedies

If a successful claim is made out in proprietary estoppel, the court's task is, according to Scarman LJ in Crabb v Arun District Council,[103] to do 'the minimum equity to do justice' to the claimant. In the same case, Lord Denning MR described that equity was at its 'most flexible'[104] in terms of awarding a remedy. In the case itself, for instance, the claimant was awarded an easement to access the new road.

In Sledmore v Delby,[105] Hobhouse LJ stated that the remedy awarded must also be proportionate to the assurance made by the defendant and the detrimental reliance expended by the claimant. Proportionality of the result was described as the 'most essential requirement'[105] of the court's task to achieve justice between the parties. It is a question of doing justice for both parties, not just the claimant.

Robert Walker LJ analysed the appropriate remedy available to the claimant in Jennings v Rice. He thought that the cases could be broken down into two areas:

(a) where the assurance and the claimant's detrimental reliance are essentially consensual, for instance, an elderly person promising a younger individual their house if they cared for them. The benefit to the defendant and the claimant are roughly equal. The remedy should reflect that by providing the claimant with the specific property promised to them. For example, in Inwards v Baker, the Court of Appeal held that the son was entitled to a licence of the bungalow and could remain in the bungalow for however long he wished to do so; or

(b) where the claimant's expectation is not focused on any particular property. It is uncertain. Alternatively, the claimant's expectation is much higher than the assurance given to him.

---

102 Lloyds Bank plc v Rosset [1991] 1 AC 107.
103 Crabb v Arun District Council [1976] Ch 179 at 198.
104 Ibid at 189.
105 Sledmore v Delby [1996] 72 P & CR 196 at 208.
106 Per Aldous LJ in Jennings v Rice [2003] 1 P & CR 8 at [36].

In such a case, the court cannot award any specific property to the claimant and the claimant's expectations are a mere starting point to assess his remedy. The remedy will then be more limited than the clearly described property promised to the claimant in (a).

In the majority of cases, the claimant's remedy will either be equitable compensation, or a proprietary interest in the property itself. The aim of the court is also, where possible, to achieve a clean break between the parties, so as not to encourage further litigation.[107]

Equitable compensation

A compensatory award was made in *Jennings v Rice*. The Court of Appeal agreed with the trial judge that an award of £200,000 was the minimum required to achieve justice for all the years of work by Mr Jennings in the care of Mrs Royle.

In *Gillett v Holt*, the court considered the extent of Mr Holt's property from the period when he first made an assurance to Mr Gillett to the time that the assurance was repudiated. The extent of Mr Holt's property changed considerably during that 20-year period. The court again had to decide the minimum award necessary to do justice between the parties. On the facts, Mr Gillett was awarded the freehold estate of the farmhouse, together with £100,000 to compensate him from being excluded from the farming business.

Proprietary interest

It is important to stress that whilst the remedy is the minimum required, such minimum must still do justice between the parties. This was shown in *Pascoe v Turner* where Ms Turner was awarded the freehold interest in the house. The defendant argued that the minimum required to do justice was to award her a licence to occupy the property but the Court of Appeal rejected this. The Court of Appeal took into account the defendant's conduct throughout the proceedings and felt that the defendant may not keep the property in good repair or permit the claimant quiet enjoyment of the house if only a licence was granted. Such a licence could not be registered as a land charge to protect the claimant's interest,[108] thus meaning that a *bona fide* purchaser of the legal estate for value without notice of her licence could purchase the house free from her licence. To address these issues, the entire freehold interest had to be transferred to her which was, after all, no less than the defendant had promised.

❖ ANALYSING THE LAW

The earlier cases place more emphasis on the promisee's expectations than the more recent decisions. For example, the promisee in *Pascoe v Turner* was awarded in full what she expected to receive.

Look again at the facts of *Jennings v Rice*, *Gillett v Holt* and *Thorner v Major*. Would you say the claimant in each case was awarded their full expectation? Is the court shifting towards what may be classed as a 'fair' result nowadays? And is fairness capable of ever being defined satisfactorily?

---

107 *Pascoe v Turner* [1979] 1 WLR 431 at 438–439 per Cumming-Bruce LJ.
108 Nowadays, in registered land, an interest arising by proprietary estoppel is an interest capable of binding successors in title: see Land Registration Act 2002, s 116.

Proprietary estoppel v the constructive trust

In *Thorner v Major*, the majority of the House of Lords held that David was entitled to a remedy in proprietary estoppel. That remedy was, as the trial judge declared, to the freehold of the farm, its livestock, chattels and working capital of the farming business.

Whilst agreeing with the overall remedy, Lord Scott expressed a different view with how the court should reach that remedy. He would have confined proprietary estoppel to a case where a claimant had been promised an immediate interest in certain property, such as occurred in *Crabb v Arun District Council*.

For assurances relating to potentially inherited property, Lord Scott did not believe proprietary estoppel was the appropriate means of achieving a remedy. That was because, as in this case, it was not necessarily the case that the assurance was sufficiently clear and unequivocal. It was not set out entirely clearly by Peter that David would inherit a particular farm and, even if he did, the extent of the farm was unclear. Second, as Lord Scott explained, in every case where proprietary estoppel is raised for inherited property, the assurance may be made many years before the defendant's death. Suppose the defendant promises the claimant his entire farm but then circumstances change so that the defendant needs costly nursing care before his death. It would be difficult to say that the defendant should be bound to adhere to his assurance and not use the property to pay for his nursing care, even after he had promised it to the claimant. As Lord Scott pointed out, 'it is an odd sort of estoppel that is produced by representations that are, in a sense, conditional.'[109]

Instead, Lord Scott thought that the remedial constructive trust would be the appropriate vehicle to use to provide the claimant with a remedy for assurances concerning inherited property. The remedial constructive trust would be created by the parties' common intention. On the basis of this common intention, the claimant acted to his detriment.

Lord Scott was in a minority in this view in *Thorner v Major* itself. It would, of course, be difficult to recognise the remedial constructive trust in this area of law when it seems to have been otherwise more generally rejected in English law in cases such as *Re Polly Peck International (No. 2)*.[110] His constructive trust approach would seem to have more theoretical sense to it with regard to assurances for inherited property than an approach based on proprietary estoppel but, pragmatically, it must be questioned whether it would add anything to the overall result in such cases. The remedies awarded by the courts under the existing doctrine of proprietary estoppel are very flexible and could not arguably become more flexible by the development of a remedial constructive trust in this area.

Points to Review

You have seen:

- how equity developed a series of bespoke remedies to act to prevent wrongs occurring, rather than righting wrongs that have already occurred, as damages at common law tend to do. Such remedies are awarded comparatively rarely by the courts and in all cases, the claimant must prove that damages are not an adequate remedy for him;
- that proprietary estoppel has developed greatly over the last 40 years and can be used to be awarded a flexible remedy to a claimant who has acted to his detriment on an assurance given to him. Yet proprietary estoppel cannot be developed further on rather loose

---

109 *Thorner v Major* [2009] 1 WLR 776 at 784.
110 *Re Polly Peck International (No. 2)* [1998] 3 All ER 812.

equitable principles such as conscience, as the House of Lords pointed out in *Cobbe v Yeoman's Row Management Ltd.* The key ingredients of assurance, reliance and detriment remain necessary for a claimant to establish a successful claim; and

- that a glimmer of hope still shines for the development of the remedial constructive trust in English law in the form of a dictum of Lord Scott albeit at the expense of conditional claims in proprietary estoppel. It will be interesting to see if the courts develop the remedial constructive trust in this area.

Making connections

In a sense, you have now come full circle in your study of equity and trusts. As has been suggested, equitable remedies are only awarded if the claimant is able to come to equity with clean hands. This maxim is discussed further in Chapter 1 and you should re-read it for further knowledge.

The debate about the future of proprietary estoppel and whether the remedial constructive trust should take its place develops the argument for the remedial constructive trust, which is discussed at the end of Chapter 3.

 ## Useful Things To Read

The best reading is contained in the primary sources listed below. It is always good to consider the decisions of the courts themselves as this will lead to a deeper understanding of the issues involved. A few secondary sources are also listed, which you may wish to read to gain additional insights into the areas considered in this chapter.

Primary sources

American Cyanamid Co v Ethicon Ltd [1975] AC 396.
Cobbe v Yeoman's Row Management Ltd [2008] 1 WLR 1752.
Co-Operative Insurance Society Ltd v Argyll Stores (Holdings) Ltd [1998] AC 1.
Gillett v Holt [2001] Ch 210.
Jennings v Rice [2003] 1 P & CR 8.
Shepherd Homes Ltd v Sandham [1971] Ch 340.
Thorner v Major [2009] 1 WLR 776.

Secondary sources

Mischa Balen and Christopher Knowles, 'Failure to estop: Rationalising proprietary estoppel using failure of basis' [2011] 3 Conv 176–190. An interesting article which looks at whether unconscionability or unjust enrichment is needed to succeed in a claim in proprietary estoppel.

Guy Fetherstonhaugh, 'Is rectification in need of rectification?' [2012] 1211 EG 90. This article considers alleged deficiencies in the law of rectification.

Alastair Hudson, *Equity & Trusts* (7th edn, Routledge-Cavendish, 2012) ch 13 and Part 9.

Mark Pawlowski, 'Revocable gifts and estoppel' [2012] 18 (1) T & T 64–67. An article which examines the decision in *Gillett v Holt* and considers the interesting question of whether proprietary estoppel might be used to support a beneficiary of an interest under a secret trust which has since been revoked.

Mohamed Ramjohn, *Text, Cases and Materials on Equity & Trusts* (4th edn, Routledge-Cavendish, 2008) pp. 86–90 and chs 22–25.

Solene Rowan, 'For the recognition of remedial terms agreed *inter partes*' (2010) 126 LQR 448–475. This article looks at how the law tends to be reactive in nature in the event of a breach of contract by imposing damages on a 'guilty' party and considers whether the law should be more proactive by obliging parties to negotiate a solution to their difficulty.

David Schmitz, 'Not such a good bargain' (2008) 152/37 SJ 18–19. A useful summary of the decision of the House of Lords in *Cobbe v Yeoman's Row Management Ltd*.

Index

Page references in italics refer to figures